Wome
Social Re
Modern India

To

UMA CHAKRAVARTI AND MUKUL MANGALIK

in appreciation of what they have been in Delhi University

Women and Social Reform in Modern India

A Reader

VOLUME I

edited by

SUMIT SARKAR

&

TANIKA SARKAR

permanent black

Published by
PERMANENT BLACK
'Himalayana', Mall Road, Ranikhet Cantt,
Ranikhet 263645
Email: perblack@gmail.com

Distributed by
ORIENT BLACKSWAN PRIVATE LIMITED
Bangalore Bhopal Bhubaneshwar Chandigarh Chennai
Ernakulam Guwahati Hyderabad Jaipur Kolkata
Lucknow Mumbai New Delhi Patna
www.orientblackswan.com

First published in hardback 2007
First paperback printing 2011

Third impression 2014

ISBN 81-7824-327-X (for set of 2 vols)

Printed and bound by Sapra Brothers, New Delhi 110092

Contents

Introduction

Tanika Sarkar and Sumit Sarkar

Colonial social reforms have long been a routinized part of our school, college, and university syllabi, written and taught more or less on similar lines at all three levels. Reforms conjure up, inevitably, the names of a few great individuals, almost invariably Hindu: upper-caste educated men from metropolitan cities, and one or two memorable women. This galaxy of remarkable persons identified and abolished abuses in social life, and their efforts ushered in more progressive gender relations—although we must remember that even though the reforms largely related to women and family relationships, the word 'gender' rarely occurs in the more conventional textbooks. We find little about reforms among Muslims or among 'lower castes'. Attention is centred on upper-caste women's education and on their marriage practices—which were altered largely through new laws: in particular those that banned widow burning, allowed widow remarriage, restricted child marriage.

To explain the emergence of reformers precisely from the early nineteenth century, three kinds of reasons are invoked in these historical writings: a new colonial education, purveyed through the state and Christian missionaries, that altered and modernized traditional social perceptions; new religious movements that revived and consolidated older humanitarian impulses; and, of course, the sudden availability of a pool of human greatness, eager to save the weak and the helpless. Little significant change has inflected such presentation of this theme over the years, and the social reform chapter usually occurs as a boring though easy interlude, interrupting the more exciting or taxing chapters on nationalist struggle and the colonial economy.

Even within its own terms, such a perspective on social reform could have broadened into an engagement with a number of connected themes. The invocation of the great reformist individuals could, for instance, have expanded into a discussion of their regional, class, and caste specificities, or of the way in which the variations in their social particulars shaped distinctive styles of work or varied the patterns of their social concerns. This, in turn, would have led into a consideration of variations within the new intelligentsia, and of the characteristics of the public spheres that emerged in metropolitan centres with the development of print culture, newspapers, and new modes of communication and association, all of which allowed the reformers to engage in sustained conversations and arguments with one another and with their orthodox opponents in the public domain. A description of the situation in the metropolitan centres would, then, need to expand into a discussion of how, over time, and with the progressive enlargement of the public sphere, smaller towns and new regions were incorporated within the larger debates on the 'women's question', leading to the development of new modes of argument and presentation. We need to know, moreover, what exactly was written about reforms in the newspapers, novels, and tracts, how the matter was performed in the public theatre, how public opinion was formed, pluralized, made contradictory and fractured, swerving people away, finally, from the rule of prescriptive texts and commands that may have been diverse but which, certainly, were authoritative and compelling.

The term 'middle class', so commonly deployed in textbook histories, is also surely in need of some problematization. The term has been in fairly wide use from the nineteenth century, in Indian-language equivalents such as *madhyabitta* in Bengali. It used to invoke, in those days, an optimistic analogy with the history of the English middle class as the presumed harbinger of economic and social progress. Paradoxically, in striking contrast with the English middle classes, the emergent Indian educated 'middle class' was rooted primarily in rent income from land, where production relations were far from capitalistic. This was combined with professions and office jobs in government or European business firms. The gap between that social group and indigenous entrepreneurship actually widened over time, most notably in Bengal.[1] The middle class, again, would have varied across regions and times, its links with commerce and industry being much more evident in Bombay—and to some extent in the United Provinces—for instance. Recent research also uncovers a kind of lower stratum, a 'low-life of literature' (to borrow a phrase by Robert Darnton about eighteenth-century France), typically clerical in its ambience, its values somewhat at odds with those of the well-known established reformers, writers, journalists, and politicians. The proliferation of cheap print resulted in a mass of tracts, plays, farces, and manuals which disclosed the characteristics of this more plebeian underworld. Little of this research, however, has found its way as yet into textbooks.[2]

We have moreover a recurrent use of the word 'debates' in connection with social reforms, without acquiring an understanding of how public debates—a very new historical development—could take place: Among whom? Through what concrete communication practices and technologies?

Second, when we discuss what was being done for women in those times, we rarely connect the 'abuses' to enduring systems or traditions of gender practices and their internal variations across times, classes and castes, labour patterns, and regions. For instance, when we address changes in widow immolation or widow remarriage practices, we do not study the larger domain of gender relations which sanctified immolation or which outlawed widow remarriage: What arguments were used? What else went with these specific norms that reformers did not address, what was said by the orthodox practitioners who defended such traditions? In other words, an exclusive focus on reformers—once they had already been installed as reformers—obscures the milieu they came from, and the large, powerful context of orthodoxy that they had to contend with. The focus on the specific achievements of reformers thus obscures the larger horizon of gender norms and practices.

Third, there is a very curious omission. Most reforms passed through the grid of state legislation. Yet, there is little engagement even with the law-making machinery and with the state under colonial governance, far less with the judicial courts that enforced the laws and dealt with disputes around the new laws. Most surprisingly, there is seldom any mention of the fact that the reforms related to the sphere of 'personal laws', Hindu, Muslim, Christian, and, later, Parsi. The colonial state had marked these out as parts of a domain that would be governed by the religious scriptures and customs of the various Indian communities, within which the state would only intervene if it could be definitively demonstrated that present practices deviated from more authentic norms. The state had demarcated a sphere of personal laws from the late eighteenth century, based on clear-cut assumptions about religious divisions. Colonial courts were instructed to apply such personal laws, and colonial lawmakers, too, rarely stepped out of such boundaries. Even though the entire domain was supposedly governed by both scripture and custom, in cases of conflict between the two, scripture was generally privileged in Bengal: which explains why Rammohan Roy and Ishwarchandra Vidyasagar scoured ancient scripture to locate citations for their views. In Bombay Presidency, on the other hand, local custom was taken far more seriously from the late eighteenth century. Case law was compiled through detailed investigations among various caste heads; they were also compiled carefully as precedents. In the South, there was a recurrent vacillation between Sanskrit and brahmanical texts, and old vernacular texts, the latter sometimes seen as non-textualized custom. The separate marriage practices of Nayars and Tiyyas, for instance, and their matrilineal residential and property-owning traditions, could be jettisoned as corrupt forms when, from the late nineteenth century, the community men themselves began to agitate for changes in marriage and property relations. In Punjab, customary laws of landholding 'tribes' were clearly privileged over the different textual traditions of Hindus, Muslims, and Sikhs. Similarly, the version of Shariati law—derived from a twelfth-century Arabic text, the Hedaya—that was made the paradigmatic Islamic law in the country provided no space for different marriage practices among Muslim communities like the Khojas, the Momins, and the Mapillas. It has often been said that the newly codified colonial laws stamped out customary variations and pluralities and froze the legal system. What emerged, rather, was a combination of centralization with sharpened distinctions, not a single uniform pattern.

The legal framework, thus, set limits to the reformist enterprise. Reformers had to invent supple stratagems to bypass or manipulate the boundaries of the law, and so did the orthodoxy. It is pointless, as has often been done, to condemn the reformers for constantly appealing to old texts instead of going beyond them. What we find, instead, is a recurrent tension and play over varied texts, plural interpretations, and the invocation of custom. Instead of a permanent closure, therefore, there were repeated contestations within the realm of the various personal laws, and they never completely settled into a particular mould. By the mid-nineteenth century, for instance, Khoja and Memon marriage practices came to be recognized as a subdivision within Islamic law. Low-caste Hindu widows challenged inheritance regulations under the law of 1856 in the name of plural caste custom. In the interests of stable revenue flow and the quality of recruits from Punjabi Jat landholding communities into the British Indian Army, widows in Punjab were not allowed to marry outside the matrimonial family and were often coerced into levirate marriages even when they would have wanted to retain their widowhood with some property inheritance rights.

This, again, takes us into the problems of codification of scriptural citations and of customary usages, of judicial interpretations under the guidance of Brahman pandits and maulavis officially appointed by courts, and of the variety of contentious interpretations that would, eventually, alter the legal-judicial parameters that had been set initially. It should also lead us to a consideration of who exactly manned the courts and the legislatures: what happened when Indians finally pierced these preserves of colonial governance.

Finally, even apart from the invocation of the few remarkable women reformers that there were—like Pandita Ramabai—the theme of social reforms should take us into the zone of women's own intervention in the public sphere.[3] It is generally argued that male nationalists separated the two domains, public and private, into male and female spheres, respectively, achieving a resolution regarding the distribution by allotting the home to the woman and the world to the man with a seeming but counterfeit equity.[4] Actually, women—however few and exceptional—did begin to shape public opinion by writing about their lifeworlds even from within the domestic seclusion. Educated at home by fathers or husbands, and benefiting from the growth of print culture and vernacular prose that made writing easier for them, they published their views on women's entitlements, or the lack thereof, often with remarkable criticality. We also have the instance of Rashsundari Debi, an upper-caste rural housewife, who very secretly and fearfully taught herself to read and write, and later in the century published an autobiography—the first such venture in the Bengali language—to recount the history of her self-earned mastery over words. Tarabai Shinde of Maharashtra disclosed the hidden world of women with passionate anger, berating even liberal reformers for failing to address some of the crucial lacks in women's lives.

What is interesting is that such writings found a popular market in the new world of print, and the corpus grew. It was evidently thought that women did possess privileged knowledge about the domestic sphere, and, since social reforms revolved so much around the home, their views were eagerly read, if not always approved of. What is also important is the way in which the pattern of their concerns would be allied to, yet somewhat dislocated from, the major preoccupations of male reformers. By and large, male reformers addressed issues of marriage and widowhood, whereas a lot of women writers talked about the pain of premature patrilocality, of the need to acquire an education so that they could be independent of male intellectual tutelage, of the oppressively insensitive relatives that child brides found in their new matrimonial homes. Focusing on these figures—who do not constitute front-ranking reformers—we enter into the details of the domestic sphere and of women's experiences. We are also introduced to a new social category that was a crucial sign of modern times: that of the woman writer.

By the turn of the century, and precisely around the time when the male nationalist resolution into the 'home' as distinct from the 'world' was reaching its zenith with the rise of Extremist nationalism, women were doing even more unusual things. They attended schools which began to develop in the metropolitan cities from the mid-nineteenth century, and which took them away from the domestic confines and the control of kinship networks, giving them a public identity beyond the familial. They were also admitted into colleges and universities, receiving degrees in the sciences and arts, much earlier than English women were allowed those in Britain. Some of them went abroad for medical training and a few of them took up employment as teachers and doctors. Of course, they were fortunate to have exceptionally supportive families and they were blessed with class privilege. The vast majority of girls—like their male counterparts—were deprived of literacy because of dire poverty. At the same time, these upper- and middle-class women would earlier have been the most closely guarded of people, repositories of lineage honour, specially obliged to faithfully observe orthodox prescriptions of conduct. The new paradigm of female behaviour not only breached brahmanical and sharif lifeworlds. However modestly, it created an alternative trajectory of social respectability for women of lower castes and classes who often tended to emulate the behaviour of their social superiors—when they could afford it at all.

In the early decades of the twentieth century, their numbers had multiplied to the point when they set up networks among themselves. Gradually, women emerged as leaders in social reform, banding together, writing and petitioning for better health and childcare facilities, female education and maternal benefits, improved marriage and inheritance laws, suffrage. The trajectory of social reforms thus blends into the new world of women's political activism.

So we find that the hoary theme of social reforms takes us into entirely new domains which, in their turn, get reconfigured through their association with reforms. We enter into older prescriptive texts and schools of law and the regime of gender discipline that they prescribed. We consider the variations that caste practices would have introduced into the textual domain. We turn to new modes of public argument and their presentation in literary, journalistic, and performative genres: and into the spheres of legislatures and courts, of lawmaking and judicial disputes. And finally we move away to take a broad look at the new thrusts that develop into thinking, arguing, writing, and relating to the state. In other words, we revision colonialism and modernity in the light of the broad discussion of social reforms.

II

It is surprising that textbook presentations of social reform have not changed much over the years. Outside the classroom, a number of very significant historiographical shifts and debates have actually changed the nature of the field. We used to have an old, positive teleology about the nature of Indian modernity deriving predominantly from social reforms: their intention and their impact. Concerned with beating the West at its own game, the historian Jadunath Sarkar had proclaimed in the 1940s that Indians enjoyed a Renaissance far nobler than anything that had happened in Europe, for the Indian version was inflected by deep moral concern and was hence far more than a mere aesthetic efflorescence. The Marxist historian S.C. Sarkar traced back impulses of social and political freedom to nineteenth-century social-reform movements, which unfolded steadily into national emancipation and promised to eventuate into socialism.[5] Till the 1960s, when a new corpus of histories of the nationalist movement bloomed—largely as a reaction against the Cambridge School denigrations of nationalism—social reforms were a central axis of historical writings, especially in Bengal, supposedly the nerve centre of the reform movements.

In the early 1970s, largely in the light of contentions with the Cambridge School, and motivated by fresh and urgent critiques of colonial rule and of the 'development of underdevelopment' in intellectual and social life that imperialism inflicted, a new group of leftist historians turned to a review of social reform. They found much to dispute with: the elite subject position of reformers appeared significant, along with their compromises with colonialism, their investment of hope in its liberal promises. The distance of reformers from popular, low-caste religious movements with composite cultural styles and critiques of religious establishments was seen as crucially limiting their agenda and causing a severe social restriction of its reach among common people. Finally, the colonial context that reformers had to work within was underlined, along with the way its logic inverted the liberal possibilities that reform could amass in the imperial metropolis.[6] In the 1980s, a new and more final critique was added. Not only did the colonial context limit the social acceptance or even the content of the reformist agenda, but the endeavour was doomed in a more profound way. Had it fully succeeded, it would only have consolidated imperial mastery over Indians, since every modern enterprise for change and progress was suffused with Western knowledge forms and Enlightenment influence.[7]

In the late 1980s, finally, a feminist survey of reforms was initiated, partly under the influence of these postcolonial theories, and partly deriving from certain notions within feminist critiques of modernity. The new approach argued that modern notions of gender rights in the public domain were premised on a public–private split whereby private disempowerment and the subordination of women were masked and reinforced by the bestowal of public rights. More influential, however, was the Marxist–feminist influence, reworked in the Indian colonial context. It was argued that colonial rule introduced a capitalist regime into India and produced a modern but dependent bourgeoisie. This class recast its women and its gender practices to align itself more closely with the domesticity of the colonial masters and the ways of modern capitalists. A new form of patriarchy thus evolved which provided the rationale for reforms, not seriously questioning, but merely 'recasting', male domination.[8]

There is much truth in the new negative teleology of reforms—as there was in the older positive teleology. Certainly, the reforms were the first clear signs of guilty and self-critical introspection by a privileged, male, upper-caste, middle-class intelligentsia, compromised with colonial governance and yet convinced that the present order was not a just one, even when it benefited them. If they took no political risks, as later nationalists would, they took huge and painful social risks. Made outcaste by their families, kin groups, and community, threatened by an outraged orthodoxy, they often watched reformist gains peter out in the face of social ostracism and hostility, even when they had been enacted as state laws. We can map a trajectory of broadening social and political criticism, if not social change, from the time of reforms. If not directly connected with or created by the reforms, and even when contradicted by the class, caste, and political limits of the early reformers, there were complex, parallel, interanimating movements for rights: for self-determination against colonialism, for social justice for low castes, for the human rights of the labouring poor.

At the same time, the later critics of reform pointed out crucial and valid limits, both in reformist understanding and in their historical context. The criticism enriches our understanding of modernity as a complex and contradictory formation, not a linear model of steady progress.

Where the Left, postcolonial, and early feminist versions converge is over two shared absences in all three discourses. None of them has cleared any space for women's investment, agency or political activism in the reform agenda. It has, in fact, been suggested that nationalism imposed a closure on the 'women's question' by dividing up the world into female/home and male/world domains. However, a growing volume of research indicates that, increasingly, women assumed initiatives in leading reforms, as well as in forcing openings into the male and public sphere of politics of all sorts.

The other absence relates to a virtual ignoring of the world of the orthodoxy which exerted decisive influence on gender relations throughout the colonial era. Reforms inevitably ran into an impossible impasse, since orthodoxy ruled the social world. Reforms, when refigured in the light of orthodox discourses and discipline, begin to look very different from the timid, pallid and imitative agenda they are often made out to be.

Apart from a few significant works, there is a similar crucial absence of historical writing on the Hindu revivalism of the late nineteenth century.[9] A form of cultural nationalism, revivalism glorified older, pristine Hindu traditions uncritically and chauvinistically, attributing existing abuses to 'Muslim misrule' or to British misunderstanding. It would accept no colonial legislative intervention in Hindu gender practices. At the same time, movements with strong revivalist leanings did carry out certain reforms. The Arya Samaj, notably, espoused many of the reformist measures, not as legal change but as change effected within and by the new community of Aryas: widow remarriage, female education, a higher age of marriage. It had moreover to strenuously argue on behalf of such changes in the face of a rejuvenated North Indian orthodoxy embodied in the Sanatanist movement for a rigidly brahmanical gender and caste discipline. Why then do we distinguish revivalist from liberal reformers?

Many liberal reformers too, in order to gain social acceptability, had justified reforms as part of an older and more authentic scriptural tradition, reassuring the state that no genuine religious norm was being violated. In so far as they still asked for legal change, however, they sought to provide the woman with a legal personhood, with legal rights. Revivalists, on the other hand, offered the same kinds of changes as coming from the hands of male community leaders and the scriptures. The woman, recipient of social change, did not relate to the change as a right-holder. Moreover, the basis for revivalist change was quite different from that of liberal reform. It did not talk much about the sexual double standards that forbade female education or widow remarriage. It did not refer to the sexual and intellectual needs of the woman. It talked, rather, of the need to populate the community and to educate the girl child properly at home. The entire discourse gradually came to be framed within antagonism and competition *vis-à-vis* other Indian religious communities. In the Sikh reformist movements, too, women were encouraged to educate themselves and take a more active part in community life—not in the name of their own needs and rights but in order to invigorate the inevitably male-dominated community.

The last decades of the nineteenth century saw a political shift from Moderate nationalism, which criticized colonial policies but which asked for reforms and improvements within the existing framework of governance; this shifted to more strident and militant nationalist critiques. It often relied on revivalist Hinduism, and resisted social reform as well as any changes through interventions by the alien state. Traditional women came to be glorified as the last refuge of a threatened indigenous culture. Revivalism and a more militant nationalism thus fed on each other. Tilak, who had supported revivalists in their opposition to the Age of Consent Act of 1891, forced a split between the Congress and the National Social Conference in 1895 by disrupting the earlier practice of the two organizations holding conferences in the same physical space.

With the growth of the popular politics of the Gandhian Congress and mass movements under the leadership of radical men and women like Nehru, Subhas Bose, and Sarojini Naidu, the intimate interdependence between cultural nationalism and militant political nationalism waned. Gandhi himself was opposed to the practice of child marriage and accepted women's decision to enter Congress movements. Women acquired an equal place in all forms of struggle and women from all social strata joined such movements. Bose encouraged the formation of women's brigades within the Congress and even recruited women soldiers for his Azad Hind Fauj. Nehru promised universal franchise after Independence. Women's organizations, such as the All India Women's Conference—worked in a close relationship with the Congress movement. In the transformed political environment, Indian legislators in the Assembly moved a resolution against child marriage and, in 1929, the Child Marriage Restraint Act was passed without any great difficulty: a significant change from the anti-Age of Consent agitation only thirty years earlier, when a curtailment of premature conjugal cohabitation was seen as a destruction of faith and nation. The new legislative departure was a conjoined effect of the power of women's organization, a more liberal and activist Congress leadership, and the embarrassment and anger caused by a very racist account of Indian marriage practices by the American journalist Katherine Mayo. Significantly, the anger now led to reform initiated by nationalist Indians, not social conservatives.

The nineteenth century had been especially clamorous about Hindu social reforms. The main themes that characterized Hindu social reforms did not constitute problems within Muslim personal laws. These did not demand widow immolation and contained no strictures against widow remarriage. In fact, Faraizi reformers of the mid-nineteenth century attributed the prevalence of such norms among Muslims to Hindu influence, and encouraged Muslims to popularize widow remarriage. Similarly, the opening up of female education in Urdu in North India was undertaken largely to integrate women in seclusion with authentic Islamic teachings and to eradicate female rites and customs that Muslims shared with Hindus. Effects, however, outran original intentions, and, by the turn of the century, Muslim women in North and East India emerged as noted reformers in their own rights, introducing girls' schools, and criticizing absolute female seclusion. Later, a curious and ironic political development enabled further reforms. In the 1930s, as communalism gained ground, the Muslim League sought an entry into Punjab, then governed by the Unionist Party, by espousing scriptural female inheritance rights which, in Punjab, had been undermined in the name of 'tribal custom' among landholders (Hindu, Muslim. and Sikh), which denied land inheritance rights to women. Similar communal motives, once again, granted the right to initiate divorce to Muslim women in 1939. Faced with the threat of female apostasy, religious leaders chose to adopt elements from the Maliki School of Islamic law which was not otherwise practised in India. Communalism created competitive mobilization whereby women emerged as a significant constituency.

Recent historical work offers increasingly wide and complex perspectives, working into their analyses women's agency and the possibilities and constraints that the legal framework simultaneously held. Reforms are reviewed in the light of political change, class and labour patterns, caste movements, and literary and religious processes within the public sphere. Whereas the earlier focus was exclusively on Hindus, the new explorations are undertaken into gender relations and ideologies among all Indian religious communities. So, this is a felicitous moment to reopen discussion of social reforms in the area of gender relations.

We intend to follow up this collection with a subsequent volume on caste and social movements. For that reason, major subordinate-caste and Dalit reformers like Phule, Periyar, and Ambedkar find little or no place in the present work, which remains deliberately centred on middle-class reform. Our focus is on debates and movements around reform, and readers will not find here a comprehensive account of the broader dimensions of gender relationships, women's conditions, and sexuality. Our intention has been for the present to publish a selection of research articles, along with some excerpts from contemporary sources. The Introduction has been kept to a bare minimum to allow space for as large a volume on the subject as seemed possible.

III

The volume consists of research papers (Part A), and excerpts from contemporary documents (Part B).

Part A begins with two essays on widow immolation. Anand Yang provides a thick description and analysis of the practice of sati on the eve of the legal ban in 1829, on the basis of a careful study of the sources. This is followed by one of Lata Mani's very influential, if controversial, contributions, marked by an emphasis on certain basic similarities underlying the premises of British officials, Indian reformers, and Conservatives alike. For all of them, she suggests, the condition of women provided the site, or occasion, for developing a new stress on the textual basis of Hindu religious notions and practices.[10] Readers at this point have been given an opportunity to have a look at some excerpts from Rammohan's tracts against sati (Part B 1). It will be seen that one of these tracts moves away in conclusion from a purely textual exigesis to a powerful, humanistic critique of the everyday conditions of women in Hindu society, utterly remarkable for its times.

The extract by Geraldine Forbes which is placed next is about the education of women, and its far-reaching, and sometimes unexpected, consequences. It includes three case studies of pioneer educationists, two of them women, all of whom, unlike many others, worked independently of religious reform organizations.

This is followed by several essays on the thorny issue of widow marriage, possibly the central theme in the history of reform through much of the nineteenth century. Lucy Carroll studies the way in which the law permitting widow marriage unwittingly restricted the already existing rights to property of widows who remarried among certain subordinate castes, for whom there was no taboo on such unions. It provides data about alternative paths followed subsequently by law courts in various provinces while adjudicating the issue.

Two essays then focus on Vidyasagar and his times. Sekhar Bandopadhyay highlights the strength of orthodox opposition to Vidyasagar's efforts, a dimension which, as already mentioned, has generally been little studied in the historical literature on social reform. Sumit Sarkar attempts a detailed analysis of Vidyasagar's position within Brahmanical society and his reformist endeavours. Prem Chowdhry, like Carroll, focuses upon regional distinctions, where a peculiarly restricted kind of widow marriage was actually encouraged in the Punjab region by officials and menfolk alike, coercing women into levirate practices.

We then come to an essay woven around the outstanding figure of Pandita Ramabai. Gauri Viswanathan provides a sensitive account of the complexities of religious conversion and how these could at times lead to a certain embattled agency for a woman in the interstices between two orthodoxies.

With Chowdhry's essay on the Haryana region (then part of Punjab) and the excerpt about Ramabai, the volume has moved out from its earlier primary focus on Bengal. This widened spatial perspective continues through Madhu Kishwar's study of the specific features of Arya reformism, and John and Karen Leonard's evaluation of the leading Andhra reformer Viresalingam.

We are coming now towards the end of the nineteenth century, when the Age of Consent issue revealed a widespread shift in moods in a revivalist, anti-reform direction. Two essays deal with this controversy. Tanika Sarkar highlights the linkages between the Age of Consent furore and the emergence of an aggressive cultural nationalism which defined itself, from the perspective of women, as a realm of unfreedom rather than of liberty. Padma Anagol looks at the same theme from the perspective of the Bombay Presidency, and, like Carroll and Tanika Sarkar, highlights the importance of judicial archives in the study of social reform.

Five essays that follow move beyond the boundaries of Hindu society. Extracts from Kenneth Jones's survey of socio-religious movements look briefly at a range of late-nineteenth-century movements among Sikhs: the reformist Nirankaris and Namdharis, the Dev Samaj, and the Singh Sabha, the latter similar to the Aryas in its incorporation of reform within a basic emphasis on the purity and distinct identity of Sikhs. This is followed by four papers on Muslim social reform—a largely neglected subject. Gregory Kozlovski looks at rights to property of Muslim women under colonial Anglo-Muslim law. C.M. Naim examines the kind of values being sought to be inculcated among Muslim women through Urdu novels which combined encouragement of education and reading habits with correct morality. Gail Minault probes the rebellious figure of Sayyid Mumtaz Ali (editor of *Tahzib ur-Niswan*), the associate of Sayyid Ahmad Khan who did not share the Aligarh movement founder's conservatism on women's issues. The last essay in this group, by Faisal Devji, attempts an analysis of late-nineteenth-century Muslim movements for women's reform in terms of a *sharif* discourse aimed at setting up firm spatial boundaries around the community.

Four ensuing essays move to new regions and social spaces. Two articles on the South, by S. Anandhi and G. Arunima, deal with the women's question as foregrounded by the early phase of the Dravidian movement in Tamilnadu, and the marked specificities of the situation in Kerala, where the existence of matriliny among the Nairs and the prevalence of the custom of *sambandham* sexual relations meant that reform concentrated on the establishment, rather than the reform, of the patrilineal conjugal family. Virginius Xaxa offers a survey of gender relations among *adivasi* groups in Central and North East India, entered through a review of the historiography around that subject. The article by Saroj Parratt and John Parratt is a case study of a women's movement in the 1940s in Manipur, a region remarkable, down to present times, for the level of initiative and militancy displayed by women in popular movements for freedom and human rights.

Our selection has focused primarily on the nineteenth century, in that way sticking to the conventional stress in the literature so far. But Xaxa and the Parratts have already taken us into the twentieth, and indeed to some extent postcolonial times, and this temporal shift continues through the concluding two articles of Part A. Both focus upon legislative changes and their settings. Mrinalini Sinha looks at the contexts of the 1929 Sarda Act raising the minimum age for marriage. Reba Som examines parliamentary debates in the early postcolonial years and offers a critical review of the legislation that eventually became the present code of Hindu marriage and succession law, a significant advance shot through with the compromises that Nehru eventually agreed to make.

Part B comprises extracts from historical documents. Spatial constraints, along with the obvious problem of language, have made us restrict the number. The most interesting writings, particularly by women, were generally in the vernaculars, and the limits of time and absence of translation facilities have compelled a restriction to articles already in English translation. Within these constraints, and keeping in mind that there is a general, but quite misleading, common sense that women's reform in the nineteenth century consisted entirely of efforts by philanthropically motivated men, we have tried to include articles by reformist women rather than men: three of the extracts, therefore, are by women.

The first, from Rammohan's tracts on *sati*, is followed by passages from a remarkable pamphlet written in the early 1860s in Bengali, by Kailashbasini Devi. This illustrates the point made in the Introduction that women's writings advocating reform were often distinctive in seeking to cover a much wider area of the everyday lives of women and did not rest content with advocating marriage practices reformed through legislation. The next extract is from a work by a much better-known woman polemicist, Tarabai Shinde's *Stripurusha Tulana*. Then there are excerpts from the premier late-nineteenth-century reformer of western India, Mahadev Govind Ranade, who made the Indian Social Conference the main space for his endeavours, seeking to raise the reform question from the provincial to an all-Indian platform. The volume ends with a remarkable essay by Begum Rokeya, 'Nari-puja', 'The Worship of Woman', brilliantly ridiculing the widespread assumption that women have been held in high honour in traditional Hindu and Muslim society through the insistence on seclusion.

Notes

1. The dualism here was neatly expressed by the *Amrita Bazaar Patrika* of 9 December 1869: 'madhyabitta people are always considered the most useful group in any society. Our country's welfare depends to a large extent on this class. If there is ever to be a social or any other revolution in this country, it will be by the middle class. All the beneficial institutions or activities that we see in our country today have been started by this class . . . The livelihood of middle-class people comes from landed property and the services. Middle-class people are often "*gantidars*" [A form of intermediate tenures common in the central Bengal region from which the newspaper was then being published].'
2. Recent research highlighting distinctions within the middle class includes Veena Naregal, *Language Politics, Elites, and the Public Sphere* (Delhi: Permanent Black, 2001); Sumit Sarkar, 'Renaissance and Kaliyuga: Time, Myth and History in Colonial Bengal', in *Writing Social History* (Delhi: Oxford University Press, 1997); Tanika Sarkar, *Hindu Wife, Hindu Nation* (Delhi: Permanent Black, 2001), chapters 1, 2; Tithi Bhattacharya, *The Sentinels of Culture: Class, Education and the Colonial Intellectual in Bengal* (Delhi: Oxford University Press, 2005); Judith Walsh, *Domesticity in Colonial India: What Woman Learned When Men Gave Her Advice* (Delhi: Oxford University Press, 2004); and Anindita Ghosh, *Power in Print: Popular Publishing and the Politics of Language and Culture in a Colonial Society* (Delhi: Oxford University Press, 2006).
3. For Maharashtra, this zone is explored in Meera Kosambi, *Crossing Thresholds: Feminist Essays in Social History* (Delhi: Permanent Black, 2007).
4. This is the very influential argument put forward by Partha Chatterjee, in his 'The Nationalist Resolution of the Woman's Question', in Kumkum Sangari and Sudesh Vaid, eds, *Recasting Women* (New Delhi: Kali for Women, 1989), and *The Nation and Its Fragments*, chapters 6, 7 (Delhi: Oxford University Press, 1994).
5. Jadunath Sarkar, *Dacca University History of Bengal* (Dacca, 1948); S.C. Sarkar, 'Notes on the Bengal Renaissance' (1946), and 'Rabindranath Tagore and the Renaissance in Bengal', reprinted in Sarkar, *Bengal Renaissance and Other Essays* (Delhi: Peoples' Publishing House, 1970).

6. See the essays of Barun De, Asok Sen, Sumit Sarkar, and Pradyumna Bhattacharya in V.C. Joshi (ed.), *Rammohan Roy and the Process of Modernization in India* (New Delhi, 1975); Asok Sen, *Iswarchandra Vidyasagar and His Elusive Milestones* (Calcutta: 1977).
7. Partha Chatterjee, *Nationalist Thought and the Colonial World: A Derivative Discourse?* (Delhi: Oxford University Press, 1986); Chatterjee, *The Nation and Its Fragments*, op. cit.
8. *Recasting Women*, op. cit., particularly its Introduction, by Kumkum Sangari and Sudesh Vaid.
9. One important exception here is Amiya P. Sen, *Hindu Revivalism in Bengal* (Delhi: Oxford University Press, 1993).
10. Lata Mani subsequently developed her argument through her contribution in *Recasting Women*, and finally in her book *Contentious Traditions: The Debate on Sati in Colonial India* (Berkeley: University of California Press, 1998).

PART A

Historical Research

1

Whose Sati?

Widow Burning in Early-Nineteenth-Century India*

ANAND A. YANG

Intentionally interrogatory, the title of this essay emphasizes the speculative nature of my remarks regarding the phenomenon of sati. Derived from the Sanskrit term for pure or chaste (*sat*)—the very term 'sati', therefore, is a misnomer—sati has come to signify both the act of immolation of a wife on the funeral pyre of her husband (in some areas a widow was buried with her deceased husband or took poison) and the victim herself rather than its original meaning of a 'a virtuous woman'.[1] Generally, a woman was burnt together with her deceased husband, a practice termed *sahamarana* or *sahagamanan* (dying together with). But if concremation was not possible, such as when a husband died in a distant place or a woman's pregnancy required that she wait till after delivery, a sati conformed to the practice of *anumarana* or *anugamana*: burning with the husband's ashes or with some other memento representing him, for example, his sandals, turban, or piece of clothing.[2]

The title also has another meaning, a double trajectory: an interrogation of the historical literature on the subject and an interrogation of sati as a practice involving women of different times, places, and backgrounds. Both lines of inquiry seek to converge on the same objective: better questions *and* answers regarding the phenomenon of sati.

*From *Journal of Women's History*, vol. I, no. 2 (Fall 1989): 8–33.

Hitherto, much of the literature on sati has tended to favour an institutional approach.[3] Not surprisingly, the most familiar aspect of sati is the British campaign against it culminating in the promulgation of Regulation XVII in 1829 'declaring the practice of suttee, or of burning or burying alive the widows of Hindus, illegal and punishable by the criminal courts.'[4] Viewed from this angle, the history of sati has been appropriated by some scholars to represent the beginnings of 'a deliberate policy of modernizing and westernizing Indian society', as embodied in the person and policies of Governor-General Lord Bentinck who directed the official campaign against sati, and in the emergence of a Bengal 'Renaissance' under the guiding hand of the 'Father of Modern India', Raja Rammohun Roy, who acted as the Indian architect of this and other social reforms.[5]

The legislative prohibition of sati has also 'become a founding moment in the history of women in modern India.' To continue in the words of this scholar,

> colonial rule, with its moral civilizing claims, is said to have provided the contexts for a thoroughgoing re-evaluation of Indian 'tradition' along lines more consonant with the 'modern' economy and society believed to have been the consequence of India's incorporation into the capitalist world system. In other words, even the most anti-imperialist amongst us has felt forced to acknowledge the 'positive' consequences of colonial rule for certain aspects of women's lives, if not in terms of actual practice, at least at the level of ideas about 'women's rights'.[6]

But as Lata Mani's deconstruction of the colonial discourse on sati reveals, women were neither the subjects nor the object of this discourse, 'but rather the grounds of the discourse on *sati*. . . . For the British, rescuing women becomes part of the civilizing mission. For the indigenous elite, protection of their status or its reform becomes an urgent necessity, in terms of the honor of the collective—religious or national.'[7]

For the political and ideological context in which the government campaign for social reforms was waged, whether focusing on sati, infanticide, *thagi* (ritual murder), or human sacrifice, aimed at entitling the British with the right to proclaim the superiority of their own values, and ultimately, to justify their right to rule. Only they could usher in the morality they found wanting in the indigenous civilization. Consider the tenor of the following government pronouncement on sati:

> Of the rite itself, of its horror and abomination not a word need be said. Every rational and civilized being must feel anxious for the termination of a practice so abhorrent from humanity. . . . But to the Christian and to the Englishman, who by tolerating sanctions, and by sanctioning incurs before God the responsibility of this inhuman and impious sacrifice not of one, but of thousands of victims, these feelings of anxiety must be and ought to be extreme. The whole and sole justification is state necessity—that is, the security of the British empire, and even that justification, would be, if at all, still very incomplete, if upon the continuance of the British rule did not entirely depend the future happiness and improvement of the numerous population of this eastern world.[8]

In part, the prevailing modes of inquiry have fashioned their own blinders because they have not until recently sought to penetrate the purdah of rhetoric imposed on sati, whether that made out of the fabric of discourse woven from the religious ideology sanctioning its practice, or that stitched together from the doctrines of policy makers and reformers seeking its abolition. In part, the peculiar emphases in the literature on sati reflect the predominant orientation of South Asian studies towards conventional political history rather than the 'new' social history.[9]

No wonder the history of sati is still being written—or perhaps better stated, being revised. And the fact that its full reconstruction is only now being attempted reflects not only the biases and limitations of the historical record but also of historians. Enough has been uncovered by the new scholarship to establish, as does the discussion below of sati as 'an invented and reinvented tradition', that the practice can no longer be merely ascribed to and explained away as a 'tradition' rooted in an immemorial past. On the contrary, recent scholarship has treated it more as an 'invented tradition' whose origins can be roughly dated and whose construction, institution, and development can be traced over historical time.

Another perspective, largely absent in the literature, is the focus of the human face of sati: neither the identities of those who committed sati, nor their reasons for seeking 'virtue' in death has received much attention. A notable exception—although raising more questions than providing answers—is the work of Ashis Nandy which unequivocally states that not only did the incidence of sati rise sharply in the late eighteenth century because of the effects of the British presence on certain sectors of Bengali society but also that the considerable surge can be traced to the upper-caste Bengali gentry (*bhadralok*) who resorted to sati as a means of compensating for the social and cultural price they paid for abiding by the new rules established by the British system rather than the traditionally prescribed norms. According to this psychocultural interpretation, 'the rite had anxiety-binding functions in groups rendered psychologically marginal by their exposure to western impact. These groups had come under pressure to demonstrate . . . their ritual purity and allegiance to traditional high culture. To many of them sati became an important proof of their conformity to older norms at a time when these norms had become shaky within.'[10]

This essay will attempt to identify the faces of sati victims by highlighting their social and economic conditions and circumstances. Such a characterization intends to examine the practice of sati as part of the fabric of the local society in which the widows lived, and such a portrait seeks to draw us closer to the subjects themselves and their subjectivity in playing out their lives as satis. Because of limitations of data, however, a complete portrait of the victims is not possible; the best close-up of these otherwise invisible women can only put faces on them, faces whose features can be partially filled in by considering their act as an 'option' bound by economic, social, and religious constraints.[11] The specific reasons for their sacrifice, however, cannot be fully determined from their perspective because their voices have not been preserved in historical documents; in fact, they appear largely as mute objects even in the most detailed of sources—colonial records of the early nineteenth century. Indeed, even their names have been 'grotesquely mistranscribed'. To continue in the words of Gayatri C. Spivak, 'one never encounters the testimony of the women's voice-consciousness. Such a testimony would not be ideology-transcendent or "fully" subjective, of course; but it would have constituted the ingredients for producing a counter sentence. As one goes [through] the records of the East India Company, one cannot put together a "voice".'[12]

In order to develop a more sharply focused portrait, this essay will rely on a local-level perspective based on data from the Bengal Presidency, an area which returned the highest reported cases of sati in British India. An extensive territory stretching across northeastern and northern India, this area (then encompassing the present-day Indian states of West Bengal, Bihar, Orissa, Uttar Pradesh [UP], and the new nation of Bangladesh) also represented a diversity of local contexts because it included several distinct cultural, linguistic, historical, and structural regions. Most studies regarding sati in Bengal have concentrated their attention on Bengal proper, particularly the area focusing on the metropolitan centre of Calcutta—Calcutta Division reported the highest number of satis in the Presidency. This essay, however, will also consider the local contexts of sati in the Gangetic plain area in the western peripheries of the Presidency, the Bhojpur-speaking region. In the Bhojpur districts of Gorakhpur and Ghazipur in UP, Saran and Shahabad in Bihar, and, to a lesser extent, in the premier city of the region, Banaras, the incidence of sati reached such significant proportions that only in Calcutta Division were there a greater number of cases.[13]

The Documentary Basis of Sati

Data exist to compile a portrait, albeit incomplete, of the many faces of sati in the early nineteenth century. As Bayly notes, 'the British obsession with sati was boundless. Thousands of pages of Parliamentary papers were given up to 4,000 immolations while the mortality of millions from disease and starvation was only mentioned incidentally.'[14] But these accounts 'cannot be read as photographic representations of reality' because they reflected the 'anxieties of the new rulers as much as of a practice of the people . . . ruled'.[15]

The documentary basis for this essay is the data collected annually on sati in British India prior to its prohibition in 1829. Drawn from local-level police records, much of the information for the period between 1815 and 1829 was compiled into parliamentary papers for the scrutiny of the authorities in England. District judicial and police records, were they to exist in their entirety, of course, would offer the most comprehensive official inventory of sati cases. Eyewitness accounts of sati can be found both in official reports and in contemporary memoirs and travelogues.

To track the growing British interest in documenting the phenomenon of sati is not only to comprehend the biases of the source materials but also to see the gradual development of a policy. From Poona in western India, from Banaras, and from Shahabad, in 1787, 1788 and 1789, respectively, came the first official reports of widow burning.[16] In response to the Shahabad administrator who had informed the authorities of his intervention in a sati case because he had mistakenly thought that the practice had been disallowed in the Calcutta area, the government spelled out its initial position on sati. Although approving his actions, the government directed him, in future, to 'exert all his private influence to dissuade', but not 'to prevent the observance of it by coercive measures, or by any exertion of his official powers'.[17]

Because official documentation was only kept if a sati raised questions relating to government policy and procedure, or to other matters requiring administrative attention,[18] systematic data do not exist for the early years of British rule although some local officials kept records of incidents they encountered in the course of their administrative rounds. Some sati reports also appeared in other guises. For instance, an 1801 account of a 'desperate affray' involving several hundred armed men in Shahabad, although filed as a record of a 'heinous crime', reports not only of the death of 16 men in the fighting but the subsequent satis of four widows.[19]

Sati surfaced again as an issue in 1803–4 when the missionary William Carey produced reports documenting the incidence of sati in the Calcutta area. Although appalled by the missionary accounts, and eager to prohibit the practice, Governor-General Lord Wellesley deferred taking decisive action in 1805 by turning the matter over for the consideration of the legal authorities.[20]

Until the promulgation of Regulation XVII of 1829, the main principles of the official policy on sati emanated from a directive issued by the Nizamat Adalat (head criminal court) in 1805. In providing the 'guidance' sought by a district magistrate who had rescued a 12-year-old girl from burning with her deceased husband, the Nizamat Adalat refused to outlaw sati on the grounds that such a step was 'impracticable at the present time' and inconsistent 'with the principle invariably observed by the British government, of manifesting every possible indulgence to the religious opinions and prejudices of the natives'. This court also expressed concern about stirring up 'alarm and dissatisfaction in the minds of the Hindoo inhabitants of these provinces'.[21] Nevertheless, it asked judicial officials to secure advance notice of the occurrence of a sati, *then* to depute police officers to proceed personally to the site of the burning in order to ensure that the rite was performed voluntarily and not under the influence of intoxicants or drugs, and to establish that the 'youth' or the 'state of pregnancy' of a widow did not violate the norms of 'tradition'.[22]

In enacting these procedures, however, the government invariably played its hand cautiously, consulting with its Hindu pandits before setting up any rules regulating sati. Thus, the parameters of a 'legal' sati were drawn with the assistance of Pandit 'Ghunesham Surmono' who informed the court: 'Every woman of the four cast[e]s (brahmin, khetry, bues, and soodur) is permitted to burn herself with the body of her husband. . . . No woman having infant children, or being in a state of pregnancy, uncleanness, or under the age of puberty is permitted to burn with her husband; with the following exception, namely, that if a woman having infant children can provide for their support, through the means of another person, she is permitted to burn.'[23]

The issue of sati returned to the political limelight in 1812 when a local administrator sought instructions on 'whether a magistrate ought to take any and what steps to prevent Hindoo females from sacrificing themselves on the funeral piles of their husbands'.[24] The Nizamat Adalat's rejoinder was to revive its 1805 statement—largely a dead letter until then—to redraft the earlier instructions into 'Directions to be issued by Magistrates to the Police Daroghas', and to insert an additional proviso into the Draft specifying 16 years as the age of puberty.[25] The government also took this opportunity to remind local officials of its earlier orders enjoining them to gather information on satis occurring in their jurisdictions.

From a statistical and documentary viewpoint, systematic records begin in 1815 when annual reports on satis indicated name (of widow), age, caste, name and caste of husband, date of burning, name of police jurisdiction, and in a separate column entitled 'Remarks', 'any particular circumstances in the report of the police officers, which may appear to deserve notice'.[26] The 'Remarks' column allowed local officials to note whether or not a sati was legal by government's definition. Beginning in 1821, information was also gathered on the kind of sati committed: sahamarana or anumarana. The purpose behind this directive was to ensure that the customary and legal prohibition (first enacted in 1817) against Brahmin widows committing sati by anumarana was being enforced. Prior to the outright ban in 1829 the British strategy was to restrict the practice by tightening up the definition of a 'legal' sati—a definition for which they invariably sought and received the sanction of their 'authoritative' Indian advisers. In 1821 information on the economic backgrounds of the deceased husband was also collected; by 1824 data on husbands became a regular feature of sati reports.[27]

After the prohibition of sati in 1829, no doubt its practice did not fall into disuse entirely, although government vigilance and enforcement of severe punishments for offenders must have sharply reduced the number. Cases of sati also tapered off dramatically because the official ban on it—notwithstanding the fact that the implementation of legal sanctions was entrusted to a weak administrative infrastructure—proved to be enough of a blow to shake the foundations of an institution that enjoyed greater support in the spirit than in the actual practice; the number of widows who resorted to immolation never amounted to a sizeable proportion of the population. Furthermore, the attack on sati was launched with the active cooperation of Indian reformers. Thus, in the initial years after its prohibition, as police and crime reports indicate, the numbers were quickly down to only one or two in districts where there had formerly been considerably more.[28]

Sati: An Invented and Reinvented Tradition[29]

The Vedas, the religious hymns constituting the earliest literature of the Aryans who arrived in India in the centuries after 1700 BC, reveal no evidence of sati. The Rig Veda, however, refers to an act, appropriately termed a 'mimetic ceremony' where a 'widow lay on her husband's funeral pyre before it was lit but was raised from it by a male relative of her dead husband'.[30] A later, and probably deliberate, mistranslation (perhaps in the sixteenth century) was made in order to attain 'Vedic sanction for the act [of sati] by changing the word *agre*, to go forth into *agneh*, to the fire, in the specific verse.'[31]

That sati was not a practice in vogue in the early Vedic period is also suggested by the occurrences of widow remarriages which, apparently, were not uncommon. Vedic texts, furthermore, indicate the existence of a system of *niyoga* or levirate whereby a widow without male heirs was allowed to marry her husband's brother, an act designed to consolidate property.[32]

Nor is sati featured in the literature that developed in the wake of the Vedas, whether the Hindu expository texts stemming from the period 1,000 to 500 BC or the early Buddhist literature. Sati makes an occasional appearance in the popular religious texts of early Hinduism, the epics, but these are works that developed by continuous accretion over a thousand-year period beginning in the fifth century BC; some of the references to sati, moreover, have been attributed to later interpolations. Nor is there a clear-cut endorsement of sati in the prescriptive literature dating to the beginning of the Christian era. The codes associated with the names of Manu and Yajnavalkya, considered among the most authoritative of Hindu law books, for instance, prescribe austere and chaste lives for widows but issue no specific injunctions for them to become satis. Increasingly, however, in the first millennium AD, for instance, in the popular texts of later Hinduism, the Puranas, sati is mentioned as an option for widows. But so is a life of asceticism; other texts of this period, however, glorified sati.[33]

The 'virtue' of this practice was ostensibly defined by a religious logic that deemed a widow inauspicious for having outlived her husband—an abnormal circumstance said to have been brought about by her sinful nature in this, or a previous, life. A life of ascetic discipline could diminish the stigma with which widowhood branded her, but she was, nevertheless, considered a spiritual hazard to all around her except her own children. Closely related to this idea was the belief that an unattached woman, a woman without a husband, for instance, constituted a grave danger to her community because of the supposedly irrepressible sexual powers she possessed, a capacity which always had the potential to disrupt her ritually prescribed life of austerity. No wonder at least one writer has considered sati 'an expression of the perceived superfluity of women who were considered unmarriageable in a social context where marriage was the only approved status for women'.[34] By becoming a sati, furthermore, a widow not only ended the threat she posed to the spiritual welfare of others but also reaped honour and merit—according to some religious texts enough to last 35 million years—for herself, her husband, and the families of her husband, her mother, and her father.[35]

The fact that sati is not featured in the earliest religious texts and is referred to infrequently in the later literature leading up to the Christian era is supported by historical information that tracks the first instance of sati only back to the fourth century BC. Such a chronology also reflects the changing status of women in Indian society. Although the characterization of the Vedic Age between 1700 and 500 BC as a 'golden age for women' is debatable, the decline in their status in the centuries thereafter is less a matter of dispute. As a recent review of the literature on women in South Asia notes, 'by 500 BC women were increasingly assigned the same low status as *sudras*, forbidden to wear the sacred thread, and excluded from the performance of sacrifice either as priests or as partners with their husbands'.[36]

But to attribute the rise of sati solely to the declining status of women—a position that eventuated ideologically in the model of a dutiful wife and of sati as the ultimate wifely act of duty—is to overstate the equation; nor does it adequately explain its uneven geographical spread. Just as sati lacked clearcut scriptural authority, so too did the paradigm of dutiful wife that represented only one construct of the feminine in Hindu ideology and, at that, one emanating from the priestly tradition of Brahmanic Hinduism. Hinduism, 'a composite of religious traditions in which diverse philosophical, sectarian, and cultic movements are loosely associated', has historically comprised two distinct ideological traditions: 'brahmanic Hinduism [that] has tended to objectify and exclude women . . . [and] nonbrahmanic Hindu traditions [that] have tended to provide for full recognition and active participation by women'.[37]

Furthermore, as Romila Thapar states, although the beginning of sati can be 'traced to the subordination of women in patriarchal society', changing 'systems of kinship and inheritance' and '[c]ontrol over female sexuality' were also factors in the rise of widow immolation. Moreover, the 'practice may have originated among societies in flux and become customary among those holding property such as the families of chiefs and kshatriyas. Once it was established as a custom associated with the kshatriyas it would continue to be so among those claiming kshatriya status as well'.[38]

Principally associated with high status and rank during its early history, particularly with families of kingly or warrior (Kshatriya) status or those aspiring for such status, sati, according to another version, became more widespread during the Muslim period when invasions and conquests precipitated its development as a means of preserving the honour of Hindu women. Its rise, in this interpretation, is therefore typically linked to 'wars of conquest and their inevitable toll on the women of the defeated groups'.[39] But evidence exists from western and southern India indicating that women were becoming satis in appreciable numbers well before the advent of Muslim rule; in some areas, the peaks in numbers were reached in the pre-Islamic period. According to one scholar, inscriptional and archaeological sources, including sati stones erected at the sites of immolation, suggest that the practice was increasing towards the end of the first and the beginning of the second millennium AD. This rise, moreover, occurred in areas characterized by internal conquests and competition, often involving traditional castes, newly emergent castes, and tribal groups. In this setting, competition for status may have made upper-caste practices such as sati more prevalent. That is, sati became valorized as a practice—a practice emphasizing the subordination of women—as groups with different conceptions regarding the status of women encountered one another. Thus, widow immolation 'may have been . . . a method of demarcating status'.[10]

The spread of sati across caste boundaries must also have been generated by Sanskritization—the process whereby lower castes aspire for higher position by emulating the 'customs, rituals, ideology, and way of life' of higher castes. Although the effect of Sanskritization is evident from the enormous range of castes who performed sati, the practice never became generalized throughout the subcontinent but was confined to certain areas: in the north, particularly to the Gangetic Valley, Punjab, and Rajasthan; in the west, to the southern Konkan region; and in the south, to Madurai and Vijayanagar.[41]

Whether its rise can be attributed to groups aspiring for Kshatriya status or of lower castes emulating the rituals of higher castes, sati clearly developed as a reinvented tradition, a tradition no longer confined to warrior widows whose husbands had died in battle. A crucial development in this regard may have been its adoption by Brahmins who, according to some religious texts, were specifically prohibited from taking up this practice.[42] Perhaps the Brahmin appropriation of this warrior practice represented yet another round in the ongoing 'inner conflict of tradition' that J.C. Heesterman regards as the 'pivot of Indian tradition': the 'irreconcilability of "brahmin" and king", who yet are dependent on each other, for the king will need the transcendent legitimation that only the brahmin can give. But the brahmin, however much he may need the king's material support, cannot enter into relations with the king, for this would involve him in the world of interdependence—a situation that would be fatal to the brahmin's transcendence.'[43] Surely, with the practice rooted in both the kingly and Brahmanical traditions, its constituency must have grown rapidly across spatial and social boundaries.

Certainly, in Bengal, where sati dates back to at least the twelfth century AD, Brahmins figured prominently among its practitioners. But from very early on, as vernacular sources indicate, it was not restricted to Brahmins, but observed by both upper and lower castes.[44] Perhaps its rise in Bengal was not unrelated to the growing reliance on marriage in the period between 1450 and 1800 as 'the way to sustain rank and the path to fame [for upper castes—Brahmins and Kayasths]'.[45] And, as the emphasis on marriage intensified, so must have the importance of sati as its structural concomitant. Not surprisingly, Brahmins took to this practice in great numbers; so did merchants and the writer caste of Kayasths who sought to emulate the ritual observances of the Brahmins. And once elevated to new heights as a status-conferring ritual, the next step was its practice by lower—artisan and entrepreneurial—castes who saw it as an avenue for attaining prestige and status in society.[46]

A practice once tied to the warrior ideal of the Kshatriya thus became a tradition appropriated by all of society. But in the process of widening its constituency, as the evidence from Bengal shows, sati emerged as a reinvented tradition. How novel the reinvented tradition was—assuming that the old tradition really was guided by a heroic ideal—is apparent from looking at sati in its 'new' context, a context in which it figures as an 'option' bound by the economic, social, and religious constraints of widowhood.[47]

Sati: Subjects and Subjectivity

Abraham Caldecott, writing in 1783, stated that had he not seen a sati with his own eyes he would 'have been apt to doubt the veracity of it, but the fact is so well established, and so many instances of the like nature have occurred . . . as leaves no doubt of the generality of the Practice all over Bengal'.[48] A few 'hard' estimates reinforce this impression of the 'generality of the Practice' for the pre-1815 period. William Carey's investigations in a 30-mile radius of Calcutta in 1803–4 showed that as many as 438 widows had committed sati over a 12-month period.[49] District records can also provide some information for the pre-1815 years, but if the numbers for Saran are any indication, these may not be reliable. For 1812, 1813, and 1814, Saran returned one, two, and five cases—a far cry from the 15 noted for 1815 when the administrative machinery was geared to the task of collecting such information. In the magistrate's words, the police did not pay attention 'to cases of this nature, and it is most probable that a small part only of those that actually took place . . . were reported.'[50] Much more consonant with later statistics is the estimate for Burdwan district that 114 cases occurred in 1811–12 and 1812–13.[51] Statistical investigations conducted in Bengal at roughly this same period reported an average of 25 satis a year for Shahabad and 13 for Gorakhpur.[52]

In the 10 years between 1815 and 1824, 6,632 cases of sati were reported for the three Presidencies of Bengal, Bombay, and Madras. Of these, 5,997 (90.4 per cent) occurred in Bengal.[53] In the 14 years between 1815 and 1828 (Table 1), a grand total of 8,134 cases of satis were reported for the Bengal Presidency. But as the data reveal, the practice was not uniformly observed across the region but predominated in specific areas. The division of Calcutta alone accounted for 5,119 cases, or almost 63 per cent of the Presidency total, followed by Banaras, Dacca, and Patna divisions in a distant second, third, and fourth position, respectively.

Further geographical breakdown of these figures shows (Table 2) that sati was practised throughout the districts of Calcutta Division,

Table 1: Sati Cases in Bengal Presidency, 1815–28

Division	1815	1816	1817	1818	1819	1820	1821	1822	1823	1824	1825	1826	1827	1828	Total
Calcutta*	253	289	442	544	421	370	392	328	340	373	398	324	337	308	5119
Dacca	31	24	52	58	55	51	52	45	40	40	101	65	49	47	710
Murshidabad	11	22	42	30	25	21	11	22	13	14	21	8	9	10	260
Patna†	20	29	49	57	40	42	59	70	49	42	38	43	55	55	689
Banaras	48	65	103	137	92	93	114	102	121	93	64	70	49	33	1153
Bareilly	15	13	19	13	17	20	15	16	12	10	17	8	18	10	203
Total	378	442	707	839	650	597	654	583	575	572	639	518	517	463	8134

Source: Compiled from Great Britain, Parliament, *Parliamentary Papers* (hereafter *PP*), *1821*, *1823*, *1824*, *1825*, *1826/27*, *1830*; Amitabha Mukhopadhyay, 'Sati as a Social Institution in Bengal,' *Bengal Past and Present* 76 (1951): 106.

*Includes the numbers for the Orissan 'districts' of Cuttack, Khurda, Puri, and Balasore, which then formed part of Calcutta Division. The totals for these districts varied from 9 in 1815 to a high of 45 in 1825.

†The tallies for Gorakhpur have been retained in the Banaras totals although that district was transferred to Patna Division in 1824.

Table 2: Sati Cases in Districts of Bengal Presidency, 1815–26

Presidency Division	1815	1816	1817	1818	1819	1820	1821	1822	1823	1824	1825	1826	Average
Burdwan	50	67	98	132	75	57	62	40	45	56	63	45	66
Hughli	72	51	112	141	115	93	95	79	81	91	104	98	94
Jessore	7	13	21	23	16	25	31	21	14	30	16	3	18
Jungle Mehals	34	39	43	61	31	18	39	24	27	16	9	11	29
Midnapur	4	11	7	22	13	12	6	16	15	22	22	15	14
Nadia	50	56	85	80	47	59	59	50	59	79	60	44	61
Suburbs of Calcutta	25	40	39	43	52	47	39	43	46	34	48	35	41
24-Parganas	2	3	20	31	39	26	33	25	21	22	26	20	22
Cuttack†	9	9	14	11	33	33	28	27	30	24	30	45	24
Dacca Division													
Dacca City	4	6	18	25	15	18	26	9	14	7	18	12	14
Tipperah	20	7	13	22	21	17	11	6	9	6	8	4	12
Bakarganj	no figures available				6	3	3	18	11	28	63	45	21
Patna Division													
Saran	12	16	25	23	10	11	15	12	7	12	15	10	14
Shahabad	4	9	14	25	17	19	39	36	30	18	20	22	21
Banaras Division													
Banaras City	13	12	16	15	18	11	12	10	18	16	17	15	14
Ghazipur	8	15	27	43	26	34	35	48	55	33	21	19	30
Gorakhpur	14	23	24	50	23	32	44	28	32	17	9	22	26

Source: Compiled from *PP, 1821, 1823, 1824, 1825, 1826/27, 1830.*

but unevenly elsewhere. In the predominantly Muslim Dacca Division in east Bengal, it was primarily confined to Dacca City, Tipperah, and Bakarganj—areas with large Hindu populations; in Banaras, the highest incidence was in Ghazipur and Gorakhpur; and in Patna Division, in Saran and Shahabad. Indeed, 90 per cent of the total cases reported for the Presidency occurred in the nine jurisdictions of Calcutta Division (which included Cuttack at this time) and the above-mentioned areas of east Bengal, UP, and Bihar.

Notwithstanding the bold arguments of Ashis Nandy, little evidence exists to suggest that a considerable surge in the incidence of sati occurred beginning in the late eighteenth century. That sati increased with the coming of the British rests on a statistical inference for which Nandy can muster little evidence other than to refer to a few contemporary observations to that effect. Not only is the pre-1815 data scanty, but even the usable 'hard numbers' are fraught with problems. Although sati was by its very nature a public art—for 'virtue' in that practice lay in part in exposing it to the gaze of a crowd—the emerging colonial government simply did not possess the administrative apparatus to extend far into any locality and, certainly, not to maintain a regular presence in the interior. Furthermore, with much of the personnel of the incipient Raj lodged in cities, and in a major town or two in localities where there were no cities, reporting was only as good as the administrative infrastructure. In short, the inherent biases built into the system of reporting favoured better coverage for towns than countryside, and, not surprisingly, nowhere was official representation better than in the heart of the emerging empire—Calcutta. Indeed, in some districts, away from metropolitan centres, local officials did not even make their first visit into the interior until 1815![54]

The social geography of sati (see Table 2) also indicates that the practice was not confined to the Calcutta area, but also prevailed in such districts far removed from the seat of the Presidency as Ghazipur, Gorakhpur, Saran, and Shahabad. Furthermore, to consider sati as an urban-based phenomenon centred on Calcutta ignores the sizeable territorial dimensions of Calcutta Division. Nandy's critics have rightly noted that even Raja Rammohan Roy's family village 'which may nowadays feel like "greater Calcutta" . . . is about sixty miles away as the crow flies, and before the railway age, when that distance took many hours to traverse, it was considered quite another area'.[55]

To explain the higher incidence of sati in the Calcutta area, Nandy offers a cultural analysis emphasizing that city's close integration into the British system and its urbanness, characteristics he contrasts with other parts of India where the practice was less common. Thus, he concludes that 'the rite was prevalent among passive people and not among the "bold and manly" type', an assertion which prompts him to emphasize 'the difference between the exposed easterners [Bengalis], feeling increasingly impotent ritually, and the unexposed northern and western parts of India, still mainly outside direct British rule and yet undisturbed in their traditional life style. It was also noticed by others that there had been only one instance of the wife of a dead Indian soldier of the colonial army committing sati.'[56] In elaborating on why he considers only one case of sati by a sepoy's wife 'crucial', Nandy writes:

> given that (1) traditionally sati had been associated with the so-called martial races, (2) the British Indian Army was drawn almost entirely from these races, and (3) the earlier epidemics of sati (such as the one in Rajasthan towards the end of the Mughal period and the one in South India during the decline of the Vijayanagar kingdom) had a clear kshatriya (martial or princely caste) connection. Offset these against the facts that Bengal did not have a proper kshatriya caste and that the region was marginal to mainstream Hinduism, and one is forced to conclude that the eighteenth century epidemic of sati was not a pure product of traditions and that it drew upon a different configuration of political, cultural and psychological forces.[57]

The post-1823 sati reports, which contain information on the profession of deceased husbands, however, do not support the assertion that only one dead sepoy's wife committed sati. Since the 'martial races' recruited into the Bengal Army were drawn not from the heart of the Presidency but from the Bhojpur region, it is in the data for those areas that the best prospects lie for finding cases of sati among the widows of sepoys. The information for Shahabad—a district which supplied a considerable number of men for the military—does not disappoint. Names of sepoy widows who burnt themselves appear repeatedly on its sati rosters: in 1824 Mussamut Dela, wife of Naik Tiwari, Brahmin, and M. Somerin, wife of Sahi Rai; in 1825 Nagbansi, wife of Adhir Singh, Rajput, Jethun, wife of Bissambhar Ojha, Brahmin and Hisabea, wife of Raghubans Rai, Bhumihar Brahmin; in 1826 Musst. Fakania, Rajput, Musst. Dhupia, Rajput and Musst. Abhi Lakhi, Brahmin.[58]

Nandy may be right, however, in insisting that sati was rooted in a different tradition in the region of Bengal focusing on Calcutta. Certainly, the notion of sati in the Bhojpur region seems to have had much of a 'kshatriya connection' as evidenced not only in the roster of victims above but also in the above-mentioned account of a 'desperate affray' in Shahabad in which 16 men were killed and four widows committed sati subsequently. Consider also the place of pride given to the tradition of sati in the Choudhary family, a Patna family of Bhumihar Brahmins with a long history of military service.[59]

Some scholars have also sought to relate the high incidence of sati (and female infanticide) in Bengal to the extreme hypergamy of the higher castes (*kulinism*), the practice whereby women of high castes had to marry men of equivalent or higher status. Presumably, this practice so restricted the pool of appropriate bridegrooms that a few eligible high-caste males were able to accumulate many, often young, wives for whom the demise of their husband left no choice but for them to commit sati. The evidence regarding the geographical distribution of sati in Bengal, however, offers little conclusive proof because rates of sati were higher in the west than in the east (more in Calcutta than in Dacca Division), whereas kulinism was more predominant in the east than in the west.[60]

Another argument has been to relate the high incidence of sati to the existing system of law in Bengal, the Dayabhaga school of law. In contrast to the Mitakshara school of law, the Dayabhaga school allowed widows greater access to their deceased husbands' property for support although it did not favour their rights of inheritance. Whereas this 'might have encouraged heirs to do away with widows or to pressurize them into suicide' and may therefore explain the 'numbers of satis in Bengal by comparison with other parts of India . . . it hardly explains the great variation of incidence between the different districts and cities of Bengal'.[61]

Some correspondence can be established, however, between the incidence of sati and mortality rates: 'There is no doubt that the rite was a primitive Malthusian means of population control in famine-ridden Bengal. Previously, high mortality rates and prohibition of remarriage of widows had helped the society to limit the number of mothers to below the level of available fertile women. However, at times of scarcity, these controls became inadequate and . . . the widows at certain levels of consciousness seemed "useless" drags on resources.'[62] But if sati were 'a Malthusian form of population control, stimulated by a series of crop failures and widespread famines', as G. Morris Carstairs notes, 'it would surely have resulted in higher rates among the poorer castes, less well protected against starvation, than among the gentry.'[63]

Much more significant is the correlation between changing rates of sati and shifts in mortality rates due to epidemics. Consider especially the increase in numbers of sati during peak years of cholera epidemics: in Bengal this occurred in 1817 and 1818 when cholera had a devastating effect on mortality rates (see Table 1). The close correspondence between the geography of the epidemic and sati rates in affected districts further demonstrates this correlation. Note that the unusual rise in cases of sati in 1817 and 1818 was registered primarily in Calcutta Division—in and around Calcutta, Burdwan, Jessore, Nadia, and 24-Parganas—precisely those areas that were also the most seriously afflicted by cholera.[64] In other parts of the Presidency, too, where increases, although not on a par with those for Calcutta Division, were registered for 1817 and 1818, local officials attributed the rise 'to the mortality occasioned by the epidemic'.[65] Much the same conclusion was reached by the Banaras magistrate who plotted the rise in sati cases in his city in 1823, 1824, and 1825 with the 'extreme sickness and mortality' of those years.[66] Similarly, the noticeable increase in satis in Dacca Division in 1825, especially in Bakarganj (see Table 1), was attributed 'to the excessive mortality which occurred in the district, owing to the prevalence of cholera morbus'.[67]

According to an official report in 1824, the annual death rate in the Bengal Presidency (total population 50 million people) was one in 33, that is, approximately 1,500,000 people. A sixth of this total, or 250,000, represented the number of Hindu women who became widows. Rounding out to 600 the figure for those who burned themselves that year, the number of immolations constituted only 0.2 per cent of the overall number of widows.[68] By this calculation, the incidence of sati in Hughli, the district consistently reporting the highest number of cases in British India, added up to 1.2 per cent.[69]

Perhaps Banaras provides the best illustration of the limited incidence of sati, especially when the practice of sati is viewed against a backdrop of that city's reputation as a place to which 'large numbers of elderly people . . . [came] specifically to die . . . and so achieve immediate salvation'.[70] Thus, the Banaras magistrate noted with surprise—and in an obvious ethnocentric manner—that only 125 cases had occurred in the nine years between 1820 and 1828.

> Benares is one of the most sacred homes of Hinduism . . . in it the bigotry of the people is nurtured . . . it is peopled by the wealthiest and most scrupulous of Hindus . . . inhabited by crowds of every description of religious enthusiasts, the place where every Hindu is anxious to die, and the resort of all classes of rank of all ages, more especially those whose earthly career is drawing to its close. . . . At such a place then it would be expected the performance of this most inhuman rite would be frequent, and that its frequency would be in proportion to the peculiar sanctity of the spot, a sanctity immemorially acknowledged.[71]

The practice of sati, in short, was not only peculiar to certain regions of the subcontinent, but within those particular areas, taken up by only a small fraction of the widows. Although difficult to verify because the data say little about kinship ties between satis, this restricted scope of the rite probably indicates, as many scholars suspect, that it was a practice that must have been a tradition only in certain lineages.[72] The Choudhary family of Patna, for instance, honour and worship, 'along with their family gods', two satis, wives of one of their ancestors who 'immolated themselves on the funeral pyre at their Patna house on hearing of the death of their husband on the battlefield. . . . It is still believed that the lineage which was threatened at that time with extinction continues through their blessing.'[73]

Another aspect of the identity of sati victims in the early nineteenth century that explains the phenomenon better is their caste and economic backgrounds. Contrary to the conventional wisdom regarding the high-caste status of sati victims, a different portrait emerges from a close examination of the detailed information. Of the 575 cases reported in 1823, 234 were Brahmins (41 per cent), 35 Kshatriyas (six per cent), 14 Vaishyas (2 per cent), and 292 Sudras (51 per cent).[74]

That this configuration of nearly even representation of both high and low castes was not uncommon is also borne out by the figures for individual districts. Of the 52 victims in 24-Parganas in 1819, 20 were Brahmins, 10 Kayasthas, and two Vaidyas, and the rest comprising such low castes as Sadgope, Jogi, Kaivarta, Kansari, Suri, and Ahir (Goalla). The 141 cases enumerated for Hughli district in 1818 reveal a similar composition: other than 40 Brahmins, 26 Kayasthas, and 4 Vaidyas, the remaining 71 were of the lower castes.[75] The diversity of caste backgrounds of sati victims also shows up clearly in the details regarding the Bhojpur districts of Ghazipur, Gorakhpur, Saran, and Shahabad. While Saran's numbers include a disproportionately higher percentage of high-caste women among its satis, the figures for the other three districts conform more closely with those for the rest of the Presidency. But in Saran, too, lower-caste women followed the practice. Noticeably present among the 168 satis in that district between 1815 and 1826 are two Harijans (Untouchables): in 1816 Punbosia Chamar, the wife of Jodhi, and in 1818, Dukhni Chamar, the wife of Dohari. Such diversity in the caste composition of sati victims certainly does not authenticate Nandy's characterization of sati as the expression of a rudderless upper-caste Bengal gentry seeking to anchor themselves in a period of flux by resorting to the 'traditional' practice of sati.

The caste backgrounds of satis in Banaras city, however, add up to a different picture. An overwhelming majority were upper caste, particularly Brahmins. In 1821 all 12 satis were upper caste (11 Brahmins and one Rajput); only in 1816 and 1820 did the proportion fall below 70 per cent (66 and 63 per cent, respectively). No doubt, the caste profile for this city is skewed by the fact that people from other areas of the subcontinent converged on it to die there. Not surprisingly, then, many 'foreigners' stand out among the roster of sati victims, including such typically Bengali names as Biswas, Mukherjee, Chakravarty, Bhattacharya, and Banerjee, as well as the well-known Maratha name of Joshi and even a 'Moorleedhur', identified as a former resident of Nepal.[76]

Table 3: Caste Composition of Sati Victims in Bhojpur Districts, 1815–1826

	1815	1816	1817	1818	1819	1820	1821	1822	1823	1824	1825	1826
Ghazipur Upper Caste	2	7	13	19	14	17	13	16	32	25	13	13
% of total	(25)	(46)	(48)	(42)	(50)	(50)	(37)	(34)	(54)	(75)	(61)	(68)
Gorakhpur Upper Castes	8	16	14	28	14	16	24	15	18	14	7	16
% of total	(57)	(69)	(58)	(56)	(60)	(50)	(54)	(53)	(56)	(82)	(77)	(72)
Saran Upper Castes	8	12	11	3	6	7	12	9	6	6	12	6
% of total	(73)	(63)	(79)	(57)	(60)	(64)	(80)	(75)	(86)	(50)	(80)	(60)
Shahabad Upper Castes	1	5	9	13	9	11	29	21	18	10	13	12
% of total	(25)	(56)	(64)	(52)	(50)	(58)	(51)	(58)	(60)	(55)	(65)	(55)

Source: Compiled from *PP*, *1821*, *1823*, *1824*, *1825*, *1826/27*, *1830*.

A different light on the practice of sati is also cast by analysing the ages of its victims. Whereas many studies have tended to emphasize the young ages of widows in any given year, almost half of them were 50 and over, and two-thirds 40 years and more (see Table 4). In 1818, out of 839 cases 123, or 14.6 per cent, were 70 and over; but only 98, or 11.6 per cent, aged 25 or under. The overwhelming majority, as in other years, were 40 years and more. As the official report concluded in presenting these statistics, 'a great proportion of these acts of self-devotion have not taken place in youth, or even in the vigor of age; but a period when life, in the common course of nature, must have been near its close'.[77]

Almost every district also yields examples of women who had not only reached a ripe old age but who immolated themselves long after their husbands' demises. To draw on illustrations from Ghazipur's 1822 cases: 60-year-old Jhunia committed sati 15 years after her husband passed away; 70-year-old Karanja 40 years after her husband's death; 80-year-old Bhujagan 25 years after her husband's death; and 70-year-old Hulasi immolated herself on the funeral pyre of her son, 16 years after her husband Niamdhar Tiwari had died.[78] Equally striking are cases from other Bhojpur districts: Lagni burnt herself at the age of 90, 25 years after the death of her husband; Namao ascended the funeral pyre at the age of 80 following the absence of her husband, presumed dead, for a period of 15 years.[79]

Such characteristics of its victims suggest that sati was a form of ritual suicide[80] conditioned at least in part by personal considerations. The economic conditions of many widows further underscores this colouring. Data collected on satis from 1822 onwards reveal that many widows came from impoverished families. Of the 40 cases reported for Burdwan in 1822, only three or four of the deceased 'left any considerable property . . . the greater proportion were in a state of poverty'. Similar observations were filed for other districts that year: Hughli's 79 satis followed 25 husbands who had died in 'opulent circumstances, thirteen in middling, and forty-one in poor circumstances'; Bakarganj's 18 cases involved only five deceased husbands who were 'in respectable circumstances, all the rest died indigent'.[81]

The high representation of poor widows who took their lives after the demise of their husbands is again borne out by the statistics for

Table 4: Age Composition of Sati Victims in Bengal Presidency in 1825 and 1826

	0–19	20–9	30–9	40–9	50–9	60–9	70–9	80–9	90–9	100+	Total
1825	17 (2.7)	98 (15.3)	104 (16.3)	122 (19.1)	110 (17.2)	112 (17.5)	46 (7.2)	26 (4.1)	3 (.5)	1 (.1)	639 100%
1826	20 (4)	104 (20)	70 (13.5)	77 (14.9)	84 (16.2)	81 (15.6)	53 (10.2)	24 (4.6)	3 (.6)	2 (.4)	518 100%

Source: Compiled from *PP*, 1830, vol. 28, pp. 113–18, 208–13.

1823. Hughli's 81 cases involved 37 husbands who were 'poor, sixteen in middling, and twenty-four in opulent circumstances'; Jessore's 14 incidents involved six husbands in 'good [condition], three in middling, and five in bad circumstances'; Jungle Mehals' 27 cases included 10 said to be 'poor, the rest were generally in moderate circumstances'; and 'the greater part' of the 31 cases in Cuttack 'appear to have been in low circumstances'.[82]

Much the same conclusions regarding the advanced age and impoverished conditions of sati victims emerges from the information collected for 1826 when almost every district report turned in full details on these subjects. Burdwan's report on 45 satis referred to women who 'generally speaking . . . have attained mature ages, and their deceased husbands to have been in low circumstances'; Hughli's 98 cases evoked the observation that the 'greater proportion of the husbands appear to have been in poor or middling circumstances'; Nadia's 45 'female sacrifices . . . [involved] parties . . . for the most part . . . in poor circumstances; and the widows were, generally speaking, of an advanced age'.[83]

Furthermore, even in the best of circumstances, the practice of sati was shaped by other considerations. For it existed in a milieu in which widowhood was regarded as the final and lowest stage in the life of a woman, a stage sometimes termed 'cold sati'.[84] In other words, a widow was regarded as 'a marginal entity in society':

> She was not allowed to wear the insignia of her active married state, that is, her clothes and her jewelery, but wore rags. In some cases her hair was shorn. She was not permitted to partake in family meals, could only sleep on the ground and in all ways was kept separate from the active social world of the living. She was treated by the family and the rest of society as unclean, and polluting, and her marginality was enforced by these pollution taboos. She was expected to devote the rest of her life to asceticism and worship of the gods, especially Siva, and her dead husband.[85]

Thus, viewed from the perspective of widows in early nineteenth-century India, the 'option' of becoming a sati was not only conditioned by their economic and social circumstances but also by the 'virtue they earned in gaining long-term spiritual rewards for themselves and their families and by the deliverance they attained by closing out their lives as the 'symbolically dead,'[86] a role to which they were consigned. As an alternative to life as a 'cold sati', a life of marginal existence and symbolic death that was made more precarious for many by advancing age and poverty, self-immolation was an act of ritual suicide that terminated their 'after lives' of certain misery as widows.[87]

Notes

This is a much travelled essay that has benefited from many readings and suggestions. An excerpt from an earlier version appeared in *Manushi* 42–3 (1987): 26–9.

1. This essay follows the now common usage of the term to refer to both the act of widow burning as well as the woman victim. To differentiate between the two, some writers use suttee, the Anglicized term for sati, to refer to the practice and sati to the victim. E.g., see V.N. Datta, *Sati: A Historical, Social and Philosophical Enquiry into the Hindu Rite of Widow Burning* (New Delhi: Manohar, 1988), 1. See also Datta, *Sati*, 2, regarding the prevalence of widow immolation in other parts of the world.
2. Edward Thompson, *Suttee* (Boston: Houghton Mifflin, 1928), 15; Upendra Thakur, *The History of Suicide in India: An Introduction* (Delhi: Munshiram Manoharlal, 1963), 141–2.
3. E.g., see Thompson, *Suttee*; R.K. Saxena, *Social Reforms: Infanticide and Sati* (New Delhi: Trimurti Publications, 1975); Amitabha Mukhopadhyay, 'Sati as a Social Institution in Bengal', *Bengal Past and Present* 76 (1951): 99–105.
4. 'Sati: Regulation XVII, AD 1829 . . . ',in *The Correspondence of Lord William Cavendish Bentinck, vol. 1: 1828–1831*, ed. C.H. Philips (Oxford: Oxford University Press, 1977), 360.
5. John Rosseli, *Lord William Bentinck: The Making of a Liberal Imperialist, 1774–1839* (Brighton: Sussex University Press, 1974), 208–14; Rajat K. Ray, 'Introduction', in *Rammohun Roy and the Process of Modernization in India*, ed. V.C. Joshi (Delhi: Vikas, 1975), 1–20.
6. Lata Mani, 'Contentious Traditions: The Debate on Sati in Colonial India', *Cultural Critique* (1987): 119–20.
7. Ibid., 153. British attitudes towards sati were also characterized by a 'deep ambivalence'. See Veena Das, 'Gender Studies, Cross-Cultural Comparison and the Colonial Organization of Knowledge', *Berkshire Review* 58 (1986): 68.
8. 'Government circular on sati addressed to military officers', 10 Nov. 1828, in *Correspondence of Bentinck*, 91.
9. Hanna Papanek, 'False Specialization and the Purdah of Scholarship—A Review Article', *Journal of Asian Studies* 44 (1984): 127–48. A significant

departure from the conventional modes of interpretation is the work of Lata Mani (cited in notes 6 and 47).

10. Ashis Nandy, 'Sati: A Nineteenth Century Tale of Women, Violence and Protest', in *Rammohun Roy*, ed. Joshi, 174–5.
11. See Helena Znaniecka Lopata, ed., *Widows*, 2 vols (Durham: Duke University Press, 1987), for a study emphasizing the significance of the social context of widowhood in shaping the 'after life' of widows in positive or negative ways. Also see Betty Potash, ed., *Widows in African Societies: Choices and Constraints* (Stanford: Stanford University Press, 1986) for an anthropological analysis of the lives of widows and their options, choices, and strategies.
12. See Gayatri C. Spivak, 'Can the Subaltern Speak? Speculations on Widow-Sacrifice', *Wedge* 7/8 (1985): 120–30, for a provocative discussion of the 'muting' of subaltern women in the colonial discourse.
13. On the Bhojpur region, see Gyan Pandey, 'Rallying Round the Cow: Sectarian Strife in the Bhojpur Region, c. 1888–1917', in *Subaltern Studies II: Writings on South Asian History and Society*, ed. Ranajit Guha (Delhi: Oxford University Press, 1983), 60–129. See also Robert I. Crane, ed., *Regions and Regionalism in South Asian Studies: An Exploratory Study* (Duke University, Monograph and Occasional Paper Series, Monograph No. 5, 1967).
14. C.A. Bayly, 'From Ritual to Ceremony: Death Ritual and Society in Hindu North India since 1600', in *Mirrors of Morality: Studies in the Social History of Death*, ed. Joachim Whaley (New York: St. Martin's Press, 1981), 174.
15. Das, 'Gender and Colonial Knowledge', 69.
16. Great Britain, Parliament, *Parliamentary Papers* (hereafter *PP*) (Commons), *1821*, vol. 1, 3–22.
17. Ibid., 22.
18. See, e.g., Magistrate, Nadia, to Secty., Judicial, 30 Oct. 1803, Bengal Criminal Judicial Consultations, 5 Nov. to 29 Dec. 1803, 3 Nov., no. 10.
19. Collector, Shahabad, to Board of Revenue, 29 Sept. 1801, Bengal Revenue Consultations, 2 Sept. to 29 Oct. 1801, Oct. 22, no. 13.
20. Thompson, *Suttee*, 61.
21. Acting Register of the Nizamat Adalat (N.A.) to Secty., Judicial, 5 June 1806, in *PP, 1821*, vol. 18, 27.
22. Police officers were also ordered to submit information on sati cases in their monthly reports to the magistrates, ibid., 28.
23. In the four-fold division of Aryan society, Brahmins or priests constituted the highest order followed by Kshatriyas or warriors, Vaishyas or merchants and artisans, and Sudras or serfs. According to this pandit, if a woman reneged on her intention to commit sati before pronouncing the *sankalpa*, or resolution to die, she faced no punishments. However, if she had already announced her sankalpa and performed other ceremonies but refused to

ascend the funeral pyre, then her decision could only be rectified by her 'undeıgoing a severe penance'. 'Question to the Pundit the Nizamut Adawlut', in ibid., 28–9.

24. Magistrate, Bundelkhand, to Register, N.A., 3 Aug. 1813, ibid., 32.
25. Register, N.A., to Chief Secty., 11 March 1813, ibid.
26. *PP, 1821*, vol. 18, 44.
27. *PP, 1823*, vol. 17, 7–26; *PP, 1824*, vol. 23, 76; *PP, 1825*, vol. 24; *PP, 1826/27*, vol. 20. A column entitled 'Profession, and Circumstances of the Husband' was added to the 1824 report.
28. Commissioner, Patna, to Secty., Judicial, 15 Oct. 1834, Bengal Criminal Judicial Consultations, 26 Jan. to 9 Feb. 1836, 26 Jan, no. 22.
29. This section draws on the highly suggestive and provocative ideas of Eric Hobsbawm, 'Introduction: Inventing Traditions', in *The Invention of Tradition*, ed. Hobsbawm and Terence Ranger (Cambridge: Cambridge University Press, 1983), 1–14.
30. Romila Thapar, 'In History', *Seminar* 342 (1988): 15. See also the other essays in this important and informative special issue on sati.
31. Ibid. Whether or not sati was referred to and endorsed by the Vedas is a subject of some disputation. See, e.g., Datta, *Sati*, 2–3.
32. Thapar, 'In History', 15; A.L. Basham, *The Wonder That was India* (New York: Grove Press, 1959), 186–7.
33. P. Thomas, *Indian Women through the Ages* (Bombay: Asia Publishing House, 1964), 217–24; Datta, *Sati*, 3–4; Benoy Bhusan Roy, *Socioeconomic Impact of Sati in Bengal and the Role of Raja Rammohun Roy* (Calcutta: Naya Prokash, 1987), 1–2; Thapar, 'In History', 15–16.
34. Dorothy Stein, 'Burning Widows, Burning Brides: The Perils of Daughterhood in India', *Pacific Affairs* 61 (1988): 465, and her 'Women to Burn: Suttee as a Normative Institution', *Signs* 4 (1978): 253–68; and Richard Lannoy, *The Speaking Tree: A Study of Indian Culture and Society* (London: Oxford University Press, 1971), 114–18, regarding the belief that women have a greater need of sexual satisfaction than men.
35. Thakur, *Suicide in India*, 126–45; Basham, *The Wonder That was India*, 186–8.
36. Barbara N. Ramusack, 'Women in South and Southeast Asia', in *Restoring Women to History* (Bloomington: Organization of American Historians, 1988), 4. Sudras were said to be the servants of the three higher orders.
37. Sandra P. Robinson, 'Hindu Paradigms of Women: Image and Values', in *Women, Religion and Social Change*, ed. Yvonne Yazbeck Haddad and Ellison Banks Findly (Albany: State University of New York Press, 1985), 183. See also Susan S. Wadley, 'Women and the Hindu Tradition', *Signs* 3 (1977): 113–25.
38. Thapar, 'In History', 15.

39. Vina Mazumdar, 'Comment on Suttee', *Signs* 4 (1978): 273. See also Sanjukta Gupta and Richard Gombrich, 'Another View of Widow-burning and Womanliness in Indian Public Culture', *Journal of Commonwealth and Comparative Politics* 22 (1984): 255–6 for an argument that Hindu emphasis on the chastity of women was reinforced under Muslim rule because Muslim rulers posed a threat to the purity of Hindu women and because Muslim culture placed an even higher premium on chastity as 'virtually the sole repository of family honor'.
40. Thapar, 'In History', 16.
41. Mukhopadhyay, 'Sati in Bengal', 100; Kenneth Ballhatchet, *Social Policy and Social Change in Western India 1817–1830* (London: Oxford University Press, 1957), 291. See also Ray, 'Introduction', 3–5 regarding the 'spread of sati as a Sanskritizing rite'; and M.N. Srinivas, *Social Change in Modern India* (Berkeley: University of California Press, 1969), 6 for a standard definition of Sanskritization.
42. Thapar, 'In History', 17.
43. *The Inner Conflict of Tradition: Essays in Indian Ritual, Kingship, and Society* (Chicago: University of Chicago Press, 1985), 15.
44. Mukhopadhyay, 'Sati in Bengal', 99–101; Zakiuddin Ahmad, 'Sati in Eighteenth Century Bengal', *Journal of the Asiatic Society of Pakistan* 13 (1968): 149–50; Thompson, *Suttee*, 15–43.
45. Ronald B. Inden, *Marriage and Rank in Bengali Culture: A History of Caste and Clan in Middle-Period Bengal* (Berkeley: University of California Press, 1976), 82.
46. Bayly, 'From Ritual to Ceremony', 175; Thapar, 'In History', 17.
47. No wonder the practice in the eighteenth and nineteenth centuries is often seen as an involuntary act, more akin to murder than ritual suicide. E.g., Datta, *Sati*, 216–19. Note also that in the nineteenth-century debate over sati the British followed legal and Brahminical precedents and ignored the multivocal nature of the discourse on sati. See Lata Mani, 'Production of an Official Discourse on Sati in Early Nineteenth Century Bengal', *Economic and Political Weekly* 21 (1986): 32–40.
48. Caldecott to Petter, 14 Sept. 1783, Caldecott Manuscript, Eur. Mss. D. 778, India Office Library and Records, London.
49. S. Pearce Carey, *William Carey* (London: Hodder & Stoughton, 1923), 209.
50. Acting Magistrate, Saran, to Acting Suptd. of Police, Lower Provinces, 20 Feb. 1819, Saran District Records, Letters Issued, 11-4-1816 to 17-6-1819, Bihar State Archives, Patna.
51. Magistrate to Register, N.A., 18 Dec. 1813, *PP, 1821*, vol. 18, 37.
52. Francis Buchanan, *An Account of the District of Shahabad in 1812–13* (Patna: Patna Law Press, 1934), 213; Montgomery Martin, *Eastern India*, vol. 2,

Bhagalpur, Gorakhpur (1938; reprint ed., Delhi: Cosmo Publications, 1976), 475.

53. Mukhopadhyay, 'Sati in Bengal', 105. These numbers do not include satis occurring in such areas as Punjab and Rajasthan that were then territories not completely under British control but where the practice was prevalent. On Rajasthan, see Saxena, *Social Reforms*, 57–147. On sati in the Bombay Presidency, see Ballhatchet, *Social Policy in India*, 275–91.
54. Anand A. Yang, *The Limited Raj: Agrarian Relations in Saran District, India, 1793–1920* (Berkeley: University of California Press, 1989); Basudeb Chattopadhyay, 'The Penetration of Authority in the Interior: A Case-study of the Zamindari of Nakashipara, 1850–1860', *Peasant Studies* 12 (1985): 151–69. See also Nandy, 'Sati', 174–5.
55. Gupta and Gombrich, 'Another View of Widow-burning', 254.
56. Nandy, 'Sati,' 175.
57. Ashis Nandy, 'Cultures of Politics and Politics of Cultures', *Journal of Commonwealth and Comparative Politics* 22 (1984): 265.
58. Wherever possible, I have attempted to correct the 'grotesquely mistranscribed' names. Compiled from *PP, 1826/27*, vol. 20, 108; *PP, 1830*, vol. 28, 30, 93–100, 189–91. The 1830 identifications of sepoy widows also lists Musst. Una of Ghazipur and Musst. Gurua of Kanpur. See also Buchanan, *Shahabad*, 153 for an estimate that at least 4,680, and as many as 12,000 men from Shahabad were serving in the military in 1812–13.
59. 'A Short History of the Chaudhary Family, Patna City (translated from the Hindi of Pandit Rampratap Pandey)', in Babu Ramgopal Singh Chowdhary, *Select Writings and Speeches of Babu Ramgopal Singh Chowdhary* (Bankipur: Express Press, 1917), ii. Bhumihar Brahmins, a dominant landholding caste in the region, sometimes termed Kshatriya Brahmins, have historically valorized their military and kingly identities. See M.A. Sherring, *Hindu Tribes and Castes* (1872; reprint ed., Delhi: Cosmo Publications, 1974), 39–54.
60. Gupta and Gombrich, 'Another View of Widow-burning', 256; Mukhopadhyay, 'Sati in Bengal', 108. Infanticide is said to stem from the same dynamic because the dearth of men of appropriate status also meant that high castes were faced with the dreadful prospect of raising unmarriageable daughters.
61. Bayly, 'From Rituals to Ceremony', 174. Such pressures have also been cited as reasons why many satis in Bengal should be seen as involuntary, i.e., as murder. E.g., see Ahmad, 'Sati in Bengal', 161–3.
62. Nandy, 'Sati', 171, goes on to argue that large-scale scarcities occurred in Bengal, such as the disastrous famine of 1770, after a period of about 150 years of relatively famine-free existence.
63. 'Ashis Nandy on the Inner World', *Journal of Commonwealth and Comparative Politics* 22 (1984): 259. Perhaps this was another dynamic in

the generalization of the practice across social and economic liens.

64. James Jamesson, *Report on the Epidemic Cholera Morbus* (Calcutta: A.G. Balfour, 1820), 3–32, 167–74.
65. Magistrate, Patna, to Suptd., Police, 21 Dec. 1818, *PP, 1821*, vol. 18, 233.
66. Robert Hamilton to Captain Benson, 1 March 1829, in *Correspondence of Bentinck*, 175. For a similar trend in western India, see Ballhatchet, *Social Policy in India*, 275.
67. 'Extract from . . . suttee report . . . for the year 1825', *PP, 1830,* vol. 28.
68. 'Mr. Harington's Minute', with Governor-General's, 3 Dec. 1824, *PP, 1825,* vol. 24, 11.
69. I have used an 1822 population estimate of 1,239,150. See Durgaprasad Bhattacharya and Bibhavati Bhattacharya, eds., *Census of India, 1961: Report on the Population Estimates of India (1820–1830)* (New Delhi: Government of India, 1963), 71.
70. Bayly, 'From Ritual to Ceremony', 161.
71. Hamilton to Benson, 1 March 1829, *Correspondence of Bentinck*, 172.
72. Elizabeth Leigh Stutchbury, 'Blood, Fire and Meditation: Human Sacrifice and Widow Burning in Nineteenth Century India', in *Women in India and Nepal,* ed. Michael Allen and S.N. Mukherjee (Canberra: Australian National University Monographs on South Asia No. 8, 1982), 41.
73. 'History of the Chaudhary Family', in *Writings of Chowdhary*, ii.
74. *PP, 1825,* vol. 24, 153.
75. Mukhopadhyay, 'Sati', 108–9. Although upper-caste victims comprised approximately half the total number of satis in most districts, in proportion to the percentage of high to low castes in the overall population, they, of course, constituted a substantial proportion. Interpolating on the basis of the systematic census data of the late nineteenth century, one can assume that high castes typically represented eight to 20 per cent of the total population of most Bengal districts, their numbers standing higher in Bihar than in Bengal proper.
76. E.g., see *PP, 1821, 1823, 1825*. Nearly eight per cent of the population of Banaras, a centre of pilgrimage, were Marathas in 1820. See Bayly, 'From Ritual to Ceremony', 164–5.
77. 'Remarks . . . for the year 1818', 21 May 1819, *PP, 1821*, vol. 18, 222. For a different emphasis—on the youth of the victims—see Gupta and Gombrich, 'Another View of Widow-burning', 256.
78. *PP, 1825,* vol. 24, 67–70.
79. *PP, 1821,* vol. 18, 166–8.
80. For a discussion of sati as suicide and particularly Durkheim's views on this subject, see Raj S. Gandhi, 'Sati as Altruistic Suicide', *Contributions to Asian Studies* 10 (1977): 141–57; Arvind Sharma, 'Emile Durkheim on Suttee as Suicide', *International Journal of Contemporary Sociology* 15 (1978): 283–91.

81. *PP, 1825*, vol. 24, 76–7.
82. Ibid., 140–1. For a different profile, see the details regarding the 46 cases from the suburbs of Calcutta where the majority of the deceased husbands of satis were said to have 'been in good [economic] circumstances' (141).
83. *PP, 1830*, vol. 28, 138–9.
84. Susan Hill Gross and Marjorie Wall Bingham, *Women in India* (Hudson, Wisconsin: GEM Publications, 1980), 30.
85. Stutchbury, 'Widow Burning in India', 37; Stein, 'Women to Burn,' 254–5.
86. See Lina M. Fruzzetti, *The Gift of a Virgin: Women, Marriage, and Ritual in a Bengali Society* (New Brunswick: Rutgers University Press, 1982), 103–7 for an excellent discussion of the present-day status of the widow. Also Manisha Roy, *Bengali Women* (Chicago: University of Chicago Press, 1975), 146–7.
87. Nor have the conditions and ideologies favouring sati completely disappeared in twentieth-century India. Thousands were present at the recent burning of 17-year-old Roop Kanwar, a bride of eight months, who immolated herself on her husband's funeral pyre in Rajasthan on 4 Sept. 1987. For the literature—and some shocking pronouncement—on this incident, see, e.g., the special issues of *Manushi* 42–3 (1987); *Seminar* 342 (1988); and *Economic and Political Weekly*, 7 Nov. 1987 and 14 Nov. 1987.

2

Production of an Official Discourse on Sati in Early-Nineteenth-Century Bengal*

LATA MANI

Nineteenth-century British India was marked by a series of debates on reforming the status of women. The first, and most sensational public debate, was concerned with outlawing sati: the practice, prevalent predominantly among high-caste Hindus, of the immolation of widows on the funeral pyres of their husbands. These immolations were sometimes voluntary and at other times coerced. The official debate centred around the issue of the tolerance of such a practice in a 'British India'.

The literature on sati[1] and more generally on social reform in the colonial period has largely adopted the framework of modernization theory. Reform here is conceptualized as a product both of the impulse to 'moderate' that supposedly characterized the officials of this period and the demands of a small but increasingly vocal 'westernized', urban indigenous male elite. Officials who initiated and defended 'progressive' legislation like the abolition of sati, have been loosely called 'Anglicists'. They have been marked off from their 'Orientalist' forerunners and colleagues, said to have been more 'Hindooized' and wary of interventions in indigenous culture not prompted by the needs of colonial rule. The abolition of sati in 1829 is said to signal the rise of Anglicists

*From *Economic and Political Weekly*, vol. XXI, no. 17, 'Review of Women Studies' (April 1986): WS 32–40.

whose victory is seen to culminate in the great debate on English *versus* vernacular education in the mid 1830s.[2]

However, I will argue that a number of important issues are obscured in a characterization of the official debate on sati as one between 'preservationists' and impatient westernizers. Firstly, the fact that the debate was primarily about the feasibility rather than the desirability of abolition is overlooked. Secondly, that which is common in the analyses of Indian society in the arguments of those for and against abolition remains hidden. Finally, I will argue the case for abolition is not, in fact, elaborated on the grounds that such a characterization implies. Rather than arguing for the outlawing of sati as a cruel or barbarous act, as one might expect of a true 'modernizer', officials in favour of abolition were at pains to illustrate that such a move was entirely consonant with the principle of upholding indigenous tradition. Their strategy was to point to the questionable scriptural sanction for sati and to the fact that, for one reason or another, they believed its contemporary practice transgressed its original and therefore 'true' scriptural meaning.

I. Discourse as an Ideological Tool

In this paper I have treated the debate on sati as a discourse. My use of the term and a discussion of the value of this approach is presented below. Briefly, however, in analysing the debate as discourse, I focus on how knowledge about sati was produced. In particular, I examine assumptions about sati, Indian society and colonial subjects on which this discourse depended and also the role of indigenous people in its production. Several interlocking assumptions informed this discourse. Chief among these was the hegemonic status accorded by colonial officials to brahmanic scriptures in the organization of social life. The corollary to this was to assume an unquestioning submission of indigenous people to the dictates of scripture and thus to posit an absence of conscious individual will. Widows in particular are represented as having no subjectivity and as doubly victimized by their ignorance of the scriptures and its consequence, their reliance on brahmin pundits. The latter are portrayed as self-interested interpreters of the sacred texts. As for sati itself, there is a repeated insistence on a scriptural sanction for the practice, although this claim is increasingly contested as the debate develops.

Analysis of the discourse also clarifies how selected natives, especially brahmin pundits, were deeply implicated in its production, albeit in a subordinated role. As I will illustrate, pundits' statements were interpreted and deployed in ways that produced a distinctively colonial concepton of sati.[3] Examining the production of discourse clarifies what was privileged and what was marginalized in the process. Thus it becomes possible to contest the conclusions about sati drawn by colonial officials.

This paper falls within the category of historical studies that is concerned with the contribution of imperialism to what is known about colonial and ex-colonial societies; with reconstituting what B.S. Cohn has called a 'colonial sociology of knowledge'.[4] Building on the work of Foucault on the collaboration of power/knowledge in the production of discourse[5] and Said[6] with specific reference to discourses on the Orient, this study begins with the premise that what is known about colonial and ex-colonial societies is itself a colonial legacy. This problem is not merely confined to knowledge of what is designated 'the colonial period'. As Romila Thapar states: 'A major contradiction in our understanding of the entire Indian past is that this understanding is derived from the interpretations of Indian history made in the last two hundred years.'[7] Needless to say such understandings were forged in situations that reflect the vicissitudes of a 'colonial' representation of reality and the needs of colonial power.

Acknowledgement of the complex history of received ideas is not new. The production in recent years of 'workers' history', 'women's history' or 'subaltern studies'[8] implies the partiality, even bias, of existing accounts. An argument for women's history, for instance, is based on the need to remedy a situation in which history has largely meant the history of men. Obviously, accounts of women or workers do not function only in an additive way but transform our understanding of society as a whole.

I suggest, however, that an analysis of discourse is a different proposition, which goes beyond producing 'indigenous' or 'oppositional' accounts, whether nationalist, Marxist or feminist. Rather, discourse analysis focuses on that which is stable and persistent in the ordering of social reality in each of these accounts. Thus it can point to assumptions shared by those who claim to be opposed to each other or are conceptualized in this manner, whether nationalists and colonialists or Orientalists and Anglicists.

In a sense the term discourse as used by Focault and Said is similar in scope to the Marxist notion of ideology: a public, institutionalised set of constraints on what is 'truth' and 'knowledge'. Discourse is, however, the more useful analytical tool: for it retains the dialogical processes implied by speech and requires at least two parties. I believe it is useful to speak of a 'colonial discourse' on sati rather than a colonial ideology, precisely because knowledge about colonial society was produced through interaction between colonialists—officials, scholars, missionaries—and certain selected natives. The 'interaction' was often 'interrogation' and always transversed by power. Discourse signals the back-and-forth of these power-laden encounters more sensitively than ideology, for the latter seems to have gathered about it notions of rigidity and monological, even hegemonic, production. The concept of discourse also embodies the possibility of several simultaneous discourses. It makes for the analysis of missionary, official and indigenous discourses as autonomous although engaged with each other in relations of dialogue and struggle.

In this paper I examine the production of an official discourse on sati. A complete analysis of colonial discourses on sati would require, in addition, attention to missionary and indigenous discourses for both were important in the debate on abolition. This essay represents only the beginning of such an enterprise.

Such a critical reading of historical materials is not the province of intellectual history alone. Given that these discourses were spawned by considerations of social policy and informed practice, they are of equal concern to social historians. As for colonial subjects confronting the colonial legacy, such a critical reading offers a way of reinterpreting tradition, history and identity.

II. Sati: A Legislative History?

As a subject covered by criminal law, colonial policy on sati was formulated between the Governor General and Council and officials at various levels of the criminal justice system in Bengal: magistrates, police officials, the provincial court—Nizamat Adalat—and the superior court—Sadr Nizamat Adalat. Also involved was the Privy Council at the apex of East India Company hierarchy in London. Finally, given the supposed scriptural sanction for sati, brahmin pundits also became crucial participants. Appointed to the civil courts under Warren Hastings in 1772 to interpret scriptural law in civil matters—marriage, divorce, inheritance, succession—pundits were called upon to elaborate the dictates of scripture on all aspects of sati. Residents of Calcutta were beyond the purview of this debate since the city fell under the jurisdiction of British law and sati had been outlawed there in 1798.

The history of legislation on sati is relatively straightforward. In all, only one regulation and three circulars were actually promulgated between the first recorded query on the official position on sati in February 1789 and its prohibition in December 1829. The first official position on sati was articulated in response to a clarification sought by M.H. Brooke, Collector of Shahabad District. In the absence of any official instructions on the subject, and on the strength of its illegality in Calcutta city, Brooke had prohibited the burning of a widow and sought government approval for his decision. The Governor General commended his action but urged him to use private influence rather than official authority in dissuading natives from sati, claiming:

> The public prohibition of a ceremony authorised by the tenets of the religion of the Hindus, and from the observance of which they have never yet been restricted by the ruling power would in all probability tend to increase rather than diminish their veneration for it.[10]

He continued that he hoped in the course of time natives would 'discern the fallacy of the principle which have given rise to this practice, and that it will of itself gradually fall into disuse'.[11] The Governor General cites no support for his claim of a religious sanction for sati.

The issue was raised again in 1805 when Elphinstone, acting magistrate of the Zillah of Behar, reported his intervention in a case where an intoxicated 12-year-old was being coerced into the pyre. Like Brooke, he sought instructions from the Governor General and his Council. The secretary of the government referred the issue to the Nizamat Adalat, asking how far and in what ways the practice of sati was founded in the scripture, stating that if scriptural sanction precluded abolition, measures might be taken to prevent coercion and such abuses as the intoxication of widows.

The Nizamat Adalat in turn referred the matter to its pundit, Ghanshyam Surmono. The pundit responded in March 1805 but not until 29 April 1813, some eight years later, was his exposition of the scriptural position on sati issued in the form of instructions to the District Magistrates.

Based on an official reading of Surmono's interpretation of the texts, the instructions declared sati to be a practice founded in the religious beliefs of Hindus. It was clarified that the practice was intended to be voluntary and, if performed, was expected to ensure an after-life together for the widow and her husband. The circular also stated that a widow who had taken a vow to commit sati was permitted to change her mind without loss of caste, providing she performed a penance. The preface to the instructions clarified that given the scriptural status on sati and the government's commitment to the principle of religious tolerance, sati would be permitted: 'in those cases in which it is countenanced by their religion; and [prevented] in others in which it is by the same authority prohibited.'[12] Sati was thus to be prohibited in all cases in which the widow was less than 16 years of age, or was pregnant or intoxicated or in any other way coerced. Magistrates were also instructed to transmit to the Nizamat Adalat details of each sati committed in their jurisdictions, including any prohibitive measures they might have taken.

This circular, promulgated on 29 April 1813, was the only significant regulation introduced until the practice was outlawed. Three more circulars were issued, but these were merely further refinements prompted by the queries of District Magistrates on what constituted a legal sati. Its 'legality' supposedly conferred by its scriptural origin had been confirmed by the regulation of 1813. Queries were forwarded by the Nizamat Adalat to their resident pundits, requesting them to provide *vyawasthas* in conformity with the scriptures.[13] Thus a circular was promulgated in September 1813 that authorized *jogis* (a tribe of weavers supposedly the survivors of wandering mendicants) to bury their dead, since the scriptures reportedly forbade burning in their case.[14]

It was similarly decreed in 1815 that women with children under three might commit sati only if arrangements had been made for the maintenance of their children. The 1815 circular also specified that brahmin women could only burn along with their husbands by performing the rite of *sahamarana*, while women of other castes were also permitted *anoomarana*, in which the widow burned at a later date together with an article belonging to the husband. Finally, this circular instructed magistrates to submit an annual report of satis in their districts to the Sadr Nizaṃat Adalat, specifying for each sati: the name of the widow, her age, her caste, the name and caste of the husband, the date of burning and the police jurisdiction in which it occurred. An additional column was provided for recording any remarks that the magistrate thought deserving of attention. A third circular, issued in 1822, instructed that information on the husband's profession and circumstances also be included for each sati.[16] Although no further regulations were issued, the following years witnessed intense debate on abolition. The debate was rekindled every year when the Nizamat Adalat analysed the annual returns of sati and examined for each incident the conduct of the district magistrate and police officers.

The question of abolition raised the related issues of desirability and feasibility. Colonial officials were unanimous on the desirability of abolition in the abstract, although they were fearful of violating the principle of religious tolerance. Needless to say, the latter concern was itself linked to the feasibility or political costs of intervention. Given their belief in the centrality of religion in the lives of Hindus, officials feared that any interference would produce repercussions that might endanger the East India Company's economic and political stakes in India. The tactic of gathering scriptural evidence was thus an attempt to challenge sati in such a way as to preclude a threat to public order. Indeed it had become clear in consulting with the pundits that the older scriptures made no mention of sati, but rather glorified ascetic widowhood. Even more recent texts did not enjoin sati but merely recommended it. The use of scriptures by officials for and against abolition will be discussed more fully below.

Meanwhile, a dramatic increase in sati lent urgency to the debate. In the first three years of data collection alone the number of satis nearly tripled from 378 to 839. Although the figures declined after 1819–20, they never fell to the levels first recorded in 1815, but fluctuated between an annual incidence of 500 and 600.

Over the years the Nizamat Adalat proposed various explanations for this rise. Initially it claimed that the rise could merely reflect more refined counting. In 1817–18 it argued, somewhat weakly, that the figures reflected the cholera epidemic that had ravaged parts of Bengal. Some officials, however, proposed a more convincing, albeit sinister, explanation pointing out that the government circular might have made people aware of more circumstances under which sati might be performed. Suspicion grew that the rise was somehow linked to government interposition. W. Ewer, Acting Superintendent of Police in the Lower Provinces, argued that 'authorising a practice is not the way to effect its gradual abolition'.[17] Courtney Smith, Nizamat Adalat judge, echoed Ewer's sentiment that government attention had given 'a sort of interest and celebrity to the sacrifice'.[18] He recommended that all circulars be rescinded since they had a tendency 'to modify, systematise or legalise the usage' and made it appear as though 'a legal suttee was . . . better than an illegal one'.[19]

Not all officials agreed with Ewer and Smith. Some Nizamat Adalat judges like C.T. Sealy and A.B. Todd resisted the implication that the circulars were interventionist and insisted that they merely implemented the law as embedded in the scriptures. Others asked for an even more rigorous enforcement of scriptural law. For instance, in 1828 Cracroft, Magistrate of Dacca, even went so far as to recommend that only widows from families with pure caste status be permitted to perform sati. Cracroft suggested that such a rigorous interpretation of caste would reduce sati by ninety per cent since few families if any would meet this standard.[20] In 1823, Harrington proposed circumventing the scriptures, suggesting that sati need not be outlawed outright but that brahmin pundits and relatives might be prosecuted as principals or accomplices in homicide.

Officials advocating further legislation, however, were in a minority. The general view was that in the context of a sustained high incidence of sati, anything short of total prohibition would be unwise. Yet this appeared out of the question. In the meantime, it was hoped that the spread of education and the example of the high caste, educated, westernized Hindus would serve to make the practice unpopular. Indigenous opposition to sati had been growing since 1818, when Rammohun Roy, chief campaigner and symbol of the native lobby against sati published his first tract against the practice.

However, in general, faith in the progressive influence of higher caste, better educated Hindus was misplaced, for the practice was predominantly theirs.[21] The regional distribution of sati also made it difficult to sustain in the hope that a great exposure to western influence would result in its popularity declining. For 63 per cent of satis between 1815 and 1828 were committed in the Calcutta Division around Calcutta city, the seat of colonial power. Indeed this high figure may in part be accounted for by Hindu residents of Calcutta going outside the city to commit sati, which was illegal within its boundaries.

The regionally skewed distribution of satis prompted some magistrates like H.B. Melville in 1823 and W.B. Bayley in 1827 to propose abolition in certain districts. Others used the regional variation as evidence that sati was a localized, temporal phenomenon and not a universal religious one. Further, already by 1818, it had become evident that the scriptural sanction for sati was not clearcut. In March 1824, the Court of Directors sitting in London, drawing almost exclusively on official correspondence and Nizamat Adalat proceedings on sati, came to the conclusion that these papers themselves were replete with arguments on the basis of which abolition could be justified. In particular, the directors highlighted the following: the questionable scriptural status of sati, the violation of scriptural rules in its performance, the inefficacy of current regulation, the support for abolition among Indians, the confidence of some magistrates that sati could be abolished safely, the incompatibility of sati with principles of morality and reason. The Court of Directors however conceded that the final decision must rest with the authorities in India since only they could evaluate the political consequences of such action.

Indeed it was in India that legislation to outlaw sati was finally initiated by Governor General Lord William Bentinck in December 1829. Bentinck had little more information than his predecessors, either on sati or on the probable effects of such legislation, although he had gathered military intelligence that such legislation would not provoke disquiet among the armed forces. What Bentinck did possess was a combination of the will to outlaw sati and the benefits of a greater political stability of the East India Company whose control had now been extended across Rajputana, Central India and Nepal. A new confidence and energy was reflected in Bentinck's Minute on sati: 'Now that we are supreme, my opinion is decidedly in favour of an open, avowed and general prohibition, resting altogether upon the moral goodness of the act and our power to enforce it'.[22] The desirability of abolition had never been at issue. Its feasibility had proved to be the thorny question, Bentinck settled the issue once and for all.

Sati either by burning or burial was outlawed and made punishable by the criminal courts. *Zamindars* and *talukdars* were made responsible for immediate communication to the police of intention to perform sati, any lapse being made punishable by a fine or imprisonment. The Nizamat Adalat was authorized to impose the death sentence on active participants in sati if the crime was gruesome enough to render them unworthy of mercy. It is not known to what extent the legislative act succeeded in putting out the flaming pyres. Statistics were no longer collected and thus it is impossible to evaluate the effects of abolition. What abolition did achieve was an official resolution in one instance of the conflict between political expediency and the civilizing mission of colonization.

III. The Discourse and Its Assumptions

The one feature that is clear even from this brief legislative history is that the abolition of sati was complicated by official insistence on its scriptural status. Whatever their views on the feasibility of abolition, all colonial officials shared to a greater or lesser degree three interdependent ideas: the centrality of religion, the submission of indigenous people to its dictates and the 'religious' basis of sati. Those against abolition argued that prohibition of sati was likely to incite native resistance. As the Nizamat Adalat put it: 'Such a measure would, in all probability, excite a considerable degree of alarm and dissatisfaction in the minds of the Hindoo inhabitants of these provinces.'[23] Officials in favour of abolition also developed arguments reflecting the view of Hindu society generated by these same assumptions. For instance, Judge E. Watson's argument for the feasibility of abolition rested on the precedent of Regulation 8 of 1799 which, by declaring female infanticide, child sacrifice and the burial of lepers capital offences, had similarly, in his view, violated religious principles. It is in this sense that I assert that officials on both sides of the debate shared the same universe of discourse.

Walter Ewer, Superintendent of Police in the Lower Provinces, made a different kind of argument for abolition. As a thorough and systematic analysis which sums up the arguments of officials over the years, it is worth detailed attention.[24] Ewer took the position that the contemporary practice of sati bore little resemblance to its scriptural model as a voluntary act of devotion carried out for the spiritual benefit of the widow and the deceased. Rather, in his view, widows were coerced and sati was performed most often for the material gain of surviving relatives. Ewer suggested that relatives might save the expense of maintaining the widow and 'irritation' of her legal right over the family estate. Also said to apply pressure on the widow by extolling the virtues and rewards of sati were 'hungry brahmins' greedy for the money due to them for officiating on such occasions.

Even if the widow succeeded in resisting the combined force of relatives and pundits, Ewer held that she would not be spared by the crowd. According to him, 'the entire population of the village will turn out to assist in dragging her to the bank of the river, and in keeping her down on the pile'.[25] For the crowd, sati was said to offer the lure of a spectacle. 'None of the holy exultation that formerly accompanied the departure of a martyr, but all the savage merriment which, in our days, accompanies a boxing match or a full-bait.'[26] Ewer thus concludes that 'the widow is scarcely ever a free agent at the performance of the suttee'.[27] According to Ewer, such scriptural transgressions as the coercion of widows or the performance of sati for material gain could either be the result of ignorance of scriptures or reflect conscious design on the part of relatives and pundits: in the former case sati could be abolished without provoking indigenous outrage; in the latter case, sati could not be considered a sacred act and could safely be abolished.

It is clear that, according to Ewer, when Hindus acted 'religiously', they did not act consciously. In other words, true 'religious' action was synonymous with a passive, unquestioning obedience. Thus, if the widow is construed as a victim of pundits and relatives, they in turn are seen by Ewer to act in two mutually exclusive ways: either 'consciously', that is 'irreligiously', or 'passively', that is 'religiously'. Hence Ewer nowhere suggests that pundits and relatives could manipulate religion to their own ends. As for the widow, she is not offered any possibility of ever exercising her will. Ewer submitted that left to herself, the widow would 'turn with natural instinct and horror from the thought of suttee'.[28] However, in his view, given her ignorance and weak mental and physical capacity it took little persuasion to turn any apprehension into a reluctant consent.

Ewer resolved the issue of the feasibility of abolition further by problematizing the assumption of a scriptural sanction for sati. He pointed to the heterogeneity of the scriptures on the issue; Manu 'the parent of Hindoo jurisprudence' did not even mention sati, but instead glorified ascetic widowhood. It is important to note that what unites both the 'temporal' and 'scriptural' aspects of Ewer's arguments is the privileging of religion and the assumption of a complete native submission to its force.

This analysis was not that of Ewer alone. Maloney, Acting Magistrate of Burdwan, similarly emphasized that the decision of widows to commit sati stems not 'from their having reasoned themselves into a conviction of the purity of the act itself, as from a kind of infatuation produced by the absurdities poured into their ears by ignorant brahmins.'[29] For Maloney, as for Ewer, the widow is always a victim and the pundit always corrupt. Maloney, like Ewer, also concedes the possibility of a 'good' sati that is voluntary and the product of reason; but only in the abstract. In reality, the widow is uneducated and presumed to be incapable of both reason and independent action.

This accent on 'will' in the analyses of Ewer and Maloney, testifies to the ambivalence which lies at the heart of the colonial attitude to sati. It suggests that within the general and avowed disapproval of the practice, there operated notions of 'good' and 'bad' satis. 'Good' satis were those that were seen to be true to an official reading of the scriptures. And the critical factor in determining official attitude was the issue of the widow's will. Thus the Nizamat Adalat instructed magistrates to pay close attention to the demeanour of the widow as she approached the pyre so that officials could intercept at the merest suggestion of coercion. Magistrates accordingly recorded in the annual returns on sati such remarks as the following: 'the widow voluntarily sacrificed herself', 'ascended the pyre of her own free will', burnt 'without in anyway inebriated and in conformity with the Shaster'.

Such guarded acceptance of 'good' satis is also evident in the suggestions of Harrington and Elliot that legislation should cover not the widow, who should be left free to commit sati, but brahmins and others who aided or unduly influenced her. Such an act it was argued would prevent coercion, with the additional merit that: 'No law obligatory on the consciences of the Hindoos will be infringed, and the women desirous of manifesting the excess of their conjugal love will be left at liberty to do so.'[30] Officials like Elliot, quoted above, approved of sati as long as it was an act of free will. This view also reflected in a non-horrified announcement of two satis in the *Calcutta Gazette* as late as 1827, by which time it was officially maintained that feasibility was the only reason for tolerating sati. It described the widows respectively as 'having abandoned with cheerfulness and her own free will, this perishable frame', and as 'having burnt herself with him in their presence with a swelling heart and a smiling countenance'.[31] Other officials dismissed out of hand the possibility of such voluntary satis and insisted with Ewer that widows were incapable of consenting and must therefore be protected.

It is evident that the arguments in favour of prohibiting sati were not primarily concerned with its cruelty or 'barbarity' though many officials did maintain that sati was horrid, even as an act of volition. It is also clear that officials in favour of legislative prohibition were not interventionists, contemptuous of indigenous culture, nor advocates of change in the name of 'progress' or Christian principles. On the contrary, officials in favour of abolition were arguing that such action was consistent with the policy of upholding indigenous religious tradition, even that such a policy necessitated intervention. And indeed this was how the regenerating mission of colonization was conceptualized: not as the imposition of a new Christian moral order but as the recuperation and enforcement of the 'truths' of indigenous tradition. In this regard, it is interesting that Elliot suggested a preamble to the legislation outlawing sati, explaining government policy on indigenous customs and appealing to scriptural authority for abolition through apposite quotations from the texts. In his opinion this would:

> . . . remove the evil from the less learned, who would thus be led to lament the ignorance in which they have hitherto been held enslaved by their bigoted priests, and at the same time to rejoice in the mercy and wisdom of a government which blends humanity with justice, and consults at once the interests and prejudices of its subjects, by recalling them from practices revolting, and pronounced erroneous even by their own authorities.[32]

This conception of colonial subjects held the majority to be ignorant of their 'religion'. Religion was equated with scripture. Knowledge of the scriptures was held to be largely the monopoly of brahmin pundits. Their knowledge was however believed to be corrupt and self-serving. The civilizing mission of colonization was thus seen to lie in protecting the 'weak' against the 'artful'; in giving back to the natives the truths of their own 'little read and less understood Shaster'.[33]

The arguments of abolitionists were thus developed within the ambit of 'religion'. The pros and cons of sati were systematically debated as doctrinal considerations. In this sense the debate on abolition might be fruitfully interpreted as, in part, a conflict over scriptural interpretation. In employing scriptures to support their view the abolitionists in effect resurrected the vyawasthas of pundits that had been marginalized in earlier official readings of the scriptures. In particular, they re-examined the discussions between officials and pundits leading to the formulation of the 1813 regulations. These previously marginalized vyawasthas were now reactivated by officials both as testimony of the safety of abolition and as index of the ignorance of natives. Official debt to the pundits in interpreting the texts was not acknowledged. This gives us a clue to the role of the pundits in the production of official knowledge about sati, a theme that will be taken up in the next section.

In the meantime, as we already know, official commitment to enforcing indigenous faith and penalizing its violation in the practice of sati did not lead to a decline in its incidence. This was regarded as native misunderstanding of colonial intention and construed as further evidence of Hindu 'bigotry'. Proposals were made for closer supervision although in the event none were implemented. It is striking that officials did not acknowledge the 'inconsistencies' between their interpretation of the place of scripture in native life, and natives' own behaviour, let alone revise their view. If anything, it appears as though such inconsistencies served to reaffirm their assumptions.

In summary, the official view of sati rested on three interlocking assumptions: the hegemony of religious texts, a total indigenous submission to their dictates and the religious basis of sati. However, a re-examination of Parliamentary papers makes it possible to contest each of these assumptions.

To begin with, the insistence on textual hegemony is challenged by the enormous regional variation in the mode of committing sati. The vyawasthas of pundits had elaborated differences by village and district, even caste and occupation in the performance of sati. 'In certain villages of Burdwan a district in Bengal the following ceremonies are observed.'[34] Or, 'In some villages situated in Benares, the following practices obtain among the widows of merchants and other traders.'[35] Local influence predominated in every aspect of sati. For instance the pundits pointed out, 'She then proceeds to the place of sacrifice . . . having previously worshipped the peculiar deities of the city or village.'[36] In the face of such diversity the pundits concluded, 'The ceremonies practically observed, differ as to the various tribes and districts.'[37] Colonial officials acknowledged these differences and instructed magistrates to allow natives 'to follow the established authority and usage of the province in which they reside'.[38] However, such diversity was regarded as 'peripheral' to the 'central' principle of textual hegemony.

Similarly, regional variation in the incidence of sati was not taken as a challenge to the assumption of the hegemony of religion even though it did count as evidence of a material basis for sati. Colonial officials did not completely ignore the fact of such variation. The regulation of 1813 recognized that in some districts sati had almost entirely ceased while in others it was confined almost exclusively to certain castes. Despite this, colonial officials decided to pursue a course of tolerance because in their opinion, in most provinces, 'all castes of Hindoos would be extremely tenacious of its continuance'.[39] Whatever the justification for concluding thus in 1813, such insistence was hardly tenable once systematic data collection on sati was begun in 1815.

For it quickly became apparent that 66 per cent of satis were carried out between the districts surrounding Calcutta city and the Shahabad, Ghazipur and Sarun districts. This indicates either that sati was not a solely 'religious' practice as the officials maintained, or that religion was not hegemonic—another colonial assumption—or both. However, officials interpreted regional variation to imply that although sati was primarily a religious practice, other factors might be at play. Therefore, as late as 1827, with 11 years of data at hand, W.B. Bayley could continue to be puzzled by what he called 'anomalies' in the annual report of satis. He wrote to the court seeking an explanation 'in regard to the following extraordinary discrepancies in the results exhibited by the present statement. In the district of Backergunj 63 instances of suttee are reported, and in the adjacent district of Dacca Telalpore only 2.'[40] These could only be 'extraordinary discrepancies' because Bayley, like other officials continued to maintain, despite evidence to the contrary, that religion had a uniformly powerful influence in native life.

If the hegemony of religious texts and its corollary, an unthinking native obedience to scripture, is called into question by regional variation in the incidence and mode of performing sati, the representation of widows as perennial victims is similarly debatable. For one thing the Parliamentary papers contain several accounts of women acting on their own behalf. Some of them did so when they resisted being coerced into the pyre. The annual reports of sati include many instances of women being coerced. Representations of such incidents, however, stress not the resistance of women but the barbarity of Hindu males in their coercion.

Women also expressed their will when they resisted being prevented from jumping into the flames. One such case reported by Magistrate W. Wright in 1819 is worth recounting. A child widow, Mussummat Seeta had suddenly decided at age 15, some nine years after her husband's death, to commit sati. She resolved to die through the rite of anoomarana with a stringed instrument that had belonged to her husband. According to Wright, her parents, in-laws and police officers sought in vain to dissuade her. Wright records that the widow 'continually made use of the expression: "All your remonstrances are perfectly unavailing; it is now necessary for me to become suttee; if you persist in your remonstrances I will curse you."[41] The relatives, supposedly fearing the legendary curse of the sati, are said to have complied with her wishes and built the pyre. Her parting words were reported to have been, "Set fire to the pile; if you refuse to do so, I will curse you".'[42] Colonial officials systematically ignored such evidence of the widows as subjects with a will of their own. Although they conceded the possibility of a 'voluntary' sati, these were interpreted not as evidence of the will of the widow, but testimony of her subjection to religion. The widow thus nowhere appears as a full subject. If she resisted, she was considered a victim of Hindu, male barbarity. If she appeared to consent, she was seen to be a victim of religion. Colonial representations further reinforced such a view of the widow as helpless by 'infantilizing' the typical sati. The widow is quite often described as a 'tender child'. Analysis of sati by age fails to confirm such a picture, for a majority of satis were undertaken by women well past childhood. In 1818, for example, 64 per cent of satis were above 40 years of age.

In highlighting the absence of women's subjectivity in colonial representations of sati, my intention is not to imply that women acted voluntarily or argue that sati could be an act of 'free will'. Their subjectivities were probably complex and inconsistent. In any case they are not accessible to us. As for whether or not relatives were self-interested or brahmins bigoted, such questions can also only be addressed with reference to specific cases. My purpose in raising the issue of the widow's subjectivity is rather to point out that the ubiquitous characterization of the widow as victim was not borne out by the experience of colonial officials as recounted by them in the Parliamentary papers.

It is not the widow alone who is represented as passive, for all colonial subjects, male and female, are portrayed as finally subordinated to religion. The Nizamat Adalat stated this view quite dramatically in the context of discussing the Hindu practice of burying lepers. Reviewing a case that had come to their notice, they exclaimed, 'no example can be of any avail. Their motives were above all human control.'[43]

IV. Production of Knowledge about Sati: Interaction and Interrogation

Information about sati was generated at the instance, one is tempted to say insistence, of colonial officials posing questions to pundits resident at the courts. The pundits were instructed to respond with 'a reply in conformity with the scriptures'.[44] The working of colonial power is nowhere more visible than in this process. It is worth examining one such interaction in detail.

In 1805, as noted earlier, the question of scriptural sanction for sati was first put to the pundits of the Nizamat Adalat. Specifically they were asked 'whether a woman is enjoined by the Shaster voluntarily to burn herself with the body of her husband, or is prohibited; and what are the conditions prescribed by the Shaster on such occasions?'[45] The pundit responded as follows:

> Having duly considered the question proposed by the court, I now answer it to the best of my knowledge:- every woman of the four castes (brahmin, khetry, bues and soodur) is permitted to burn herself with the body of her husband, provided she has no infant children, nor is pregnant, nor in a state of uncleanness, nor under the age of puberty; or in any of which cases she is not allowed to burn herself with her husband's body.[46]

The pundit specified that women with infant children could burn provided they made arrangements for the care of such infants. Further, he added that coercion, overt or subtle, was forbidden. In support of his opinion, he quoted the following texts:

> This rests upon the authority of Anjira, Vijasa and Vrihaspati, Mooni.
>
> 'There are three millions and a half of hairs upon the human body, and every woman who burns herself with the body of her husband, will reside with him in heaven during a like number of years.'
>
> 'In the same manner, as a snake-catcher drags a snake from his hole, so does a woman who burns herself draw her husband out of hell; and she afterwards resides with him in heaven.'
>
> The exceptions above cited, respecting women in a state of pregnancy or uncleanness, and adolescence, were communicated by Oorub and others to the mother of Sagar Raja.[47]

The question posed to the pundit was whether sati was enjoined by the scriptural texts. The pundit in effect responded that the texts did not enjoin but merely permitted sati in certain instances, drawing on quotes which spoke of the rewards sati would bring to widows and their husbands. That the scriptures permit sati can only be inferred from the above passage. Nevertheless on the basis of this rather elusive response the Nizamat Adalat concluded:

> The practice, generally speaking, being thus recognised and *encouraged* by the doctrines of the Hindoo religion, it appears evident that the course which the British government should follow, according to the principle of religious tolerance . . . is to allow the practice in those cases in which it is countenanced by their religion; and to prevent it in others in which it is by the same authority prohibited (emphasis mine).[48]

Two moves have been made from the pundit's actual words to arrive at this conclusion. The pundit claims that he has answered the question 'to the best of my knowledge'. However, his response is treated as an altogether authoritative one. Further, permission by inference is transformed into scriptural 'recognition' and 'encouragement' of sati. Colonial policy on sati was thus formulated on the basis of an interpretation of the pundit's replies by the officials who put the questions. It was a result of this encounter which produced the only legislative enactment on sati until its eventual abolition. The statement itself was also repeatedly recalled by officials arguing against abolition. Certainly, permission to commit sati was more explicit elsewhere in the scriptures. However, at issue here is not the scriptural accuracy of the pundit's response so much as the arbitrariness so typical of the official interpretation of vyawasthas.

This example embodies many of the basic principles by which a body of information about sati generated. Questions to pundits were intended to establish clarity on all aspects of sati. Pundits were required to comb the scriptures and produce unambiguous scriptural support. For instance, in April 1813, a pundit was required to specify the meaning of the phrase 'tender years' in his statement that 'a woman having a child of tender years is wholly inhibited from becoming a suttee'.[49] Inferential conclusions were only acceptable where explicit documentation was impossible. Thus, for example, the Sadr Nizamat Adalat had to be content with inferential scriptural support for the burial of *jogis.* The matter had been referred to the Sadr Nizamat Adalat by the magistrate of the provincial Dacca court, since the pundit at that court had in their view unsatisfactorily claimed that 'This is an act which is founded merely on practice'.[50] The Sadr Nizamat Adalat pundits produced inferential support in their response. In this context they also argued that the scriptures themselves gave equal support to custom and usage. However, despite official insistence on faithfulness to the scriptures, colonial officials continued to prefer explicit scriptural injunction.[51] It was for this reason that the Sadr Nizamat Adalat reprimanded a district pundit for referring 'to the custom of a country, upon a point which is expressly provided for by law'.[52]

Over the years, through such continual and intensive questioning, criteria for an officially sanctioned sati were generated. It had to be voluntary. Brahmin women were permitted only sahamarana. Non-brahmin women could burn through sahamarana or anoomarana. Sati was forbidden to women under 16 and to women with infants less than three years. Women of the jogi tribe were permitted to bury themselves.

Although scriptural authority was claimed for this model, a careful reading of the Parliamentary papers tells quite another story. For example, colonial officials treated vyawasthas as truthful exegeses of the scriptures in an absolute sense and enforced them legally. By contrast, it is clear from reading these vyawasthas that pundits issuing them believed them to be interpretive. However, not all vyawasthas were accorded such legitimacy; rather, colonial officials selectively privileged some and marginalized others.

Pundits attested to the interpretive nature of vyawasthas in several ways. Vyawasthas were often prefaced with such declarations as:

> Having inspected the paper drawn up by the chief judge of this court we proceed to furnish a reply *to the best of our ability* (emphasis mine).[53]
>
> Having considered the question proposed by the court I now answer it *to the best of my knowledge* (emphasis mine).[54]

Similarly, they characterised their replies as opinions: 'The authorities for the above opinion are as follows'. The interpretive character of the *vyawasthas* was also evident from the way in which the scriptures were used:

> In support of the above *may be adduced* the following authorities (emphasis mine).[55]
>
> In the above sentence by using the words 'she who ascends', the author *must have had in contemplation* those who declined to do so (emphasis mine).[56]
>
> From the above quoted passage of the Mitateshura, *it would appear that* this was an act fit for all women to perform (emphasis mine).[57]

It is clear from the above that vyawasthas did not claim to pronounce either scriptural truth or the only possible response to a given question.[58]

The corpus of texts designated 'the scriptures' also made such a claim difficult to maintain. The scriptures were an enormous body of texts composed at different times. They included the *srutis*, the *dharmashastras* or *smritis* and *nibandhas*. The *srutis* were believed to be a pre-scriptural transcription of a revealed oral discourse anterior to the category of historicity. The *dharmashastras* or *smritis* were mnemic and historico-social texts supposedly transcribed by the sages under the authority of Hindu kings. The principal *shastras* are products of named and thus 'historical' subjects: Manu, Yajnavalkya and Narada. The commentaries and digests were treatises interpreting and expounding the *shastras* and mainly produced between the eleventh and eighteenth centuries. Different commentaries were held to be authoritative in different regions. It is no wonder then that two pundits could issue vyawasthas on the same point and quote different texts or different passages from the same text to support their statements.

The fact that the various texts were authored at different periods also accounted for their heterogeneity on many points, not least of which was the scriptural sanction for sati. Colonial response to such heterogeneity took three forms. Sometimes diversity was selectively recognized, as in the determination and enforcement of the appropriate modes of committing sati for brahmin and non-brahmin widows. At other times it was acknowledged for practical reasons but not 'resolved', as in the considered tolerance of regional variation in the mode of conducting sati: whether the widow's body was placed to the left or right of the corpse, the direction of the pyre, and so on. A third response was to marginalize certain vyawasthas. A telling example of such strategic marginalization is the fate of Mrityunjoy Vidyalankar's vyawastha, relegated to the appendix of the Nizamat Adalat proceedings of 1817, with no more than a mention in the main text. This vyawastha systematically called into question the colonial rationale of a scriptural sanction for sati and questioned its status as an act of virtue. Vidyalankar pointed out that as a form of suicide it was debatable whether sati was consonant with the *srutis* which forbade any wilful abridgement of life. Further he noted that the ultimate goal of all Hindus was selfless absorption in a divine essence, a union which was said to flow not from action like sati, performed with a view to reward, but from devotion and contemplation of the divine. Given this a life of austerity and sexual abstinence, as implied by ascetic widowhood, emerged as an equally if not more meritorious act.

Vidyalankar's vyawastha contained sufficient scriptural justification for prohibiting sati. It was however ignored. Continual reinscription of sati into a scriptural tradition despite evidence to the contrary points to the arbitrariness of meanings imposed by a colonial reading of vyawasthas. If the construct of sati thus produced is specifically 'colonial', it can also be argued that 'religion' in this discourse emerges merely as that part of culture that colonial power chooses not to interdict. If for some reason it was decided to prohibit a practice the strategy was to discount its claim to being 'religious' in a colonial reading of the scriptures. In the end this is what happened in the case of sati. Of course it was not quite as simple as this for as we have seen, sati's scriptural status was problematized long before the practice was prohibited. Ultimately abolition was legislated when it was deemed feasible. However, this was not the basis on which the discourse was articulated.

In the meantime, while sati was still conceptualized as 'religious' official policy, whatever its claim to non-interference, was to ensure adherence to the official conception of a 'true' sati. A coherent, unambiguous definition of sati was an essential prerequisite to this policy. We have already traced how such clarity was achieved. Attentiveness to the details of practice was another aspect of this policy. Official watchfulness was made possible by the systematic collection and tabulation of data on each sati. In addition to personal data on the widow and her deceased husband, the time, place and mode of burning, magistrates were also given explicit instructions to 'not allow the most minute particular to escape observation'.[59] Such details ensured that no infraction, whether on the part of officials or natives, could escape the official eye. Thus, for instance, in the review of satis for 1819, the magistrate of Shahabad was reprimanded for preventing an illegal sati by persuasion where he could have employed force. Magistrates were also censured for being over-zealous. Thus in 1819, the magistrate for Bheerbhoom district was criticized for requiring previous intimation for performing sati when there was no order to this effect on the statute books. Given the importance of detail to such 'a penal mapping of the social body',[60] magistrates were compelled to record details and reprimanded for reports that were 'totally destitute of remark'.[61] The consistency of the Nizamat Adalat on this score drew the approval of the Governor General and his Council who commended them in 1820 on the 'minuteness with which the Nizamat Adaulut have entered on the examination of the returns from the several districts'.[62]

There is no doubt that despite the professed colonial policy of religious non-interference, the process by which knowledge on sati was produced for legal enforcement ensured that the concept of sati generated was distinctly 'colonial'. As the examples above indicate, despite the involvement of brahmin pundits, the privilege of the final authoritative interpretation of their vyawasthas was appropriated by colonial officials. For it was Nizamat Adalat judges, the Governor General and his Council who determined which vyawasthas were 'essential' and which 'peripheral'. The position of the brahmin pundits was ambiguous. The fact of being native simultaneously privileged and devalued them as reliable sources. They were critical to making the scriptures accessible to colonial officials. But they were also the 'artful classes' against whom it was the mission of colonization to protect 'the simple'.

This process by which this construct of sati was produced exemplifies the textualized nature of the discourse. Here I draw on the work of Paul Ricoeur.[63] Ricoeur illustrates the process of textualization, analysing what happens to 'discourse' or 'speech' when it becomes 'textualized' for instance, in language, action or ritual. Contrasting discourse with language, Ricoeur points out that discourse is realized temporally, it has a subject who speaks, 'a world which it claims to describe, to express or to represent',[64] and a person who is being addressed. In the example at hand, the pundit's vyawastha is analogous to discourse. Vyawasthas, like speech, had as their reference a specific context, as opinions expressed by the pundits on specific situations which took into account particular needs.

The textualization of such discourse, according to Ricoeur, results in the fixation of meaning, its dissociation from any authorial intention, the display of non-ostensive references and a universal range of addresses. The colonial rewriting/reinterpretation of the pundits' vyawasthas as invariant scriptural truths and their enforcement as law is analogous to the textualization of discourse. Opinions pronounced on particular cases became rules applicable to all cases. Thus the meaning of sati became 'fixed'; in other words, a sati that met certain criteria could be identified as authentic. Once 'textualized', in this instance through systematic writing, colonial officials could and did interpret the vyawasthas in ways that both reflected and did not reflect the intentions of pundits. Given that a statement of the particular became generalized, it obviously no longer had as its reference the initial interaction that produced it. Finally, the enforcement of vyawasthas as law automatically extended their relevance beyond those whose situation had initially elicited them.

The textualization of the pundits' discourse on sati also had as a consequence the elimination of human agency. If vyawasthas grounded in specific contexts were made autonomous the result was also to create an 'imaginative construct' that did not represent any particular sati. This ideal typical representation of sati denied the possibility of sati as the conscious enactment of a social practice. Such erasure of human agency effectively put the operation of Hindu culture into a timeless present in which passive natives remained eternally yoked to religion. In this context it is interesting that many of the descriptions of sati written and used by abolitionists in their arguments are narratives of sati the phenomenon, not of any specific incident.

The following description of a 'typical sati' by the magistrate R.M. Bird is a perfectly textualized example:

> If it were desired to portray a scene which should thrill with horror every heart, not entirely dead to the touch of human sympathy, it would suffice to describe a father, regardless of the affection of his tender child, in having already suffered one of the severest miseries which flesh is heir to, with tearless eye leading forth a spectacle to the assembled multitude, who with barbarous cries demand the şacrifice, and unrelentingly delivering up the unconscious and unresisting victim to an untimely death, accompanied by the most cruel tortures.[65]

Bird here describes sati in which the widow, relatives and spectators all play parts which are predictable given what has been said here about colonial representation of each of their roles. That such textualization also denies the widow subjectivity has also been noted.

In Ricoeur's expanded sense of the term 'textualization', cultures are 'textualized' in a number of ways. Myths, folklore, epics, rituals and other artifacts express and reiterate to a society its cultural values. Ricoeur and Geertz[66] among others have interpreted such cultural expressions in the manner of texts. In arguing that the colonial discourse textualized sati, I am not suggesting that Indian society was not textualized in the pre-colonial period, merely that the colonial mode of textualizing was one that privileged writing and that such writing produced consequences of domination, including those discussed in this paper.

Finally, of course, the discourse on sati is a discourse of power. It illustrates dramatically Foucault's compelling thesis that knowledge is produced within the matrix of power and that power operates through the deployment of knowledge. The relationship between the colonial official and pundit was clearly interwoven by power while the production and accumulation of knowledge about sati enabled both attention to detail and the redefinition and redistribution of sati into its 'legal' and 'illegal' forms.

V. Conclusion

In this paper I have examined the first of the nineteenth-century debates on the status of women in India. These debates arose in the context of determining an appropriate colonial policy on such matters as sati which were seen to mark the depressed position of women in Indian society, the reform of which was held to be part of the regenerating mission of colonization. I have treated the debate as discourse and focused on the assumptions about Indian society crucial to this analysis—the hegemony of religious texts, native obedience to its injunctions, and a scriptural sanction for sati—all of which are problematized by material in the Parliamentary papers.

For instance, diversity in the mode of carrying out sati and regional variation in its incidence highlight the fact that textual tradition was actively negotiated. Similarly, both the resistance of some widows to coercion and what appears as the willingness of others to commit sati signal the fact that women had a will of their own and acted on their own behalf. Finally, whatever the official claims for sati as a practice founded in the Hindu faith, attention to the process by which knowledge about sati was produced illustrates that officials interpreted the responses of pundits in particular ways, with the consequence that the construct of sati that was legally enforced was specifically 'colonial'. Officials employed a number of tactics in reading the vyawasthas of pundits. Among these are the following: they privileged vyawasthas based on religious texts over those that drew on custom. They also insisted that pundits produce explicit scriptural injunction and would accept inference only where such unambiguous support could not be generated. Of course, such tactics were not used with any consistency. Some vyawasthas (like that of Vidyalankar) were simply ignored. Thus, whatever their insistence on having arrived at a concept of sati that was true to the scriptures, we can state with assurance that the process attests mainly to the arbitrariness of meanings imposed by official reading of vyawasthas.

However arbitrary or contingent nineteenth-century official interpretations might have been, some of these assumptions remain with us today, both in the scholarship on sati or more generally in our understanding of Indian society. It is the remarkable endurance of some of these ideas that confirms the contemporary relevance of this investigation. For example, much of the scholarly work on sati reproduces the notion of sati as an essentially religious practice.[67] One consequence of this is to assume a transhistorical significance for the phenomenon, a perspective that precludes the possibility of sati being the product of different factors at different times. Dorothy Stein even goes so far as to suggest that the concept of sati might be more important than its practice.[68] Such an approach lacks explanatory value; it cannot, for example, explain regional variation in the incidence of sati. Not all academic work shares this perspective. Although he does not say so himself, Sharma's article on the history of western response to sati conclusively documents first, that the meaning of sati was historically variable and second, that its meaning was bitterly contested in the nineteenth century.[69] Also, in Ashis Nandy's work, we have the beginnings of an analysis of sati as a practice rooted in temporal and spatial contexts.[70]

The discourse on sati was by no means the first time colonial officials accorded primary significance to religion. The codification of scriptural law as civil law in 1772 had already enshrined its importance.[71] The enforcement of scriptural law as civil law had extended the applicability of brahmanic scripture hitherto limited to the twice-born castes to all colonial subjects. Thus was established a particular relationship between scripture and society, a relationship which was bolstered each time, as in the case of sati in Bengal, colonial officials privileged as authentic the scriptural tradition and marginalized the importance of custom.

I suggest that this designation of the scriptural tradition as 'true' was to have an important bearing on the nineteenth-century debates on the status of women. For these debates were a mode through which colonial power was both enforced and contested. Colonial officials sought to justify interference in indigenous tradition, even colonial rule itself, on the basis of women's low position in indigenous tradition as also in contemporary society. Divergent indigenous male elite responses to this challenge were to argue either that such poor treatment was contrary to tradition—Roy's strategy in the case of sati—or that women approved of their traditional lot—the conservative Hindu response—or that this tradition was bankrupt—the view among others of Henry Derozio. In all three instances, the official equation of tradition with scripture was reproduced. In other words, arguments for and against social reform were articulated, at least in part, upon a peculiarly colonial construction of tradition. Put another way, official discourse shaped the nature of indigenous counter discourses in quite specific ways.

Finally, analysis of the official discourse on sati suggests a less sharp distinction than has hitherto been proposed between Orientalists and Anglicists. The commonalities underlying their perspectives are significant. As such, the issue is raised of the extent to which the Anglicist programme for social engineering was determined by the Orientalist analysis of Indian society.

Notes

1. For a straightforward history of colonial state policy, A. Mukhopadhyay, 'Sati as a Social Institution in Bengal', *Bengal Past and Present*, 75, pp. 99–115; K. Mittra, 'Suppression of Suttee in the Province of Cuttack', *Bengal Past and Present*, 46, pp. 125–31; G. Seed, 'The Abolition of Suttee in Bengal', *History*, October 1955, pp. 286–99. For a 'colonial' account, E.J. Thompson, *Suttee: A Historical and Philosophical Enquiry into the Hindu Rite of Widow Burning*, London, Allen and Unwin, 1928. For a general but very suggestive history of western responses, A. Sharma, 'Suttee: A

Study in Western Reactions', in his *Threshold of Hindu-Buddhist Studies*, Calcutta, Minerva, 1978, pp. 83–111. For a provocative psycho-social analysis, A. Nandy, 'Sati: A Nineteenth Century Tale of Women, Violence and Protest', in V.C. Joshi (ed.), *Rammohun Roy and the Process of Modernisation in India*, Delhi, Vikas, 1975, pp. 168–94. For contemporary feminist analyses, D.K. Stein, 'Women to Burn: Suttee as a Normative Institution', *Signs*, 4(2), 1978, pp. 253–68; M. Daly, *Gyn/Ecology*, Boston, Beacon, 1978.

2. For a succinct formulation of this perspective as it relates to sati, C.A. Bayly, 'From Ritual to Ceremony: Death Ritual in Hindu North India', in J. Whaley (ed.), *Mirrors of Mortality: Studies in the Social History of Death*, London, Europa, 1981, pp. 173–4.
3. I am arguing that this conception was distinctly 'colonial' not by means of comparison with some pre-colonial conception of sati but rather, as will become clear in the course of the paper, with reference to the way a particular knowledge about sati was produced under colonialism.
4. B.S. Cohn in a lecture at University of California, Santa Cruz, February 1981.
5. M. Foucault, *Discipline and Punish*, New York, Vintage, 1979.
6. E. Said, *Orientalism*, New York, Vintage, 1979.
7. R. Thapar, *The Past and Prejudice*, National Book Trust of India, 1975, p. 3.
8. R. Guha (ed.), *Subaltern Studies I: Writings on South Asian History and Society*, Delhi, Oxford University Press, 1982.
9. There is a substantial literature on the history of law under colonialism, a discussion of which is beyond the scope of this paper. See especially: J.D.M. Derrett, *Religion, Law and the State in India*, London, Faber and Faber, 1968, chs 8, 9; Lloyd I. Rudolph and Suzanne H. Rudolph, *The Modernity of Tradition*, Part III, Chicago, University of Chicago Press, 1967, B.S. Cohn, 'Anthropological Notes on Disputes and Law in India', *American Anthropologist*, 67, December 1965, pp. 88–122; D.A. Washbrook, 'Law, State and Agrarian Society in Colonial India', *Modern Asian Studies*, 15(3), 1981, pp. 649–721. Also noteworthy is A. Appadurai's discussion of law in his *Worship and Conflict under Colonial Rule*, Cambridge, Cambridge University Press, 1981.
10. Parliamentary Papers on Hindu Widows (hereafter *PP*), 1821, xviii, p. 316.
11. Loc. cit.
12. Ibid., pp. 322–6.
13. *Vyawasthas* were the written legal opinions submitted by pundits in response to such questions. See also Note 58.
14. *PP*, 1821, pp. 332–3.

15. Ibid., pp. 335–8.
16. *PP*, 1824, xxiii, p. 353.
17. *PP*, 1821, p. 513.
18. *PP*, 1824, p. 378.
19. Loc. cit.
20. *PP*, 1830, xxviii, pp. 1009–11.
21. Analysis of sati by caste for 1823 is as follows: brahmin: 234; kayasth: 25; vaisya: 14; sudra: 292 (*PP*, 1825). It is clear that the practice was disproportionately high among the numerically smaller brahmin caste.
22. J.K. Majumdar (ed.), *Raja Rammohun Roy and Progressive Movements in India: A Selection from Records, 1775–1845*, Calcutta, 1941, p. 141.
23. *PP*, 1821, p. 321.
24. Ibid., pp. 521–3.
25. Loc. cit.
26. Loc. cit.
27. Loc. cit.
28. Loc. cit.
29. Ibid., p. 529.
30. *PP*, 1830, p. 918.
31. *PP*, 1828, xxiii, p. 169.
32. *PP*, 1830, p. 918.
33. *PP*, 1821, p. 532.
34. Ibid., p. 410.
35. Ibid., p. 411.
36. Loc. cit.
37. Ibid., p. 412.
38. Ibid., p. 424.
39. Ibid., p. 321.
40. *PP*, 1830, p. 906.
41. *PP*, 1821, p. 506.
42. Ibid., p. 507.
43. Ibid., p. 404.
44. Ibid., p. 400.
45. Ibid., p. 322.
46. Loc. cit.
47. Loc. cit.
48. Ibid., p. 325.
49. Ibid., p. 322.
50. Ibid., p. 406.
51. The undermining of custom and customary law was not particular to sati but was a general feature of colonial rule and has been noted among others by Derrett, op. cit.; Rudolph and Rudolph, op. cit.; Appadurai, op. cit.

52. Ibid., p. 134.
53. Ibid., pp. 408–9.
54. Ibid., p. 322.
55. Ibid., p. 407.
56. Loc. cit.
57. Loc. cit.
58. In this context it is interesting to note that the dictionary definition of vyawastha tells its own tale of colonial legacy. Vyawastha is variously defined as 'settlement', 'decision', 'statute', 'rule', 'law', 'legal decision' or opinion applied to the written extracts from the codes of law or adjustment of contradictory passages in different codes. Source: A Sanskrit–English Dictionary compiled by Sir Monier Williams.
59. *PP*, 1821, p. 327.
60. Foucault, op. cit., p. 78.
61. *PP*, 1821, p. 344.
62. *PP*, 1823, xvii, p. 354.
63. P. Ricoeur, 'The Model of the Text: Meaningful Action Considered as a Text', *Social Research*, 1971, 38, p. 3.
64. Ricoeur, op. cit., p. 531.
65. *PP*, 1825, xxiv, p. 243.
66. C. Geertz, 'Deep Play: Notes on the Balinese Cockfight', *Daedalus*, 1972, 101, pp. 1–37.
67. Mitra, Mukhopadhyay, Seed, Stein, Thompson, op. cit.
68. Stein, op. cit.
69. Sharma, op. cit.
70. Nandy, op. cit.
71. B.S. Cohn, 'Notes on the History and Study of Indian Society and Culture', in *Structure and Change in Indian Society*, Singer and Cohn (eds), Chicago, Aldine, 1968, p. 10.

3

Education for Women*

Geraldine Forbes

Among the earliest women's memoirs from the nineteenth century are stories of a passionate desire to learn to read. Rassundari Devi, born *c.* 1809, taught herself to read by stealing precious moments from her housework and the responsibilities of caring for 12 children. Later, she described her craving for knowledge:

> I was so immersed in the sea of housework that I was not conscious of what I was going through day and night. After some time the desire to learn how to read properly grew very strong in me, I was angry with myself for wanting to read books. Girls did not read . . . That was one of the bad aspects of the old system. The other aspects were not so bad. People used to despise women of learning . . . In fact, older women used to show a great deal of displeasure if they saw a piece of paper in the hands of a woman. But somehow I could not accept this.[1]

Rassundari's progress was slow but she learned to read, to write, and finally wrote about her own experiences.

Haimavati Sen (*c.* 1866–1932), born a half-century later, recalled her childhood in Khulna District of East Bengal:

> The outer quarters were my resort, that is where I spent all my time; during the office hours I stayed in the school room. The teacher was very fond of me. I greatly enjoyed listening to the lessons. But I had no right

*From Geraldine Forbes, *Women in Modern India* (*New Cambridge History of India*, vol. IV, no. 2) (Cambridge: Cambridge University Press, 1996), pp. 32–63.

> to education. Though I lived like a boy in every respect, in matters of education I remained a woman. It is a popular superstition in our country that women, if educated, have to suffer widowhood; hence that path was entirely closed for me. But I was inspired by an eager wish God had planted in my heart.[2]

Fortunately, a sub-inspector visited the school and heard Haimavati answer the questions her brothers missed. The sub-inspector spoke to her father and Haimavati became a regular pupil.

Pandita Ramabai (1858–1922) was awarded the title 'Pandita' in recognition of her great learning. Ramabai's first teacher was her mother. Anant Padmanabha Dongre, Ramabai's father, was a great Vedic scholar who decided to educate his wife over the objections of the community. Ramabai's rigorous education began at age eight and continued until she was 14. She memorized the *Bhagavata Purana* and the *Bhagavad Gita*; then studied Sanskrit grammar and vocabulary. At this time her family was travelling from one pilgrimage site to another and Ramabai learned first-hand how various sects practised Hinduism.[3]

One cannot generalize from these three cases about women's desire to learn. But given conventional notions about the impropriety, even danger, of women's education we can be certain these headstrong women were a minority. In his Report on the State of Education in Bengal (1836) William Adam wrote: 'A superstitious feeling is alleged to exist in the majority of Hindu families, principally cherished by the women and not discouraged by the men, that a girl taught to read and write will soon after marriage become a widow.' Adam also commented on the fear, shared by Hindus and Muslims, that a 'knowledge of letters' might facilitate female intrigue.[4] Because Hindu women were totally dependent on fathers, then husbands, and finally sons for support, they said prayers and performed rituals to ensure longevity for these men. If learning to read would lead to a husband's death, then pursuing knowledge was tantamount to suicide. This was a sex-segregated world; men and women did different work and occupied separate spaces. Women interacted primarily with women and it was women who enforced the prohibition against female education. Many of the women who learned to read before the 1870s have reported hiding their accomplishments from other women. Even if mothers were lenient with daughters, mothers-in-law and the other women in the father-in-law's home were seldom as kind. It is difficult to impute motives to the women who vehemently opposed education. Subjects of a harsh patrilineal, patriarchal system they were not in a position to oppose prevailing codes. Their survival depended on upholding the status quo and an educated stranger in their midst posed an obvious threat. Those women and girls who were eager to learn had no recourse but to look to the men who controlled their lives.

Missionaries began the first girls' school but their efforts were soon rivalled by Indian reformers. Despite their valiant efforts, there were no real advances in female education until the second half of the nineteenth century when the government offered financial support. Even then, efforts to organize girls' schools languished until the urban professional elite joined reformers in supporting formal education for girls. In the last quarter of the nineteenth century, institutions proliferated and the number of educated women grew steadily. The debate then turned to what was the most suitable type of education for women. Before the century was over a few women came forward to articulate their ideas about female education. By the twentieth century women were ready to design a curriculum and set up schools for girls.

Traditional Education

Traditionally education meant learning to read sacred literature. Among Hindus, members of the priestly caste, brahmins, were learned in all branches of sacred knowledge, while the other twice-born castes (kshatriyas and vaishyas) were given a less rigorous programme but also learned practical skills. Shudras and most women were not taught the sacred books but some women were taught to read. Some women from upper-class Vaisnavite families learned to read puranic literature.[5] Muslims girls were expected to learn the Quran and some accounting skills but the strict seclusion observed by upper-class families prohibited their daughters from attending schools. Consequently, what they learned about their religion they learned at home, either from their families or through tutors.[6] At the turn of the century there were only 11 Quran schools for girls in Bengal with 142 pupils.[7]

At the beginning of the nineteenth century, female literacy was extremely low in relation to male literacy. Male literacy, ranging from approximately 6 per cent in Bengal to 20 per cent in the Deccan, was also low in comparison with Western nations or Japan. Moreover, indigenous schools for boys were on the decline.[8] Boys attended three kinds of schools: small village schools which taught elementary reading and accounting; higher schools for Hindus, primarily brahmins, which taught Sanskrit grammar, lexicography and literature; and Persian and Arabic schools for Muslims. We do not know how many of these schools there were throughout India, but in Bengal there were approximately 100 traditional institutions per district with a total of 10,800 students. There were 164 Hindu schools in Poona in the 1820s. Aparna Basu contends that 'the state of higher learning among Hindus and Muslims resembled that which existed in Europe before the invention of printing'.[9]

Female education was informal and largely limited to practical matters. Women from respectable families often studied classical or vernacular literature as 'a pious recreation', and girls from propertied families received some education in keeping accounts.[10] But most females learned only the household arts.

English Education in India

English education was introduced into India because the East India Company needed clerks and translators. From 1813 the Company set aside some money for education, and after the Charter of 1833 English became the official language. In 1844 Lord Hardinge announced that English-educated Indians would be given preference for government appointments. Free-traders voiced their support for this policy believing it would help develop an Indian population loyal to the British. The missionaries joined the chorus of approval. Eager to convert Indians from influential families, missionaries recognized how much easier it would be with English as the language of professional advancement. Liberals believed in the civilizing influence of Western philosophy and literature. It was only at the end of the century that these men saw the dangerous side of education, that is, its tendency to promote nationalism and political unrest. Then, the government made attempts to control and even curtail education.[11]

Long before the government decided to sponsor English education, Indian gentlemen set up Hindu College in Calcutta. Opened in 1816,

Hindu College was designed to prepare young Indian men for lucrative positions with the East India Company. In the first three decades of the twentieth century Hindu College and similar schools throughout British India depended on the patronage of wealthy Indians and were in direct competition with traditional schools teaching Sanskrit, Persian and Arabic. As economic patterns changed, patronage for traditional schools disappeared. At about the same time, bright young men decided to study English.[12]

In contrast to support for boys' schools, there was little interest in the education of girls. The colonial government, despite pressure exerted by missionaries and liberals, was unconcerned with female education. The missionaries were interested in female education and schools for girls because, they argued, women needed to be brought into the fold to make conversions permanent. But since men made the decisions, female education was ancillary.[13]

Unmarried female missionaries arrived in India in the 1840s and were assigned to work with women and children. These missionary women, educated and eager to prove their worth, concentrated on converting adult married Indian women to Christianity.[14] They gained entry to households as teachers where they read stories, taught needlework, and attempted to bring their charges to Christ. Rarely were they successful in gaining converts. When it became apparent that these zenana projects were unproductive, the mission authorities substituted girls' schools. Missionary women continued to teach and it was their students, Indian women from Christian families, who became teachers in a number of the new girls' schools.[15]

Early Schools for Girls

The opening of Hindu College in 1816 was closely followed by the founding of the Calcutta School Society to promote female education. Radha Kanta Deb, the secretary of this society, became a patron of female education and assisted in the formation of the Calcutta Female Juvenile Society (founded in 1819 by Baptists). In 1821, the School Society brought Miss Mary Anne Cooke to Calcutta but could not raise the money to open schools. The Church Missionary Society stepped in, employed Miss Cooke, and opened 30 schools for 'respectable' Hindu girls. These schools enjoyed the patronage of Hindu gentlemen and were staffed by brahmin pundits, but they failed to attract girls from the higher castes. The religious instruction deterred prestigious families while pupils from the lower classes or Christian families were lured to the school by gifts of clothing and other items.

The Church Missionary Society was more successful in South India where it opened its first boarding school for girls in Tirunelveli in 1821. By 1840 the Scottish Church Society could claim six schools with a clientele of 200 Hindu girls. By mid-century the missionaries in Madras were instructing nearly 8,000 girls, the majority of whom were Christians, in day schools and boarding schools.[16]

One of the most important schools for girls was the Hindu Balika Vidyalaya opened in 1849 in Calcutta by J.E. Drinkwater Bethune, legal member of the Governor-General's Council and president of the Council of Education. The school was secular, instruction was in Bengali, and the girls were transported in a carriage emblazoned with a Sanskrit verse declaring that a daughter's education was a father's religious duty. Pandit Vidyasagar was appointed school secretary. Bethune persuaded several prominent families to endorse this experiment and by 1850 there were eighty pupils. When Bethune died in 1851, support for the school declined. In 1863 the school had 93 girls aged five to seven, three-quarters of whom were the 'lowest class', a clear indication of continuing upper-caste prejudice against female education.[17]

Government Support of Female Education

Lord Dalhousie, Governor-General of India from 1848 to 1856, declared that no single change was likely to produce more important and beneficial consequences than female education.[18] Sir Charles Wood, president of the Board of Control from 1853 to 1855, issued an education despatch in 1854 that detailed a shift in government policy, from providing higher education for the elites to support for mass education in the vernacular. This new focus on a total system of education was to include both sexes. The despatch read:

> The importance of female education in India cannot be over-rated; and we have observed with pleasure the evidence which is now afforded of an increased desire on the part of many of the natives to give a good

education to their daughters. By this means a far greater proportional impulse is imparted to the educational and moral tone of the people than by the education of men.[19]

The moral and financial support of the colonial authorities was essential to the spread of female education, but did not guarantee schools for girls. Unlike education for males, education for females did not automatically enhance the prestige and financial standing of the family. In fact, the opposite may have been true.

Indian norms and social customs made the British model of schooling difficult, if not impossible. Deeply ingrained notions of sex segregation and, in some areas, of complete seclusion, meant girls had to have female teachers and study in separate institutions. The widely accepted ideal of youthful marriage limited a girl's school-going years. Moreover, the demands on women for food production and nurturing left little time for lessons and studying.

There was a third set of problems associated with the institutions for female education. Indians were unaccustomed to sending their daughters to 'schools' yet this was the only practical method of accomplishing the task. Zenana education—education given in the home—was expensive, cumbersome, and largely ineffectual. Schools were the answer but what kind of schools? Who would teach? What would be taught? Which families would choose to send their daughters to school and for how long? If girls were married prior to puberty, could they continue their education as married women? The leaders of Indian society had to respond to these questions—a far more difficult task than providing moral and material support.

Reformed Hinduism and Female Education

The breakthrough came with the establishment of government schools, such as Bethune's, and schools sponsored by reformist religious institutions. First the Brahmo Samaj, and later the Prarthana Samaj, Arya Samaj, and Theosophical Society all supported female education.

In 1854 there were approximately 626 girls' schools (Bengal: 288, Madras: 256, Bombay: 65, and NWFP and Oudh: 17) with a total of 21,755 students.[20] Obviously these schools were very small and the total number of girls receiving this education was minuscule in relation to the total population. Yet, a shift in attitudes towards female education had taken place.

Indians supported female education because they wanted social and religious reform, or social and financial mobility, or both. The founders of Hindu College and other early schools for boys wanted to advance the opportunities of their own class. In the case of female education, early supporters saw opportunities for social mobility as the demand for educated brides increased. They were also motivated by a desire for social reform, possible only if women as well as men were educated. Many Western-educated Bengali gentlemen undoubtedly wanted to 'wean away their own wives and daughters' from various forms of popular culture regarded as licentious and vulgar. This increased the social distance between the 'new women' and their less educated sisters and deprived educated middle-class women of an avenue of protest offered by street performers and popular songs.[21] The concern here was not with women as individuals, but with their development as companions to men, as 'scientific' nurturers, and as members of civil society.

Members of the Brahmo Samaj, the Bengal-based reform society, led the movement for female education and equality between the sexes. Keshub Chandra Sen, a Brahmo leader, lectured on the importance of female education in 1861 and the following year organized a society for males who supported reforms for women. In 1865, the Brahmo Samaj sponsored the first organization where women met for religious instruction, sewing lessons, and discussions of social issues.[22]

The topic of women's education led to a split in the Brahmo Samaj in 1866. That year, Navabidhan (Keshub Sen's breakaway group) welcomed Miss Mary Carpenter to Calcutta. Carpenter's mission was to encourage female education and she was quick to notice the shortage of suitable teachers.[23] She spoke publicly about the problem, presented her proposals to the Governor-General, and helped establish the National Indian Association to promote mutual understanding between Indian and English people. In 1872 Carpenter, Keshub Sen, and another English woman, Annette Akroyd, set up a normal school.[24] Later Akroyd broke with Keshub and worked with another group of Brahmos to establish the Hindu Mahila Vidyalaya (Hindu Girls' School). By 1878 this school had merged with the older Bethune

School to become Bethune College, an affiliate of Calcutta University. In 1883 Kadambini Basu and Chandramukhi Basu received their BAs from Bethune, becoming the first women graduates in the British Empire.[25]

In Madras it was the Theosophical Society that encouraged female education. Speaking as a leader of the society, Annie Besant (1847–1933) asserted that in ancient times Hindu women were educated and moved freely in society. She urged a return to this 'golden age'. In England Besant had been identified with women's emancipation since her public lecture on women's suffrage in 1874.[26] Besant had been associated with a number of other movements in England before she read Madame Blavatsky's *Secret Doctrine* in 1889. She then decided to join the theosophists and make India her home. Madame Blavatsky, a founder of the Theosophical Society, viewed child marriage, child widowhood, and sati as perversions of the original Hindu doctrine.[27] When Besant first spoke in India in 1893, she spoke of the greatness of the Indian past and the need to regain that past. Later she focused on specific problems and by 1901 had written an article for the *Indian Ladies Magazine* on the 'Education of Women'. Besant warned that India's fate would be sealed if women were not educated. But Western education was not the answer; it would 'unsex' women. Indians should look to their own ideal of womanhood—the Goddess Durga.[28] Besant pledged her efforts to this reform and founded a women's college based on these principles.[29]

In North India female education was encouraged by the Arya Samaj, a reformist Hindu sect which followed the teachings of Swami Dayanand Saraswati. By the end of the nineteenth century, progressive Arya Samajists recognized the importance of involving women in their reform efforts. The Jullundar Samaj opened the Arya Kanya Pathshala (Girls' School) in 1890 with a lady principal in charge.[30]

The Kanya Mahavidyalaya (Girls' Higher School) of Jullundar was opened somewhat later. Both this high school and the elementary girls' school, firmly established by 1892, owed their existence to the efforts of Lala Devraj. He opened his first school for girls in the family home, supported it through the sale of 'waste paper', and staffed it with teachers who were partially compensated with food from his mother's kitchen. As public acceptance for the idea of female education grew so did the school's enrolment. Before long a cadre of experienced women teachers and school administrators had designed special instructional materials. This institution occupied a special place in the community and 'became a catalyst for various kinds of change relating to women in [the] Punjab'.[31]

The Progress of Women's Education

Between 1849, when Bethune School opened, and 1882, when the Indian Education (Hunter) Commission reviewed the progress of education in India, serious efforts had been made to develop primary schools for girls and teacher-training institutions. Higher education for women and co-education were still contentious issues.[32] Faced with the fact that 98 per cent of school-age girls were not in school, authors of the Hunter Commission Report recommended more liberal grants-in-aid for girls' schools than for boys' and special scholarships and prizes for girls. In the next two decades higher education expanded rapidly; whereas there were only six women in Indian universities in 1881–2, by the turn of the century there were 264. During the same time period secondary school enrolment rose from 2,054 to 41,582.[33]

The story of women's education in the period following the Hunter Commission and the end of the century can be told through the work of three pioneer educationalists—Pandita Ramabai Saraswati, founder of the Sharada Sadan in Bombay and Poona (1889), Mataji Tapaswini who began the Mahakali Pathshala of Calcutta (1893), and D.K. Karve who began a school for widows in Poona (1896). These three examples are particularly significant because they represent efforts to build female schools distinct from those of the religious reform organizations. These were not secular public schools in the contemporary sense; in fact, they were all narrowly caste-, class- and community-based. These three examples are especially worthy of attention because they highlight the involvement of women in structuring and defining female education.

Pandita Ramabai

Pandita Ramabai was truly remarkable as a pioneer in women's education and rebel champion of women's rights. Her father supervised her education and allowed her to remain unmarried. When her father and mother died, Ramabai was 16 years old, unmarried, and able to read Sanskrit. She and her brother travelled throughout India lecturing on female education and social reform. The Calcutta elite were enchanted and bestowed on her the name 'Saraswati'—the Goddess of Learning—and called her 'Pandita' because she seemed as learned as other brahmin pandits. Other audiences were outraged and they jeered and booed when she attempted to speak.[34]

Ramabai's brother died in Calcutta and she married his close friend, Bipen Behari Das Medhavi (a shudra by caste). The next year, at age 23, Ramabai gave birth to a daughter. Unfortunately her husband died the following year.

Returning to Poona, Ramabai began to work with reformers to educate women through the Arya Mahila Samaj (Aryan's Women's Society).[35] While in Poona she gave evidence before the Hunter Commission and stressed the urgent need for women doctors and teachers. Determined to learn English and study medicine, Ramabai sought help from members of the Anglo-Catholic Community of St Mary the Virgin whose mother house was at Wantage in Oxfordshire, England. They were able to give her some assistance while the balance of her expenses were met through the sale of *Stri Dharma Neeti* ('Morals for Women'), her book urging women to take charge of their own lives. Ramabai, her young daughter, and a travelling companion, Anandibai Bhagat, left for England in 1883. Soon after the three of them had settled at Wantage, Ramabai declared she was unwilling to convert to Christianity. Some months later Anandibai committed suicide (the records here become very elusive) leaving Ramabai extremely shaken.

Ramabai was only 25 years of age and had already watched her parents, her brother, her husband, and her closest friend die. It was at this time, alone with her small daughter in a strange country, that Ramabai decided to accept baptism.[36] She continued her studies until 1886 when she decided to sail for America to attend the graduation ceremonies of her cousin Anandibai Joshi.

To finance this trip and popularize her cause Ramabai wrote *The High Caste Hindu Women*. Ten thousand copies of this book were sold before Ramabai had left America. In 1887 Boston admirers set up a Ramabai Association to support her work in India. She travelled throughout the United States and Canada studying educational, philanthropic and charitable institutions and lecturing to various groups. By May of 1888, she had collected over $30,000 in the name of her association.[37]

In India Pandita Ramabai established Sharada Sadan (Home of Wisdom), a school for widows, in Bombay. This was to be a non-sectarian school where all the caste rules of brahmins were scrupulously observed. It attracted some high-caste Hindu widows, among them Godubai (renamed Anandibai after her marriage to D.K. Karve) but generally the Hindu community remained suspicious of Ramabai's motives.

Ramabai attempted to forestall criticism by forming an Executive Committee composed of reformers who were known as staunch Hindus. This plan did not work and less than one year later Bombay newspapers carried articles critical of Ramabai and her school. When financial problems forced her to move the school to Poona, the newspaper *Kesari* charged her with converting widows to Christianity. Ramabai's admitted crime was allowing widows to attend her personal prayer meetings. By 1893, 25 girls were withdrawn. But there was no dearth of widows in need of shelter and before long Ramabai had other students. By 1900 the Sharada Sadan had trained 80 women who were able to earn their own living through teaching or nursing.[38]

Ramabai's second school, Mukti, was established 30 miles outside of Poona at Kedgaon following the famine that began in 1897. She began taking women and children who were victims of famine into Sharada Sadan where she fed and clothed them, and enrolled them in her school. Attempting to control the plague, the government placed restrictions on the movement of people; in Poona the city magistrate placed a limit on the number of inmates in Sharada Sadan. Since she could not keep famine victims in Poona, Ramabai took her charges to Kedgaon where she had purchased 100 acres of land. By 1900 this venture had grown into a major institution housing 2,000 women and children attending school and involved in industrial training and production. Financing for Mukti came from an American committee which willingly approved all her schemes.[39]

Given a free hand, Ramabai urged the inmates of her home to become Christians and developed a unique educational programme to suit their needs. Her own version of Christianity was doctrinally eclectic, combining ideas she had learned from the sisters at Wantage, and from Roman Catholic, Jewish and Indian Christian friends. Ramabai saw caste as the great flaw in Hindu society. It led to false valuing of the intellect and denigration of physical work. Caste association promoted narrow self-interest and inhibited the development of a democratic spirit.

Ramabai designed a remedial curriculum. Literature selected for its emphasis on moral models would engender a spirit of caring; classes in physiology and botany were included to teach students about their own bodies and the physical world in which they lived. Industrial training was included—in printing, carpentry, tailoring, masonry, wood-cutting, weaving and needlework—as well as training in farming and gardening. All students were required to join 'unions' or societies such as the Temperance Union or the Christian Endeavour Society in an effort to break down caste barriers and develop new loyalties based on interest. As members of these societies, the children learned simple parliamentary rules and were encouraged to take charge of their own affairs.[40]

Ramabai's educational work impressed contemporaries, but her connection with Christianity has obfuscated her contribution to women's education. An acknowledged Christian when hatred of the ruling power was growing daily, her work angered some of the most powerful men in western India. Ramabai believed the intensity of their anger was related to the fact that many of her pupils came from the higher castes. She argued that these men would have remained unconcerned if her work were confined to low caste women.[41]

There were many issues that provoked Ramabai's sharp and unpopular comments. When she heard about the Rukhmabai case, she exploded in angry denunciations of both the British and Indian men. Rukhmabai, married as a child, had been tried and sentenced to prison (but was never imprisoned) because she refused to have a conjugal relationship with her husband. Ramabai wrote:

> Our only wonder is that a defenceless woman like Rukhmabai dared to raise her voice in the face of the powerful Hindu law, the mighty British Government, the 129,000,000 men, the 330,000,000 gods of the Hindus; all these have conspired together to crush her into nothingness. We cannot blame the English Government for not defending a helpless woman; it is only fulfilling its agreement made with the male population of India.[42]

Ramabai's greatest legacy was her effort, the first in India, to educate widows and the pupils she left behind to carry on her work.

Mataji Maharani Tapaswini

The Mahakali Pathshala (Great Mother Kali School) of Bengal stands in sharp contrast to Pandita Ramabai's school, with its missionary connection and foreign support. Founded in Calcutta in 1893 by Her Holiness Mataji Maharani Tapaswini, this school and its many branches has been styled a 'genuine Indian attempt' at developing female education.[43] This school received no financial assistance from foreigners and employed no foreign teachers. Founders of the institution accepted the 'school' model for female education, but opposed co-education and the use of one syllabus for both sexes. Their aim was to educate 'girls on strictly national lines in the hope that they might regenerate Hindu society.' This was a project consistent with those of nationalist 'revivalists', who, in the historian Tanika Sarkar's view, did not automatically oppose reform 'in the name of resisting colonial knowledge'.[44] Despite their differences with the liberal reformers, they too believed in the relationship between progress and female education and looked to a future where Indian women would play a large role in the affairs of the country.

Gangabai (Mataji Maharani Tapaswini), a brahmin woman of the Deccan who had learned Sanskrit and studied sacred literature, opened her first school with 30 pupils.[45] She had come to Calcutta with a mission: to promote female education in harmony with Hindu religious and moral principles. Unlike Pandita Ramabai, Gangabai believed that Hindu society could be regenerated from within. Her notion of an ideal education for women was translated into a syllabus which included: knowledge of sacred literature and history; an understanding of the myths and legends that spoke of the duties of the daughter, wife, daughter-in-law and mother; and practical skills such as cooking and sewing.[46] This syllabus was praised by 'Hindoo gentlemen of the middle-class' who believed that much of the female education then in existence 'demoralized and denationalized' young Hindu women.[47] Cooking lessons were especially popular in light of the prevalent belief that educated girls avoided the kitchen. Financial support for this institution grew rapidly and within 10 years there were 23 branches with 450 students. As the school expanded it published its own Bengali and Sanskrit textbooks. Gangabai turned more and more to supervision while the actual administration of the school was left in the hands of an illustrious board of trustees presided over by the Maharaja of Darbhanga, Bengal's largest landlord.

This school proved immensely popular. Patrons approved of the emphasis on religious injunctions, domestic skills, and strict purdah. Although the original curriculum included very little formal reading and writing, this gradually changed. In 1948 the Mahakali Pathshala was affiliated to Calcutta University and by that time all that remained of the original curriculum was the performance of a few pujas (religious rituals).[48] In the early years of the twentieth century the existence of this school and its popularity were regarded as indicators that the conservative elements of society, at least in Bengal, had given their approval to the concept of female education.[49]

Dhondo Keshav Karve

In the 1890s Dhondo Keshav Karve established a number of female schools in Poona. In his autobiography, *Looking Back*, Karve reconstructs his personal history to explain how his experiences led him to build a school for widows in 1896. Other accounts tell the story of Godubai Joshi (later Anandibai), a child widow who became Karve's second wife. She dreamed of setting up a widow's home soon after she became Pandita Ramabai's first pupil. What may well have been the culmination of the life-long dream of two people has been known as 'Karve's Home'. Anandibai joked about this when she was very old:

> Sometimes in fun I tell him that although people call him Maharshi, some of the credit is due to me. For if I had not managed the family affairs and set him free to carry out his public activities, he could not have achieved to much.[50]

Karve's association with reform movements dated back to his college years. After graduation from Elphinstone College he taught mathematics in three different high schools in Bombay before accepting a position at Fergusson College in Poona. Here he was elected a life member of the Deccan Educational Society.[51] When his wife died, he decided he would marry a widow and chose Godubai, the 22-year-old sister of his college friend. People in his home town excommunicated him and persecuted his mother. These actions shocked Karve and caused him to question remarriage as a way of helping child widows. At the same time he became increasingly interested in education as a way of assisting widows to become financially independent. In 1896 he opened a shelter for widows that became a school.

The curriculum in this school was designed to make young widows employable and self-sufficient. Because schools for girls were scarce, Karve was asked to admit unmarried girls as well. To accommodate this new clientele, Karve set up the Mahila Vidyalaya (Girls' School) to develop 'good wives, good mothers, good neighbours'. He believed that widows needed an education 'that would make them economically independent and would enable them to think for themselves'[52] but unmarried girls needed an education that would reinforce their dependence.

Parvatibai Athavali, Anandibai's widowed sister, played an important role in the growth and expansion of Karve's schools. Married at age 11, Parvatibai became a widow at age 20, the third widowed daughter in her father's home. Rejecting all discussion of remarriage, Parvatibai declared her wish to study and 'do some work of importance'.[53] After receiving her education in Karve's school, she became a teacher and then the superintendent. Parvatibai, a voluntarily tonsured widow, orthodox in her food habits, spoke publicly against widow remarriage.[54] Through her, Karve gained credibility with conservatives who had previously characterized him as a radical because of his own remarriage. In her public lectures, Parvatibai insisted a woman's true mission in life was to marry. She supported the curriculum of Karve's school with instruction in the vernacular languages and emphasis on childcare and homecraft. Traditionally, these subjects had been taught by the older women in the households, but the increased complexity of women's work made formal education necessary.[55] Parvatibai warned women against rejecting their 'natural roles' to enter the tyrannical market place. Yet she had entered the market place and from her own account not unwillingly. She explained her own life as follows:

> I felt that a widow who had one or two children and who had had some actual experience of the happiness of domestic life, if she were able to do some work of importance would not be tempted to enter again into the duties of a married life. In accordance with this idea, I settled on my ideal of life.[56]

In her description of the ideal education for a woman and the ideal life-course, Parvatibai seemed to ignore the lesson of her own life. Like Karve, she regarded public roles for women as an aberration rather than the norm.

Karve spent much of his money on his institutions and even cashed in his life insurance policy of Rs 5,000 to raise funds for the home. Anandibai, now the mother of his child, was alarmed because she knew that if Karve died she would be refused even domestic employment. Many brahmin widows found employment as cooks or maidservants but if they married a second time they were considered unclean. By her own account Anandibai, 'cried, quarrelled with him, abused him' but could not get him to budge. Karve was similarly neglectful of their day-to-day needs. Finally Anandibai realized that for survival she would have to seek employment. She completed a course in midwifery and earned enough to provide for the family's needs.[57]

Karve's third institution for women was the Women's University founded in 1916. He had heard of the Women's University in Japan and concluded that this model would be more suitable for India than the Western co-educational university. As president of the National Social Conference in 1915 he said: 'we must recognize that both national and social economy require that women should occupy a station of their own distinct from that of men . . . but that the office they have to fill is different, though equal—perhaps greater in importance.'[58] All courses at the Women's University were conducted in the vernacular, special subjects like home science were included, and it was 'possible for women to avoid difficult subjects like mathematics and physical science'.[59] This institution limped along for the first few years until it was adopted by Sir Vithaldas Thackersey who contributed Rs 1,500,000 in 1920 with the stipulation that the university be named after his mother (thereby becoming Shreemati Nathibai Damodar Thackersey Indian Women's University or SNDT) and relocated in Bombay.[60]

The Early Twentieth Century

By the turn of the century the number of schools for girls and school enrolment had risen dramatically. By the end of World War I, there were educational institutions for women in all parts of the country, and enrolments tripled at the school level and quintupled in universities.[61] Parents now had more options: they could choose the type of institution, the curriculum, even the language of instruction. These alternatives assuaged the fears of conservatives and liberals, the religious and the non-religious, those who desired radical change and traditionalists, anglophiles and anglophobes. Institution-builders like Karve had effectively argued that female education was the ideal method of smoothing over the rough spots in the transition from tradition to modernity and his successors continued to echo his reasoning:

> In the eyes of men of forethought and ambition, a woman trained on these lines to the profession of wifehood, is a far more desirable companion than an amateur wife. The training which a girl gets in her own home and under her own mother in India is admirable as far as it goes, but modern life has introduced many complexities to deal with for which a regular and systematic training is necessary.[62]

Maharani Tapaswini and K.D. Karve were educating young women from conservative homes to become, as they argued, better wives and mothers in a modern world. To gain the support of conservative communities, they developed curricula dominated by home science and religious lore. And their rhetoric matched their curricula. Karve may have educated young widows to be self-supporting but he was clear that unmarried girls needed to be taught how to become good wives and mothers. Maharani Tapaswini was not at all interested in education for employment.

Pandita Ramabai stands in direct contrast to these two educators. She was critical of her own society and renounced Hinduism to become a Christian. She built a successful school in terms of numbers but she relied for both material and psychological support on foreign missionaries. They sent her money and praised her while her own community ostracized her. Ramabai wanted to make women capable of supporting themselves. It was an appealing idea as long as her focus was lower-class women; upper-class/caste families were unwilling to contemplate economic independence for their wives and daughters.

Between 1900 and 1920 'new women', that is, women who were the beneficiaries of the social reforms and educational efforts of the nineteenth century, stepped forward to begin their own schools. They too were aware of conservative attitudes towards female education, but the picture had changed considerably. The demand for female education was growing steadily and what parents wanted, it seemed, was reassurance that these new schools observed 'traditional' customs. To illustrate the change I will sketch the educational effort of two women: Begum Rokeya and Sister Subbalakshmi.

Begum Rokeya Sakhawat Hossain

In 1909 Begum Rokeya Sakhawat Hossain (1880–1932) began an institution for Muslim girls in the district town of Bhagalpur, Bihar. She set up this school soon after her husband's death but his relations were offended. Driven out of her home by her step-daughter, Begum Rokeya closed the school and moved to Calcutta where she opened another school, Sakhawat Memorial Girls' School, in 1911. Although this was not the first school set up by a Muslim woman for Muslim girls, Begum Rokeya's systematic and undaunted devotion to this project has earned her the title of pioneer. This school, with Urdu as its language of instruction, was designed and organized for students who observed purdah even though Begum Rokeya wrote and spoke publicly about the evils of this custom.[63]

Begum Rokeya was fortunate, by her own account, in having an elder brother and a husband who encouraged her interest in education. Her elder sister Karimunnessa had not been so lucky. When it was discovered that Karimunnessa had learned to read English, she was sent to live under the watchful eye of her grandmother until her marriage could be arranged. To be on the safe side, Rokeya's elder brother taught her to read English in the dead of night. Syed Sakhawat Hossain, her husband, was a widower who had been educated in the West. He looked to his young wife for companionship and soon after their wedding gave her lessons in English and encouraged her to write essays. At age 21, only three years after their marriage, Rokeya was publishing articles about women's condition. Over the years she wrote a number of articles, short stories, and novels in which she developed her ideas on the need to awaken women to their oppression and the role of education in this process.

In three of her essays, 'Ardhangi' ('The Female Half'), 'Griha' ('The House'), and 'Borka' (or *burqah*—'The Veil'), Rokeya commented on women's asymmetrical development, lack of economic means, and confinement for the sake of male honour. In 'Sugrihini' ('The Ideal Housewife') she pointed out that education would help women fulfil their traditional roles knowledgeably and professionally and hence contribute to the progress of the nation. Additionally, education would make it possible for women to grow and develop in step with their menfolk.

Begum Rokeya's school conformed, in curriculum and purdah restrictions, to the schools for Muslim girls in the Punjab and United Provinces.[64] Emphasis was placed on literacy and practical subjects such as handicrafts, home science and gardening. The curriculum in Begum Rokeya's school also included physical fitness training. But this was the only deviation from an educational programme designed to produce good wives and mothers: companions and help-mates to their husbands and teachers for their children.

The strictest rules of female seclusion were observed in transporting the girls to and from the school and there was only slight modification (curtains replacing closed shutters) when the young pupils vomitted and fainted in the hot, airless carriage.[65] Inside the school the girls covered their heads. This was a new form of modest attire, suitable for the modernizing women now entering new spaces where neither the burqah, designed as outdoor wear, nor the clothes worn inside the home were suitable. The new head coverings signified concern with both modesty and modernity.

While Begum Rokeya's school conformed to rules of female seclusion, she wrote stinging criticisms of the practice. In addition to her essay on the burqah, she wrote *Sultana's Dream* (1905), a short story in which women ran the world and men hid indoors, and *Avarodhbasini* ('The Secluded Ones') (1929), 47 serialized reports documenting the custom of purdah. Her satirical writings on female seclusion were meant to inform an audience ignorant of the real tragedy of purdah (her own aunt was killed by a train because she would not cry out for help). Seclusion, Begum Rokeya, wrote, 'is not a gaping wound, hurting people. It is rather a silent killer like carbon monoxide gas.'[66] She denied this custom had any basis in the Quran or Shari'ah (the Muslim religious law).

Rokeya's campaign was unpopular. Accused of being both pro-Christian and a Europhile, Rokeya attracted more hostility when she endorsed Katherine Mayo's *Mother India*. But her school remained open, attended by Muslim girls from good families. Apparently her central argument, that neglect of female education would ultimately threaten Islamic culture, struck a responsive chord.

Sister Subbalakshmi

At about the same time that Begum Rokeya opened her school for Muslim girls in Calcutta, Sister Subbalakshmi (1886–1969) established a school for young high-caste widows in Madras. Sister Subbalakshmi's concern was society's discarded child widows. Her plan was to transform these unfortunate and inauspicious women into useful and valued members of society.[67]

Prior to her own marriage at age 11, Subbalakshmi had received four and a half years of formal schooling. Her husband died shortly after their wedding and she returned to her parents' home in Rishyiyur, Tanjore District. Her parents decided not to burden her with all the restrictions normally placed on widows and instead arranged to send her to school. Their community reacted so violently that Subramania Iyer, Subbalakshmi's father, decided to move. In Madras, Subramania Iyer taught his daughter English at home and then sent her to a convent school. The nuns' dedication so impressed the young Subbalakshmi that she resolved to devote her life to educating widows. Although she never became a Christian, she was affectionately known as 'Sister Subbalakshmi' in recognition of her dedication to her chosen work.

Subbalakshmi completed her matriculation and enrolled in Presidency College, Madras University. As the first Hindu widow in Madras to study for a BA, she was threatened with excommunication, harassed in the streets, and ostracized in the classroom. By 1911 she had completed her BA degree and was ready to begin her life's work. She set up her first school in her father's home in a Madras suburb and began with a class of four brahmin widows.

Subbalakshmi's interest in helping widows coincided with that of Miss Christina Lynch (later Mrs Drysdale), the Irish feminist who was appointed inspectress of female education in Coimbatore. Miss Lynch was deeply troubled by the difficulty of finding 'suitable' (high-caste) teachers for the schools. At the same time she was aware that Madras had over 22,000 widows between the ages of five and 15, many of them brahmins. Meeting with Subbalakshmi's father, Miss Lynch explained that she had worked out a plan whereby the government would support a home for young brahmin widows willing to be trained as teachers. Meanwhile, Sister Subbalakshmi was pursuing the same scheme with her friends and relations. In 1912 the Sarada Ladies Union was formed as a women's club to provide its members with an opportunity to hear lectures, discuss new ideas and collect money for a brahmin girls' school.

In 1912 the government agreed to support a boarding school for training teachers. The government would pay the rent and give scholarships to three girls; the remainder of the operating expenses had to be met through donations and fees. In order to make this plan more acceptable to critics of education for Hindu widows, Miss Lynch proposed shifting the school from a liberal section of the city to the more orthodox Triplicane. This meant Subbalakshmi had to locate a 'home' for the widows. After an extensive search she finally settled on the Ice House, the old warehouse along the beach once used to store ice from Boston. The Ice House was slowly made habitable for the 35 girls who by this time had joined Subbalakshmi. As Sister Subbalakshmi commented, 'There was a lot of gossip and ill-talk' about the large number of girl widows and female staff who occupied the Ice House without male protection. The presence of so many inauspicious women walking about forced local people to modify their schedules. Subbalakshmi wrote:

> I remember how the orthodox elders in a well-to-do family wanted the bride-groom's procession either before 9 a.m. or after 10 a.m. so that there would be no contact (seeing) the widows on their way to school.[68]

The school's curriculum was set by the government. The aim was to train these women as teachers: first, they were prepared for regular classes, then they completed the syllabus for matriculation, and finally, they entered Queen Mary's College (begun in 1914 as the first college for women in Madras). In 1922 the Lady Willingdon Training College and Practice School, an institution for teacher training, opened with Sister Subbalakshmi as principal. At this institution Sister Subbalakshmi was able to implement some of her ideas on education. The college offered three programmes: post-graduate training for potential high-school teachers, secondary training for teaching through the eighth grade, and training for elementary teachers. English was emphasized (because teachers who knew English were in demand), some vocational subjects were required to instil the value of working with the hands, a training course in physical education was available and popular, and Hindu and Christian priests offered moral and religious instruction. Before long Sister Subbalakshmi was compelled to open Sarada Vidyalaya, a high school and boarding school for adult widows. This facility was necessary because the Ice House did not accept widows over age 18 even though the age of marriage was gradually shifting upward and the concept of widows working as teachers was gaining acceptance.

The boarding school was run in strict conformity with orthodox Hindu customs. In the early days of the school, Sister Subbalakshmi denounced remarriage. Her widowed aunt, V.S. Valambal Ammal, was described by a visitor to the home as a woman in 'disfigured [shorn hair] condition' wearing a white sari and performing a traditional puja (act of worship). Mrs Drysdale utilized her inspection tours to locate high-caste widows and would often pay the train fare of reluctant fathers who wanted to see for themselves how the institution was run.[69]

Sister Subbalakshmi understood the importance of running the boarding school for widows in accordance with orthodox customs and caste rules. At the same time her own life was one of rebellion against the accepted role for a widow. She defied caste rules by opening a school for the fisherfolk in the area of the Ice House. When she was warned that as a government servant she could not join the Women's Indian Association, Sister Subbalakshmi continued to attend branch meetings while scrupulously avoiding the more public annual conferences. When the Women's Indian Association and the All-India Women's Conference began their campaigns in support of the Child Marriage Restraint Bill, Sister Subbalakshmi lectured against the custom and gave evidence before the Joshi Committee about the harmful effects of youthful marriage. Her activities suggest that she was idealistic yet shrewd. She was willing to compromise as long as it served her long-range goals.

Spiritually, Sister Subbalakshmi was deeply attracted to Swami Vivekananda and the Ramakrishna Mission. She regarded Ramakrishna and his disciple Vivekananda as the first religious reformers to be deeply concerned with the woman question. Although the model of the Catholic nun attracted her in her childhood, as an adult Sister Subbalakshmi drew her spiritual sustenance and philosophy of action from reformed Hinduism.

Conclusions

What these examples accentuate is the extent to which successful experiments in female education were a product of the labour of educated Indian women. Many of the schools were geographically limited, communally bound, and caste-sensitive. They were schools for females only, the teachers were females, and curricula were geared to gender-specific socialization.

Looking at female education and its products in the second decade of the twentieth century one can begin to answer the question of how far female education had achieved the results desired by the three groups who had promoted it: the British rulers, Indian male reformers, and educated Indian women.

The British wanted their civil servants to have educated wives to further ensure their loyalty. Uneducated wives (or wives who were educated only in the vernacular and traditional subjects) would split the household into two worlds. Just as the British were certain that rebellious plots were hatched and nurtured in inaccessible zenanas, they believed English-educated Indian women would raise their children to be anglophiles. Despite this dream, education did not promote loyalty among women except those married to civil servants. They became help-mates to their husbands but there were some renegades even among this group. Many women became critics of British policy in India.

Reform-minded Indian men were interested in developing a progressive society. If women were educated, Indian society could no longer be characterized as decadent and backward. On a personal level, these men yearned for companionship and the support an educated woman could give them as they advanced professionally. They wanted women to take responsibility for helping the less fortunate members of their communities. On the national level, they envisioned women in charge of social reform while men pursued politics.

Educated women accompanied their husbands to their civil service postings, joined husbands who had left their ancestral homes, opened schools and entertained district magistrates. The two-person career was finally possible with the appearance of the carefully groomed, English-speaking wife. Women took over the task of social reform at a time when men were becoming obsessed with political action and worried that social reform might complicate the task of arousing the masses. While men feared education might cause women to 'go too far', female educators promised to graduate 'professionalized housewives.' The educational system was overwhelmingly conservative, but the education of women had unexpected and unanticipated consequences.

The first generation of educated women found a voice: they wrote about their lives and about the conditions of women. The second generation acted. They articulated the needs of women, critiqued their society and the foreign rulers, and developed their own institutions. That these institutions were often as conservative as those designed by men should not be taken as a sign that these women wished to preserve the status quo. Rather it should be taken as evidence that they understood their subordinate position very well.

Through their efforts to develop institutions women learned the limits of their power. Deviant behaviour was severely punished. Within households girls who wanted to learn were teased and ostracized. Those who attended schools were stoned in the streets and marginalized in the classroom if they attended boys' schools. They were harassed when they sought to practise their professions. By straining for new lives, 'new women' learned where the boundaries were and just how far they could go. But this was a dynamic process; women were becoming educated and then becoming the educators. The boundaries of the early nineteenth century had been stretched considerably by the early twentieth century. What was deviant behaviour for one generation was acceptable behaviour for the next. What is more important, by the early years of the twentieth century Indian women were full participants in the redefinition of their futures.

Notes

1. *Women Writing in India*, vol. I, ed. Susie Tharu and K. Lalita (New York, Feminist Press, 1991), p. 199.
2. 'The Memoirs of Dr Haimavati Sen', trans. Tapan Raychaudhuri, ed. Geraldine Forbes and Tapan Raychaudhuri, unpublished ms., p. 15.
3. Nicol Macnicol, *Pandita Ramabai* (Calcutta, Association Press, 1926), pp. 11–13; 'Ramabai Pandita', *DNB*, vol. III, pp. 457–9.
4. Syed Nurullah and J.P. Naik, *History of Education in India During the British Period* (Bombay, Macmillan, 1943), p. 21; Meredith Borthwick, *The Changing Role of Women in Bengal, 1849–1905* (Princeton: Princeton University Press, 1984), pp. 60–1.
5. Aparna Basu, 'Mary Ann Cooke to Mother Theresa: Christian Missionary Women and the Indian Response,' *Women and Missions: Past and Present: Anthropological and Historical Perceptions*, ed. Fiona Bowie, Deborah Kirkwood and Shirley Ardener (Providence, R.I./Oxford, BERG, 1993), p. 190.
6. Sonia Nishat Amin, 'The Early Muslim Bhadramahila: The Growth of Learning and Creativity, 1876–1939', ed. Bharati Ray, *From the Seams of History: Essays in Indian Women*, ed. Bharati Ray (Delhi, Oxford University Press, 1995), p. 112.
7. Usha Chakraborty, *Condition of Bengali Women Around the Second Half of the Nineteenth Century* (Calcutta, Usha Chakraborty, 1963), p. 52.
8. Aparna Basu, *Essays in the History of Indian Education* (New Delhi, Concept Publishing Co., 1982), pp. 31–2; Syed Nurullah and J.P. Naik, *History of Education in India During the British Period*, pp. 12–13.
9. Basu, *Essays*, p. 33.
10. Kalikinkar Datta, *Survey of India's Social Life and Economic Condition in the Eighteenth Century (1707–1813)* (Calcutta, Firma K.L. Mukhopadhyay, 1961), pp. 23–4.
11. Basu, *Essays*, pp. 7–9.
12. Ibid., p. 14.
13. Harihar Das, *Life and Letters of Toru Dutt* (London, Humphrey Milford, 1921), p. 8.
14. Geraldine Forbes, 'In Search of the "Pure Heathen": Missionary Women in Nineteenth Century India', *EPW*, 21, no. 17 (26 April 1986), pp. ws2–ws8.

15. Glendora B. Paul, 'Emancipation and Education of Indian Women Since 1829', Ph.D. dissertation, University of Pittsburgh (1970).
16. Dr (Mrs) R. Vishalakshmi Nedunchezíar, 'Education of Girls and Women in Tamilnadu,' *Status of Women Souvenir 1973* (Madras, Task Force Sub-Committee on Education, Tamil Nadu, 1975), no page numbers.
17. J.C. Bagal, *Women's Education in Eastern India: The First Phase* (Calcutta, The World Press Private Ltd., 1956), pp. 77–95; N.S. Bose, *The Indian Awakening and Bengal* (Calcutta, Firma K.L. Mukhopadhyay, 1969), pp. 188–9; 'Hindoo Women', *Calcutta Review*, 40 (1864), pp. 80–101; 'The Bethune Female School', *The Bengalee* (13 January 1863), p. 13; Borthwick, *Changing Role*, pp. 73–7.
18. Y.B. Mathur, *Women's Education in India, 1813–1966* (Bombay, Asia Publishing, 1973), p. 25.
19. Ibid., p. 29.
20. Ibid., p. 26.
21. Sumantha Banerjee, 'Marginalization of Women's Popular Culture in Nineteenth Century Bengal', *Recasting Women: Essays in Colonial History*, ed. Kumkum Sangari and Sudesh Vaid (New Brunswick, Rutgers University Press, 1990), pp. 130–1.
22. Borthwick, *Changing Role*, p. 219.
23. Mary Carpenter, *Six Months in India*, 2 vols (London, Longman, Green and Co., 1868), vol. II, pp. 142–5.
24. Lord Beveridge, *India Called Them* (London, George Allen and Unwin, 1974), p. 83.
25. David Kopf, 'The Brahmo Idea of Social Reform and the Problem of Female Emancipation in Bengal', *Bengal in the Nineteenth and Twentieth Century*, ed. J.R. McLane (East Lansing, Mich., Asian Studies Center, 1975), pp. 47–50.
26. Annie Besant, *The Political Status of Women*, 2nd edn. (London, C. Watts, 1885), pp. 1–11 (pamphlet).
27. H.P. Blavatsky, 'Hindu Widow-Marriage', *A Modern Panorama: A Collection of Fugitive Fragments* (London, T.S. Publishing Society, 1895), vol. I, p. 243.
28. 'Mrs. Besant on Indian Womanhood', *ILM*, 1, no. 7 (January 1902), pp. 195–7; 'Indian Women', *MR*, 25 (1919), pp. 271–2.
29. Arthur H. Nethercot, *The Last Four Lives of Annie Besant* (Chicago, University of Chicago Press, 1963), pp. 17, 55, 73; 'Annie Besant,' *DNB*, vol. I, pp. 51–3.
30. Kenneth W. Jones, *Arya Dharma: Hindu Consciousness in Nineteenth Century Punjab* (Delhi, Manohar, 1976), pp. 104–5.
31. Madhu Kishwar, 'Arya Samaj and Women's Education: Kanya Mahavidyalaya', *EPW*, 21, no. 17 (16 April 1986), pp. ws9–ws24; Kumari

Lajjavati, 'A Pioneer in Women's Education', *ISR*, 45 (June 1, 1945), pp. 134–5.

32. Premila Thackersey, *Education of Women: A Key to Progress* (New Delhi, Ministry of Education and Youth Services, 1970), p. 6.
33. Thackersey, *Education of Women*, pp. 1–11; Mathur, *Women's Education in India*, pp. 40–4.
34. Jyotsna Kapur, 'Women and the Social Reform Movement in Maharashtra', M.Phil. thesis, Delhi University (1989), p. 79.
35. *The Letters and Correspondence of Pandita Ramabai*, compiled by Sister Geraldine, ed. A.B. Shah (Bombay, Maharashtra State Board of Literature and Culture, 1977), pp. 15–18; Rajas Krishnarao Dongre and Josephine F. Patterson, *Pandita Ramabai: A Life of Faith and Prayer* (Madras, Christian Literature Society, 1969), pp. 6–10; Muriel Clark, *Pandita Ramabai* (London, Paternoster Bldg., 1920), pp. 24–5; 'Pandita Ramabai', *Men and Women of India*, 1, no. 6 (June 1905), pp. 316–19; Meera Kosambi, 'Women, Emancipation and Equality: Pandita Ramabai's Contribution to Women's Cause', *EPW*, 23, no. 44 (29 October 1988), pp. ws38–ws49; Meera Kosambi, *At the Intersection of Gender Reform and Religious Belief* (Bombay, SNDT, Research Center for Women's Studies, Gender Series, 1993).
36. *Letters and Correspondence*, p. 14.
37. Ibid., pp. xx–xxi.
38. Ibid., pp. 257–362.
39. Ibid., pp. 342–416.
40. Ibid., p. 412.
41. Ibid., p. 257.
42. Ibid., p. 257; Kosambi, 'Women, Emancipation and Equality', pp. ws44–ws45.
43. Minna S. Cowan, *The Education of the Women of India* (Edinburgh, Oliphant, Anderson and Ferrier, 1912), p. 113.
44. Tanika Sarkar, 'Rhetoric Against the Age of Consent', *EPW*, 28, no. 36 (4 September 1993), pp. 1869–78.
45. M.M. Kaur, *The Role of Women in the Freedom Movement* (*1857–1947*) (New Delhi, Sterling, 1968), p. 85. Kaur claims that Maharani Tapaswini was a niece of the Rani of Jhansi.
46. Kaur, *The Role of Women*, p. 145.
47. 'The Mahakali Pathshala', *The Statesman* (3 February 1985), p. 7.
48. Latika Ghose, 'Social and Educational Movements for Women and by Women, 1820–1950', *Bethune School and College Centenary Volume, 1849–1949*, ed. Dr Kalidas Nag (Calcutta, S.N. Guha Ray, 1950), p. 146; Cowan, *The Education of Women in India*, p. 113; 'The Mahakali Pathshala', p. 7.

49. *ILM*, 3, no. 1 (July 1903), p. 16; *ILM*, 3, no. 6 (December 1903), pp. 194–5.
50. D.D. Karve, ed. and trans. *The New Brahmins: Five Maharashtrian Families*, ed. assistance, Ellen E. McDonald (Berkeley, University of California Press, 1963), p. 79.
51. '(Maharshi) Dhondo Keshav Karve', *DNB*, vol. 1, pp. 299–301.
52. Quoted in D.D. Karve, *The New Brahmins*, p. 51.
53. Parvati Athavale, *My Story, The Autobiography of a Hindu Widow*, trans. Revd. Justin E. Abbott (New York, G.P. Putnam, 1930), p. 30.
54. Dhondo Keshav Karve, *Looking Back* (Poona, Hinge Stree-Shikshan Samastha, 1936), p. 75.
55. Athavale, *My Story*, p. 133.
56. Ibid., p. 30.
57. Karve, *Looking Back*, pp. 77–82.
58. Ibid., p. 104.
59. Ibid., pp. 95–106; D.D. Karve, *The New Brahmins*, p. 56.
60. G.L. Chakravarkar, *Dondo Keshav Karve* (New Delhi, Publications Division, Government of India, 1970), pp. 169–87.
61. Basu, *Essays*, p. 14.
62. 'Thackesay (*sic*) Women's University Convocation', Sir Visvesvaraya's convocation address, 29 June 1940, *IAR*, (January–June 1940), (Calcutta, Annual Register, n.d.), p. 438.
63. Sources on Begum Rokeya include *Inside Seclusion: The Avarodhbasini of Rokeya Sakhawat Hossain*, ed. and trans. Roshan Jahan (Dhaka, Bangladesh, BRAC Printers, 1981); Ghulam Murshid, *Reluctant Debutante* (Rajshahi, Bangladesh, Rajshahi University, 1983); Amin, 'The Early Muslim Bhadramahila', pp. 107–48; Sonia Nishat Amin, 'The World of Muslim Women in Colonial Bengal: 1876–1939', Ph.D. dissertation, University of Dhaka (1993); Sonia Nishat Amin, 'Rokeya Sakhawat Hossain and the Legacy of the "Bengal" Renaissance', *Journal of Asiatic Society*, Bangladesh, 34, no. 2 (December 1989), pp. 185–92; Sonia Nishat Amin, 'The New Woman in Literature and the Novels of Nojibur Rahman and Rokeya Sakhawat Hossain', *Infinite Variety: Women in Society and Literature*, ed. Firdous Azim and Niaz Zaman (Dhaka, University Press Limited, 1994), pp. 119–41.
64. Gail Minault, 'Purdah's Progress: The Beginning of School Education for Indian Muslim Women', *Individuals and Ideals in Modern India*, ed. J.P. Sharma (Calcutta, Firma K.L. Mukhopadhyaya, 1982), pp. 76–97.
65. Jahan, *Inside Seclusion*, pp. 33–5.
66. Ibid., p. 20.
67. Monica Felton, *A Child Widow's Story* (London, Victor Gollancz, 1966); *Women Pioneers in Education (Tamilnadu)* (Madras, Society for the

Promotion of Education in India, 1975); interview with Mrs Soundarain, Madras (22 January 1976); letter from Rabindranath Tagore to Miss M.F. Prager, Eur. Mss., B 183, IOOLC; interview with Sister Sublakshami (*sic*) (10 December 1930), RWC, box 28; Malathi Ramanathan, *Sister R. Subbalakshmi: Social Reformer and Educationalist* (Bombay, Lok Vangmaya Griha, 1989).

68. By Sister Subbalakshmi, n.d., enclosed in a letter from R. Tagore, Eur. Mss., B 183, IOOLC.
69. Ibid.

4

Law, Custom and Statutory Social Reform

The Hindu Widows' Remarriage Act of 1856*

Lucy Carroll

Second marriages, after the death of the husband first espoused, are wholly unknown to the Hindu Law; though in practice, among the inferior castes, nothing is so common.—Sir William Hay Macnaghten, 1862.[1]

When the British assumed judicial responsibility in India, there were several diverse systems of law existing. Not only were there literary traditions of Hanafi and Ithna Ashari Muslim Law and the Dayabhaga and Mitakshara schools of Hindu Law, but there were also numerous practical traditions of Customary Law, applicable to caste, tribe, lineage or family group. In assuming judicial powers and responsibilities over Indian territory in the late eighteenth century, the British rulers promised their Indian subjects that the personal laws administered to them would be those of their own respective religious community—a promise reiterated in every act establishing further courts and expanding the jurisdiction of the legal system. For the Hindus (particularly upper-caste Hindus) this meant

*From *Indian Economic and Social History Review*, vol. 20, October–December 1983, pp. 363–88.

that the British-Indian courts assumed the responsibility of administering textual Hindu Law (Dayabhaga or Mitakshara as appropriate) in suits concerning such matters as marriage, adoption, succession, and legitimacy to which the parties were Hindus. In order to fulfil this promise, the British appointed Indian pandits to expound the Hindu Law and advise the courts on questions concerning Hindu Law coming before them; and undertook to collect, compile, and translate standard legal texts which were then recognized by the British-Indian legal system as authoritative. By the mid-nineteenth century the texts had replaced the pandits as the repositories of Hindu Law.

What about Customary Law, which by definition rests not in literary works but in the mores and behaviour of the people? The British-Indian courts gave lip-service to Customary Law, but in actual practice it was extremely difficult in most cases to prove custom in the face of the judicial presumption that Hindu (book) Law applied. The history of the British administration of Hindu Law is largely the story of the erosion of Customary Law in the face of a judicial preference for law that could be found in the (judicially recognized) texts.

At the same time, because the Government of India possessed legislative powers sufficient to change this personal law, Hindu Law as administered in the British-Indian courts could be altered by statute. The Hindu Widows' Remarriage Act of 1856 (Act XV of 1856) is an example of such statutory social reform. The judicial controversies that arose over the interpretation and application of this Act set in clear relief three different categories of law—Hindu Law, Customary Law, and Statutory Law—and illustrate the role of the judicial branch of the British Raj in the process of propagating values of orthodox Hinduism and 'Hinduizing' castes and tribes on the fringes of Hinduism.[2]

The Hindu Widows' Remarriage Act was enacted by the British-Indian government in response to the social reform agitation organized by Pandit Vidyasagar and others. Legislation was required because under the Hindu Law, as administered by the British-Indian courts, widow remarriage among higher-caste Hindus was prohibited and children of such a remarriage were illegitimate: the social reform movement thus required legal sanction.

The problem of widows—and especially of child widows—was largely a prerogative of the higher Hindu castes among whom child marriage was practised and remarriage prohibited. Irrevocably, eternally married as a mere child, the death of the husband she had perhaps never known left the wife a widow, an inauspicious being whose sins in a previous life had deprived her of her husband, and her parents-in-law of their son, in this one. Doomed to a life of prayer, fasting, and drudgery, unwelcome at the celebrations and auspicious occasions that are so much a part of Hindu family and community life, her lot was scarcely to be envied.

On the other hand, the lower, particularly Sudra, castes and the (so-called) 'Untouchables'—who represented approximately 80 per cent of the Hindu population—neither practised child marriage nor prohibited the remarriage of widows.

The Hindu Widow's Right of Succession

Before proceeding to a consideration of the Hindu Widows' Remarriage Act, it is necessary to establish a few general propositions concerning the Hindu widow's right of succession prior to the modifications introduced by the Hindu Women's Rights to Property Act (Act XVIII of 1937) and the Hindu Succession Act (Act XXX of 1956).

Prior to 1937, under both the Dayabhaga and the Mitakshara schools of Hindu Law, the widow only succeeded to her husband's estate in the absence of a son, son's son, or son's son's son of the deceased; and the estate which she took by succession to her husband was an estate which she held only for her lifetime; at her death it went not to her own heirs but to the nearest living heir of her deceased husband. According to the Dayabhaga school, the widow (given the absence of a son, son's son, or son's son's son) succeeded to her husband's share whether or not he was a member of an undivided coparcenary: according to the Mitakshara school, she succeeded to his estate only if he were separate and had simply a right to maintenance if he were a joint coparcener.

Under Hindu Law of both schools, it is only the chaste wife who is entitled to succeed to her husband's estate. It is further a rule of Anglo-Hindu Law, as laid down by the Privy Council in 1880, that once a widow has succeeded to her deceased husband's estate, she does not forfeit her right to the enjoyment of that estate until her death by living an unchaste life.[3]

The Hindu Widows' Remarriage Act (Act XV of 1856)

The preamble and sections 1, 2, 5, and 6 of the Hindu Widows' Remarriage Act are as follows:

> Whereas it is known that, by the law as administered in the Civil Courts established in the territories in the possession and under the Government of the East India Company, Hindu widows with certain exceptions are held to be, by reason of their having been once married, incapable of contracting a second valid marriage, and the offspring of such widows by any second marriage are held to be illegitimate and incapable of inheriting property; and
>
> Whereas many Hindus believe that this imputed legal incapacity, although it is in accordance with established custom, is not in accordance with a true interpretation of the precepts of their religion, and desire that the civil law administered by the Courts of Justice shall no longer prevent those Hindus who may be so minded from adopting a different custom, in accordance with the dictates of their own conscience; and
>
> Where it is just to relieve all such Hindus from this legal incapacity of which they complain, and the removal of all legal obstacles to the marriage of Hindu widows will tend to the promotion of good morals and to the public welfare;
>
> It is enacted as follows:
>
> 1. No marriage contracted between Hindus shall be invalid, and the issue of no such marriage shall be illegitimate, by reason of the woman having been previously married or betrothed to another person who was dead at the time of such marriage, any custom and any interpretation of Hindu Law to the contrary notwithstanding.
> 2. All rights and interests which any widow may have in her deceased husband's property by way of maintenance, or by inheritance to her husband or to his lineal successors, or by virtue of any will or testamentary disposition conferring upon her, without express permission to remarry, only a limited interest in such property, with no power of alienating the same, shall upon her re-marriage cease and determine as if she had then died; and the next heirs of her deceased husband or other persons entitled to the property on her death, shall thereupon succeed to the same. . . .
>
> 5. Except as in the three preceding sections is provided, a widow shall not by reason of her re-marriage forfeit any property or any right to

which she would otherwise be entitled; and every widow who has remarried shall have the same rights of inheritance as she would have had, had such marriage been her first marriage.

6. Whatever words spoken, ceremonies performed or engagements made on the marriage of a Hindu female who has not been previously married, are sufficient to constitute a valid marriage, shall have the same effect, if spoken, performed or made on the marriage of a Hindu widow; and no marriage shall be declared invalid on the ground that such words, ceremonies or engagements are inapplicable to the case of a widow.

However clear the intent of the legislature may appear to the lay reader of the statute, when called upon to interpret these provisions, the judges of the British-Indian courts found the language of the legislature 'somewhat embarrassing';[4] 'somewhat ambiguous';[5] 'to some extent misleading';[6] 'not free from difficulty';[7] and 'curious'.[8] Substantiation of these characterizations of the wording of the Act is found in the fact that this humanely-inspired statute was responsible for more than three-quarters of a century of dramatic judicial controversy among the High Courts of the British-Indian legal system.

The main point of contention in the judicial controversies arising from the differing interpretations placed upon Act XV of 1856 by the various High Courts concerned the effect of the statute in regard to those castes which had, according to their own pre-existing customs, permitted widows to remarry. Although section 6 of the Act prescribes the ceremonies which would be regarded as solemnizing a valid widow marriage (thus indicating that the legislators believed themselves to be writing on *tabula rasa*, innovating a practice where none had existed before); and although the ceremonies so prescribed differed significantly from those observed among castes which had a custom of widow marriage, the High Courts of Bengal, Bombay and Madras held that section 2, involving forfeiture of the deceased husband's estate on remarriage, applied to all Hindu widows, whether or not the validity of their remarriage derived from the Act, and whether or not their marriages were solemnized by the ceremonies prescribed in section 6; or, alternatively, that if section 2 did not apply, the same forfeiture was enjoined by Hindu Law. The exception of this judicial trend was the High Court of Allahabad, which held consistently—and in the face of contrary rulings and open criticism from the other High Courts—that the Act of 1856 was inapplicable to individuals who were, prior to the passing of the Act, permitted by Customary Law to remarry.

Customary Law

The case of *Har Saran Das v. Nandi*,[9] decided by the Allahabad High Court in 1889, established what was to become the scrupulously observed precedent for this High Court and those lower courts subject to it.[10]

Nandi, the widow of a sweeper, succeeded to her deceased husband's interest in two *kothas* of land and subsequently remarried. Her deceased husband's brothers contested her right, following her remarriage, to the property. Two lower courts held that under section 2 of Act XV of 1856 all rights and interests which the widow had acquired from her deceased husband had been forfeited upon her remarriage. Justice Straight, writing the decision of the High Court, overruled the lower courts:

> It is admitted that the woman Nandi was of the sweeper caste, and in that caste there is no legal obstacle or hindrance, either by law or custom, or otherwise, nor is any suggested, against remarriage, and it must be taken that this condition of things has been existing in the caste for years past, and was existing in the year 1856. Accordingly, when Musammat Nandi married Bhujo, she did what in her caste never had been and was not prohibited by the law to which she was subject, and her marriage was a good and valid marriage. I do not think that, looking to the preamble to Act XV of 1856, which refers to Hindu widows, it was ever intended to apply to persons in the position of Musammat Nandi, or to place under disability or liability persons who could marry a second time before the Act was passed. The Act was passed for the purpose of enabling persons to marry who could not remarry before the Act, and s. 2 only applies to such persons. By her second marriage Musammat Nandi, in my opinion, did not forfeit her interest in the two kothas.[11]

The Allahabad High Court thus decided in favour of the remarried sweeper widow on the basis of Customary Law ('the law to which she was subject'). It was proved before the Court that custom sanctioned the remarriage of sweeper widows. The Court, however, neither heard nor asked for evidence on the Customary Law as to whether such a remarried widow retained her interest in her deceased husband's property; it simply ruled that she did not forfeit that interest under section 2 of Act XV as had been alleged in the suit.

On the other hand, in *Ranjit v. Radha Rai*[12] a custom entailing forfeiture upon remarriage among Kurmis was alleged but held not proved on the evidence; while in both *Ram Devi v. Kishen Dei*[13] and *Mangat v. Bharto*[14] it was proved that among the castes in question (Grihast Goshain and Jat, respectively) it was customary for a remarried widow to retain her interest in her deceased husband's estate.

It was, indeed, very rarely contended in cases before the Allahabad High Court that castes which permitted widow remarriage by Customary Law, by that same Customary Law deprived a remarried widow of her first husband's property. And, in the absence of proof of a custom of forfeiture, the Allahabad High Court refused to enjoin it. Chief Justice Sulaiman in 1932 summed up the Allahabad position on Customary Law as applied in widow remarriage cases as follows:

> When nothing more than a mere custom of remarriage is established, there is not presumption that under the Hindu Law she [i.e., the remarried widow] forfeits the estate. The party who is alleging that there has been a forfeiture must establish a further incidence of the custom that forfeiture is a necessary consequence [of remarriage]. Wherever such additional custom is established, she would, of course, lose the estate. . . . But where nothing more is established than a mere right to remarry under a custom, it cannot be presumed that forfeiture is a necessary consequence. The burden to prove a custom involving forfeiture is on the party asserting it, and in the absence of such proof, it must be held that she could remarry and retain the estate and not forfeit it. . . . [U]nless it is affirmatively established that in addition to the custom of remarriage there is the further custom of forfeiture of the husband's estate, she is entitled to retain the estate even after remarriage and till her death.[15]

The Allahabad position was therefore: (*a*) that Act XV of 1856 was not applicable to castes where Customary Law had permitted widow remarriage prior to 1856; and (*b*) that in order for a remarried widow subject to Customary Law to be deprived of property to which she had succeeded as heir of her first husband, a custom decreeing such forfeiture must be proved.

Individual judges of the Calcutta and Madras High Courts were willing to agree that Act XV of 1856 did not apply to widows 'who could without the aid of the Act marry according to the custom of their castes',[16] and that 'the word "remarriage" in the section [2] must be taken as meaning remarriage contracted under the Act'.[17] Nevertheless, these High Courts refused to follow the Allahabad precedent of *Har Saran Das v. Nandi* on the ground that 'although section 2 might not apply the same result might follow from an application of the fundamental rules of Hindu Law',[18] a fact which 'for some reason not apparent' the Allahabad High Court had not considered at all.[19]

Hindu Law

Judges of the British-Indian courts—judges both British and Indian—expounded freely on 'the Hindu Law', creating the impression that such an indigenous creation existed fully complete and ready to hand. This was really not the case, not only because statute had the power of changing Hindu Law as applied and enforced by the British-Indian courts (e.g., after Act XXI of 1850 excommunication from caste or religious apostasy no longer barred rights of inheritance under Hindu Law); but, even more importantly, because what was meant by the term 'Hindu Law' was altered by accretions of case-law (e.g., after the Privy Council ruling in *Moniram Kolita v. Keri Kolitani*[20] a Hindu widow did not forfeit her estate in her deceased husband's property by leading a notoriously unchaste life). Hindu Law as administered by the British-Indian courts was a mixture of Shastric Law, custom, and case-law, with a hardy dose of English legal concepts and notions, simplified and standardized for ease of application and administrative convenience. Not surprisingly, the end result contained several anomalies.

The case which provided the occasion for the exposition of what became the Calcutta precedent in regard to Act XV of 1856 and widow remarriage cases, *Matungini Gupta v. Ram Rutton Roy*,[21] arose out of somewhat unique circumstances. A childless widow, who had succeeded to her husband's property and subsequently converted to the reformist Brahmo Samaj sect, remarried under the provisions of Act III of 1872 (Special Marriage Act), having declared as required by that statute, that she did not profess the Hindu religion. The reversioner (next heir) sued for possession of the estate of the deceased husband, alleging that by her remarriage the widow had forfeited her interest in the property under section 2 of Act XV of 1856.[22]

The Court (Wilson, Prinsep, Banerji, JJ., referring opinion; Petheram, C.J., Wilson, Pigot, Ghose, and Prinsep, JJ., Full Bench) ruled, with Justice Prinsep dissenting,[23] that the widow forfeited. The majority disagreed, however, on whether the forfeiture occurred by virtue of the statute or by virtue of Hindu Law. Chief Justice Petheram interpreted section 2 of Act XV as applying to 'all persons who being Hindus become widows'; any person who had succeeded to property as a Hindu widow fell under the scope of the section when she remarried, regardless of whether or not she remarried as a Hindu. Justice Wilson held that both Hindu Law and Act XV applied and that both decreed forfeiture. Justice Banerji held that section 2 applied only to a widow who was a Hindu both at the time of succession and at the time of her remarriage and only to such widows as remarried under the Act. Nevertheless, according to Justice Banerji, although the widow had remarried independently of the Act and as a non-Hindu, she forfeited her interest in her deceased husband's estate by virtue of Hindu Law independently of the statute.

What then, precisely, was the Hindu Law that decreed the forfeiture? 'We cannot expect to find express texts on this point in the usual authorities on Hindu Law,' observed Justice Wilson, 'because second marriage was a thing they did not contemplate.'[24] Certainly all the texts speak of the widow enjoying the property until her death; indeed, the passage from Vrihaspati relied upon so heavily by Justices Wilson and Banerji ('Of him whose wife is not deceased half the body survives. How then should another take his property while half his person is alive?') speaks of the widow's right during her life, that is, until her death. But, arguing from this text that the widow inherits under Hindu Law because she is regarded as the surviving half of her deceased husband's body, Justice Wilson found it impossible to reconcile the idea of a widow continuing in the enjoyment of property so inherited when she 'ceases to be the wife or half the body of her late husband, and becomes the wife and half the body of another man'.[25] He supported his inference that under Hindu Law the estate of a widow must be forfeited on remarriage by remarking that 'where second marriages are sanctioned by custom, the further rule seems almost always to have been followed, that such remarriage entailed a forfeiture of the first husband's estate'; and concluding that the forfeiture section of Act XV indicated that the legislature considered forfeiture on remarriage 'to be in accordance with the principles of Hindu Law'.[26]

Of course, section 1 of Act XV was directly contrary to orthodox, textual Hindu Law; the necessity for legislative action derived from this very fact. Why then should it be assumed that section 2 was in accordance with Hindu Law? The observation that when custom permitted remarriage, it almost always also decreed forfeiture is not supported by the findings of fact in the courts of upper India where the question was actually considered.

Justice Banerji also based his contention of what the Hindu Law was concerning widow remarriage and forfeiture on inferences drawn from the 'half-his-body' metaphor:

> The widow's right of succession is based, according to the Dayabhaga, on the ground that she is half the body of her deceased husband, and is capable of conferring by her acts spiritual benefit on him. The widow takes her husband's estate, not because of past relationship, not because she was the wife of the deceased, but because of the continuing relationship, because she is still the *patni* (wife) of the deceased. . . . [I]t follows, as a necessary consequence, that the estate of a Hindu widow can last only so long as she continues to be the wife and half the body of her deceased husband; that is only so long as the relationship, by reason of which she inherits, continues, and the estate must be held to determine when she must cease to be the wife of her late husband and half his body by marrying another person.[27]

Although the 'half-his-body' metaphor is a quaint legal fiction, it is not the only text on the widow's right of succession to her sonless husband. Much more mundane is the statement of the law given in the Yajnayavalkya Smriti:

> Wife (widow), daughter, father, mother, brother, their sons, gotraja (of the same family), bandhus, disciple and Brahmacharias of the same school, each succeeding one is heir in the absence of the person immediately preceding him in the order of enumeration—this is the law in respect of the inheritance to the property of a sonless deceased person of whatever caste.[28]

Statutory Law

In 1896 a Full Bench of the Bombay High Court considered the application of Act XV of 1856 and overruled the decision of the same Court in *Parekh Ranochor v. Bai Vakhat.*[29] In the latter case it had been held that Section 2 of Act XV had no application to the case of a widow belonging to a caste among whom widow remarriage was permitted and the case had been remitted for determination as to whether the caste custom which permitted the widow to remarry also permitted her to retain her interest in the property of her first husband, or whether by custom such interest was forfeited upon remarriage.

The 1896 case, *Vithu v. Govinda*,[30] concerned a Sudra widow whose infant son had succeeded to her husband's/his father's property. The infant subsequently died and the estate passed to his mother, the widow. The mother, after succession to the estate, remarried (*c.* 1875); she and her alienee had been in possession since the death of the son. It was common ground that the caste of the widow permitted remarriage of widows; it was further found by the Subordinate Judge that according to the custom of the caste, remarriage did not entail forfeiture of property held by succession to the first husband.[31]

The Full Bench of the Bombay High Court (Farran, C.J., referring opinion; Farran, C.J., Parsons and Ranade, JJ., Full Bench) took its stand neither on Customary Law nor Hindu Law but on a very literal view of the wording of the enacting clauses of Act XV of 1856. In his referring judgment, Chief Justice Farran characterized Section 2 as a law which 'plainly extends to all Hindu widows irrespective of the castes to which they belong and to the special customs of such castes. It reads as a law of universal applicability.' He found nothing in the words of section 2 to support the notion that the legislature did not intend that section to be generally applicable, or that it intended it to apply only to those widows who were for the first time permitted to contract valid second marriages under the Act. Although the preamble indicated that the legislature, aware that some Hindu widows were permitted to remarry and some prohibited from doing so, desired to remove the disability affecting those widows prohibited from remarrying, he saw no reason for assuming that the Act applied only to those widows standing in need of such relief. The legislature might have chosen either of two means to secure their object of relief for widows barred from remarrying: 'First by passing a general act applicable to all Hindus alike, or secondly by passing an enabling act which would be applicable to such widows only as chose to avail themselves of its provisions. The Legislature has, we think, adopted the former method.' It was, the Chief Justice asserted, difficult to argue that the broad language of sections 1 and 2 'does not extend to all Hindus alike, whatever their caste or the interpretation of the Hindu Law authorized by their caste may be'.[32]

As to the Allahabad position, Chief Justice Farran had two comments:

> (1) that it is an assumption without basis to attribute that absence of intention [i.e., the absence of intention 'to place under disability or liability persons who could marry a second time before the Act was passed'[33]] to the Legislature; it is equally probable that they intended to assimilate the Hindu Law in this particular in all castes and to make the law as administered accord with the true principles of Hindu Law; and (2) that it is not allowable to cut down the express provisions of a law by a consideration of the supposed intention of the Legislature in passing it.[34]

It could be argued, of course, that as between conflicting interpretations of a statute, it is a matter of prudence and justice to select that construction which is the least disabling, leaving it to the legislature to extend the liability if it so chooses in view of the judicial interpretation. The 'express provisions of the law' being, as every court dealing with the Act noted, ambiguous, a prudent construction might appear even more strongly enjoined; the remedy, if the legislature failed to secure its intention under such an interpretation, would lie with the legislature, not the courts.

In the decision of the Full Bench, Justice Ranade expanded upon the position taken by the Chief Justice in the referring opinion. Although Justice Ranade found that the preamble implied that the Act was not intended to apply to all classes of Hindu widows, nonetheless the enacting clauses 'are as general as they can well be, and there is no special section preserving to the castes in which remarriage was permitted full recognition of their customary rights'.[35] The apparent discrepancy between the preamble and the enacting clauses, Justice Ranade considered deliberate: while it was true that some castes permitted widow remarriage and some did not, it was, he considered, equally the case that in all castes where widow remarriage was permitted, forfeiture of the remarried widow's rights and interests in her first husband's property was the rule. In his view, the legislature had declared in the general language of section 2 what was in fact a rule already in force, and no new disability was thereby created. In support of the universal custom of forfeiture, Ranade cited Arthur Steele's *Law and Custom*,[36] a study confined to the castes of the Brahmin-dominated region around Poona, and ignored the finding of fact by the Subordinate Judge that according to the custom of the caste of the widow whose case was actually before the Court, remarriage did *not* entail forfeiture.

Justice Ranade conceded that the legislature had been mistaken in some of their assumptions underlying the Act: that is, (*a*) in assuming that the castes permitting remarriage were exceptions to a general rule of prohibition, while in fact the prohibition was confined to the upper castes or about 20 per cent of the population; (*b*) in assuming it necessary to prescribe ceremonies for celebrating a second marriage (*vide* section 6 of the Act); and (*c*) in prescribing remarriage ceremonies in the terms they did, for 'in this part of the country the customary ceremonies observed at a *pat* [second] marriage are different from those observed at a *lagna* or first marriage'. Nevertheless, he held that the legislature had been correct in its wording of section 2 and had in that section 'only declared what was a universal practice'.[37]

The difficulties and mistaken assumptions pointed out by Justice Ranade, however, only arise if one assumes that the legislature in Act XV was legislating for the whole of the Hindu population, and not simply providing an enabling act for the benefit of those sections of the population who, prior to 1856, neither recognized widow remarriage nor had available any ceremonial practices appropriate for such an occasion.

And, finally, Justice Ranade suggested that the legislature actually had before it the information from Steele's *Law and Custom* concerning the practice of widow remarriage in the Poona area and the custom of forfeiture among remarrying castes, and that it was on the basis of this information that the legislature enacted section 2 in broad general terms. It is, however, hardly likely that, if the legislature had studied Steele's volume and based section 2 on it, it would have at the same time confused *pat* and *lagna* marriage observances (*vide* Ranade's comments earlier).

Following the Farran/Ranade argument to its logical conclusion, the Madras High Court explicitly ruled that a custom of non-forfeiture could not be pleaded in the face of the statutory forfeiture enjoined by section 2 of Act XV: '[N]o plea of custom can prevail to violate an express statutory enactment to the contrary and any custom repugnant to such enactment will be held to have been swept away thereby.'[38]

The Allahabad Rejoinder

The dramatic conflict among the High Courts over the interpretation of Act XV—which really resolved into a conflict between the Allahabad High Court and the High Courts of Calcutta, Bombay, and Madras (the latter following both Calcutta and Bombay precedents)—continued until the question itself was superseded by the Hindu Code legislation of independent India, almost exactly a century after the passage of the Hindu Widows' Remarriage Act.

In 1908 (*Gajadhar v. Kaunsilla*),[39] 1910 (*Mula v. Partab*),[40] and 1926 (*Mangat v. Bharto*),[41] individual judges of the Allahabad High Court appeared personally less impressed with the Customary Law position of their own Court than with the Hindu Law/Statutory Law traditions of the Presidency Courts. The power of precedent, however, served to overcome personal idiosyncrasies and to pull the wavering judges into line with the legal traditions of the bench on which they, for the moment, sat. The Allahabad tradition was maintained intact; no decision contrary to that tradition issued from any judge serving on the Allahabad High Court. The personal reservations of Justices Stanley, Banerji, Dalal and Pullan were more than compensated for by the strength and vigour of the Full Bench defence of the Allahabad tradition in 1932.

When *Bhola Umar v. Kausilla*[42] came before a Divisional Bench of the Allahabad High Court, the following question was referred to the Full Bench for decision: 'Does a Hindu widow, who remarried in accordance with a custom of her caste, forfeit thereby her rights in the estate of her first husband?' In reply, Chief Justice Sulaiman and Justices Mukerji and King picked up the gauntlet and proceeded to lecture those of the Wilson/Banerji and Farran/Ranade schools on the subjects of Hindu and Statutory Law.

While Justice Wilson had had difficulty in reconciling the notion of a widow retaining her inheritance from her first husband when she remarried and the assumption that under Hindu Law the widow inherited because she was regarded as the surviving half of her husband's body, Justice Mukerji had even greater difficulty in reconciling the notion that a widow inherited because she was half her husband's body with the actual practice of widow remarriage prevailing among many Hindu castes.

> If these people believed that a wife was one-half of the body of her husband and on the death of her husband one-half of his body survived in the widow, how could they possibly have allowed the widow to remarry. . . . It must follow that those people who allow their widows to make a valid remarriage *never believe* in the doctrine that a wife is one-half of the body of the husband and that the widow survives as one-half of his body.[43]

Was Hindu Law to be invoked and enforced by the British-Indian courts to penalize those who acted contrary to the religious ordinances of orthodox Hinduism because they were outside the charmed circle of the twice-born, for whom alone the sacred law was intended anyway? The textual Hindu Law was never intended for the Sudras.

> It was only the privilege of the first three classes, the Brahmins, the Kshatriyas and Vaishyas to read the Shastras and the sacred laws and to abide by them. . . . Indeed, Manu himself says in the clearest terms that his laws were meant mostly for the benefit of the three regenerate or higher classes and not for the Sudras.[44]

As the castes which permitted remarriage of their widows were generally Sudras, it was inappropriate to apply reasoning based on the general principles of Hindu Law—a law intended only for the upper castes—to decree forfeiture of the property the widow had inherited from her first husband.

On the other hand, Justice Mukerji continued, if it were assumed that 'the strict rule of Hindu Law applies to a caste which does not recognize the strict Hindu Law . . . the remarriage of a widow can only be regarded as an immoral act. The orthodox Hindus *would not recognize the marriage as valid*', although the caste and the British-Indian courts may do so.[45] According to the Privy Council Unchastity Case

(*Moniram Kolita v. Keri Kolitani*[46]), unchastity in a widow does not divest her of her inheritance from her deceased husband once she has succeeded to the estate.

> Can it be an act of justice to say that living as the wife of one single man would be followed by a punishment, while the grossest immorality cannot be? It was argued that this may be so, but such is the Hindu Law. I, as a Hindu Judge, refuse to believe that such is the Hindu Law. I emphatically deny that such is the Hindu Law. The Hindu Law lays down, not at one place, but at many places, that the Shastras can never be interpreted apart from the dictates of conscience and reason.[47]

Chief Justice Sulaiman, concurring, denied both that the 'half-the-body' metaphor was the sole basis for the Hindu widow's right of succession, and that the efficacy of her acts of spiritual benefit to her deceased husband was a condition necessary for her continued enjoyment of his estate. The unchaste widow did not forfeit the estate vested in her, although her unchastity rendered her unable to secure through her acts spiritual benefit to her husband's soul. Relying upon the Privy Council's decision in the Unchastity Case, Chief Justice Sulaiman found it impossible to accept the situation whereby the courts would put 'a premium on unchastity' by holding that the widow 'can retain the property so long as she remains notoriously unchaste, but the moment she remarried she will forfeit it'. Particularly in the absence of an express text enjoining forfeiture on remarriage, 'the Hindu Law should be interpreted so as not to cause a shock to one's moral conscience'. Hindu Law did not contemplate remarriage and would not regard a remarriage as a valid marriage, but as a case of unchastity; under Hindu Law, as interpreted by the Privy Council, a widow's unchastity did not entail forfeiture of an estate once vested.[48]

The texts of Vrihat Manu and Katyayana, so much discussed in the Unchastity Case, established a clear right for the widow to hold the property until her death:

> The widow of a childless man, keeping unsullied her husband's bed, and preserving in religious observances, shall present his funeral oblation and obtain his entire share.
>
> Let the childless widow, keeping unsullied the bed of her Lord, and abiding with her venerable protector, enjoy with moderation the property until her death. After her let the heirs take it.

As interpreted by the Privy Council, the conditions contained in these texts concerned the right of succession to the estate and did not lay down conditions for its retention when once vested; violation of any or all of the conditions subsequent to succession did not involve forfeiture. Therefore, argued the Chief Justice, if the forfeiture section of Act XV did not apply, a correct application of Hindu Law did not entail forfeiture.

Justice King endorsed Mukerji's views on the application of strict Hindu Law:

> It appears to me that the general principles of strict Hindu Law could not be properly applicable to a caste in which a custom of remarriage is admitted. If the members of the caste recognized the remarriage of a widow as valid, then it follows that they do not accept the theories of orthodox Hinduism which would make a legal remarriage impossible. If such theories are rejected by the caste for the purpose of permitting remarriage, it seems illogical to invoke the very same theories for the purpose of holding that if the widow does remarry, then she must forfeit her rights in her deceased husband's estate.[49]

And he took particular issue with Justice Ranade's Statutory Law position and his assumption, based on Steele's *Law and Custom*, that the custom of forfeiture among castes which permitted remarriage was universal and that the legislature, aware of this universal custom, had recognized it in section 2 of the Hindu Widows' Remarriage Act.

> I do not think it can safely be inferred that even if the Legislature knew that among the tribes or castes of the Bombay Dekhan a custom was in force that a Hindu widow should forfeit her rights in her husband's estate upon her remarriage, this would furnish an adequate ground for enacting, in a statute applicable to the whole of British India, the rule that forfeiture of interest in her deceased husband's estate must be a necessary consequence of the remarriage of every Hindu widow, whatever the custom of her tribe or caste may be.

At least as far as the Northwestern Provinces were concerned, the rule of forfeiture was 'by no means universal . . . among those castes in which widows are permitted to remarry.' In the long series of Allahabad cases, where a custom of remarriage was alleged, it was seldom pleaded that custom decreed forfeiture; 'when it has been pleaded it has never been proved and in some cases a contrary custom has been proved affirmatively.'[50]

Social Consequences

By definition, social reform legislation is intended to have social consequences, to serve and facilitate ends deemed desirable. Obviously the social consequences of the Hindu Widows' Remarriage Act varied according to the geographical jurisdictions of the High Courts. Within the jurisdictions of the High Courts of Calcutta, Madras, and Bombay, the result was undoubtedly the displacement of Customary Law as regards remarriage and the establishment in its stead of Brahminical values which held widow marriage in disrepute and insisted on some penalty (in this case forfeiture of inheritance rights) being imposed for a breach of the preferred norm of the chaste, prayerful widow. I believe that this forms but a chapter in the much larger drama of the Brahminization of the low castes and the Hinduization of tribals that was an unintended, but, given the nature of the system itself, almost an inevitable consequence of the British administration of Hindu Law. An example of this process is conveniently provided by the Calcutta High Court in regard to the Rajbansis.

In 1885 *Fanindara Deb Raikat v. Rajeswar Dass*[51] reached the Privy Council on appeal from the Calcutta High Court. The case involved succession to the *gaddi* of the Baikantpur Raj. It was common ground that the family were descended from the Koch tribe, that they had been subject to Hindu influence, and that they had adopted some Hindu customs. The extent of this process of Hinduization was the point at issue: were they sufficiently Hinduised to be subject to Hindu Law or were they ruled by tribal and family custom?

The succession contest was drawn between the adopted son of the late Raikat and the nearest male agnate, whose claim was clear providing the late Raikat died sonless. Hindu Law recognizes succession by adoption; for the adopted son it was contended that the family was governed by Hindu Law. Against this it was contended that although the family had come under Hindu influence, they did not observe the Shastras, and had retained and were 'still governed by many tribal and family customs inconsistent with that law', including the custom of exclusion of an adopted son from inheritance.[52] The District Judge held that adoption was contrary to the custom of the Baikantpur family and found in favour of the agnate. The Calcutta High Court (Morris and Tottenham, JJ.) held that Hindu Law was applicable to the case and that succession passed to the adopted son. Both the Indian courts held that the burden of proof rested with the agnate claiming the existence of a custom prohibiting adoption, although they differed in their judgments as to whether or not he had conclusively proved such a custom. In apportioning the onus of proof in the way they did, both Indian courts implicitly or explicitly took the position that Hindu Law applied unless and until a contrary family custom were proved in law.

The Privy Council turned the matter the other way up; given the non-Hindu origin of the family, the Privy Council refused to accept that the family was 'generally' governed by Hindu Law and threw the burden of proof upon the adopted son, who was then required to prove that the Hindu practice of adoption had been accepted by the non-Hindu family. On the basis of the history of the Raj family, which in 16 devolutions of the estate had seen no successions by adoption, 'though in three instances the circumstances were such [i.e., the Raja died sonless] as usually move Hindus to make an adoption', the Privy Council had no difficulty in holding that 'whatever Hindu customs may have been introduced into . . . [the family], the custom of succession by adoption has not been introduced'.[53]

Seven years later the Calcutta High Court heard another case involving Rajbansis, *Ram Das v. Chandra Dassia*,[54] on appeal from Rangpur. This involved an inheritance dispute between a daughter and her uncle (father's brother). The Bengal school of Hindu Law recognized the daughter's inheritance rights; tribal custom did not. The Calcutta High Court, which had held that Hindu Law applied to the Baikantpur Raj family, had no hesitation in holding this family likewise subject to Hindu Law—and no difficulty in distinguishing this case from the Baikantpur decision in the Privy Council. The Privy Council decision had been reached 'having regard to the origin and history of the family'; in the present case, 'of the history of the family nothing is known, and it is not likely that it has a history'! Witnesses called to testify to the law and custom of the family 'were ignorant, illiterate people who could not distinguish one system [of Hindu Law] from the other'.[55] The High Court held that the family were subject to Hindu Law and the daughter secured her inheritance.

A third Rajbansi case, *Santala Bewa v. Badaswari Dasi*,[56] reached the Calcutta High Court in 1923 and involved the question of widow remarriage. A daughter sued her deceased father's second wife, who had succeeded to his property, on the ground that as the widow had taken a dangua and thereby allegedly contracted a remarriage, she had forfeited the inheritance, and the daughter, as next heir of her father, was entitled to the property. The widow contended that among the Rajbansis custom decreed that a widow keeping a dangua did not forfeit property inherited from her deceased husband.

The Munsiff of Siliguri held that the family was non-Hindu by descent and origin and was governed not by Hindu Law but by custom. He further held that among the Rajbansis a widow may keep a dangua and that a widow so doing is permitted by custom to retain her former husband's property. The Deputy Commissioner of Darjeeling reserved the Munsiff's decision on the ground that the Calcutta High Court had previously held the Rajbansis to be Hindus and subject to Hindu Law. And Hindu Law, as interpreted in the strictly 'orthodox' tradition of the Calcutta High Court, divested remarried widows of any inheritance they had received from their first husbands, regardless of a custom of remarriage among the tribe or caste concerned.

The case was appealed to the Calcutta High Court. For the widow it was contended that: (*a*) Rajbansis were not Hindus and were not governed by Hindu Law but by custom; (*b*) according to Rajbansi custom a widow may keep a dangua and by such an action she does not compromise her interest in the property of her deceased husband; and (*c*) keeping a dangua is not equivalent to remarriage; at most such action may amount to unchastity but it is established in law that subsequent unchastity does not divest a widow of property already vested in her.

For the daughter it was urged that: (*a*) the Rajbansis were Hindus and governed by Hindu Law as held in previous decisions of the Calcutta High Court; (*b*) keeping a dangua was equivalent to remarriage; and (c) given the previous decisions of the Calcutta High Court on the forfeiture of property by remarried widows, a Rajbansi widow by keeping a dangua forfeited her interest in her first husband's property, even though there be a custom of remarriage and non-forfeiture.

The Calcutta High Court noted that widow remarriage was prevalent among the Rajbansis and that it took place without any ceremonies whatever.

> The peculiar circumstances under which widows are received by men as wives, amongst Rajbansis, have given rise to different names by which such women are known, such as *dangua* wife, *dhoka* wife, *pashua* wife. *Dang* means a stick or a blow dealt with a stick; when a widow lives by herself and a man goes to the house with a *dang* or stick in his hand and strikes a blow with it on the roof of the house, and so enters in and takes possession of the woman, such a woman is called a *dangua* wife.[57]

This is certainly a far cry from the provisions of section 6 of the Hindu Widows' Remarriage Act![58]

Writing in 1891 Risley had stated concerning the Rajbansis in the Darjeeling Terai that they

> make no secret at all of allowing a widow to remarry outside the degrees prohibited to her before her marriage, and subject to the further condition that she may not marry any of the elder relations of her late husband. Where a widow happens to be the head of the family, she enjoys the further privilege of choosing any man not within the prohibited degrees to live with her as her husband without going through any ceremony whatever. This looks like a survival, and may possibly furnish an explanation of the statement made by Buchanan about the Pani-Kochh that 'women who happen to be unmarried after they have grown up select a husband according to their own discretion', which by itself seems rather unlikely. If, however, we suppose the privilege to have been limited to women who had control of the property of their family, it bears a different aspect, and falls into line with several points of primitive practice in matters affecting property.[59]

These observations are particularly relevant as the parties to the suit before the Calcutta High Court were Rajbansis of Darjeeling and the widow who took a dangua had control of her late husband's property.

The Calcutta High Court, however, held that Rajbansis were governed by the 'ordinary Hindu Law, although there may be a custom prevailing amongst them which renders remarriage of widows possible'.[60] The Rajbansi widow was divested of her first husband's property, although the custom of her community allowed and permitted widow remarriage and although the Munsiff had found that custom also permitted a remarried Rajbansi widow to retain her first husband's property. In criticizing this decision, Justice Mukerji of the Allahabad High Court stated, quite rightly, that the Calcutta High Court, in coming to the decision it did, 'was not administering the law of the parties before the Court, but the law of a different people'.[61]

The judicial view of Indian society expounded by the Calcutta High Court appears to have been fundamentally incompatible with existing ethnographic evidence. Certainly such judicial imposition of Hindu Law must have been a potent force in expediting the centuries-old process of Brahminization and Hinduization among the castes and tribes on the cultural and geographical fringes of Hinduism. Particularly where, as among the Rajbansis, Hinduization (or 'Kshatriyization', or 'Sanskritization', if one prefers either of these terms) was a contemporary process actually in progress, judicial sanction of this nature amounted to partisan interference in the internal affairs of the group-category. Again the limitations of the 'caste-category'[62] approach to Indian social reality are illustrated. To quote further from Risley on the Rajbansis:

> The Rajbansis profess to marry their daughters as infants . . . but this custom has only recently been adopted, and it is difficult to ascertain to what extent it is really followed even among those sub-castes which profess to be pure Hindus. In the more primitive groups adult-marriage still prevails, and a breach of chastity before marriage is already condoned, though the tendency is continually towards the adoption of what is believed to be more orthodox usage. The same remark applies to the remarriage of widows. The Rajbansis in Rangpur if questioned on this point aver most positively that nothing of the sort is permitted; while their brethren in the Darjiling Terai make no secret of allowing a widow to remarry. . . . Curiously enough, the Rajbansis, who prohibit widow-marriage, nevertheless recognize divorce—a fact sufficient in itself to show, if further proof were wanting, that the former prohibition cannot have been long in force among them.[63]

Whether or not the decision to apply Hindu Law to the Rajbansis of Rangpur (*Ram Das v. Chandra Dassia*[64]) could possibly have been justified, the Rajbansis of Darjeeling were clearly a different cultural and social group, in spite of the fact that the same broad ascriptive designation was applied to both.

The partisan nature of the judicial attitude towards groups like the Rajbansis is illustrated by the fact that to prove a custom derogating from the textual, orthodox Hindu Law, strong and convincing evidence was required to prove to the satisfaction of the court that the custom pleaded was ancient, certain, and of invariable application. However, no such evidence was required to establish a 'custom' that coincided with (or approximated towards) the textual law. Even among the Rajbansi groups which observed it, the custom prohibiting widow remarriage was clearly far from 'ancient'; it was equally clearly far from being of 'invariable application' among the Rajbansi category as a whole. By the tests applied to prove custom, this supported 'custom' would have failed. But tests of custom were only applicable to customs in opposition to orthodox, textual law; they were not applicable to customs which were not at variance with that law. Among other things, this meant that, particularly in regard to matters which involved questions of personal legal status (e.g., marriage, divorce, adoption) and many aspects of property law (e.g., inheritance, succession, property rights of women), there was only one avenue of autonomous social change open, that is, change in the direction of conformity with the tenets of orthodox Hinduism. Change in any other direction required official sanction; the door to change could only be opened by legislation, such as the Hindu Widows' Remarriage Act. Yet even this Act in its application by the British-Indian courts, with the exception of the Allahabad High Court, was transformed into an instrument for the propagation and imposition of orthodox Hindu values.

It seems a fair comment to observe that the majority of the judges of the British-Indian courts—judges both British and Indian—shared a very Brahminical view of Indian society, derived in the one case from the legal texts which they studied and in the other from the texts as well as from family traditions and social circumstances, as most Indian judges were themselves Brahmins. Sitting on the High Court benches and moving in the society of the political and social elite, judges were far removed from the lives of the lower orders of society, from the beliefs and practices of the Sudra castes which permitted and recognized widow remarriage regardless of what the Brahminical texts might have to say on the matter of proper conduct befitting a widow.[65]

A second factor which undoubtedly contributed to the preference for orthodox Hindu Law was simply ease and convenience: it was much simpler for a busy court to refer to texts at hand than to undertake empirical investigations into the various and sundry local systems of Customary Law. Certainly the 'orthodox' tradition of the Calcutta High Court was, at least in part, a response to the difficulties inherent in a centralized judicial system attempting to deal with disputes arising in a social system characterized by a multitude of localized, largely autonomous groupings governed by their respective customs and *kulachar* (family practice). Coupled with a strong disinclination to decide cases on the basis of custom at variance with Hindu Law was an equally strong inclination to integrate these multitudinous groupings into a less complicated (and more easily administered) system of law, into a single overarching legal code.

That there was a vigorous and consistent alternative to the orthodox tradition of the Calcutta High Court is apparent from the long series (remarkably totally free of dissenting opinions) of decisions emanating from the up-country Allahabad High Court. In contrast to the Calcutta High Court's invocation of inferences from ancient texts which admittedly did not deal directly with the question in hand, and to the heavy-handed literalism of the Bombay High Court, the Allahabad decisions appear not only just and humane, but down-to-earth, in touch with what was actually going on down on the ground, with the lives, customs, and traditions of living people.

Within the jurisdiction of the Allahabad High Court, Customary Law was preserved—but it was also frozen. This was but an inevitable consequence of the codification or judicial recognition of custom. Once custom is recorded, it loses its ability to change, to evolve new refinements in the face of new situations. Within the jurisdiction of the Allahabad High Court 1856 became an arbitrary cut-off date. To prove a valid custom of widow remarriage, it was absolutely necessary to prove that the custom had existed prior to July 1856. No more recent custom of remarriage could be legally recognized. At least theoretically, for families and groups among the lower social strata, who as the Calcutta High Court had noted in regard to the Rajbansi family, might well be ignorant, illiterate, and possessed of no (literary or documentary) history, the problem of proving a custom preceding the cut-off date became more difficult with every passing year.

It is also possible, of course—indeed, it is usually the desired objective of the legislators, particularly when the enactment relates to a social reform objective—that a consequence of legislation will be a change in the way people behave. Thus a new pattern of behaviour may be introduced which derives its legal validity not from recognized Customary Law but from the innovations introduced through changes in Statutory Law gradually influencing the way people actually conduct themselves and their affairs. In such a situation, a custom or pattern of behaviour going back three or four generations may be invalid under Customary Law. Such a problem of the validity of a new custom under Customary Law was presented to the Allahabad High Court in 1933 and 1937, that is, after Act XV had been in operation for approximately 80 years.

In *Bhola Umar v. Kausilla*[66] it was alleged that the remarried widow had forfeited all rights in her deceased husband's estate 'according to the custom of the caste [Umar Banya]'.[67] The Subordinate Judge held that the burden of proof of a custom of forfeiture lay on the party alleging it and that he had failed to prove the point. On appeal, the High Court held that the lower courts had failed to determine whether the validity of the widow's marriage derived from Customary Law or from Act XV, it only having been determined that the marriage was valid. The High Court commented:

> The practice of widow remarriage after 1856 in this community or in any other section of the Hindus may well be referrable to the provisions of the Hindu Widows' Remarriage Act and would not necessarily be indicative of an ancient custom existing before the passing of that Act. Unless, therefore, it is shown that the present practice is in pursuance of an ancient custom and not under the Act, the marriage of a widow cannot be held to be under the custom of the caste.[68]

If the custom were a 'new' custom, that is, one that came into existence after 1856 (or could not be proved to have existed before 1856), the assumption would be that the marriage derived its validity from

Act XV of 1856 and the forfeiture clause of section 2 would apply. If the custom pre-dated 1856, there would be no forfeiture unless a further custom entailing forfeiture were proved. The High Court accordingly remitted the case for trial of the following issues:

(1) Whether, according to ancient custom, a widow belonging to the community of Umar Banyas could contract a valid remarriage before the passing of the Hindu Widows' Remarriage Act; and
(2) If the first issue is found in the affirmative, does such a widow forfeit her right in the property of her first husband according to the custom prevailing in the said community before 1856?[69]

The 1937 case, *Narain v. Mohan Singh*,[70] involved a Jat widow who had succeeded to her husband's property and subsequently remarried. She remained in possession of the property until her death. The suit arose following her death and the plaintiff, who was admittedly not the nearest reversioner at the time of her death, claimed that his ancestor had been the nearest reversioner at the time of her remarriage and had been from that date legally entitled to the property; and that he, as heir to this ancestor, was now its rightful owner. The lower courts held that the plaintiff had failed to prove a caste custom involving forfeiture on remarriage.

On appeal, the High Court was dissatisfied with the evidence in regard to both the alleged custom of remarriage and the alleged custom of forfeiture. On the one hand, the evidence as to a custom of remarriage was

> . . . nothing but a repetition of instances of remarriages deriving their validity from the Hindu Widows' Remarriage Act. To show that the custom now obtaining is not the result of the Act, but wholly apart from it, some evidence ought to be forthcoming to prove that the custom was in existence before the Act was passed.[71]

On the other hand, there were the plaintiff's 'allegations of forfeiture coming into existence in consequence of the Act [of 1856]'.[72] Accordingly, the High Court remitted the case to the lower court for retrial of the relevant issues of Customary Law.

Further findings in both these cases are unavailable.

In spite of the provocative suggestion in these two Allahabad cases that some castes may have accepted widow remarriage as a consequence of the Hindu Widows' Remarriage Act, it is difficult to come to any other conclusion than that, outside the jurisdiction of the Allahabad High Court, this humanely inspired statute was retrogressive in its social effects. Few women of the upper castes availed themselves of their new right to remarry, while those widows who, in the exercise of their customary rights, remarried independently of the Act, found themselves now subject to the forfeiture clause of section 2, regardless of their Customary Law which permitted a widow to remarry and certainly in many, if not most, cases permitted her also to retain property inherited from her first husband.

Postscript: The Law Today

The Hindu Women's Rights to Property Act (XVIII of 1937) gave the Hindu widow, who had previously been excluded from inheritance by the son, agnatic grandson, or agnatic great-grandson of her husband, a right to intestate succession equal to a son's share in regard to her husband's property liable to devolution by succession (i.e., separate and joint property under Dayabhaga and separate property under Mitakshara) and to the whole of her husband's interest in property liable to devolution by survivorship (i.e., Mitakshara joint family property). The estate which the widow took under this Act was a limited (life) estate, held during her lifetime with limited powers of alienation and descending on her death to the heirs of her deceased husband. This estate was subject to forfeiture on remarriage—unless the widow lived within the jurisdiction of the Allahabad High Court and was a member of a caste which by Customary Law permitted its widows to remarry and where it could not be proved (as it generally could not) that this same Customary Law divested remarried widows of the property of their first husbands.

The Hindu Succession Act (XXX of 1956) converted the limited (life) estate of a Hindu female into an estate of which she was the full and absolute owner (section 14). Although the Act specifically provides that heirs who are related to an intestate deceased by reason of being the widow of a predeceased son, the widow of a predeceased son of a predeceased son, or the widow of a brother are not entitled to succeed to the property if they have remarried at the time the succession opens (section 24), the Act does not provide for divesting such a widow, or the widow of the deceased himself, of the property to which she has succeeded if the widow should contract a remarriage after succeeding.

A widow succeeding to her husband's property after June 1956, or a widow who, having succeeded before this date, was in possession of such property when Act XXX of 1956 came into effect, became by virtue of that Act absolute owner of the property which prior to June 1956 she would have held as a limited estate.[73] Any such absolute estate held by a woman descends upon intestate succession in the first instance to her heirs, rather than to the closest living heirs of her husband as had been the case with the limited estate and was the course of succession prescribed in section 2 of Act XV of 1856.

The courts have held that section 2 of the Hindu Widows' Remarriage Act contemplates the forfeiture only of property held by the widow as a limited (life) estate and not of property of which she is absolute owner.[74] As the limited estate has for all practical purposes disappeared from intestate succession (it may still be established by will or gift), the applicability of the forfeiture clause of Act XV of 1856 has been severely curtailed.

Indeed, it would seem that the Hindu Widows' Remarriage Act, although not actually repealed, has been superseded by the Hindu Code legislation of independent India. Nothing in the Hindu Marriage Act (XVIII of 1955) restricts the remarriage of widows—section 5 provides that a marriage may be solemnized between any two Hindus if neither has a spouse living; the fact that one or both parties may have been betrothed or married previously is not listed among the factors preventing a valid marriage. Thus, there is no necessity for a widow wishing to remarry to have recourse to Act XV of 1856. Further, nothing in either the Hindu Marriage Act (1955) or the Hindu Succession Act (1956) provides for the forfeiting of property inherited by a woman from her first husband upon her subsequent remarriage.

The far-reaching legislative enactments of independent India have revolutionized the Hindu woman's rights in regard to succession and inheritance. Many of the prescriptions of the Shastric Law have been superseded by an emphasis on modernity, social emancipation, and equality of the sexes, and by the social exigencies of a new era. It is perhaps a sign of the times that a High Court judge, in holding that the forfeiture section of Act XV of 1856 did not apply to the absolute estate created by the Hindu Succession Act of exactly a century later, observed:

> In the present conditions women do earn and acquire property and husbands are entitled to inherit partially or wholly the property of their wives. There is no process providing for the forfeiture of the property inherited by a husband from a deceased wife on his contracting a remarriage.[75]

Although Hindu society and Indian public opinion are far from equating the remarriage of a widower with the remarriage of a widow, at least in law the remarried Hindu widow, after a century of penalty and forfeiture, is no longer in a worse legal position than the widow who lived in 'notorious unchastity' but wisely did not permit her paramour to make her an honest (and property-less) woman.[76]

Notes

1. *Principles of Hindu and Mohammadan Law*, London, William and Norgate, 1862, p. 60.
2. See also Lucy Carroll, 'Colonial Perceptions of Indian Society and the Emergence of Caste(s) Associations', *Journal of Asian Studies*, 37 (1978): 233–50.
3. *Moniram Kolita v. Keri Kolithani*, ILR 5 Cal. 776 (P.C.).
4. L.S. Jackson, J., *Akora Suth v. Boreani*, 2 Bom. L.R. 199, p. 206.
5. E. Jackson, J., ibid., p. 203.
6. Ranade, J., *Vithu v. Govinda*, ILR 22 Bom. 321, p. 331.
7. Wallis, C.J., *Vitta Tayaramma v. Chatakondu Sivayya*, ILR 41 Mad. 1078, p. 1091.
8. Coutts, J., *Mst. Suraj Jote Kuer v. Mst. Attar Kumari*, ILR 1 Patna 706, p. 710.
9. ILR 11 Allah. 330; Straight and Brodhurst, JJ.
10. See also *Ranjit v. Radha Rani*, ILR 20 Allah. 476; *Khuddo v. Durga Prasad*, ILR 29 Allah. 122; *Gajadhar v. Kaunsilla*, ILR 31 Allah. 161; *Mula v. Partab*, ILR 32 Allah. 489; *Bhagwan Din v. Mst. Indrani*, AIR 1921 Oudh 233; *Narpat v. Mst. Janaka*, AIR 1921 Oudh 130; *Mangat v. Bharto*, ILR 49 Allah. 203; *Ram Lal v. Mst. Jawala*, ILR 3 Luck. 610; *Gajadhar v. Mst. Sukhdei*, ILR 5 Luck. 689; *Bal Krishna Sharma v. Paij Singh*, ILR 52 Allah. 705; *Bhola Umar v. Kausilla*, ILR 55 Allah. 24; *Ganga Saran Singh v. Mst. Sirtaji Kuer*, AIR 1935 Allah. 924.
11. ILR 11 Allah. 330, p. 332.

12. ILR 20 Allah. 476; Blair and Aikman, JJ.
13. AIR 1916 Allah. 193; Banerji and Piggott, JJ.
14. ILR 49 Allah. 203; Dalal and Pullan, JJ.
15. *Bhola Umar v. Kausilla*, ILR 55 Allah. 24, p. 49.
16. Wilson, J., *Matungini Gupta v. Ram Rutton Roy*, ILR 9 Cal. 289, p. 293.
17. Banerji, J., ibid., p. 296.
18. *Ganga Pershad Sahu v. Jhalo*, ILR 38 Cal. 862, p. 871; Mookerjee and Casperaz, JJ.
19. *Vitta Tayaramma v. Chatakondu*, ILR 41 Mad. 1078, p. 1085; Krishnan, J., referring opinion.
20. ILR 5 Cal. 776 (P.C.).
21. ILR 19 Cal. 289. See also: *Murugayi v. Viramakali*, ILR 1 Mad. 226; *Rasul Jehan Begum v. Ram Surun Singh*, ILR 22 Cal. 589; *Nitya Madhav Das v. Srinath Chandra Chuckerbutty*, 8 Cal. L.J. 542; *Gouri Churn Patni v. Sita Patni*, 14 Cal. W.N. 346.
22. For other cases involving conversion of a widow prior to remarriage see: *Ganga Saran Singh v. Mst. Sirtaji Kuer*, AIR 1935 Allah. 924; *Mohan Lal v. Mst. Bhudevi*, AIR 1954 Allah. 588; *Vitta Tayaramma v. Chatakondu Sivayya*, ILR 41 Mad. 1078; *Raghanath Shankar Dixit v. Lakshmibai*, ILR 59 Bom. 417; and *Abdul Aziz Khan v. Nirma*, ILR 35 Allah. 466.
23. Justice Prinsep, dissenting, held that as the remarriage was under Act III of 1872 and not as a Hindu widow under Act XV of 1856, section 2 of the latter Act was not applicable; and he was unable to accept the 'half-his-body' argument as ground for forfeiture when the widow remarried as a non-Hindu, given that neither change of religion (*vide* Act XXI of 1850) nor unchastity (*vide Moniram Kolita v. Keri Kolitani*, ILR 5 Cal. 776, P.C.)—either of which actions destroyed her ability to secure through her acts spiritual benefit to her deceased husband's soul—compromised her right to enjoyment of his estate (*Matungini Gupta v. Ram Rutton Roy*, ILR 19 Cal. 289, p. 300).
24. Ibid., p. 291.
25. Ibid., p. 292.
26. Ibid.
27. Ibid., p. 295.
28. Quoted by Seshagiri Aiyar, J., dissenting opinion, *Vitta Tayaramma v. Chatakondu Sivayya*, ILR 41 Mad. 1078, pp. 1095–6.
29. ILR 11 Bom. 119; Sargent, C.J., and Birdwood, J.
30. ILR 22 Bom. 321.
31. For other cases involving the widow who succeeded to her deceased husband's property as heir to their son, see *Akora Suth v. Boreani*, 2 Ben. L.R. 199; *Chamar Haru Dalmel v. Kashi*, ILR 26 Bom. 388; *Basappa v. Rayava*, ILR 29 Bom. 91; and *Lakshmana Sasamallo v. Siva Sasamallayani*, ILR 28 Mad. 425.

The distinction which was made by the Bombay, Calcutta, and Madras High Courts depended on whether or not the widow's remarriage preceded the son's death: the mother could inherit from her son if she had remarried during the son's lifetime; but if she remained a widow during her son's life, succeeded to the property on his death, and then remarried, she forfeited the property. Put another way, if the widow were actually in possession of the property of her deceased husband at the time of the remarriage, either as heir to her husband or to her son, she forfeited the property; if the property were vested in the son at the time of the remarriage, she did not compromise her rights as heir to the son in the event of his dying without wife or child surviving him.

32. *Vithu v. Govinda*, ILR 22 Bom. 321, pp. 326–7.
33. *Har Saran Das v. Nandi*, ILR 11 Allah. 330, p. 332.
34. *Vittu v. Govinda*, ILR 22 Bom. 321, p. 327.
35. Ibid., p. 300.
36. *The Law and Custom of Hindu Castes Within the Dekhun Provinces Subject to the Presidency of Bombay*, London: W.H. Allen and Co. (new edition, 1868). The Preface indicates that the original report was submitted in 1826.
37. *Vithu v. Govinda*, ILR 22 Bom. 321, p. 331.
38. *Gajapathi Naidu v. Jeevammal*, AIR 1929 Mad. 765; Pandalal, J.
39. ILR 31 Allah. 161; Stanley, C.J., and Banerji, J.
40. ILR 32 Allah. 489; Stanley, C.J., and Banerji, J.
41. ILR 49 Allah. 203; Dalal and Pullan, JJ.
42. ILR 55 Allah. 24.
43. Ibid., p. 36; italics in original.
44. Ibid., p. 38.
45. Ibid., p. 41; italics in original.
46. ILR 5 Cal. 776 (P.C.).
47. *Bhola Umar v. Kausilla*, ILR 55 Allah. 24, p. 42.
48. Ibid., pp. 46–8.
49. Ibid., pp. 59–60.
50. Ibid., pp. 56–7.
51. LR 121A 72 (ILR 11 Cal. 463 P.C.).
52. Ibid., p. 74.
53. Ibid., p. 87.
54. ILR 20 Cal. 409; Macpherson and Beverley, JJ.
55. Ibid., pp. 412–13.
56. ILR 50 Cal. 727; Ghose and Panton, JJ.
57. Ibid., p. 735.
58. See also *Ram Pearey v. Mst. Kailasha*, AIR 1930 Oudh 426; and *Tapoo v. Emperor*, AIR 1937 Sind 42.

59. H. Risley, *The Tribes and Castes of Bengal*, vol. I, Calcutta, Bengal Secretariat Press, 1891, p. 495.
60. *Santala Bewa v. Badaswari Dasi*, ILR 50 Cal. 727, p. 735.
61. *Bhola Umar v. Kausilla*, ILR 55 Allah. 24, p. 40.
62. See Lucy Carroll, 'Colonial Perceptions of Indian Society and the Emergence of Caste(s) Associations', loc. cit.; Bernard S. Cohn, 'Notes on the History of the Study of Indian Society and Culture', in M. Singer and B. Cohn, eds., *Structure and Change in Indian Society*, Chicago, Aldine, 1968.
63. H. Risley, op. cit., pp. 494–5.
64. ILR 20 Cal. 409; see note 63 above, pp. 37–8.
65. It is one of the many ironies of British India that while the Raj was morally justified by contrasting the alleged cultural superiority of western civilisation with the alleged social barbarism of India which the Europeans saw evidenced by such unenlightened practices as child marriage and the deplorable institutions of the child widow, nonetheless at the same time the judicial system of the Raj was sanctioning and enforcing Brahminical norms upon castes and tribes which were at best only marginally committed to these norms, and commonly actively committed to quite contrary norms.
66. ILR 58 Allah. 1034; Young and Naimat-ullah, JJ.
67. Ibid., p. 1035.
68. Ibid., p. 1038.
69. Ibid., p. 1040.
70. AIR 1937 Allah. 343; Naimat-ullah, J.
71. Ibid., p. 344.
72. Ibid. It may be noted that the Allahabad High Court, consistently with its entire approach to customs and Customary Law, here clearly implies that the same standard of proof would be required to prove an alleged custom which conformed with textual Hindu Law as to prove one derogating from that law.
73. *Punithavalli Ammal v. Ramalingam*, AIR 1970 S.C. 1730.
74. *Thangavelu Asari v. Lakshmi Ammal*, AIR 1957 Mad. 534; *Mst. Bhuri Bai v. Mst. Champi Bai*, AIR 1968 Raj. 139; *Pandurang Narayan Saluke v. Sindhu*, AIR 1971 Bom. 413; *Chinnappavu Naidu v. Meenakshi Ammal*, AIR 1971 Mad. 453; *Sasanka Bhowmick v. Amiya Bhowmick*, 78 CWN 1011; *Jagdish Mahton v. Mohammad Elahi*, AIR 1973 Pat. 170; *Smt. Sankaribala Dutta v. Smt. Asita Barani Dasi*, AIR 1977 Cal. 289.
75. *Mst. Bhuri Bai v. Mst. Champi Bai*, AIR 1968 Raj. 139, p. 145; L.N. Chhangani, J.
76. See *Parvati v. Bhiku*, 1867 Bom. HCR 25.

5

Caste, Widow-Remarriage, and the Reform of Popular Culture in Colonial Bengal*

Sekhar Bandyopadhyay

Social reforms in Bengal in the nineteenth century affected many aspects of human relations and existential realities, the most important of them being gender relations and the condition of women. Yet, towards the close of the century a large section among the latter who were widows by civil status were still being 'forced' to live celibate and austere lives, despite the reform endeavours of men like Rammohun Roy, Iswar Chandra Vidyasagar and others. As the realities stand, while the former had succeeded in achieving his goal, the latter's mission ended in what has been described as an 'unavoidable defeat'.[1] Sati, the eradication of which was on Rammohun's reform agenda, was abolished by Regulation XVII of 1829. Widow-burning was made a penal offence, any violation of which would immediately invite the regulating hand of the state. Rammohun could thus save widows from being immolated with the help of the constant presence of state power and the law-enforcing apparatus. But Vidyasagar failed to see many widows remarried, as in this case the Act of 1856 only legalized their marriage, but could not make it socially acceptable; nor was it possible to enforce it with the help of the police force. So Vidyasagar had to depend ultimately on social consent, not on the power of the state, and it was here that his 'defeat' was quite manifest. But one might ask whether this was in fact avoidable or not.

It may also be argued that in retrospect the movement does not appear to have failed. That widow-remarriage has gained in social legitimacy today is partly due to this nineteenth-century reform endeavour. But it may be pointed out also that this legitimization has taken place only among the educated sections of the community and, even within that limited social sphere, it is not widespread. 'Everyone feels the evil and wishes that it could be removed', wrote *Hindu Patriot* in 1855, 'but the difficulty is how to meet the lion in his den.'[2] Widow-remarriage remains exceptional among the educated even today, as it was in the nineteenth and the early twentieth centuries. And contrary to the existing stereotypes, the uneducated and the lower orders are also ardent defenders of the taboo just as their social superiors are. This compels us to re-think this reform movement as a 'defeat', since the problem was complex and not one of education alone.

The existing literature[3] seeks to explain this 'defeat' by focusing mainly on the structural weaknesses of the reformist effort, but does not adequately emphasize the power of tradition that refused to be reformed. This paper is concerned mainly with the traditional culture of the Bengali Hindus, as it was to the realm of culture that the issue of widow-remarriage ultimately belonged. Culture, according to Peter Burke, is 'a system of shared meanings, attitudes and values, and the symbolic forms . . . in which they are expressed and embodied'.[4] Forms of marriage or social organization of human sexuality and relationship are therefore to be understood in terms of their cultural connotations and imputed social meanings. But culture is also multi-layered, different social groups have different cultures. Usually, we assume a simple dichotomy between the two broad cultural traditions, the 'elite culture' and the 'popular culture', or to use E.P. Thompson's Marxian phraseology, between 'patrician' and 'plebeian' cultures.[5] But we need not assume a clinical disjunction between these two traditions, as there are constant interaction and overlapping, though of an unequal nature, between them. As a result of this process popular culture often accepts and internalizes the ideologies of the elites and assumes in some respects a common interface with their culture. This process of the 'reform of popular culture', which Peter Burke first talked about in relation to early modern Europe,[6] implies an imposition of certain elite cultural forms on the masses from above, rather than voluntary emulative behaviour of the socially mobile groups from below, as suggested in our familiar 'Sanskritization' discourse.[7] Martin Ingram has more recently defined the process in the following words:

> . . . the world of popular culture came under attack from elite groups (clergy, nobility and some middle class groups in town and country) who gradually attenuated and transformed many aspects of social life among the mass of the people. This 'reform of popular culture' combined attempts to suppress many popular activities and to modify the behaviour of the common people, . . . and the sponsoring of a new 'popular' or 'mass' culture which embodied the ideologies of the ruling elites.[8]

This concept[9] can be a useful tool for understanding and explaining the success or failure of the reforms proposed by men like Vidyasagar. The present paper will try to show that the taboo on widow-remarriage, which was adhered to by more people than is usually believed, was in itself the result of a 'reform of popular culture'. This first process of reform was so effective and of such antiquity, that the subsequent attempt at counter reform was bound to fail, given the weakness of the reform ideology and the vulnerability of the strategy to promote it.

II

One of the major contentions of the most recent feminist critique of the nineteenth-century reform movements is that the issues which had been picked up concerned mainly a small section of women. The reform endeavours therefore reflected only the paternalism of the elitist male reformers, concerned exclusively about their own class, and their eagerness to retain their patriarchal control over the private spheres of life.[10] The first premise of this feminist discourse, however, needs to be re-examined, for compulsory widow-celibacy, like many other similar customs, was more widely practised than indicated by the available cultural stereotypes, both old and recent.

In Bengal widow-remarriage was strictly forbidden among the upper castes and most of the middle-ranking castes in the nineteenth century. The 1891 list of castes that forbade widow-remarriage included, apart from the Brahmans, Kayasthas and Vaidyas of the upper stratum, the various trading castes, as well as the Sadgops, Sundis, Mahishyas, Telis, Mayras and Napits.[11] It was allowed among the lower castes, but they too appear to have shared the values of their social superiors. Widow-remarriage even when permitted, was looked down upon and was disparagingly referred to as *sanga* marriage, a practice prevalent in many other parts of India as well. Among the Namasudras of Bengal, for example, the married couples of a widow-remarriage occupied a lower place in the estimation of their caste fellows and were referred to as *Krishna-Paksha* (dark fortnight after full moon), while those married in a regular way were described as *Sukla-Paksha* (bright fortnight after new moon).[12] The very use of the terms 'dark' or 'bright' indicates the respective values attached by the community to the two forms of marriage. And by the beginning of the twentieth century, they too, like many other *antyaja jatis* around them had almost completely discontinued the practice and begun to conform to the traditional upper-caste behavioural norms of widowhood.[13] At the turn of the century, therefore, it was perhaps only the lowest menial groups like the 'Doms, Boonas, Bagdis and "low people" of various kinds' and the so-called 'aborigines' who practised widow-remarriage without any stigma attached to it, while the rest of the Bengali Hindu society strictly forbade this custom.[14] Nothing can be a better indicator of the failure or 'defeat' of the reform movement to introduce widow-remarriage.

Side by side, we also come across another social phenomenon the importance of which need not be minimized. And that was the increasing social legitimacy of widow-remarriage among the educated *bhadralok* who had been constructing in the nineteenth century new 'models of womanhood' to suit the socio-psychological as well as political needs of the time.[15] Even during Vidyasagar's lifetime, important groups in Calcutta, in addition to Young Bengal, and a significant section of the native press, like *Hindu Patriot, Tattvabodhini Patrika, Sambad Purnachandroday* or *Bamabodhini Patrika*, had lent full support to his reform movement.[16] As the bhadralok category kept on expanding across caste and local boundaries, this legitimacy became more and more broad-based. The Bengali bhadralok was never a closed status group incorporating only the members of the three traditional upper castes. In reality, as John McGuire's quantitative study has shown, in the latter half of the nineteenth century the Calcutta bhadralok community included individuals belonging to as many as 18 different castes.[17] In the early twentieth century, as there was further extension of education and literacy down the caste lines,[18] there were fresh entrants into this category. As the newcomers got access to the new literate culture of the educated urban bhadralok, they also began to accept and imbibe the reform ideology of the latter. To them widow-remarriage now appeared to be good conduct or *sadachar* while its prohibition became *kadachar* or bad conduct.[19] A symbolic acceptance of this innovation was taken as a signifier of their entrance into the new status groups. Certain sections of the Sadgops, Baruis, Gandhabaniks, Jogis, Rajbansis and Namasudras therefore sought to promote widow-remarriage at least for the minors. The educated Mahishyas also advocated remarriage of widows, though only for those who would be found incapable of practising *brahmacharya* or self-abnegation. And some of the progressive Jogis and Sadgops went even beyond such oral acceptance of the reform, and actually organized a few such marriages.[20] Such symbolic actions did not however mean that the innovation had acquired popular acceptance among such communities. The newly educated sections of these communities, the recent entrants into the bhadralok category, shared with the old members of the group the same dilemma as regards the actual practice of the reform. Since Vidyasagar himself had failed in his mission, a Sadgop rationalized his dilemma, what else could they be expected to achieve![21]

Thus as a direct legacy of the reform movement started by Vidyasagar to introduce widow-remarriage what we find during the decades immediately following his death are two parallel situations. Prohibition of widow-remarriage became a far more widely shared popular custom, while the innovation of widow-remarriage gained wider social legitimacy among the educated sections of society. But even those who had accepted the innovation refrained from practising it. This paradoxical situation constitutes a problematic that can be explained only with reference to the dynamics of popular culture in Bengal in the nineteenth and the early twentieth centuries.

III

Public control over private life as a dominant feature of Bengali Hindu society has had a long history. In this cultural milieu, marriage was not a consensual union between two individuals. It was indeed a concern of the whole community, as endogamy was one of the fundamental aspects of the caste system with a bearing on social rank. Transactional modalities, rituals and rites in a marriage were therefore parts of a public spectacle, supervised and often monitored by the community. The slightest deviation from the established norms invited public censure, while major violations meant more severe punishments, which usually took the form of social boycott of the erring families. Popular Hinduism in other words inculcated an ideology of discipline, which was enforced or maintained through a hierarchized structure of social authority that expressed itself through the idiom of caste. The caste system represented, according to a recent commentator, a cultural construction of power in Indian society.[22] That it was a system connotative only of a structure is essentially a colonial ethnographic stereotype. It was also a normative system which defined, determined and also legitimized the structure,[23] and this relationship is crucial for understanding the failure of the reform movement advocating widow-remarriage.

The *Hindu Patriot* in 1855 recognized without any reservation the rationality of the proposed reform of widow-remarriage. But for it the major problem was how 'to bring about so desirable an end as the removal of miseries of our helpless females without incurring the risk of losing caste with all its concomitant disadvantages. . . .'[24] The widow of the first proposed remarriage, who was subsequently let down by the prospective bridegroom, also complained that 'she had by such refusal lost her position in society and is now an outcast. . . .'[25] Even the observers who had participated in the first widow-remarriage ceremonies organized by Vidyasagar, 'were completely outcasted' by the large majority of bhadralok in Calcutta.[26] Social rebels like Dakshinaranjan Mukhopadhyay, who had committed a double sin by marrying outside his caste and by marrying a widow, also had to acquiesce ultimately to this social tyranny and had to migrate and seek refuge in a completely different and distant social environment of Awadh.[27] What appears to be crucial is the fear of 'losing caste', of being excommunicated by society, which intimidated people into surrendering to dominant social norms. The question therefore is what were the social implications of this phenomenon of 'losing caste' and how was the terror that it generated organized.

Caste as a normative system prescribed for each group in society, according to its rank, certain codes of conduct or *jati-dharma*,[28] which every individual had to perform in real life. This performance was believed to be the chief determinant of the quality of 'body spiritual', which determined a person's ritual as well as social rank and therefore took precedence over both the 'body individual' and 'body social'. Any deviation from such codes would lead to the fall from the ascribed rank, or loss of caste, which implied the denial of interaction with the local community and sometimes even of essential social services. The codes varied from group to group, but always there was a tendency of the lower groups changing and remoulding their behavioural patterns with reference to the elite model. The process which Alfred Lyall had once described as 'the gradual Brahmanisation of the aboriginal non-Aryan or casteless tribes' had reached such a point in Bengal in the mid-1880s that Herbert Risley could not detect any variance in customs and ceremonies of the different castes, high and low. He had to adopt, therefore, the method of anthropometric measurement in order to determine the origin of the intermediary and lower castes, who could thus be separated, somewhat arbitrarily, from the upper castes, to fit into his racial model of the Aryan–non-Aryan dichotomy in Hindu society.[29] The phenomenon which Lyall and Risley had observed in the nineteenth century was no doubt the reflection of the process of reform of popular culture, which had taken place apparently by volition and not by any visible application of power.

But this acculturation was not entirely voluntary; there was, as it appears, an element of compulsion in it. In order to get access to Hindu society and to move up in its status-ranking scale, acceptance of its behavioural norms was mandatory. These norms were essentially based on an ideology of hierarchy that legitimized the prime position of the Brahmans who, because of their monopoly over knowledge, both used to define such normative standards of social behaviour, as also arbitrated in cases of their violation. But the maintenance of social discipline, or the actual execution of the Brahmans' mandate, depended on an elaborate power structure within which every single individual had his or her own location. The primary unit within this structure was the extended family, which was always patriarchal, as patriarchy alone corresponded to the hierarchical ethos of Hindu society. The family household, as it appears from the late-nineteenth-century evidence, was organized in a hierarchical structure of obedience, in which every member was situated according to age, generation and gender, the supreme position of authority being held by the eldest male member, the patriarch or the *karta*.[30]

The lowest position, in terms of entitlement to rights and resources of the family, was held by the women, who were expected only to obey their husbands. An anonymous author wrote in a popular treatise entitled *Hindudharmaniti* (Principles of Hindu Religion) in 1794 Saka: 'The wife should follow her husband like his shadow; she should be like his friend in performing all religious duties; and like his maid she should carry out all his orders . . . The wife who retains her smile in spite of the harsh words and angry looks of her husband, is considered to have properly performed her sacred duties.'[31] What was thus defined as the dharma or the duties of an ideal wife virtually meant her unconditional surrender to the dictates of the husband, and this subjection would continue even beyond the death of the husband, as marriage was conceived to be a relationship of eternal bondage. As another pamphlet called *Hindu Narir Kartabya* (Duties of Hindu Women) noted in 1916: 'The duties of a widow are included among the duties of a wife. For marital relations among Hindus continue even beyond death.'[32] It was this eternalist concept of marriage which rationalized prohibition on widow-remarriage. But such restrictions were not applicable to the widowers. In Bengali Hindu society of the nineteenth century polyandry was unthinkable but polygamy was acceptable and in certain cases a legitimate social practice. A widower was therefore often encouraged to remarry, particularly for procreating progeny for the patriliny. Twentieth-century Bengali literature bears ample testimony to the existence of this social mentality.[33]

In the traditional social hierarchy of the Hindus, women and Sudras were the two lowest categories, as both were denied access to Vedic religious rites. Later on as sections of the Sudra *jatis* became socially mobile, gained access to elite culture, and became claimants to higher ritual status, they too began to conform to the patriarchal norms of the upper-caste elite families. Even the women of these castes were so deeply socialized into this essentially elite (or upper-caste) and male worldview that they too accepted without any question this patriarchal standard of morality. 'Devoted wives must always follow their husbands dead or alive,' wrote *Mahishya Mahila*, the journal of the Mahishya women, in 1911. 'If the husband was dead', it continued further, 'the widow, until her own death, should observe self-abnegation and should never even pronounce the name of any other man during her life time.' Because, 'it is only by serving the husband that a woman can reach the heaven'.[34] The prohibition on widow-remarriage, which thus virtually implied a total control over the mind and body of women by their husbands during their lifetime and even after, had become, as we have noted already, an almost universal practice in Bengal by the beginning of the twentieth century. This near-total acceptance of the moral code of widow celibacy was not just due to an imitative urge from below. It resulted from a long-drawn and often imperceptible process of the 'reform of popular culture' imposed from above.

The question that we had begun with, that is, how were these moral behavioural codes enforced, should now be answered. At an ideological level, these codes of behaviour derived their legitimacy from the injunction of the *shastra* or scriptures as interpreted by the Brahmans, who enjoyed, till the advent of print culture, a near-total monopoly over Sanskrit textual knowledge. Even when the printing press allowed a broader section of the people access to the scriptures, it was not the texts as such which were taken to the people,[35] but the commentaries written by these pundits which became more popular and widely read. Thus paradoxically, the spread of education or literacy in Bengal had led to a further traditionalization of society. The modernizing impact of education depends on its content, or as Bernard Cohn remarked on 'what people read after they have become literate'.[36] Even a cursory glance at the list of vernacular publications in the late nineteenth and the early twentieth centuries[37] would at once reveal that the average reading public in Bengal was more interested in traditional lore or the knowledge of the shastra, than in the new secular humanistic knowledge.

The educated Bengalis' infatuation with the shastra was, however, due mainly to the Orientalist tradition which had attached supreme importance to scriptures for understanding Indian society. Consequently, during the debate over sati, the competing discourses established the 'centrality' of brahmanic scriptures in determining the legitimacy of social customs.[38] Vidyasagar, an inheritor of this tradition and a Sanskrit scholar by training, also recognized the power of the shastra, from which he believed all social behavioural codes derived their legitimacy. His innovation of widow-remarriage would therefore acquire social acceptance, as his contention was, only if it could be supported by some scriptural maxims; because, as he noted, 'in this country people behaved in accordance with the dicta of the *shastra* and only the *shastra*'.[39] In his first treatise of widow-remarriage we find a massive effort to hunt for a supportive text from the available corpus of scriptural knowledge. But Vidyasagar by going according to the Orientalist tradition misunderstood his own society.

The shastra constituted only one element among many on the basis of which the moral-behavioural codes were constructed. The other elements were oral traditions and longstanding customary usages that gave Hinduism the character of a folklorized religion. Thus when Vidyasagar discovered in *Parasarasamhita* a maxim in support of his reform, the *Hindu Intelligencer* immediately pointed out that

> the views of Parasara, if they were such as have been interpreted to us by the author of the brochure under notice [i.e. Vidyasagar's first treatise on widow-remarriage], have never been adopted by the Hindus, and will continue to be discarded by the people of this country for a long time to come.[40]

Samachar Sudhabarshan also observed around the same time:

> Since the beginning of the Kali Yuga till date, the remarriage of Hindu widows has never been *heard of, nor seen*. And it is for this reason that people believe that widow-remarriage is against the *shastras* and the codes of good conduct.[41]

This statement needs to be emphasized as it implied that the popular perception that widow-remarriage did not conform to the accepted standards of moral conduct was not derived from any written tradition. It was based on hearsay or a longstanding oral tradition which a citation from an obsolete text could not invalidate. To the Hindus 'established custom is law' and in this case, the age-old, often believed to be 'eternal', custom was to debar widows from re-entering connubial relations.[42] An editorial in *Bamabodhini Patrika*, while discussing the futility of Vidyasagar's reform endeavour, very aptly summarized this situation:

The common people neither follow reason, nor understand *shastra*; local customs also follow more or less the established tradition. These people hate widow-remarriage as a great sin, as they find it to be alien to their tradition.[43]

Vidyasagar had also realized, though much later, the power of oral tradition and customs and admitted it in his second treatise on widow-remarriage:

> . . . Most of the people in this country are ignorant of the *shastra*. Therefore when there is a debate on any issue concerning the *shastra*, they cannot evaluate the arguments of both sides to get at the actual truth.

As they remained 'slaves of local customs' or '*desachar*', they continued to prohibit widow-remarriage and thus 'ignored the injunctions of the *shastra*'. But local customs in this country changed from time to time and therefore Vidyasagar hoped that this inhuman custom could be changed, provided there was the right type of social consciousness.[44] But he himself failed to promote this consciousness, as neither he nor his associates were able to offer a radically new ideology—and they did not challenge the power structure that sustained the old custom.

But before we go into the limitations of the reform movement, it is essential to discuss the power structure that maintained social discipline and punished the errant in Bengali society. At the primary or family level, it was the karta who enforced the prescribed codes of behaviour on the individual members of his family. If he failed to do so, the family as a collective was held responsible for the violation or deviation and was liable to be excommunicated or ostracized. It could also be absolved, if the violation was involuntary, through the performance of *prayaschitta* or penance.[45] Such matters affecting families were the concerns of their immediate larger body, the clan or *goshthi* headed by the *goshthipati* who often adjudicated, with the advice of the clan elders, in such social disputes.[46] But the more serious matters, particularly those involving the possibility of excommunication, were referred to the higher authority, the caste council or the *jati panchayat*. Each caste had its own council which settled disputes relating to caste and family affairs and acted as the custodian of public morality. All these councils were however subservient to the larger *samaja*, which actually meant the hierarchy of castes living within a particular territory. In medieval Bengal, with minimum interference from the central state authority, the territorial chiefs or the Rajas, and below them the Zamindars, controlled the samajas. The Raja was the headman of his own caste council, as well as the head of all the councils in his chiefdom. He provided protection for his subjects, maintained law and order, settled caste and family disputes, and enforced the appropriate codes of social and moral behaviour. Thus, as Ronald Inden has shown, in a medieval Bengali Hindu chiefdom there existed different levels of leadership for social control. But all these levels were tied to each other in fixed vertical relationships and at the apex stood the Raja, the most powerful patron in the whole chiefdom.[47]

This medieval system of control possibly continued into the early British period, as it was present in the living memory of Bengalis even in the early twentieth century. A social historian of Bengal wrote in 1911:

> Previously some Brahman rajas like the Raja of Nadia, the Raja of Tahirpur, the Raja of Natore or the Raja of Susung, exerted immense influence on the Bengali Hindu society. The rules which they prescribed, in consultation with the chief *pundits* of the country, regarding ritual and social behaviour were obeyed by everybody.[48]

This Raja-pundit nexus, with one group enjoying monopoly over political power and the other a monopoly over scriptural knowledge, controlled popular culture in the medieval and early colonial periods. These power elites retained their control at the local level even in the nineteenth century, by adjusting themselves to the changes in the political structure of the country and in the organization of its social production. The nexus now started operating through a new institution called *dal*, which S.N. Mukherjee found to have, in the late eighteenth and the early nineteenth centuries, the same functions as those of the samajas in the earlier time.[49] The only difference was that while the control of the samajas was local or at the most territorial, that of the dal system was regional. Led by the absentee landlords and Rajas and guided by the priests and pundits, these dals operated from the colonial metropolis of Calcutta and stretched their controlling hands over the countryside. As a late-nineteenth-century observer notes, the dal in many respects performed the functions of the Rajas of the pre-colonial days.[50] The caste questions, which were theoretically under the jurisdiction of the colonial courts, remained for all practical purposes the prerogative of the *dalapatis*. It was on them that the interpretation, arbitration and modification of the customary laws depended almost entirely; only, they were advised in such matters by the knowledgeable pundits. While the dals usually operated at the local level, there emerged what McGuire has called a number of *supra-dals*, which were referred to variously as *sabhas* or samajas. Each consisted of a number of local dals and thus cut across the territorial boundaries of Calcutta and linked the city to the country. This dal system, which was generally used by the traditionalist elites as an apparatus of control over popular culture, continued to operate till about the end of the nineteenth century. Then, as McGuire has noted, it 'became increasingly more diffuse as capitalist development broke down the relationships upon which it was based. Yet this process of disintegration was long and complex.'[51]

The dal was gradually replaced by the various exclusive caste associations which began to emerge in Bengal in great numbers after 1905. These organizations, as recently discussed,[52] were also responsible for the process that has been described earlier as the 'reform of popular culture'. Through them more and more of upper-caste behavioural norms and notions of morality found acceptance and wider currency among people of the lower orders. The hegemonic culture set the limits for the imagination of the upwardly mobile lower-caste groups, who could not think of subverting the ritual order or repudiating its moral behavioural codes. Instead of inversion, which was rare and exceptional, we usually find co-option of these groups into the hegemonic cultural order and their acceptance or appropriation of upper-caste cultural symbols, which was mandatory, as we have discussed earlier, for being recognized as respectable in Hindu society. Any deviation from the prescribed norms led to the fall from the ascribed rank and this was monitored, as we have seen, through an efficient and ubiquitous control mechanism. As the *Hindu Patriot* had noted in 1855: 'Conservatism forms a principal feature in the character of the Hindu . . . The slightest breach of the established rules and practices is attended with serious consequences—the rash innovator is branded with infamy and discarded from all social intercourse.'[53] It was for this innate 'conservatism' of popular culture that even those who recognized the desirability of widow-remarriage could not actually practise it.

The power structure within Hindu society, together with its normative system, both based on the concept of hierarchy and expressed through the cultural idiom of caste, operated as a 'massive chain' that kept the entire society bound together. Important changes in the socio-economic structure were accommodated, but this was a gradual or slow and long-drawn process; the Sudra jatis, for example, were given more and more rights towards the turn of the century. Deviations from moral behavioural codes, on the other hand, were usually dealt with individually and were often pardoned after the performance of penance. The system, in other words, made piecemeal adjustments, but lacked the capacity to cushion and absorb the shock of any sudden or radical organizational reform. Like a 'massive chain', as a correspondent of the *Friend of India* had observed in the middle of the nineteenth century, 'Caste must exist in its entirety, or gradually cease altogether. . . .'[54] Destruction of any particular component of that chain would mean its losing the binding capacity and that would imply the loss of power and privilege for a traditionalist elite who had so long ruled society and controlled popular culture. Therefore, when the prohibition of *koolin* polygamy had been proposed, a panicky 'defender' of the system wrote a letter to the editor of the *Reformer* stating that if it was dropped by authority, it would lead to 'nothing short of great confusion and breach of peace. . .'.[55] Vidyasagar himself had to call in the police a number of times so that the widow-remarriage ceremonies which he organized could pass off smoothly.[56] The conservative press at the same time continued to threaten widows willing to remarry with the consequences of being ostracized.[57] The battle over widow-remarriage had thus become for the traditionalist elites a fight for a symbol of authority and domination. To lose the battle would mean the destruction of that 'massive chain' which had ensured their hegemony.

To fortify their position further, the traditionalist elites now began to argue that the caste system, both its structural and normative aspects taken together, was the essence of Hinduism, and so the destruction of the one would mean the annihilation of the other. In 1883, Shib Chandra Bose had observed in a cautious tone that '. . . though in every sense of the word an anti-social institution, it (caste) is nevertheless the main support of the Hindu religion. Take away this support and you destroy the very life and vitality of that religion. . . .'[58] Within a quarter of a century this sentiment came to be shared by a wide range of people in Bengal, from Chintaharan Chattopadhyay, a Brahman pundit of village Sundisar in Dacca district, to Sakharam Ganesh Deuskar, the celebrated history teacher of the Bengal national school. In 1910 Deuskar wrote in a little-known pamphlet: 'These days, to the people of this country, destruction of caste system has become synonymous with the destruction of Hinduism.'[59] Within a few months, Chattopadhyay noted in the same tone: 'Casteism is integrally related to Hinduism. For maintaining family life and Hindu identity, it is essential to preserve the caste system.'[60] Both of them belonged to the same elite group that was carefully building up this notion of an organic connection between caste and Hindutva. It was done to force people to adhere to the moral behavioural codes that legitimized the social hierarchy.

People down the ladder had also internalized this concept of hierarchy that imposed limits on their imagination. Talking about the caste feeling of the lower-caste people, an early-twentieth-century observer noted: 'A sort of instinctive dread of breaking caste puts the idea of doing without caste absolutely beyond the range of possibilities to their minds.'[61] Indeed, how their minds were conditioned becomes more clear from another observation of the same period:

> Each caste considers itself as only a petty member of a mighty body and it never entered into its head even in dreams to set itself in opposition to the central authority. Humble as it might be it was content to share the glory of belonging to the proud hierarchy. A man had no place unless he belonged to a caste; everyone therefore looked upon his caste as a valuable privilege, and no one would be foolhardy enough to lose this by offending the Brahmanical authority. . . .[62]

To lose caste would further mean losing religion, that is to say, a forced uprooting from the familiar social and cultural environment—a terrifying prospect for any individual or family. Some people braved the consequences, as there are instances of widows being converted to Islam or Christianity before actually getting remarried.[63] This meant that they had to get out of the control mechanism of Hindu society, before defying its cultural norms. But most people could not afford to do so because of the dreadful implications. *Samachar Sudhabarshan* could therefore boast: 'Widow-remarriage would mean violation of a part of the Hindu *shastras*, which we do not think most of the religious minded people would be courageous enough to risk.'[64]

IV

Vidyasagar was aware of and had consciously accepted this power structure of Hindu society and its ideology of hierarchy. In other words, he neither challenged the power structure, nor offered any radically different ideological alternative. This becomes apparent if we look at his two treatises on widow-remarriage as texts.

To some of his traditionalist contemporaries, Vidyasagar was the representative of the western educated intelligentsia. For the *Hindu Intelligencer*, he was 'the learned Principal of the Sanscrit [*sic*] College, who is regarded by foreigners as a man of enlarged views and deep research . . .'[65] And to the *Sambad Prabhakar*, his only achievement was the Anglicization of the Sanskrit College, which was not allowed to develop in the way that would have been most appropriate for it.[66] But whatever his popular image might have been, Vidyasagar's reformist ideology was not derived from the so called 'western' concepts of rationality or equality, as opposed to the traditionalist Hindu concept of hierarchy. At the very outset, in his first treatise on widow-remarriage, he had discarded the use of reason, for he believed that people were not amenable to reason and were only governed by shastra. So he went on interpreting and reinterpreting the shastra, trying to prove that his reform had sanctions within the corpus of traditional religious texts. In this he was not perhaps doing anything qualitatively very different from what the Nabadwip and Bhatpara pundits did when they issued *vyavastha* on various social issues.[67] The difference was only of degree: the vyavastha was applicable to individual cases, while Vidyasagar's reform had implications for the entire society.

When this method of referring to shastra failed, Vidyasagar in his second treatise appealed for a change of the local custom or *desachar*. While doing this, he argued.

> No one can prove that there has been no change in our customs since the first day of creation. . . . If an example is cited, you will be able to realize more easily to what extent the customs have changed in our country. In olden times, if a Sudra sat with a Brahman, there would have been no end to his crime. Now those very Sudras take the higher seats, and the Brahmans like obliging servants sit below.

This was, as Vidyasagar's footnote goes, 'against the *shastra*'. So at the end of his treatise he laments: 'Oh shastra! What a misfortune has befallen you! People who live their lives by indulging in activities which you have repeatedly identified as destructive of religion and caste are hailed as wise and pious, while those who even mention, not to speak of performance, the duty which you prescribe as an appropriate *dharma* [referring to widow-remarriage] are endlessly rebuked as atheist, irreligious and unwise.'[68] There could be no clearer statement vindicating the hierarchic ethos of the traditional Hindu society. It was essentially within this discourse of hierarchy, despite occasional references to equal rights for women,[69] that Vidyasagar situated his reform proposal.

The notion of patriarchic control over women in Hindu society, as we have discussed earlier, emanated from this concept of an all-encompassing hierarchy. Vidyasagar had also accepted and internalized this notion. The language in which he phrased his reform proposal clearly revealed his concern to maintain the patriarchic control over female sexuality and family discipline. What we find in his two treatises is first of all a definite and honest statement of paternalistic sympathy for the miserable plight of the widows. But side by side, what is also writ large is a concern for the falling standards of public morality and the increasing social tendency towards adultery and foeticide, all due to the unsatiated sexual appetite of widowed women. Unable to lead a life of self-denial, they indulged in illicit sex and thus put to shame all the three lineages of their husband, father and mother. So it was necessary to regulate and direct this unbridled and wayward female sexuality into a socially legitimate channel, that is, marriage, and for this it was essential to remove the prohibition on widow-remarriage.[70] The reform, in other words, was meant to ensure social discipline and patriarchic control over women's bodies and desires.

Most of the educated contemporaries of Vidyasagar who supported his cause shared this basic hierarchic assumption of gender inequality and expressed the same concern for public morality. The growing sexual anarchy in society was attributed only to the inability of the widows to restrain their libido which, as even the more progressive *Tattvabodhini Patrika* apprehended, would affect other women in society and thus would completely destroy the family structure. The plea for widow-remarriage was no doubt coated in a language of equality. If men could remarry after the death of their wives, the *Patrika* asked, why could not widows do the same? But in the same breath it also argued in a sexist language that widow-remarriage was all the more necessary, as the libidinal urge of women was eight times greater than that of men. It was for this reason that all of them could not restrain their desires and brought infamy to Bengal.[71] A biological dimension was thus added to the concept of innate gender inequality. Other proponents of the reform also shared the same concern for falling standards of public morality and believed that what had further contributed to this social disorder were the other two evil institutions of child marriage and *koolin* polygamy,[72] which were also on the nineteenth-century reform agenda.

This assumption of innate and uncontrollable feminine sexuality, as James Mill had already shown, was embedded in Hindu cultural traditions.[73] And therefore, the ideology of reform as Vidyasagar and his supporters had defined it, appeared not as an alternative to but as a derivative from the ideology of hierarchy which the traditionalist elites of Hindu society had been propounding. It was natural therefore that this new reformist position would not find popular acceptance, unless sanctioned by these elites. Even those who had realized that the reform was a social necessity, could not raise their voice, as the *Tattvabodhini Patrika* commented, for fear of either offending the dalapatis or inviting public censure.[74] This was because Vidyasagar and the other protagonists of reform, instead of trying to subvert the power structure of Hindu society, sought the patronage of both the dalapati and the pundit themselves. Vidyasagar, for example, had accepted quite resignedly, that in this country people had to behave according to the words and dictates of the great men who were the interpreters of *dharma-shastra*.[75] So he went to Radhakanta Deb and his dal for support and appeared in a public debate to argue his case against the rival pundits. He won the first round and got a shawl and favour from the almighty dalapati. Victory would have been his if the situation had not changed further. But soon the other dalapatis approached Deb and requested him to revise his decision to promote widow-remarriage. Vidyasagar was called for a second round of debate and here he lost, or he was perhaps meant to lose. The decision of the dalapati was reversed[76] and with this the fate of the reform movement was also sealed. Even those pundits who had earlier given a vyavastha in support of the marriage of the widowed daughter of Shyamcharan Das of Calcutta, now changed their minds and became opponents of widow-remarriage.[77] And the common people could hardly muster the courage to go against the shastra as interpreted to them by the pundits or defy the established customs as imposed upon them by the dalapatis.[78] No legislation had the power to break this massive chain.

Vidyasagar, in other words, had opted for the traditionalists' method of reforming popular culture, that is, of initiating and imposing reform from above. Crucial for the success of this method was the support of the hegemonic power of the traditionalist elites, in which he too had reposed his faith. The movement against koolin polygamy was successful as it received the support of some influential leaders of Hindu society, like the Maharaja of Burdwan, the Raja of Nadia and the Raja of Dinajpur. As *Friend of India* had noted, the Raja of Nadia was 'to Hinduism what Sir Harry Inglis was to Church of England' and the Raja of Dinajpur was 'a Hindoo of Hindoos'.[79] But widow-remarriage seemed to be too exotic a deviation from the established moral-behavioural codes of Hinduism to enjoy the favour of these elites. In the nineteenth-century cultural stereotype it appeared as a custom that violated the shastra; and it was complemented by another stereotype, that it was prevalent only among the lower orders. The *Hindu Intelligencer* wrote in 1855: 'This custom no longer prevails among the natives of the higher orders, . . . but it is still followed by those of the lower grades.'[80] For the *Samachar Sudhabarshan*, it was more specifically a custom of the '*antyja*' (low born) castes, 'prevalent only among the Hari, Methar, Dom, Chandal etc.'[81] Vidyasagar appeared to be proposing the adoption of the values of the unclean castes, who were at the bottom of society, by the Brahmans and the clean Sudras, who were the elites among the Bengali Hindus. He was asking the bhadralok to adopt a social practice that the *chotolok* had been pursuing since time immemorial. This must have looked like a reform of popular culture in the reverse direction—a 'counter reform'. The elites could only be expected to resist this effort.

The only alternative now left for Vidyasagar, which indeed he had already opted for, was to rely on a higher authority, that is, the colonial state. He had been pleading for a legislation, perhaps with the assumption that the state and social authority were the two mutually validating reflections of the same hierarchy. But this was a crucial misunderstanding of the relations of power in nineteenth-century Bengal, where the colonial state and the leaders of Hindu society still held sway over two mutually exclusive domains of power. The former occasionally tried to encroach upon the territory of the latter, but could never completely control it. Therefore, even if there was a law, there was no prospect of its being enforced without social consent. And this consent or cultural acquiescence of the people could only be ensured either through the support of the traditionalist elites or by completely breaking what we have described as the 'massive chain' of caste. Vidyasagar was denied the first, and his mind, like that of most of his contemporaries was culturally so conditioned that he could not even think of opting for the second alternative. He operated essentially within the ideological and functional boundaries imposed by the dominant power structure of Hindu society. The roots of his tragedy lay here; the reasons for the 'unavoidable defeat' of the reform movement.

V

However, as a result of Vidyasagar's campaign for reform, the question of widow-remarriage became an issue of public concern as well as a subject of controversy. This had long-term implications for Bengali society, as it became a symbol for the traditionalist elites, the acceptance or rejection of which was thought to have been inversely related to the diminution or continuance of their power. By taking the issue to the legislature, Vidyasagar had renewed the conflict over definition of boundary between the two domains of power of state and society. The traditionalists had already lost the first battle when Rammohun had the custom of sati abolished through the intervention of the state. As the *Hindu Patriot* had observed, the practice was discontinued only because it became 'penal at law'.[82] The leaders of Hindu society were no longer prepared to concede any further ground and the result was a stubborn resistance which sometimes even lapsed into violence. This critical response to the bill pending before the Legislative Council was adequately reflected when the *Eastern Star* noted:

> that the proposed legislative interference . . . is improper and quite uncalled for. The legislative body of the country, not being a representative assembly of the people for whom it legislates, is under the necessity of using great care and circumspection in the enactment of laws. . . . The legislative council cannot compel the natives to marry their widows, but it proposes to fix the stamp of legitimacy on the children born of Hindu widow. . . . The community will continue to look upon them as bastards, and as persons not born in lawful wedlock. The legislature cannot coerce the opinions of men, nor influence their social relations, at least not directly.[83]

The statement clearly questions the legitimacy of state power within the domain of social relations, where the will of the community was held to be the supreme authority. But this social opinion, as we have seen, was effectively manipulated by the powerful traditionalist elite group. And therefore, even when there was a law validating widow-remarriage, just as the *Samachar Darpan* had predicted four years before it was actually passed, there was no way to enforce it.[84] In the case of sati, what was being proposed was the abolition of an evil custom, which could be ensured through the intervention of the state. But widow-remarriage was an innovation, indeed a revolutionary one, which could not be introduced by government fiat. The law therefore remained a dead letter for several decades after Vidyasagar's death.

What was worse, widow celibacy gradually became a much more widely practised popular custom. The elites portrayed it as one of the most authentic symbols of the culture of the respectable, and the socially mobile sections of the lower orders readily appropriated it. There were some among the educated members of the lower castes who had notionally accepted the innovation, but they too shared the same patriarchal and moralist concerns[85] and refrained from practising it in real life. Neither could they popularize the reform among their respective communities, because of the obvious socio-cultural compulsions to adopt the dominant elites' behavioural codes, defined by the ideology of hierarchy. This was the ongoing or the usual process through which the traditionalist elites had been extending their hegemonic control over popular culture. It was beyond the power of Vidyasagar or his reformist compatriots to make a dent in their sphere of influence. This situation continued till about the middle of the twentieth century, when the war, the famine and Partition disrupted social bonds and destroyed in many cases the structure of the patriarchal family, making way for new values and fresh adjustments within the relations of power in Bengali society.

The final point to be mentioned about this reform movement is the marginality of women in the whole process. While Vidyasagar had started his crusade out of a sense of compassion for young widows, what followed subsequently was a battle for a cultural symbol, in which the plight of the widows had become a subsidiary concern for both the contending parties. It was never a concern for the opponents of the reform; even Vidyasagar's sympathetic self often got superseded by the orthodox social disciplinarian in him. And in the scriptural polemics, women did not even figure as objects. In the nineteenth- or the early-twentieth-century social world of Bengal, women had not as yet emerged as conscious subjects of history, trying to assert their own rights. If *Bamabodhini Patrika* represented the only feminine voice raised in support of the reform, it too accepted in a resigned mood the futility of the endeavour.[86]

On the other hand, women at the intermediate and bottom layers of the ritual hierarchy appear to have been so thoroughly socialized into the orthodox male worldview, that they not only accepted and promoted the dominant Hindu stereotypes of womanhood, but also opposed the idea of widow-remarriage. The *Mahishya Mahila*, a monthly journal for Mahishya women, edited by Krishnabhamini Biswas, is an ideal example at hand.[87] Even the Subarnabanik Mahila Sammilani, the first ever conference of about 500 women of the Subarnabanik caste, held in December 1925 under the supervision of the male leaders of their community, discussed strategies for the spread of female education and other issues concerning women, but did not dare to include widow-remarriage in their agenda.[88] This also explains the differential success achieved by the two reform programmes. The first reform for the spread of higher education had been relatively more successful, because its proponents, Vidyasagar included, had succeeded to a large extent in mobilizing female opinion in support of it. Some of the caste associations, as that of the Subarnabaniks mentioned above, had also ensured the active participation of women in this organized drive for female education. The *Mahishya Mahila* urged its literate women readers to educate their female neighbours and thus to spread literacy among the womenfolk of their community.[89] But none of the champions of widow-remarriage ever thought of mobilizing women's opinion in favour of the reform, not to speak of involving them as active participants in the actual reform process. This explains to a large extent the failure of their reform endeavour. And individual or independent voices of women, either in support of the reform or against it, have remained totally unrecorded, confirming only their marginality in this crucial social debate in colonial Bengal.

Notes

1. Asok Sen, *Ishwar Chandra Vidyasagar and His Elusive Milestones* (Calcutta, 1977), p. 6.
2. Benoy Ghosh, ed., *Selections from English Periodicals of 19th Century Bengal* (Calcutta, 1979), vol. III, p. 116 (hereafter *Selections*).
3. Asok Sen, *Ishwar Chandra Vidyasagar*; Amales Tripathi, *Vidyasagar, The Traditional Moderniser* (Calcutta, 1976).
4. Peter Burke, *Popular Culture in Early Modern Europe* (London, 1978), p. xi.
5. E.P. Thompson, 'Patrician Society, Plebeian Culture', *Journal of Social History*, vol. VII, 1974, p. 395.
6. Peter Burke, *Popular Culture*, pp. 207–43.
7. See M.N. Srinivas, *Social Change in Modern India* (Bombay, 1977), pp. 1–45.
8. Martin Ingram, 'The Reform of Popular Culture: Sex and Marriage in Early Modern England', in Barry Reay, ed., *Popular Culture in Seventeenth Century England* (London, 1988), pp. 129–30.
9. For more details, see Barry Reay, ibid., Introduction, pp. 17–22; also David Hall, Introduction, in S.L. Kaplan, ed., *Understanding Popular Culture* (Berlin, 1984).
10. For a comprehensive discussion of this recent critique, see Barbara N. Ramusack, 'From Symbol to Diversity: The Historical Literature on Women in India', *South Asia Research*, vol. 10, no. 2, November 1990, pp. 154ff.
11. *Census of India*, 1891, vol. III, The Report, p. 267.

12. Risley Collection, Eur. MSS. E. 295, vol. 3, pp. 258–9, vol. 4, p. 95, India Office Library, London.
13. Shyamlal Sen, *Jatitattva-Vivek* (The Caste Ethics, Barisal, 1797 Saka), p. 111.
14. H.H. Risley, *The Tribes and Castes of Bengal* (Reprint, Calcutta, 1981), vol. I, p. lxxxiv.
15. For details on the construction of these models, see Uma Chakrabarti, 'Whatever Happened to the Vedic *Dasi*? Orientalism, Nationalism and a Script for the Past', in Kumkum Sangari and Sudesh Vaid, eds, *Recasting Women: Essays in Indian Colonial History* (New Brunswick, New Jersey, 1990), pp. 27–87.
16. *Selections*, vol. III, p. 116; Benoy Ghosh, ed., *Samayikpatre Banglar Samajchitra* (Reflections of Bengali Society in Journals, Calcutta, 1980) (hereafter *Samajchitra*), vol. III, pp. 70–1, 166–7, vol. IV, pp. 157–66.
17. John McGuire, *The Making of a Colonial Mind: A Quantitative Study of the Bhadralok in Calcutta, 1857–1885* (Canberra, 1983), p. 22.
18. *Census of India*, 1911, vol. V, Part I, p. 373, Subsidiary Table VI.
19. Madhusudan Sarkar, 'Abar Bidhaba Bibaha Keno?' (Why Widow-Remarriage?), *Navyabharat*, vol. 25, no. 12, Chaitra, 1314 BS.
20. *Jogisakha*, Baisakh, Jaistha, Ashadh, Sraban, 1312 BS; *Bangiya Tili Samaj Patrika*, Chaitra-Baisakh 1332–3 BS, Magh-Falgun 1333 BS; *Kshatriya*, Chaitra 1332 BS; *Sadgop Patrika*, Baisakh 1330 BS, Sraban, Paush 1337 BS; *Tilir Gaurab*, Ashwin 1326 BS; *Bangiya Vaisya Barujibi Sabhar Chaturdas Barshik Karya-Bibaran* (Jessore, 1915), p. 55; *Subarnabanik Samachar*, Magh 1327 BS; *Gandhabanik*, Kartik-Agrahayan 1330 BS; *Mahishya Samaj*, Falgun 1328 BS, Jaistha 1329 BS.
21. *Subarnabanik Samachar*, Magh 1323 BS.
22. See Nicholas B. Dirks, *The Hollow Crown: Ethnohistory of an Indian Kingdom* (Cambridge, 1990), pp. 5–7.
23. For a detailed discussion on this aspect, see Sekhar Bandyopadhyay, *Caste, Politics and the Raj: Bengal 1872–1937* (Calcutta, 1990), pp. 1–51.
24. *Selections*, vol. III, p. 116.
25. Quoted in Asok Sen, *Ishwar Chandra Vidyasagar*, p. 58.
26. John McGuire, *The Making of a Colonial Mind*, p. 37.
27. Ibid., p. 40.
28. Ronald B. Inden, *Marriage and Rank in Bengali Culture* (New Delhi, 1976), pp. 14–21.
29. On the Application of Dr Toppinard's Anthropometric System to the Castes and Tribes of Bengal', by H.H. Risley, 8 March 1886, Government of Bengal, Financial (Miscellaneous) Proceedings, March 1887, pp. 83–5, West Bengal State Archives, Calcutta.
30. Shib Chandra Bose, *The Hindoos As They Are* (Second edition, Calcutta, 1883), pp. 2–3.

31. Anonymous, *Hindu Dharmaniti* (The Hindu Code of Ethics, Calcutta 1794 Saka), p. 8.
32. Jatindramohan Gupta, *Hindu Narir Kartabya* (The Duties of Hindu Women, Calcutta, 1323 BS), p. 108.
33. Cited in Bharati Ray, 'Do We Have a Choice? Widows of India with Special Reference to Bengal, 1900–1956', paper presented at the Berkshire Conference of Women Historians, June 1990 and at the Seventeenth International Conference of the Historical Sciences, August–September 1990.
34. *Mahishya Mahila*, vol. I, no. 3, 1318 BS.
35. Basumati Sahitya Mandir was one of the pioneering organizations responsible for the publication of such Smriti, Nyaya and Darshana texts published since the time of Rammohun Roy.
36. Bernard S. Cohn, *India: The Social Anthropology of a Civilization* (New Jersey, 1971), p. 100.
37. See, for example, National Library, India, *Author Catalogue of Printed Books in Bengali Language*, vols I–IV (Calcutta, 1959–63); also J.F. Blumhardt, ed., *Catalogue of the Library of the India Office*, vol. II, Part IV (London, 1905).
38. For a recent and excellent discussion on this aspect, see Lata Mani, 'Contentious Traditions: The Debate on Sati in Colonial India', in Kumkum Sangari and Sudesh Vaid eds, *Recasting Women*, pp. 88–126.
39. Iswarchandra Vidyasagar, *Bidhaba-Bibaha Prachalito Haoya Uchit Kina Etadbishayak Prastab* (Should Widow-remarriage be Introduced?), in Gopal Haldar, ed., *Vidyasagar Rachana Sangraha* (The Collected Works of Vidyasagar, Calcutta, 1972), vol. 2, pp. 21–2.
40. *Hindu Intelligencer*, 12 February 1855, *Selections*, vol. III, p. 112.
41. *Samachar Sudhabarshan*, 29 December 1855, *Samajchitra*, vol. III, p. 140.
42. *Hindu Patriot*, 15 February 1855, *Selections*, vol. III, p. 115; *Samachar Sudhabarshan*, 6 November 1855, *Samajchitra*, vol. III, p. 137.
43. *Bamabodhini Patrika*, Sraban 1277 BS, *Samajchitra*, vol. III, pp. 166–7.
44. Iswarchandra Vidyasagar, *Bidhaba-Bibaha Prachalito Haoya Uchit Kina Etadbishayak Prastab: Dwitiya Pustak*, in *Vidyasagar Rachana Sangraha*, vol. 2, pp. 36, 160–1.
45. Bani Chakraborti, *Samaj-Sanskarak Raghunandan* (Raghunandan, A Social Reformer, Calcutta, 1970), pp. 246–55, 259.
46. Umeshchandra Gupta, *Jatitattva-baridhi-dwitiya bhaag ba Ballal-Mohamudgar* (Calcutta, 1905), p. 441.
47. Ronald Inden, 'Hindu Chiefdom in Middle Bengali Literature', in Edward C. Dimock, Jr. ed., *Bengal: Literature and History* (East Lansing, Michigan, 1967), pp. 25ff.
48. Durga Chandra Sanyal, *Banglar Samajik Itihas* (The Social History of Bengal, Calcutta, 1317 BS), p. 450.
49. S.N. Mukherjee, *Calcutta: Myths and History* (Calcutta, 1971).

50. Shib Chandra Bose, *The Hindoos*, p. 167.
51. John McGuire, *The Making of a Colonial Mind*, pp. 30–5 (quotation from p. 35).
52. Sekhar Bandyopadhyay, *Caste, Politics*, Chapter III.
53. *Hindu Patriot*, 15 February 1855, *Selections*, vol. VIII, p. 116.
54. *Friend of India*, 5 June 1851, *Selections*, vol. III, pp. 44–5.
55. *Reformer*, 7 April 1833, *Selections*, vol. I, p. 170.
56. Subal Chandra Mitra, *Iswar Chandra Vidyasagar* (in Bengali) (Calcutta, 1902), p. 319.
57. *Samachar Sudhabarshan*, 29 December 1855, *Samajchitra*, vol. III, p. 140.
58. Shib Chandra Bose, *The Hindoos*, p. 163.
59. Sakharam Ganesh Deuskar, *Bangiya Hindujati ki Dhangsonmukh* (Is the Hindu Community in Bengal on a Path of Decline, Calcutta, 1317 BS), p. 116.
60. Chintaharan Chattopadhyay, *Brahman* (The Brahmin, Faridpur, 1317 bs), p. 19.
61. N. Sengupta, 'The Census and Caste', *The Dacca Review*, vol. 1, no. 6, September 1911, p. 200.
62. Jatindra Chandra Guha, 'Reform in the Hindu Society', *The Dacca Review*, vol. 1, no. 9, December 1911, pp. 284–5.
63. *Bamabodhini Patrika*, Jaistha 1277 BS, *Samajchitra*, vol. III, p. 165; *Census of India*, 1901, vol. vi, Part I, Appendix II.
64. *Samachar Sudhabarshan*, 6 November 1855, *Samajchitra*, vol. III, p. 137.
65. *Hindu Intelligencer*, 12 February 1855, *Selections*, vol. III, p. 112.
66. *Sambad Prabhakar*, 21 April 1265 BS, *Samajchitra*, vol. II, p. 177.
67. Indeed, some time before Vidyasagar wrote his first treatise, some of the *pundits* had given a *vyavastha* sanctioning the marriage of the widowed daughter of one Shyamacharan Das of Calcutta. See Iswarchandra Vidyasagar, *Bidhaba-Bibaha . . . Etadbishayak Prastab*, pp. 14–17.
68. Iswarchandra Vidyasagar, *Bidhaba-Bibaha . . . Dwitiya Pustak*, pp. 161, 164.
69. Iswarchandra Vidyasagar, *Ratnapariksha* in *Vidyasagar Rachana Sangraha*, vol. 2, p. 538.
70. Iswarchandra Vidyasagar, *Bidhaba-Bibaha . . . Etadbishyak Prastab*, p. 32 and *passim; Bidhaba-Bibaha . . . Dwitiya Pustak*, pp. 164–5 and *passim*.
71. *Tattvabodhini Patrika*, no. 140, Chaitra 1776 Saka, *Samajchitra*, vol. IV, pp. 158–62.
72. *Sangbad Purnachandroday*, 17 June 1851, *Sarbasubhakari Patrika*, no. 1, Bhadra, 1772 Saka; *Samachar Sudhabarshan*, 31 December 1855, *Samajchitra*, vol. III, pp. 70–1, 89, 140.
73. Uma Chakrabarti, 'Vedic *Dasi*', p. 35.
74. *Tattvabodhini Patrika*, p. 157.

75. Iswarchandra Vidyasagar, *Bidhaba-Bibaha . . . Etadbishayak Prastab*, p. 16.
76. For details, see John McGuire, *The Making of the Colonial Mind*, p. 33.
77. Iswarchandra Vidyasagar, *Bidhaba-Bibaha . . . Etadbishayak Prastab*, pp. 15–16.
78. *Sarbasubhakari Patrika*, no. 1, Bhadra 1772 Saka, *Samajchitra*, vol. III, pp. 82–3, 88.
79. *Friend of India*, 17 July 1856, *Selections*, vol. III, p. 93.
80. *Hindu Intelligencer*, 12 February 1855, *Selections*, vol. III, p. 113.
81. *Samachar Sudhabarshan*, 10 July 1855, 15 September 1855, *Samajchitra*, vol. III, pp. 134, 137.
82. *Hindu Patriot*, 15 February 1855, *Selections*, vol. III, p. 117.
83. *Eastern Star*, 8 December 1855, *Selections*, vol. III, p. 137.
84. *Samajchitra*, vol. III, p. 71.
85. Balaram Sarkar, *Namasudra Jnanabhandar* (About the Namasudras, Faridpur, 1911), pp. 80–3.
86. See note 43 above.
87. See note 34 above; for a more detailed discussion on *Mahishya Mahila*, see Chandrima Sinha, 'Mahishya Jatir Samajik Andolan O Mahishya Nari' (The Social Movement of the Mahishya Community and their Women), *Aitihasik*, vol. 3, no. 2, April–June 1981.
88. *Subarnabanik Samachar*, Paush 1333 BS.
89. *Mahishya Mahila*, vol. 1, no. 9, 1319 BS, pp. 108–12.

6

Vidyasagar and Brahmanical Society*

Sumit Sarkar

Vidyasagar never wrote a systematic treatise on education. The precise significance of his extremely innovative ideas and projects has to be reconstructed from scattered texts—official letters and notes,[1] school primers and textbooks written by him, and documents relating to Vidyasagar in the files of the government education department and archives of Sanskrit College.[2]

The changes Vidyasagar sought to make in Sanskrit College, as Assistant Secretary (1846–7) and later as Principal (1850–3), were not just about reforms in a particular institution, for they can be seen to imply ultimately a distinctive educational-cum-social philosophy. Even the innovations that might appear trivial today, such as Vidyasagar's insistence on punctuality and regular attendance by students and teachers,[3] acquire greater meaning when one remembers that clock time was no more than a generation or two old in India in the 1840s, having been a belated, colonial import. Its history has been surprisingly neglected in studies of colonial India. Bound up, as elsewhere, with new pressures for regularity and tighter work schedules, clocks and watches acquired somewhat distinct and varied implications through their links with structures of colonial power. The three principal early sites for time-discipline in colonial Bengal were educational institutions, government and mercantile offices and the railways.[4] Indigenous responses to it clearly had a differential character. Vidyasagar is a reminder that systematized, rule-bound education governed by clock time was widely perceived as indispensable for middle-class self-improvement under colonial conditions. Punctuality no doubt often remained a burden, but its normative role in schools and colleges was not questioned. Things were quite different in the alienated world of *chakri* or office work under foreign bosses, where disciplinary time entered into a distinctively late-nineteenth-century vision of Kaliyuga.[5]

Vidyasagar's plan of 16 December 1850 suggested a series of changes in the syllabus of Sanskrit College, all in a recognizably modern, rationalistic direction. It simultaneously sought to bring Sanskrit teaching into close contact with the development of both Bengali and English education. Thus, for Sanskrit grammar, which students so long had been forced to memorize through the very difficult *Mugdhabodha*, Vidyasagar suggested the learning of the basic rules 'dressed in the easiest Bengali', followed by graduated Sanskrit readings. (He would himself soon supply the appropriate Sanskrit grammar in Bengali, the *Vyakarana-Kaumudi*.) Training in English, too, was necessary, but only in the higher classes, to avoid the danger of getting swamped by it at the expense of the vernacular. Sanskrit College students, the plan emphasized, must 'acquire great proficiency in Bengali' and 'derive useful information' through it (for which he was already providing the wherewithal, through textbooks like *Jivancharit* and *Bodhoday*), 'and thereby have their views expanded before they commence their English studies'. They could also learn Jyotish (mathematics and astronomy) much more profitably through Bengali translations of contemporary English texts, instead of Lilavati and Bhaskaracharya, which Vidyasagar thought 'very meagre' by modern standards. Even more striking is the evident attempt to reduce the importance in the syllabus of the Smriti teachings of Raghunandan (whose texts constituted the principal barrier to reforms like widow remarriage or a higher age of consent throughout the nineteenth century) and the Navya-Nyaya of Raghunath Shiromani (whose logic Vidyasagar thought had been 'similar to that of schoolmen'). Along with Navya-Nyaya, the philosophical portions of the pre-Vidyasagar syllabus had a strong tilt towards Vedanta, characteristic of high-Hindu metaphysics since medieval times. It included texts specifically refuting 'the Bouddha or atheistical doctrine' and all other non-Vedantist schools. In their place, Vidyasagar wanted to introduce the *Sarvadarshanasangraha*, through which, he argued, the student would be able to see how 'the different systems have attacked each other, and have pointed out each other's errors and fallacies. Thus he would be able to judge for himself'—particularly since some courses in European philosophy would also be introduced.[6] In 1858 Vidyasagar brought out a critical edition of this fourteenth-century text of Madhavacharya, which he said had become a very rare manuscript.[7] It may not be irrelevant to note that the *Sarvadarshanasangraha* remains the primary source for the little information we have about the suppressed ancient Indian materialist tradition of Lokayata, associated with Carvaka.[8]

That the implications of Vidyasagar's reform plan went very much beyond mere syllabus revision becomes clear from his *Notes on the Sanskrit College* (12 April 1852), which summed up with admirable precision and logic the core of his educational perspectives. 'The creation of an enlightened Bengali Literature', Vidyasagar now declared, 'should be the first object of those who are entrusted with the superintendence of Education in Bengal.' This required the 'exertions of those . . . competent to collect the materials from European sources and . . . dress them in elegant, expressive and idiomatic Bengali.' But for this, Vidyasagar felt, mastery of Sanskrit was also essential, as 'more English scholars are altogether incapable of expressing their ideas in elegant and idiomatic Bengali. They are so much anglicized that it seems at present almost impossible for them to do so even if they later learn Sanskrit.' It is very clear then that 'if students of the Sanskrit College be made familiar with English Literature, they will prove the best and ablest contributors to an enlightened Bengali Literature'.[9]

In September 1853 Vidyasagar had to defend his syllabus against criticisms made of it by J.R. Ballantyne, Principal of Benaras Government Sanskrit College. In course of that exercise he had to formulate its underlying assumptions with greater clarity and polemical sharpness. Ballantyne had suggested a greater emphasis on the 'correspondences' between select aspects of European and Indian philosophical traditions as a way of reconciling the Brahmanical literati to the coming of Western ideas. This involved a very different pattern of choice between philosophical schools, than Vidyasagar's. The Benaras principal wanted less of Mill's *Logic*, the inclusion of Bishop Berkeley's *Inquiry*, and the introduction of a commentary written by Ballantyne himself which had emphasized the alleged similarities between that classic text of European philosophical Idealism, and Vedanta and Sankhya. This was the specific context for Vidyasagar's blunt and aggressive statement about Vedanta and Sankhya being 'false systems of philosophy': a remark that has been often torn out of context to indicate either Vidyasagar's laudable Westernized modernity, or (with some justice) his philosophical naivete and dogmatism. But Vidyasagar's position, it must be emphasized, was not an uncritical preference of Western to Indian thought, for Vidyasagar was equally dismissive of Berkeley. The really interesting thing about the reply to Ballantyne is the way it anticipated, and sought to refute, what by the late nineteenth century would become a central strategy of much Hindu revivalism, as well as of a brand of Orientalism from which it was often highly derivative.[10] 'Lately a feeling is manifesting itself among the learned of this part of India, specially in Calcutta and its neighbourhood, that when they hear of a Scientific truth, the germs of which may be traced out in their Shastras, instead of shewing any regard for that truth, they triumph and the superstitious regard for their own Shastras is redoubled.' Vidyasagar went on to make a most uncomplimentary characterization of the 'learned of India' as a 'body of men whose longstanding prejudices are unshakeable'—referring presumably to the traditional Brahman literati, not the Sanskrit College students he was trying to train in a new way. He went on to reiterate and expand the alternative cultural perspective he had outlined in April 1852. Instead of trying 'to reconcile the learned of the Country',

> what we require is to extend the benefit of education to the mass of the people. Let us establish a number of Vernacular schools, let us prepare a series of Vernacular class-books on useful and instructive subjects, let us raise up a band of men [who] should be perfect masters of their own language, possess a considerable amount of useful information and be free from the prejudices of their country. To raise up such a useful class of men is the object I have proposed to myself and to the accomplishment of which the whole energy of *our* Sanskrit College should be directed.[11]

Beginning, then, in 1844 with the suggestion for tackling the employment problem facing Sanskrit College graduates through giving them jobs in Hardinge's experimental village schools, Vidyasagar in course of a decade had progressed to an integrated plan for cultural renovation of the literati of Bengal. Considered in the perspective of conventional histories of education, Vidyasagar's scheme may be seen as a bringing together of Orientalist, Anglicist and Vernacularist positions, achieved through significant changes within each of them. Translated more meaningfully into social terms, it needs to be understood as an attempt to bridge the growing gap between the traditional pandits and the Westernized, English-educated intelligentsia: not through some kind of eclectic compromise, however, which roughly had been Ballantyne's advice, but by a determined effort to transform and get beyond both poles. Vidyasagar hoped to impart a fundamentally new vernacular-cum-rural turn to pandits and English-educated alike, and considerably broaden the social basis of the intelligentsia as a whole. That such a trend could unfold in mid-nineteenth-century Bengal, it needs to be added, should considerably complicate the Westernist–traditionalist dichotomy in terms of which so much colonial middle-class history has been conceptualized.

Vidyasagar had had ample opportunities of watching this rupture grow at first hand, for classes in Sanskrit College in his time took place in the same building as Hindu College, with the two institutions, however, carefully segregated from each other by walls. His class-friends would all be Brahmans (plus a few Vaidyas), mostly poor. Hindu College was catering to a more multi-caste clientele, including many sons of the relatively low-born Calcutta nouveaux riches, but it was at the same time considerably more exclusive in economic terms. Vidyasagar himself had managed to straddle both worlds, through mastering English and developing personal ties with a host of Hindu College products (including many of the Young Bengal variety), but he would have realized how insuperable the barriers might soon appear to many. And indeed the long-term consequences of the failure of Vidyasagar's dream have been very far-reaching. The logical implication of his educational strategy was a reunification of the literati on a basis oriented towards modernistic change, which would be at the same time geared towards mass vernacular education, and therefore at least potentially more democratic than pre-colonial Brahmanical culture. Instead, as the rift widened, the world of the old-fashioned pandits became increasingly narrow, immersed in futile grumbling about the many evils of Kaliyuga, often blindly conservative—while the 'Anglicized' have often swung between complete alienation and recurrent searches for 'roots' in (largely invented or spurious) 'traditions'. In total contrast to Vidyasagar's vision, the occasional unificatory moments have tended to develop around revivalist-nationalistic programmes—right down to our own times, one is tempted to add, in Hindutva's twin base among Vishwa Hindu Parishad sadhus and a Non-Resident Indian-oriented elite that is highly Westernized in a consumerist sense.

Two things were indispensable if Vidyasagar's plans were to succeed. There was the need for an 'enlightened Bengali Literature', in particular a vernacular discursive prose capable of tackling in a creative and attractive manner a much wider range of themes than had been possible or necessary in pre-colonial times. The other, interrelated, prerequisite was the rapid spread of vernacular education. The two together could help to constitute a public space open to argumentation, and based on expanding literacy and print culture.

The first condition was largely met, for this was an autonomous area where the intelligentsia could operate on its own, and where the coming of print culture enabled wide dissemination and created some possibilities for financial independence. Western education on the whole was a stimulus rather than hindrance to the development of indigenous languages, in significant contrast to what happened in some other parts of the colonized world. Vidyasagar's own seminal and multiple contributions to the development of modern Bengali prose have of course been very widely recognized. They ranged from mundane but necessary things like the introduction of standardized punctuation[12] and syntax, the careful compilation of glossaries of new terms for modern concepts,[13] to the creation of a style that was chaste, dignified, yet free from the inaccessible and excessively Sanskritized ornateness of the Bengali which many pandits still liked to use.[14] Rabindranath even felt this to have been Vidyasagar's greatest single achievement, and described it as an emancipation of the language simultaneously from 'rustic barbarism' and 'parochial scholasticism'.[15] And for a man capable of the considerable literary qualities of a text like *Sitar Banobas*, it must have been a major sacrifice to devote one's writing talents al-most entirely to composing, as part of a deeply felt social commitment, school textbooks, adaptations and reform tracts.[16]

The expansion-cum-improvement of vernacular schools in villages required, however, considerable financial inputs from the state and/or the rural gentry, as well as active support from the literati, old and new. For a brief period in the mid 1850s the conjuncture appeared favourable for Vidyasagar's dream. Colonial educational policy was not quite the monolith, determined solely by Macaulay's notorious Minute of 1835, that is sometimes assumed nowadays. Bengal officials in the early 1850s had been impressed by the apparent success of the 'circle' experiment started in the North-Western Provinces under Thomason that had tried to set up a model school in each revenue district as a way of improving vernacular education. Wood's Education Despatch of 1854, though in the end contained within the 'filtration' framework, had also visualized some expansion in vernacular education through the grants-in-aid system by which costs would be shared between the government and local patrons.

Around 1855–6—the peak years also of his social reform drive—Vidyasagar was enjoying excellent relations with many high British officials in Bengal, from Lieutenant-Governor Halliday downwards. This had helped him to develop links with a number of prominent zamindars, in particular some 'improving' landlords like Joykrishna Mukhopadhyay of Uttarpara, who had recently acquired large estates in Hooghly district, and who around 1855 was combining efforts to promote new crops like potatoes and sugarcane with the establishment of both English and vernacular schools in the areas under his control.[17] Vidyasagar, finally, had become a major figure by the mid-1850s among the literati, both traditional and new: active in the Brahmo-led Tattwabodhini Sabha and Patrika, friends of many with Young Bengal antecedents, and yet numbering among his closest associates pandits like Madanmohan Tarkalankar, who helped him start the Sanskrit Press Depository, and Taranath Tarkavacaspati, who combined running a *tol* at Ambica-Kalna with far-flung business interests. The peak of Vidyasagar's educational and reform campaign seems to have coincided in fact with a last flurry of enterprising landlordism and middle-class entrepreneurship in Bengal.[18] Vidyasagar's, in other words, was not quite a lone venture in the Bengal society of the 1850s. A British Inspector of Schools would note in April 1859 that 'the learned Pundits of Sanskrit College have, as a body, been seized with a love of publishing books'. They had become interested 'in European Science and Literature' and 'were writing in a language that ordinary people may read'. Through their efforts, and particularly 'under the able superintendence of Ishur Chunder Vidyasagar', the Bengali language was becoming 'capable of being the elegant vehicle of scientific and other information'.[19]

In May 1855, Halliday appointed Vidyasagar Assistant Inspector of Schools for the four districts of Hooghly, Burdwan, Midnapur and Nadia, conjointly with his principalship of Sanskrit College, with a combined salary of Rs 500 a month. By the end of that year he had already established some 20 model schools, applying to Bengal Thomason's circle system, and also started a normal school to train village headmasters at Sanskrit College under the superintendence of his close friend, the rationalist Akshoykumar Dutta. In a parallel move Vidyasagar, who had already displayed his commitment to women's education by enthusiastically backing Bethune's school for daughters of respectable families in Calcutta in 1849, utilized his new official position to start 40 girls' schools in villages between November 1857 and June 1858.

Precision is needed about what exactly was new in these two initiatives of Vidyasagar, for it is possible both to exaggerate or unduly downplay their significance. The surveys made in 1835–8 by William Adam, Rammohan's Unitarian friend, had found a fairly widespread system of indigenous vernacular education in the villages, with some 100,000 *pathshalas* for the 'indigent classes' in Bengal and Bihar, mostly under non-Brahman (often Kayastha) *gurumohasayas*. Adam discovered 'the desire to give education to their male children' to be 'deeply seated in the minds of parents even of the humblest classes', and thought that the pathshalas, of course quite radically modified and improved, could be 'the institutions—through which primarily, although not exclusively, we may hope to improve the morals and the intellect of the Native population'.[20] Vidyasagar's plan of normal and model schools can be seen, therefore, as in a way a belated effort to implement Adam's suggestions.

The impressive number and apparent absence of direct Brahman control has led to an occasional romanticization of these pre-colonial schools, which in some ways fitted in better with rural conditions than the new system which colonial rule, actively helped by reformers like Vidyasagar, eventually established.[21] Poromesh Acharya has recently provided an important corrective here, emphasizing both the extremely limited nature of the education supplied by these schools even at their best, as well as the split-up and hierarchized nature of the entire indigenous educational system which allowed little scope for social mobility. Pathshala education, of course entirely in Bengali, was basically confined to writing, arithmetic, and a bit of revenue and commercial accounting. Reading was less important, since there were no printed textbooks and a necessarily very limited number of manuscripts—which put a premium on memorizing.[22] The pathshalas, in other words, were geared to the everyday needs of would-be petty zamindari officials, traders and better-off peasants: a source of strength, but also a limit. Adam's Reports were actually quite critical of the very limited content of indigenous elementary education.[23] The village school structure had little or nothing to do with the tols, *chatuspathis* and *madrasas*—centres of Sanskrit and Arabic or Persian learning which were the preserve of Brahman males and other learned groups. The educational apparatus consisted of 'separate classes of institutions without any link or relation of any kind, each catering to a distinct class or community'.[24] The relative absence of high castes from village schools was thus a mark of inferiorization and hierarchy (a crucial instance of *adhikari-bheda*, in fact, the principle which Ramakrishna had extolled and Vidyasagar questioned in their only conversation), not autonomy. The *Chanakya-slokas*, for instance, which pupils were often made to memorize in the pathshalas, combined maxims of worldly wisdom with frequent reaffirmations of Brahmanical supremacy: the Brahman was the guru of all other castes, it declared, just as the husband was guru to his wife.[25]

The changes Vidyasagar and other mid-nineteenth-century colonial officials sought to introduce in the pathshala involved expansion of its curriculum to include history, geography, ethics and natural philosophy (i.e. elementary science), much greater use of textbooks, promotion through examinations, and in general an integration within the theoretically 'complete and continuous' system that was being worked out for colonial education.[26] Hierarchies did not end, of course, particularly those based on economic or class differentials, and may even have been sharpened at times, both through the dichotomy in medium of instruction (English at higher levels) and by some of the changes brought about in the pathshalas.[27] At the same time, there was a new theoretical equality of opportunity independent of caste status, a chance for talented boys of families with some but not much resources to climb up a uniform educational ladder through personal grit, determination and self-discipline.

There was much more gradual and limited, but still strikingly new, opening for some girls, too, against formidable opposition, The widespread belief was that educated wives became widows, and while daughters in high-caste families could be occasionally taught a little within their parents' homes, the idea of sending them out to school was deeply shocking, and a very early marriage anyway obligatory. Conditions were no different in the villages: Adam's First Report made the categorical statement that 'there are no indigenous girls' schools'.[28] It is true that Radhakanta Deb, the great champion of sati against Rammohan and Bentinck and of ascetic widowhood against Vidyasagar, had been at the same time a promoter, of a kind, of the education of girls and is even said to have published a tract about it. This had specified, however, that only girls of poor parents could be sent out to school, while respectable families should have their daughters taught within the home—in both cases only till they were married off. A number of girls' schools were set up in Calcutta in the early 1820s, mostly at missionary initiative, but they were, significantly, located in the poorer parts of the city. The initiative then seems to have died out for a generation, and we may speculate whether the conservative consolidation against the ban on sati and Derozian iconoclasm may not have had something to do with this hiatus. What was striking about Bethune's endeavour in 1849 was that daughters of respectable families were now being encouraged to go out to a school, being transported there in a carriage that displayed a Sanskrit quotation said to have been hunted up by Vidyasagar.[29] In course of his drive for girls' schools in villages, too, Vidyasagar took special pride in those being attended by daughters of respectable, high-caste families, thus once again challenging directly conservative bhadralok prejudices.[30]

The characteristic features—and limits—of Vidyasagar's pedagogy are revealed most clearly through a glance at his primers and textbooks.[31] Three themes stand out. There is the motif of the poor boy making good through diligence, devoted effort, and single-minded pursuit of learning. *Jivancharit* and *Charitabali* use material from William and Robert Chambers' *Exemplary and Instructive Biography* (Edinburgh, 1846) to present brief life-histories of leading Western scientists, along with those of Grotius, Valentine Duval (a shepherd boy who rose to become a historian), and Jenkins (son of an African prince who managed to get a British education). The concentration on scientists (Copernicus, Galileo, Newton, Herschell Linnaeus) indicates Vidyasagar's rationalist preferences, and so perhaps is the insertion here of Grotius—founder of an international law which theoretically puts the same limits on the powers of all states, big or small, and prominent advocate of toleration in an age of religious bigotry. The life-histories are adaptations from English, yet a revealing displacement seems to be at work in many of the comments: diligence, which in the Western exemplars is by no means constricted to formal book-learning alone, tends inevitably, in the conditions of colonial, middle-class Bengal, to get focused solely on a single-minded pursuit of education. The biography of Duval ends with Vidyasagar remarking that *yatna* and *parisrama* (devoted effort and exertion) would have led the shepherd-boy nowhere had he not harnessed that devotion to learning.[32] The *Varnaparichay* and, even more, *Bodhoday* made the point sharper: 'Those who are diligent about becoming educated will live happy lives because they will be able to earn money.'[33]

The theme of improvement through education is inextricably bound up with a tremendous insistence on discipline, connoting both rigorous self-control and strict obedience to the commands of parents and teachers. The *Varnaparichay*, as Sibaji Bandopadhyay has emphasized in an important study, is structured throughout by a binary contrast between disciplined diligence and errant disobedience, culminating at the end of Part I in the opposition of Gopal who will succeed in life, and Rakhal who will never learn to read.[34] This is a discipline, it should be added, that is presented in terms utterly stark and bleak, abstracted from human affect and paternalistic glosses. Children are actually told in one lesson that they should always try to please their parents, for if the latter had not been kind enough to feed and clothe them, their sufferings would have known no limit.[35] The Utilitarian, materialistic tone of Vidyasagar's textbooks in fact provoked some contemporary criticism from both orthodox Hindus and some Christian missionaries.[36] These are understandable enough, but the peculiar bleakness of the world of *Varnaparichay* remains a bit puzzling: it is almost as if Vidyasagar sometimes is fighting a part of himself, suppressing an inner Rakhal, projecting the path of discipline and obedience as something made necessary by a heartless world.[37] *Varnaparichay* ends with a really strange and cruel tale, quite out of place one would think in a children's primer. Bhuban, an orphan boy spoilt by his loving aunt, becomes a thief, is condemned to be hanged, and as a parting 'gift' bites off his aunt's ear while saying goodbye.

Improvement, or social ascent, through stern discipline: but only up to a point, within limits set by existing property relations. *Bodhoday* affirms a highly status quoist version of a kind of labour theory of property: 'The things we see around us must belong to one or other person. An object belongs to whoever has worked to produce it, or has inherited it from his forefathers. No one else has any right to it. Whoever owns an object should continue to own it.' No respectable (*bhadra*) person should be a beggar, while having property is conducive to continuous effort. Vidyasagar's school texts are full of warnings about the immorality of theft: 'One shouldn't lay one's hand on something belonging to another person, even if one's life is at stake.'[38] There was, then, a clear class limit—and sometimes a caste frontier, too, though here it was more a question of expediency than believed-in principle. Vidyasagar had insisted in 1851 on opening Sanskrit College to Kayasthas, and in 1854 to other 'respectable castes'. But in 1855 he rejected as inexpedient a suggestion that a Subarnabanik student should also be admitted.[39] Though often very prosperous, he argued, 'in the scale of castes the class stands very low', and he did not want to further 'shock the prejudice of the orthodox Pundits of the Institution.'[40] Despite a concern for primary education in the countryside very rare among members of his class, Vidyasagar, it needs to be added, was probably not the unqualified advocate for mass enlightenment that later admirers have at times made him out to be. Hatcher has cited a letter of his written in September 1859, which argues that educating 'one boy in a proper style' was preferable to providing a smattering of learning to large numbers, for poor children would be taken out of school and put to work by their parents in any case.[41] Vidyasagar did set up a night school for 'sons of the cultivating class' in Birsingha in 1853, but this seems to have been a special gesture made for his home village, and not part of his overall schemes.[42]

Still it is possible to be over-harsh about Vidyasagar. Ranajit Guha has described his schoolbook morality as nothing but 'hard-baked, bourgeois individualism',[43] and certainly there are not only similarities but obvious connections (through Chambers, for instance) with nineteenth-century middle-class British ideologies of improvement as moulded by amalgams of Evangelicalism and Utilitarianism.[44] Texts like *Varnaparichay* comprise the part of Vidyasagar's work that might appear readily assimilable to today's very influential emphasis on 'disciplinary' projects, either derived from colonial discourses or running parallel with them.[45] Hatcher's book has effectively drawn attention, in significant contrast, to the possibility of the more indigenous roots of Vidyasagar's pedagogical values, in particular the traditions of *nitishastra*, embodied in texts like *Chanakya-slokas* and *Hitopadesha*, which also contained elements of an ethic of this-wordly improvement through strenuous learning.[46] But Hatcher, like the analysts of colonial discourse, remains within the parameters of a search for 'influence' or origins. What tends to remain unasked is the question of the precise social contexts which made the emphasis on discipline appear unavoidable. (Not necessarily pleasant or attractive: the bleak world of *Varnaparichay*, its almost Machiavellian realism and ruthlessness, perhaps signifies a recognition of necessity rather than blithe imitation or enthusiastic acceptance.) With the closing of opportunities for military careers and the decline of indigenous business enterprise, education in Bengal was, by the mid-nineteenth century, becoming virtually the sole channel for respectable upward mobility: education, further, of a far more formal, examination-centred kind, for which the old kind of pathshala, however much in tune with earlier conditions, was quite unsuited. Recruitment into services and professions was becoming increasingly dependent on examinations and educational degrees. The informal patronage that Vidyasagar could still distribute through his personal relations with top British officials would soon become a thing of the past. And, once again, instead of a homogenized 'middle class', a focus on its poorer elements seems helpful for situating Vidyasagar's initiatives. The strenuous moods of his school texts were not primarily meant for the gilded youth of Calcutta. They become meaningful only when placed in a context of genteel poverty, and here Vidyasagar's projects implied a striving for a real though limited expansion, an attempt, in the words of Asok Sen, to extend 'opportunities of education for the poorer gentry in small towns and villages of Bengal'.[47]

The attempt went some distance beyond them, perhaps, in terms of long-term appropriations by groups about whom Vidyasagar himself had shown little or no concern. Recent research has unearthed a mass of early-twentieth-century vernacular tracts composed by an emerging literati of Muslims and lower-caste authors located in obscure villages or small towns of rural Bengal.[48] They are imbued with an improvement ethic reminiscent often of Vidyasagar's combination of education with puritanical virtues and discipline, though there is also a greater focus on life outside the classroom, in particular on agricultural development. Given the continued, massive circulation of texts like *Varnaparichay*, one might even suspect a certain amount of direct, if unintended, influence.

Such developments lay much in the future in the 1850s. For Vidyasagar, the tragedy was that the favourable conjuncture that he had sought to utilize for major educational and other initiatives proved extremely short-lived. Educational administration was getting more bureaucratized under a brash young ICS Director of Public Instruction, Gordon Young, who did not get on with Vidyasagar. Much more important was a new mood of financial stringency, fairly obviously connected with counterinsurgency expenses in the wake of 1857. Vidyasagar had gone ahead in the early summer of 1857 in starting girls' schools in his four districts, on the strength of a verbal assurance from Halliday that if 'the inhabitants would provide suitable school houses, the expenses for maintaining the schools would be met by the Government.' In the next year 'the Supreme Government . . . refused their sanction to their establishment except under the Grants-in-aid Rules. My labours have thus become fruitless and the interesting little schools will have to be closed immediately.'[49] Towards the end of 1858 Vidyasagar resigned in disgust from all his official posts.

Barriers of another kind, relating to the development of vernacular education for boys, become evident from an earlier report of Vidyasagar in January 1857. He had pointed out then that 'the success of Vernacular Education will depend materially upon the encouragement given in the way of providing the Alumni of these institutions with offices under Government'. Vidyasagar suggested that vernacular students should therefore be nominated 'to lower posts in the Judicial or Revenue Departments'—a proposal, needless to state, that was entirely ignored.

Colonial constraints—in the form of very material considerations and structures, not abstract ideas—are therefore entirely clear in the case of Vidyasagar's educational ventures. They had coalesced with the elite Brahmanical traditions of high castes, sometimes strengthening, but hardly creating them: for there is no evidence whatsoever of any major attempt at mass education (or organized efforts to improve the conditions of women, for that matter) by bhadralok men in pre-colonial times. The philanthropy of the more enterprising zamindars, on which too Vidyasagar had thought he could depend in the 1850s, was often a bit double-edged at its best,[50] and died away as enhancement of rent became more difficult with the tenancy acts of 1859 and 1885. And deepening employment problems clearly constricted middle-class attitudes over time. Bhadralok protests poured in when Lieutenant-Governor Campbell suggested some diversion of funds from higher towards primary education in 1870.[51] Even anti-colonial nationalism did not change attitudes fundamentally. The 'national education' of the Swadeshi era concentrated on trying to float an alternative university, and certain interesting experiments in districts like Barisal and Faridpur to start autonomous nationalist-oriented village schools among Namashudras and Muslims, which had worried the government considerably, soon died away.[52]

A report of an inspector of schools just a few months after Vidyasagar's resignation can serve as an appropriate, if depressing, epitaph for this section. At Jowgong village near Boinchee, Burdwan district, where a girls' school founded by Vidyasagar was still getting an official grant of Rs 32 per month, 'not a girl, boy or pundit was in attendance' when it was visited on 25 January 1859. The inspector went from there to the neighbouring village of Koolingram, which, as we have seen, Vidyasagar had singled out for special mention in December 1857 as an instance of successful overcoming of the initial hostility of 'respectable men'.[53] A few girls could be seen there in January 1859, but 'the poor Pundit of the Girls' School had . . . no friends'. The headmaster of the boys' school was leading the opposition, and the girls' school had had to shift to another village a mile away.[54]

II

Many stories have been current about the origins of Vidyasagar's passionate concern for the plight of women, in a society where child marriage was normative, widow remarriage prohibited, austere widowhood stringently enforced among high and most intermediate castes, and polygamy considered prestigious among Kulin Brahmans, Kayasthas and Vaidyas. His mother first advised him to take up the cause of widows—according to one account. Others refer to first-hand experiences during visits to Birsingha in his college days: seeing a child-widow of his own age having to fast on *ekadosi*, and hearing about another forced into infanticide by parental command. He was particularly shocked when a favourite teacher of his at Sanskrit College, the elderly Vedanta scholar Sambhuchandra Vacaspati, married a child to run his household for him a few months before his death. (Vidyasagar is said to have wept on meeting the child-bride, doomed to early and lifelong widowhood, and walked out of his teacher's house, refusing to touch water there henceforth.[55]) Two widows are prominent, as we have seen, in his own autobiographical fragment, but as exemplars of warmth and compassion rather than suffering.

What is common to all these anecdotes is an emphasis on personal experience that can be read as a confirmation of the inference I had drawn from Maheshchandra Deb's essay.[56] There are no references at all to any stimulus provided by Western models of marital relations. And, contrary to an interpretive model which today is very influential, all biographies about Vidyasagar agree that the counterposing of shastra against *deshachar*, texts versus customs, eventually the core of his widow remarriage and anti-polygamy tracts, came as deliberate strategy, formulated after he had become convinced that certain practices were harmful and evil.[57] Vidyasagar's reform tracts hardly bear out the assumption so often made nowadays that 'the discursive struggle in which the social reformers were engaged was over tradition and culture; women were simply the site of this contestation'.[58]

Vidyasagar's first essay on social reform, *Balyabibaher Dosh* (Evils of Child-Marriage, 1850), was marked in fact by a total absence of textual exegesis. Partly for that reason, it was also his most radical statement on gender relations, and it was able within the space of a few, brilliantly written pages to unfold an integrated, comprehensive critique of child marriage, arranged marriages, marital oppression, taboos against educating women, and the horrors and evils of austere widowhood.[59]

The essay began with a trenchant denunciation of *both* text and custom, shastra and *laukik vyavahara*. The two in combination have produced, and sustain, all that Vidyasagar found objectionable in existing marital practices. Throughout the essay, he judged the existing institutions and practices against an ideal norm of companionate conjugality based on adult mutual love (*pronoy*)—and that, Vidyasagar says, can flow only from a 'unity of minds'.[60] This is impossible if girls are married off at eight, nine, or ten—which happens because *smritishastras* have promised some imagined other-worldly boons from such action, and people are also afraid of flouting long-continuing custom. All marriages, further, are arranged by parents as advised by often corrupt *ghataks* (professional go-betweens), and the couple do not even see each other before the ceremony—and so 'in our country sincere marital love is rare: the husband is merely the breadwinner, the wife a domestic servant (*grihaparicharika*)'. Child marriage, again, is directly connected with women being kept without education, for, even if they had been taught a little at their parental homes, after marriage will begin life in an 'alien house (*paragriha*)', totally subjected to the authority of fathers and mothers-in-law, and filled with an endless round of 'cleaning the house, preparing beds, cooking, serving food, and other duties which would have to be learned with perfection'. The early marriage of girls also increases the number of widows, 'and who has not witnessed first-hand the unbearable sufferings of widows? . . . All chance of pleasure must end as soon as their husbands die . . . they will not be allowed a drop of water, even if critically ill, on days of ritual fasting.' Never again would Vidyasagar condemn so uncompromisingly the rules of austere widowhood, identify patrilocal marriage for women as life in an 'alien' home, or indeed critique child marriage directly. These did not become part of his action programmes, nor did he return to the interconnections he had worked out here between the need to raise the age of marriage, promotion of women's education and improving the lot of widows.

The major plank of Vidyasagar's argument in this pamphlet is thus individual and conjugal happiness—but there is also a second register, of morality and social welfare—that on the whole has figured more in social reform literature but remains somewhat low-key here. The rigours of lifelong widowhood, imposed often on young girls, cause much immorality and lead to abortions and infanticide. Children born of too early marriage tend to be weak and unhealthy, nor can they get proper training from mothers who have been kept uneducated. Young men married off in their teens neglect their studies and are overburdened by the financial responsibilities of maintaining wife and children: earning money has to become the sole aim of life, leading, once again, to immoral ways. Vidyasagar, interestingly, comes close for a moment here to what became a standard late-nineteenth-century Kaliyuga theme, and figured often in Ramakrishna's conversation as the link between *kamini*, *kanchan* and *chakri*—but then his argument moved in a very different direction, prioritizing this-worldly happiness and welfare, not devotion or asceticism. Ramakrishna would certainly not have shared his enthusiasm for conjugal love.

Did the later, and very much better known, tracts advocating widow remarriage and criticizing Kulin polygamy on largely textual grounds then mark a retreat for Vidyasagar, with gender injustice becoming no more than a site for arguments about valid and invalid tradition? Such a critique would be less than fair, for it fails to analyse the options that were open (or not open) to Vidyasagar when formulating a specific programme of reform and trying to organize a movement on its basis. The tract against child marriage could be daringly radical and reject shastric exegesis, precisely because it was more of a consciousness-raising exercise than a specific proposal for an immediate, concrete reform. It raised no demand for a new law: did not need to, in strict logic, for of course there was no law prohibiting adult marriage—as widow remarriage was prohibited and its issue illegitimate till 1856. The basic point that has to be made is that under British Indian law personal and family matters were supposed to be regulated in accordance with the shastras for Hindus, and the shariat for Muslims.[61] Reform through external state legislation, and reform-from-within through scriptural exegesis and community debate, which today often get counterposed against each other (as in current controversies about Muslim Personal Law, for instance), were actually interdependent in Vidyasagar's time. He had to find shastric justifications for widow remarriage, if it was to become legal under 'Anglo-Hindu' law: reason and humanity alone would not be sufficient. The intertwining of Brahmanical tradition and colonial law becomes clear when seen from the opposite side, too. The petition organized by Raja Radhakanta Deb against the Widow Marriage bill in March 1856 combined alternative interpretations of the shastras and appeals to age-old custom with the argument that 'the proposed law is also at variance with the several Statutes of the British Parliament and the Regulations of the East India Company'.[62]

The author of *Balyabibaher Dosh* was not yet particularly important in official or elite Indian circles. The widow-remarriage tracts, in contrast, were published in 1855–6, at the peak of Vidyasagar's influence, and the plunge into shastric exegesis was obviously in significant part an attempt to convince leading pandits who, through their importance in the *sabhas* of big zamindars and at high-caste ritual occasions, could in turn help him get the support of the big men of Hindu society. Vidyasagar in other words was trying to utilize and manipulate, for reformist purposes, the traditions of the medieval raja–pandit nexus that had spilled over in modified forms into the Calcutta-based *dals* of the nineteenth century.[63] Soon after publishing his first tract justifying widow remarriage, Vidyasagar even tried to win over the Sobhabazar Raj, approaching Radhakanta Deb through a nephew who had become an ally of his. That attempt failed,[64] but he was able to get a substantial section of leading zamindars, along with a number of pandits like Taranath Tarkavacaspati and some Sanskrit College teachers, to line up with Brahmos and Young Bengal intellectuals in the petitions that were organized from October 1855 onwards asking for the legalization of widow remarriage.[65] Vidyasagar's subsequent campaign against Kulin polygamy in 1856-7 also got the support of many prominent zamindars: probably more easily, for in its extreme forms (Kulins with a hundred wives or more, many of whom never saw their husbands after marriage) this was an undeniable scandal, confined moreover to a limited circle of high-caste families claiming a peculiarly high status.[66] A law on the subject may well have been enacted but for the 1857 rebellion. In the late 1860s, when Vidyasagar revived the demand and published his two tracts against polygamy, support was forthcoming for a time even from the Sanatan Dharmarakshini Sabha that had lately been organized to defend Hindu orthodoxy.[67]

As Sekhar Bandopadhyay has emphasized, Vidyasagar's reform campaigns thus included an element of continuity with earlier ways of seeking change through *vyavasthas* (authoritative rulings on social matters) from prominent pandits.[68] There had been several attempts earlier to get individual widow marriages sanctioned in this way, notably one by Raja Rajballabh of Dacca in the mid eighteenth century, which had been blocked by the pandits of Maharaja Krishnachandra of Nadia. Shortly before Vidyasagar published his first tract on widow remarriage, Shyamacharan Das, a man of intermediate-caste (Nabasakh) status living in North Calcutta, had managed to get a favourable vyavastha for the remarriage of his widowed child from a number of leading pandits. (The ruling used a passage from Manu but was careful to limit permission for remarriage to Shudra widows who had remained virgins.[69])

Vidyasagar's tracts, then, were in a sense sophisticated vyavasthas, geared to an audience of fellow pandits and their patrons. But this was only one register among several on which he was playing. Right at the beginning of the first *Bidhaba-bibaha* pamphlet, there is a memorable appeal to a conception of public, vernacular space that is fundamentally new. This was the space that he was simultaneously trying to create, through vernacular prose and reformed elementary education, in endeavours that, like widow remarriage, attained their climax precisely around 1855–6. Tired of the endless controversy on the matter that had been so long confined to pandits animated by mutual jealousy, Vidyasagar declares he has decided to present his views 'in the language spoken by the people, to bring it to the notice of the general public [*sarbasadharan*]. Now let everyone read and discuss, in an impartial manner, whether widow marriage should be introduced or not.'[70] The shastric passages are therefore always translated, and the discussion, though inevitably complicated, is conveyed through a prose far simpler than what had been current in scholarly discussion in Bengali before Vidyasagar. And textual exegesis, ever so often, is interrupted by passages marked by deep compassion for suffering womankind, anger and a profound sense of male guilt. The best known of these is of course the eloquent condemnation of deshachar at the close of the second *Bidhaba-bibaha* tract, highlighting (in that order) the sufferings of widows and the flood of immorality and abortion which is caused by male cruelty sanctioned by that custom. As in the *Balya-bibaha* pamphlet, an implicitly positive recognition of the naturalness of physical, sexual needs underpins Vidyasagar's polemic: 'You think that with the death of the husband, the woman's body becomes like a stone.' The tract ends with the famous lines:

> Let not the unfortunate weaker sex [*abala*] be born in a country where the men have no pity, no dharma, no sense of right and wrong, no ability to discriminate between beneficial and harmful, where preservation of what has been customary is considered the only duty, the only dharma . . . By what sin do women come to be born in Bharatvarsha at all?[71]

There are other, less-known passages, too, that outstrip the limits of shastric interpretation. Space permits only one more reference. The first *Bahubibaha* pamphlet begins with the general proposition that women everywhere are subordinated to men, because 'they are physically weaker, and because social rules are so bad': 'But in no country are the conditions of women so bad as in our unfortunate land, due to the excessive barbarism, selfishness, and thoughtlessness of men.' And the long lists of Kulin men with many wives that Vidyasagar goes on to offer, giving precise names and locations, are interspersed with an angry sarcasm: 'The younger [of two Kulin sisters] has a husband aged 25–26. He has not so far managed to marry more than 32 times.'[72]

The more purely textual sections of the widow-marriage and anti-polygamy tracts are unlikely to attract many readers today: a pity, for they have a brilliance of their own. Vidyasagar displayed here a mastery over text and interpretive logic that was able to subvert, or appropriate for his own purposes, a number of standard orthodox arguments. The example of 'Kali-varjya' is particularly relevant for us, for once again we see Vidyasagar come close to the trope of Kaliyuga, and then move off in a completely different direction. Kali-varjya had been the method by which ancient texts had been modified or pruned, almost always in socially restrictive ways, and often with reference to controls over women, by medieval Smriti experts like Raghunandan.[73] Vidyasagar appropriated the same scholastic tool to prise open a textual space for widow marriage. The lynchpin of Vidyasagar's argument, as is well known, is a passage in *Parasara-samhita*, permitting the remarriage of women in five specific cases, one of which is the death of the husband.[74] But there were many contrary texts which had to be got out of the way. Vidyasagar eliminated the *puranas* among these through the argument that Parasara as a dharmashastra had to be given precedence over them, and then made maximum use of the claim, made in the *Parasara-samhita* itself; that this was the text specifically applicable to Kaliyuga: the other texts, where they contradict it, are Kali-varjya. Vidyasagar's use of Parasara, and not, say, Manu, which had been cited by pandits to allow the remarriage of Shyamacharan Das' daughter, indicates his desire to open the space for widow remarriage to the maximum degree possible within the shastric mode of argument. (Manu, it will be recalled, had been read by the pandits to permit only the remarriage of Shudra widows who were also *akshata-yoni*, i.e. *virgo intacta.*) Vidyasagar's second tract specifically controverted the argument that remarriage is only permitted for low-caste widows, and he also quietly dropped all reference to virginity as a prerequisite.

The shastric rejection of polygamy seems to have been a more difficult task. With all his obvious enthusiasm for monogamous conjugality, Vidyasagar could not prove a complete case for strict monogamy from the Hindu scriptures. All that he could establish, mainly on the basis of Manu, was that the texts had laid down a number of specific conditions under which a man could take more than one wife—there was no unlimited and arbitrary right to multiple wives, as had become the practice among Kulins in Bengal.[75] The argument in the first tract against polygamy then shifts rather quickly to non-shastric grounds: a highly derogatory sketch of the history of Kulinism in Bengal, followed by statistics giving the names, ages, number of marriages, and locations of prominent polygamous men in Hooghly district.[76]

Vidyasagar's shastric arguments justifying widow remarriage and restricting polygamy provoked a flood of attempted refutations from pandits, mostly it seems from the Nadia-Jessore and 24 Parganas belt of solid Brahmanical orthodox scholarship, but joined in later by some erstwhile allies, notably Taranath Tarkavacaspati. Vidyasagar plunged with zest into the scholastic debate, making his sequels far longer than the initial tracts, and carrying on the battle right into his last days. Leafing through his voluminous replies to critics (the second tract against polygamy runs to nearly 200 closely printed pages in the edition I am using), one does at times get the impression of the reformer trapped in a scholastic morass, lost in an endless polemic of interest to fellow pandits alone, moving away in fact from that vision of widening, lay, public space that had animated him in 1850 and 1855. There is a sense of helpless anger, too, finding vent perhaps in bouts of violent, even vulgar, abuse that Vidyasagar sometimes published under pen-names, replying in kind to no doubt equal or greater scurrility on the other side.[77]

A more crucial problem lay in the built-in limits of a strategy of reform 'from within', by shastric exegesis. A number of areas dear to Vidyasagar's heart, as revealed by the 1850 pamphlet (notably, child- and arranged marriages) had to be left out as clearly validated by the scriptures, and the scholastic method also had a tendency to create problems for other, subsequent, reform agendas. Rammohan may have unwittingly added to Vidyasagar's difficulties by hunting up and publicizing the texts praising austere widowhood in order to controvert those that insisted on sati. Vidyasagar sought to eliminate one kind of polygamy which Manu had permitted (marrying a woman of lower caste) by emphasizing that in Kaliyuga intercaste marriage was strictly prohibited.[78] His polemic against Kulinism also used the argument that it often led to delayed marriages for girls in the absence of suitably high-status bridegrooms—and this, Vidyasagar emphasized, clearly contradicted the shastric command that marriage had to be consummated before the first menses.[79] Perhaps it was this passage in his own earlier writing that contributed to Vidyasagar's surprising ambiguity on the Age of Consent issue, when his opinion was officially asked for shortly before his death.[80] And finally, as Bankimchandra acutely pointed out in 1873 in a critique of Vidyasagar's demand for a law against polygamy, scriptural arguments were in a sense redundant, as Hindus guided themselves far more by customs, and texts at times prescribed rules which it would be quite impossible to implement strictly.[81]

We have been looking at Vidyasagar's reform initiatives so far in terms of texts and polemics. But this can be no more than a partial view, for with all its obvious limitations the issue of widow marriage did become for a time something like a movement, not confined to pandits or even always only to highly literate people. Vidyasagar, as is well known, did not stop with getting widow marriage legalized. From November 1856 onwards he went to enormous trouble, expenditure and sometimes real physical danger to organize widow marriages, and by 1867 had personally arranged about 60 of them.[82] Most of the big names, the rajas and zamindars who had joined him in petitioning the government for the law, quickly backed out, often defaulting on earlier commitments of financial help. He did continue to get enthusiastic and active support from a number of young men, most of them Brahmos, through the late 1850s and 1860s and beyond, and much of the information we do have about specific widow-marriage cases in fact comes from Brahmo biographies and histories.[83] During and just after the campaign for legalization of widow remarriage, interest and excitement was high enough to generate a large number of poems and songs, some ridiculing the move, others hailing it, and even 'cultivators, street-porters, cab-men and other lower-class people' indulged in them.[84] The best known of the verses is of course the one wishing long life to Vidyasagar, which appeared on the borders of some saris woven at Santipur. (As weavers have been a low-status group in caste society, this in itself is an indication of a reach beyond the bhadralok.) But more significant perhaps than such momentary excitement, yet peculiarly difficult to recuperate, are the long-term personal experiences into which a movement like widow marriage necessarily translated itself. For widow marriage meant, above all, young men, and girls growing up into young women, entering into a domesticity that flouted traditions, in the face of an enormous amount of everyday petty slander, persecution, ostracism.

Here our sources tend to fail us, for nearly all accounts stop with the first few highly publicized marriages in Calcutta, followed by some discussion of Vidyasagar as lonely, tragic hero. The flood of anecdotes, so voluminous on philanthropy, also narrows down quite suddenly. Indramitra's *Karunasagar Vidyasagar*, which brings together the largest number of anecdotes, is a collection of 737 pages: only 62 of them deal with widow marriage.

We can get a few stray and momentary glimpses, however, of developments that should have called into question a number of very well-established assumptions but have been almost entirely ignored.

Vidyasagar has usually been seen as a reformer of urban, educated bhadralok society, whose work had Calcutta as its focus. Yet the *Tattvabodhini Patrika* of Bhadra (August–September) 1858 contrasted the five widow marriages that had been achieved in Calcutta over the 20 months since the wedding of Srishchandra Vidyaratna in November 1856 with the seven in just two months in Hooghly villages (or very small towns) around Birsingha, beginning in June 1858. It mentioned Ramjibanpur, Khirpai, Chandrakona, Basuli; there were two more at Chandrakona next month, and the first widow marriage in Vidyasagar's home village in July 1852. By August 1862 *Somprakash* could report some 20 to 22 marriages in three years in this fairly small corner of Hooghly district, where Vidyasagar clearly had established some kind of a rural base.[85] Widow marriage, further, was not an entirely high-caste matter: thus Sambhuchandra Vidyaratna describes the '20–25' marriages that took place during 1864–5 as involving 'Brahmans, Kayasthas, Tantubay (weavers), Vaidyas, Telis, etc.'[86]

Vidyasagar's letter in *Hindoo Patriot* of July 1867 gives some hints about how the movement had been organized in the villages—as well as the kind of problems it was facing. Explaining why widow marriage had proved so expensive, Vidyasagar stated that apart from the heavy sums he had spent on the first wedding to establish its respectability, '*dals* or parties' were being 'maintained in several villages in the Mufassil', and anyone 'acquainted with the constitution of Hindoo society' would know that this was an expensive proposition 'even ordinarily'. But this was not an ordinary situation: many cases had been brought against 'the promoters of the movement in the Mufassil', and sometimes physical force was also being deployed. All this was demanding heavy litigation expenses.

Most remarkable of all, illuminating in concrete detail one instance of what Vidyasagar described in general terms in his letter, are the notes he had kept (in English) among his papers about a series of incidents in Kumarganj village, adjoining Birsingha. Long extracts from these are tucked away in a corner of Subolchandra's biography, but seem to have somehow gone unnoticed by later scholars.[87] The party at Kumargunj supporting widow marriage had been excluded from the ceremonies in the village Shiva temple at the time of 'Churrukpooja', at the end of the Bengali year. When they tried to enter the temple to offer puja separately, they 'were beaten back with great violence', and local police officials at first refused to record their complaints. Worse was to come, for then the 'Zamindar of the village Baboo Shib Narain Roy' of Jurul began 'oppressing with impunity those of the Royots of his Talook Comergunj who belong to the widow marriage party'. Shib Narayan sent durwans to forcibly round up the pro-reformers, who were dragged to his presence and 'dismissed with 10 strokes of shoes and a fine of Rs 10 each. . . . Several of them have left the village with their respective families.' The terror had a wider impact: 'The news having reached the inhabitants of pergonnas Burda and Chandrakona, those who are willing to marry their sons and daughters have fallen back, through fear of consequences.' Further, the zamindar was clearly being backed by not only subordinate police officials but the Deputy Magistrate of Jehanabad: the local state apparatus, in other words. Numerous complaints to the latter, including several lodged by Vidyasagar himself, had had no result. The Deputy Magistrate passed orders against continuation of the acts of oppression, but Vidyasagar had learnt from a friendly police *amla* that 'the Khan Bahadur' had told his subordinates to ignore these, render no help to the widow marriage party, but 'endeavour to give them trouble if possible. . . . It is notorious that Baboo Shib Narain Roy often calls on the Deputy Magistrate at an advanced hour of the night.' The net result was that 'the party at Coomergunge' which had 'consisted of about 60 families' was reduced to four or five. Vidyasagar concluded his notes in a mood of complete despair. As 'those who joined the cause at my solicitation and are suffering from their act' are not being relieved and their oppressors are going unpunished, 'I must leave the world, for what is the good of my remaining in it when there is no chance of success of the cause. I have resolved to devote my existence to it and if it fails, life would have no charm to me and existence would be useless.'

There is a little bit of data also in Vidyasagar's notes about the social composition of the two parties in the Kumargunj region. The Deputy Magistrate would of course be high caste, and the zamindar probably also so. Some names are given of Vidyasagar's 'Royot' supporters: Damoo, Sriharee, Nilcomal, Gopal and a 'Sreenibas Doss'. The one surname, as well as its absence in the other cases, suggests a subordinate, probably lower-caste status. But the peasants are clearly divided, for Vidyasagar's supporters at one point get beaten up by the 'Goallas [Sadgops] of the opposite Party'. An anthropological study of Birsingha in the 1950s located the Sadgops as an upwardly mobile jati, dominant in the neighbouring villages and becoming so in Vidyasagar's home village, where the other major groups were Brahmans and Bagdis.[88] One is tempted to speculate about a link between the 'Goalla' hostility to widow marriage and possible Sanskritizing aspirations at work already in the 1860s, but of course this is no more than guesswork.

The Kumargunj affair certainly raises some questions regarding the common stereotype about nineteenth-century social reform being an affair of the English-educated high bhadralok alone, generally backed by the foreign rulers and confined to issues which did not affect the rural masses. Despite Vidyasagar's contacts with leading British officials, an informal alliance between the state machinery at the local level and landlord power evidently frustrated all his initiatives in an area where he would have been most influential.[89] The implicit caste dimensions are equally interesting. In an important article some years ago, Lucy Carroll pointed out that for lower castes already practising widow marriage Act XV of 1856 could have been unwittingly retrogressive, and indeed in some ways represent a paradoxical extension of Brahmanical norms. It deprived widows who married of all succession rights to the property of the deceased husband, even though lower-caste customs had been more liberal in that respect at times.[90] But, at least in Bengal where Brahmanical norms had penetrated fairly deep into lower-caste society, it is dangerous to associate the 'popular' with any unqualified realm of freedom from upper-caste taboos and restrictions. The Kumargunj data seem rather to indicate that the ambiguities and divisions on reform issues could have their counterparts at other social levels, too, with some of the upwardly mobile seeking to 'Sanskritize' themselves by imposing greater controls on women, while at the same time the problems and misery caused by the widow-marriage ban could also stimulate quite contrary tendencies. In 1922, a big Namashudra conference broke up partly through a bitter controversy as to whether widow marriage should be prohibited or encouraged, and during the mid 1920s Digindranarayan Bhattacharya, the rebel Brahman closely identified with lower-caste movements, revived and indeed extended Vidyasagar's programme by campaigning against the practice of widows being made to go without water on ekadosi.[91]

Vidyasagar had sought respectability for widow marriage by making their forms as conventional as possible, and in his letter of July 1867 claimed to have spent no less than Rs 10,000 on the marriage of Srishchandra, giving massive presents to pandits, ghataks and kulins. The reference to go-betweens confirms the obvious: these were presumably all arranged marriages, independent of the bride's consent. Yet despite this strategic emphasis on conventionality, something entirely unconventional was happening, with implications that could at times go a bit beyond the norms set by the founder of the movement. In 'normal' marriages, the child or very young girl was doing what every rule and custom of her society told her to do: in widow marriage she, along with the man she was marrying, was engaged in a violation of norms which no amount of apparent conformity could really disguise. And though the emphasis was always on getting child-widows remarried, neither Vidyasagar's arguments nor the law itself made any mention of age of virginity being a condition. In practice, widows marrying again would have been likely to be of somewhat maturer age than first-time child-brides. It is unlikely that a socially dangerous second marriage could have been imposed on them.

Some of the verses composed during the height of the agitation do convey a real sense of rebellion: mostly in ridicule and outrage, but just occasionally in what seems to be celebration. Take some of the lines of the song said to have been inscribed on Santipur saris, of which only the first is commonly remembered. 'O when will that day dawn, when the law will be proclaimed/Orders will be passed in every district and region/Widow marriages will come in a rush/We will live happily, with husbands of our own choice/When will the day come, when the sufferings of widows will end.'[92]

That, of course, was optimistic imagination, not reality: but an autobiography by a little-known Brahmo from Bikrampur, Gurucharan Mahalanobis (1833–1916), does reveal an instance of woman's agency. Gurucharan, unusual among Brahmos in never having formal English education, married a widow in 1862. Remarkably, as described in detail by Gurucharan, he had known her for some time before the marriage, and it was she who had taken the initiative. Indeed, there is a hint of a bit of romantic competition over the young man between her and another young girl who had also lost her husband. Vidyasagar, Gurucharan reports, was quite pleased when told of these unusual happpenings, and commented that an intelligent person should never agree to marry someone s/he had never seen. He did not come to the wedding—for Gurucharan, as a fervent young Brahmo who had discarded his sacred thread, refused to follow the Hindu forms—but remained close to the Mahalanobis family.[93]

The limits of Vidyasagar's ideas and reform activities still remain clear, particularly from today's feminist perspectives. The problems did not consist only in the kind of inconsistencies that we have seen emerging from his reform-through-texts strategy. The fundamental impulse, as in all nineteenth-century male *stri-swadhinata* (women's freedom—'freeing women' would perhaps convey the implicit meaning better) initiatives, was 'protectionist' rather than egalitarian.[94] It sought through legal reform to improve the lot of the abala (weak), a term much in use in reformist discourses. Paternalist concern certainly differed from conventional patriarchal discipline, but it could slide towards ideologies of control. Vidyasagar was not entirely free, perhaps, from a certain fear of the 'over-independent' woman going beyond the bounds of (reformed and humanized) conjugality. All his tracts do have a moralizing strand, though to be sure usually on a minor key, which portrayed theoretically austere widowhood as in practice a realm of sexual license. (A license, it should be added immediately, that basically men enjoyed at the expense of widows, who would be left to bear the costs in terms of illicit abortion, infanticide and scandal: Vidyasagar's moralism did also have a point.) Such fears probably help to explain the most obvious limit, even contradiction, in Vidyasagar's programme. It made no attempt at all (unlike Digindranarayan later on) to improve the lot of the widow who could not, or maybe did not wish to, marry again. When his own daughter returned home as a widow, Vidyasagar is said to have imposed the same austerities on himself for some time. A moving tale, within limits: there is no report that Vidyasagar ever asked her to defy the traditional rules, the inhumanities of which had been a major impulse behind his entire reform drive. There are also a few indications that by the late 1860s and 1870s an increasingly frustrated and cynical Vidyasagar was falling behind some of the younger Brahmos in the extent to which he was prepared to endorse radical patterns of behaviour. He rejected Miss Carpenter's proposal for starting a normal school to train women teachers on the grounds that 'respectable Hindus' would not allow 'their grown-up female relatives to follow the profession of tuition', while 'unprotected and helpless widows', whose services might be available, might not be 'morally . . . fit agents for educational purposes'.[95] A last, very personal, inconsistency: there are many instances of husbands educating their wives in the nineteenth century, but Dinamoyee Devi, wife of the great educator and champion of companionate conjugality, seems to have remained virtually illiterate, spending much of her time looking after Vidyasagar's parents in Birsingha.

The failure, indeed absence of effort, to modify the conditions of most married women, as well as of widows who did not remarry, may help us to understand the somewhat paradoxical appeal of a figure like Ramakrishna by the closing decades of the century. The saint's conversations were full of references to the dangers flowing from womankind: yet middle-aged and elderly wives and widows flocked to Dakshineswar. Like the men caught in the toils of chakri, they sought solace from the burdens of household routine in the message of *grihastha bhakti*, which promised a certain distancing through the cultivation of an inner devotional space, even while remaining immersed outwardly in the mundane everyday. Similarly, the withering of hopes in the transformative potential of education, as pressures on the middle class increased, may have had something to do with the resonance of Ramakrishna's denigration of formal learning found precisely among the educated.[96]

The biggest limit of all, so far as prospects of change in gender relations were concerned, was of course the absence, as yet, of autonomous, organized women's initiatives. Domestic domination and injustice—located 'within the precincts of their own respective domiciles', to use again Maheshchandra Deb's clumsy but expressive phrase—has always been peculiarly difficult to organize against, which is one reason why self-conscious feminist movements and even perceptions have been fairly rare in history. A few of the preconditions for them did start to emerge in Vidyasagar's times, however, sometimes as distant consequences of his work.

The spread of women's education, combined with the questioning of norms that Vidyasagar had provoked, led on towards the beginnings of a female literary public sphere in the decade that immediately followed the peak of his educational and reform initiatives. Three instances will have to suffice. The *Bamabodhini Patrika* was founded in

1863, run by reformist Brahmo men but greatly stimulating writings by women.[97] The same year saw the publication of Kailasbashini Devi's *Hindu Mahilaganer Heenabastha*. Kailasbashini had initially become literate at the behest of her husband, but her learning process still included an element of subversion, for it had to be kept a secret from her parents-in-law. Its results, as her husband confessed in his preface to the book, had surprised him, for the text by this neo-literate woman had needed no correction from her erstwhile teacher. In the sheer range of its survey of women's disabilities *Hindu Mahilaganer Heenabastha* rivals Vidyasagar's polemic against child marriage, for it includes within its sweep unequal treatment from childhood onwards, keeping girls uneducated and immersed in female rituals (*vratas*) which Kailasbashini considered meaningless, marrying them off in childhood into loveless conjugality, and exposing them to the miseries of Kulin polygamy. The accounts of married life and austere widowhood are especially poignant: child-brides torn from parental homes live as if in a prison, she says, caged like birds and animals. The agony of widows observing ekadosi provoked Kailasbashini to remark that only God can understand the wonders of the Hindu religion.[98] And then in 1868 there was Rashsundari Devi's *Amar Jivan*, the product of the lone, heroic efforts of an obscure, otherwise entirely conventional housewife, who had learnt her letters in fear and secrecy and gone on to publish the first autobiography in the Bengali language.[99]

Vidyasagar failed, in so far as the number of widows daring to remarry has remained almost negligible, and much social obloquy persists even today. But the legal reform he was able to push through, and even more the debates he provoked, did unsettle grossly unjust gender norms that had been part of a doxa of common sense, immune from rational debate and questioning. That, maybe, is where reformist efforts to change laws can help, even when they remain largely unimplemented, or much misapplied.

There is also a paradoxical way in which the extent of resistance to widow remarriage itself bears witness to the significance and radical implications of Vidyasagar's crusade. Whatever the degree of their continued prevalence in practice, child marriage and polygamy are no longer considered normative, but the widow who remarries still generally invites criticism or worse. Widow remarriage was, and remains, disturbing, because it had implications that went some distance beyond what is quite often assumed in feminist circles today to have been the outer limit of nineteenth-century male reformism; a notion of companionate marriage that in essence represented yet another form of control over feminine sexuality. Vidyasagar's campaign, and the law it was able to push through, implicitly challenged the basic Hindu notion of the pure woman as *ardhangini*, half her husband's body even after the latter's death (and hence entitled to a share in his property as long as she does not remarry), who is permitted to have sex in the entire course of her life with one male partner, her husband, alone. (Here lay also the core of the double standard in Hindu conjugality, for there was no corresponding restraint on men.) The subversion implied in Vidyasagar's work was that he achieved the legalization of the remarriage, not of child widows or virgins alone, but of adult women who would have had full-fledged sexual relations with their husbands, and may have borne children. The 'Great Unchastity Case' of 1873 drove the point home more sharply. It decided, going against general Hindu public opinion, that a widow who had not remarried but was proved to have committed 'adultery' subsequently (i.e. been 'unfaithful' to her deceased husband after his death) would retain her share of her husband's property. Vidyasagar, somewhat hesitantly, supported the majority judgement: 'I do not want to condone immorality. But how can property, once inherited, be taken away again?'[100] Bourgeois property right clearly triumphed in his mind in this case over customary norms of chastity.[101] It is also noteworthy that Vidyasagar's tracts on marriage sedulously avoided the standard language of describing the husband as the supreme, near-divine, preceptor of the wife. It emphasized repeatedly, rather, the dimension of mutuality, the meeting of adult minds and bodies. Vidyasagar obviously remained far from any questioning of the limits of ideal monogamous marriage, but he was still an uncompromising critic of double standards, and the weight he was prepared to give to theoretical equality of rights remains quite remarkable.[102]

The protectionist compassion of Vidyasagar was recuperable into socially innocuous philanthropy, and that quickly became, and remains, the dominant way of representing him. But his was a compassion associated above all with anger, and a deep sense of male guilt. It is this which distinguishes his widow-marriage campaign from apparently similar later moves, notably under Arya Samaj auspices, where there was a shift in emphasis to the need for breeding faster and better for religious community and/or country. Anger and guilt, too, have been often diffused or displaced on to external targets, in the heyday of anti-colonial nationalism, but also in much more recent times, through writings where Western 'post-Enlightenment modernity' becomes the primary polemical target.

We cannot afford to lose touch with Vidyasagar's anger and guilt, directed primarily towards gender relations in his own society. For we live in times when wives are regularly burnt for dowry, a lower-caste woman activist is raped for campaigning against child marriage, and the murderers of Roop Kanwar, burnt as sati at Deorala in 1987, are acquitted in court.

Notes

1. The most important of these are Vidyasagar's proposals for reorganizing Sanskrit College (16 December 1850), his notes on the Sanskrit College, drawn up at the request of Lieutenant-Governor Halliday (12 April 1852), and the controversy with J.R. Ballantyne, Principal, Benaras Sanskrit College, in 1853.
2. These have been usefully collated and published in Arabinda Guha, ed., *Unpublished Letters of Vidyasagar* (Calcutta, Ananda Publishers, 1971).
3. Vidyasagar introduced a pass system for students wanting to go out during college hours, and tried to shame latecomers among teachers by standing at the gate every morning 10:30. Chandicharan Bandopadhyay, *Vidyasagar* (Calcutta, 1895, 1969), pp. 92, 104–5.
4. Modern factories start getting important only in the later decades of the nineteenth century, and much of the workforce even then consisted of immigrants. Relatively few Bengali-speaking people were recruited into that other site of time-discipline—the modern colonial army.
5. For a fuller discussion, see Chapters 6 and 8 [of Sarkar's *Writing Social History*].
6. The full text of Vidyasagar's plan for the reorganization of Sanskrit College, submitted to F.J. Mouat, Secretary, Council of Education, on 16 December 1850, is included in Debkumar Basu, ed., *Vidyasagar Rachanabali*, vol. I (Calcutta, 1966, 1974), pp. 376–92. The quotations in this paragraph are taken from this report.
7. Ibid., pp. 364–5.
8. S.N. Dasgupta, *A History of Indian Philosophy*, vol. I (Cambridge, 1922); Debiprasad Chattopadhyay, *Lokayata: A Study in Ancient Indian*

Materialism (New Delhi, People's Publishing House, 1959, 1978), Chapter I.

9. The text of the *Notes* has been reprinted in many places: I am using Indramitra, *Karunaisagar Vidyasagar* (Calcutta, 1969, 1992), pp. 652–4.
10. Ballantyne as Principal of Benaras Sanskrit College, interestingly, contributed quite directly to the later development of Hindu revivalism by insisting on the need to evolve a Sanskritized Hindi, distinct from Urdu. As early as 1847, he was advising his pupils that they should try to make the Hindi used by the pandits of the 'holy city' of Benaras 'the standard of all India'. 'It was the duty of himself and his brother Pundits not to leave the task of formulating the national language in the hands of the villag–ers, but to endeavour to get rid the unprofitable diversity of provincial dialects—.' This was in reply to a rather puzzled interjection of a student of his that it was difficult to understand 'what you Europeans mean by the term Hindi, for there are hundreds of dialects . . . and what you call the Hindi will eventually merge in some future modification of the Oordoo, nor do we see any great cause of regret in this prospect'. Christopher R. King, 'Forging a New Linguistic Identity: The Hindi Movement in Banaras, 1868–1914', in Sandria B. Freitag, *Culture and Power in Banaras* (Delhi, Oxford University Press, 1990), pp. 184–5.
11. Vidyasagar to F.I. Mouat, replying to Ballantyne's observations, 7 September 1853. Text in Benoy Ghosh, *Vidyasagar o Bangali Samaj*, vols I, II, III (Calcutta, 1957, 1958, 1959; combined volume, Calcutta, Orient Longman, 1973), pp. 525–30.
12. Vidyasagar's introduction of commas and semi-colons made Bengali prose both more rigorous and more accessible, as a comparison, say, with Rammohan, immediately reveals. On the importance of punctuation, see the perceptive comments of Carolyn Steedman, who reminds us that even for written English, rules for punctuation were still 'in the process of being established' in the second half of the nineteenth century. *The Radical Soldier's Tale* (London, Routledge, 1988), p. 73, and *passim*.
13. Vidyasagar's *Jivancharit* (1849) included a list of the Bengali terms he was coining for words like 'colonial', 'prejudice', 'museum', 'natural law', 'theatre', 'revolution' and 'university'. Debkumar Basu, vol. I, pp. 234–6.
14. Many among the old-fashioned literati disliked Vidyasagar's Bengali. Chandicharan Bandopadhyay, p. 178, relates a story of Sanskrit scholars at a shastric debate in the palace of the zamindar of Krishnanagar ridiculing a pandit who had given a vyavastha (opinion on a point of religious law) in Bengali that seemed too close to Vidyasagar's: 'What have you done? This can be too easily understood!'
15. Rabindranath Tagore, *Vidyasagarcharit*, 13 Sravana 1902/1895; reprinted *Charitvapuja* (1907); *Rabindra-rachanabali*, vol. IV (Calcutta, Vishwabharati, 1940, 1975), p. 478.

16. Bankimchandra's remark in 1871 that 'beyond translating or primer-making Vidyasagar has done nothing' therefore appears peculiarly uncharitable. *Calcutta Review*, April 1871, quoted in Swapan Basu, *Samakale Vidyasagar* (Calcutta, 1993), p. 157.
17. In June 1855, for instance, Joykrishna and his brother proposed the starting of 14 village vernacular schools, and were able to obtain from the Lieutenant-Governor a grant-in-aid of Rs 189 a month for each. Nilmoni Mukherjee, *A Bengal Zamindar: Joykrishna Mukherjee of Uttarpara and His Times, 1808–1888* (Calcutta, Firma K.L. Mukhopadhyay, 1975), pp. 102, 160.
18. Thus the prominent Derozlan Ramgopal Ghosh had prospered through rice trade with Burma, while Taranath Tarkavacaspati around 1860 was supplying imported yarn to 1200 weavers in Ambica-Kalna and Radhanagar, and exporting cloth to many places in north India. He was connected also with trade in timber and ghee. Such literati connections with successful business enterprise would become very rare after the 1850s. Benoy Ghosh, pp. 161–2.
19. H. Woodrow, Inspector of Schools, East Bengal, in General Report of Public Instruction, 1858–9, Appendix A, p. 30, cited in Arabinda Guha, ed., *Unpublished Letters of Vidyasagar*, p. 19.
20. William Adam, *First Report on the State of Education in Bengal, 1835*, ed. Anathnath Basu (Calcutta, Calcutta University, 1941), p. 7.
21. Thus the pathshalas used to have classes from early morning to ten, and again from three to sundown, and were often closed during the harvesting season: certainly arrangements far better suited to rural conditions and a hot climate than the 'modern' system. The changeover to a ten-to-four schedule was in the 1860s, after Vidyasagar had resigned his official positions, but it came about through the influence of the Normal School for gurus which he had started. Kazi Shahidullah, 'The Purpose and Impact of Government Policy on Pathshala Gurumohashoys in Nineteenth-Century Bengal', in Nigel Crook, ed., *The Transmission of Knowledge in South Asia* (Delhi, Oxford University Press, 1995), pp. 120, 122, 125.
22. One might recall in this context the terms which Vidyasagar's village teacher is said to have used when advising Thakurdas that his son should be taken to Calcutta and taught English: 'His handwriting is very beautiful.' Chandicharan Bandopadhyay, p. 23.
23. 'There is no text or schoolbook used containing any moral truths or liberal knowledge. . . .' Adam, p. 9.
24. Poromesh Acharya, 'Indigenous Education and Brahmanical Hegemony in Bengal', in Crook, p. 98.
25. Poromesh Acharya, pp. 105–11.

26. Brian A. Hatcher, *Idioms of Improvement: Vidyasagar and Cultural Encounter in Bengal* (Calcutta, Oxford University Press, 1996), p. 106; Poromesh Acharya, p. 98.
27. In 1863, a British official noticed a 'marked difference' in the appearance of pupils of 'improved', as compared to unreformed pathshalas. In the latter, cultivators' children were prominent, those of 'the better class of villagers' relatively rare. Normal school pupils in contrast were largely 'the Brahmin and writer-caste boys'. Report of Inspector Medlicott, Government of Bengal Educational Proceedings, No. 51, January 1863, cited in Kazi Shahidullah, p. 125. School fees in the new system were rigorously collected, and payable in cash only; school timings no longer made adjustments for agrarian rhythms; and the curriculum had become more abstract, detached from labour processes (e.g. the shift from zamindari and *mahajani* accounting to formal Western mathematics).
28. Adam. p. 7.
29. The above paragraph is based on Chandicharan Bandopadhyay, Chapter VII, and Benoy Ghosh, Chapter IV.
30. Vidyasagar's report to H. Woodrowe, Officiating Director of Public Instruction, 10 December 1857, emphasized the importance of the girls' school he had managed to start at Koolingram, Burdwan district, as those sending their daughters there 'are, for the most part, respectable men'. A later report of his claimed that with consistent government support he could have started girls' schools 'in almost every village in the districts under me, except perhaps the District of Nuddea'. The qualification is revealing, for Nadia was the citadel of Brahmanical learning and orthodoxy. Arabinda Guha, pp. 35, 36.
31. The key texts here include *Jivancharit* (1849), *Bodhoday* (1851), *Nitibodh* (1851: published in the name of Vidyasagar's close friend Rajkrishna Bandopadhyay, but with the first seven sections written by himself), *Charitabali* (1856), and, of course, *Varnaparichay* in two parts (April, June, 1855). *Varnaparichay* went through 152 editions totalling 3,500,000 copies in Vidyasagar's lifetime, and remained the standard Bengali primer right down to contemporary times. Sibaji Bandopadhyay, *Gopal-Rakhal Dvandvasamas: Upanibeshbad o Bangla Shishusahitya* (Calcutta, Papyrus, 1991), p. 135.
32. I owe this point to Hatcher, p. 181, who does not, however, make this distinction between Western exemplar and Indian adaptation explicit.
33. *Bodhoday*, in Gopal Haldar, ed, *Vidyasagar Rachanasangraha* (Calcutta, 1972), vol. I, p. 182. The theme, of course, has become a Bengali proverb: 'Lekhapara kore je garighora chare se.'
34. Sibaji Bandopadhyay, pp. 134–42, and *passim*.

35. *Varnaparichay*, Part ii, in T. Datta, ed., *Vidyasagar Rachanabali*, vol. I (Calcutta, 1994), p. 1264.
36. Biharilal Sarkar, *Vidyasagar* (Calcutta, 1895, 1900, 1910, 1922; ed., Asit Bandopadhyay, 1986), p. 153, was critical of *Bodhoday*, which had declared that sense impressions constitute the only source of knowledge, and defined matter as objects that can be perceived. The missionary leader John Murdoch objected to the use of the 'secularist' *Varnaparichay* in Christian schools. Swapan Basu, p. 130.
37. Vidyasagar's autobiographical fragment begins by recalling how disobedient he had been in his childhood and how often his father had had to scold or beat him: a relevant personal detail, but which does not, I feel, fully explain this tone.
38. *Bodhoday* (1851, 1886), in Debkumar Basu, ed., *Vidyasagar Rachanabali*, vol. I, pp. 282–3.
39. Subarnabaniks were a prosperous trading community in Bengal who had a surprisingly low-caste status: supposedly because they had offended Ballal Sen, eponymous founder of the specific caste structure of Bengal.
40. Letters dated 28 March 1851 and 21 November 1859, in Benoy Ghosh, pp. 542–5.
41. Letter to Rivers Thompson, 29 September 1859, cited in Hatcher, p. 111.
42. Vidyasagar also ran a free day-school and a girls' school at Birsingha, along with a charitable dispensary. His total expenses for these came to as much as Rs 500–600 a month. Subolchandra Mitra, *Life of Pandit Isvarchandra Vidyasagar* (Calcutta, 1902, 1975), pp. 240–1.
43. Ranajit Guha, *An Indian Historiography of India* (Calcutta, K.P. Bagchi, 1988), p. 61.
44. For later generations, Samuel Smiles' *Self-Help* has come to epitomize this ideology: here, however, there can have been no direct influence, since that text was published only in 1859.
45. See, for instance, Partha Chatterjee, ed., *Texts of Power: Emerging Disciplines in Colonial Bengal* (Calcutta, Samya, 1996). For a more nuanced version of a similar argument, see Sibaji Bandopadhyay.
46. A prize-winning Sanskrit poem by Vidyasagar in his student days, composed at a time (1838) when he had not mastered English, had already announced that 'though a man be weak, poor, or of low birth, through learning he earns the respect worthy of a king'. Hatcher, pp. 165–7.
47. Asok Sen, p. 42.
48. I am indebted for this point to the very original research of Pradip Kumar Dutta: 'Hindu–Muslim Relations in the Bengal of the 1920s' (unpublished thesis, Delhi University, 1996), Chapter II, and *passim*.
49. Extract from General Report of Public Instruction, 1858–9, Appendix A, in Arabinda Guha, p. 36.

50. There had been complaints in 1847 that Joykrishna Mukherjee was funding his Uttarpara English school by enhancing the rents of his tenants at Boinchee. Nilmoni Mukherjee, p. 108.
51. Asok Sen, pp. 38–9.
52. Sumit Sarkar, *Swadeshi Movement in Bengal 1903–1908* (New Delhi, 1973), Chapter IV.
53. See n. 21 above.
54. Report of E. Lodge, Inspector of Schools, South Bengal, 10 March 1859, cited in Arabinda Guha, pp. 50–1.
55. Chandicharan Bandopadhyay, pp. 59–61, rejects as inauthentic the story about his mother, and relates the tales about infanticide and Vacaspati. Subolchandra Mitra, p. 262, gives the story about ekadosi.
56. See above, footnote 39 and corresponding text [of Sarkar's *Writing Social History*].
57. Chandicharan Bandopadhyay, pp. 237–8, vividly describes sleepless nights spent by Vidyasagar hunting for shastric arguments to prove the case for widow remarriage, before he came across the Parasara passage he would make famous. The story may be overdramatized, as it seems unlikely that Vidyasagar would not have known about the passage earlier (see n. 73 below), but the essential point regarding the primacy of personal experience over text is reiterated by Subolchandra Mitra, p. 262, who adds that he 'rightly' took no public step before discovering the shastric justification.
58. Ratna Kapur and Brenda Cossman, *Subversive Sites: Feminist Engagements with Law in India* (New Delhi, Sage, 1996), p. 47, a pioneering feminist study of Indian legal discourse which unfortunately accepts at this point a little uncritically Lata Mani's thesis about the debate around sati. I have stated elsewhere my difficulties with Mani's argument, namely that nineteenth-century debates about the conditions of women were primarily a means to the end of establishing textualized versions of tradition, even when applied to Rammohan: see my 'Orientalism Revisited: Saidian Frameworks in the Writing of Indian History', *Oxford Literary Review*, 16, 1994.
59. *Sarvasubhakari*, 1850; Gopal Haldar, ed. *Vidyasagar Rachanabali*, vol. II (Calcutta. 1972), pp. 3–9. This was an article in a short-lived monthly brought out by some Hindu College friends of Vidyasagar; it was published anonymously, but there is complete unanimity among biographers and critics that the author was Ishwarchandra.
60. I intend to argue below that this implicit recognition of ideal conjugality as necessarily based on the union of adult minds and bodies is quite central to a proper assessment of Vidyasagar.
61. Warren Hastings' Regulations had laid down, in 1772 and again in 1780, that 'inheritance, marriage, caste and other religious usages or institutions were to be administered to Hindus according to the laws of "Shaster".'

Numerous changes were made, of course, but in consultation with indigenous experts (hence the need for 'judge-pandits' in courts)—till the 'assumption', made in 1864, that judicial knowledge of Hindu law was complete. In practice, occasional consultations continued even afterwards. J.D.M. Derrett, *Religion, Law and the State in India* (London, 1968), p. 233, and *passim*.

62. The petition, which obtained 36,764 signatures, went on to cite regulations enacted in 1772, 1793 and 1831, and the unanimous opinion of the judges of the Sadr courts given to the Law Commission of 1837 that legalization of widow remarriage would 'at once dislocate the whole framework of Hindu jurisprudence'. A similar combination is visible in the petition made by the 'Professors of the Hindu law' of 'Nuddea, Tribeni, Bhatpara, Bansberia, Calcutta, and other places' denouncing the efforts of a '*Modern* pandit, Vidyasagar', 'in conjunction with a few young men of the rising class'. For the texts of both these documents, see Subolchandra Mitra, pp. 302–17.
63. See the excellent discussion in Sekhar Bandopadhyay, pp. 22–3.
64. Radhakanta organized two shastric debates, but at the end of the second awarded the shawl that traditionally signified victory at such occasions to Brajanath Vidyaratna, leading Smriti expert of Nabadwip. Subolchandra Mitra, pp. 268–9. Brajanath remained one of Vidyasagar's most bitter and formidable antagonists down to the 1880s.
65. The signatories included the Maharajas of Burdwan and Nadia, and the heads of both branches of the Tagore family Debendranath and Prasannakumar), and the first petition was headed by the unimpeachably respectable and orthodox Joykrishna Mukherjee of Uttarpara. Altogether some 25,000 signatures could be collected for reform: less than the number collected by its opponents, but still fairly impressive. Chandicharan Bandopadhyay, pp. 255–6; Nilmoni Mukherjee, pp. 142–3.
66. Polygamy had become rampant because it often became the principal source of livelihood for Kulin young men, who would be paid handsome sums by the parents of daughters eager to move their families up in the hypergamous scale.
67. A support that Vidyasagar cited as a particularly telling argument in his favour in the introduction to his first *Bahubibaha* tract (1870). This also gives a brief history of the earlier campaigns against polygamy. Haldar, ed., *Vidyasagar Rachanabali*, vol. II, pp. 167–9.
68. Sekhar Bandopadhyay, p. 28.
69. Vidyasagar reprinted this vyavastha in the second edition of his initial widow-remarriage tract (1857), at the same time pointing to its subsequent repudiation by most of the signatories as a crass instance of opportunism. Haldar, ed., pp. 15–19. Chandicharan Bandopadhyay, pp. 224–5, lists a number of earlier attempts to get widow marriage accepted.

70. Ibid., p. 21.
71. Haldar, ed., pp. 164–5.
72. Ibid., pp. 171, 218–19.
73. Raghunandan had listed, among practices allowed by some dharmasastras but no longer permissible in the Kaliyuga, sea voyages, twice-born jatis marrying women of lower castes, going on too-distant pilgrimages, Brahmans using Shudra cooks—as well as a practice which had often been interpreted as widow marriage. The relevant passage was quoted, and glossed differently, by Vidyasagar in his first widow-marriage tract. Haldar, ed., p. 28.
74. 'A woman is permitted by the shastras to remarry if her husband has disappeared, has died, been found impotent, has abandoned the world, or has been outcasted.' Haldar, ed., p. 26. Biographers like Chandicharan Bandopadhyay, p. 237, present Vidyasagar's discovery of this text in dramatic terms, as coming in a revelation after many nights of sleepless study of the shastras. This seems a bit unlikely, as the Derozian journal *Bengal Spectator* had already referred to the passage in July 1842 while advocating widow remarriage. Indramitra, *Karunasagar Vidyasagar* (Calcutta, 1969, 1992), pp. 242–3. A Sanskrit scholar like Vidyasagar would surely have known his Parasara anyway: the real problem was how the texts contradicting this passage could be shown to be irrelevant.
75. The permitted grounds in Manu are nearly all highly gender-unequal: the husband could marry again, not only if his wife dies, but also if she is barren, bears daughters only, drinks, is unfaithful, extravagant, always ill and even if she talks back at him. Contrary to today's widespread communal stereotype which somehow associates Islam uniquely with many wives, the scriptural-cum-customary grounds for monogamy in Hindu traditions have been quite remarkably weak, and only postcolonial legislation has made a (partial) change. See the passages cited in Vidyasagar's two *Bahubibaha* tracts (1870, 1873), reprinted in Haldar, ed., pp. 173–5, 413–15.
76. One hundred and thirty-three are listed for Hooghly district, with the number of marriages ranging from 80 to five. A list follows for the single village of Janai, near Calcutta, with 64 names of men having from two to ten wives. Ibid., pp. 201–12.
77. See for instance the passage in *Ratnapariksha* (1886) where Vidyasagar, writing under the alias of 'Worthy Nephew', expresses regret that his earlier polemic has led to the death of 'Uncle Vidyaratna' (Brojobilas Vidyaratna, the Nadia Smriti scholar who had been opposing him from 1855), and now he doesn't know whether this should be classed as Brahman-slaughter or cow-slaughter. Haldar, ed., p. 512.
78. Ibid., p. 176.
79. Ibid., p. 188.

80. Vidyasagar found it impossible to support the bill in its existing form, as he thought fixing the minimum age of consent at 12 could go against the *garbhadan* rite immediately after menses. His alternative suggestion was to make consummation before first menses a penal offence, irrespective of age. As girls can menstruate very early, this would not have given protection against physical and emotional injury in many cases. Subolchandra Mitra, who enthusiastically gives long extracts from this note of 16 February 1891, rejects however a widespread opinion that it represented a kind of recantation of earlier attitudes: for two months before his death Vidyasagar warmly welcomed the marriage of the Brahmo activist Durgamohan Das (who had earlier tried to get his own widowed stepmother remarried) with a widow with several children. Mitra, pp. 652–5.
81. Bankim, however, used this potentially radical argument to reject Vidyasagar's demand for an anti-polygamy law, which he thought to be unnecessary. A passage in his article was quite prophetic in the way it anticipated what later became, and remains, a recurrent argument: it was unfair to pass a law curtailing Hindu (male) rights unless a similar restriction was imposed on Muslims too. *Bahubibaha* (*Bangadarshan,* 1280/1873), reprinted in Jogeshchandra Bagal, ed., *Bankim Rachanabali*, vol. II (Calcutta, 1954, 1969), pp. 314–19.
82. Vidyasagar mentioned this figure in a letter published in *Hindoo Patriot*, 1 July 1867, in connection with a proposal that had been made to raise a public fund to help him repay the debts he had incurred while organizing these marriages. He rejected the offer, but evidently felt it necessary to explain how so much had been spent.
83. In his preface to the third edition (1863) of his first widow-marriage tract, Vidyasagar referred to the excitement and agitation generated in the Dacca region by his pamphlet, necessitating the reprint. Vidyasagar is not known to have had many contacts in East Bengal, but the Brahmo movement acquired some of its principal bases in the areas of bhadralok concentration there, like Bikrampur, Barisal, and parts of Mymensingh and Sylhet.
84. Subolchandra Mitra, p. 279.
85. Indramitra, p. 292. Sambhuchandra Vidyaratna mentions 'nearly fifteen' widow remarriages organized in Jehanabad villages like Ramjibanpur, Chandrakona, Sola, Srinagar, Kalikapur and Khirpai in Asar-Sravana 1265 (June–July 1858). Numerous such marriages, he states, took place in this area down to 1865. Sambhuchandra Vidyaratna, *Vidyasagar-Jivacarit* (Calcutta, 1891; reprinted, ed. Kumud Kumar Bhattacharya, Calcutta, 1992), p. 104.
86. Sambhuchandra Vidyaratna, p. 116.

87. Subolchandra Mitra, pp. 511–16. There is a passing reference to the Kumarganj developments also in Biharilal Sarkar, p. 282. From Vidyasagar's autobiographical fragment, we learn that Kumarganj was the weekly market-place (*hat*) for Birsingha, located in Chandrakona police-station, Jehanabad (Arambag) sub-division. There is no indication of date, but it must have been before 1869, when Vidyasagar left Birsingha permanently. Subolchandra places the extracts just after his account of Vidyasagar's relief work during the 1866 famine, and a date, *c.* 1867, seems indicated also by the reference in general terms to similar developments in the letter of 1 July 1867.
88. The study, made incidentally by a descendant of Vidyasagar, found the village Siva temple controlled by a Brahman family, surnamed Ray (a relation of Shib Narayan Roy, perhaps), who had land granted by the Maharaja of Burdwan. Village religious festivals were still the foci of social conflict. Gouranga Chattopadhyay, *Ranjana: A Village in West Bengal* (Calcutta, 1964).
89. There seems to have been a brief spell earlier where the local authority at Jehanabad had been helpful. Interestingly, the deputy magistrate who Sambhuchandra remembers as helping Vidyasagar then was the well-known Muslim intellectual Abdul Latif. Sambhuchandra Vidyaratna, p. 104.
90. Lucy Carroll, 'Law, Custom and Statutory Social Reform: The Hindu Widow Remarriage Act of 1856', in J. Krishnamurty, ed., *Women in Colonial India: Essays in Survival, Work and the State* (Delhi: Oxford University Press, 1989).
91. Sekhar Bandopadhyay, 'Social Mobility in Bengal in the Late-19th-Early-20th Century' (unpublished thesis, Calcutta University, 1985), p. 480; Digindranarayan Bhattacharya, *Bidhabur Nirjala Ekadosi* (Serajgunj, 1923, 1926).
92. The full text of this song is given in Subolchandra Mitra, pp. 279–80.
93. Gurucharan Mahalanobis, ' Atmakatha', manuscript, *c. 1913:* pub. and ed. Nirmalkumari Mahalanobis (Calcutta, 1974), pp. 46–53.
94. See the useful theoretical distinctions drawn in Ratna Kapur and Brenda Cossman, pp. 22–33.
95. Vidyasagar to William Grey, 1 October 1867, reprinted in Subolchandra Mitra, p. 466.
96. See Chapter 8 of this book [*Writing Social History*].
97. Bharati Ray is editing a valuable collection of extracts from this journal: Ray, ed., *Sekaler Narishiksha: Bamabodhini Patrika, 1270–1329/1863–1922* (Calcutta, 1994).
98. Kailasbashini Devi, *Hindu Mahilaganer Heenabastha* (Calcutta, Gupta Press, 1863).

99. For Rashsundari, see Tanika Sarkar, 'A Book of Her Own, A Life of Her Own: Autobiography of a Nineteenth-Century Woman', *History Workshop Journal*, 36, 1993.
100. Biharilal Sarkar, p. 332.
101. My assessment of the significance of widow marriage has been greatly helped by Tanika Sarkar.
102. The second widow-remarriage tract, for instance, did some skilful bending of the shastras to reach the conclusion that 'carefully studied, the makers of the shastras may be seen to have wanted the same rules for men as for women'. Haldar, ed., p. 156.

7

Customs in a Peasant Economy
Women in Colonial Haryana*

PREM CHOWDHRY

In Haryana the control of women's behaviour through certain customs has been central to the affirmation of the solidarity of the dominant Jat peasant group. Such customs, emerging from the growth and demands of a patriarchy and interacting with specific geo-economic needs, have been largely constrictive for women. Further, when such customs came to be buttressed with the force of law by the colonial government, who became conscious agents in their perpetuation, the customs naturally became more binding upon Jat and other social groups in Haryana, making it either difficult or impossible for a woman to break out of their confines. The tenacious persistence of historically crystallized customs and attitudes made a mockery of attempts by women to contest these and often involved them in prolonged legal battles and open confrontations.

There is a peculiar contradiction in the dominant emergent customs and attitudes in rural Haryana in relation to women in the colonial period. On the one hand, the agrarian milieu shows the generally accepted indices of high status for women, that is, bride-price, widow-remarriage, polyandry or its own sexual variants and full economic participation in agricultural activities resting on a relatively greater similarity of function with men. On the other hand, it shows the region as also having indices of women's backwardness, that is, female infanticide in different forms resulting in an extremely unequal female sex ratio as compared to the male, purdah (seclusion) and the *ghunghat* (veil) custom, total neglect of and prejudice against female education, and the complete absence of women from any positions of power and decision making. This paper takes up the socio-economic aspects of such mutually contradictory indices, social customs and attitudes and analyses the dominant peasant cultural ethos which has accepted and sanctified them. In this connection, British administrative policy decisions as well as those of a reformist movement like the Arya Samaj, both of which sustained these customs, have also been examined. This paper also attempts to explore the social implications of these customs and the reasons behind the ostensibly 'liberal' attitudes towards women in the context of marriage, remarriage, sexuality, etc. All these factors are seen in the historical context of overall colonial domination, the adoption of certain policies which, although not directly connected with women, nevertheless had profound effects on issues specifically relating to women. As such, this study also highlights the role of the colonial administration and its attitudes in retaining and reinforcing the emergent dominant social ethos of the Haryana peasantry.

I. The Dominant Caste and the Peasant Ethos

In the agrarian milieu of the Haryana region of Punjab, the socio-cultural ethos came to be coloured and determined generally by the agriculturist castes, and in particular by the land-owning classes. Among the agriculturist castes, the Jats emerge as the 'dominant caste'.[1] The model of the dominant caste in a given region as described by M.N. Srinivas is apposite for the Jats in Haryana.[2] Economically and numerically stronger than any other caste, the Jats satisfied yet another norm of the 'dominant caste', that is, they did not occupy a low ritual status. Numerically they were found in very large numbers in the five districts of this region, viz., Ambala, Gurgaon, Hissar, Karnal and Rohtak, forming nearly one-third of the total population. They also held the bulk of agricultural land as proprietors. For instance, in Rohtak district in 1910, the Hindu Jats emerged as the owners of 60 per cent of the total cultivated land. In a very large number of 'Jat villages' of this region, they held a near monopoly of landownership ranging between 88 and 99 per cent. Besides, most other castes were in a relation of servitude to the landowning Jats who stood as the single largest receivers of services from the other castes. And, although the social status of Jats is somewhat difficult to define in terms of the ritualistic framework of caste hierarchies, the accepted social superiority of the Brahmin did not exist here or elsewhere in Punjab. The Brahmin could certainly be sacerdotally superior yet socially he was described as the 'lowest of the low'. Whatever superiority the Brahmin may have enjoyed declined severely by the early 1920s with the propagation and acceptance of the Arya Samaj, especially among the landowning Jats of this region. On the other hand, regarding the Jats, who ritually ranked in Punjab after the Brahmin, Rajput and Khatri, the Punjab Census of 1901 laid down 'there is no caste above the Jat'. In this agrarian society, the norms as seen to be operating and also as encouraged by the British did not conform to ritualistic concepts and were necessarily related to the amount of land that was in the possession of a particular caste. Seen as such the Jats clearly emerge as the 'dominant caste' in social, economic and numerical terms, as well as in the emerging politics of this region.[3]

This ubiquitous domination by a single caste (despite internal economic disparities) set the tone and shaped the customs and attitudes that became common in rural Haryana. The emergent customs followed by most Jats came to be accepted and projected for the entire region, especially as many of these customs could be seen to be followed by nearly all lower castes as well as classes.

II. Socio-economic Conditions: Their Significance for Women

Haryana remained one of the most backward and underdeveloped regions of Punjab under the British. The needs of imperialism gave a very low priority to any improvement of agriculture in Haryana.[4] This region in any case had poorer resources as compared to most other parts of Punjab. Irrigation was extremely limited and British irrigational policies kept the region starved of this basic requirement which was the crucial determinant of agriculture. Apart from limited irrigation, precarious rainfall, recurrent floods due to periodic overflow of the river

Jamuna, seasonal excesses and frequent *akal* (famines) spelt devastation for this region and its economy. Throughout, the official emphasis remained on low-value food-cum-fodder crops and the region continued to be seen as primarily suited for the supply of draught animals to the rest of Punjab as also to certain other parts of India.

In this chronic famine-ridden region, where large sections of the peasants tended to be subsistence or deficit producers, only a comparatively large holding could be economically viable. For example, in Rohtak district, a holding of at least 12 acres could be taken as an economic one.[5] This meant that only about 28 per cent of landholdings fell in this category.[6] The same was true, more or less, for the entire Haryana region. The *barani* (dependent on rainfall) nature of the region with its concomitant low-yielding inferior crops and chronic crop failures made for a subsistence economy and hand-to-mouth living for an overwhelming majority of landowners. Deficient in any kind of resources, the small landowners relied mostly upon their family labour and some hired labour, if the need arose. Such an economy reinforced covetousness for male progeny. A male child came to be as essential as the life-giving rain. A popular local saying maintained:

> *meehn aur bettya te koon dhappya sai*[7]
>
> (Who can be satisfied without rain and sons; for cultivation both are necessary.)

Moreover, given uncertain conditions, family labour requirements, and the high mortality rate, it was not considered either safe or sufficient to have only one male child:

> *ek ankh ka ke sulakshana,*
> *ek poot ka ke sapoota*[8]
>
> (Just as a one-eyed man can hardly be called lucky, so also a man with only one son.)

Another proverb went on to maintain:

> *chohra mure nirbhag ka*
> *chohri mure bhagwan ki*[9]
>
> (The son of an unfortunate dies, the daughter of a fortunate dies.)

This local proverb showing a marked preference for boys over girls, reflects the dominant social ethos. In very real terms this ethos manifested itself in the favourable male sex ratio. There was a great deal of difference in the male–female sex ratio at any given age not only in Haryana but all over Punjab.[10] The British administration ascribed this imbalance to a distant past, before the annexation of Punjab, when female infanticide had been practised to a large extent.[11] However, by the time of the 1901 Census they were not willing to give it any significant contributory role and ascribed the uneven sex ratio to other reasons like neglect of female children in earlier times (both precolonial and in the early years of British rule in Punjab), the high rate of mortality due to frequent child-bearing starting at a very early age, and the neglect of women of advanced age. Additionally, in the all-too-frequent famines, droughts and epidemics, the first casualty were women.[12] All these factors undoubtedly combined to enable a different form of femicide to continue in order to keep the female ratio down, and resulted in Punjab having the smallest proportion of females as compared to the major Indian provinces under the British.[13]

The socio-economy of this region has been emphasized because of its special significance for women and not merely to rationalize or explain the low female sex ratio. The hard subsistence-level economy with total dependence on family labour for cultivation made women an economic asset. W.E. Purser and H.C. Fanshawe recognizing this, commented in their report on the revised land revenue settlement of the Rohtak district in 1880:

> Enquiry from people themselves, in almost every village of the district has shown that as long as a family has its proper complement of workers, male and female, it is well-to-do . . . where there is no woman in the family, the house is certain to fall into difficulties.[14]

Another graphic description of women's work showed:

> The women work as hard as the men if not harder. The heavy tasks of bringing in wood and fuel and water fall on them; they have to cook the food, and carry it daily to the fields; they have to watch the crops; to them the peeling of the sugarcane and picking of the cotton belongs; and when there is nothing else to do, they must always fill up the time by tasks with the spinning wheel.[15]

A large number of local proverbs show that certain agricultural tasks such as weeding fell exclusively on women. Two proverbs from Karnal can be cited here as examples:

main koli nahin duppatti
keya chugegi kuppatti

(Cotton says you did not weed me when I had two leaves above the ground, what do you expect to pick now, bad woman.)

jo wahin nalaye do patti
to kya kamae kuppatti[16]

(If weeding be not done when there are but two leaves, then what will you earn, worthless woman.)

To this may be added the extensive animal husbandry work. Animal husbandry was a necessary supplement to this region's subsistence-level economy. It meant tending, feeding, milking the cattle and making *lassi* (buttermilk) and *ghee* (refined butter). All this was the special preserve of women.

III. The Colonial View of Women: Utility to Agriculture

Hard work was a general feature all over rural Punjab. Yet, relatively speaking, due to the harsh, unyielding geo-economic conditions of Haryana, the women worked harder than elsewhere in the Punjab province. The British officials' observations bear this out:

> It can be safely said that proportionately a large number of women are engaged in economic work in the Himalayan natural division than in the plains, and that in the latter the women of South-eastern districts such as Hissar, Rohtak and Gurgaon take a greater share of such work than the women of the Central districts with one or two exceptions. In the Himalayas, as well as in the South-east of the province, women take a large share in agricultural work and in some locations are believed to do it even better than their husbands. Women of North-western districts are also fairly active workers.[17]

Among these regional variations, women of certain caste groups were specially singled out for praise. For example, the Jatni (Jat woman) was hailed as an 'economic treasure' by British officials, who wrote a great deal applauding the 'help' she rendered to 'an ideal cultivator and a revenue payer', that is, the Jat.[18] The Jatni was universally praised thus:

bhali jati jatni ki khurpi hath
khel nivare apne khavind ke sath[19]

(Good kind Jatni, hoe in hand, weeds the fields in company with her husband.)

Another proverb maintained:

ran jatti, te hor sab chalti[20]
(A Jat wife for me, as all other women are a mere waste of money.)

The Rohtak Assessment Report of 1909 mentioned that a Jatni did not plough, dig or drive a cart, but there was no other form of agricultural labour which she did not perform. The women from other agricultural castes were also said to do as much work as the Jatni if not more.[21] Here one may include the women from lower castes as well. In fact, these women showed a higher number of female workers than the other castes.[22] Those specially mentioned were from among the Chamars, Chuhras and Jhimars. They were described by the officials as 'hard working',[23] but because they did not belong to the landowning castes their being 'economic assets' found no expression in official British accounts.

The caste groups who did not encourage their women to work outside home were the Bania, Khatri and Rajput among the Hindus, and the Pathan, Biloch, Sayyad, Shiekh and Ranghar or Rajput among the Muslims.[24] The colonial administrators' comments on these caste groups which were 'conspicuous' for having 'the smallest number of female workers' reveal their own attitude. For example, the Rajputs, both Hindu and Muslim, by the 'common consent' of various British officials were considered to be 'the worst cultivators in the Punjab' whose 'land revenue dues remained frequently in arrears'; the Rajput's regard for his *izzat* (honour) forbade him to take any help from his wife who remained in purdah and was generally considered to be 'an economic burden'.[25] The Brahmins were also considered to be 'inferior cultivators', because their women gave little or no assistance to the men in the fields beyond bringing them their meals.[26] For the same reason, the Pathans were considered 'bad cultivators' and 'very bad revenue payers'; the Biloch were described as 'poor cultivators and heavily indebted'.[27] The other castes being 'non-agriculturist castes', however, merited no mention.

Obviously, the British criterion for judging women was their usefulness to agriculture which was of supreme concern to them not only in terms of land revenue but also in terms of the general socio-economic stability and utility of this region. In fact, even the custom of purdah was seen from the point of view of women's non-availability for tasks other than the domestic as it led to women's seclusion and severely curtailed their availability for agricultural labour.[28] The British support to the social reformers' struggle against purdah therefore may well have emanated out of such concerns. Interestingly, this non-utilization of female labour was not only considered a handicap to the Indian peasant but was also considered to be one of the chief causes of Punjab poverty.[29] This fact made them take a very serious view of a social custom which prohibited women from sharing the work of their men. It was this custom which they felt could be substituted by the 'more progressive' western social norm. Comparing the two norms, British officials maintained in 1921:

> There is a vast waste of female labour, due primarily to custom and prejudice. In most other countries the proportion of female labour to the whole is high; while its efficiency is equal to the tasks performed; the contribution to the national dividend resulting from this forms an appreciable part of the whole. If there were in western countries a movement aiming at the exclusion of female labour for all except purely domestic tasks, that movement would endanger the whole economic fabric, and, if successful would involve those countries in ruin. The Punjab discards what in England and elsewhere is an absolutely necessary element in the maintenance of their civilization. The fact that there are tribes such as Brahmans and Rajputs which do not allow their womenfolk even to work in the fields is alone sufficient to explain their poverty. . . . In the course

> of generations the loss from the waste alone must have made material progress almost impossible. No European country could maintain its present standard of living without the assistance derived from female labour.[30]

The British officials' attempt to make 'deeply ingrained Indian minds' see the need for involving women in agricultural work by projecting their own western example of 'high present economic standards' was vastly frustrating. They confessed to experiencing 'great difficulty' in making Indians accept their reasoning and getting the desired results.[31]

IV. Marriage and Bride-price

The importance of women in the agrarian economy made marriage an acknowledged 'economic necessity'.[32] So much so that a man's inability to pay his revenue dues was put down to his unmarried status, since an '*akela adami*' (single man) was not expected to perform well agriculturally; and a widower was considered to be 'half paralysed'.[33]

Significantly, the so-called 'work qualities' of a prospective bride were looked for at the time of arranging marriages, the acknowledged requirement being, '*hath-paer ki mazboot honi chahiye, take khet-kivar ka kaam thik treh ho sake*'[34] (she should be physically strong, so that agricultural work can be performed well). The emphasis on these 'work qualities' also led them to disregard the girl's age, he,ight etc., with the result that the girl was quite frequently older and sometimes taller than the boy. This fact was made a virtue of and a local proverb eulogizing it maintained:

> *badi bahu bade bhag*
> *chhota bandra ghane suhag*[35]
>
> (An older or taller wife brings luck, as also a shorter or younger bridegroom.)

The important role played by women in the economy led to a wide acceptance of the prevalent custom of sale and purchase of brides among the economically hard-up peasantry. In the nineteenth century, except among a few better-off families, this custom was observed to have been universal among the agriculturist castes as well as the lower castes.[36] Among the lower castes bride-price was well signified in a local proverb:

> *nai kis ka bhai*
> *chhori bech leyava lugai*[37]
>
> (The *nai* [barber] is no one's friend, he sells his daughter to buy himself a wife.)

Although looked upon as a 'disgraceful custom' and admitted by Jats with a 'certain amount of apology and obvious sense of shame', it was a practice that was gaining ground everywhere in the first decade of the twentieth century.[38]

Regarding the price of brides, Malcolm Lyall Darling, one of the most distinguished of Punjab officials who made a thorough and comparative study of varied aspects of social life in different regions of Punjab, maintained that it rose steadily with the rise in prices:

> In the fifties a bride could be had for Rs. 50, but nowadays in neither hill nor plain can anything worth having be got for less than three or four hundred rupees, and a serious epidemic may considerably raise the price. In Rohtak, for instance, where in 1918 influenza carried off 10 percent of the people, the price rose from Rs. 500 to Rs. 2000. In Hissar, on the other hand, the prolonged drought of 1919–21 reduced it from Rs. 2000 to Rs. 500.[39]

In individual cases 'fancy prices' were paid, especially if the boy was handicapped in some way, or if he was considerably older or had an obvious defect of body or limb.[40]

It may be pointed out that payment of bride-price was one of the reasons why British officials denied that female infanticide existed in this region in any substantial way and offered other reasons for the low sex ratio of females. The situation was indeed apparently contradictory, especially as the official perception of bride-price conceived it as 'a compensation . . . for the family authority which was transferred to the husband'.[41] Similarly a recent article interprets bride-price as a 'compensatory payment to the family for the production loss they suffer on her departure'.[42] Yet, even this apparent economic worth did nothing to raise her status. In practice, bride-price was most common among the lower economic strata of agriculturists. It was this factor which was responsible for not elevating the custom to respectability. The middle-level agriculturist with some standing had to pay bride-price to marry his son (the bride generally came from the poorer families who charged a price) and gave a dowry to marry his daughter, as a better alliance within the caste was always sought.[43] No girl was allowed to marry outside the caste, the norm being '*Jat ki beti Jat ko*' (A Jat girl must marry a Jat). Since there were no recognized 'socially superior' clans as such, status was determined by the amount of land held, and in the arid Haryana region the coveted wish was to get daughters or sisters married where canal irrigation existed.[44] This combination of bride-price and dowry made the existence of females a financial drain. Those accepting bride-price were looked down upon for this very practice and consequently could hardly effect a change in the dominant attitude of the others towards women. In turn, they blamed the female species for being there at all, as a woman's existence meant bride-price and bride-price spelt ultimate shame to the family; izzat among the agriculturists scored over economics, even in financially deprived households. Females therefore meant drain—financial for some and moral and ethical for others. It is small wonder that bride-price even in its positive aspects could not represent high status for women in any real terms.

V. Widow-Remarriage or the Custom of *Karewa*

The agrarian needs which allowed bride-price also sanctified widow-remarriage. Like the former, this was also a feature which the agriculturist castes shared in common with the lower castes. However, the custom of widow-remarriage as followed here had special features of its own. Known as *karewa, karao*, or *chaddar andazi*, the custom was a throwback to the old Rig-vedic *niyog* (levirate marriage) which was prevalent in the geographical region of Haryana–Punjab and associated with the early Vedic Aryan settlements.[45] Karewa, a white sheet coloured at the corners, was thrown by the man over the widow's head, signifying his acceptance of her as his wife. This custom represented social consent for cohabitation. There could be certain variations.[46] For example, it could take the form of placing *churis* (glass bangles) on the widow's wrist in full assembly and sometimes even a gold *nath* (nose ring) in her nose and a red sheet over her head with a rupee tied in one of its corners. This could be followed by the distribution of *gur* (jaggery) or sweets. Significantly, this form of remarriage was not accompanied by any kind of religious ceremony, as no woman could be customarily married twice, that is, could go through the ceremony of *biah* (religious wedding). After karewa the widow merely resumed her jewels and coloured clothes which she had ceased to wear on her husband's death. So much so that sometimes mere cohabitation was considered sufficient to legitimize the relationship and it conferred all the rights of a valid marriage. However, for cohabitation to be accepted as remarriage it had to be cohabitation in the man's house. Mere visits to the woman were considered 'adulterous'.[47]

The Jats, as in other customs, led in the practice of karewa and other agriculturist castes (except the Rajputs) followed suit. Interestingly, among the Brahmins, the reports indicate that karewa was being followed.[48] Even in a far-flung district like Muzaffargarh, the Brahmins had declared their adherence to the Jat custom. The settlement officer of this district pointed out that there was scarcely a Brahmin there who had even the slightest knowledge of the Hindu law books or was acquainted with their names.[49] The Brahmins of this province, who were not a priestly class but were mostly landowners, consequently followed the dominant social custom of this region in preference to the sanskritic model of the other Brahmins who brooked no remarriage at all and upheld *sati* (widow immolation) instead. Among other Hindu castes, the 'low grade Khatris'[50] also followed this practice but others like the Bania and Kayastha did not do so, and among the Muslims nor did the Sayyads.[51] Castes that did not admit widow-remarriage were contemptuous of this practice and looked down upon those who practised it.[52]

The widespread acceptability of karewa is reflected in local proverbs:

aja beti lele phere
yo mergaya to aur bhotere[53]

(Come daughter get married, if this husband dies there are many more.)

Another one maintained:

ek kanya sabansar var[54]

(There are several bridegrooms available for one bride.)

Karewa, however, as a rule, was a levirate marriage in which the widow was accepted as wife by one of the younger brothers of the deceased husband; failing him the husband's older brother; failing him his agnatic first cousins, etc. In 1934, in the Ambala district there was also the case of a Jat who claimed validity of custom regarding karewa marriage with his widowed daughter-in-law.[55] The case was lost by the father-in-law, who then appealed to the Lahore High Court. The High Court also rejected it and maintained that the custom of karewa marriage between a Jat and his widowed daughter-in-law was invalid, 'being repugnant to the ideas of Jats'. However, this judgement did not apparently lay down a general rule of custom applicable to the entire province. In another case decided shortly afterwards in 1936, the Hoshiarpur district judge took a totally opposite view and held, on the evidence, that such a remarriage was valid by custom.[56] Significantly, it may be noticed that the customs could and were sought to be extended specially as they had come to have legal sanction. The father-in-law's claim to the karewa custom has to be seen as an attempt to retain the widow within the family for a variety of reasons (given later) ranging from control of property and of her sexuality to control of her options regarding marriage partners. The reigning ideology behind this control, recorded by E. Joseph, significantly laid down:

> A female, minor or adult, is always under guardianship, while single she is under the guardianship of her father, if he be dead, of other relatives, in the order given [all male members]. So too when married until her *muklawa*, when she comes under the guardianship of her husband; on his death until remarriage she is under the guardianship of his family, whether she be minor or major.[57]

Therefore, the widow's right as to whom she could marry was not only severely restricted, it could be settled only by her late husband's family. And although the widow could not be compelled to remarry, she was not free to marry without their consent. So complete was the control over the woman and on the question of her remarriage that it was freely admitted that the widow was often practically forced and made to yield to their wishes.[58] Any assertion to the contrary would be difficult to believe in a region which advocated:

zamin jor zoi ki
zor ghati hor ki[59]

(Land and wife can only be held through the use of force, when this fails they become another's.)

Karewa and the Question of Inheritance

The popularity of karewa among the overwhelming majority of land-owning classes emanated out of the need for retaining landed property within the family. The main reason for making the marriage arrangements inside the family was to transfer control of her deceased husband's land from the widow (who succeeded to a life estate in the absence of male lineal descendants) to his brother or to a patrilineal family member, because a widow who remarried lost all her rights to property, even if she married her husband's brother.[60] Remarriage therefore deprived her of even the limited right to land which she came to possess after her husband's death, that is, only a lifelong interest; ultimately the property passed to her husband's male line. In case she had children, her sons succeeded to the property and she had right only to suitable maintenance; her daughters and their issue had no right to inherit from the father. It was essential to deny the daughters any share in the inheritance in order to retain land within the immediate kinship group. The daughters were only entitled to maintenance and to be 'suitably betrothed and married'.[61]

However, even this limited right of the widow was seen as a menace, because she could claim a partition of the property on certain grounds, that is, when she could not secure the required maintenance.[62] But the onus of proving this was on her. This meant that the court either implicitly or explicitly took the position that the required maintenance was indeed being granted to her by her deceased husband's agnates. However, the fact that this view was contrary to reality was even acknowledged by the revenue officials. In their considered opinion the widow found it difficult to obtain her 'fair share of produce' as long as the holding remained undivided.[63] A separate possession meant that the widow could get it cultivated through someone else as she was customarily not allowed to undertake full agricultural operations herself. A popular proverb from Karnal maintained:

ikh ne bowen rand
aur paden sand[64]

(A widow may be able to sow sugar-cane, but it needs a strong man [literally a bull] to press out the cane.)

A separate possession also produced a fear, 'often well founded', that it would lead to an 'attempt to alienate' the property.[65] The widow could alienate the property, though not sell it, for her own maintenance, for her daughter's wedding or for payment of revenue, all the reasons dubbed as 'strict necessity'. That a lot of women had started to utilize this proviso can be seen from the constant appeals made to the Deputy Commissioner, protesting against widows who were accused of alienating their property 'without necessity'.[66]

This self-assertion by widows in taking control of the economic resources after their husbands' death must have assumed such a proportion that, for a variety of reasons, government action against it became essential. J.M. Douie, compiler of *The Punjab Land Administration Manual*, advised the revenue officials that the widow's attempts to partition the land 'should be disallowed'.[67] (The widow's right to control land had been legalized under the Land Revenue Act because after her husband's death she was held responsible for the payment of government revenue dues.) However, since legally such advice could not have held much weight, the only solution to the fast growing claims to partition was, according to official instruction, to be sought in 'a firm anchoring of the widow in remarriage.' This, the *Manual* instructed, could be the 'only satisfactory arrangement against which she had no appeal'.[68]

Strengthening Karewa: Colonial Perception and Policy

Such advice was an inevitable outcome of the colonial policy followed in Punjab, because of its economic, political and military importance, too well known to bear a recount here. The imperial government had, right from the beginning, adopted the 'preservation of village community' as a settled policy for Punjab, To this end it advocated 'co-hering tribes' (rather than 'their break up') through the operation of their customary law as an essential prerequisite for controlling Punjab.[69] The general argument of British officials was that the mass of the agricultural population in this province did not follow either the Hindu or the Muslim law. Therefore, a general code of tribal custom was prepared by the settlement officers, who at each settlement had compiled the *rivaj-i-am* (record of customs and rights), in consultation with the village headmen of each principal landowning tribe in the district; these being acknowledgedly 'men of most influential families in the village'. Consequently the customs of the landowning class in regard to civil matters like succession, alienation, marriage, tenure of land, adoption and the like came to be settled primarily by the Punjab customary law, which then became the first rule of decisions.[70] However, the British perception of these customs, which they also made legally binding, is significant. For karewa they held:

> . . . most officers conversant with this tract of country have entertained, in the existence *sub rosa* of a system of polyandry. This institution is probably the first stage in development of a savage people after they have emerged from a mere animal condition of promiscuity. It is the concomitant of female infanticide. . . . The family is the first organisation, when all things, including the wife are owned in common. The eldest brother is the head of the house, but the younger brothers have their rights, and the universal survival of the karewa custom of widow-remarriage among the Jats shows how the younger brother (though now it is not necessarily always the younger brother or any real brother) succeeds to the headship of the family on elder's death.[71]

In Punjab, the fundamental political interest of the British transcended their less well-defined concern for 'social progress'. This 'low level' of civilization as signified by karewa had to be retained because the British concern lay in strengthening the hold of the existing peasant society over land; its break-up was inevitable if the widow was allowed to have her way.

The apprehension regarding the danger of social disequilibrium in Haryana was sharper because this region, with its insecure agricultural conditions, had provided the best recruiting ground for the British Indian Army. For example, in World War I, this region had contributed one-fifth of the total recruitment from the whole of Punjab.[72] And although the karewa custom contributed significantly to the unceasing heavy recruitment (despite the insecurity of life and the equally heavy rate of mortality) the agricultural interests of the recruits' families could not be allowed to be jeopardized by the ever-growing number of widows' claims. This could prove to be very costly to the imperial government and not only unsettle its military recruitment, but also the social equilibrium upon which its rule in the state was founded.

Moreover, even economically, such a demand, if conceded, would have only added to the fragmentation and sub-division of holdings and consequently to the fast-growing smaller uneconomic holdings in this region, as elsewhere in Punjab,[73] which were posing a direct threat to the agricultural prosperity of the province and so to the collection of revenue. In fact, the fast-spreading problem of the fragmentation of landholdings was serious enough for the Viceroy to order an inquiry in June 1936.[74] This fact had also led to government attempts at consolidation of holdings, the results of which were not noticeably fruitful.[75] The growing demands of the widows in this socio-economic milieu combined with an ever-growing population dependent on agriculture, was certain to further compound the problem. It became necessary to issue instructions and give out administrative guidelines in this connection. The district officials were therefore instructed: 'Often a young widow will present a petition to the Deputy Commissioner for sanction to marry a man of her choice, but with such application he is wise to have nothing to do.'[76]

A woman's resistance to the peasant culture of remarriage which was designed to retain her within the family of her deceased husband was not allowed to surface. Petitions nevertheless continued to be made. Petitions were also made by widows, and even courts moved, to deny that karewa had taken place. This resistance shows that many peasant women perceived the karewa custom to be a repressive one. So common was this resistance that British officials noted in 1921 that criminal proceedings were most frequently resorted to by the deceased husband's brother by lodging a complaint under section 498 of the Indian Penal Code to counter the widow's attempts to escape by asserting that a marriage by karewa or chaddar andazi had taken place whereas it was firmly denied and challenged by the widow.[77] It was very difficult for a widow to prove the contrary for, as pointed out earlier, even cohabitation could be and was recognized as karewa. Once marriage or remarriage status was accepted, on no account could a Hindu woman claim release from it.[78] As against this, there was no limit to the number of wives a man could have either through *shadi* (a caste marriage) or by karewa. He could also expel his wife for unchastity through a practice called *tyag* (renunciation) which practically amounted to divorce, and also for change of religion which was said to automatically dissolve the marriage.[79] The customary law of the land, backed by the full force of the colonial administrators, safeguarded the landed property from a woman's possession. Interestingly, not allowing women to inherit property was a view which found a sympathetic and even an enthusiastic chord among many British officials. A curious parallel observation about the situation of women prevailing 'back home' as compared to that in Punjab discloses the ambivalent attitude of British officials towards women:

> . . . the proportion of females to males in England and Wales rises continuously from childhood to old age, indicative of the excessive care lavished on women in England qua women, and not merely qua child bearer. Social reformers may well stand aghast at the neglect of and the contempt for female life shown by all religious groups in the Punjab, but no less extensive, and, possibly fraught with serious consequences to the future of the race, is the excessive pampering of females in England. . .[80]

An attempt on their part to understand this 'great disproportion among females and males' resulted in the following conclusion:

> During the past half century there has been a steady tendency for females to acquire property and sums of money in their own right. Now, whereas, a man has through the force of tradition and social custom, a tendency to spend his money for the benefit of the woman, the woman has no traditional tendency to spend her money for the benefit of the man. The consequence is that, in enjoying the benefits of little comforts and luxuries, woman in England is steadily increasing her advantage over the man, and the effect of this process on the relative male and female mortality can hardly be negligible. In the Punjab the independent woman, i.e., the orphan daughter or widow, has under the customary law, only the right to maintenance, and she may never alienate the ancestral property except for necessity, the onus of proving which is put upon her.[81]

The 'dangers' of women inheriting and controlling property were evidently clear to those brought up in the British cultural milieu; they wanted no repetition of it in Punjab, The fact that the custom of karewa snatched away whatever little right of possession women in Haryana–Punjab had come to acquire as widows, was well known to them. They were fully aware of the nature and operation of this custom in relation to women. This can be seen from a perceptive observation of F. Cunningham, a British Barrister at Law; who compiled a draft gazetteer of Rohtak district in 1870–4. He wrote: '*Karewa* under these conditions may be called remarriage with reference to reasons affecting the women; but such unions often take place for causes which have regard to the men only.'[82] Widow-remarriage—a seemingly progressive feature—continued to be applauded by the British administrators. The practice, however, as it was encouraged to exist, merely reinforced the social ethos which safeguarded the land in the family, clan and community. The British administrators' own attitudes regarding female inheritance were closely identified with the primary concern of the colonial government which did not want to disturb the existing rural society of Punjab.

Widow-Remarriage: The Arya Samaj and the Brahminical Code

The Arya Samaj made its own contribution to the practice of karewa in this region. It provided a justification drawn from the most ancient Hindu texts and offered protection to those who accepted it. In actual practice, the Arya Samaj Jat *updeshiks* and *bhajniks* (preachers and singers) emphasized the Vedic derived niyog, that is, the levirate aspect of it, whereas widow-remarriage per se hardly formed a part of the programme they actually adopted. In fact, one of the major reasons for the popularity and acceptability of the Arya Samaj in this region was the legitimacy that it provided to this custom, which was looked down upon with great prejudice, and even horror, by the other upper-caste Hindus, especially by commercial castes. In fact the widow-remarriage programme of the Arya Samaj remained extremely restricted elsewhere in Punjab.[83] Among the followers of the Arya Samaj in Punjab, predominantly the commercial castes, a distinction was drawn between virgin widows and those widows who had lived with their husbands or had children, The remarriage of the latter evoked very strong opposition, and remained socially unacceptable to many of the Arya Samajis themselves. In Haryana alone where the Arya Samaj merely legitimized its peculiar form (karewa), could widow-remarriage be called a huge success.

The peasant ethos of Haryana-Punjab sanctified widow-remarriage for reasons of its own and even celebrated it by maintaining:

titar pankhi badli
bidhwa kajal rekh
wuh barse yue ghar kare
ya mari nahin bisekh[84]

(Just as a cloud shaped like a partridge feather means that it is going to rain, so a widow using *kajal* [kohl] or paying attention to her toilette means that she is going to remarry.)

This was in sharp contrast to the high-caste Hindus who under the brahminical code prohibited widow-remarriage completely and considered the children of such a marriage as illegitimate. They had instead adopted an extremely repressive system for widows which condemned them to a living hell. Such a state, especially among the child-widows, had led to a wide-scale social reform agitation in Bengal, Maharashtra and the south as a response to which the Widow Remarriage Act, XV of 1856 was passed by the imperial government which legalized widow-remarriage. For rural Punjab this Act had no significance, as a form of widow-remarriage was not only being observed but was also legally recognized under the customary law of the land operable in the courts. As such this Act made no difference. However, like the generally forced levirate marriage of the peasant culture which successfully kept landed property intact in the family and within the patrilineal clan, the Widow Remarriage Act also successfully retained patrilineal hold over property by taking away from the widow her limited right over it in case of remarriage.[85] Interestingly, the social reformers, whether the Arya Samajis in the north, or the others in the east or south of India, were unanimous in emphasizing the remarriage of child-widows or virgins and were also unanimous in keeping a studied silence where inheritance and property matters were concerned.

VI. 'Liberal' Attitudes?

The agrarian milieu of Haryana which necessitated widow-remarriage, with its own peculiar features, also imparted a somewhat flexible attitude and wide social acquiescence to certain emergent practices involving women. In the given geo-economic background (the adverse female sex ratio, the prevalence of bride-price with the wife as an agricultural-labour asset) emerged the concept of the woman being married to a family rather than to an individual. Translated in terms of hard reality this concept meant that two or three brothers would share a wife;[86] thus began a systematic and extensive sexual exploitation of women. In 1904, P.J. Fagan, a district-level British official observed: 'It is not uncommon among Jats and lower castes for a woman to be shared in common by several brothers, though she's recognised as the wife of only the eldest of them.'[87] M.L. Darling, writing about the prevalence of this custom in the 1920s and identifying it as 'polyandry', similarly observed that the latter was not 'unknown'.[88] However, this kind of sexual exploitation did not always go unchallenged and at least one criminal case of adultery came up in the early twentieth century in which the accused cited in his plea the existence of this social custom which allowed him sexual access to his brother's wife.[89] Cases of worse sexual exploitation were also known. E. Joseph, recording the customary law of Rohtak district, observed:

> In point of fact the girl is often older than the boy. This is not an infrequent source of trouble that comes to the courts. . . . Certain villages which need not be named, have the evil reputation of deliberately getting girls older than their boy husbands in order that the father of the latter may have illicit enjoyment of them.[90]

From the sexual point of view, the two cases cited earlier, fathers-in-law wanting to marry their widowed daughters-in-law, may be taken as attempts to legitimize an already existing relationship.[91]

An oft-repeated story of those days, popular even now,[92] not only reveals this sexual exploitation to be common knowledge but also its acceptance, albeit in a humorous and highly exaggerated manner. The story concerns a new bride who had four or five *jeths* and *devars* (older and younger brothers-in-law). All of them had free sexual access to her.

After 15 to 20 days of her marriage, the bride requested her mother-in-law to identify her husband from among them. Upon this the mother-in-law came out in the *gali* (narrow street) and started to howl loudly. When questioned, she replied: 'It's difficult for me to live in this house any more. I have been married for 40 years, yet even now I have never asked anyone to determine the identity of my husband. This bride of 15 days is already asking about hers.'

There were two other factors which seem to have provided grounds for the general acceptability of this custom. One was the emigration of men to seek work especially in the canal colonies (which offered better agricultural opportunities) as tenants or even as labourers and second, the wide-scale recruitment into the British Indian Army from this arid and famine-hit region. Both these factors meant that many married women had to live without their husbands for long stretches of time. On such occasions a man handed over his wife to his brother till he returned.[93] E. Joseph, the Deputy Commissioner and Settlement Officer of Rohtak district during 1905–10, writing about the 'liberal attitude' operating behind the acceptance of this practice, which also conveniently transferred the onus of desiring sexual favours on women, disclosed:

> A most respectable Jat of my acquaintance procured his son's resignation from the army because his wife could not be trusted alone, as he explained, all his younger sons were too small to assist in dealing with the difficulty.[94]

It was also considered a 'common practice' to beget children from a devar or jeth while the husband was away serving in the army.[95] This fact, a logical corollary of the sexually exploitative custom, had to be accepted in the rural society of the time. A popular local story is illustrative of this acceptance. The dialogues proceed as follows:

First man	:	After how many years have you come home?
Second man	:	After three years.
First man	:	And how old is your child?
Second man	:	Two years.
First man	:	How come . . .?
Second man	:	(mildly) Well I had sent home my *dhoti*.[96]

Such is the reason why despite severe war casualties among the pick of the population and the absence of so large a proportion of the able-bodied men from their homes, the birth rate was not affected.

The sexual exploitation of menial (low-caste) women by other agriculturists was a common feature which does not need much comment. However, interestingly, the difficulties experienced in obtaining a wife for the reasons explained above, led many agriculturists of this region to take wives from among the lower castes as well. Although it never became a norm as such nor was practised on a wide scale, the economically hard-up agriculturists were known to take recourse to it. For example, a Jat was stated to marry almost any woman he could.[97] Frequently these were women from the Chamar caste.[98] However, a faint pretence was kept that the girl was of his caste and an equally faint acceptance followed. A local belief maintains:

Jat ek samunder hai aur jo bhi dariya es
samunder mein patti hai woh samunder ki hi bun jati hai[99]

(The Jat is like an ocean and whichever river falls into this ocean loses its identity and becomes the ocean itself.)

The children of a Churhi or a Chamaran, whoever was accepted as a wife by a Jat, were called Jats though many times they were ridiculed as *churhi ke* or *chamaran ke.*[100] Such general social acceptance, despite derogatory references, is due to the fact that these social groups could not afford to, and indeed did not, attach undue importance to caste purity in case it was breached by the man; a woman, as pointed out earlier, was not allowed this freedom. This is aptly referred to in a local proverb:

beeran ki kai jaat[101]

(Women have no caste)

Moreover, within this subsistence economy the social practice was rationalized by maintaining that '*roti to bun jagi, naam to chul jaga, dono ka guzara ho jaga*'[102] (at least the food will be cooked; the family name will be carried on, both will somehow manage to live together). This practice of taking wives from lower castes was greatly frowned upon by British officials who declared it 'a kind of disreputable matrimonial agency'.[103] Given to applauding the 'magnificent physique' of the so-called superior agriculturist castes in agrarian and military professions, they actually bemoaned its biological 'deterioration' because of this practice.[104]

VII. Some Further Indices of the Low Status of Women

Clearly, in Haryana a woman had come to be recognized and coveted as an economic necessity though only as a part of a man's property, and she was equated with food, a house and animals. A local proverb from Rohtak showed this:

santhi chaoul, bhains dudh, ghar kulwanti nar,
chauthe tarang ki, bihist nishani char[105]

(Red rice, buffalo milk, a good woman in the house, and a horse to ride, these four are heavenly things.)

Women provided labour for the peasant household, as well as for cultivation and for animal husbandry, all the while operating inside the male-dominated norms of the purdah culture—a culture of secluding women.[106] This culture represented a spatial boundary between man and woman, and was visible in Haryana in the normal six inches to a yard long ghunghat for the woman. However, the peasant economy, in which women provided an indispensable source of labour and thus could not be kept secluded, accommodated it by allowing her to work 'shoulder to shoulder' with her man, but only in a ghunghat. Even the progressive Arya Samaj was not known (in this region) to preach against women observing ghunghat.[107]

The ghunghat culture, as perhaps somewhat distinct from the purdah culture, accepted and took for granted women's extreme labour without affording them any freedom. This attitude can be seen to be operating in other spheres as well. For example, in education, a region which had considered literacy to be useless ('*kala akshar bhains barobar*',[108] that is, lack of literacy), was slowly realizing the importance of education, but only for boys. For the women it maintained:

beerbanni ghar kibanni[109]

(A woman who remains at home adorns it.)

Generally used in reference to education, it emphasized that a woman should remain a housewife only and not jeopardize her position by stepping out of the house. Education therefore was looked upon with suspicion and was associated with an inevitable crumbling of the social structure.[110] Even the Arya Samaj which did a great deal for women's education in Punjab,[111] was quiet in its Haryana region. The Arya Samaj established Gurukuls but primarily for boys. The Kanya Pathshalas for girls were negligible in number and experienced a perennial shortage of both teachers and students.[112]

This social attitude also kept women away from any decision-making process whether it was at home or in the wider sphere of *jaat-biradari* (caste-brotherhood), or in the village itself. At home they were never consulted even in matters of buying or selling of milch cattle, though cattle tending was generally an exclusive work domain of women.[113] And although women put in an equal if not larger share of work in the earning of money, its expenditure was the special and exclusive reserve of men, and was dictated to the minutest detail. An Ambala proverb maintained:

lekha mawari dhianda
bakhshisha lakh laketi[114]

(Even if one gives away lakhs in charity, a wife and a daughter must be held accountable.)

All that a woman had control over was merely a few rupees which her visiting relatives might have gifted to her.[115] Summing up this social milieu, the compiler of local customs in this region maintained:

> . . . in the present phase of customary law, especially among the Hindu Jat tribes, there is a strong disinclination to admit any independent power of the wife even over movables, however acquired by her, apart from the wishes of her husband, who generally exercises an unfettered control over her estate.[116]

The customary law prevailing among the agriculturists regarded the wife and anything associated with her, whether her ornaments or her earnings, if they existed, as the property of her husband, about which she had no independent voice at all.

The attitude of keeping women secluded from all decision making, as reflected at home, was also projected outside. The women were never a part of the caste or the village *panchayat* (village council) although certain issues relating to them were frequently brought to it for decision making. These matters concerned women who had made runaway marriages with other caste men or had simply run away with someone belonging to their own village.[117] Such self-assertion broke too many social norms and customs and was never accepted. The women were also not allowed to enter the village *chaupal*, that is, the place where the panchayat customarily sat. The guarding of the chaupal as forbidden ground for women symbolized their complete seclusion, subordination and inferiority.

VIII. Conclusion

From the above account emerges a picture of Haryanavi peasant women perhaps best exemplified in their high visibility as the full working partners of men—but only in a ghunghat. The reality of ghunghat culture exposes the apparent contradiction in the co-existence of indices of high status and of low status for women in the region. The indices of high status like bride-price, widow-remarriage, equal economic work partnership and a 'permissive' sexual climate, all emerge as customs evolved, dictated and enforced by the dominant peasantry of this region to suit its own peculiar socio-economic needs. They hardly had any relation to the needs of women. Therefore, in reality these indices were bereft of all validity as markers of high status and value. The customs encouraged by the British administrative policies, usually interpreted as indices of high status when combined with the discriminating practices also already operating, that is, the low-status indices, together became responsible for lowering the status of women in the colonial period. However, even within this tightly controlled peasant culture, as aided and abetted by the colonial government, occurred women's self-assertion and protest against a system in which they shared the work but not its fruits. This can be seen in the widow's determination to hold on to her limited right over landed property and the challenge which the women posed to her marriage or to her remarriage in its levirate form. Women's perception of peasant customs as repressive also exposes the claims of high-status indices. So outwardly the women of Haryana who have been projected as equal work companions of men and whose role has been celebrated by the British administrators, continued to remain men's inferior and subordinate counterparts—their status not above that of unpaid agricultural labourers.

It is perhaps needless to emphasize that once the socio-economic forces changed, the cultural ethos and the resultant customs and attitudes which these forces had moulded and determined also changed. This can be seen quite clearly in the wide-scale changes which have occurred in Haryana in the post-colonial period which have catapulted this region from a backward subsistence-level economy to the second richest state in India in the wake of the Green Revolution. These changes have had deep rooted socio-cultural effects especially in relation to women, in either completely or partially diluting many of the customs and social attitudes described above, in retaining or sharpening many others, or in introducing new ones. Apart from the wide-scale changes in the socio-economic sphere the role of the independent Indian state may also be underlined. Just as the colonial state's policies had selectively reinforced social norms and customs, the post-independence state policies have had a revolutionizing effect on rural society. A single example, the introduction of the Hindu Code Bill of 1956, is illustrative.

Two of its provisions had a direct bearing on Haryana's rural society. One was the Hindu Succession Act which gave equal right of succession to male and female heirs and the second was the divorce clause which allowed Hindu women for the first time the right to seek divorce on a variety of grounds. The effects of these acts, which reversed the hitherto carefully maintained traditions and customs of society, need to be studied in the framework of wider socio-economic changes. Briefly speaking, their effects can be seen, on the one hand, in the violent reaction of a greatly strengthened patriarchal society forging newer weapons for the social control of women involving even physical violence and bloodshed, and on the other hand, in the greater intensification of women's resistance seen, apart from other evidence of self-assertion, in the large influx of court cases involving inheritance, property and divorce. An understanding of the post-colonial period would require a separate study, which I propose to undertake later. Such a study alone would determine the extent and direction of change in various spheres involving women that is visible in the Haryana of today as compared to what existed in the colonial period.

Notes

This is a substantially revised version of my article, 'Socio-economic Dimensions of Certain Customs and Attitudes: Women of Haryana in the Colonial Period', *Economic and Political Weekly*. I wish to thank Uma Chakravarti, Sudesh Vaid and Kumkum Sangari for suggesting certain points for elaboraton.

1. The agriculturist castes of Haryana, as notified under the Punjab Alienation of Land Act, 1901, were: Jat, Rajput, Pathan, Sayyed, Gujar, Ahir, Biloch, Ror, Moghal, Mali, Taga, Saini, Chauhan, Main, Gaud Brahmin and Qoreshi.
2. For the concept and features of a 'dominant caste', see M.N. Srinivas, 'The Dominant Caste in Rampura', *American Anthropologist*, 61 (Feb. 1959), pp. 1–16. M.N. Srinivas specifically mentions Jats as the 'dominant caste' in Punjab-Haryana in his *Caste and Modern India and Other Essays* (Bombay: Asia Publishing House, 1962), p. 90.
3. For a detailed discussion on 'Jat dominance' in Haryana and for the different sources consulted, see Prem Chowdhry, 'Jat Domination in South-East Punjab: Socio-Economic Basis of Jat Politics in a Punjab District', *Indian Economic and Social History Review*, 19, nos. 3 & 4 (Oct.–Dec. 1983), pp. 325–46.
4. For details, see Prem Chowdhry, 'The Advantages of Backwardness: Colonial Policy and Agriculture in Haryana', *Indian Economic and Social History Review*, 23, no. 3 (Oct.–Dec. 1986), pp. 236–88.
5. *Rohtak District Gazetteer, 1910*, vol. 3 A (Lahore, 1911), p. 68.
6. Calculated from the Board of Economic Inquiry, *The Size and Distribution of Agricultural Holdings in the Punjab* (Lahore, 1925), p. 16.
7. Jainarayan Verma, *Haryanavi Lokoktiyan: Shastriye Vishaleshan* (Delhi: Adarsh Sahitya Prakashan, 1972), p. 123.
8. Ibid., p. 96.
9. Ibid., p. 30. The birth of a daughter was regarded as the equivalent of a decree of Rs 2000 against her father. See M.L. Darling, *The Punjab Peasant*

in Prosperity and Debt, 2nd ed. (1925; rpt. New Delhi: Manohar Book Service, 1978), p. 5.

10. For details of female–male sex ratio, see *Census of India: Punjab, 1931*, vol.17, pt. I, Report, p. 157.
11. The British officials agreed that among Jats, especially the Sikh Jats and Rajputs, female infanticide had been widely prevalent at the time of annexation of the province, but by 1901, it had dwindled to insignificant numbers. By 1931, it was confined to some individual families or groups of families which, according to them, did not influence the sex ratio as such. See *Census of India: Punjab, 1931*, ibid., p. 154.
12. For details of these factors and other contributory reasons, see *Census of India: Punjab, 1931*, ibid., p. 156.
13. Ratio of females per thousand males in different provinces of British India in 1931:

    Punjab: 831; North West Frontier Provinces: 843; United Provinces: 906; Bihar and Orissa: 909; Bengal: 924; Madras: 1025; Bombay: 909; Central Provinces: 1000; Central India Agency: 948; Rajputana: 908. Although the proportion of the sexes was not uniform in different parts of Punjab or in the different castes (for example, the proportion of females among Jats had always been lower than among other castes), by and large the figures given for the whole of Punjab correspond to the detailed figures available for the different districts of Haryana. Source: *Census of India: Punjab, 1931*, ibid., p. 159. For the exact number of females per thousand males in different districts of Haryana, see sub-table no. 1, p. 163.
14. W.E. Purser and H.C. Fanshawe, *Report on the Revised Land Revenue Settlement: Rohtak District, 1873–79* (Lahore, 1880), p. 65; hereafter *Revised Land Revenue Settlement, Rohtak.*
15. *Rohtak District Gazetteer, 1910*, p. 96.
16. R. Maconachie, ed. *Selected Agricultural Proverbs of the Punjab* (Delhi: Imperial Medical Hall Press, 1870), p. 264.
17. *Census of India: Punjab, 1931*, p. 217.
18. Darling, *Punjab Peasant*, p. 35.
19. *Revised Land Revenue Settlement, Rohtak*, p. 53.
20. Darling, *Punjab Peasant*, p. 35.
21. Ibid., p. 33.
22. *Census of India: Punjab, 1931*, p. 217.
23. Ibid., p. 217.
24. Ibid.
25. Darling, *Punjab Peasant*, p. 35. See also *The Settlement Report of the Ambala District*, 1893 (Lahore, 1893), p. 12.
26. *Rohtak District Gazetteer, 1910*, p. 77.
27. *Census of India: Punjab, 1931*, p. 217.

28. See Rushbrook William, Director, Central Bureau of Information, Govt. of India, *India in 1921–22* (Calcutta, Govt. Printing, 1922), p. 222.
29. *Census of India: Punjab and Delhi, 1921*, vol. 15, pt. I, Report, p. 363. Also see, *India in 1929–30* (Calcutta, 1931), p. 117.
30. *Census of India: Punjab and Delhi, 1921*, p. 363.
31. *India in 1929–30*, p. 119.
32. Darling, *Punjab Peasant*, p. 53.
33. Ibid., p. 53.
34. Personal interview with R.M. Hooda, Rohtak, 1 June 1986. Born in 1933, village Makrauli-Kalan, Rohtak Dist., a graduate from Jat College Rohtak (BA, LLB) R.M. Hooda has been practising law since 1962 at the district level. He has ancestral land, 4–5 acres, in the village.
35. Verma, *Haryanavi Lokoktiyan*, p. 43. The fact of the wife being older than the husband also arose out of levirate marriages, described later on, in which a much older widow married her *devar* (husband's younger brother), who could be younger than her by four to ten years.
36. Darling, *Punjab Peasant*, p. 49.
37. Shanker Lal Yadav, *Haryana Pradesh Ka Loksahitya* (Allahabad: Central Book Agency, 1960), p. 423.
38. *Rohtak District Gazetteer, 1910*, p. 85.
39. Darling, *Punjab Peasant*, p. 50.
40. *Rohtak District Gazetteer, 1910*, p. 91.
41. W.M. Rattingan, *A Digest of Civil Law for the Punjab Chiefly Based on the Customary Law as at Present Ascertained*, revised by Harbans Lal Sarin and Kundan Lal Pandit, 2nd ed. (1880; rpt. Allahabad: The University Book Agency, 1966), p. 737.
42. For an analytical study of bride-price and its socio-economic aspects, see Indira Rajaraman, 'Economics of Bride Price and Dowry', *Economic and Political Weekly* 18, no. 8 (19 Feb. 1983), pp. 275–9.
43. For details of similar cases in Gujarat, see Alice Clark, 'Limitation on Female Life Chances in Rural Central Gujarat', *Indian Economic and Social History Review*, 20, no. 1 (March 1983), pp. 1–25.
44. *Revised Land Revenue Settlement, Rohtak*, p. 49.
45. Niyog was a practice of levirate marriage. Later, as during the Mahabharata times, niyog came to signify cohabitation by the wife with men other than her husband under certain specific conditions like impotency of the husband and the 'moral' and 'religious duty' to beget sons to continue the family line. See, for instance, the case of Kunti.
46. For details, see C.L Tupper, *The Punjab Customary Law* (Calcutta: Govt. Printing, 1881), vol. 2, pp. 93, 123; see also E. Joseph, *Customary Law of the Rohtak District, 1910* (Lahore: Govt. Printing, 1911), p. 45.
47. Joseph, *Customary Law of Rohtak*, p. 46.

48. *Karnal District Gazetteer, 1976* (Chandigarh, 1976), p. 85.
49. Rattingan, *A Digest of Civil Law*, p. xvii.
50. *Census of India: Punjab and Delhi, 1911*, vol. 17, pt. I, Report, p. 219.
51. *Karnal District Gazetteer, 1976*, p. 85.
52. *Rohtak District Gazetteer, 1910*, p. 85. All those who were interviewed for this article also confirmed this.
53. *Revised Land Revenue Settlement, Rohtak*, p. 53. Generally said in relation to the Jats, this proverb highlights the social ease about widow-remarriage.
54. Verma, *Haryanavi Lokoktiyan*, p. 43.
55. Rattingan, *A Digest of Civil Law*, p. 82.
56. Ibid. Nothing more is known about this case.
57. Joseph, *Customary Law of Rohtak*, pp. 54–5. Until puberty a child-bride stayed on with her natal family; *muklawa*, which customarily took place several years after the wedding ceremony, was the entry and establishment of the wife in her husband's home when the marriage was consummated.
58. Ibid., p. 45.
59. Maconachie, *Agricultural Proverbs*, p. 280. This proverb is from Kangra, but according to R. Maconachie it revealed 'a universal sentiment' of Punjab.
60. *Rohtak District Gazetteer, 1910*, p. 90. In certain areas and among specific agricultural castes of Haryana and Punjab different forfeiture customs applied. The customary norm which was to be operative in a particular case had to be decided by the court, on the basis of the custom applicable to the concerned parties. In any case the final result was the same, since the customary law prevailing amongst agricultural castes of Punjab regarded the wife's personal property as merged with that of the husband; he was also deemed entitled to all the wife's earnings and even her ornaments. In other words, the woman both by marriage and by remarriage lost all control over moveable and immoveable property. See Rattingan, *A Digest of Civil Law*, pp. 204, 427, 747.
61. *Hissar Dist. Gazetteer, 1907*, vol. 2 A (Lahore, 1907), p. 229.
62. Joseph, *Customary Law of Rohtak*, pp. 136–7.
63. Ibid., p. 40.
64. Maconachie, *Agricultural Proverbs*, p. 253.
65. J.M. Douie, *The Punjab Land Administration Manual*, 2nd ed. (1908; rpt. Chandigarh: Govt. of Punjab, 1971), pp. 270–1.
66. Joseph, *Customary Law of Rohtak*, pp. 70–1.
67. Douie, *Punjab Land Administration*, pp. 270–1.
68. Ibid.
69. Tupper, *Punjab Customary Law*, vol. 1, pp. 17–19.
70. Ibid., vol. 2, pp. 86–8, 99–100.
71. *Rohtak District Gazetteer, 1910*, p. 88.

72. M.S. Leigh, *The Punjab and the War* (Lahore: Govt. Printing, 1922), pp. 61–2.
73. See Inquiry conducted by M.L. Darling, Financial Commissioner of Punjab, dated 3 June 1936, *Darling Papers* (South Asian Centre, Cambridge), Box 5, F. No. 1.
74. Ibid. See letter of Laithwait, Private Secretary to the Viceroy, 3 June 1936. The village surveys undertaken by the Punjab Board of Economic Inquiry 1920–40, also showed that in seven out of eight villages, in different districts of this region, the average area per owner had decreased noticeably in the last 30 years.
75. Darling, *Punjab Peasant*, pp. 240–1, 251–3.
76. *Rohtak District Gazetteer, 1910*, p. 90.
77. *Census of India: Punjab and Delhi, 1921*, p. 244.
78. Joseph, *Customary Law of Rohtak*, pp. 40–1. See also *Gurgaon District Gazetteer, 1910* (Lahore, 1911), p. 58.
79. Joseph, *Customary Law of Rohtak*, pp. 35, 40.
80. *Census of India: Punjab and Delhi, 1921*, p. 234.
81. See views of Col. Forster, Director of Public Health, Punjab, in f.n., ibid., p. 234.
82. Cited in *Rohtak District Gazetteer, 1883–84* (Calcutta, n.d.), p. 51.
83. For details, see Kenneth W. Jones, *Arya Dharma: Hindu Consciousness in Nineteenth Century Punjab* (Delhi: Manohar Book Service, 1976), pp. 218–19.
84. Maconachie, *Agricultural Proverbs*, p. 46.
85. For the effects of customary law and Hindu law on widows and the remarriage question, see Lucy Carroll, 'Law, Custom and Statutory Social Reform: The Hindu Women's Remarriage Act of 1856', *Indian Economic and Social History Review*, 20, no. 4 (Oct.–Dec. 1983), pp. 363–89.
86. Darling, *Punjab Peasant*, p. 51. K.L. Rathi also confirmed the 'sharing of women among brothers' to be a 'common phenomenon' in the 1920s. He cited several cases in different villages in which there was only one married brother, but other brothers had free access to his wife. (Personal interview with K.L. Rathi, New Delhi, 24 May 1986. Born in 1912, village Rajlugarhi, Sonepat, K.L Rathi is currently practising law in the Supreme Court. His large joint family had been in possession of 100 bighas of land.) R.M. Hooda was also of the same opinion. He saw the stark poverty of the region as responsible for this practice (personal interview with R.M. Hooda).
87. *Hissar District Gazetteer, 1904* (Lahore, 1908), p. 65.
88. Darling, *Punjab Peasant*, p. 51.
89. *Rohtak District Gazetteer, 1910*, p. 88. Verdict given not known.
90. Joseph, *Customary Law of Rohtak*, p. 19.

91. R.M. Hooda also confirmed that this practice was widespread in the past. He, however, put the onus on the 'inability of the young immature husband to satisfy his fully physically mature wife'. According to him there were always some women who protested against the sexual demands of their fathers-in-law. Such women, he commented, were generally 'packed-off' to the parents—an act which was considered to be a matter of 'ultimate shame' for the natal family of the woman in question (personal interview with R.M. Hooda).
92. Personal interview with Smt. Chhotu Devi, village Dujjana, Rohtak district, 6 June 1986. Born in 1921, Chhotu Devi's late husband was a big landowner in Dujjana.
93. Darling, *Punjab Peasant*, p. 51.
94. *Rohtak District Gazetteer, 1910*, see f.n., p. 88.
95. Personal interview with R.M. Hooda.
96. Personal interview with Smt. Shanti Devi, Delhi, 9 June 1986. Born in 1921, Sonepat, Shanti Devi married a soldier who rose to the rank of a colonel in the Indian Army. A *dhoti* is a length of cloth worn as a lower garment by men.
97. Darling, *Punjab Peasant*, p. 51,
98. Joseph, *Customary Law of Rohtak*, p. 60. According to R.M. Hooda, low-caste women, especially from among the Chamars, worked shoulder to shoulder with the Jats in the fields. This led to 'sexual promiscuity' due to the innumerable opportunities for close physical proximity. Because of this a large number of children among the Chamars came to be fathered by Jats and an equally large number among Jats by the Chamars. This fact also led many Jats to take wives from among the Chamars. According to Hooda, this practice continues to this day (personal interview with R.M. Hooda). E. Joseph, the British Settlement Officer of Rohtak district, also mentions a case brought to his notice in which a Jat woman was physically involved with a Chuhra (menial), and she was thrown out of the house for this reason. See Joseph, *Customary Law of Rohtak*, p. 42.
99. Personal interview with K.L. Rathi.
100. Personal interview with Shamsher Singh, Rohtak, 23 May 1986; a Jat agriculturist, Shamsher Singh is the owner of 12½ bighas of good cultivable land in Haryana.
101. Verma, *Haryanavi Lokoktiyan*, p, 120.
102. Personal interview with Shamsher Singh.
103. *Census of India: Punjab and Delhi, 1911*, vol. 17, pt. I, Report, p. 216.
104. Darling, *Punjab Peasant*, p. 51.
105. *Land Revenue Settlement, Rohtak*, p. 54.
106. For details of purdah culture, see Uma Chakravarti, 'Pativrata', *Seminar*, no. 318 (Feb. 1986), pp. 17–20.

107. Personal interview with K.L. Rathi.
108. Verma, *Haryanavi Lokoktiyan*, p. 46.
109. Ibid., p. 46.
110. *Karnal District Gazetteer*, p. 87.
111. Kenneth W. Jones, *Arya Dharma*, pp. 107–8, 215–19. For the nature of education imparted to women by the Arya Samaj, see Madhu Kishwar, 'Arya Samaj and Women's Education: Kanya Mahavidalya, Jallandar'. Review of women studies in *The Economic and Political Weekly*, 21, no. 17 (26 April 1986), pp. 9–24.
112. Personal interview with K.L. Rathi.
113. Personal interview with R.M. Hooda.
114. Maconachie, *Agricultural Proverbs*, p. 209.
115. Personal interview with R.M. Hooda.
116. W.M. Rattingan, *A Digest of Civil Law*, p. 747.
117. Significantly, no marriage alliance was possible in the same village and consequently such cases were greatly frowned upon (personal interview with R.M. Hooda).

8

Silencing Heresy*

Gauri Viswanathan

Feminist Struggle and Religious Dissent

Pandita Ramabai (1858–1922), Christian convert and renowned social reformer, lived a life that was a prototype of feminist aspiration to succeeding generations of Indian women, but to her own generation her career appeared confusing, inconsistent and even contradictory. As a scholar of Hinduism who had profound quarrels with its philosophical premises, particularly with regard to women, and later as a Christian convert who rebelled against Christian dogma, Ramabai seemed always to be outside the system of which she was ostensibly a part. The travails of her early life reinforce this impression.

Born in 1858 to an upper-caste Chitpavan Brahmin family of Maharashtra, she survived a series of deaths in her immediate family, including the deaths of her parents, sister, brother, and husband, with a resilience steeled by her determination to turn misfortune into salvation for herself and other similarly afflicted women. (Years later, in 1921, she was to lose her only child Manorama, whose death would soon be followed by her own in 1922.) A peripatetic Sanskrit scholar for much of her early life, Ramabai's years of pilgrimage through the length and breadth of India mirrored the tragic rootlessness of her orphaned status, culminating eventually in her happy though brief intercaste marriage, then early widowhood, and finally espousal of women's causes—especially the plight of child widows—as her own personal mission. If, over the years, her life has tended to inspire hyperboles, such as A.B. Shah's extravagant description of her as 'the greatest woman produced by modern India and one of the greatest Indians in all history', such high praise is undoubtedly prompted by her achievement as an exceptionally learned woman and outspoken champion of women's rights and social reform.[1]

One of the few women of her time whose voice found its way into male-controlled public discourse, Ramabai quickly shot to fame as a passionate and enthusiastic spokeswoman for the amelioration of women's status in Hindu society. Publicly honoured by the Sanskrit scholars of Calcutta as a 'Pandita', or learned woman, she is nonetheless better known for influential works like *Morals for Women* (1882) and *The High Caste Hindu Woman* (1888), which are devastating critiques of Hindu patriarchy and the circumscribed lives to which upper-caste women were doomed. These diatribes earned her the wrath of orthodox sections of the Hindu public and the admiration of modernizing elites and social reformers. Both works express Ramabai's extreme disillusionment with the religion of her birth, particularly the false views of sublime philosophy that, to some extent, western Orientalism had helped promote. She importuned women in the west to resist the seductive subtleties of Hindu philosophy and resolutely look beyond them to unmask the thralldom in which Hindu women were held.

> I beg of my Western sisters not to be satisfied with the looking on the outside beauties of the grand philosophies, and not to be charmed with the long and interesting discourse of our educated men, but to open the trapdoors of the great monuments of the ancient Hindu intellect, and enter into the dark cellars where they will see the real working of the philosophies which they admire so much. There are thousands of priests and men, learned in the sacred lore, who are the spiritual rulers and guides of our people. They neglect and oppress the widows and devour widows' houses. . . . Thousands upon thousands of young widows and innocent children are suffering untold misery and dying helpless every year throughout the land, but not a philosopher or Mahatma has come out boldly to champion their cause and to help them. . . . Let not my Western sisters be charmed with the books and poems they read. There are many hard and bitter facts we have to accept and feel. All is not poetry with us. The prose we have to read in our lives is very hard. It cannot be understood by our learned brothers and comfortable sisters of the West.[2]

Refusing to be intimidated by accusations that such remarks merely confirmed the colonialist and missionary criticism of Hinduism's moral bankruptcy, Ramabai directed her ire against the guardians of a priestly tradition who obscured what she called the 'prose' of Hinduism's social hierarchy by turning it into a 'poetry' of refined moral sensibility.[3] Her disgust with Hinduism over its treatment of women made it impossible for her to accept religion as an exclusively philosophical system. This was an attitude to religion that would stay with her even when she had formally renounced Hinduism; even Christian missionaries never fully appreciated how repugnant she found a purely philosophical approach to religion. Thinking they had a better chance in winning her over by appealing to her logic and intellect, they turned to a view of Christianity as philosophy rather than historical revelation. In the long run, this approach bore consequences detrimental to their own interests.

Nor could Ramabai ever see religious devotion as purely personal salvation or search for solace in light of the ideological deployment of such a notion of religion for rationalizing women's subordination. *The High Caste Hindu Woman*, for instance, meticulously takes apart the various philosophical underpinnings of Hinduism and shows how they have succeeded in maintaining the low status of women in Indian society, such as propagating 'the popular belief among high-caste women that their husbands will die if they should read or should hold a pen in their fingers'.[4]

The path to Ramabai's rupture with Hinduism, however, was by no means a straightforward one, nor did her conversion to Christianity immediately follow her disillusionment with Hinduism. Attracted briefly while in Calcutta to reformist organizations like the Brahmo Samaj and the Prarthana Samaj, which had a practical agenda but were still focused on ridding Hinduism of outdated superstitions and rituals, Ramabai found that she could make her most enduring contributions not to debate and disputation but, rather, to the social welfare of women. That brought her back to her own native Maharashtra, where she revived a number of contacts with people active in establishing institutions for the benefit of women. She even appeared before the Hunter Education Commission in 1882 to offer detailed recommendations for the improvement of female education. The momentum for reform certainly grew after her arrival in Maharashtra, but not quickly enough. Her plans to start a home and school for child widows and child wives in Poona received little support, and she was driven by a desire to go abroad to seek wider assistance from sympathetic organizations in the west.

While in Poona, she came in contact with Sister Geraldine, who had come to India from an English missionary order at Wantage, the Community of St Mary the Virgin. There were other missionaries from the same order in Poona who saw, in Ramabai, an eager and alert young woman intent on learning as much as she could about Christianity. Ironically, in these first few encounters with the missionaries, Ramabai's openness to Christian teaching came about primarily because she was interested in learning English in order to promote the education of women. With the missionaries' encouragement, Ramabai left for England on 20 April 1883 with her young daughter Manorama and, on her arrival there, was received by the sisters of the Wantage order, who welcomed her into St Mary's Home. Within five months of her arrival in England, Ramabai received baptism along with her daughter.

The simplicity of this chronology, however, does not come near to revealing the complex relationship Ramabai had to both Christianity and the missionaries in England. Some sense of this is already apparent in her initial interest in Christianity for pragmatic reasons, but the complexity extended to profound conflicts with Protestantism's position in England and the doubts that it engendered in her about the promise of Christian liberty offered by the scriptures, a promise that she found vitiated by the hierarchical government in which it was deeply mired. After all, it was the gender hierarchy of Hinduism that alienated her from the religion of her birth. Though Ramabai claimed she had no intention of converting to Christianity or any other religion at the time she went abroad, she had already begun to turn her back on Hinduism, decrying its cruel and heartless attitude to women. Yet when she joined the Wantage sisters and accepted their baptism, she discovered that the Christianity they propagated gave her little room to develop the sensibilities and spiritual inclinations that drove her flight from Hinduism.

Critical representations of Ramabai's feminism have tended to obscure the depth and intensity of her own spiritual struggle, either glossing over it as an incidental aspect of her feminism or as the instrumental medium through which she expressed her critique of Hindu patriarchy. Her anguished search for a personal God who is also a source of justice and love rarely finds a place in accounts of her battles with the Maharashtrian elite society. These accounts also invariably omit her protracted effort to define a conception of divinity that satisfied her craving for interpretive freedom. Ramabai's spirituality is accorded relevance only to the extent that it illuminates her protest against brahmanical ritualism and codification of women's social roles.

Receiving even less critical attention is the fact that Ramabai's developing religious sensibility enabled her also to critique the philosophical contradictions of British colonialism. Ramabai's search for a moral and theological framework of social critique did not merely serve her immediate purposes in disputing the gender disparities of brahmanism, but also provided her a point of entry into a devastating analysis of British colonialism. Her growing distance from the Trinity and other focal points of Anglican doctrine was compounded by her perception that other religious groups like Jews, Nonconformists, Wesleyans, Congregationalists, and Methodists were left outside the Anglican fold as decisively as were colonial subjects. That she was able to attain this insight through a questioning of the theological inconsistencies in British Christianity—even as she affirmed her own faith in Christianity independently of the pressures of the English church—places her critique of colonialism uniquely in the framework of both Indian nationalism and English religious dissent.

It would be a mistake to regard Ramabai's Christian conversion as motivated entirely by assimilationist motives or to suggest that she was essentially rejecting her own cultural background in an act of identification with Western traditions of thought. Her learned readings in the religious literature of those who colonized her country helped her to see the divide between two possible meanings of religion as the source of cultural and national identity on the one hand and, on the other, as universal moral value. She reached startling insights about the distinctions between these meanings in a long and fractious correspondence with Sister Geraldine, her chief mentor in England. At one point, warned by the missionary that she was in danger of forfeiting divine grace through her arrogant questioning, Ramabai retorted that 'the door of the Universal Church of God is not shut against me, and I believe the Universal, the Holy Catholic Church is not confined within the walls of the Anglican Church'. Her response disaggregates religion from political, national institutions,[5] even as it also seeks out a subjective location for belief beyond the circumscribed world of Anglican doctrine. And though her use of the term 'Catholic Church' might lead one to conclude she was still narrowly focused on interpreting religion in institutional terms, the context of the passage as well as the repetition of the word 'Universal' suggest that she had a metaphorical and expansive understanding of Catholicism as an analytical concept signifying unity, as opposed to the divisions that produced institutions historically ranged against each other. This is further apparent in her attempt to detach religion from all forms of territorial associations, whereby 'Catholic' and 'universal' become interchangeable terms: 'Baptism and the solemn oath which we take before GOD do not belong exclusively to one person or to one church with particular belief or customs. They are Catholic, i.e., universal.'[6]

In her own critical practice, by which we must understand both her writing and her conversion, Ramabai further drove a wedge between these two ways of conceiving religion and, by converting, asserted a moral scale of values independent of the cultural systems of both her native and adopted religions. The warning issued to Ramabai by the missionary sisters 'against making . . . a self-chosen religion' reminds one that conversion is not necessarily a mode of assimilation to a predetermined reality, identity or system of thought.[7] Rather, conversion is a dynamic process that *creates* the ideal system to which the convert aspires. The self-styled construction of such a system is precisely what renders it heretical, and conversion's instrumentality in producing heresy marks it off dramatically from assimilationist goals.

In the absence of a perspective that accepts religious dissent as resistance not only to dogmatic interpretations but also the political structures that support them, Ramabai's conversion to Christianity is invariably written off as the source of a divided consciousness that alienated her from the nationalist stirrings of her fellow Indians. If Ramabai was considered a disloyal Indian by her Hindu peers because she converted, that impression has not been substantially countered by subsequent critical commentaries, which focus on her conversion as the axis along which she realigned herself with a colonialist agenda for women's reform. First, one will have to be deeply sceptical about the primary source for such a charge, which happens in this case to be missionary records. These reveal that Ramabai was clearly being trained, in true filtration style, to take up the task begun by missionaries in redeeming Hindu widows from their situation of destitution and social disgrace. Yet for this reason it is important to fragment and disperse the monumentality of the missionary archives in order to locate the dissonant voice of the subject herself. Does Ramabai see herself participating in a colonial reconstructionist scheme? Does her conversion signal her acceptance of missionary objectives for Indian women? Or does she place her conversion in the service of other objectives that, although focused on ameliorating women's position, did not necessarily partake of the missionaries' agenda for reform?

Although Ramabai's spiritual battles may have appeared to culminate in her conversion to Christianity in 1883, they never ceased, even with her apparent discovery of a more satisfying religious ethic. Her religious conversion was less a turning point than an intermediate stage in her pursuit of a moral goal that she believed Hinduism obscured by its denial of parity to women. Ramabai's search for religion encompassed a framework for her social activism that went far beyond the moral imperatives of contesting patriarchal oppression. In her restless striving for an ideal of human perfection she refused to accept that such an ideal could emerge either through institutional measures or from a system of philosophical thought based exclusively on human rationalism. Unlike other Hindu social reformers, such as Keshab Chander Sen in Bengal or M.G. Ranade in Maharashtra, she did not believe that Hinduism's egregious record in ensuring basic rights for women and other oppressed groups could be rectified by a materialistic ethic, professed by such reformist organizations as the Brahmo Samaj and the Prarthana Samaj. On the contrary, Ramabai rejected purely rational approaches to religious reform. Though she was initially drawn to these groups in her early gropings for religious alternatives to orthodox Hinduism, she was convinced they could not adequately illuminate pathways to basic philosophical dilemmas regarding such things as the apperception of supreme godhead. Since it was still necessary to deal with human authority as a mediating factor in perceiving divinity under these systems, Ramabai was persuaded that such dilemmas could only be resolved by private exertions of conscience and independent judgement. Her studious discrimination between the planes of the human and the divine meticulously separated obedience to the word of God (which she implicitly believed offered the path to salvation and liberty) from obedience to the law (which she considered to be the source of human enslavement). Her search for religion was essentially a search for viable ways of defining and realizing liberty far outside the boundaries of priestly intervention.

Ramabai's explicit quest for unconstrained spiritual freedom brings her squarely within an antinomian tradition of dissent particular to English history. For her careful distinction between two forms of obedience—to God and to the law—rehearses the antinomian rejection of 'Moral Law' as a product of institutional and priestly repression. Antinomian literature describes such repression as having the effect of removing the believer further and further from God's divine mercy and love; consequently, restoration to a position prior to one's estrangement from God means a repudiation of all forms of legal authority. As E.P. Thompson points out in his brilliant study of Blake and Muggletonianism, the term 'antinomian' itself means *against the law*, and is broad enough to include a range of oppositions to prescriptive dogmas. Primarily, antinomian doctrine takes its inspiration from Paul's letters to the Romans and to the Galatians. Apart from the fact that the Pauline emphasis on justification by faith resists a purely regulated form of worship involving ceremonial observances and rituals, its distinguishing attribute is its contestation of the imperatives of Mosaic Law. In its injunction to believers to obey moral commandments and follow the letter rather than the spirit of the law, Mosaic Law turns these commandments into what Thompson calls 'the necessary rules of government imposed upon a faithless and unregenerate people'.[8] Ramabai's admonition to her missionary mentors in England to respect her as a student 'not of letter alone but also of the spirit of religion' reproduces the language of Paul and salvages religious belief as personal testimony from the crude pit of religious ideology, which Ramabai came to see as a product of the instrumental rationality of the colonial English state.

Ramabai's disillusionment with the reduction of religious belief to a form of cultural and national identity is further aggravated by Sister Geraldine's comparison of the Christian kingdom to the English nation. By bringing the two within the same frame of reference, Geraldine establishes a bureaucratic worldliness in Christianity matching the complex requirements of the modern state:

> A corporate body . . . [such as] a nation, a municipality, a regiment, school or anything you like to name . . . must have its rulers, officers and discipline. If any member, or members, refuse to submit to its officers or otherwise set discipline at nought, they would be free to give up the rights and privileges of membership and go elsewhere. Now the Church is an invisible Kingdom with a visible and delegated Government. Christ is its King, and the Government which He has ordained for His Kingdom is that of Apostles or Bishops. We as members of Christ's Kingdom are not free to choose any other form of religious Government than this. If therefore any set up a self-chosen organisation or depart from His teaching, it is they who cut themselves off from the Church our Lord has founded and refuse to be governed in the way which He has appointed, and not the church which separates itself from them.[9]

The most interesting remark in this passage, of course, is the one that relates excommunication to civil disenfranchisement. In Sister Geraldine's presentation of the argument, what naturalizes the withholding of citizenship rights to non-Anglican groups, just as much as to colonial subjects, is their willing estrangement from the undivided community of God because of their refusal to submit to church authority. Heresy is an offence not pardonable by any but God; therefore, if non-Anglicans fail to be included in the body politic, the fault is theirs alone for stubbornly persisting in their misguided pride and false judgement. In Geraldine's stern reworking of church–state relations, the issue of obligatory citizenship rights is made irrelevant by a religious discourse that attaches criteria of sworn national allegiance to the practice of religious belief.

The antinomian rejection of 'Moral Law' laid the foundations for an antistatism that was to persist in English history. It also confirmed that challenges to English political life would invariably come from dissenting religious groups like the Anabaptists of the sixteenth century, to whom Pandita Ramabai is at one point disapprovingly compared by Sister Geraldine. The Anabaptists, declares Geraldine, 'taught polygamy and an entire freedom from all subjection to the civil as well as the ecclesiastical law'.[10] This allusion to an antistatist movement of English history—one that was not even contemporaneous but went back at least three centuries—suggests that Ramabai's rejection or authority is much greater than resistance to colonial subjection. Indeed, it is a rejection of the entire structure and content of civil and ecclesiastical law, which leaves no space for the articulation of belief outside doctrinal content or institutional constraints. Ramabai's repeated insistence on belief as inalienable choice openly repudiates the usurpation of her subjectivity by law or creed: 'When people decide anything for me, I call it interfering with my liberty, and am not willing to let them do it. I have a conscience, and mind, and a judgement of my own. I must be allowed to think for myself.'[11]

Ramabai's outsider position enables her to say this. Coming to an established religion from the outside allows her and other converts to interpret the new religion with a freedom not necessarily available to those already within the fold. She complains to Sister Geraldine that 'you have never gone through the same experience of choosing another religion for yourself, which was totally foreign to you, as I have. You, wise and experienced and old as you are, you cannot interpenetrate my poor feelings.'[12] Ramabai articulates a viewpoint that is not often heard in missionary literature: the convert's conflicted sense of cultural and spiritual change is compounded by the inability of missionaries to understand the reorientation of the convert's subjective reality. From the perspective of the missionaries, the challenges posed by choice are interpreted as wilful refashioning of reality. If Ramabai is typically seen as crossing a fine line between conversion and heresy and moving towards a 'diluted Christianity without Christ'—her spirited independence convinces her detractors that conversion, in her case, *is* heresy.

Ramabai's refusal to accept the command of law, coupled with her embrace of God as the only uncreated deity and Christ as a messenger but not surrogate of God, brought her into sharp conflict with her English mentors. The sisters, like many an Anglican divine who lambasted antinomianism as a smug recapitulation of the Calvinist heresy promising unmerited grace to the elect, warned Ramabai that she was reposing far too much confidence in her salvation without exerting any effort towards winning it through service and obedience to authority.

Quoting Ruskin on unlimited liberty as being no different from licentiousness, Sister Geraldine turned the statement into its obverse to suggest that true liberty really implied obedience to law. Shortly after Ramabai's conversion, noting that she had grown more distant from her friends and community, Sister Geraldine and other missionaries concluded that her alienation was a mark of her developing pride. But Ramabai's own words suggest that the narrowly defined Christianity in which she had been trapped caused her to feel estranged from the spiritual longings she had been experiencing. The sisters' use of alienation as a metaphor for pernicious rootlessness and lack of meaningful community is transformed by Ramabai into a metaphor for the loss of intimate communion with God brought about by institutional regulation.

Ramabai's disagreement with Sister Geraldine regarding the existence of the Church before the Bible, however, is more than a young convert's refusal to accept a new religion on other people's terms.[13] Ramabai's often intemperate language appears to personalize her conflict with her mentor and sponsor, but the idiosyncratic tone of her responses is belied by her own careful, close reading of English religious history. But this kind of meticulous attention to church history is vehemently denied by Sister Geraldine, who interprets as pride what Ramabai puts forth as legitimate intellectual inquiry. Bishop Westcott, when informed of Ramabai's vexing recalcitrance, counsels Sister Geraldine that 'those dealing with her should seek to get her to believe rather than define'.[14]

The clash of perspectives between teacher and pupil is further exacerbated by the heady novitiate's refusal to allow a description of her turbulent state of mind as intransigent self-absorption; rather, by painting her situation as involving a loss of self, she castigated obedience to law as the source of a tragic self-estrangement. If Ramabai is accused of being smug, she turns the charge of complacency into a point of doctrine that distinguishes between divine election and personal belief—that is, between an offer of salvation on predestined grounds, as supported by Calvinism which Ramabai roundly rejects as disparaging of individual effort, and Pauline mysticism whose promise of salvation requires the believer to seek out personal truth in Christ's word. Ramabai thus overturns the charge that she is proud by denying

Calvinist predeterminism and, instead, emphasizes the depth of her struggle for spiritual salvation as itself a process of Christian understanding.

On the other hand, the Anglican sisters, perceiving Ramabai's stance as dangerously presumptive in challenging the foundations of both Anglican doctrine and English law, remind her ominously that 'you have by your Baptism looked into this Law of Liberty'.[15] Their stress falls pointedly on the word *this*, which narrows down liberty to a prescriptive law sanctioned by church authority alone. Refusing to accept the regulated logic of such admonitions, which reduced liberty to an obligatory contradiction that included constraint as part of its self-definition, Ramabai heaped contempt on the missionaries' qualified notion of liberty as typifying 'the will of those who have authority to speak as expressing His will'.

> It seems to me that you are advising me under the WE to accept always the will of those who have authority, etc. This however I cannot accept. I have a conscience, and mind and a judgement of my own. I must myself think and do everything which GOD has given me the power of doing. . . . I am, it is true, a member of the Church of Christ, but am not bound to accept every word that falls down from the lips of priests or bishops. If it pleases you to call my word liberty as lawlessness you may do so, but as far as I know myself, I am not lawless. Obedience to the law and to the Word of God is quite different from perfect obedience to priests only.[16]

Ramabai's meticulous dismantling of her mentors' logic set up private interpretation not as an exalted alternative to institutional authority but rather a means of recapturing a lost affinity to God. Her God is less a product of human rationality (as the Brahmo Samajists believed) than a source of self-empowering reason. What ought to have been a point of little dispute between Ramabai and the missionaries, however, turned into a major disagreement because she used her God-given reason to construct her own religious system in which the Christian God is then placed (arbitrarily, according to the shocked sisters). Furthermore, her new system empties deity of established gender attributes as the first step towards an egalitarian order ensuring liberty. This is in contrast to the hierarchical religious scheme upheld by the missionaries, who acknowledge that 'in Christ she had learned that there was perfect liberty, and though there was necessarily a church order and subordination, yet in the Spirit, there was in Christ neither male nor female. It seemed going back to what she had been delivered from.'[17]

Yet, despite the obviously heretical components of Ramabai's Christianity, few critics are willing to see her conversion—or what Geraldine haughtily dismissed as her 'self-chosen religion'—as the site from which she chose to fight both British colonialism and Hindu patriarchy. Ram Bapat, for instance, who has written with considerable perspicacity about Pandita Ramabai's negotiation of the dialectics of faith and reason, sees her Christian conversion as a transitional moment in her fight against Hindu orthodoxy. He views her conversion as a crucial turning point in her resistance to the tradition that shaped her early life and established the foundations of her own deep learning in Sanskrit texts. In Bapat's reading Ramabai's point of reference for converting to Christianity remains Hinduism, despite her apparent attraction to the tenets of monotheism and the claims of mystical faith. He thus views her conversion as a reactive gesture against the retrograde features of Hinduism and patriarchal society, rather than as an act of will directing the self toward an exploration of the spiritual realm. If, however, the latter proposition is considered more seriously, it leads to the consideration that Ramabai's spiritual restlessness has less to do with Hindu religious reform than seeking out existential conditions of freedom from temporal bondage—conditions leading to the creation of a selfhood released from social restrictions. It is to this trajectory that we shall now turn our attention.

Ramabai's Early Upbringing

Ramabai's conversion to Christianity could not have been predicted from her early religious behaviour. Critics make much of her repeated insistence that she never intended to convert to Christianity, especially to a religion that she initially described as composed of meaningless and empty rituals. Perceiving no substantial difference between Christian and Hindu ceremonial worship, she writes sarcastically of the Christians she encountered in India, 'We did not see any image to which they paid homage but it seemed as though they were paying homage to the chairs before which they knelt.'[18] Christianity's own mysticism and ritualism appeared to be no more than a Westernized form of Hinduism. Ramabai's view that Christianity lacked a lively tradition of disputation on doctrine and dogma drew her initially to the Brahmo Samajists, who, as avowed social reformers, were dynamically engaged with debates on the nature of divine substance and theistic ideality. Certainly the instruction in Hindu religious texts that she received from her father did not prepare her for the questioning that later led her to reject Hinduism. Her father, Anant Shastri Dongre, believed it was imperative for women to read sacred texts, but he scrupulously excluded the Vedas as one of the required texts in Ramabai's Sanskrit education. As Meera Kosambi points out, it was not until Ramabai had encountered the monotheistic system of the Brahmo Samaj that she began to consider alternatives to the tradition-bound practices of Hinduism.[19] Yet not even the new attractions of a monotheistic faith can explain why Christianity should have so compelled her attention, particularly when there was every likelihood that, by converting, she would jeopardize her respected standing amongst her Hindu peers as a reformer and thinker.

The answer to this vexed question requires one to take a brief biographical detour, particularly in the circumstances of Ramabai's growing distance from a sense of affiliation to community, which her spiritual mentors in England noted as culminating in crisis around the time of her conversion: 'She was less free with her early friends, less confidential [*sic*]. She seemed somewhat less cordially disposed towards us, and to have a sense of distrust.'[20] Ramabai's utter isolation following the loss of all members of her family was certainly a factor contributing to her gradual detachment from community feeling. In the years following her parents' deaths, Ramabai travelled extensively across India with her sole surviving sibling, her older brother. Together, as pilgrims, they wandered from temple to temple, impressing people with their deep knowledge of Sanskrit texts and holding their own in learned conversations with pandits. Educated in the classical religious texts by her father, who was officially censured by a village council for exposing his wife and his daughters to the sacred texts, Ramabai was brought up in an atmosphere that was essentially oriented to the

Dharmashastric Vedic tradition of Hinduism, the scriptural tradition of moral codes and precepts.

However, though providing the primary textual bases for legal and social identity, this tradition of moral precepts is only one of the many presentations of Hinduism, yet Ramabai remained fairly oblivious to popular expressions of other religious forms. Her subsequent disenchantment with Hinduism was entirely on the basis of the scriptural texts in which she received instruction from her parents, among which are the *Bhagavatapurana*, the *Bhagavad Gita*, the *Kaumudi*, the *Amarokosha* and other works in the oral tradition.[21] Thus, in spite of the fact that there were varying sets of religious scriptures, practices, and beliefs among Hindus, Ramabai held on to the conviction that 'no woman as a woman can get liberation' in the Hindu tradition, since she assumed that all the Hindu traditions treated the knowledge of the Veda, Vedanta, and Brahma as a necessary condition for religious salvation.[22] Her learning, though deep and wide, was limited largely to Sanskrit Bhagavata literature, and her impressions of the possibilities of female emancipation were confined to what this literature offered. Until she moved to Calcutta, where she acquired a new set of acquaintances in the reform-oriented Brahmo Samaj, Ramabai had not studied the Vedas, the Upanishads, the six systems of thought other than the *nyaya* (or analytical) system, nor the Dharmashastras. Nor was she familiar with the literatures even of the Varkari, the Lingayat or the northern Sant *sampradays* which offered the promise of salvation to the lower caste of shudras, women outcastes, and sinners, in total defiance of the Vedic scriptures and the Smritis (traditional texts). Thus, as Bapat argues, 'in spite of her bitter, pertinent and acute attacks on the fundamentals of the modernizing Hindu elitist world-views, she continued to operate within the confines of the same privileged discourse which was set up, first, by Western students of Hinduism, and then appropriated by the nationalist elites in India to meet their colonial or class interests and which valorized the Vedas and Smritis as the authoritative texts governing a monolithic Hindu order'.[23]

Ramabai's assessment of her early instruction helps explain her later antagonism to the reform of Hinduism along purely secular lines. Ramabai writes in her autobiographical tract, *My Testimony*, about the strictly religious emphasis of her classical training:

My parents did not like us children to come in contact with the outside world. They wanted us to be strictly religious, and adhere to the old faith. Learning any other language except Sanskrit was out of [the] question. Secular education of any kind was looked upon as leading people to worldliness which would prevent them from getting into the way of *moksha* [salvation]. To learn the English language and to come into contact with *mlecchas* [non-Hindus, or foreigners] was forbidden on the pain of losing caste and all hope of future happiness. So all that we could and did learn was the Sanskrit grammar and dictionaries with the Puranic and modern literature in that language. Most of this, including the grammar and dictionaries which are written in verse form, had to be committed to memory.[24]

Ram Bapat reads this passage as unassailable evidence of Ramabai's restrictive outlook within what he calls a 'high caste, high form of Hinduism'. And to some extent this is true. Anant Shastri's rejection of Shankara's monist philosophy of Advaitism and acceptance of Vaishnava doctrines did not necessarily mean that he welcomed dissenting traditions of low-caste protest, nor did it indicate his openness to other interpretations of Hinduism. As Bapat rightly points out, 'his revolt was rather expressive of the age-old contradictions and confrontations within the high caste, high form of Hinduism, rather than that of the emancipatory, egalitarian, popular Bhakti ethos emerging from below'.[25] Yet Bapat's evaluation of the 'patrician' aloofness of Anant Shastri's Vaishnavism assumes too quickly that bhakti, as an expression of religious dissent, is synonymous with anticasteism and low-caste protest, whereas in fact the mystical leanings of bhakti are perfectly consonant with the rigid orthodoxies of hierarchical brahmanism. Indeed, the accent on mystical unity in the *bhakti* tradition of worship does not preclude either the appropriation of bhakti by caste Hinduism or its accommodation by the requirements of upper-caste privilege.

In 1883 Pandita Ramabai, by then already a widow with a small child, set out for England. At the time of her departure she had already acquired a formidable reputation not only as a woman of profound classical learning but also as a social reformer of great perseverance and courage. But Ramabai had to pay a heavy price for her reformist activity: her espousal of widows' causes and her mobilization of (an essentially conservative) social conscience against child marriage earned her the wrath of Maharashtrian brahman society. Though it would not be accurate to say that she was driven out of India, nonetheless conditions in her home state of Maharashtra were too hostile for her to continue her relief efforts unhampered. Determined to study medicine, in order that her moral impulses for reform would be amply buttressed by a professional degree, Ramabai eagerly took up an offer made by the Community of St Mary the Virgin at Wantage, which promised to finance her higher studies. She paid her passage to England by publishing a book in Marathi, *Stree Dharma Niti*, translated into English as *Morals for Women*, which earned her both money and fame—far more than she or anyone else anticipated.

However, Ramabai's professional plans to study medicine abroad were quashed by her acute hearing problems, and she was instead channelled into a course of studies in English and natural science. The sisters of the Wantage community who sponsored her stay in England arranged for her to teach Marathi and Sanskrit at the Cheltenham Ladies College. In return for her own education in Western learning, Ramabai was expected to offer missionaries setting out for Poona the training in vernacular languages they needed for their proselytizing work. Here undisputedly was the case of the imported native informant, a prototype for upcoming generations of Indians travelling to England and America for higher studies, absorbing Western knowledge in exchange for 'native' languages. The exact terms of the exchange were to play a significant part much later, when Ramabai defied the accepted conventions and insisted on teaching missionaries more than the obligatory native languages. Far more shocking was her request that she also be allowed to teach English—and that, too, to young men, no less.

The Community of St Mary the Virgin was a small order of missionary sisters that had branches in western India, the largest and most important of which was in Poona. We have little information about the circumstances of their operation in England, though brief allusions in the letters indicate that they were in frequent communication with the Society for the Propagation of the Gospel, to whom they often sent novices and initiates from their own, much smaller order. Again, from the correspondence one has an impression that the order was challenged severely by the personal trials of missionaries: of failing health, inadequate resources, and the psychological demoralization caused by recalcitrant converts. At least one of the missionary sisters freely confessed that she suffered a nervous breakdown while working in the Indian missions. The frantic, almost hysterical tone of the correspondence between the missionaries—and between them and Pandita Ramabai—is partially explained by the stress these missionaries experienced in their effort to gain the most useful (that is, the most socially respectable) converts to continue mission work in India. Hence, the extraordinary investment in a high-caste learned woman like Pandita Ramabai, whose conversion was a prize acquisition and one not to be lost easily. Hence also the almost fastidious deference to her volatility and a willingness to mollify her at all costs, even when it clearly meant compromising the sisters' own Anglican principles.

Ramabai's ostensible motive in going to England for studies was to break what she called 'the bondage of social prejudice'—restrictions that were so great within India that 'higher principles of action' could only be pursued elsewhere.[26] But as her correspondence with the Wantage sisters shows, even as she disparaged the many strictures of Hindu patriarchy, she was no less critical of the orthodoxies governing the missionaries' conduct. Her letters reveal her alienation not only from Hindu society but also from the institutional culture of the religion to which she had converted. The letters further provide powerful insights into the lonely world of the convert, struggling to resist cooptation by both Hindu and Christian culture, even as she strove to recreate herself within a restrictive space offering little or no room for private manoeuvre. Sister Geraldine, Ramabai's chief mentor, was clearly aware that Ramabai was refashioning Christianity to her own requirements, far beyond what her sponsors desired for this young woman whom they aimed eventually to embrace within their fold: 'I fear she is willingly accepting a religion which has no claim to the name of Christianity, as she thinks it will commend itself more to the intelligence of her countrywomen than the revealed Truth, which latter will require for them a higher standard of moral and spiritual perfection than they would be willing to accept.'[27]

Because the correspondence between Ramabai and the missionaries elucidates Ramabai's construction of a belief system more systematically and coherently than any of her other better-known works, including her celebrated book *The High Caste Hindu Woman*, the primary text

I shall focus on is A.B. Shah's edition of *The Letters and Correspondence of Pandita Ramabai*, a comprehensive collection of the correspondence between Ramabai and her missionary sponsors exchanged almost entirely during the time Ramabai spent in England. Unlike many missionary–convert interactions that form the basis for most scholarly analysis, this work registers the impressions of a new Christian convert writing from her location not in the colonies but in England. Ramabai's residence in England at the time she debated the missionaries gave her a closer perspective on English ecclesiastical history and its impact on the English state. Her letters powerfully reveal the fissures and dissensions within Anglican England, just as they also shed light on well-entrenched divisions in church history, which were by and large glossed over by the Anglican self-presentation of unity and strength required for efficacious missionary instruction. Ramabai's puncturing of the false certainties and presumed stability of mainstream Anglican orthodoxies paradoxically gave her an uncanny sense of release from the social constraints that bound her as a Hindu. Partly sensing this, the sisters with whom she was in communication found their own proselytizing ambitions uncomfortably compromised. For it was evident that, although to her English mentors' approving eyes Ramabai was loosening her ties with Hinduism and turning a suspicious and sceptical eye upon her native religion, yet her repudiation of Hinduism was accompanied at the same time by an intellectual resistance to accepting a version of Christianity handed down as scriptural authority. Chided by the sisters for her 'arrogant' independence, Ramabai angrily retorts that 'I have just with great efforts freed myself from the yoke of the Indian priestly tribe, so I am not at present willing to place myself under similar yoke by accepting everything which comes from the priests as authorised command of the Most High.'[28]

Ironically, Ramabai's departure from Hinduism is brought on by an independence the missionaries now wish to curb. Though the Wantage sisters initially believed that Ramabai's orphaned status and unencumbered situation would help them to transform her into whatever shape and form they desired, they found her rootlessness to be the source of an obstinate refusal to accept institutional will and authority. Their view that she offered 'fair promise of good at the outset of her career, but in consequence of having no restrictions is unprofitable to the world' disparaged her unattached status as the source of a pernicious intellectual ('heretical') independence. Their insistence on familial ties as the basis of temporal authority established dependence on a community or a family as a measure of one's usefulness, thus also confirming the family as a primary source of traditional, dependable and sustaining values. Unfettered liberty is the antithesis of a communitarian vision that Sister Geraldine locates at the heart of Christian enterprise, as she remarks in a pointed aside: 'The most unhappy person of my acquaintance, and one who has made shipwreck of her life is one who in independent circumstances and without family ties can do pretty much as she pleases.'[29]

If the single woman as a danger to society persists in the resolutely Victorian consciousness of Sister Geraldine, it was Ramabai's special insight that the persistently negative perceptions of women who chose to remain outside the family structure provided a rationale for the passing of retrograde British legislation, both in England and India. Referring to the infamous Rakhmabai decision of 1887 passed by the British Indian courts, which ordered a young woman Rakhmabai to return to her husband against her wishes, Ramabai remarked with great bitterness, 'A Hindu woman—*unless she be a widow and destitute of friends and relatives*—cannot follow even the dictates of her own conscience.'[30] Clearly Ramabai did not see widowhood as a condition of deprivation but rather understood that the absence of social ties also loosened obligatory ties to prevailing orthodoxies.

However, Ramabai's orphaned and widowed situation made her extremely culpable in the eyes of the missionaries. For her capacity of private judgement, which made her such a prime candidate for conversion, contributed at the same time to a questioning of all received notions and undercut the conceptions of priestly authority favoured by the Anglican order to which the Wantage missionaries belonged. In the absence of parents, husband, kinsfolk or community, Ramabai appeared to have the mobility that was the substance of heterodoxy. With the family as the undisputed touchstone of stable, orthodox values, the missionary order proceeded to turn into heretics single, unattached women like Ramabai, whose lack of ties to family or community made her extremely susceptible to the 'pride' of interpretative freedom. Not only did Ramabai's rejection of moral commandments puncture the family-based, community-oriented patriarchal authority of Mosaic Law, which the missionaries' beliefs affirmed, but such rejection was enabled by a slackening of all connections with a filiative order of things.

In other words, disruption of an affiliative model of the family becomes the source of a new and powerful assertion of antinomianism, in which unmediated faith in God challenges the moral prerogatives of obedience to law. The communitarian vision informing the missionaries' perspective required a web of alliances between women, family and community for the efficacious administration of religious law. The selflessness of community service is the norm of Christian liberty. Because this so clearly contradicted Ramabai's own sense of liberty as self-inspired devotion, her assertions cast a cloud of suspicion over the reasons for her conversion if, as seemed to be the case, she did not intend to serve Christianity in the same spirit as did the Wantage sisters. An early exchange between Ramabai and Sister Geraldine reveals that they had been talking at cross-purposes for a tragically long time, with Geraldine lauding Ramabai's conversion as having been inspired by the 'holy unselfish life' led by the missionaries. Ramabai breaks her silence on this representation of her conversion by finally responding to Canon William Butler:

> This is her opinion. I held my silence when I heard this, thinking that it was not of much consequence to discuss upon such points of question but now I see that the misunderstanding is growing too formidable not to be corrected.
>
> I was indeed impressed with the holy life of the Sisters, and their sublime unselfishness, and am so impressed to this moment, but I must say for the sake of truth that their life was not the cause of my accepting the faith of Christ. It was Father Goreh's letter that proved that the faith which I professed (I mean the Brahmo faith) was not taught by our Veda as I thought, but it was the Christian faith which was brought before me by my friends disguised under the name of Brahmo religion. Well, I thought if Christ is the source of this sublime faith, why should not I confess Him openly to be my Lord and my Divine teacher?[31]

Phrased in these terms, 'heresy' is at once a condition of Christian conversion as well as of its subversion. The form and content of *The Letters and Correspondence of Pandita Ramabai* have particular salience in relation to the dual, contradictory function of heresy. Originally compiled by Sister Geraldine of the Community of St Mary the Virgin as vital source material for writing the history of conversion in India, the epistolary exchange between Ramabai and other sisters of the order was preserved in the hopes that it would contribute one day to the writing of her biography.[32] But Sister Geraldine's proposed biography was not necessarily intended in the spirit of hagiography, nor was it meant to record the inspiring story of a great Indian woman who had witnessed and received God's truth and then returned to India to translate Christian truth into social service, Indeed, most missionary accounts of Christian conversions among natives are written as celebrations of achievement—that is, the acquisition of one more soul for the proselytizing enterprise. Pandita Ramabai's story was an exception to the principle of missionary biographies, for Sister Geraldine had a much more cautionary tale in mind when she decided to preserve Ramabai's often volatile letters. She believed her subject, Pandita Ramabai, had historical importance as an imperfect, erring sinner whose quarrels with certain doctrinal aspects of Christianity constituted an allegorical tale of warning to true believers.

If Ramabai is relegated to the ranks of a heretic by the very people who seek her conversion, their refusal to accept her conversion as a final event condemns as heretical the spiritual questioning they would have otherwise welcomed as a definitive step towards conversion. Thus, as long as Ramabai continued to probe into the varieties of Christian belief found in English sects, her receiving of Christian grace was deferred indefinitely and she remained disqualified from being accepted as a true Christian convert. From the missionaries' perspective, conversion is the affirmation of a given set of propositions. For Pandita Ramabai, on the other hand, conversion is a form of self-fashioning, the right to 'have a voice in choosing my own religion'.[33] Ramabai keeps drawing attention to her 'own free will: by it we are to decide for ourselves what we are to do, and fulfill our intended work'.[34] When Ramabai claims the right of free will and choice, she conjoins a theological point with a political and cultural one. She is making the argument, contrary to the missionaries' wish or liking, that Indians have to make their own country, and that the free will, independent conscience, and judgement demonstrated in their religious choices strengthen the kind of moral society Indians must make for themselves.

Ramabai recognizes that the missionaries' attempt to restrict her thinking about religious questions is also a form of colonial control, and it is a central feature of her own critique that she makes independent conscience a matter of national reconstruction.

The narrative organization of *Letters and Correspondence* suggests that not only did Ramabai's questioning epitomize wilful pride but, more importantly, it also elucidates why she failed to achieve real conversion and hence justified the missionaries' refusal to acknowledge her baptism. Sister Geraldine writes:

> I have found the most interesting and edifying biographies to be those where the faults of the person under review are not withheld. Shadows shew up the light and help to give true proportion. Secondary lives which are brought onto the stage are often brought into high light and become an inspiration by a truthful narration. A life with all the faults suppressed is dazzling, but tends to depress. Where the opposite plan is followed, that life simply told is bracing and heartening.[35]

The extraordinary point of this passage is that the containment of Ramabai's heresy is possible only by presenting her conversion as a failure. Such an objective goes completely against the customary rationale of missionary writing, which was driven by a compulsion to record successes not only in order to commemorate the certain spread of Christianity but also to satisfy those who were subsidizing missionary efforts abroad. But in this particular case, the recounting of Ramabai's life story as a rough passage through a variety of theological quarrels and controversial arguments—none of which, by the way, was satisfactorily resolved—is seen to offer a more valuable lesson if her conversion is understood *as never having occurred at all.* Ramabai's conversion, presented by the missionaries as incomplete, irresolute, and endlessly deferred, takes place on so many different sites, so many different levels of meaning, that the multiplicity of its occurrence—the distended repetition of her conversion as performative gesture—is taken as definitive proof by missionaries of its lack of credibility. The conflict between Geraldine and Ramabai was most pronounced on the issue of baptism. When Geraldine insisted that Ramabai could not assume her baptism implied full conversion to Christianity, in the absence of her complete acceptance of church tenets, Ramabai was forced to re-enact her conversion by other intellectual means, which took her through a cycle of religious introspection, dialogue and disputation.

The Unitarian Heresy, or Sectarian Options

Pandita Ramabai's correspondence with the missionaries is noteworthy in another respect. The religious controversies and intellectual debates of the nineteenth century are rehearsed not in the Oxford classroom as in John Henry Newman's *Loss and Gain*, but in an often heated exchange between English missionaries and their Indian Christian initiate—an exchange that is consciously framed by the reality of colonial relationships. Two historical positions—that of colonial subject and religious dissenter—dramatically collapse into a single one in the missionaries' representation of Ramabai's questioning. The blurring of Ramabai's colonized status with the position of those coming out of a dissenting religious tradition in England produces a description of colonial acculturation as a process not significantly different from the containment of English religious dissent. Ramabai's refusal to accept the main tenets of the Anglican church put her firmly in the subject position of England's hated Dissenters. Her rejection of the Thirty-Nine Articles, coupled with an insistence on her own five articles of faith, aligns her unmistakably with several dissenting groups falling outside the Anglican fold. In asserting her faith on the grounds of direct scriptural interpretation unmediated by institutional authority, Ramabai affiliates herself to a tradition of protest that claims the autonomy of religious subjectivity from church intervention:

> I shall tell you my Articles of Faith which I am so far able to draw from the Scripture, as my limited knowledge of the Word of God enables [me to do]. I have of late, as you know, after realising the sublime truths of Christ's teaching, become one of the least of his disciples, and believe in Him as the Messiah of God, and therefore am bound to receive every word which falls from His lips as the command of God which comes to me through His meditation. I am baptized according to His direction in the name of the Father, of the Son and of the Holy Ghost; and, therefore, I call myself a Christian, though I do not know if after hearing my creed my fellow Christians would call me so.[36]

In this last line, Ramabai enters the unambiguous ground of heresy by calling her faith 'my creed' and setting aside the doctrinal creeds considered pivotal to Anglican worship. Though she may declare herself a Christian, she does so in defiantly subjective terms, marking the distance between herself and a community of Anglican believers by her claims to the sanctity of private interpretation. Rewriting the Thirty-Nine Articles of the English church into her own five articles of faith, Ramabai denied the terms of membership by which alone, at one time, she would have been accepted as a subject of both England and Christianity. As instruments of enforcing allegiance to the Church of England, the Thirty-Nine Articles also historically established the terms of inclusion in the English nation. This fact did not escape Ramabai, who read as emotional blackmail the sisters' condition that she had to subscribe to the Thirty-Nine Articles if she were to remain attached to St Mary's Home in Wantage. The drama being played out between Ramabai and the sisters turned Wantage into a microcosm of England itself.

Ramabai's increasing attraction to Unitarianism accompanied her inquiry into sectarian differences. Her Unitarian sympathies came from a range of popular religious literature that missionaries denounced as distortions of Christian doctrine. Their indictment of mass-based pamphlet literature as sources of heretical thinking is suggestive of the deep sectarian divide in English society, just as Ramabai's intellectual resistance to religious authority allies her, as a colonial subject, with the English masses' disaffection from a rule that represented only landed and clerical interests. Indeed, Unitarian heresy becomes, for Ramabai, the means of contesting colonial authority. Her reaction against Trinitarianism stems from her perception that it is the very foundation of Englishness; axiomatically, anti-Trinitarianism lends itself to strong expressions of anti-colonialism.

The major obstacle in Ramabai's acceptance of the missionaries' faith was that pillar of Trinitarianism, the Athanasian Creed. No issue caused greater bitterness between the missionaries and Ramabai than the doctrine of the Trinity, and when Ramabai virtually ordered the sisters not to teach her daughter 'anything about the mysterious Trinity, and about the deity of our Saviour, until you quite convince me that these doctrines are according to the Bible',[37] she pushed them to the point where they were no longer willing to humour her claims to individual interpretation ('She is altogether off the lines,' complained an exasperated Geraldine).[38] In reality Ramabai's primary objection against praying to Christ, and to the Holy Ghost, as a person separate from the godhead had less to do with a close, sustained reading of anti-Trinitarian literature than with a deep-seated reluctance to accept Christ as a metonym for the godhead in its entirety, a reluctance that she attributed to her own dissatisfaction with a religion like Hinduism where godhead is dispersed among different icons. When she asserts that 'I am not commanded by Christ (in the New Testament) to address my prayers either to Himself or to the Holy Ghost alone',[39] her statement has shock value because not only does it deny that Christ partakes of the divinity of God but it also implies that the claim to being the son of God is a declaration of faith that can be made by others in totally non-blasphemous ways, as long as God is recognized as the only true divinity. In other words, the importance of Christ lies in his being the messenger of hope, divine mercy and salvation, rather than in any specific identification with God or in having attributes that are interchangeable with God's.

To a large extent there was a certain literalness in Ramabai's understanding of the Trinity, since she appeared to believe it referred to three separate aspects of divinity, whereas the crucial historical issue that failed to engage her in any sustained way was whether Christ the Son was of similar substance (*homoiousios*) as God the Father, or of the same substance (*homoousios*). This was, of course, the fundamental conflict that had led, in AD 325, to the adoption of the Athanasian Creed by Constantine to resolve the dispute. Not only did the creed assert that Christ is identical with God and, together with the Holy Ghost, constitutes the Trinity, but it emphasized that the Trinity comprises three aspects of a single, *uncreated* unity, with God the Father being the one underived or unbegotten principle. Because the godhead is uncreated, Christ the Son is not considered to have been begotten in human fashion but rather is an image of the godhead. 'To be begotten', therefore, simply means completely to share in the entire nature of God the Father.

To insist otherwise, as did the fourth-century bishop of Antioch, Arius, who asserted that 'the Son is an unrelated and an independent being totally separated from, and different from the substance or nature of the Father',[40] was to invite public condemnation as a heretic, and Ramabai was sufficiently well acquainted with church history to know the dangers of recapitulating the Arian heresy even in nineteenth-century England. With a religious history still haunted by the hangings and public prosecutions of anti-Trinitarians, England was not yet a place for the open expression of Unitarian feeling. The Athanasian Creed pronounced Arianism a heresy and condemned those who were guilty of professing it. As late as 1695 a Scottish student Thomas Aikenhead was hanged for declaring the Trinity an absurdity and Christianity an illusion. Such events occurred despite the fact that a leading religious figure like Archbishop John Tillotson (1630–1694) complained about the Athanasian Creed (albeit privately): 'I wish we were well rid of it.'[41] Nor were institutions of higher learning exempt. William Whiston (1667–1752), who succeeded Isaac Newton to the chair of mathematics at Cambridge, lost his professorship because of his Arianism.

Even efforts at compromise aroused parliamentary disapproval, and those who tried to accommodate Arianism to Anglican doctrine suffered the consequences. David Lawton provides an absorbing history of some of these developments which culminated in the radical Unitarianism of such figures as the great scientist Joseph Priestley and William Frend. Frend was dismissed from Cambridge for his disavowal of the Athanasian Creed and for putatively authoring an influential pamphlet, *An address to the members of the Church of England and to Protestant Trinitarians in general, exhorting them to turn from the false worship of three persons to the worship of One True God* (1788). Lawton's conclusion that 'enforcement of orthodoxy against Unitarianism extended into the highest ranks of Church and University—and continued to do so into the nineteenth century' reveals that there was virtually no space in public life to discuss Unitarianism without repeating an offence against both English Christianity and the English state.[42] For the close identification of Trinitarianism with English nationhood was certainly not lost sight of even by an intrepid inquirer like Pandita Ramabai, who in her sporadic attacks on Anglican church doctrine quickly discovered that impugning the Trinity was tantamount to inveighing against the English Crown itself.

Ramabai's attraction to a Unitarian conception of divinity sprang from what she perceived as its clearcut demarcation of the divine from the human. In the absence of such necessary distinctions in its own religious system, Hinduism was reduced to a mindless pantheism, and Ramabai turned to Unitarianism because it offered an ideal expression of a religious faith in which the divine could be steadily contemplated as a pure entity. When Ramabai is faulted for saying human beings are not perfect, she defends herself by saying that perfection implies an absence of distinction between humans and God: the virtue of Unitarianism, in her opinion, was that it preserved this distinction. The Wantage missionaries were correct to conclude that Ramabai's dissatisfaction with pantheistic expressions of worship drew her compulsively to the Brahmo Samaj, a reformist branch of Hinduism that resisted the facile blurring of human and divine features.

But as in so many other instances, where Ramabai's 'heresy' produced an ambivalence in the missionaries' attitudes to her intellectual probings, the sisters were simultaneously aware that Ramabai's resistance to Trinitarianism had a positive aspect, because her rejection of godhead in three figures reinforced her rejection of the polytheism of Hinduism and its blurring of human and divine. A letter by Dorothea Beale, principal of Cheltenham Ladies College, to Canon William Butler reflects the missionaries' ambivalence: 'She will never perhaps think exactly as we do, but if she did, she would not so well be a teacher for India. I am now beginning to see why she does not so readily accept sacramental teaching as we do. She is afraid of its being confused by native thought with their own pantheism. She sees dangers, which would not occur to us.'[43]

Though Ramabai may not have engaged directly with the historical debate on the substance of godhead, she did engage quite conspicuously with two related issues: the possibilities of perfection and the Incarnation. Her seemingly innocuous discussions with Sister Geraldine about the impossibility of human perfection led her to make some of her strongest statements about Christ as an independent being totally distinct from the substance of God the Father, and thus to reveal her own developing position as a Unitarian. Ramabai's argument may be summarized as follows: proceeding from the dictionary definition of perfection as 'not defective, completed, unblemished, possessing every moral excellence', she maintained that if human beings are describable in these terms, they would have foregone the progressive condition of souls and become not merely transfixed in time but God himself, since only God can be outside time, Since this is theologically impossible, the maximum state to which human beings can aspire is to be *like* God but not *as* God. Therefore, the real translation of Christ's 'Be ye perfect', is to strive for perfection and approximate God, but remain substantially distinct from God and therefore imperfect. Trying to be perfect *like* God and *becoming perfect* are thus two totally separate arguments, the first signifying a paradox of necessary imperfection and the second a theological cul-de-sac:

> If we understand 'Be ye perfect,' etc., literally and in its fullest sense, then 'As the Father' also must be taken literally and full[y] which I know according to Christian teaching cannot be. For if we were to become *like* or *as* or equally perfect with the Father, we should undoubtedly be so many supreme Gods, as the Vedantists say. There would not be any difference between us and the Father in perfection. Such a thing is an impossibility to me at least. I do not at the same time say that we shall not be perfect like the Father in a certain degree, but I object to saying that we shall be as perfect (not defective) as the Father is.[44]

Ramabai had less to say about the Incarnation, but her chief difficulty lay in reconciling immaculate conception with the doctrine of the Trinity: three beings are either separate from each other or they are one, but they cannot be both. Similarly, one is either born the way that human beings are, or one is uncreated; one cannot have both a human birth and be uncreated at the same time. To her mind, the entire idea of God emptying himself of omnipotence and omniscience in order to undergo human birth as Christ and suffer human travails is simply incompatible with the perfection and oneness of godhead.

The subject of the Incarnation roused Ramabai to new heights of theological argumentativeness. Whereas she was incredulous about the Trinity because the concept of three deities made Christianity no different from Hinduism, discussions of the Incarnation left her much more defensive about Hinduism. One might even say she was perverse in her defence, since her reason for wishing to leave Hinduism was precisely its free mixing of human and divine attributes. Earlier, she had expressed great doubts in believing that the boundless and pure essence of godhead could ever be limited or mixed with the impurities of the lower human nature, though it may be everywhere and remain boundless and pure in every limited thing.[45] Her dissatisfaction with Hinduism sprang from its erratic combinations of divine and human elements. But Christianity fared no better in her analysis, and she mercilessly lampooned some of its more salient contradictions. For instance, if the traditional Christian objection to Hinduism lay in the latter's conception of God as alternatively incarnate (that is, many persons) *and* One, Christianity itself could not claim to be exempt from the same tendency. 'If Christian teachers laugh at the Hindoos because they want to reconcile these two opposite natures, on what ground, may I ask, they can establish their doctrine . . . that Jesus Christ although omnipotent and omniscient emptied himself for a time of his qualities[?]'[46] Needless to say, her conclusion that no religion could base its theology on the Incarnation did not win much favour with the missionary sisters.

To Ramabai, the intermixture of human and divine was not merely a problem of substance; it had as much to do with the capacity to distinguish good from evil. In fact, Ramabai disparaged discussions of the Trinity in terms of substance alone by showing how foolish Hinduism had been made to appear because substance overtakes morality, as when incarnation is described as air filling up different rooms, 'so the three persons being one fill three persons, yet they are one [like] air, and that at last these different vessels or bodies will be broken up and the whole essence of God will be again united.'[47] If Hinduism was pilloried for treating deity as substance, neither could Trinitarianism be exempt from the same charge, and Ramabai mercilessly applied what appeared to the sisters as cold logic to dismantle their arguments.

Similarly, if human birth is irreconcilable with unchanging essence, so too is the narration of national history with the scheme of spiritual redemption. Indisputably, no point of doctrine in Christianity has created more problems for narrative than the Incarnation, which symbolizes the uneven, discontinuous relationship between human history and scriptural revelation. When Ramabai asks, 'How could Christ be called the offspring of David if He had not a human father', her question not only voices scepticism about the coexistence of opposites in the figure of Christ, but it also interrogates the construction of universal religion as a counterpart to national hagiography.[48] Ramabai's insistence on the exceptionalism of human birth also emphasizes the particularism of national history, and resists all attempts to accept the birth of Christ as simultaneously signalling the rise of a new nation.

Despite the missionaries' obvious outrage at Ramabai's persistent questions, it is partly out of a sense that she would be useful to her people only when she was able to discuss Christianity dispassionately as one among many other religious systems that led Dorothy Beale to advise Sister Geraldine that

> she must study Christianity as a philosophy. She cannot receive it merely as an historical revelation, it must also commend itself to her conscience. *We say* (who are brought up as Christians),—'Such things *were* and they reveal to us such and such truths.' She *can* only say, 'Such and such things are metaphysical necessities, therefore I am ready to receive evidence.' And it was thus that St. Paul often spoke to the Greek-thinking converts. 'It was *necessary*, is common in his mouth; and so our Lord spoke to His disciples.'[49]

The sisters rationalize Ramabai's resistance to the Trinity as in fact a healthy sign of her determination to distinguish all aspects of Hinduism from her faith. Yet, although the missionaries recognized that Ramabai's Unitarianism was logically the only way she could justify leaving Hinduism, the fact remained that it brought her simultaneously to the brink of heresy. The sisters were caught in a position where they wished Ramabai at once to think and *not* think like themselves.

Ramabai's objections to praying in the name of Jesus Christ were not only on the grounds that Trinitarian worship blurred the divide between human and divine. Her reluctance must also be linked to her acute awareness that the ascription of full deity to Christ meant the exclusion of Jews from the community of Christ. Her opposition to the exclusionary character of Trinitarianism mounted with Sister Geraldine's declaration that 'the Apostles distinguished the faithful from Infidels and Jews in that the former called on the name of the Lord Jesus Christ'.[50] 'In the name of Christ' functions, for Ramabai, as a cue for a politics of exclusion that England had come to symbolize. Although Ramabai's own probings into the fabric of English social life led her to recognize the plurality of England—that there existed, besides Anglican believers, a whole host of other religious communities including Jews, Dissenters, Methodists, Wesleyans, and Nonconformists—she was also made fully aware that such central pillars of the Anglican church as the Athanasian Creed and swearing by the Thirty-Nine Articles historically denied an inclusive role to these other groups. Under the cloak of heresy, non-Anglican groups had for long been deprived of citizenship rights.

Early in Sister Geraldine's text we are told that Ramabai was 'dangerously inflated by her getting hold of points of controversy from her non-Conformist friends and dragging them clumsily and offensively into her letters'.[51] These friends are not named, but elsewhere Geraldine reveals that Ramabai's reading includes a great deal of 'popular religious literature' from which she derived ideas deemed to be distortions of Christian doctrine, though it was also the case that some of these ideas were no more palatable to Ramabai than they were to the missionaries. At other times, the sisters would not even countenance the fact that Ramabai's inquiry extended into some of the leading heresies of English history, and they obstinately concluded that her questions must come 'from a *native* source'.[52] This directly contradicts their earlier perception that she had derived 'heretical' ideas from English popular pamphlet literature. Significantly, Ramabai's reading indicates her interest in a comparative perspective between and within religions, particularly in those books that compare 'Heathen philosophy' with Christianity. We learn, for instance, that she had bought *History of Different Sects in India* 'by an Indian gentleman and also Max Müller's "Biographical Essay" '.[53]

Ramabai's intellectual interest in, if not close identification with, a mass-based religious ideology contained in English popular pamphlet literature curiously links her spiritual probings with the religious dissensions of English working-class radicalism. We do not know the full extent of Ramabai's acquaintance with English Nonconformity, especially in its lower-class expression, but her marked interest in the forms of religious controversy that were most specifically coming from the English working classes is not easily reconcilable with standard interpretations of Ramabai as an elitist, upper-caste Brahmin woman who had little interest in or contact with lower-class movements in India.[54] How then does one explain the uneven pattern of her class consciousness? Was her inability to connect with movements across class and caste in India—with non-elite women, shudras, and other low-caste groups—a product of her own Sanskritic, Dharmashastric background, a background that she was never able to surmount despite her Christian conversion? By the same token, did her conversion to Christianity open up a transnational space of identification that was impossible within the more narrowly defined caste structure of India? Could Ramabai, a high-caste Brahmin woman, indeed find unlikely points of contact with English working-class radicalism through her conversion?

A starting point for answering these questions is the course of English sectarianism as a whole and its relation to Ramabai's discovery of English Nonconformity. The decline of the established churches by the middle of the nineteenth century saw a new polarization developing in English religious life. On the one hand, there was renewed interest in established religion among the upper classes, particularly among conservatives who sought to remobilize the well-entrenched system of established churches to preserve a paternalistic, hierarchical society. On the other hand, the conservatism that favoured maintaining the status quo was countered by movements for political reform, which saw in the proliferation of new religious sects and ideologies the opportunity for conveying new ideas of political change. The dissenting churches were among the most significant institutions in nineteenth-century British society, partly because they revived the hopes of those who believed the collapse of the French monarchy and the weakened power of the papacy augured a new era of equality and social justice.

Theological controversy may have deepened the divide within the established church, but it also opened up a much more heterogeneous set of religious ideas. For instance, the 1790s saw a great acceleration in the growth of Nonconformist religion. In a society where theological controversy provoked widespread engagement, the range of religious options to choose from was reflected in a bewildering array of descriptive labels, which signified hairsplittingly different doctrines and believers such as Calvinist, Arminian, Socinian, Anabaptist, Baptist, Paedobaptist and the like. These tags of religious identification were seen by many in England as reflecting fundamental choices, and the definitions played an important part in the way the key players saw themselves and others. As a number of historians of English religion have pointed out, the structure of English society was such that sectarian identity influenced most areas of life; even those least interested in religion found that there were occasions when such an identity was forced upon them.[55]

If it was customary in nineteenth-century English discourse to place colonial subjects in the same frame of reference that included England's working classes, it is equally the case that resistance to the rule of empire by colonized peoples evoked comparisons to another oppositional group internal to England: the heterogeneous group of religious dissenters, atheists and sectaries. The effect of such comparisons was to revive memories of an odious history of rank divisiveness in England's past. The bloody battles between Catholics and Protestants, and the subsequent fracturing of these two main groups and the proliferation of various subsects, remained too vividly etched in the English national consciousness for the questionings of a young native convert like Pandita Ramabai to go unnoticed. For her spiritual probings had the effect of recalling England's highly divisive past and threatening the return of the suppressed memory of fissures in English religious history. The sisters' grave apprehensions about Ramabai's questioning are due in part to the fact that she was beginning to learn about sectarian differences in English history, for these differences provide the various subject-positions from which Ramabai launches her critique of Anglicanism. At various points in their often virulent correspondence the Wantage sisters describe Ramabai successively as a Wesleyan, a Nonconformist, an Anabaptist, and an English Dissenter. Interpellated in these terms, Ramabai is identified with sectarian tendencies in England and charged with the crime of repeating, through her questioning, the violent schisms that tore England apart in earlier times.

Not only did the English missionaries seek to present a unified version of Christianity but they also fiercely resisted Ramabai's inquiry into sectarian differences—an inquiry that culminated in her realization that she had a choice in the precise form of the Christianity she embraced. Ironically, Ramabai's recognition of the splintered, sectarian history of English Christianity brought her to the insight that the existence of religious differences creates the option of choosing a particular idea of religion in which to believe. Ramabai commented disparagingly that 'missionaries who want to convert the Hindoos to their own religion would do well to take care not to call themselves the only inheritors of truth, and all others "the so-called false philosophers", for the Hindoos as a rule will not be content to look or hear only one side'.[56] Such a sense of choice radically transformed her prospective identity as a convert into that of a heretic.

This leads one to surmise that Ramabai's modernity derives less from her repudiation of Hindu tradition than from her embrace of an ideology of free will and choice. Ramabai's understanding of religious choice as a byproduct of English sectarianism suggests a line of thought that allows one to rethink the conventional polarization between tradition and modernity. As the details of Ramabai's conversion emerge more precisely, we learn that the proliferation of sects in English religious history impressed itself on her imagination in intellectually enabling ways. As Ramabai engaged in an animated exchange with her English sponsors, she began to see that there existed a fractured Christianity which the missionaries, for their part, were trying to present as an undivided religion identical with Anglican England. Hence, their unusual description of the Anglican church as Catholic Christianity, 'the holy, apostolic Christianity', which Ramabai learned was a misnomer only long after she had parted company with the missionaries. Remarked an amused but also bemused Ramabai in 1886, 'The Roman Catholics say the Protestant interpretation (including the English Church) of the word "Catholic" is purely imaginary'; she then taunted Geraldine by sarcastically pointing out that 'she had no right to call the Dissenters heretics, because she herself belonged to a Church which is but a Dissenting sect of the Roman Catholic'.[57]

Recent scholars have drawn attention to the crucial role of choice in distinguishing conditions of modernity from those of premodernity. Christopher Queen describes the exercise of individual choice based on reason, careful deliberation and historical consciousness as defining characteristics of modernity. If modernity comprises a complex range of ideas, philosophies and systems, the ability to process them calls for not only reason to make the requisite discriminations between them but also the skill to evaluate the quality of their respective demands on one's attention. Such evaluation is itself a form of choice, but the important point is that choice is possible only when the heterogeneity of belief-systems is made visible. Such acts of conscious selection account for new types of conversion narratives, which reflect the individual subject's greater access to a range of traditions, ideas and doctrines.[58] In this context, the more empowering aspects of English sectarianism for a young convert like Ramabai take on new meaning, for religious choice is as much a part of the logic of modernity as an increasingly differentiated individual subjectivity. If Ramabai is repeatedly accused of indiscriminately exercising reason in areas where faith took precedence, in her defence it would have to be said that the varieties of Christianity practised historically in England required that she respond not with faith but with reason—that is, with the mental acuity to respond to minute distinctions between creeds, as well as the judgement to assess their relative importance within their respective branches of Christianity.

As Ramabai progressively moves towards defining her idea of religion from the sectarian options offered by English Christianity, her own status as a convert undergoes radical change. Sister Geraldine's description of English dissent emphasizes the dilution of religious truth as a product of rank sectarianism. In her earnest yet anxious correspondence with Ramabai she attempts to persuade the impressionable young Indian convert that the Anglican church represents a healthy syncretism, in sharp contrast to the dogmatism of individual sects:

> Since [Wesleyanism] sprang into existence it had split up into 80 different sects drifting farther away from the Truth [which] shewed that their original separation from the Church was in itself a wrong act. This led to a conversation on dissent generally . . . *that all dissent was the undue stretching-out of one doctrine so as to hide or overshadow the other doctrines of the Christian Faith.* I said that in the Church's teaching, a perfect harmony was kept between all the dogmas of the Christian Faith: each had its due value given and helped to form a perfect texture; whereas in dissent an undue importance being given to one doctrine, the symmetry of the whole was marred.[59]

Geraldine's account of Anglicanism is nothing short of an aesthetic description of religious utility. If dissent signifies the attenuation of truth by competing hegemonies, which assert the dominance of one doctrine above all others, then Anglican orthodoxy represents that essential syncretism by which all creeds are kept in perfect aesthetic balance. Anglicanism does so not by manifesting a plurality of difference but by merging into oneness. Not entirely dissimilar to the Arnoldian idea of culture as a containment of disparate forces by filtering the 'best that is thought and known', Geraldine's aestheticized religious ideal explains why sectarianism is as disruptive to the perfect balance represented by Anglican England as working-class anarchy is to English culture.

Silence and Heresy

'The silence of a thousand years has been broken, and the reader of this unpretending little volume catches the first utterances of the unfamiliar voice. Throbbing with woe, they are revealed in the following pages to intelligent, educated, happy American women.'[60] These are the words of Rachel Bodley, dean of the Women's Medical College in Philadelphia, as she introduced Pandita Ramabai to the Western world. These resonant words open Bodley's preface to Pandita Ramabai's hugely successful book, *The High-Caste Hindu Woman* (1888), and establish the terms for the evaluation of Indian women's emancipation as emergence into 'utterance'.

If Ramabai is known at all in the West, it is precisely because she heralded a new, yet unknown voice whose calm, dispassionate presentation of a patriarchal religion from a female point of view ruptured the Orientalist celebration of Eastern philosophy as a repository of sublime mysteries. Rachel Bodley's account locates the hitherto suppressed narrative of the Hindu woman within a continuum of silence that it was Ramabai's particular achievement to disrupt. If Ramabai is remembered as a Hindu social reformer of great note, her outspokenness about the conditions of women's oppression stands out above all other characterizations of her social activism. Her access to public forums such as the print media and the lecture platform allowed her to make the necessary interventions that gained a 'hearing' for her 'voice'. Thus, according to Bodley's rhetorical stance, it stands to reason that if silence is oppression, then speech is liberation.

Yet the fearless Ramabai also confessed that she 'was obliged to keep silence', especially on the subject of church doctrine.[61] This is a strange admission, given that *The Letters and Correspondence of Pandita Ramabai* leaves no doubt in any reader's mind that Ramabai was not one to suppress her scepticism about received notions of religious faith, nor refuse engagement in the most forthright manner with ideas that she found unacceptable. Indeed, thus far I have been arguing just the reverse: that Ramabai declined to accept Christian faith as a given, especially on other people's terms, and was willing to carry on her quarrels with received notions right up to the highest authorities in the Anglican church.

Why then did she resolve on numerous occasions to 'hold my tongue . . . and not say one single word' but 'read the Bible by myself, and follow the teaching of Christ?'[62] Is her withdrawal into silence a surrender to the impossibility of free intellectual debate on questions of religious worship? Or rather does her preferred choice of following Christ's teachings reflect a growing Pauline inclination to replace scriptural exegesis with the practice of private faith? But does that then suggest Ramabai's retreat into spiritual isolation, producing a rhetoric of self-fashioning of the sort that characterizes John Henry Newman's final conversion as an intensely private experience, contrary to the worldliness of his engagement with belief? As we observed earlier about Newman's conversion, his antipathy to large-scale dissemination of convictions arrived at through a laborious process of intellectual dissent grew out of a sense that the compulsion to proselytize masked an intellectual anxiety about the durability of hard-won convictions. Hence his willingness to slip into silence, or what he calls a 'state of repose . . . a tranquil enjoyment of cerittude.'[63] Does Ramabai's retreat into silence signify a comparable withdrawal into the self-enclosed world of private experience?

First, the pattern of Ramabai's silences reveals a curious feature. She claims that she ceases to argue further on doctrinal issues whenever she feels the futility of doing so, especially when she is misunderstood by the missionaries or accused of being difficult and proud: 'I see I cannot make you understand what I mean, nor can you make me believe in all your doctrines exactly as you believe in them.'[64] Ramabai is told in no uncertain terms that her heresy must remain unspoken, or otherwise it will result in the sisters' severing of their relation to her ('I feel my duties as your teacher are now at an end,' cautions Sister Geraldine ominously).[65] Yet while Ramabai recedes into silence on crucial theological points, she continues her resistance to missionaries on other fronts. Disarmed by the charge of sinful pride in her theological quarrels with the missionaries, who equate her speech with wilfulness and thus effectively muffle her probings into religious questions, Ramabai's alternative method of expressing her disagreement with official interpretation is to 'talk back' to the sisters, angrily challenging them in their control of her and in the matter of her daughter's religious upbringing. As an expression of colonial insubordination, the petulance and shrillness of her retorts displace blasphemy as an offence against religious doctrine and sentiment. Even when she is evidently impugning prevailing creeds, her 'heresy' takes the form of a stern tongue-lashing:

> Am I to submit to this kind of teaching? Am I to submit to the teaching of the clergy like Canon Butler, who denies that I have a voice in choosing my own religion, or to you who say that my conscience is no conscience at all and who say that outside your Church no truth can be bound, and if I tolerate with all the bodies of Christian people, I cannot be truthful? . . You or rather some of the clergy of your church think that they could make many converts to their faith in India by telling them the Anglican Church only teaches the true religion, but I think it otherwise.[66]

This passage nicely illustrates the thin line separating heresy—as an offence against orthodox doctrine—from rank verbal assault ranging from sheer impertinence to outright insubordination. The most striking quality of Ramabai's alternating silence and speech is her uncanny ability to mix intellectual interrogation with insolence, as she strategically blurs the boundaries between the two and shifts the focus of her transgression from heresy to effrontery. In the above passage, for instance, it is significant that nowhere does she attack points of doctrine; there is no engagement with ideas—only retort, condescension and retaliation. Similarly, ordering Sister Geraldine to desist from teaching her daughter Manorama the rudiments of Trinitarian belief, including the Athanasian Creed and the Thirty-Nine Articles, Ramabai's rebuke is more noticeable for its sharply reprimanding tone than for an analytical objection to Trinitarianism. If Ramabai is disarmed by the charge of pride, she in turn immobilizes the missionaries by the grating vehemence of her response.

Because the severity of Ramabai's tone conveys the uneven quality of a relationship presumed to be built on pedagogical trust but now exposed as paternalistic in fact, the missionaries are unable to reduce her recalcitrant posture to pride alone. Indeed, Ramabai's tone creates a context for her challenge of church doctrine—a context that includes the colonial conversion of subject peoples, the imposition of a religious creed which is interchangeable with imperialist hegemony, and the whole structure of unequal relationships that these presuppose. Her 'heresy' is transformed from a repudiation of specific points of doctrine into a sharp questioning of the rationale of colonial expropriation, culminating in an unequivocal denunciation of the arbitrary imposition of one people's will on others.

The missionaries' attempt to control Ramabai by curbing her speech is consistent with what Gyan Prakash has described as a general colonial attempt to normalize what cannot be named or recognized—in this case, her intellectual independence and spiritual integrity.[67] Ramabai was fully aware of the terror and fear that filled the missionaries in the face of her transgression's unnameability. That is why she could scornfully rebuke them for making 'the word "pride" almost meaningless by applying it to everything that you see in me'.[68] And there was a certain truth in her accusation, for vastly conflicting kinds of verbal behaviour—be it a lack of communication or persistent questioning—were all attributed to the same cause; pride assumed an explanatory power that far exceeded the behaviour that it putatively described. Apparently for missionaries and colonial officers alike, it was much easier to deal with their native subjects' outright rebellion and even 'heathenish' superstition than with Indians' rewriting of Christianity to suit their own purposes. What were administrators and missionaries to do when subjects claimed belief as entitling them to independent judgement? As an unmanageable part of colonial rule, belief was resistant to the space that was sought for it in programmes of governance and reform. Indeed, colonial manipulations were actually far more successful in creating a space for English culture than in regulating belief. The successful introduction of English literature is a case in point.[69]

Yet it is also the case that Ramabai oftens turns to silence as a form of resistance to doctrinal coercion. Silence in such instances is preparatory to the private interpretation that made her so subversive in missionaries' eyes. The missionaries in their turn read this as evidence of her 'alienation from her friends'—in other words, as conclusive proof of her ever-present, errant pride distancing her further and further from divine mercy. And so the circle of accusation continues. Given that it was unlikely Ramabai would easily change her mind about central doctrinal points, how could she be brought to a situation where she would refrain from uttering views that the church declared to be heresies, yet at the same time not withdraw into a silence that had equally heretical outcomes?

Indeed, the missionaries' dilemma centred around the complex, even contradictory function of silence. In her refusal to speak, Ramabai was as transgressive as when she committed herself to speech. For as Dorothea Beale, principal of Cheltenham Ladies College where Ramabai was a student and instructor, confides in a private letter to Sister Geraldine, 'If she does not find someone to whom she can speak freely, she will be silent, and might easily pass into Unitarianism.'[70] The relation between silence and heresy is clearly more complex than can be understood by descriptions of heresy hunting as a matter of policing by silencing alone. As the last-quoted remark makes clear, complete suppression of speech is no more effective in stemming the tide towards heterodoxy than the threat of punishment or ostracism from community. Though curbs may be effectively placed on speech to prevent unacceptable utterances, the ferment from which those utterances are produced remains unchecked. Therefore, speech must be allowed, but only in such ways that its influence will be confined to a carefully circumscribed space and not extend beyond it.

It is of no small significance that the limited space offered to Ramabai for voicing her religious doubts is that of an enlightened but enclosed community of women. The sisters' repeated declaration that Ramabai could not speak to a man about certain religious subjects—'there are some subjects that she could only discuss with a woman'—offers the construction of a feminist community as a counterpoint to existing barriers in social interaction between men and women.[71] Sister Geraldine's assurance that 'to a woman she can speak on the Incarnation as she could not to a man' discovers in the confessor relationship not only a practice for maintaining institutional authority but also a convention for forging sisterly bonds.[72] The conditions for the possibility of speech have a gendered aspect that merges with the boundaries of acceptable theological doctrine. For, of course, the missionaries' refashioning of community is not aimed at establishing sisterhood but, instead, at containing heresy. The feminist bonding offered by the Wantage order leaves intact the structure of patriarchal authority derived from church tradition, even as it encourages the new convert to enact her heresies on a stage especially constructed for her via feminism. The difference, of course, is that on this particular stage Ramabai's heresies will be restrained and rendered harmless, even though they are articulated freely as sisterly communication.

Yet here too the missionaries failed to meet their objectives entirely. Though the sisters assumed that the inhibitions a woman might be expected to feel about discussing the virgin birth would be naturally applicable to Ramabai, a Hindu widow, they were not prepared for her obstinate refusal to avoid questions about immaculate conception, nor did they have a ready answer to her blunt remark that 'as far as we know of the history of mankind told in the Scripture, and from other sources, as well as by our experience, we know that no man except the first couple was ever born without the natural course'.[73] Amid these scattered remarks is a refusal by Ramabai to accept a community of women as her sole interlocutors in theological debate.

Nowhere is this refusal more apparent than in her translation of 'conversion' into the sphere of gender relations. Of her many actions that so chagrined her mentors, none was as aggravating as her insistence on teaching English to both men and women. Other teachers attached to the Wantage order were known to instruct men at the Working Men's College, so her request was not an unusual one. Yet the alarm bells that it set off exposed the Orientalist assumptions about Hindu women that still guided missionary policy. In her caustic response to Sister Geraldine's disapproving letters, Ramabai reminds her that in the course of their numerous pilgrimages she and her brother habitually addressed communities of male scholars, as a result of which she earned the title of Saraswati, or goddess of learning.

> It surprises me very much to think that neither my father nor my husband objected [to] my mother's or my teaching young men while some English people are doing so. You can call some of my countrywomen 'hedged' but you cannot apply this adjective to Marathi Brahmin women. You have

> yourself seen that Marathi ladies are neither hedged nor kept behind thick curtains. . . . Can I confine my work only to women in India and have nothing to do with men?[74]

When reprimanded that it was indelicate of her—a Hindu widow—to teach men or visit 'gentlemen friends', especially given her own orthodox background, Ramabai rebuts with one of the most sustained anti-Orientalist diatribes in nineteenth-century letters. Simultaneously, she punctures almost all the cherished notions of women's reform held by English missionaries and claims a more privileged status as a Hindu woman by virtue of exposure to indigenous reform movements (like the Brahmo Samaj). Is this backsliding or sheer perversity? That question worries the missionaries, and Ramabai's determination to set her own agenda for women's reform coalesces into the 'objectives': 'Unless I begin to have a regular and pure intercourse with men, I shall in vain hope and try to help my countrywomen.'[75] For the feminist community proposed by Sister Geraldine is akin to the secluded *purdahnasheen*, zenana-style arrangement from which Ramabai and other Indian women had determined to emerge. By the time Geraldine perceives that the source of Ramabai's vehemence is a retrograde feature of caste society missionaries had long sought to remedy, Geraldine realizes she has no choice but to permit the transgressions that her attempt at forging sisterly bonds sought to contain.

> I see now why she makes this a matter of principle. I think we must remember that God seems to have anointed her with power to throw down the pernicious caste restrictions and those barriers which wrongly separate men and women. In this she has worked with all whom God set over her—father, mother, brother, husband. She would feel herself disloyal to their memory, who approved of her (a young girl) speaking in mixed assemblies if she gave in to any rules which said a woman should not teach boys. . . . It seems to me a matter in which we ought not to bind her conscience.[76]

Producing inevitable conflict and ambivalence in the Wantage sisters' dealings with Ramabai is their representation of England as at once a desirable symbol of modernity and a source of corruption. Although the learning contained in Western knowledge has the power to dispel

Hindu superstition, the sisters fear that it also fosters a superciliousness taking the form of either self-estrangement or a false sense of independence.[77] Either way, separation from earlier patterns of understanding and behaviour complements the alienation brought about by Ramabai's loosening of ties to family and community. If the missionaries object to the self-sufficiency of Ramabai's posture, they cannot help concluding that English education contributed in no small way to it. Ramabai recognizes the inherent contradiction in such a representation and, in her counterattack, forces the missionaries to peer into the mirror of modernity as the source of human depravity, displacing biblical explanations of depravity as the result of original sin. When challenged by the sisters who trace Ramabai's and other colonized Indians' arrogance to the detrimental effects of Western education, Ramabai turns the customary missionary explanations of human pride and sinfulness adroitly against them: 'I believe it is not learning or wisdom that makes people either proud or idle. It is their own nature that makes them so.'[78] Ironically, Sister Geraldine's ponderous words on Ramabai's proud nature return to haunt the nervous missionary, and it is Ramabai who, in deflecting them back towards her, has the decisive word on the subject.

Notes

1. A.B. Shah, ed., introduction to *The Letters and Correspondence of Pandita Ramabai* (Bombay: Maharashtra State Board for Literature and Culture, 1977), p. xi. Hereafter cited as *Correspondence*.
2. Letter from Pandita Ramabai, Poona, to Sister Geraldine, C.S.M.V., Wantage, 11 December 1893, in *Correspondence*.
3. In *Home and Harem: Nation, Gender, Empire, and the Cultures of Travel* (Durham: Duke University Press, 1966), Inderpal Grewal points out the difficulties of positioning Ramabai within the critiques of Hindu patriarchy, since this discourse was also deployed by English missionaries to achieve their own aim of Christian conversion (p. 180). Arguing that there were no 'neutral spaces' for articulating the problems and oppressions of Hindu women, Grewal maintains that Ramabai's genius lay in appropriating the rhetoric of the colonial state and missionaries to construct her own independent agency. Much the same is argued by Antoinette Burton in *Burdens of History: British Feminists, Indian Women, and Imperial Culture, 1885–1915* (Chapel Hill: University of North Carolina Press, 1994): resistance to the imperialist gestures of British women, she maintains, spurred Ramabai

to an acute self-consciousness (p. 32). Teresa Hubel, in *Whose India? The Independence Struggle in British and Indian Fiction and History* (Durham: Duke University Press, 1996), also conjoins Ramabai's critique of imperialism and Hindu patriarchy. My own argument has a considerably different focus, for my suggestion is that Ramabai's agency is constitutive of her developing religious sensibility, and not a mere strategy appropriated from her colonial mentors. Her critiques of colonialism not only aimed to dismantle Hindu patriarchy but also served to create her own ideal religious system in which her critical sensibility remained intact.

4. Pandita Ramabai, *The High-Caste Hindu Woman* (Philadelphia: Press of the J.B. Rogers Printing, 1988), p. 103. See also Meera Kosambi, 'Women, Emancipation, and Equality: Pandita Ramabai's Contribution to Women's Cause', *Economic and Political Weekly*, 29 October 1988: WS38–WS49, for a thorough treatment of Ramabai's social activism.
5. Quoted in S.M. Adhav, *Pandita Ramabai* (Madras: Christian Literature Society, 1979), p. 15. It is interesting that four decades earlier, in 1841, John Henry Newman made the argument that a completely Protestant document like the Thirty-Nine Articles still made room for the English clergy to accept their vocation on the authority of the Church of Rome. In denying the exclusionary intents of the articles, Newman made the claim that the interpretive possibilities of the document allowed for its being brought in harmony with the Book of Common Prayer. 'The Protestant Confession was drawn up with the purpose of including Catholics; and Catholics now will not be excluded. What was an economy in the reformers, is a protection to us. What would have been a perplexity to us then, is a perplexity to Protestants now. We could not then have found fault with their words; they cannot now repudiate our meaning.' John Henry Newman, 'Remarks on Certain Passages in the Thirty-Nine Articles', in *Religion in Victorian Britain: Sources*, vol. 3, edited by James R. Moore (Manchester: Manchester University Press, 1988), p. 13.
6. Letter from Pandita Ramabai to Sister Geraldine, 22 September 1885, in *Correspondence*, p. 88.
7. Letter from Sister Geraldine to Pandita Ramabai, October 1885, in *Correspondence*, p. 104.
8. E.P. Thompson, *Witness against the Beast: William Blake and the Moral Law* (Cambridge: Cambridge University Press, 1993), p. 10.
9. Letter from Sister Geraldine to Pandita Ramabai, October 1885, in *Correspondence*, p. 103.
10. Letter from Sister Geraldine to Pandita Ramabai, in answer to objections she made to the Catholic faith, 5 October 1885, in *Correspondence*, p. 91.
11. Letter from Pandita Ramabai to Sister Geraldine, 12 May 1885, in *Correspondence*, p. 61.

12. Letter from Pandita Ramabai to Canon Butler, 3 July 1885, in *Correspondence*, p. 74.
13. See letter from Sister Geraldine, in Wantage, to Pandita Ramabai, in Poona, 14 December 1896, in *Correspondence*, p. 339: 'It is that I *hold* the Faith which the Church has taught for nearly nineteen centuries, and *you choose* for yourself a spurious production: that *I have been willing to learn from the Church*, and you are unwilling to "hear the Church". And our Lord says of such: "If any man neglect to hear the Church, let him be unto thee as a heathen man and a publican." ' Emphasis in original.
14. Letter from the Rev. Mother, C.S.M.V. to an Exterior Sister, C.S.M.V., 1 November 1883, in *Correspondence*, p. 20.
15. Letter from Sister Geraldine, Wantage, to Pandita Ramabai, Cheltenham, 10 May 1883, in *Correspondence*, p. 53.
16. Letter from Pandita Ramabai, Cheltenham, to Sister Geraldine, Wantage, 12 May 1885, in *Correspondence*, p. 59.
17. Letter from Dorothea Beale, Cheltenham, to Sister Geraldine, Wantage, 8 May 1885, in *Correspondence*, p. 49.
18. Pandita Ramabai, *My Testimony* (1907: 10th ed. Kedgaon: Ramabai Mukti Mission, 1977), p. 17; quoted in Meera Kosambi, 'Indian Response to Christianity. Church and Colonialism: Case of Pandita Ramabai', *Economic and Political Weekly*, 24 October 1992, p. WS-62.
19. Ibid.
20. Letter from the Rev. Mother, C.S.M.V., to an Exterior Sister, C.S.M.V., 1 November 1883, in *Correspondence*, p. 19.
21. Ram Bapat, 'Pandita Ramabai: Faith and Reason in the Shadow of the East and West', in *Representing Hinduism: The Construction of Religious Tradition and National Identity*, edited by Vasudha Dalmia and H. von Stietencron (Delhi: Sage Publications, 1995), p. 226.
22. Pandita Ramabai, *My Testimony*, pp. 18–20; quoted in ibid., p. 227.
23. Bapat, 'Pandita Ramabai', p. 228.
24. Ramabai, *My Testimony*; quoted in Bapat, p. 227.
25. Bapat, 'Pandita Ramabai', p. 227.
26. Letter from Dorothea Beale to the Bishop of Bombay in England, 22 May 1884, in *Correspondence*, p. 42.
27. Letter from Sister Geraldine, London, to Dorothea Beale, Cheltenham, January 1886, in *Correspondence*, p. 114.
28. Letter from Pandita Ramabai, Cheltenham, to Sister Geraldine, Wantage, 12 May 1885, in *Correspondence*, p. 59.
29. Letter from Sister Geraldine, Wantage, to Pandita Ramabai, Cheltenham, 19 May 1885, in *Correspondence*, p. 53.
30. Letter from Pandita Ramabai, U.S.A., to Dorothea Beale, Cheltenham, 22 May 1887, in *Correspondence*, p. 176. Emphasis added.

31. Letter from Pandita Ramabai, Cheltenham, to Canon Butler, Wantage, 3 July 1885, in *Correspondence*, p. 74. A Sanskrit and Marathi scholar, Father Nehemiah Goreh (Nilakanta Shastri) was, like Ramabai, a Chitpavan Brahmin who converted to Christianity. Ramabai had occasion to know him in Poona in the years prior to her departure for England. She often claimed that he was one of the few people to whom she could confide her religious doubts and questions; while in England, she frequently corresponded with him for clarification about points of Christian doctrine.
32. Sister Geraldine, 'Apologia Pro Opere' (1917), in *Correspondence*, p. 3.
33. Letter from Pandita Ramabai, Cheltenham, to Sister Geraldine, Wantage, 7 November 1885, in *Correspondence*, p. 112.
34. Letter from Pandita Ramabai to Sister Geraldine, July 1884, in *Correspondence*, p. 25.
35. Sister Geraldine, 'Apologia Pro Opere', in *Correspondence*, p. 4.
36. Letter from Pandita Ramabai to Dorothea Beale, 21 June 1885, in *Correspondence*, p. 157.
37. Letter from Pandita Ramabai to Sister Geraldine, 20 September 1885, in *Correspondence* p. 86.
38. Letter from Sister Geraldine to the Dean of Lincoln, 1 July 1885, in *Correspondence*, p. 71.
39. Letter from Pandita Ramabai to Sister Geraldine, 20 September 1885, in *Correspondence*, p. 87.
40. Shah, introduction to *Correspondence*, p. xxxiii.
41. David Lawton, *Blasphemy* (Philadelphia: University of Pennsylvania Press, 1993), p. 126.
42. Ibid.
43. Letter from Dorothea Beale to the Rev. Canon William Butler, Wantage, July 1885, in *Correspondence*, p. 78.
44. Letter from Pandita Ramabai to Sister Geraldine, June 1885, in *Correspondence*, p. 70.
45. Letter from Pandita Ramabai to Dorothea Beale, 1 September 1885, in *Correspondence*, p. 136.
46. Letter from Pandita Ramabai to Dorothea Beale, 30 June 1885, in *Correspondence*, p. 128.
47. Ibid.
48. Letter from Pandita Ramabai to Dorothea Beale, 29 November 1885, in *Correspondence*, p. 160.
49. Letter from Dorothea Beale to Sister Geraldine—Proposal for Ramabai to leave at midsummer, 22 April 1885, in *Correspondence*, p. 32. Emphasis in original.
50. Letter from Sister Geraldine to Pandita Ramabai, October 1855, in *Correspondence*, p. 96.

51. Sister Geraldine, 'Apologia Pro Opera', in *Correspondence*, p. 4.
52. Letter from Dorothea Beale to the Rev. Canon William Butler, Wantage, July 1885, in *Correspondence*, p. 79. Emphasis in original.
53. Letter from Pandita Ramabai to Sister Geraldine, 25 March 1885, in *Correspondence*, p. 37. Ramabai came to know Max Müller quite well when she was in England, and was invited to visit his home at Oxford, where he was then a professor of comparative philology. Though he admired her vast learning in Sanskrit and Hinduism, he deplored her Christian conversion, writing in an 1895 letter from Oxford: 'What I feared when Ramabai became a Christian, has happened: She has impaired her power of doing useful work among her countrymen. Her native friends do not quite trust her, her European friends do not always remember what they owe to her. In all essentials, Ramabai had been a Christian even while she was still a Brahmin; and when she openly professed herself a Christian, it was because she felt the necessity of belonging to some communion, to be one with her friends. . . . I did not persuade Ramabai to become a Christian, because I know she *was* a Christian in heart, which is far better than a Christian by profession'. Quoted in Adhav, *Pandita Ramabai*, p. 12.
54. Bapat, 'Pandita Ramabai', p. 227.
55. Hugh McLeod, *Religion and the Working Class in Nineteenth-Century Britain* (London: Macmillan, 1984), p. 36.
56. Letter of Pandita Ramabai to Dorothea Beale, February–March 1886, in *Correspondence*, p. 170.
57. Ibid.
58. See, for instance, Christopher Queen, 'Ambedkar, Modernity, and the Hermeneutics of Buddhist Liberation', in *Dr Ambedkar, Buddhism and Social Change*, edited by A.K. Narain and D.C. Ahir (Delhi: B.R. Publishing, 1994).
59. Letter from Sister Geraldine, Bath, to Pandita Ramabai, October 1885, in *Correspondence*, p. 102. Emphasis added.
60. Rachel Bodley, introduction to *The High-Caste Hindu Woman*, p. i.
61. Letter from Pandita Ramabai, Cheltenham, to Canon Butler, Wantage, 3 July 1885, in *Correspondence*, p. 74.
62. Ibid. p. 76.
63. John Henry Newman, *An Essay in Aid of a Grammar of Assent* (Notre Dame: University of Notre Dame Press, 1979), p. 166.
64. Letter from Pandita Ramabai to Sister Geraldine, 15 October 1885, p. 107.
65. Letter from Sister Geraldine, at Bath, to Pandita Ramabai, October 1885, in *Correspondence*, p. 106.
66. Letter from Pandita Ramabai to Sister Geraldine, 7 November 1885, in *Correspondence*, p. 112.

67. Gyan Prakash, introduction to *After Colonialism: Imperial Histories and Post-colonial Displacements* (Princeton: Princeton University Press, 1995), p. 6.
68. Letter from Pandita Ramabai to Sister Geraldine, 15 October 1885, in *Correspondence*, p. 108.
69. See my *Masks of Conquest: Literary Study and British Rule in India* (New York: Columbia University Press, 1989).
70. Letter from Dorothea Beale, Penshurst, to Sister Geraldine, 22 April 1885, in *Correspondence*, p. 32.
71. Letter from Dorothea Beale, Cheltenham, to Sister Geraldine, April 1885, in *Correspondence*, p. 33.
72. Letter from Dorothea Beale, Penshurst, to Sister Geraldine, April 1885, in *Correspondence*, p. 32.
73. Letter from Pandita Ramabai to Dorothy Beale, 29 November 1885, in *Correspondence*, p. 159.
74. Letter from Pandita Ramabai to Sister Geraldine, 12 May 1885, in *Correspondence*, pp. 60–1.
75. Ibid.
76. Letter from Dorothea Beale, Cheltenham, to Sister Geraldine, Wantage, 8 May 1885, in *Correspondence*, p. 49.
77. British administrators themselves feared that the introduction of English education created self-alienation and false independence in the colonized population. See my *Masks of Conquest*, pp. 142–65.
78. Letter from Pandita Ramabai, Cheltenham, to Sister Geraldine, Wantage, July 1884, in *Correspondence*, p. 25.

9

The Daughters of Aryavarta*

MADHU KISHWAR

The nineteenth-century social reform movements were the first organized, all-India response to the challenges posed by colonial rule. They were initiated by the urban educated elite who, although they were a small proportion of the population, made extensive use of modern means of communication and thus came to acquire a widespread social, political and ideological hegemony. In this paper, I will focus on the hegemony this elite acquired in defining the 'women's question' in large parts of north India.

While focusing on the women's reform movement in Punjab, led by the Arya Samaj, I will address the question of why the women's issue came to be one of the central issues for reformers; why women's education came to occupy such an important place in the social reform movement; and the state of women's education in Punjab before the Arya Samaj started its reform activity. I will also deal with the question of women's own response to the process of social change. I have tried to show that women were not mere passive recipients of welfare activity, as most of the available historical literature suggests they were, but that their participation in the questioning process gave rise to self-generated activity by individual pioneers and by women's organizations.

Dayanand's call to purge Hinduism of distortions by restoring its Vedic purity and to defend it from attack by colonial Christianizing forces received a ready response from the educated elite which emerged

*From *Indian Economic and Social History Review*, vol. 23, 1986, pp. 151–86.

from the ranks of small businessmen, traders and money-lenders situated in urban and semi-urban areas. This elite adapted his teachings to their own needs and aspirations.

The Arya Samaj movement was, on the one hand, an attempt by the educated elite to reform Hinduism and, on the other, to defend itself from ideological onslaught by the colonial rulers. Through this movement, the elite tried to evolve new forms of organization to promote its own interests.

The Arya Samaj was not meant as a radical challenge to the existing structures of society. Even while it represented an assertion of indigenous culture, it picked up for reform precisely those issues which British rulers had pointed to as evidence of the degenerate state of Indian society. Operating within the parameters of the given social structure, the Arya Samaj sought to reform only those features which they thought acted as obstacles in the way of the economic and social advancement of the educated elite. Nowhere is this more evident than in its programme concerning caste discrimination and the low status of women—the twin foundations of Hindu society.

The First Phase

Since Dayanand Saraswati acted as the intellectual mentor of the Arya Samaj, an evaluation of his ideas on the question of women's status in society provides interesting insights into the nature of the reform movement undertaken by his followers and the educational institutions developed by them. Revivalism, based on the authority of the Vedas as interpreted by Dayanand, was the salient feature of and the prime sanction behind the movement. The depressed condition of women was also seen in the context of the presumed degeneration of Hindu society because of its departure from Vedic ideals.

However, Dayanand, in his writings, does not seem concerned with women as individuals. He recognizes women only in their familial roles as wives and mothers.[1] Since marriage was seen as the key institution of society, women were seen as essential acquisitions for men. However, even though Dayanand tried to argue in favour of relatively more humane treatment of women, his views on the importance of monogamous marriage show clearly the conservative social functions he wanted it to serve: (*a*) hierarchical relations which teach one group to serve another; (*b*) imposition of sexual restraint on women in order to ensure that they produce 'healthy' legitimate children for their husbands; (*c*) preservation of private property which can be inherited only by rightful successors:

> If the institution of marriage did not exist, all amenities of domestic life will come to an end. None will serve another. Downright adultery and illicit connections will increase, all men and women will be afflicted with disease, physically and mentally weakened, and will consequently die young. . . . No one will have a title to succeed to another's property, nor will any person be able to retain possession of anything for any great length of time.[2]

However, in the sphere of religion, unlike Manu, Dayanand's interpretation of the Vedic tradition upheld the right of all individuals, including those from the most oppressed groups in Hindu society—women and Shudras—to enter into direct communion with god. It was from this premise that Dayanand went on to champion the cause of women's education: 'All men and women (i.e., the whole mankind) have a right to study.'[3] An ignorant wife could not participate as an equal partner with her husband in social and religious duties as women in the Vedic age did. Other reasons advanced in favour of women's education included: 'If the husband be well-educated and the wife ignorant or vice versa, there will be a constant state of warfare in the house.'[4]

Moreover, he felt that without education, women could not distinguish right from wrong, behave themselves agreeably towards their husbands and relatives, beget children properly, train, nurture and bring them up well, do or see domestic duties done as they ought to be done.[5] He advocated compulsory education for all boys and girls.

Dayanand believed that men and women were created to unite in wedlock and propagate the human species. He advocated certain reforms in marriage customs which became an integral part of the Arya Samaj creed. Dayanand envisaged an ideal marriage as one in which both parties freely exercised their choice: 'The best form of marriage is that by choice (*swayamvara*), after the education of the contracting parties is finished and their *brahmacharya* . . . periods completed'.[6]

Marriage and procreation were seen as the primary duties of every woman, but an ill-matched marriage was worse than no marriage at all.[7] Women were to exercise their choice in marriage, not only because Dayanand advocated some form of individual freedom for women but also because 'when people choose their partners for life themselves . . . the children born of such a union are also of a superior order.'[8]

Remarriage for the twice-born was totally ruled out, except in the case of virgin widows and men who had had no sexual experience[9] because if remarriage was freely allowed, 'on the death of one party, the other will take away the property of his or her deceased consort, when he or she marries again. This will give rise to family disputes.'[10] Moreover, 'if a widow remarries, many a noble family will be blotted out of existence, and its property destroyed (by constant alienation)'.[11] He felt that 'remarriage involves loss of true conjugal love and infraction of duty towards the departed husband or wife'.[12]

However, widowed men or women without children could enter the *niyoga* form of alliance for the sole purpose of begetting children. They were to meet only in the 'season of women', 'once a month'.[13] The institution of niyoga would help counter evils like prostitution wherein men of 'noble' families were 'spoilt' by harlots and fallen women.[14]

Adultery and prostitution were condemned on the grounds that

> whoever wastes this invaluable fluid [spermatic fluid] in illicit intercourse with other people's wives, prostitutes, or lewd men, is the greatest fool, because even a farmer or a gardener, ignorant though he be, does not sow the seed in a field or a garden that is not his own but belongs to another man.[15]

However, this whole scheme of rules of conduct had to pay due regard to and be attuned to the expected frailties of men: 'If a man be not able to control his passions while his wife is pregnant, he may contract *niyoga* with (a widow) and beget offspring on her, but let him never misconduct himself with a prostitute or commit adultery.'[16]

Even when formally granting men and women the right to choose marriage partners, very strict rules about male and female segregation were advocated, making nonsense of their formal freedom.

> The boys' school should be at least 3 miles distant from that of the girls'. The tutors and other employees, such as servants, should, in the boys' school, be all of the male sex, and in the girls' school, of the female sex. Not even a child of 5 years of the opposite sex should be allowed to enter the school.[17]

A life of absolute celibacy and austerity had to be lived till adulthood, so as to avoid any excitation of passions and senses before marriage and to preserve the vital energy of the body. Dayanand's suggestion was that 'the king [should] encourage the practice of *brahmacharya*. Let him put a stop to prostitution and the custom of plurality of wives.'[18]

The basic message of Dayanand's reform movement was that 'women must not be ill treated' because they are the custodians of the family and the repositories of its honour. But there was absolutely nothing new in this message. Manu had said the same thing, yet the problem had remained. In fact, it may have become more acute with time. Why then was this message suddenly being resurrected with such vigour?

The answer is provided if one looks at the low status of upper-caste Hindu women, whose life condition the Arya Samaj tried to uplift, as well as at the dynamics of social change that Punjab underwent as a result of its integration into the colonial system. That the urgency of the women's question felt by the Samajists was not just a matter of a new-found spirit of 'liberal humanism' or sudden 'enlightenment' of the Hindu male reformer becomes obvious when we take note of the contemporary situation to which they were responding.

In Punjab, in 1881, 24.8 per cent of women over 15 years of age in all communities were widows. The figure for Hindus and Sikhs was 25.8 per cent.[19] In 1901, 1,363 out of every 10,000 females of all ages in Punjab were widows (as against 623 widowers per 10,000 men).[20] The phenomenon of child widowhood and ban on widow remarriage was almost exclusively confined to certain upper castes and classes. The 1901 Census observes: 'the higher their [the castes'] social position, the lower is the age of betrothal and marriage.'[21]

To the reformers, the dangerous repercussions of the oppressive institution of compulsory widowhood seemed uncomfortably apparent:

> In such cases, their situation becomes one of utter helplessness, and the result is, as well it might be, that they generally yield to temptation, and many of them become women of abandoned character, and thus swell the ranks of prostitutes, leaving thereby an indelible blot on the honour of those who even claim any relationship whatever with them.[22]

Even though the evidence put together by the reformers of a large increase in the number of urban higher-caste widows who became prostitutes is scanty and difficult to draw definite conclusions from, they seem to have taken whatever information they had as a warning signal of danger to all women of upper caste and class status as well as to widows. For example, on 13 May 1900, *The Indian Social Reformer* reported that between 1893 and 1897, the average number of convicts imprisoned in British India for the offence of 'causing miscarriage, exposing children and concealment of birth of child' was 15 in Madras, 38 in Bombay, 48 in Bengal, 116 in the North Western Provinces and Oudh, 32 in Punjab and 12 in the Central Provinces.[23] These are not large numbers but *The Indian Social Reformer* drew its own conclusions, saying that for every one such case 'that is brought to light . . . there may be many thousands behind the veil. . . . Even taking into account the most utilitarian ideas, the need of widow marriages is the more observable and felt by witnessing these gruesome cases.'[24] The 'gruesome case' referred to here was that of the murder of a 25-year-old widow and her newborn child.

In the reformers' view, there was an increasing incidence of abandonment of widows by their families, leading to a large increase of vice in the cities. The reformers were deeply perturbed by the increase of open prostitution in the new large towns. Among well-off families, *nautch* girls were an integral feature of entertainment at all festive occasions. Men of this class traditionally resorted to prostitutes, as a way of life and a mark of status. However, the newspapers of the times, especially those that became vehicles of the reform movement, were full of self-righteous outcries against this 'evil'.

The reformers thought that upper-caste widows were becoming more vulnerable because the undivided family, which was supposed to shelter helpless women, was on the decline. They conveniently forgot that the worst forms of exploitation of women usually happened within the family, and were perpetrated by the women's male relatives.

Unlike most low-caste women, many upper-caste deserted wives who were forced to earn their own living could neither seek nor get any employment outside the house and generally employed themselves in spinning cotton and grinding corn.[25]

The few occupations available to upper-caste women were especially threatened by colonial intrusion. For instance, the destruction of the handicraft industry due to the large-scale flooding of the Indian market with foreign mill-made cloth had a severely adverse effect on women.[26]

Whatever little employment was available to women was available mostly to lower-caste women because they had fewer restrictions on their mobility and suffered from fewer ritual caste taboos regarding the kind of work they were allowed to do. In certain ways, the upper-caste *pardanashin* women, if widowed or abandoned by their families, were rendered even more vulnerable than lower-caste women. The 1901 Punjab Census reported:

> . . . women are only employed in relatively large numbers, in the indefinite and disreputable occupations. Out of all females in these provinces, only 13,09,182 or only 10.6 are actual workers and their employments are practically confined to personal and household services, the preparation of food and drink, light and firing, dress and general labour including earth-work—in other words, to menial occupations. . . . In other words, women when employed at all, or allowed to earn a living must work at the most degrading and roughest occupation.[27]

Trained only for a life-time of dependence, both mental and physical, enclosed in a world whose limits were exceedingly narrow, the upper-caste widow or deserted wife was helpless if maltreated. The only options available were prostitution, conversion to Christianity (and thereby finding of shelter in a Christian mission) or going to a pilgrimage centre to survive on charity. The first two options do not seem to have been frequently chosen. But even stray cases evoked a near-hysterical response because even the threat of prostitution or conversion posed a serious challenge to those who had an interest in preserving the traditional family as an institution. Rejection and social ostracism of such women was not enough. This form of defiance had somehow to be stopped.

The famine of 1896–97 seems to have further aggravated the plight of pardanashin widows and this was also commented upon by the 1901 Punjab Census. The vernacular papers were full of reports about missionaries taking advantage of the situation and trapping women into Christianity. For instance, the *Chaudhvin Sadi* of August 1896, from Rawalpindi, complained that great injustice had been done to one Abdul Rahman in Peshawar district when his wife, Babboo Jan, was lured by a missionary lady. Apparently, the woman had complained that her husband severely maltreated her because she could not bear a child.[28]

During the famine years, reports of the sale of women and children became frequent. *Rahbar-i-Hind* of 19 November 1896 sounded the alarm by reporting that missionaries had purchased some Indian children for five annas each for the purpose of conversion.[29] *Siraj-ul-Akbar* of December 1896 reported that people had been reduced to such straits by the famine that parents were beginning to sell girls to a missionary lady for one seer of oats per child.[30] The *Punjab Samachar* from Lahore, of 9 January 1897, concluded that 'the prevalence of the famine, on the one hand, and the poverty of the people, on the other, are helping the missionaries in their work, and if this state of things continues, all indigent people will embrace Christianity before long'.[31] Most papers at this time reported an increase in criminal offences in connection with women, as a result of the famine. The plight of parda-nashin women, especially widows, who could not seek work at relief works was stated to be particularly vulnerable, and demands were made that the government make special arrangements to help this class of sufferers.[32]

The warnings continued for many years. As late as 1918, one of the reformers said: 'One of the greatest evils today is the alarming increase in the number of prostitutes . . . in each quarter of every big city . . . we must devise some means to put a stop to further recruitment of our wives and widows.'[33]

The institution of child marriage also made education virtually impossible for upper-caste women. In a fast-changing world, purdah and illiteracy ensured the virtual isolation of these women from the reality of their husbands and sons who were adapting to the demands of colonial structures. This was slowly but definitely creating for the men a wide schism between the private world of the home and family and the increasingly Westernized public world of employment and politics. Thus, the institution of the family was experiencing new stresses. One way of absorbing the stress was to expose women to a 'feminine' version of the education that men were receiving.

The Decline of Indigenous Education

The Education Commission of 1884 found that there were 1,029 girls' schools under government inspection in 1865–66. They declined to 317 in 1881–82.[34] Indigenous schools were dying out with the destruction of the traditional elite which patronized them. The government was taking little initiative to fill the vacuum. Colonial administrators noted with regret that 'if there is any one class of natives who might be considered as practically excluded from the benefits of Government primary schools for girls, it is the higher class who keep their women in strict purdah . . .'[35]

In the Punjab of the pre-annexation days, different communities maintained their respective schools. Very little information exists about the exact nature of education in Punjab just before British annexation. According to the *Punjab Education Commission Report,* boys received secular and religious education and also some vocational training, as, for instance, at the pathshalas of the trading community, which laid special emphasis on mathematics and account keeping.

But, for girls, the *Punjab Education Report* goes on to say that learning was confined to the reading of religious texts. Among the Muslims and Sikhs, the imperative to read the sacred texts made female literacy socially acceptable. Among the Hindus of the upper castes, girls were taught in the privacy of their own homes. However, very rarely were they taught to write, for this was considered an accomplishment at which only the superior class of courtesans were supposed to be adept. The few who could write hesitated to admit the fact.[36]

The British system of education had been introduced for men with a clear purpose in mind. It aimed at creating a new social base for British rule and to produce a sub-elite which could man the colonial administrative structure. The reasons for extending education to women were not as clear even to the colonial rulers when they opened government schools for girls. However, on one point both the rulers and the reformers were in absolute agreement. Education for girls was not meant to equip them for professions or for government service; the introduction of schools for girls was an attempt to transplant into Indian soil the Victorian ideal of the woman as 'housewife', as the presiding deity of home and hearth, whose business in life was to create for her husband a pleasurable haven when he returned home from each day's tiring business in the harsh, competitive outside world.

This was the ideal posed before Indian women as a part of the effort to 'civilize' them. However, even the creation of this strange hybrid required funds and energy. Not much of either could be spared for

Indian women. Therefore, female education always remained secondary to male education. Considering how pitifully small was the amount the British spent on men's education, it is no wonder that government schools for girls came to be no more than a token effort. It was the missionaries who took a major initiative in fostering the ideology of the Victorian housewife, by aiming to demonstrate to families that girls who had been to mission schools became superior housewives and mothers.[37]

After annexation, the first initiative for female education in Punjab seems to have originated from Sir Robert Montgomery who, during his tenure as lieutenant governor, held a Grand Educational Durbar at Lahore in February 1862. He 'impressed upon the European officers and native gentlemen present the importance which he attached to the education of women, and invited their co-operation'.[38] He entrusted the cause of female education to the leaders of different communities. Committees were set up to oversee the female schools. The involvement of the community leaders was supposed to lend a certain respectability to the idea of female education. Major Birch, Deputy Commissioner, speaking about Amritsar in his report for 1869–70, remarked that there were 96 girls' schools, containing 2,300 pupils, 'whose attendance was secured solely by the influence of the gentry'.[39]

But the administration of girls' schools by British-appointed 'community leaders' led to corruption and mismanagement of finances, with the result that many schools existed only in name.[40] In 1869–70, a general survey of schools revealed many such anomalies, and resulted in the reduction of the total number of schools from 2,539 in 1868 to 2,084 in 1869–70.[41] The total number of female pupils in female government schools and aided schools at the close of the academic year 1868–69 was 17,458. By the end of the academic year 1869–70, it had fallen to 13,208, that is, by about 24 per cent.[42] The Education Department tried to justify the decline by asserting that the remaining schools would be better managed[43] and it was decided that grants should not be given to any schools not open to inspection. Yet, a few years later, the lieutenant governor observed that 'a certain amount of instruction was given to a considerable number of girls, but that little real progress was reported'.[44] At the turn of the century, the picture was still one of decline, with the brunt being borne by girls' institutions:

'The decrease in institutions was on the side of both males and females, being in somewhat greater proportion in the case of the latter; whilst the fall in scholars was confined exclusively to the males.'[45]

The half-hearted efforts of the Education Department were being supplemented by vigorous missionary activity. For instance, at Hoshiarpur Mr Perkins, the Deputy Commissioner, 'fearing to offend the natives, he never insisted on the schools being regularly visited, but left the management to a Native Committee'.[46] The schools, 'after lingering . . . for some months, were closed at last as utterly useless', after which the wife of a native missionary opened a school and enrolled 120 girls within a short time.[47] The process is an interesting one, whereby the traditional schools run by different religious communities were supplanted by supposedly 'secular' government schools. Then, the neglect of the latter made way for the overtly Christian mission schools.

The support to the mission schools was not only indirect—by leaving the field open for them. It also took the form of direct financial aid. Thus, in the year 1869–70, the average grant-in-aid spent per student in mission schools was Rs 8.3 while the average amount spent for each non-mission school student was Rs 1.9.[48] In 1884, the Report of the Provincial Committee of the Education Commission clearly stated: 'With the exception of schools for Europeans and Eurasians, and a very few under Native management, grants-in-aid, in the strict sense of the term, are drawn only by the missionary societies.'[49] From 1869 onwards, only those institutions which complied with government rules received aid, and indigenous schools were excluded. In 1869, there was a correspondence between the Government of India and the Government of the Punjab respecting the grants awarded under this article, and the Government of India decided eventually that 'Grants-in-aid from imperial funds are not admissible to purely vernacular primary schools'.[50]

Even though the Education Department tried to make-believe that 'a great effort was [being] made for the extension of female education',[51] the mechanics of grants distribution often discriminated against women's institutions: 'Municipal and district committees are not likely to give fair grants to aided female schools unless bound to do it.'[52] The officials giving evidence before the Commission also asserted that the grants given to girls' schools were on 'a larger scale and on less onerous terms than schools for boys'.[53] The Lahore Arya Samaj, in its testimony, clarified the meaning of this ambiguous phrase: 'The grants to girls' schools are not given on less onerous terms. The same conditions are required of both the boys' and the girls' schools. There is only this little difference, that while inspection is enforced in boys' schools, it is not enforced in girls' schools.'[54] The Samaj demanded that all schools be open to inspection.[55]

In other words, the special concession made by the Education Department in favour of girls' schools was the old one of allowing them to wither away, under the pretext that the community would object to inspection. That this was not likely to have been the case is clear from the report of a lady who inspected the girls' schools in the Jullundur district as early as 1861–62: 'My visits and the little presents I made them seemed to create a great excitement, and immediately after my departure some 30 or 40 girls enrolled themselves as scholars.'[56] The decision taken regarding the need for inspection in 1869–70 was obviously not being implemented.

Even when inspection began to be carried out, the casual attitude to female education was evident. The convenience of the inspectors rather than of the students seemed to be the determining factor: 'Schools should be established in localities convenient for superintendence, and in groups.'[57] The Inspector of the Lahore circle complained that because the girls in villages could not be collected for examination at one central spot (as the boys could), the Assistant Inspector was 'detained in each district much longer than would be necessary for the examination of the boys' schools' while his wife, the Inspectress, visited each female school separately.[58] The Director of Public Instruction said, 'it will be sufficient that she [the inspectress) should be in the District long enough to enable the Assistant Inspector to examine the boys' schools'.[59] Thus, the subordinate role and status of the wives of colonial administrators joining their husbands in the 'civilizing mission' reinforced the subordinate status of women's education in India.

Moreover, the infrastructure provided for government girls' schools was not conducive to a healthy development of any kind, physical or mental. The atmosphere prevailing in the schools was an extension of the confinement which girls, especially those of the upper castes, suffered at home, and the lack of space and fresh air in which those of the poorer classes lived. The Lahore Inspector noted in 1909–10: 'At present little girls have to sit for hours in dark and ill-ventilated so-called classrooms which cannot have a wholesome effect on their health.'[60] Government-aided mission institutions provided a much better atmosphere.[61]

Physical education, too, was totally neglected in government schools. Once again, the blame for this was sought to be placed on the parents who, it was said, would think 'drill or any kind of rhythmic and regular exercise rather too much like the posturing of dancing girls'.[62] However, mission schools and later, even the Arya Samaj schools, succeeded in imparting physical education. The government was not willing to admit the fact that the question of giving physical training could hardly arise when the schools' quarters were so cramped.

The neglect and lack of concern visible in government schools was in sharp contrast to the situation in mission schools, which served as more direct instruments of cultural and ideological domination. They provided better facilities, with physical education and singing as an integral part of the curriculum. To begin with, the curriculum of government girls' schools was the same as that of boys' schools, supposedly 'secular' and 'modern'. The contradiction of providing the same course of study for both boys and girls lay in the fact that the curriculum was geared towards clerical employment. The colonial structure was not capable of providing jobs even to the small percentage of educated men. There were, especially in Punjab, scarcely any employment avenues for educated women nor was the government keen to promote any.

The quality of instruction at government schools was so poor that, at best, they succeeded in imparting the barest literacy. The state of affairs in normal schools, which trained teachers, was so bad that the students were taught hardly anything more than they would have to teach the children. Therefore, there was no question of anything more than bare literacy percolating down to girls' schools. The teachers worked for miserably low salaries. In a 1899–1900, four out of five female teachers in government schools were found to be 'unqualified' and many of them to be 'quite inefficient'.[63] Arithmetic could not be taught in many of the schools because of the teachers' ignorance of the subject.[64] Mr Briggs, whose wife superintended the girls' schools in Dera Ghazi Khan district, observed: 'The teachers are nearly all of them ignorant of all subjects taught in schools save a little reading.'[65] In this respect, mission institutions were scarcely better. In the Ludhiana Mission Orphanage school, 'their acquaintance with arithmetic is as yet of an elementary nature, though quite sufficient for domestic purposes'.[66] The dominant opinion came to be that 'in all girls' schools . . . actual cooking and housekeeping should be given an importance above any book learning'.[67]

Domestic economy was the fancy name given to the science and art of household drudgery. A certain minimum efficiency and organization was necessary, even to teach this. But most government schools were in a state of listlessness with the poor, low-paid teachers applying the only method they knew—and by which they themselves had been trained in the normal schools, if trained at all—that of learning by rote. Thus developed the ironical situation described by the Inspectress of Schools in her report for the year 1910–11, long after the reform effort had entered the field and made significant changes, while government schools still stagnated:

> [Domestic economy] is not taught practically in most of the day schools, and though the text books are memorised, the girls do not appear to make any use of their knowledge in daily life. For instance, they read of the necessity of boiling milk and filtering water and keeping the air in a room fresh by opening the windows and doors frequently, yet even the teachers do not trouble to take any of these precautions in their school rooms.[68]

Mission schools, however, were performing this job more efficiently.

The education introduced by the colonial rulers was clearly not meant to expand horizons for women but to narrow them: 'In a country of female seclusion it is hardly worthwhile for girls to learn by heart the countries, cities, mountains, etc., of the world. Only such instruction should be imparted to girls as may help them in becoming good housewives. Moral education should have the first place.'[69] This orientation produced very negative consequences and left a very harmful legacy, especially considering the fact that seclusion affected only a very small proportion of the total population. It was virtually unknown among the poor 'low' castes. Significantly, it was these 'low' caste girls who were at this time flocking to government and mission schools while the upper castes deliberately avoided sending their daughters to them.

Ignoring the real needs of the 'low' caste women from poor families, most of whom were compelled to earn a living, they were to be trained according to the model of a Victorian housewife, even though they came from castes and classes wherein women could not be merely housewives and mothers. Hazi Ghulam Shah, Member, Education Commission, reported on the situation up to the 1880s: 'Only girls from the lower and middle classes are sent to these schools.'[70] Khan Ahmad Shah, Extra Assistant Commissioner, Hoshiarpur, corroborated this evidence.[71] Miss Mary Boyd of the SPC Mission, Delhi, confirmed that the caste base of the mission institutions was no different from that of government institutions.[72]

Thus, it was women of the 'lower' classes who were taking to education, just as were men of the 'upper' classes, in the hope of employment. Yet, the Education Department kept attributing the unsatisfactory state of female education to the paucity of female teachers. In 1869–70, most of the ills of female education were ascribed to 'the impossibility of obtaining suitable teachers'.[73] The Amritsar Female Education Committee anticipated that 'all objections to married girls going to the schools will be removed when female teachers are appointed to them'.[74] They put great hope in their training schools: 'The point on which the success of the whole system rests is the normal school which was commenced by Mrs Rodger in June 1869, when 40 women were admitted.' It seemed to be making 'very creditable progress'.[75] Yet, by 1899–1900, the situation seemed to them to be just as bad.[76]

The few female teachers who were available found much less favour with the upper castes than did even the male teachers, provided the men were not too young. The reason for this attitude was: 'No respectable native women have as yet taken to teaching as a means of obtaining a livelihood.'[77] The word 'respectable' invariably connotes the upper castes and classes.

It is significant that not only were most students in government and mission female schools from the lower castes but so were the majority of men and women in normal schools who were training to be primary school teachers. Primary school teaching was a low-status occupation for men because of 'so miserable a pittance' given by the government by way of a salary.[78] The three government schools at Lahore, Ambala and Rawalpindi were reported to be 'attended, as a rule, by a very inferior class of men [because of] . . . the low salaries of teachers of vernacular schools, and the insufficiency of the stipends allowed to pupils at the normal schools'.[79] In 1869–70, the salary of a village school teacher was fixed at Rs 10 a month instead of Rs 5 as previously, in the hope of obtaining a 'better class of men'.[80] But this was done by reducing the number of schools, throwing many teachers out of jobs, without being of much benefit to the rest, due to 'the great and sudden rise in the cost of all the necessaries of life, as a man on Rs 10 a month is now scarcely better off than one on Rs 7 was five years ago'.[81] During 1889–90, 46 out of 316 stipends lapsed in the normal schools, among many other reasons, 'owing mainly to the unpopularity of educational service in the primary schools, because less than the minimum salaries prescribed are frequently given by the Boards'.[82]

Since so few women teachers were available, men teachers were employed in female schools. But W.M. Holroyd of the Punjab Education Department admitted: 'Frequently an incompetent old man is employed when no female teacher is available. . . . If [salaries] were on the same scale as those provided for boys' schools, all other difficulties might perhaps be surmounted.'[83] That is, female teachers were paid even lower salaries than male teachers in boys' schools.

The Punjab Education Report of 1869–70 also noted that there was a predominance of Muslim women of low castes in female schools. 'No less than 2,793, or about four-fifths of the pupils in these schools, are Muhammadans, and 2,087 girls are learning Urdu.'[84] Muslim women of higher classes were also training at the normal schools but they belonged to aristocratic families in a state of decline. These women were often the sole supporters of their families. A breakdown of the list of women in the female normal schools of the Delhi mission, who were desirous of obtaining employment, was given in the Punjab Education Report, 1869–70. All the women were said to be from 'well connected' families.[85] It was mainly lower-caste women, and those upper-caste women who had no means of support, who were taking to education at this time, even though the education imparted in these schools had little relevance to their life conditions. They turned to these institutions for the same reasons that they accepted the charity of the missionaries. These were among the very few ways in which women could earn a meagre livelihood.

Female education was becoming an explosive issue for several reasons.

> The upper classes look upon indiscriminate extension of education with disfavour. They consider education as their sole birthright and privilege, and any extension of it to the lower classes as destroying that distinction which they formerly enjoyed. They say also that education unfits the lower classes for their position and occupation in life, and makes them discontented.[86]

A lower-caste woman who acquired a modern education and moved into a 'respectable' profession came to represent a threat to both the caste and the sex hierarchies. The lower-caste woman was even less acceptable as a teacher than was the European woman.[87] The upper-caste men would rather have European women teachers than women of their families.

G.W. Leitner, the orientalist, was even more forthright on this issue:

> The female education given by us was avoided by the more respectable, because it too closely resembled that enjoyed by a class, which, if not criminal, to which our system is now reducing it, was not reputable, although under the caste system which prevents society being gangrened, it confined vice and made it hereditary, if not respectable.[88]

For centuries, sexual exploitation, in varied forms, of lower-caste women had been the privilege of upper-caste men. Prostitutes were mostly lower-caste women. The performing arts and even the art of writing were practised only by these 'fallen women'.

The content of female education was suspect because of the danger of Christianization, and became even more so when the teacher was a low-caste woman convert. An added reason for branding her 'immoral' was that government schools, with their male teachers and inspectors, were associated with a relatively freer mixing of the sexes which was more prevalent among the lower castes but taboo among the upper castes. The colonial administrator was eager to placate this sentiment. The Assistant Commissioner of Hoshiarpur, Sardar Gurdayal Singh, argued before the Education Commission against the idea of having mixed schools: '. . . the girls who come to school are generally of poor classes. . . . No Natives, except perhaps of the lowest rank in society, will send their daughters to the same school with boys.'[89] This attitude of contempt towards a freer mixing of the sexes among the lower castes persisted even after the social reformers entered the field of female education in Punjab.

Secular or Religious Education for Girls?

The growing contradiction between the kind of education provided by government schools and their purported intention to produce educated housewives was time and again pointed out in the course of the debate on whether women's education should be secular or religious. The upper castes were averse to giving their daughters the same education as their sons. Miss Greenfield, in her evidence before the Education Commission, noted: 'The people ask, "Are our daughters to become Munshis and do "naukari" that they should learn Urdu?"'[90]

Upper-caste opinion on the right kind of education for women was summed up by Khan Ahmad Shah, Extra Assistant Commissioner, Hoshiarpur:

> With the exception of a few books especially compiled for girls, the course of instruction is the same as that followed in primary schools. Such instruction is not liked by the people, and the existing schools are not popular among the respectable classes. . . . In fact, to render these schools really useful and popular, religious instruction is indispensable. Neither would it be so impracticable, as in the case of boys, as there are separate schools for Christian, Muhammadan and Hindu girls.[91]

Orientalists like Leitner also agreed that women's education should be essentially religious. Leitner's reasons for holding this view were linked to the interests of colonialism. But the logic was not very different from that of the others operating in the field of female education.[92] Leitner felt convinced that it was the women in the joint family who were the bulwark of religion, fear of god and fear of authority. Though the nationalist ideas of the educated youth might be tolerated by his female relatives at home, the moment he challenged the supremacy of religion or god, Leitner felt he would be 'slapped on the mouth with his mother's slipper'.[93] Therefore, Leitner went on, to educate girls in the same manner as boys would be ruinous. Hence, it was better to have girls instructed in indigenous religious schools, by Pandits and Mullas or to let them pick up a smattering of education at home, so that religious dogmatism should continue to be the dominant colour of women's mental world.

The same idea was reiterated by the Punjabi elite for not very different reasons. Lala Mulraj, Extra Assistant Commissioner, said:

> As to the girls' schools for Hindus and Muhammadans maintained by the Missionaries, perhaps they are doing more harm than good to the country by trying to shake the faith of the girls in their religion, which is so intimately connected with morality, and by teaching them to sing Christian songs in the vernacular. If the primary girls' schools maintained by the Government and the Missionaries were closed, it would make a great saving of resources and be productive of no harm. Female education, at least among the Hindus, can be left alone.[94]

This tussle between the Punjabi elite, on the one hand, and the government and the missionaries, on the other, triggered off the effort of the Arya Samaj for reform in women's status, with women's education as a central theme.

Strengthening of the patriarchal family was an important motivation behind the reforms suggested. The evils of child marriage, the brutal life that came with compulsory widowhood, prostitution (especially when its tentacles began to reach the women of upper-caste homes) and the increasing estrangement between husband and wife due to the spread of colonial education, were all posing a threat to the stability of the patriarchal family of the upper castes and classes. Hence the question of reforms in the status of women from these sections of society became one of the central questions in the movement to reform Hindu society.

The Arya Samaj Response

The Samajists began their campaign by advocating the adoption of pure and simple Vedic rites instead of the elaborate, expensive rituals of orthodox Hinduism at the time of marriage. A major step in marriage reform was taken with the advocacy of widow remarriage.

The Amritsar Samaj led the drive by propagandizing in favour of widow remarriage and offering assistance whenever such a marriage was arranged.[95] Each event was conducted in a grand public manner with the maximum possible publicity.[96] For instance:

> The opponents of the Arya Samaj . . . will be greatly surprised to hear that another widow marriage has been celebrated under the auspices of the Umritsar Arya Samaj, on the 10th September 1885. This is the second widow marriage which has taken place at Umritsar through the efforts of the local Arya Samaj. In the present case the pair belonged to the Arora caste, one of the high castes of the Punjab. . . . Impressive songs suited for the occasion were first sung. . . . Great sensation prevailed.[97]

The campaign was carried on with great ingenuity. Pamphleteering was the most common method. Often dramatic in style, the literature presented Samaj ideology in numerous forms—lectures, dialogues, moral tales, poetry—offering didactic entertainment to the literate Hindu.[98] Munshi Jiwan Das in his tract *Sadah-i-Haq* (The Plain Truth), Pandit Lekh Ram in *Risala-i-Nawid-i-Begwan* (A Treatise Containing Glad News For Widows), Atma Ram in *Masala-i-Niyog* and Munshi Chatar Bihari Lal in *Risala-i-Dharm Mitra* stated the Samaj arguments in favour of widow remarriage. But it was very rarely that the arguments presented were as bold as in one of the articles in *Arya Patrika* which argued that nature had created men and women equal; therefore, if an old widower could marry a 10-year-old girl, it was necessary to allow a 60 year-old widow to marry a 10-year-old boy. The author argued that he had no doubt that if this were possible, there could be no dearth of old women wishing to marry young boys.[99] But this was a stray voice. By and large, it was the remarriage of 'virgin' and child widows which gained the approval of the Samajists. Marriages of mature widows, especially those with children, were very rare, although one such marriage was reported as early as 17 February 1894, in the *Tribune*.

As a result of the sustained campaigning, remarriage of child widows gained slight acceptance by the early twentieth century, as shown, for example, by the fact that every single issue of *Saddharma Pracharak* for 1907 and 1908 carried more than one advertisement on behalf of men desirous of marrying young widows, and of widows willing to remarry. *The Vedic Magazine* reported that between 1895 and 1901, a total of 400 such marriages were conducted by the Arya Samaj.[100] And yet, practice lagged behind precept.

It is also noteworthy that the Samaj concentrated on marriage as the most desirable way of integrating widows into society, even while they hesitated to marry widows. Thus, on the one hand, they sought to neutralize the threat to the family that these unattached women represented while, on the other, they never raised the issue of maltreatment of wives. Marriage was assumed to be the aim of woman's life and the panacea for all ills besetting her. The vision of a single, independent woman did not figure prominently in Arya Samaj ideology.

Issues, such as widow remarriage and ban on child marriage, required mainly propaganda work which entailed the condemnation of social evils prevalent in the community. Much of the constructive effort for the betterment of women came to centre around the question of women's education because through it the reformers could concretely demonstrate their vision of women's role in a reformed society. When the Arya Samajists took up the cause of female education, the upper-caste women were their main focus. The financial support came from the commercial and trading classes. The lists of subscribers and donors printed in Samaj journals testify to this. The curricula in Samaj schools catered to the perceptions of men regarding the education required by women of their castes and classes. There was a heavy dose of religion and domestic economy together with general education. The course was geared not towards employment, but towards the production of a 'modernized' educated housewife.

The Arya Samaj efforts gradually made female education more 'respectable'. A certain level of education became a desired qualification in the middle-class marriage market. With the growth of this trend, attendance at government schools also began to alter in terms of caste and class composition. The content of education in these schools also began to change along the lines laid down by Samaj schools. The Education Department encouraged this trend, and lower-caste girls were channellized into mission schools set up especially for low-caste students. These schools, as the Education Reports show, came into existence around the turn of the century.

The Arya Samaj played a crucial role in bringing about this shift in the class and caste base of women's education, linked to a corresponding shift in its content.

Arya Samaj Opens Schools for Girls—and Splits

The first initiative, it seems, was taken by the Amritsar Samaj, but it met with only indifferent success. Not only was public opinion lukewarm but actual financial support was also lacking. Various innovative measures were adopted. For instance, the Amritsar Samaj, through its appeals, managed to persuade 'all the pleaders at present practising in Umritsar . . . to pay out of their daily income a donation of two annas a day . . . which comes up to two or three rupees a day'.[101] As early as 1885, the Amritsar Samaj announced the establishment of two girls' schools in the city and a third one to be started at Kutra Dula.[102]

During the 1880s, the Amritsar Samaj remained in the forefront of this activity. The Lahore Samaj, which had a larger financial base, remained on the whole indifferent, though it did run a not very successful girls' school.[103] By 1889, the Ferozepur Samaj had also managed to organize a fairly successful girls' school. The following year, the Jullundur Samaj made another attempt after having failed the first time. In 1890, a Kanya Pathshala was established at Jullundur.

An incident related in the autobiography of Lala Munshi Ram throws light on why the Jullundur Samaj took up women's education as a priority issue.[104] One day, when Lala Munshi Ram came home, his daughter, Ved Kumari, came running to him, reciting a stanza she had learnt at the mission school: '*Ek bar Isa Isa bol, tera kya lagega mol? Isa mera Ram Ramayya, Isa mera Krishna Kanhayya*' (Try saying Jesus, Jesus, once, it will cost you nothing; Jesus is my Ram, Jesus is my Krishna). Munshi Ram was duly alarmed, especially when told by his daughter that Hindu girls were taught to despise the Shastras. There and then, he decided that Hindus would have to undertake the education of women if they wanted to preserve their culture and religion. They would have to fight the insidious influence of Christianity invading their homes through the backdoor.

On 26 December 1886, a resolution was passed in the Antrang Sabha of the Jullundur Samaj that 'a zenana school be opened for which an expenditure of one rupee per month would be sanctioned.'[105] But the same year's report of the Arya Samaj mentions that the zenana school run by the Samaj was in bad shape because a good teacher was not available.[106] Lala Devraj's mother, Kahan Devi, took charge of it and for some time, classes were held in her house under the instruction of one Mai Ladi who had earlier been working in the mission school. But after a while, the Samaj stopped the paltry grant of Re 1. Smt Kahan Devi for some time continued personally to finance the venture, but the school had to be closed down very soon for lack of students.[107]

Another attempt, made in 1888–89, proved equally disappointing. However, the third attempt made in 1890–91 proved more successful. One male and one female teacher were appointed. The school had an estimated expenditure of Rs 10 per month. The 1892 Arya Samaj Annual Report mentioned with satisfaction the progress of the school and expressed confidence that one day it would become a Mahavidyalaya. There were already 55 girls in the school which still taught only up to the primary class. With growth came financial problems but Lala Devraj devised ingenious methods of dealing with these. Apart from the *raddi* fund and the *atta* fund—techniques already in use by the DAV fund raisers—Devraj took to begging in the streets of Jullundur and neighbouring small towns.[108]

The real turning point, however, came with the proposal of Lala Dev Raj and Lala Munshi Ram to start a high school for girls—a Kanya Mahavidyalaya—at a projected cost of Rs 250,000. It was to have a girls' hostel and a *vidhwa ashram*. But as soon as a public announcement of the project was made, with an appeal for funds, a storm of protest was raised—surprisingly, by none other than the DAV wing of the Arya Samaj. This became the starting point for a prolonged and bitter controversy between the two wings of the Arya Samaj (the 'Mahatmas' and the 'college party') as to the necessity for starting a high school for girls at that particular juncture.

The debate was sparked off by Lala Lajpat Rai who, in a lengthy article in the January 1894 number of the Dayanand Anglo Vedic

College *Samachar*, argued that it was 'premature, from a practical point of view, to think of giving high education to girls'.[109] A series of letters appeared in the *Tribune* of 1894, on this subject. The opponents of higher education for girls insisted that the establishment of such an institution would be at the cost of elementary education for girls and would divert resources from the much more important task of ensuring the success of DAV institutions for boys. It was also argued that since government efforts for girls' education had not made much headway, the experiment was doomed to failure. The DAV wing dismissed the relevance of similar, even higher institutions in Bombay and Calcutta.[110] Lala Lajpat Rai was convinced that the spread of education amongst women had no important inducements behind it.[111]

The loopholes in the DAV group's arguments are obvious. First, when the government had taken measures to limit the spread of higher education among Indian men on the grounds that primary education needed to be first consolidated, it was Lala Lajpat Rai himself and others of his thinking who opposed this argument. Second, when they pointed to the failures of government efforts as an index of the impracticability of female education at higher levels, they assumed that the government had put all its resources at the disposal of women's education. As we have seen, this was far from being the case. The Lahore Arya Samaj, which opposed higher education for women when undertaken by the Jullundur Samaj, had itself, in its evidence before the Education Commission, 1883, pointed out that insufficient attention was paid by the government to the education of girls. Third, they harped on the need to destroy prejudice as a prerequisite for initiating higher education among girls, but combating these prejudices was possible only in the process of struggle for women's education.

On the other hand, the champions of women's education rightly argued that the issue could not be dealt with as a problem of 'economics' and 'statistics' alone,[112] but only in the long-term perspective of its impact on future generations. In fact, '. . . want of proper teachers, and want of schools in proper quarters, and the absence of any real improvement that these schools effect in their students are the causes of the present undesirable situation'.[113] They argued further that '. . . to deny high education to our women is to deny them, as a class, any education whatsoever'; because primary education was dependent on the availability of trained women teachers.[114]

To the argument that women could not utilize education to take up jobs as men did, none of the sections of the Arya Samaj had any answer nor did they desire to pose the question seriously. This is because even the champions of higher education for women advocated it primarily as a means to bridge the mental gap between husbands and wives, mothers and sons. Moreover, they argued that ignorant women had a 'negative influence' as wives and mothers.[115]

Female education was considered the most effective way of countering the subversive activity of the missionaries. A more practical point was that unless higher education was given to women, there would be no primary school teachers for girls. Conservative opinion regarded this problem as almost insoluble. They felt that girls should not have male teachers and that the government would not be able to induce respectable Hindu and Muslim women to study in female normal schools. In their view, with Christian women as teachers, girls' schools were likely to do more harm than good. Under such circumstances, they found it difficult to suggest the best method of providing teachers for girls' schools. The Samajists discovered 'the best method' which would also solve another grave social problem:

> Few well-to-do, even easily circumstanced parents, guardians or husbands will care to allow their girls and wives to engage in service after their marriage; but there is a class of females—at present a pest on the society, *source* of untold suffering and crime all around—who can be nicely utilised for the purpose; I mean the Hindu widows (emphasis added).

It was not possible to find '. . . purer and healthier—from a moral point of view—assylum [*sic*] for the Hindu widows, than the circle presided over by men of spotless character like Lalas Munshi Ram and Dev Raj of Jullundur'.[116]

But the fear persisted that higher education would lead to a particularly condemnable phenomenon—'overculture'—among women, which would become not only 'the cause of domestic aberration' but also of the 'annihilation of the race itself' because the effect of education would be 'physical deterioration' among women.[117]

The proponents of the women's cause admitted that higher education for girls was not an unmixed blessing, but they assured their opponents that nobody was 'seriously thinking of turning out ladies mistresses of arts'.[118] They tried to convince their opponents that 'the character of girls' education should be different from that of boys in many essential respects. . . . The education we give our girls should not unsex them.'[119]

It is obvious from this debate that neither of the two sections of the Arya Samaj addressed itself to the task of emancipating women. On the contrary, women's roles within the family as wives, daughters and mothers were re-emphasized and extended to conform with the requirements of the family in a changing situation. Women had to be able to adjust to the new style of life being adopted by men, had to come out of seclusion and act as hostesses. They had to supervise the education of children in addition to feeding them. They had to be 'managers' of the family's internal existence, which was becoming increasingly complex with the changing tempo of life in large cities. Here, there was no difference between the different sections of reformers. Even those, like Lajpat Rai, who actively opposed any effort for women's higher education, could, in the same breath, declare that '. . the nature of the duties imposed on a wife and mother in the Hindu scriptures and books of law, makes a fairly good education an absolute necessity for a wife and a mother'.[120] But

> With all the sorrow and pain that an educated Hindu feels for the present position of Indian womanhood, he would not have his daughters and sisters go out into the world in search of employment as the girls in Europe do, not to speak of other excesses to which they are all liable by virtue of their conditions of life. . . .[121]

This unwillingness to question the legitimacy of certain institutional forms of women's oppression defined the narrow limits of Arya Samaj activity. They wanted women 'enlightened' but 'dependent'; they wanted to give them 'dignity' but not 'freedom'. The contradiction was not resolvable. They could not envisage any significant change in the social role of women although a number of outstanding women were appearing all over India as professionals. The names of Anandibai

Joshi, Rukmabai, Pandita Ramabai, Cornelia Sorabjee, and their achievements, were well known among the educated in Punjab because contemporary newspapers gave frequent coverage to their activities.

Stunted Ideology

It is indeed ironical that the initiative for founding institutions for the higher education of women came from the more orthodox Gurukul wing while the so-called 'progressive' college party, headed by Lala Lajpat Rai, Lala Hansraj, Lala Lal Chand, vociferously opposed it. However, the dichotomy was only skin deep. The two groups were agreed that the main purpose of women's education was to produce good Arya wives and mothers.

One of the decisive factors in the greater concern for women's education of the Gurukul party was perhaps that after its break with the DAV wing, this section concentrated on reform of religious ritual and marriage customs according to the Samaj version of Vedic tenets. The college party, on the other hand, concentrated most of its energy on evolving a new concept of national education for men, which could equip Punjabi Hindus to compete successfully in jobs and professions. Therefore, unlike the DAV wing, the Gurukul wing faced more directly the problem of 'unenlightened' women in the family acting as obstacles in the reform campaign.[122]

The Gurukul wing needed *updeshikas* who could directly deal with women's resistance, without the mediation of men—just as the zenana missionaries had been doing. Updeshikas could not be produced unless women were equipped with learning.

However, the Arya Samaj ideology remained limited in analysing the nature and causes of the downtrodden status of women of even their own class. The myth of the golden Vedic age when women supposedly were accorded a high status provided a necessary refuge from missionary attacks. Even when they admitted deterioration in the status of women, they attributed it solely to the corruption of Hindu society by Arabic, Islamic, Greek, Buddhistic and other alien influences. 'The first stroke was directed against the personal freedom of the women by the introduction of *Purdah*.'[123] This was the farthest the Samajists went by the way of providing a 'historical' explanation for the oppression of women—as though the problem began and ended with purdah, and as though women's oppression was unique to the Islamic world.

Dayanand had set the tradition for the Arya Samaj of an eclectic interpretation of the Vedas. They could be interpreted to mean almost anything that the reformer felt was most suited to his purpose. Whatever was unsuitable could be dismissed as an aberration or a later corruption. 'The Hindu scriptures and the Hindu law as administered and understood in India, before Buddha (500 BC) assign a very high position to women in the social economy of the nation.'[124] The code of Manu was affirmed even by the most enlightened Samajists like Lajpat Rai as the 'best known code of Hindu law'. If there were certain points in it which caused embarrassment by their blatant contempt for women, they could easily be explained away: '. . . the code of Manu as known to us today, is not the code which was known as such to the pre-Buddhist Aryas (Hindus) . . . it is a manual of decadent Hinduism.'[125] However, it was felt that in spite of its corruptions '. . . even the present code assigns a very high position to women and exhibits an extraordinary solicitude for their safety, for their welfare, for their purity, and for their honour'.[126] Both males and females had to be subordinated to the male head of the family, because 'the family is *patriarchal*, and not *matriarchal*' (emphasis in original), but in all other respects, the legal position of women in the joint family was much 'better than that of men'. Even if

> she has no voice in the management of the family property, nor in its disposal, nor at the time of partition, but her right to be maintained according to the rank and position of the family out of the family property is secured against all claims, internal or external.

In denying her property rights, '. . . the principle is to keep the mother function free of all anxieties and pecuniary cares. Every woman is a mother in *embryo*. That is her supreme function in life. That is her social mission' (emphasis in original).[127]

The ancient authority was resurrected, not only to condemn the present unhappy state, but also to define the limits up to which the 'present' could go in the direction of change. It provided an alibi for halting whenever necessary. However, though the dominant ideology did not envisage a role for women outside the home, the fact of participation in the movement did open the way for Samaj women to enlarge their sphere of activity.

Women's Own Initiatives

Various Stri Samajes came into being all over Punjab under the auspices of the Arya Samaj during this period. These provided valuable support for the Kanya Mahavidyalaya (KMV) experiment during its crucial early years.

The Ludhiana Stri Samaj was particularly active. It supported a Vedic female school and an ashram for widows.[128] It held regular meetings and performed the devotional ceremonies just as the regular Samaj did.

Hariana, in district Hoshiarpur, was one of the most turbulent centres of agitation. At one lecture on 'Nari Dharma' given by Mai Bhagwati, more than a thousand women were present.[129] Women *pracharikas* were few and far between, yet even in the predominantly Muslim district of Dera Ghazi Khan, a woman addressed a meeting of women in a private house. She said: '. . . a woman should have no guru but the husband and implicit obedience to him was the first duty of a woman.'[130]

Most surprising, a woman updeshika, Pandita Surender Bala, of the Jullundur Samaj, spoke at a mixed gathering of about 800 women and 500 men in Phagwara, on the subject of female education. The *Tribune* remarked on this event, saying 'nearly the whole population of the town must have been there'.[131] The Jullundur Stri Samaj was established in 1891, and met weekly at the Kanya Mahavidyalaya.[132]

Even though the KMV management was predominantly controlled by men, the success of the venture became more and more dependent on the active involvement of the female staff and students. For instance, girls and female teachers went on a number of fund-collecting tours, both in the province and outside. In 1908, Savitri Devi toured with Devraj to Karachi. Both gave a number of lectures on women's education and collected Rs 2,000.[133] In 1916, Kumari Lajjyawati travelled all over the United Provinces and Calcutta with Lala Devraj, and collected Rs 15,000.[134] In 1917, she vowed to collect rupees one lakh, and toured India, Burma and Africa to fulfil her vow.[135]

Mai Bhagwati and Guru Bibi Devi were two of the most indispensable workers in the early days of the KMV. Mai Bhagwati was one of the initiators of the movement in Punjab. Devraj called her

> the inspiring spirit behind this great venture, at a time when we have only Rs 8 as our capital. . . . now the times have changed . . . but [she] started work at a time when great social stigma was attached to a woman who dared to go around unveiled. Hariana for us is holy as Hardwar.[136]

Mai Bhagwati was born into the eminent Mehta family of Doaba, Jullundur, and was married while she was still a child. Even though she excelled in household duties, she was more inclined towards educating herself. At the age of 14, in the face of stiff opposition from her family, she started learning to write from a Pandit in Hariana. Only her mother stood by her. She lived with her in-laws till the age of 26 but, in spite of her best efforts, did not find domestic harmony. Her husband's family abused her for her learning and often threw her books into the fire. So, at 26, she returned to her village and started studying independently, because even her own brothers ostracized her. She continued her studies and opened a Putri Pathshala in her own house.[137]

She was among the first women who went from place to place, carrying the Samaj message. The impact she had is obvious from the following *Tribune* report which, by its very exaggeration, gives an interesting insight into how the possibility of women extending their activity outside homes, however marginally, filled men with consternation: 'Of late, a correspondent says, it has become difficult to get well-cooked dishes at any house in Hariana, and few people stop at Hariana, for fear of indigestion on their way to other places.'[138]

Mai Bhagwati also had the distinction of being the Editor of *Sahayak*, the first Hindi magazine devoted to the cause of women's education to come out of Punjab. It was a sister publication of *The Regenerator of Arya Varta*. Its specific aim was to 'propagate the idea of women's education and call upon men to uplift the condition of women'. She was so respected for her learning within Arya circles that with her name as Editor, the title invariably used was Fellow of the Arya Samaj.[139]

She taught at the KMV too and Devraj gratefully refers to her support when he is tracing the history of the KMV. Her popularity is evidenced by press reports of her death and funeral:

> We do not know if Mother Bhagwati's name is much known outside boundaries of this Province, yet she has, in her own line, done more to further the cause of social progress in this country, on strictly national lines, than perhaps most of those recognised reformers whose names are constantly before the public. It is our melancholy duty today to announce her untimely death, which took place at Hariana . . . on the night of the 21st instant. Thousands of her townsmen of all classes mournfully followed her bier to the burning ground. Every member of her sex in Hariana, contributed one *thuthee* and *chanathee* each towards her *mrittyak havan*, the *hom* performed in connection with funeral obsequies. She had close relations with the Arya Samaj, which loses in her the most potent instrument it relied on in the work of raising Indian womanhood to the position assigned to her by the *Shastras*. She was broad in her sympathies, and. . . . in these days of sectional feeling and *biraderi* spirit, for her liberal views and broad-mindedness in this respect she should serve as a model.[140]

Savitri was another woman who worked with single-minded devotion for the KMV. She came there as a child widow and studied even though her family was opposed to the idea. She had only Devraj's support. Poems in *Jalvid Sakha*, the organ of the KMV, testify to her zeal. In 'Savitri Stotra', every stanza ends with the refrain 'Savitri, Savitri'. Though the virtues for which she is extolled in this poem are the traditional 'womanly' ones of patience, selflessness and cheerful devotion, they acquire a new meaning because they are not placed at the disposal of the husband and in-laws, as were the qualities of the mythological Savitri, but are devoted to the cause of women's education.[141] The use of a religious genre of poetry—the *bhajan*—to create a new symbol, a child widow who is to inspire future generations of women, is interesting,

Savitri was the first Acharya of the KMV and the moving spirit behind the foundation of the Vidhwa Ashram or Widows' Home in 1907. She devoted most of her time and energy during the last years of her short life to this Vidhwa Ashram. She also travelled all over the country, mobilizing support and resources for the KMV.

Most of these women were impelled into the movement by force of personal circumstance. All of them were unusual women insofar as they attempted to break away from the traditional roles sought to be imposed on them. The Arya Samaj provided them with a refuge. Lajjyawati remained unmarried and saw the KMV through, as it were, three eras. As an exceptionally bright little girl, she was inspired by Lala Devraj to undertake the work of spreading the KMV message far and wide. She was a powerful speaker even as a child, and devoted her life to the KMV which she later took under her wing. She remained its principal until a few years ago. The meticulous care which was a feature of Devraj's way of running the institution was carried on by her. She is one of the very few to have lived through the transition, when the KMV was opening new horizons to girls like herself, encouraging them to travel, to be independent and fearless, to the present time, when such pioneers are themselves caught up in running these institutions which have been transformed into very stultifying and repressive centres of education, wherein women are subjected to severe restrictions which often exceed those found in conservative homes.

Pandita Surender Bala was another outstanding woman, one of the most versatile of the Samaj pracharikas, and an excellent singer of bhajans. She was very successful in addressing public meetings in many different places, spreading the message of women's reform. However, despite her notable contribution, she was treated somewhat like an outcast within the Arya Samaj fold. She was not considered respectable enough, since she lived with one of the prominent Samaj reformers to whom she was not married. Had he not been so influential within the Arya Samaj she would have been, in all likelihood, thrown out of the Samaj.[142] However, his place in the movement does not seem to have been affected by the relationship.

Devraj's wife and his mother played an important role in the day-to-day functioning of the institution. Valuable help came from various other women workers and students in editing the *Panchal Pandita*, the organ of the KMV from 1897, and in devising the KMV syllabus.

In this situation Devraj's ideas of what women could and should do underwent a definite change, as his justification of his decision to introduce English at the KMV shows. The success of the experiment of introducing education among girls and bringing away girls from their homes to study collectively had a logic of its own. The attempt to prove that women could be 'equals' in certain, if not in all, respects, had unforeseen consequences. Once the movement forward had begun, it became increasingly difficult to draw the line 'thus far and no further', particularly since there had never been any definite consensus among the Samajists as to where that line should be drawn.

The KMV became a centre of gravity for educational efforts in the entire province. The *Panchal Pandita* became an instrument to carry the message far and wide. It was a 'monthly magazine of 16 pages Hindi and 4 pages English . . . solely devoted to the interests of Indian women' started by the founders of KMV in 1897.[143] It took the information about the experiments being conducted at the KMV to different Samajes, almost all of which opened pathshalas. By 1918, more than 104 pathshalas followed the syllabus laid down by the KMV. Even some government schools included the books devised by the KMV in their syllabus, as well as the *Panchal Pandita*.[144] It was thus well on the way to fulfilling the objectives with which it was launched: 'Of furnishing good reading matter to our sisters, cultivating their mental faculties by . . . widening their interests by giving them a view of the world outside the closed zenanas, and of infusing in them liberal sympathies and elevating ideas.'[145]

While the schools at Bhadod, Ludhiana and Kartarpur were opened as branch schools of the KMV, there were many other Samaj schools which had a loosely affiliative character, insofar as the KMV *pracharaks* acted as catalysts for their formation. It was common for the KMV students and teachers to visit Samajes far and near, taking with them the message of women's education. The issues of *Panchal Pandita* are full of news of KMV girls going out and delivering lectures that inspired other Samajes to follow the KMV model.

The KMV's role as a nucleus of educational activity in Punjab and North India is nowhere more apparent than in its initiative in producing literature for women, most of which was written by Devraj. Some of these books were translated into Marathi, Telugu, Gujarati and other languages. The Punjab and Central Provinces governments recommended these books for their schools. In 1904, it meant a breakthrough, and Devraj got an award of Rs 200 for his contribution in the field of children's literature. The print orders give an idea of the popularity these books enjoyed and the role they played—*Pahli Pathawali*: 70,500 copies; *Doosri Pathawali*: 43,500; *Akshar Dipika*: 4,000 (27th edition); *Patra Kaumudi*: 20,500 (11th edition); *Katha Vidhi*: 72,500 (16th edition); *Balodyan Sangeet*: 34,000.[146] The KMV ran a Sahitya

Bhandar for the distribution of such literature. Moreover, the KMV was able to play a central role in the spread of women's education because, right from the start, it had addressed itself to the task of training teachers. By 1910, the KMV had produced 50 *adhyapikas*, female teachers, who were working in different schools all over the province.[147] By 1913–14, they numbered 86.[148] Devraj's message to all his students was that 'each one of the girls should become a Pathshala by herself so that not a single girl in the country should be left illiterate'.[149] Girl students, when they went home for the summer vacation, not only collected funds for the KMV but were also encouraged to take a pledge that they would educate at least two persons.[150] Many students came back to do some honorary teaching at KMV.[151]

The Issues Left Untouched

However, it is significant that education in the KMV was not oriented towards providing employment or preparing the girls for it. Teaching was viewed more as a mission than a job so the shortage of female teachers mentioned in the Education Department Reports persisted as late as the second decade of the twentieth century.

Education in the KMV became an added qualification for girls in the urban middle-class marriage market. The issues of *Saddharma Pracharak* carried advertisements regularly which listed KMV education as a desirable qualification for young brides.

Though women's education did become the central question of the movement, it was envisaged only as a means to an end.

> The aim of all education besides booklearning, is to build up character and efficiency. . . . This is particularly so in the case of girls who have to adapt themselves to the environments into which their marriages carry them. She is a householder first and everything else afterwards. . . . She must not only live but also believe and think like her husband before she can be happy. She must realise the future of her children and must sympathise with the system of education which is to bring them up as bread earners in the modern world.[152]

This was the justification offered as late as 1935–6 when the KMV decided to introduce university examinations for its students. The literature produced by the KMV bears ample testimony to the narrow range of issues taken up. Dayanand had taken for granted that 'nature' had determined different roles and positions for men and women in social organization. These were not seen as social creations. The later Samajists used this as a major ideological weapon to contain and halt women's emancipation.

In its handling of women's issues, the Arya Samaj left certain crucial areas untouched. In the various discussions of the husband–wife relation, the emphasis is on 'love', 'tolerance', 'faithfulness'. The wife is expected to embody these virtues, and win her husband's heart with her charms and accomplishments. But the question of control over income is never raised; the underlying implication is that although the couple should discuss household affairs together, the husband will have the last word.

It is surely significant that even while expressing horror at the maltreatment of widows, the question of what a wife should do, if maltreated, was not raised. Therefore, neither in theory nor in practice did they question the power imbalance that is structured into the husband–wife relation in the existing family system.

The question of women's own choice in marriage is tentatively raised through stories but such marriages are never allowed to take place in defiance of the parents' wishes. The ideological stand on the question is pitifully clear in the item in *Jalvid Sakha* of November 1932:

> Mrs Sushila Devi, by the grace of God has done well in both the Vidyalaya tenth class exam and the Punjab University Matriculation exam. She was married this July. Though she was very anxious and eager to study further, she had to bow before the wish of her pujya [worthy to be worshipped] parents.[153]

Issues such as prostitution were not even touched, except by way of self-righteous indignation against prostitutes for 'polluting society'. The question of women's employment figured only marginally on the agenda of 'reform' even though increasing destitution was taken note of. Remarriage of child widows to save them from misery and a life of 'sin' seemed a more attractive alternative than equipping them to stand on their own feet (which was seen as a distinct threat to society).

Niyoga, advocated by Dayanand, was quietly dropped and widows who were not virgins were advised to devote themselves to social service. Extreme sexual repression and austerity were advocated for them—in the KMV widows' homes the girls were not even supposed to rest their head on a pillow. The *Panchal Pandita* carried articles which preached that widows should not live like married women but should practise self-control and determine to spend their lives in *vidya* and *dharm prachar*.[154] Not only was the question of remarriage avoided but even sati was glorified, as in the story of Ratnadevi, a queen from ancient times who burnt herself on her husband's pyre. There was also a laudatory mention of 'a real sati in Kanpur' in the *Panchal Pandita* of May 1906. Thus, the heavily patriarchal ideology tainted even the zeal for reform. All the institutions sponsored by the Arya Samaj bear its mark.

The curriculum of the KMV maintained the emphasis on subjects of 'feminine interest' until the government, after independence, put pressure on it to make the curriculum conform to the general university curriculum whereby men and women are prepared for the same stultifying examinations.

Unfortunately, the key purpose which the pioneers sought to achieve through female education left its indelible mark on the educational policy and the character of most women's educational institutions.

To Sum Up

The Arya Samaj helped remove some of the prejudices against women's education among the urban middle classes. It also fought against the more blatant forms of women's exploitation. Women's status was somewhat altered within the family. While the Arya Samaj did not address itself to the question of the emancipation of women, it created certain preconditions for the alleviation of some aspects of their oppression. Yet why did it fail to develop further?

The life histories of the Samaj women clearly reveal that women were not passive recipients of reform. Right from the beginning, they took the initiative themselves and the women's organizations and institutions that sprang up in the period were a reflection of a certain activity and unrest amongst women. But from all the literature I have so far been able to go through on the subject, it is very clear that the trend of women's thinking on the question of their own status does not reveal the development of an independent self-view. This is also true of the women's organizations and institutions that mushroomed in and around the Arya Samaj.

The Samaj movement was led and initiated by men who kept the activity of women's institutions under strict control and tutelage. For instance, around 1889, when the Stri Samaj was being founded in Jullundur, it was decided that it would be allowed to come into existence only if it accepted the jurisdiction of the Purush Samaj (men's Samaj) over it.[155]

Women, therefore, joined the movement as subordinate partners—an extension of the wifely role of helpmate—and Stri Samajes tended to play a subsidiary role. In fact, the Arya Samaj women's movement was so well contained that no subversive woman of the Pandita Ramabai variety could ever emerge out of it. Even when women were allowed to speak for themselves, they spoke the language of men and their thinking remained within the parameters carefully defined for them by the patriarchal worldview. This is amply evidenced by the famous bhajans of Mai Bhagwati, which she wrote to 'purify' the minds of women, and the short stories in *Julvid Sakha*, all of which are designed to inculcate the virtue of *pativrata*; the women who is unfaithful to her husband is usually depicted as dying an untimely death in the throes of remorse. So also, the essays written by Savitridevi in the *Panchal Pandita* advocate complete austerity as a sort of end in itself, and sublimation of all desires into Samaj activity.[156]

In some ways it can be said that the Arya Samaj movement was intended to 'reform' women rather than to reform the social conditions which oppressed them. Women were to be educated into becoming more suitable wives and mothers for the new, educated men. The conditions of seclusion under which these upper-caste women lived meant that, for the most part, they lived in a world of their own. Since they had very limited contact even with their own husbands, in some ways, they had been pretty much left to themselves to devise their own inner forms of life within the repressive culture of the zenana. In the process, their thinking had become inaccessible to men. But now, this extreme form of seclusion was creating its own problems because the needs of men seemed to have suddenly changed, making it necessary for women to change their lives and attitudes to adapt to men's requirements.

There is a remarkable continuity of anachronism in Arya Samaj ideology, starting from Dayanand for whom the rationale of women's existence was the mother function, to present-day eminent Arya Samajists, several of whom I interviewed. Even today, they feel that the movement played a very positive role in attempting to produce 'good Hindu mothers'. The conceptual framework, rooted in a strong patriarchal tradition, contained in itself the seeds of obscurantism which came to characterize the movement after its first flush of reform activity.

Therefore, it was not by accident that a movement, which pioneered the struggle for the rights of women in the North, became the arch champion of social conservatism, as soon as it began reaping the fruits of its own struggle. After the first generation of prominent Arya Samajists, succeeding generations were not only unwilling to carry the movement forward and build on the foundations laid by the first generation, but even tended to disown and recoil from the by-products of the very logic of their own reform movement.

Notes

1. *Light Of Truth* (or an English translation of *Satyarth Prakash* of Swami Dayanand Saraswati, by Chirangiva Bharadwaj), (Lahore, Kaviraj Satya Vrata Bharadwaj, 3rd edition, 1927), p. 98.
2. Ibid., pp. 126–7.
3. Ibid., p. 73.
4. Ibid., p. 74.
5. Ibid., p. 75.
6. Ibid., p. 81.
7. Ibid., p. 83.
8. Ibid.
9. Ibid., p. 117.
10. Ibid.
11. Ibid.
12. Ibid.
13. Ibid., p. 121.
14. Ibid., pp. 120–1.
15. Ibid., p. 126.
16. Ibid., p. 127.
17. Ibid., p. 29.
18. Ibid., p. 189.
19. *Census of India*, Punjab, 1901, para 40, chapter 4, p. 219.

20. Ibid., para 39, Chapter 4, p. 218.
21. Ibid., para 44, Chapter 8, p. 334.
22. *Arya Patrika*, 1 August 1885, p. 6.
23. *The Indian Social Reformer*, 13 May 1900, Editorial, 'In League Against The Widows', p. 290.
24. Ibid., 'Dekhani Notes', p. 294.
25. *Census of India*, Punjab, 1881, para 749, Chapter 8, p. 389.
26. *Appendix to Education Commission Report, Report by the Punjab Provincial Committee and Memorials Addressed to the Education Commission* (Calcutta, Superintendent of Government Printing, 1884), Evidence of the Rev. F.H. Baring (Batala), p. 159.
27. *Census of India*, Punjab, 1901, para 7, Chapter 9, p. 366.
28. *Punjab Native Newspaper Reports*, received up to 12 September 1896, vol. 9, no. 37, p. 519.
29. Ibid., received up to 28 November 1896, vol. 9, no. 46, p. 675.
30. Ibid., received up to 19 December 1896, vol. 9, no. 51, p. 723.
31. Ibid., received up to 23 January 1897, vol. 10, no. 4, p. 56.
32. *Punjab Native Newspaper Reports*, received up to 28 November 1896, vol. 9, no. 46, p. 671. See also vol. 9, no. 51, received up to 19 December 1896, p. 721, and vol. 10, no. 6, received up to 6 February 1897, p. 83.
33. Ram Chandra, 'The Problem of Fallen Women in India,' *The Vedic Magazine*, vol. 11, no. 10, May 1918, pp. 549–53.
34. *Appendix to Education Commission Report* (Punjab, 1884), op. cit., pp. 28–9.
35. Evidence of Miss Rose Greenfield, *Appendix to Education Commission Report* (1884), op. cit., p. 227.
36. G.W. Leitner, *History of Indigenous Education in the Punjab Since Annexation* (Calcutta, 1882), pp. 98, 104.
37. See Minna G. Cowan, citing documents from the World Mission Conference Report, *The Education of Women in India*, 1912.
38. *Appendix to the Education Commission Report* (1884), op. cit., p. 10.
39. *Report on Popular Education in the Punjab and its Dependencies for the Year 1869–70*, by Captain W.M. Holroyd, Director of Public Instruction, Punjab (Lahore, 1870), Lahore Circle Report, p. 31.
40. For one example, see ibid., Ambala Circle Report, p. 15.
41. Ibid., Director's Report, p. 4.
42. Ibid., p. 3.
43. Ibid., Section IV, p. 31.
44. *Appendix to the Education Commission Report* (1884), op. cit., p. 25.
45. *Report on Public Instruction in the Punjab and its Dependencies* (Lahore, 1900), Chapter 1, p. 3.

46. *Report on Popular Education in the Punjab* (1869–70), op. cit., Report of Inspector, Lahore Circle, p. 17.
47. Ibid., p. 17.
48. *Appendix to the Report on Popular Education in the Punjab* (1869–70), pp. xxx–xxxi. In this table we also find that the 24 mission schools for females received a total of Rs 5,286 for 637 students on the rolls at the close of the year 1869–70. In comparison, 405 non-mission schools with a total of 8,951 students on the rolls for the same period received Rs 17,311. The average grant-in-aid for a mission school was thus Rs 220, while the average grant-in-aid for the other schools was Rs 43.
49. *Appendix to the Education Commission Report* (1884), op. cit., p. 71.
50. Ibid., pp. 71–2.
51. Ibid., p. 8.
52. Ibid., p. 159, in 'Evidence of the Rev. F.H. Baring', pp. 156–61.
53. Ibid., p. 381, in 'Evidence of Dr. G.W. Leitner', pp. 352–402.
54. Ibid., p. 481, in 'Answer of the Lahore Arya Samaj to the Questions Suggested by the Education Commission', pp. 466–85. See also pp. 197, 464.
55. Ibid., p. 473.
56. G.W. Leitner, op. cit., Appendix VI, p. 18.
57. *Report on Popular Education in the Punjab* (1869–70), op. cit., Report of Inspector, Ambala Circle, p. 30.
58. Ibid., Section 1, p. 7.
59. Ibid.
60. *Report on Public Instruction in the Punjab and its Dependencies 1909–10* (Lahore, 1910), p. 18.
61. *Report on Popular Education in the Punjab* (1869–70), op. cit., Report of Inspector, Ambala Circle, p. 44.
62. *Report on Public Instruction in the Punjab and its Dependencies 1908–1909* (Lahore, 1909), p. 18.
63. *Report on Popular Instruction in the Punjab for the Year 1899–1900*, op. cit., p. 61.
64. *Report on Popular Education in the Punjab* (1869–70), op. cit., Report of Inspector, Lahore Circle, p. 30.
65. Ibid., Report of Inspector, Multan Circle, p. 11.
66. Ibid., Report of Inspector, Ambala Circle, p. 43.
67. *Report on Public Instruction in the Punjab for the Year 1894–95* (Lahore, 1895), p. 80.
68. *Report on Education in the Punjab for 1910–11* (Lahore, Government Press, 1911), pp. 7–8.

69. *Appendix to the Education Commission Report* (1884), op. cit., Evidence of Khan Ahmad Shah, Extra Assistant Commissioner, Hoshiarpur, p. 126.
70. Ibid., p. 115.
71. Ibid., Evidence of Khan Ahmad Shah, op. cit., p. 126.
72. Ibid., Evidence of Miss Mary R. Boyd, Zenana Missionary, SPG Mission, Delhi, p. 183.
73. *Report on Popular Education in the Punjab* (1869–70), p. 1.
74. Ibid., Report of Inspector, Lahore Circle, p. 31.
75. Ibid., p. 31.
76. *Report on Public Instruction in the Punjab for the Year 1899–1900*, op. cit., p. 61.
77. *Appendix to Education Commission Report* (1884), op. cit., Statement of Delhi Literary Society, p. 529.
78. *Report on Popular Education in the Punjab* (1869–70), op. cit., p. 1.
79. Ibid., Section VI, p. 39.
80. Ibid., Report of the Inspector, Lahore Circle, p. 1.
81. Ibid., p. 1.
82. *Report on Public Instruction in the Punjab* (1899–1900), op. cit., pp. 57–8.
83. *Appendix to Education Commission Report* (1884), op. cit., Evidence of W.R.M. Holroyd, Director of Public Instruction, Punjab, p. 254.
84. *Report on Popular Education in the Punjab* (1869–70), op. cit., Section IV, p. 31.
85. Ibid., Report of Inspector, Ambala Circle, pp. 47–8.
86. *Appendix to Education Commission Report* (1884), op. cit., in Evidence of Rev. K.C. Chatterjee, Punjab, p. 529.
87. Ibid., Statement of Delhi Literary Society, p. 529.
88. G.W. Leitner, op. cit., pp. 108–9.
89. *Appendix to the Education Commission Report* (1884), op. cit., Evidence of Sardar Gurdayal Singh, Assistant Commissioner, Hoshiarpur, p. 238.
90. *Appendix to the Education Commission Report* (1884), op. cit., Evidence of Miss Rose Greenfield (Ludhiana), p. 227.
91. Ibid., Evidence of Khan Ahmad Shah, op. cit., p. 126.
92. G.W. Leitner, op. cit., p. 42.
93. Ibid., p. 42.
94. *Appendix to the Education Commission Report* (1884), op. cit., Evidence of Lala Mulraj, Officiating Extra Assistant Commissioner, Gujrat (Punjab), p. 325.
95. Kenneth W. Jones, *Arya Dharm, Hindu Consciousness in 19th Century Punjab* (Berkeley, University of California Press), p. 101.
96. Ibid., p. 101.
97. *Arya Patrika*, 12 September 1885, pp. 6–7.

98. *Arya Dharm*, op. cit., p. 102.
99. *Arya Patrika*, 8 August 1885, p. 3.
100. 'Child Widows in India', *Vedic Magazine*, vol. 8, no. 6, Margshish, 1971, p. 462.
101. *Arya Patrika*, 12 September 1885, p. 4.
102. Ibid., 3 October 1885, p. 4.
103. *Arya Dharm*, op. cit., p. 104.
104. Cited in Satyadev Vidyalankar, *Lala Devraj* (Jalandhar City, Kanya Mahavidyalaya Prabandh Kritra Sabha, 3rd edition), (1st edition 1937), pp. 111–12.
105. *Lala Devraj*, op. cit., p. 112.
106. Ibid., p. 112.
107. Ibid.
108. *Tribune*, 16 March 1892, p. 4 and 23 April 1892, p. 4. See also *Lala Devraj*, op. cit., pp. 128–9.
109. *Tribune*, 24 March 1894, Letter of Sundar Das Suri, pp. 4–5.
110. Ibid., p. 5.
111. Ibid., 28 March 1894, Letter to the Editor by Lala Lajpat Rai, p. 5.
112. *Tribune*, 11 April 1894, Letter to the Editor by Sundar Das Suri, p. 5.
113. Ibid., 7 April 1894, Letter by Lala Harkishen Lal, p. 4.
114. Ibid., 14 April 1894, Letter by Bulaki Ram, p. 5.
115. Ibid., 7 April 1894, Letter by Lala Harkishen Lal, p. 4.
116. Ibid., 25 April 1894, Letter by Ralla Ram, pp. 4–5.
117. Ibid., 21 April 1894, Letter by Sheonarain citing Herbert Spencer, p. 5.
118. Ibid., 26 May 1894, Letter by Shiv Dayal, p. 5.
119. Ibid., 11 April 1894, Letter by Sundar Das Suri, p. 5.
120. Ibid., 18 March 1915. Lala Lajpat Rai, 'The Position of Indian Women', II, p. 5.
121. Ibid., p. 5.
122. Ibid., 9 May 1894, Letter by Lala Harkishen Lal, p. 5.
123. Ibid., 18 March 1915, Lala Lajpat Rai, 'The Position of Indian Women', II, p. 5.
124. Ibid., 7 March 1915, ibid., I, p. 3.
125. Ibid., p. 3.
126. Ibid.
127. Ibid.
128. *Arya Dharm*, op. cit., p. 107, citing *Tribune*, 24 October 1891, p. 4.
129. *Tribune*, 13 January 1892, p. 5.
130. Ibid.
131. Ibid., 17 June 1893, p. 3.
132. *Lala Devraj*, op. cit., p. 91.
133. Ibid., pp. 29–30.

134. Ibid., p. 130.
135. Ibid.
136. Ibid., p. 98.
137. 'Jeevan Charitra Mai Bhagwati Ji', *Panchal Pandita*, April 1902, pp. 17–19.
138. *Tribune*, 13 July 1892, p. 3.
139. *Panchal Pandita*, May 1902, pp. 9–10.
140. *Tribune*, 25 July 1899, Editorial, p. 3.
141. *Jalvid Sakha*, November 1933, p. 3.
142. From personal conversations with Acharya Lajjyawati at the KMV, Jalandhar, 1978.
143. From the advertisement for the *Panchal Pandita* on the inside cover of every issue of the magazine. The same advertisement also used often to appear in *Tribune* during these years.
144. *Panchal Pandita*, November 1905, p. 4.
145. Ibid., June 1900, p. 22.
146. *Lala Devraj*, op. cit., p. 198.
147. *Panchal Pandita*, May 1910, p. 24.
148. *Lala Devraj*, op. cit., p. 155.
149. Ibid., p. 180.
150. *Panchal Pandita*, September 1906, p. 23.
151. Ibid., p. 24.
152. *Vidyalaya Vindication* (Jullundur, 1933), p. 19.
153. *Jalvid Sakha*, November 1932, pp. 10–11.
154. See, for example 'Vidhwayen', *Panchal Pandita*, July 1903, p. 21. See also 'Vidhwa Dharm,' *Panchal Pandita*, December 1901, pp. 7–8.
155. *Lala Devraj*, op. cit., p. 111.
156. See, for example, Savitri, 'Indriya Daman', *Panchal Pandita*, 15 October 1901, pp. 13–21.

10

Viresalingam and the Ideology of Social Change in Andhra*

John and Karen Leonard

We argue here that religious polemic sanctioning social change became part of regional ideology in coastal Andhra during the early twentieth century. The Telugu language and communication through the vernacular were powerful shapers of that message. In Andhra, Indian nationalism had an anti-priest, anti-orthodox, anti-ritual and anti-authoritarian stance which was unusual. Nationalist ideology was modelled on Bengal's Brahmo Samaj in its commitment to religious and social reform and its neutrality to Christianity. One powerful personality, Viresalingam (1848–1919), shaped much of the thought and social reform activity of coastal Andhra as well as that region's cultural identity. Speakers of Telugu and Tamil, almost equal in number, were combined under British rule in the Madras Presidency, and both cultures flourished in the capital city of Madras. However, because of Viresalingam's work, the area's two vernacular cultures proved quite distinct.

The emphasis on regional cultural traditions, characteristic of nationalism in coastal Andhra, ultimately proved to be more significant on an all-India level than the stress on Sanskritic cultural traditions,

*From Kenneth W. Jones, ed., *Religious Controversy in British India: Dialogues in South Asian Languages* (Albany, NY: State University of New York, 1992), pp. 151–77.

which was part of social reform and then nationalism in Madras. The demands for recognition of Andhra's identity irritated the leaders of the Indian National Congress from 1913 to 1920 and the leaders of the Indian Union from 1946 to 1952, confronting the national leadership with what it considered to be a threat to the national integrity of India. The leaders eventually gave way in both cases and accepted the Andhra demands: in 1920, for the local Congress organizations based on linguistic boundaries and, in 1952, for the creation of an Andhra state. These concessions signified the recognition of a political pluralism which has since become accepted and extended throughout India.

The Coastal Andhra Region

The cultural centre of coastal Andhra was the city of Rajahmundry located in the Northern Circars[1] that stretches along the Bay of Bengal to the northeast of Madras. This area formed by the deltas of the Krishna and Godavari rivers was the traditional centre of Telugu culture. Rajahmundry was a religious centre, the most auspicious one on the Godavari River. Traditionally, every Hindu pilgrim from coastal Andhra to Banares had to stop on his return trip at Rajahmundry. The Brahmans in the town were noted for their 'great sense of devotion to sacrifices and rituals',[2] and an important element of regional Hinduism in the Circars was the Sankaracharya, or religious authority, one of several spiritual heirs of Sankara, founder of the Smarta Brahman sect. The Sankaracharyas were influential public figures respected by most Hindus, although their legal jurisdiction was limited to Smartas. Coastal Andhra Smartas owed allegiance to the Sankaracharya whose *math* (centre of learning and preaching) was at Virupaksha. He occasionally came on tour to Rajahmundry, which was famed for its learned as well as its religious Brahmans. Since the eleventh century, Rajahmundry had been the centre of the Telugu literary world.[3]

In 1769, the British assumed direct administration of the Northern Circars. They made Rajahmundry the headquarters of Godavari District; although the Collector shifted to Kakinada in 1859, other government institutions were not transferred.[4] In 1875, Rajahmundry had a District and Session Judge's Court, a Sub-Collector's office and a Tahsildar's office, a Provincial School and a Telegraph Office, the Superintendent of Police's office and two (central and district) jails.[5] Government service became a major source of employment. Several *zamindars* abandoned their family estates to live in the town. Missionaries and local Hindu merchants began schools. Rajahmundry retained its reputation as a sacred centre, and Brahmans continued to perform rituals and sacrifices, but the character of the town was irrevocably altered, not only by the addition of new institutions but by social and cultural changes which flowed from Madras, capital of the Presidency. Madras was a city of 406,000 in 1881, while Rajahmundry's population was 25,000.[6]

In Madras Presidency, as elsewhere in India, the educational system constructed by the British had a certain complementarity with the indigenous system of education, especially at the lower levels. The government's first actions were concentrated at the collegiate level, and after their unquestioned success, provincial and then lower schools were added. Education up to the second form, or through the fourth class, was in the regional languages, and neighbourhood schools performed this function. Christian missionaries established alternative schools, and these were more widespread, if less coordinated. In many towns, the missionary system was the only one, and Hindu parents sent their children despite fears of conversion, because of the incentives to acquire education. To provide what the government would not, and to avoid Christian religious instruction, Indians began to establish private schools in the various district towns. Most of these schools began as acts of charity by individuals, but then upper-caste, Western-educated urban Hindus formed committees and established Hindu secondary schools.

The chief beneficiaries of English education throughout Madras Presidency were Brahmans, traditionally the literate group. By 1891, for every non-Brahman who knew English there were eight Brahmans who did, although Brahmans composed only 3 per cent of the population.[7] The first institutions of higher education were in Madras, so Tamil Brahmans dominated the Civil Service. Telugu Brahmans played a subsidiary role in the public life of most of the Madras Presidency,[8] and until 1877 their closest college was in Madras. College classes for the first two years of the college curriculum began in Rajahmundry's

Provincial School only in 1873, and in 1877 the Provincial School became the Rajahmundry Government High School and College. This was the only school in the Telugu-speaking area to offer a baccalaureate programme, beginning some three decades after Madras. The Rajahmundry College did not entirely replace the Madras colleges for the northern districts, but by 1880–1 over 13 times as many Godavari District students obtained a collegiate education in Rajahmundry as were enrolled in Madras colleges.[9]

Christianity was represented in Rajahmundry by the time Viresalingam was growing up; although less so than in other areas of South India. Government schools and private schools set up by Indians, many of them government approved and subsidized, dominated Western education in Rajahmundry. In 1881, mission education accounted for only 7 per cent of the boys and 12 per cent of the girls in Rajahmundry schools.[10] The only missionaries in Rajahmundry were the American Lutherans, most of whose activities were conducted outside the town. Lutheran missionaries had started several schools in Rajahmundry, including a girls' school, which catered chiefly to Christian converts from the Mala, or untouchable, caste. The mission suffered from manpower and financial limitations and concentrated on evangelism, not education.[11] Some of the missionaries who served in Rajahmundry were allies of Viresalingam and some were rivals, but they played relatively minor roles in social reform and politics. They did not set the context or shape the ideology of social and political reform in important ways in coastal Andhra.

The introduction of the printing press and the consequent modification of the South Indian scripts in the early nineteenth century radically altered the conditions of creation, transmission and distribution of literature. This technological innovation was for a long time limited to Madras, which in 1875 had 48 presses and produced 616 books in English and the South Indian regional languages. Coastal Andhra in 1875 had only about eight presses and produced 31 books, and most of the presses in coastal Andhra were owned and operated by the British administration, European merchants or missionaries. Godavari District had three presses but published only two books or pamphlets in 1875.[12] This imbalance was evident also in books printed in the regional languages: in 1876 Tamil books outnumbered Telugu books 2.5 to 1.[13]

Viresalingam and His Work

The social reform movement and the rise of regional consciousness in coastal Andhra began with the activities of Kandukuri Viresalingam, and his character was indelibly stamped upon it. The reforms which he initiated were continued by his followers, and his ideas were adopted by the next generation. His central place in the formation of Andhra's modern identity was recognized by those who followed:

> Mr Viresalingam conveyed to his generation in a multitude of forms the consciousness of the power of these changing causes [from] contact with Western culture and Christianity. We are led to conclude that, if he was not the original centre and first cause of them all, he had, however, laid the foundation for many of them in a sound and secure manner. He was, as it were, the initial principle of change throughout the whole course of the Telugu advance in recent times.[14]

Viresalingam, the central figure in Andhra social reform and nationalism, was a Telugu Niyogi, or secular, Brahman whose family had migrated from Kandukur in the Nellore District to the Godavari delta area. Born in 1848, he grew up in one of only two double-storeyed houses in the old section of Rajahmundry. This large house indicated the high status of Viresalingam's grandfather. *Diwan* to a local zamindar, his position had enabled him to support many relatives, donate land to learned scholars and celebrate marriages with great pomp. Viresalingam's grandfather had spent rather than saved his money, however, and since Viresalingam's father and uncle had not obtained the same high position,[15] the house symbolized to the young Viresalingam the contrast between past and present achievements.

This sense of current decline was further enhanced by domestic troubles.[16] His father had died when Viresalingam was four, and his uncle was the sole support of the joint family. Viresalingam's mother and his uncle's wife quarrelled constantly, making a strong impression on Viresalingam that was reflected in his writing on the beneficial effects of education on women.[17] Viresalingam was married at 13 to a 10-year-old girl from a nearby village; he later educated her and drew her into his social reform activities. Continued quarrelling in the home led the uncle to partition the joint family, leaving a 15-year-old Viresalingam with his bride and widowed mother in the spacious Rajahmundry house.

Viresalingam's memories of his early religious training were not very strong. Aside from his initiation as a Brahman at age six, he recalled only the ardour of his religious devotion[18] that persisted throughout his life, despite changes in his specific beliefs. His early education was typical of boys heading for government employment. He learned the rudiments of Telugu and even memorized some Sanskrit verses in *pyal*, or neighbourhood schools. He learned to read and write classical Telugu and at age 10 was apprenticed to a relative who worked as a clerk in a government office.[19] Before he went to the office he was tutored in Sanskrit, and at night his uncle instructed him in English and arithmetic. Viresalingam persuaded his mother to let him resume studying full time, and at 11 or 12 he entered the government school at Rajahmundry. His proficiency in Telugu won him prizes that paid the school tuition.[20] Marked by his classmates as a scholar, he composed poems of exceptional virtuosity in 1868–69, one of which became a text for the Bachelor of Arts examination in Telugu. He also tutored the English principal of his school in Telugu and contributed articles to the Telugu journal that the principal established.[21] Viresalingam completed his schooling in 1870.[22]

Education in a Western-style school changed Viresalingam's ideas, those on religion first of all. Keshav Chandra Sen, the Bengali religious reformer and Brahmo Samaj leader, visited Madras in 1864. Three years later Viresalingam's curiosity led him to read Sen's speeches. That same year, a new secondary school teacher, Atmuri Lakshminarasimham, encouraged students to meet and discuss Brahmo Samaj doctrines opposing caste and idolatry and advocating education, particularly for women. The group of five or six met either at the teacher's home or at Viresalingam's,[23] and Viresalingam's earliest writings show the influence of Brahmo Samaj tenets.[24]

After his schooling, Viresalingam took teaching jobs, qualified for various government posts,[25] and, finally, chose a publishing career. Viresalingam began a monthly journal, *Viveka Vardhani*, in 1874.[26] Depending upon the press for a living was precarious, but the government adopted several of his Telugu books as school texts, which earned him substantial sums. The independent life of a publisher and author attracted him.[27] But pressure from his family, friends and relatives to take a regular job coincided with an offer from the Rajahmundry

Provincial School, which he joined in 1876 as an assistant teacher of Telugu. He remained there for the next 21 years.[28] Viresalingam's autobiography gave his motives for returning to teaching: he wanted a job which would be independent and not compromise his strict moral values. Thus he ceased looking for government or legal positions, both of which required actions that he considered repugnant and demeaning.[29]

Viresalingam's search for an independent profession rested upon his stubbornness and his inability to compromise in personal relations, which offended many and drove away all but the most devoted of his friends. He recalled an incident as he walked with a group of friends:

> While I was the only one who favoured the river path, the others preferred the market road. They all set off down that road, looking back to see if I would follow them. Then I started along the river bank and reached home. The same thing happened the next day. We disagreed about which way to go, and so I began to take the river path. Then they followed me, saying that whatever I think I follow it adamantly without caring for what others say.[30]

Viresalingam's aggressive, independent ways had certain advantages, evident in his initial reform efforts in Rajahmundry, but those same ways repeatedly deprived him of close allies and drove him from Rajahmundry to Madras and then back again at the end of his life.[31] Yet the impact of his activities and his ideas spread beyond Rajahmundry and decisively shaped the development of Telugu culture.

Viresalingam's initial impact on regional and Hindu self-consciousness among Telugu intellectuals came through journalism. His venture with *Viveka Vardhani* in 1874 was a continuation of the tradition of mixing literature, items of public interest, essays on religion and social comment, but he also reported on the news. *Viveka Vardhani's* English section had a variety of editors and reported news prominently, while much of the commentary was in the Telugu section that Viresalingam edited. He consistently criticized the government and he made his journal the leading advocate of social reform in coastal Andhra. He did so partly by attacking the policies of the leading Telugu scholar at Presidency College, Madras, Kokkonda Venkataratnam, and indulging in polemics with him on nearly every conceivable topic.

These were polemics by scholars and for scholars, written in classical Telugu.[32]

Viresalingam's early literary works conformed to scholarly traditions and were lauded for their virtuosity. He wrote poetry, and he specialized in *achcha* Telugu, or non-Sanskritic Telugu. This was a technical feat, since it restricted the writer's choice of vocabulary and made adhering to the rules for composition more difficult. In 1875, he received a silver trophy at a meeting of Telugu scholars in Madras for his literary achievements. Thus he came to know the elite among Telugu scholars, those who published books, held important positions and presented their views to the government.[33] At 27 Viresalingam was honoured by this group for excelling at the traditional tasks of Telugu scholars: making translations and writing grammars. Through his journal, however, he would realize his true literary potential and be fêted for quite different achievements: innovative literary forms and, through them, the expression of new social and religious reform ideas.

Religious reform via the Brahmo Samaj had made an impression on the young Viresalingam. The Brahmo movement was making an impact in Madras and coastal Andhra, although the nature of that impact differed substantially in the two places. The non-Brahman character of the Brahmo Samaj in Madras was established early. Although a Telugu Brahman revived and led the group from 1878, its reputation as a centre of anti-Brahman feeling grew.[34] The South India Brahmo Samaj leadership and membership had little in common with the majority of the educated elite in Madras, the Tamil Brahmans, and the movement all but disappeared from Tamil Nadu's intellectual history.[35]

In the Telugu-speaking region, however, Brahmo Samaj ideas became part of Telugu literary and political culture. In Rajahmundry, Viresalingam and a few friends met together sporadically for prayer meetings based on the model of the Brahmo Samaj of Calcutta, and in 1878 they formed the Rajahmundry Prarthana Samaj. This society was at first secret, and members sang hymns and heard lectures in Viresalingam's home. After a year, apprehensions eased. The association moved to the Maharajah of Vizianagaram's Girls' School and invited the public to join.[36] Of the eight active members, five were Niyogi Brahmans, two were Vaidiki Brahmans and one was a non-Brahman

Telaga. By occupation, five were teachers, one was a lawyer and one a government clerk.[37] Since most of the reformers were teachers, they could recruit students and keep the association going. This was the first religious reform organization in coastal Andhra that lasted for any length of time, and it served as a base from which other associations were formed.

The 1870s in coastal Andhra saw little evidence of debate over social conditions and little social reform activity. Machilipatnam, the district headquarters of Krishna District, had an outstanding journal, *Purusartha Pradayini*, but no social reform activities; in 1879 local leaders were still trying to begin an association and reading room.[38] In Kakinada, the Cocanada Literary Association was founded in 1878 and was politically oriented from its beginnings, but the Kakinada journal was not effectively tied to the association and did not campaign for the issues it discussed.[39] Elsewhere in coastal Andhra there were sporadic meetings of students and local Brahman officials to debate changing specific customs but these discussions did not produce tangible results.[40] Even in Rajahmundry, early reform activities produced few results, but journalistic activity, public meetings, organized voluntary associations and some leaders among the educated elite forged the conditions in which a social reform campaign could be waged.

Through his journal *Viveka Vardhani*, Viresalingam was developing an ideology of social reform and actively seeking an issue for a reform campaign. In the journal, he introduced himself to the public with a poem:

> I am a Brahman who learned a foreign language and passed an examination in that language.
> I have an interest in the Telugu language, and I want to aid the development of the country.
> I have some talent for writing poetry.
> I write particularly about moral questions which are universal, in an easy style, without using difficult compounds, so that everyone may understand.
> I also use foreign words.[41]

In the first line, Viresalingam identified himself as a member of the educated elite, while in the third he implied that he was a scholar in

Telugu. Then he went on to state his concern for writing prose, and writing it so that people could understand it—he wanted to write in spoken, not classical, Telugu. He linked the development of Telugu with that of the country. Elsewhere, he stated that his journal had two aims: the improvement of the Telugu language and the improvement of the country.[42]

Viresalingam wanted to develop Telugu not only by modifying the language but also by using it to reform society. Language reform was to be carried out by simplifying Telugu to increase peoples' comprehension of it. He conceived of language as a means to combat the evil conditions in society and to propagate the moral standards essential for the country's progress. These journalistic goals represented a conscious break with tradition in Telugu usage.

The documentation of his intellectual odyssey is somewhat limited, but Viresalingam distinguished three periods when discussing the evolution of his journal, *Viveka Vardhani*.[43] The first two periods fell before the first widow marriage he performed in December 1881, and the last followed that crucial event. The first period was brief, from 1874 to 1876. He wrote about social conditions that affronted him—the corruption of officials, the role of prostitutes in public life, the degraded position of women and the widespread ignorance of the masses. If there was a focus to his writings then, it was on the problem of cultural contact between India and the West and the reasons for the decline of ancient Indian civilization. Viresalingam idealized the past and contrasted it with the current degraded state of society. He was especially concerned with the role of the Brahmans, keepers of the texts and traditions.

Viresalingam's explanation for the decline of ancient India became more complex with time and touched directly on the Brahmans as preservers of India's civilizational values. How he explained this decline varied with the opposition that faced Viresalingam at any one time in his career. At first, he blamed the Muslims for the destruction of ancient India's greatness: they had shattered political unity and subjugated Indians. Loss of political independence removed morality from law and order; suspicion and mutual distrust became endemic. Brahmans were humiliated and had to take up professions like low-level civil service jobs, and some were even reduced to begging. The prevailing fact in political life was oppression, and the dominant emotion in social life was fear: Indian civilization had lost its confidence and power.[44] This attribution of the decline to external forces came as Viresalingam was just beginning to write about social reform and was still committed to the role of a scholar and teacher. Opposition to his ideas was slight and came chiefly from scholars; he had undertaken no significant reform activities.

Then came a transitional period. Scholars sharpened their attacks after Viresalingam defied orthodox burial customs and began to criticize Brahmans, and a perceptible shift occurred in his account of the decline of ancient India. Increasingly Viresalingam blamed scholars for the deterioration of knowledge and standards of morality.[45] However, this internal factor, evident in his speeches and lectures during 1875–6, still played only a subordinate role in Viresalingam's thinking.

As Viresalingam attacked current practices and beliefs, he began to attribute malpractices to scholars, pseudoscholars or teachers, basing his argument on the place of knowledge in a country's civilization. At first arguing that Muslim rule had forced Brahmans to abandon their honourable professions of preserving knowledge and had encouraged various corruptions,[46] Viresalingam began to trace the deterioration of knowledge to two new causes: one was the preference of scholars for revelation, rather than observation and inference, as a source of knowledge; the other was the scholars' concern for form rather than meaning, for Sanskrit and poetry rather than for the regional languages and prose.[47] He traced these two causes to ancient Indian civilization prior to the coming of the Muslims and saw them as precluding the rise of a scientific tradition in India. They were also the principal evils of the present day that needed to be rectified. Thus he focused on internal causes for India's decline—on scholars and their faults.[48]

During these years Viresalingam used his journal to experiment with new literary forms, farcical one-act plays about social conditions and stories illustrating moral principles specifically for women. These innovative forms set his journal off from its competitors and were significant in the development of Telugu literature. Their content was as notable as their form. Many of his one-act plays satirized Brahmans, highlighting the evils and absurdities of contemporary society. He developed social stereotypes of 'the orthodox'. Viresalingam used his farces to pillory his enemies; since his attempts at disguising the personalities he portrayed were ineffective, a target of his writing could easily find himself with a new nickname, that of a character in one of Viresalingam's plays. These farces were the first instance in modern times when the Telugu spoken dialect was employed for dramatic purposes. Viresalingam used the spoken dialect for *all* his characters, Brahmans and untouchables alike (the conventions in Sanskrit drama allowed only a few low-born characters to use spoken dialects).[49]

As Viresalingam was increasingly criticized by his fellow scholars during 1875–6, his responses in his journal pointed to ancient scholars seduced by the lure of power and wealth, confused by the urge to acquire prestige and misled into fabricating stories that the mass of illiterates believed. He began to question the later accretions to Hindu traditions, such as the *itihasa* and the *puranas*; to note the purity of thought in *Smrti* and the Vedas, including the Upanishads; and to claim inclusion of gross superstitions in *Smrti*, the *dharmasastras*, the *itihasa* and the *puranas*. Since *Smrti* was often used to confute him, it was natural that he should try to discredit it. He argued that contemporary Indians were merely continuing the prostitution of education and the adoption of debased jobs initiated by the ancient Indian scholars. Contemporary scholars seldom studied the Vedas or even the *dharmasastras*, so spurious customs based on later texts had crept in and lowered the standards of scholarship and morality.[50]

Viresalingam based his ideas about progress on the cyclical ages of Hindu cosmology, postulating that since the literal descriptions of the darkest of the four ages fit the present, contemporary society was in the last age and anything that succeeded it was bound to be better. Rejecting the inevitability of the destruction of the world, he argued that steady improvement would culminate in a future golden age, thus assimilating the Western idea of progress to traditional Hindu beliefs and making it part of his conception of societal development.[51] To justify cultural borrowing from the West, he argued that the West had first borrowed from India—mathematics, via Greece—and thus India was responsible for achievements derived from mathematics.[52] Furthermore, mutual cultural borrowing involved no subordination of one civilization to another. The leading ideas in Viresalingam's programme of regeneration were in fact indigenous scholarly ones: the ameliorative power of knowledge and the intrinsic strength of a unified people. He believed that education would instil morality in the leaders of society and create a climate of opinion favourable to reform. This education would be both moral and practical, since knowledge concerning the sciences and humanities had to be tempered with a knowledge of moral principles.[53]

Education was one remedy for India, and unity—of race, religion and caste—was the other. In his speeches and writings, Viresalingam appealed to his audience to promote unity, not just at the philosophical level of Vedantic speculation, but at a social level. He advocated the formation of debating clubs, caste organizations, trade unions, almost any kind of organization which would bind men together. These associations would be like building blocks, in themselves small and useless, but together indispensable.[54] These essentially scholarly ideas reflected his initial activities, rectifying abuses that afflicted Brahmans and combating specific corrupt practices of officials in Rajahmundry.

Viresalingam's first reform efforts had been personal and idiosyncratic. He refused to call in Brahmans for rites connected with the removal of a beehive from a roof beam in his house, although it was customary to employ them to do so;[55] and he joined Basavarazu Gavarrazu, a friend, in defying Brahman burial customs when Gavarrazu's son died. The two of them buried the corpse themselves, hoping to encourage secular Brahmans to participate in funeral processions and discourage ideas about pollution.[56] He wrote against Brahman marriage customs such as bride price, child marriage of girls and marriages restricted by sect and kinship,[57] but he found it difficult to promote changes in these even among his friends. Girls' education was a popular reform—Viresalingam had founded a girls' school in 1874 when teaching in a nearby small town and, in 1881, he began another in Rajahmundry. Finally, in 1874, Viresalingam turned his attention to the controversial issue of widow marriage.

The Widow Marriage Campaign

That Telugu-speaking reformers took the lead on the widow marriage issue in the Presidency seems indisputable. In Madras, the Hindu Widow Re-Marriage Association had been formed in 1874 but served only briefly as a forum for voicing the arguments for widow marriage before it languished. Its leaders were Brahmans but not Tamil Brahmans, and it used English, not a regional language, for its meetings. The Tamil Brahman establishment was more concerned in the 1870s with educational policy, questions of management (by government or private institutions), and the role of Indian languages (including Sanskrit). The fear that Western education would lead to secularism was strong. After Viresalingam formed the Rajahmundry Widow Marriage Association in 1879, the Madras Hindu Widow Re-Marriage Association became active again. The Rajahmundry and Madras reformers cooperated in limited ways over the next two decades.[58]

When Viresalingam began to plan a widow marriage campaign in the Telugu-speaking Circars, he spent over a year meeting with various people and scholars to discuss the question of widow marriages.[59] Because of the scholars' reluctance to agree with his textual interpretations, Viresalingam became convinced of their unwillingness to cope with change, and he began to attack them as agents and even the sources of religious authority. In the spring of 1881, he challenged his religious superior, the Sankaracharya from Virupaksha, when he came to Rajahmundry. In his journal Viresalingam attacked the Sankaracharya, claiming that he was coercing donations from people by threatening excommunication. He also denigrated the Sankaracharya's personal disciple and presumptive heir. At a March meeting, Viresalingam presented a petition signed by 30 Niyogi Brahmans asking for the Sankaracharya's approval of widow marriages. Viresalingam spoke in favour of widow marriages and another pandit spoke for the opposition. Later in the meeting the audience was informed that the Sankaracharya would sanction widow marriage only if the majority of caste Hindus in Rajahmundry approved. This meant, of course, that local custom would prevail; it cut off the debate and silenced Viresalingam. Since the Sankaracharya left the meeting without commenting on the validity of Viresalingam's interpretation, Viresalingam believed he was still free to persuade other Hindus of the correctness of his argument.[60]

This confrontation was the first of several clashes between Viresalingam and the Sankaracharya. Viresalingam continued to criticize or subvert religious authority in pursuit of his reform goals. Viresalingam was a Smarta and under the Sankaracharya's religious authority, but Brahmans from different sects joined in the appeal for approval of widow marriages. Thus the confrontation illustrated the more general religious role of the Sankaracharya and also the interest in the widow marriage issue; it cut across sectarian boundaries and united reformers of different sectarian backgrounds.

Formed in 1879, the Rajahmundry Widow Marriage Association[61] held its first widow marriage in 1881, when a secret executive committee and, in effect, a new association were formed. The Prarthana Samaj had been dominated by teachers; in this new association, there were as many officials as teachers on the executive committee.[62] Many members were students from the Rajahmundry Government College. The teachers recruited students directly from their classes for social reform activities and also served as role models for their students, who were in many cases living away from home for the first time. Viresalingam in particular was admired, since he was recognized as the foremost Telugu scholar of his age, and students remembered that he advocated social reform in his classes. He concentrated especially on exposing and ridiculing the ideas and practices of orthodox Hindus, creating in the classroom the same social stereotypes that he wrote about in his journal.[63] As the widow marriage campaign aroused controversy, students formed bodyguards for Viresalingam and other leaders in danger of physical attack from their orthodox opponents.[64] After the first marriage in 1881, students went out to villages, found widows and arranged to bring them to Rajahmundry; some became bridegrooms themselves despite threats and beatings from their parents.[65] The intense excitement and enthusiasm of the 1881–4 widow marriage campaign, when 10 marriages of widows were celebrated, deeply marked the young men who participated.[66] Some 30 more widow marriages had been celebrated in Andhra by 1919, making this the most intensive campaign in all of India.

From the time of Viresalingam's first speech on widow marriage in 1879 it took almost two years to find a widow who would remarry and a bridegroom for her. In December 1881, the first widow marriage was performed. It took the help of British officials to conduct it: to secure the bridegroom's leave from his job, depute a police detachment of Muslims and Christians from Madras, and threaten to arrest orthodox

Hindu leaders if there were overt disturbances.[67] The orthodox had persuaded Brahman cooks, water carriers and priests not to carry out their customary duties, but the reformers countered the threatened boycott by paying more for all the services.[68] Four days after the highly publicized wedding, another widow was brought by her mother to Rajahmundry and married; this event was even grander, since many British officials joined the procession and many more people came to watch it.[69]

Both the reformers and their opponents organized themselves for these controversial events. The Widow Marriage Association left the publicity to Viresalingam, whose journal made him the most effective spokesman, but the other leaders secured support from officials in the district towns. In Kakinada, Godavari District headquarters, a local merchant, Paida Ramakrishnayya, offered to donate thousands of rupees once the marriages began, and he kept his promise.[70] The opponents organized too. Before the first widow marriage, the orthodox opposition was led by Vaidiki or priestly Brahman scholars;[71] then an association against widow marriages was formed in Rajahmundry led by Western-educated men, indicating a shift in the leadership of the orthodox opposition. Although scholars still had an important place, Western-educated men holding government positions became the leaders. Similarly, their tactics shifted. Until this time, orthodox opponents would enforce traditional sanctions, withdraw essential domestic and religious services, and refuse to contract marriage relationships or fulfil kinship obligations. But now they asked the Sankaracharya to make the reformers outcastes. When the Sankaracharya complied, it was the Municipal Council President of Rajahmundry who convened a meeting to announce the expulsion of the reformers from their castes.[72] Some 30 people who attended the wedding meals were expelled, their readmission to caste dependent upon formal, public acknowledgement of the Sankaracharya's authority and a ceremony of penance.[73] Among the reformers outcasted by the Sankaracharya were non-Smartas, indicating his more general authority among Hindus.

This counterattack was very effective, and only Viresalingam and one friend, Basavarazu Gavarrazu, ultimately resisted submission to the Sankaracharya. Viresalingam had his own well; he and his wife had no children and, as a Telugu Brahman pandit, he performed the marriages himself. The worst blow to the reformers was the loss of their chief patron, the Kakinada merchant, who performed penance and swore not to give any more money to the reformers.[74] Viresalingam was bitter about the failure of the educated elite to support the reform campaign and withstand social pressure. From this experience, he concluded that education had to be extended to women and the masses; once educated, they would not be intimidated by those opposed to social change. Enthusiasm for reform in Rajahmundry declined noticeably, and it was harder to find brides and bridegrooms. Violence used by both sides during the months after the first two widow marriages—college students fought with the young disciples of priests—resulted in the filing of lawsuits by both sides, although only the priests' disciples were convicted.[75]

Another lawsuit filed as a consquence of the first widow marriage was far more significant. One of the non-Smartas outcasted by the Sankaracharya, Atmuri Lakshminarasimham, filed a court case against him. The initial decision, against the reformers, was appealed to the Madras High Court in August 1882, and this caused misgivings among orthodox and reformers alike. (The two most prominent social reformers in Madras denied any association with the appeal.[76]) Viresalingam's closest follower, Basavarazu Gavarrazu, filed the appeal, and its outcome was surprising. The Madras High Court upheld the lower court decision with respect to Sankaracharya's ecclesiastical powers—he could expel people from caste—but decided *against* Sankaracharya because of the way he had notified reformers of his action. He had sent them postcards through the mail, and this violated the laws against defamation! They fined him Rs 200.[77]

The real question here was whether or not the government had the legal power to pass judgement on a duly constituted source of Hindu religious authority. Advocates of reform in Rajahmundry supported the initial court case, although some were ambivalent about it, and they did not oppose the appeal. They were disappointed in the decision, fearing it would diminish support for social reform.[78] In Madras, the response was different. Just as they had opposed the appeal itself, without exception the Madras social reformers condemned the court's decision to fine Sankaracharya.[79] In Rajahmundry, widow marriages continued—four took place between the time of the appeal and the High Court decision seven months later, and four more took place before internal dissension led to the decline of the movement in 1884. By the time of the High Court decision, the reformers no longer needed police protection.[80]

These 10 widow marriages had an impact far beyond their numbers. Most of the child widows were from the Brahman castes,[81] but the Rajahmundry widow marriages included two Komati (merchant) couples. There were more secular Brahmans than priestly ones among the eight Brahman couples, but every Brahman sect and branch was represented in these couples, and the tenth marriage was an inter-sect Brahman marriage. The Rajahmundry Widow Marriage Association sponsored all 10 marriages and all save one were held in Rajahmundry; that one was held by Rajahmundry reformers in Madras.[82] This small group displayed remarkable diversity and involved a wide range of the educated elite and their families in controversy over the reform.

After 1884 serious dissension among the reformers caused the movement to lose momentum, although 30 more widow marriages were performed before Viresalingam's death in 1919. What is significant here is that the dissension no longer concerned whether or not widow marriages were religiously sanctioned or were a useful reform. The dissension was over how to support the married couples (many bridegrooms lost their jobs and the Widow Marriage Association provided them housing, allowances and sometimes employment),[83] and, after 1886, over the provisions of the will of Paida Ramakrishnayya. He had honoured his pledge to the Sankaracharya not to give money directly to the Rajahmundry reformers, but he had channelled money to them through the social reform leaders in Madras, and upon his death he left a trust fund containing Rs 10,000 for the widow marriage movement. This was to be administered by Atmuri Lakshminarasimham, the teacher who had first propounded Brahmo Samaj doctrines to Viresalingam. He was now a judicial official and the filer of the court case against Sankaracharya. Viresalingam's unfortunate tendency to alienate his closest allies inspired him to attack Lakshminarasimham in a farce just at this time, so that disagreements among the reformers and bridegrooms produced factions within the association. Lakshminarasimham refused to use the trust fund for new couples, preferring to keep it for those already married.[84] There had already been rivalry among the leaders—before 1881, three of them, including Viresalingam and Lakshminarasimham, had founded competing girls' schools in Rajahmundry—but it did not interfere with the widow marriage campaign until the mid-1880s.

The widow marriage campaign in Andhra showed the impact of direct, positive action; its symbolic achievements were many. The direct challenge to religious authority, in this case that of the Sankaracharya, appealed to college students and helped keep Hindu revivalism out of the social reform movement in coastal Andhra. An antipathy to religious authority appeared in later reform movements initiated by Viresalingam's students.[85] The widow marriage movement had offered direct, positive action with tremendous potential for dramatization, maximum publicity and controversy.

Despite the setback to the widow marriage campaign, reform activities proceeded. The dissension and the loss of old members through death (especially Basavarazu Gavarrazu in 1888) and dispute coincided with the initial experiments by the British in local government and with the emergence of nationalism throughout India. Thus the energies of the educated elite were drawn into new fields. There was, however, continuity in some areas. Religious reform remained an attractive alternative and was less threatening to orthodox Hindus; girls' education proceeded to grow and Telugu literary activities featured both innovations and controversy.

The vital relationships between social reform, religious reform and literary activity were recognized by contemporary social reformers. Attacks on orthodox customs and views were conducted through the widow marriage campaign, religious reform associations and literary activity. The widow marriage campaign gave an impetus to innovations in Telugu literature; it continued under Viresalingam's leadership. In 1883, he began *Sati Hita Bodhini*, a journal written for women, and he used this genre to inculcate his ideas on social reform. This type of writing was developed by his former pupils to become almost a separate field of Telugu prose.[86]

Literature as a means of reform became a cultural tradition in coastal Andhra, and literary activity became a suitable alternative field of endeavour for many social reformers. Telugu journalism was also pressed into the service of social reformers. Most significant, journal debate during the 1880s in coastal Andhra was carried on in Telugu and not in English—there was no English-language newspaper for coastal Andhra until 1921, when the Congress leader T. Prakasam published one from Madras.[87] *The Hindu*, published in English from Madras from 1878, reported little on coastal Andhra, and this neglect was, in a sense, fortunate for Telugu journalism, for the important issues of the day were discussed and analysed only through the Telugu journals. This strengthened Telugu journalism and forced the educated elite to use Telugu and solve the problems inherent in transforming the regional language. The negative aspects of this situation were that people in other parts of India were unaware of what was happening in coastal Andhra and that parochialism was encouraged among Telugu-speaking people. But by the 1890s, educated men and women in Andhra were committed to the use of Telugu as a serious medium of expression in journalism and literature, and they were engaged in transforming the regional language and its culture.[88]

Social reform proved to be the chief determinant of the direction of cultural change in the Telugu language and literature. The modification of the Telugu script for printing, the initial efforts at prose composition, and the introduction of new literary forms had occurred by the mid-nineteenth century, developed by Telugu scholars who tried to control the changes. The transition to a new phase of culture occurred in the late 1870s, when Viresalingam began employing innovative literary forms in his social reform publicity. The cultural change wrought by the social reform campaign also led to a shift in the men and institutions associated with the development of Telugu literature.

Scholars in Telugu began to be superseded by the educated elite as effective communicators, and consequently the structure of the Telugu literary culture was altered. The main motivation for this modernization of Telugu was the hope that it would bridge the gulf which the educated elite felt between themselves and those who did not know English. Viresalingam's concern with the masses developed after his disillusionment with the educated elite—he emphasized the moral benefits of education for women and the masses so that they would not hold back the educated elite and could themselves participate directly in reform efforts.[89] This modernization was also an attempt to bridge the gulf between urban and rural people, and, to some extent, between Brahman and non-Brahman.

If social reform activity accelerated cultural change, it also accelerated the process of political development in the area. Because social reform was the first organized activity initiated by the educated elite in coastal Andhra, it had a significance which transcended its success or failure in the performance of widow marriages. The educated elite started journals, organized associations, recruited supporters and planned campaigns around the idea of social innovation. The leaders of social reform recruited members and attracted sympathizers. Reform activity was an experience for students and others that accustomed them to nontraditional groups and activities. Social reform was also an arena of political activity. The centrality of the Rajahmundry Government College in the educational life of the Circars and the central position of Viresalingam in both social reform and literary activities gave a strong initial base for the widow marriage campaign and heightened its impact. But Viresalingam's stubbornness and controversial personal relations ensured that other reformers split off from him and built associations and institutions of their own. Thus reform efforts did not proceed under the direction of just one man, but through the rivalry of several major figures and the allegiance to them of many others. These shifting alignments broadened the arena for reform ideas and activities. Viresalingam's associations and institutions may have depended upon personal and financial support which sometimes proved elusive, but his ideas decisively shaped social and political concepts in coastal Andhra.

Viresalingam's Thought

Viresalingam's responses to the questions posed by Westernization changed over the years. Before 1876, he had conceived of the problems largely as arising from a confrontation between India and the West. Attributing the rise of the West chiefly to unity and a scientific tradition he harnessed these achievements to his conception of progress for India. In that period Viresalingam had been unsure about which cultural tradition or group he should favour to bring about the changes he desired in society. The second period, from 1876 to 1881, when he was actively engaged in the widow marriage campaign, was a transitional one for him in which he worked out tentative answers to these questions. From 1881 to 1888, when the first two marriages had been successfully performed, Viresalingam fully developed the ideas that he had begun to formulate during the transitional period, a period that coincided with the decline of the social reform movement and an increase of political activity at the local and national levels. Viresalingam's solutions were his ultimate intellectual response to problems that he had encountered in the early 1870s. His followers adopted many of his ideas, but faced with different tasks, they used his thought to meet the situations facing them in the late 1880s.

Viresalingam's social reform experience during the transitional period decisively shaped his intellectual development. His initiation of the widow marriage campaign in 1879 shifted his attention from assessing the reasons for India's decline to determining practical means of achieving its regeneration. Viresalingam's concerns about India's relationship to the West receded in importance as he was confronted with the immediate problems posed by Indian society. His narrowed view relegated the West to a category of 'other countries'[90] where the issues of child marriage, bride price, and prohibition of widow marriage did not exist. Viresalingam invoked 'other countries' in his arguments only to show that the situation in India was not a universal one. While stating that the elimination of undesirable social conditions was a universal goal, he was reluctant to point to the West as the specific model for India's future. He did not mind taking Western knowledge of natural science as a model for India, because he argued that Western science had originated with ideas borrowed from India.[91] It would have been difficult, however, for him to apply this same argument of cultural borrowing in the areas of social structure and social relationships. Hence he tried not to associate desirable social conditions explicitly with contemporary Western society. The development of universal goals absorbed his attention from 1880 onwards.[92]

Viresalingam's understanding of progress recurred throughout his writings in the phrase 'the development of the country'.[93] He used the word *development* to designate those activities that used rational means to improve Indian social conditions and, in the process, freed individuals from the control of traditional authorities to allow the realization of individual potential. By country he meant a local area, for he spoke of the many countries within the Madras Presidency. He did not intend it to stand for a nation or a geopolitical unit, either; he related progress to the improvement of social conditions and social classes. His 'country' is best understood as synonymous with *society*.

Believing that education was the key development activity, Viresalingam expanded his ideas about who should be educated, though he did not change his ideas about its content. His view of education was a very broad and complex one, for he approached it from a metaphysical point of view and linked it implicitly with his ideas on religion. Thus he equated education with the particular knowledge that allowed one to perceive truths about the nature of the world. The existence of divinity was one such truth.[94] This knowledge was to be derived from observation and critical reflection; Viresalingam applied these criteria to his proofs of the existence of divinity as well as to more mundane matters.[95] He placed a new emphasis on science, especially Western science based on an empirical tradition of observation and experimentation, which he grasped as being similar to his own ideas about knowledge. In the 1880s, he began to translate scientific treatises on subjects like biology, physics and astronomy into Telugu. He valued science because it was a systematic method of investigating phenomena that gave a consistent, 'true' picture of the nature of the world, unlike the accounts of creation that he read in the Hindu epic literature.[96] Science was a tool with which Viresalingam could expose superstition and ridicule the basis of existing customs. He hoped to use scientific explanations to refute the arguments of traditional scholars and win the allegiance of the educated elite for social reform.

Morality was the second major element in Viresalingam's ideas on education. He believed that science and morality were different aspects of the truth—each represented a way of perceiving divinity and each confirmed the existence and benevolence of divinity.[97] Viresalingam deprecated the contemporary equation of Western education with material advantages, because he connected education with religious training. It was chiefly the moral benefits of education that he wanted to confer on women and the masses.[98] He advocated moral teaching of a nondenominational nature that would stress the truths common to all religions: the existence of God, God's benevolence and kindness, and the individual's need to adopt appropriate moral behaviour, based on reason, in order to please God.[99]

At first Viresalingam believed the purpose of education was to create an elite group—emancipated from the inhibiting bonds of custom and tradition—to lead society to a higher level through social reform. This was his view before he tried to gain the support of the educated elite for the widow marriage campaign in 1881.[100] When he first encouraged the education of women, he was concerned only with upper-caste women, particularly those related to members of the educated elite. When this elite failed to support the widow marriage campaign and other reforms, Viresalingam understood that education for an elite group was not sufficient, because pressure from the rest of society could intimidate the few educated men and prevent them from achieving reforms. Therefore, he considered the extension of educational opportunities to the lowest levels of society as a step necessary to emancipating the educated elite.[101] He had already advocated teaching science (hygiene) and morality to high-caste women; these were now to be taught in a simplified form to the masses.[102]

With the inclusion of the masses in Viresalingam's educational goals, his concept of the elite changed, although his belief in its potential to improve the country was always a consistent strand in his thought. Even before 1876, he had praised the educated, but his essays on their role in society had conveyed a quality of ambivalence, since at that time the educated elite in coastal Andhra was small in numbers and still adhered to the lifestyle of the political elite. In that early period, Viresalingam had looked to the traditional scholars as possible promoters of change, but, from 1879 to 1881, his belief in that group's capacity to accomplish this work waned rapidly, and he turned to the educated elite as more appropriate agents of change. His hopes for support from the educated reached a high point in October 1881, when he declared that only Western-educated men should continue to write books in the regional language, since the works of traditional scholars were of no benefit to society.[103] When many of them refused to participate in social reform activities, and some even showed a reluctance to promote education, Viresalingam began to be disillusioned with them.[104] By 1884, his disenchantment was complete, but Viresalingam still believed that if change was to come it must be led by the educated, and he continually urged their commitment to social reform while he criticized them for adopting political reform exclusively.[105]

Viresalingam now envisaged a new mission for the Western-educated elite: constrained from participation in active social reform, they were to be the main instruments in the implementation of universal education. In an essay written in June 1883, he listed the tasks for the educated elite. Only one, the abolition of child marriage, was concerned with social reform; the other tasks focused on the development of education and its consequences for society.[106] After Viresalingam's redefinition of 'progress' to include the improvement of the social conditions of the masses, he began to argue for universal education.[107] He argued, as he had before, that scientific and moral training should be adapted especially for women's education and would prepare them to accept changes in society.[108] Viresalingam went on to argue that the effect of education on the masses would be the same: it would drive out superstition, inculcate morality and provide a receptive climate for social reforms. He did not expect all people to become educated, but he hoped a majority would eventually take advantage of educational opportunities and move from ignorance and poverty to a middle rank in society, a social stratum then rather sparsely occupied by the educated elite.[109] In his view, the masses occupied the lowest level of society, not for economic reasons, but because of their lack of education.

Viresalingam set several tasks for Western-educated men. He anticipated that women and the masses would not take advantage of education initially unless they were under some social pressure to do so. Therefore, the first task for educated men was to send their daughters to school and educate their wives. Next, these literate men must work to dispel the current belief that the *dharmasastras* prohibited the education of Sudras. When this was accomplished, Viresalingam wanted members of the elite to enter the villages and persuade rural people to become educated. Finally, his programme for the elite included the writing of Telugu books on science and morality for the masses. The educated elite was still to be the active agent of change in society, though Viresalingam expected help from the government in providing educational facilities.[110]

Viresalingam had called on the government school system to implement his ideas,[111] but his expectations of government assistance were actually not very great. He had difficulty obtaining approval for his girls' school, and he knew that the municipalities and the Department of Public Instruction in Madras were reluctant to expand government-managed educational facilities. Furthermore, while science classes were relatively easy to introduce or strengthen in the government schools, morality instruction (in the form of nondenominational religious doctrines) was not so easily inserted into the curriculum. Viresalingam wrote repeatedly in his journal, *Viveka Vardhani*, on this theme of introducing moral training into the school curriculum, but the opposition was great, so he considered other ways to inculcate morality in students. In his assessment, the most effective alternative was to utilize Telugu literature.[112]

Viresalingam's identification of the regional language with a Telugu culture was shared but slightly by different segments of the population in 1882. By 1884, his belief in universal education and a Telugu medium of instruction implied linking together the different levels of culture among Telugu-speaking people. This new and broader goal became included in the meaning of his phrase 'the development of the country'.[113] Thus Viresalingam's concept of Telugu as a tool in the service of the educated elite had changed drastically; he now saw it as a vehicle for the transformation of the masses. The interaction between his views on reform and his ideas concerning the people who should benefit from reform eventually led him to consider changes in the Telugu language and literature that he had not anticipated in 1874, innovations that led to the fuller development of the new cultural tradition of literature as a means of reform and eventually to a new and broader culture itself.

From 1880 to 1888 there was a clear progression in Viresalingam's thinking about Indian society. Viresalingam's earlier use of metaphor, though frequent, lacked a consistent pattern. When he discussed the masses his metaphors invariably represented them as being at a low level of development—such as a child.[114] Then, with the introduction of local self-government in 1884 and the organization of the Indian National Congress in 1885, Viresalingam's images of them emphasized their 'youth'. He envisioned society as an organism and saw its parts in anthropomorphic terms. He did not revert to the hierarchical ranking of *varnas* or castes and their approximation to parts of the body, an image featured in the Rig Veda, for he focused on the activities of society. He made his ideas explicit in the following way: social and political reform were both growths of society and, since society was organic in nature, the two had to develop evenly. Coordinated growth was healthy, while uneven growth was a sign of disease. He stated that, in political terms, Indian society was progressing from childhood to adolescence. The Government of India was the mother who would grant measures of independence as soon as the adolescent proved capable of exercising it. Viresalingam disavowed his earlier reliance on the educated elite by concluding that one segment of society should not be allowed to forge ahead of other segments, such as women or the masses.[115] This even development of all sections of society was another way in which Viresalingam expressed his idea that the unity of society was essential for progress.

Viresalingam's concept of society as an organic entity initially led him to distrust political reformers. He never quite lost this feeling, even though he came to laud the founding of the Indian National Congress. Local politicians attempted to argue that social reform was not a necessary accompaniment to progress and that contemporary customs were either admirable or impossible to change; Viresalingam reacted sharply to such assertions. He consistently criticized local political reformers for deserting social issues; yet, on another level, he praised the Indian National Congress for its work in promoting the unity of India.[116]

Ultimately, Viresalingam's thinking about the development of Indian society stemmed from two problems. The first was India's low position *vis-à-vis* the West; this led him to consider largely abstract ways to elevate a country's status. The second problem was the failure of the Western-educated elite to actively support social reform—social pressures exerted by the rest of Indian society meant that educated men were actually being used to enforce conformity to existing social practices. Thus leadership at an elite level obviously was not sufficient to change society; followers also had to be receptive to change, for all levels of the population had to progress together. Viresalingam's recognition of the power of uneducated people to subvert the implementation of socially desirable goals made him realize the magnitude of their power and the need to harness it for progress. This led him to campaign for mass education and the broadening need of the regional language and its literature. He began to equate the development of Telugu culture with the progress of the masses. Earlier he had identified the development of Telugu with progress of the country and its status; by this time he was concerned about the status of the masses as well as that of the country.[117] Viresalingam never made the final, direct equation—the identification of the people with the country—because he still believed in the leadership of an elite, the inherent inertia of the masses and the wisdom of the British administration in India.[118] Yet his intellectual development, in retrospect, represents a far-reaching attempt to build nationalist consciousness on a cultural base.

One can trace in Viresalingam's intellectual odyssey the interaction of his perceptions and actual social reform experiences through time. Viresalingam began his intellectual inquiry into the origins of the decay of Indian society when he was a young teacher in a village school. His early concern for education made him stress teaching as the key to change, although he was uncertain about exactly what to change at that time. His position as a Telugu scholar inclined him towards that language as the medium of cultural change, and his position as a member of the educated elite and as a Brahman stressed the role of an elite in guiding the country's destiny. But his experience in the widow marriage campaign modified these early ideas and led him to consider mass education as a necessary prerequisite for the inauguration of social reform. Mass education could be conducted only through Telugu, and this made him consider the further expansion of Telugu as the opener for a cultural change much greater than the one he had conceived originally. Beginning as an imitator of the traditional Telugu scholars, he ended his career as a great popularizer and prophet of cultural change for the masses.[119]

Conclusion

The relationship of social reform, literary, and political activity to regional identity forged by Viresalingam decisively shaped the character of the Indian nationalist movement there and contrasted with the lack of such a relationship in Madras. From 1879 to 1913, the educated elite established organizations at three levels—local, district and regional—and social and religious reform associations stemming from Rajahmundry and Viresalingam's widow marriage campaign were fundamental to development of these groups all over coastal Andhra. Subsequent stages of political development focused on the creation of political contacts and consciousness at the district and regional levels. In 1892, the first conference at the district level was held in Krishna District,[120] and a few delegates came from other districts too.[121] Within three years leaders initiated meetings in other districts, and social conferences were held in conjunction with these district meetings.[122] In 1905, conferences drew attendees from all of coastal Andhra.[123] Some of these gatherings were explicitly political in nature and some, like the Andhra Theistic Conference, were not. From these supra-local conferences came the impetus to inaugurate a political movement in order to secure the recognition of Andhra's separate identity.[124]

The continuing relevance of key social reform ideas to political activity in coastal Andhra, both on the regional level and eventually in the nationalist movement, was unusual, for social reform ideas became increasingly irrelevant in shaping the development of nationalism in other regions of India. But the nationalists in coastal Andhra retained the idea of attaining social modernity, social progress, with its emphasis on the educated elite as the catalyst and the Telugu language and cultural traditions as the means. Modernity was now conceived of as a series of regional political communities within the Indian nation, where law and an Indian government would be the instruments creating new social conditions. Viresalingam's rooting of the idea of progress in the regional culture and his sustained attack on Sanskritic traditions destroyed the intellectual basis for any type of Sanskritic revivalism in Andhra. Viresalingam's first attacks were on the priestly Brahmans, and then he included traditional scholars. For many years his newspaper, the leading one in Andhra, vilified priests, scholars and aspects of ancient Aryan civilization. Thus succeeding generations grew up with a declining status of priests and traditional scholars; consequently, they accepted the futility of using Sanskritic traditions to build a modern identity.

In Madras, Christians and non-Brahmans attacked Brahmans; in coastal Andhra, Western-educated Brahmans, led by Viresalingam, attacked 'the orthodox'. Discrediting the image of the orthodox

Brahman was central to the evolving ideology of social change and national progress. The 'new Brahman' conscience in Andhra questioned traditional religious authority as the social reformers sought to transform their regional culture through the modification of Telugu, the expansion of education and social and religious reform activities. Despite his history of alienating even allies in the implementation of his ideas, Viresalingam was an ideological thinker and polemicist whose ideas decisively shaped the regional culture and nationalist ideology in Andhra. He criticized the existing structure of social and political authority and provided a vision of indigenously generated social change and national progress. He reconceived of both individuals and their collective identity in coastal Andhra, insisting that educated men confront the failure of priestly Brahmans and scholars to uphold Indian society, that they commit themselves to new goals and form new associations, that they assume responsibilities for the condition of women and the masses in Andhra society. Later leaders went far beyond Viresalingam in questioning British political authority in India. Nonetheless, his emphasis on regional cultural traditions had far-reaching political implications, and his widow marriage campaign gave future leaders a direct and overwhelmingly political experience in bringing about social change.

Bibliographic Essay

The reconstruction of the social reform movement in coastal Andhra during the period 1874–91 required a synthesis of two very different types of sources: biographies and autobiographies in Telugu, and English-language newspapers. Neither type of source was sufficient by itself because events in Andhra had few connections with events of an all-India importance. Not until 1907, when Bipin Chandra Pal toured South India protesting the partition of Bengal, did Andhras participate noticeably in events whose significance transcended the regional boundaries. This isolation meant that the history of coastal Andhra during this period of social reform was not fully understood in Madras. The English-language newspapers in Madras mentioned some of the highlights of the social reform movement and thus provided a rough chronology of events in the region, a chronology which could then be linked with major events in Madras and the rest of India. Yet this chronology was at best only an outline.

For a full understanding of social reform and its significance in Andhra, the Telugu sources were crucial. Most valuable were Kandukuri Viresalingam's autobiography and collected works. For the period preceding the widow marriage campaign his autobiography was indispensable. Newspaper reports were very brief at that time, and it would be virtually impossible to describe that early social reform activity without Viresalingam's account. Once the widow marriage campaign began, the two main sources were Viresalingam's 1885 report to the Association, 'Rajahmahendravara Stri Punar Vivaha Caritramu', which he included in his collected works, and an English account by Viresalingam's ex-student, D.V. Prakasa Row. Reminiscences of Viresalingam's students and followers, especially those of Rayasam Venkata Sivudu, Valluri Suryanarayana Rau and Cilakamarti Lakshminarasimham, filled out the narrative. The opposition to social reform had to be glimpsed mainly through the eyes of the reformers themselves, for the only biography of an opposition leader, that of Vedamu Venkataraya Sastri, mentions a few relevant facts only briefly and omits any discussion of other opposition leaders or connections with them. The decline of the social reform movement in Rajahmundry coincided with the school careers of three future prominent Andhra political leaders, K. Venkatappayya, T. Prakasam and A. Kaleswara Rao, and their autobiographies furnished revealing accounts of the social reformers' participation in reform activities.

During the decades of the 1870s and 1880s the English-language newspapers relied on correspondents in coastal Andhra for news of that region. The correspondents for the British-owned newspapers were probably Europeans, since most of their news concerned the activities of British officials and missionaries. Even Indian-owned newspapers like *The Hindu* did not pay much attention to events in coastal Andhra, for reports from there were irregular and brief even at the best of times.

Other types of sources, such as records of the Madras government or missionary reports, were of little use for this topic. The general policy of the Government of India was to refrain from undertaking social reform, and, except in individual instances, the Government of

Madras did nothing to encourage social reform. This lack of interest was evident in those few cases (such as the circulation of Mr Malabari's Notes) when the government was compelled to act. Also, British administration at the local level did not pay much attention to the social reformers or include information about them in the reports to higher levels of government, since the social reformers' actions did not impinge directly upon the administration.

The lack of missionary reports for this period was disappointing. Neither the missionary college at Rajahmundry nor its affiliate in Guntur had preserved records from the nineteenth century. The most valuable missionary sources for this study were the journals published in North America. Missionary records usually dealt with the business of managing the mission, whereas the letters of some missionaries to journals provided a few insights into social reform and Viresalingam's life. Even the archives of the Lutheran Theological Seminary in Philadelphia have preserved only statements regarding itineraries and travelling expenses of missionaries and disputes within the mission. The Lutheran Theological Seminary at Gettysburg has an extensive collection of records and manuscripts for the Lutheran mission in Guntur. The journals of women missionaries were valuable for descriptions of social reform activities and missionary attitudes towards these. These Canadian Baptists had their Telugu Mission headquarters in Kakinada; archives are in McMaster University, Hamilton, Ontario. Although none of their records or journals illuminates any of Viresalingam's actions, there are a few letters in the *Canadian Missionary Link* dealing with Paida Ramakrishnayya. Another journal, *Among the Telugus*, first appeared in 1900 and is valuable for material on social conditions in Kakinada.

Sectarian histories of missionary activity in coastal Andhra, moreover, are uniform in their concentration on those activities which contributed to the growth of Christianity. Although the missionaries in coastal Andhra were pioneers in promoting education, and, interestingly enough, admired and utilized Viresalingam's writings on monotheism and the restrictive aspects of the caste system, they wrote little about Indian society except as it affected their work.

The diaries of Viresalingam, 1897–1916, are in the possession of Y. Venkat Rao, Rajahmundry, who picked them up one day when he noticed a pile of waste paper outside the Viresalingam Theistic High School. There were probably earlier diaries, but even so, their value is limited. Viresalingam recorded the events he considered important but did not comment on them. Most entries deal with the prices of food in the local market and would be valuable for an economic historian. Other financial entries were of value in tracing his supporters for his various projects.

Notes

*When John died in 1985, an outline for this article was on his desk. I have relied heavily on his two unpublished manuscripts to complete it. I am indebted to Professors G.N. Reddy and K.V. Narayana Rao of Sri Venkateshwara University (the former was John's Telugu professor) and Professor Charlotte Furth of the University of Southern California and Professor Montgomery Furth of The University of California, Los Angeles, for their helpful readings of the manuscript.

1. The other two are Rayalaseema, a slightly less populated dry area northwest of Madras (most of the present Nellore District), and Telangana, separately administered as part of the Nizam's Dominions until 1948 and of Hyderabad State until 1956.
2. Cilukurvi Virabhadra Rau, *Rajamendra Pura Caritra* (Rajahmundry: 1915), pp. 33–4); F.R. Hemingway, *Godavari* (Madras: Madras District Gazetteer, 1915), 1, p. 247; Digavalli Venkata Siva Rau, ed., *Kasi Yatra Caritra*, 3rd ed. (Bezwada, 1941), pp. 344–5.
3. K.A. Nilakanta Sastry, *A History of South India*, 3rd ed. (Madras: Oxford University Press, 1966), p. 406.
4. Henry Morris, *A Descriptive and Historical Account of the Godavary District in the Presidency of Madras* (London: Madras District Manual, 1878), pp. 244, 303–4.
5. Morris, *Godavary District*, p. 22.
6. For comparisons between Rajahmundry and Madras, see John G. Leonard, Urban Government Under the Raj', *Modern Asian Studies* 7, no. 2 (April 1973), pp. 227–51 and Susan J. Lewandowski, 'Urban Growth and Municipal Development in the Colonial City of Madras, 1860–1900', *Journal of Asian Studies* 34, no. 2 (February 1975), pp. 341–60.
7. Government of India, *Census of India*, 1891–2 (Madras, 1893), vol. 13, p. 181.
8. This was a precipitating cause of the Andhra movement—only in the Circars region did Telugus outnumber Tamils in government positions.

See John G. Leonard, 'Politics and Social Change in South India: A Study of the Andhra Movement', *Journal of Commonwealth Political Studies* 5, no. 1 (March 1967), pp. 60–77.

9. Government of India, Indian Education Commission, *Report of the Madras Provincial Committee* (Calcutta, 1884), p. 38; Government of Madras, *Report on Public Instruction in the Madras Presidency for 1880–1881* (Madras, 1881), pp. 65–7.
10. Government of Madras, *Madras Financial Proceedings*, no. 58 (10 January 1884), India Office Library.
11. Morris, *Godavary District*, p. 24; Martin Luther Dolbeer, Jr., *A History of Lutheranism in the Andhra Desh, 1842–1920* (New York: Board of the Foreign Missions of the United Lutheran Church in America, 1959), p. 14; Martin Luther Dolbeer, Sr., *The Andhra Evangelical Lutheran Church: A Brief History* (Rajahmundry: Department of Religious Education, Andhra Evangelical Church, 1951), pp. 27–30.
12. Government of Madras, *Report on Public Instruction in the Madras Presidency for 1876–77* (Madras, 1877), p. 135.
13. Government of Madras, *Report on Public Instruction for 1876–77*, p. 136. This ratio is best understood with the help of data drawn from later sources: it seems to approximate the proportion of Tamils to Telugus in Madras City, which was 2.7 to 1; see Government of India, *Census of India*, 1891–2 (Madras, 1893), vol. 14, pp. 137, 139. The ratio of Tamils to Telugus in Madras Presidency was 1.1 to 1; see Government of India, *Census of India*, 1911, vol. 12, pt. 2 (Madras, 1912), p. 140 for details.
14. J. Gurunatham, *Viresalingam, the Founder of Telugu Public Life* (Rajahmundry: S. Gunneseworao Bros., 1911), pp. 165–6.
15. Tanguturi Prakasam, *Na Jivita Yatra* (Rajahmundry: Kalahastri Tamma Rao and Sons, 1957), p. 48; Kandukuri Viresalingam, *Surya Caritramu* (Rajahmundry: Hitakarini Samaj, 1954), vol. 1, pp. 1–2, 8–9, 17; A. Ramapati Rao, 'Jivitamunandali Konni Mukhya Ghattamulu', in *Yuga Purusudu Viresalingam* (Hyderabad, n.d.), p. 223. Viresalingam's father and uncle were revenue officials for the Government of Madras.
16. The following information about family life comes from Viresalingam's recollections in *Caritramu*, vol. 1, p. 18 *passim*, pp. 30–4, and about his wife, pp. 10–11 (but he gives no details of their early years together).
17. Kandukuri Viresalingam, 'Stri Vidya', *Viveka Vardhani* (hereafter abbreviated *VV*), February 1875 in *Kandukuri Viresalingam Kavikrta Granthamulu* (hereafter abbreviated *KVKG*), 8 (Rajahmundry, 1951–2), pp. 330–2.
18. Smarta Brahmans are followers of Sankara (*c.* 788–820), believers in monistic or Advaita Vedanta who are supposed to conform to Smrti traditions. Viresalingam expressed devotion by repeating the Gayatri from one hundred to one thousand times each day and visiting the river Godavari and

the various Saivite and Vaishnavite temples for prayer. His only recollections of specific practices were of fasting on Shivaratri (fast day of the God Shiva) and of putting the three horizontal stripes of Shiva on his chest, upper arms and face while he was praying: Viresalingam, *Caritramu*, vol. 1, pp. 19, 56.

19. Viresalingam, *Caritramu*, vol. 1, pp. 15, 17. For *pyal* schools, see *The Foreign Missionary* (Philadelphia), 10, no. 2 (February 1889), p. 11, and 'South Indian Pyal Schools', *Christian Mission Intelligencer* 10, n.s. (September 1874), pp. 287–8.
20. Viresalingam, *Caritramu*, vol. 2, p. 138.
21. A. Rampati Rau, 'Pantulu Gari Grantha Racana Mudranamula Vivaramulu' (A Bibliography of Viresalingam's Writings), in *Yuga Purusudu Viresalingam*, p. 206; Viresalingam, *Caritramu*, vol. 2, p. 146.
22. Viresalingam first stated that he passed the Matriculation examination in 1871 but later gave 1870 as the date: Viresalingam, *Caritramu*, vol. 1, p. 66 and vol. 2, p. 146. Although his claim was accepted by his biographers (*The Hindu*, 19 January 1893; Gurunatham, *Viresalingam*, pp. 26–7; V.R. Narla, *Veeresalingam* [New Delhi: Sahitya Akademi, 1968], p. 18), examination of several contemporary sources does not show his name in the lists of students who passed the Matriculation; see Government of Madras, *Godavary District Gazette*, 1869–1871; Government of Madras, *Fort St. George Gazette*, 1869–1871; *Madras Times*, 1870.
23. Viresalingam, *Caritramu*, vol. 1, p. 60. At this time Keshav Chandra Sen had broken with the older Brahmo Samaj members led by Devendranath Tagore and had organized his own association; in contrast to Tagore's stress on the gradual changing of Hinduism, Sen emphasized the necessity of more drastic uprooting of old customs. S. Natarajan, *A Century of Social Reform in India* (Bombay: Asia Publishing House, 1959), pp. 48–9; The Brahmo Samaj, 'Jesus Christ: Europe and Asia' (a lecture given on 5 May 1877), *Keshub Chunder Sen's Lectures in India*, 3rd ed. (Calcutta, 1899), pp. 30–1.
24. Kandukuri Viresalingam, 'Satyamu', *VV*, November 1874, in *KVKG*, vol. 8, pp. 313–20.
25. He began in 1871 as an assistant teacher in the Rajahmundry Provincial School, then passed a government examination qualifying him to practise in the lower courts. In 1872 he accepted a job as headmaster of a village school. That same year he passed a translator's examination in English and Telugu, but he continued to teach and in 1874 became headmaster of a school in Dowleshwaram, a large village near his Rajahmundry home. He lived in the village but walked to town frequently to participate in the activities of the Provincial School Club. In 1875 he passed an English precis writing examination that qualified him for a sub-magistrate's position. Viresalingam, *Caritramu*, vol. 1, pp. 66–77.

26. He first had his journal published in Madras and then persuaded six men to finance the purchase of a press which was set up in his Rajahmundry home. After a quarrel with the Dowleshwaram school management, he left them in 1875 and began a printing business in Rajahmundry. A rupture with his partners followed and he bought them out, using funds from his books. Viresalingam, *Caritramu*, vol. 1, pp. 88, 92–5, 99.
27. Viresalingam, *Caritramu*, vol. 1, pp. 88, 94.
28. Viresalingam, *Caritramu*, vol. 1, p. 99.
29. Viresalingam, *Caritramu*, vol. 1, pp. 77, 92. Viresalingam refused a government job when one was offered to him: Viresalingam, *Caritramu*, vol. 1, p. 13. He attacked government service as the 'meanest' of jobs: Kandukuri Viresalingam, 'Aikamatyamu', *VV*, July 1875 in *KVKG* vol. 8, p. 366.
30. Viresalingam, *Caritramu*, vol. 1, p. 59.
31. For details of Viresalingam's life and career, especially his later career, which cannot be covered here in outline, see John G. Leonard, 'Kandukuri Viresalingam, 1848–1919: A Biography of an Indian Social Reformer' (Ph.D. diss., University of Wisconsin, 1970).
32. Members of the educated elite in the 1870s had difficulty following some of these essays: Nidudavolu Venkata Rau, *Andhra Vacana Vangmayamu* (Madras, 1954), p. 147; G.V. Sitapati, 'Telugu', in Nagendra, ed., *Indian Literature* (Agra: Lakshmi Narain Agarwal, 1959), pp. 53–5, 63–5; Rayasam Venkata Sivudu, *Sri Viresalinga Samsmrti* (Guntur: R.V. Sivudu, 1931); Konda Venkatappayya, *Sviya Caritra*, vol. 1 (Vijayawada: Andhra Rastra Hindi Pracara Sangham, 1952–55), I, p. 60. Classical Telugu, or the poetic dialect, differed from spoken Telugu and had a highly Sanskritized vocabulary and syntax. Poetry was the only approved form of literary creation until the last part of the nineteenth century, with grammar and rhetoric recognized as subsections of poetry. Prose was used for business or government purposes in the spoken dialect and was considered 'village' or crude Telugu. Not only did poetry have a particular structure and dialect, it was also confined to particular subject matter, much of it erotic in nature. This posed a problem to scholars looking for texts for classroom use in the new educational systems. The initial formulation of a solution to this problem for educators in Telugu had come from one of Viresalingam's scholarly predecessors, Cinnaya Suri (1809–62). This non-Brahman became head of the Department of Telugu at Madras Presidency College and standardized many of the rules for classical Telugu as applied to prose.
33. A. Ramapati Rau, 'Viresalingamu Pantulu Savimarsa Parisilanamu' (Ph.D. diss., Osmania University, 1964), pp. 37–8; A. Ramapati Rau, 'Mukhya Ghattamulu', in *Yuga Purusudu*, p. 223.

34. Following the visit of the famous Bengali Brahmo Samaj leader, Keshav Chandra Sen, a Brahman in Madras started a Veda Samaj in 1864; many members were non-Brahmans, however. The founder was Rajagopalacharlu; his friend, Subbarayalu Chetty, a non-Brahman, seems to have been the principal leader. The Veda Samaj limited its activities to preaching, although it started a Tamil journal, *Tattvabodhini*, to propagate the view of the association's leaders. Sridharulu Naidu, a non-Brahman in charge of the association from 1867 until 1874, changed the name to the Southern India Brahmo Samaj and framed regulations more in keeping with Brahmo traditions in Calcutta: Sivanatha Sastri, *History of the Brahmo Samaj*, vol. 2 (Calcutta: R. Chatterjee, 1912), pp. 456–65. After Naidu's death in 1874 the association was dormant until 1878 when a Telugu Brahman, Mannava Buccayya, teacher at a girls' school in Madras, revived it and associated it with the Sadharan Brahmo Samaj in Calcutta. Viresalingam, *Caritramu*, vol. 1, pp. 93–4. For its anti-Brahman character, see Sivudu, *Samsmrti*, p. 38; *The Madras Mail*, 24 November 1881, p. 3.
35. According to R. Srinivasan, the Brahmo movement 'has been wholly forgotten by the Tamils'. He was unable to find books or pamphlets on it in Madras libraries, Brahmo characters in Tamil novels, or more than one Tamil Brahman in the Madras chapter of the Southern Indian Brahmo Samaj. In contrast, he noted the prominence of Telugus in it and the involvement of Telugu zamindars in funding it and of Telugu school teachers in popularizing Brahmo and reformist ideals in Andhra. Citing a 1912 source, he listed six samajs in the Tamil region and 20 in the Telugu-speaking region. (The Madras Presidency had 17,038,000 Tamil speakers and 15,782,000 Telugu speakers in 1911 [*Census of India*, 1911, vol. 12, pt. 2 (Madras, 1912), p. 140].) Finally, he remarked on the appearance of missionaries in Tamil novels in the proselytizing roles given to Brahmos in Bengali literature (and, we add, Telugu literature) of that period: R. Srinivasan, 'The Brahmo Samaj in Tamilnadu', *Journal of the University of Bombay*, arts nos. 44–5 (1975–76), pp. 80–1, 213–25.
36. Viresalingam, *Caritramu*, vol. 1, pp. 138–9; Sastri, *Brahmo Samaj*, vol. 2, pp. 494–5. Despite its name, this association was not derived from the Prarthana Samaj movement in western India.
37. One's occupation was unknown. Viresalingam, *Caritramu*, vol. 1, pp. 135, 159.
38. *The Madras Mail*, 27 October 1880, p. 2.
39. *The Hindu* (Madras), 19 November 1885, and 1 December 1884, p. 5.
40. *The Madras Standard*, 17 November 1879, p. 3, and 13 June 1881, p. 3.
41. Viresalingam, *Caritramu*, vol. 1, p. 79.
42. Viresalingam, *Caritramu*, vol. 1, pp. 79–80.
43. Viresalingam contributed several early articles to journals in Masulipatnam

and Madras, but his earliest surviving writings are from *VV*, the articles which he reprinted in the volumes of his collected works: Viresalingam, *KVKG*, vol. 8, pp. 31–47.

44. Viresalingam, *VV*, February 1875, in *KVKG*, vol. 8, p. 335.
45. Although Viresalingam attacked contemporary 'false' scholars as early as January 1875, he began criticizing ancient Indian scholars in April 1875, and he accentuated this criticism in October 1875 and July 1876. See the following articles by him: *VV*, January 1875, in *KVKG*, vol. 8, pp. 325–9; *VV*, April 1875, in *KVKG*, vol. 8, pp. 347–8; 'Brahmanavicaramu', *VV*, October 1875, in *KVKG*, vol. 8, pp. 400–1; 'Brahmanulunu, vari vrttulunu', *VV*, July 1876, in *KVKG*, vol. 8, p. 431.
46. Viresalingam, *VV*, January 1875, in *KVKG*, vol. 8, p. 326; Viresalingam, *VV*, July 1875, in *KVKG*, vol. 8, pp. 36–8; Viresalingam, 'Pramanavicaramu', *VV*, October 1875, in *KVKG*, vol. 8, pp. 392–404.
47. Viresalingam, *VV*, April 1875, in *KVKG*, vol. 8, pp. 348–9.
48. Viresalingam, *VV*, July 1876 in *KVKG*, vol. 8, pp. 428–38.
49. The one-act farce 'Brahma Vivahamu' he published in his journal's supplement, *Hasya Sanjivani*, in July 1876 and he republished this in 1878 as a separate piece. It ridiculed the logic used to justify Brahman marriage customs: Ramapati Rau, 'Pantulu Gari Grantha Racana', in *Yuga Purusudu*, p. 207; Viresalingam, 'Brahma Vivahamu', in *KVKG*, vol. 2, pp. 1–67. He developed the farces to attack social evils: Viresalingam, *Caritramu*, vol. 1, p. 140. His use of colloquial speech offended critics: letter of G.V. Appa Rao, 2 June 1912, as quoted in Vedamu Venkataraya Sastri, *Vedamu Venkataraya Sastrulavari Jivita Caritra Sangrahamu* (Madras, 1949), p. 121. In Madras, however, attacks on Brahmans were deprecated by social reformers: *Athenaeum and Daily News*, 3 June 1874.
50. Viresalingam, *VV*, July 1876, in *KVKG*, vol. 8, pp. 428–38.
51. Viresalingam, *VV*, January 1875, in *KVKG*, vol. 7, p. 329; Viresalingam, *VV*, April 1875, in *KVKG*, vol. 8, pp. 347–9; Viresalingam, *VV*, July 1875, in *KVKG*, vol. 8, p. 364; Viresalingam, 'Aikamatyamu', in *KVKG*, vol. 7, pp. 8, 9.
52. Viresalingam, *VV*, July 1876, in *KVKG*, vol. 8, pp. 431–9.
53. Viresalingam, *VV*, April 1875, in *KVKG*, vol. 8, pp. 343–9.
54. Viresalingam, *VV*, July 1875, in *KVKG*, vol. 8, pp. 363–71; Viresalingam, 'Aikamatyamu', in *KVKG*, vol. 8, pp. 4–13.
55. Viresalingam, *Caritramu*, vol. 1, p. 69.
56. Viresalingam, *Caritramu*, vol. 1, pp. 143–5. Burial rather than cremation prevailed among Telugu Brahman Virashaivites of the Aradhya sect.
57. Viresalingam, *Caritramu*, vol. 1, pp. 140–3.
58. A detailed comparison of the Andhra and Madras social reform movements is in John G. Leonard, 'Viresalingam and the Making of Modern Andhra:

Social Reform in Rajahmundry and Madras, 1874–1891' (MS, 1968). A summary appears in Karen I. Leonard and John G. Leonard, 'Social Reform and Women's Participation in Political Culture: Andhra and Madras', in Gail Minault, ed., *The Extended Family: Women and Political Participation in India and Pakistan* (Columbia, Mo.: South Asia Books, 1981), pp. 19–45.

59. Viresalingam, *Caritramu*, vol. 1, pp. 152–8, 277. Kandukuri Viresalingam, 'Rajahamahendravara Stri Punar Vivaha Caritramu', in *KVKG*, vol. 7, pp. 6–8. The latter was an unofficial report presented to the Rajahmundry Widow Marriage Association by Viresalingam on 9 June 1885. It contained a description of the widow marriage campaign and Viresalingam included it in his collected works. Hereafter it will be cited as 'Vivaha Caritramu'. For an example of an orthodox Hindu argument, see Vedamu Venkataraya Sastri, *Stri Punar Vivaha Durvada Nirvapanamu*, 2nd ed. (Madras, 1924).
60. Viresalingam, *Caritramu*, vol. 1, pp. 163–6; *Indian Law Review* 6 (Madras Ser.): pp. 382–3.
61. Viresalingam, *Caritramu*, vol. 1, p. 159; Viresalingam, 'Vivaha Caritramu', in *KVKG*, vol. 7, pp. 11–12.
62. Viresalingam, *Caritramu*, vol. 1, pp. 159, 161–2. D.V. Prakasa Row, 'The Widow Marriage Movement in Madras', *Kayastha Samachar* (Allahabad), vol. 7, no. 6 (1903), p. 540.
63. Sivudu, *Samsmrti*, pp. 2–4, 135–43; Subba Rao, *Memories*, pp. 19–25; *Sundara Rao*, pp. 3–13; C. Cilakamarti Laksminarasimham, *Sviya Caritramu* (Vishakapatnam, 1957), p. 51; Valluri Suryanarayana Rau, *Suryanarayaniyamu* (Kovvuru, 1936), p. 165.
64. Viresalingam, *Caritramu*, vol. 1, pp. 166–8, 170, 252–4; Venkatappayya, *Caritra*, vol. 1, p. 36.
65. Suryanarayana Rau, *Suryanarayaniyamu*, pp. 166–7; Viresalingam, *Caritramu*, vol. 1, pp. 158–62, 171; Viresalingam, 'Vivaha Caritramu', in *KVKG*, vol. 7. p. 11; Prakasa Row, 'Widow Marriage', p. 540.
66. Suryanarayana Rau, *Suryanarayaniyamu*, pp. 166–7.
67. A Deputy Tahsildar found a mother willing to have her widowed daughter remarried and Viresalingam sent a college student to go to the village and bring the girl in the night to his home. Then Viresalingam found a bridegroom, a young man who had been educated for many years in his house, was enthused about widow marriages and was of the right sect. Viresalingam, *Caritramu*, vol. 1, pp. 158–9, 181–4, 188; Viresalingam, 'Vivaha Caritramu', in *KVKG*, vol. 7, p. 17; Prakasa Row, 'Widow Marriage', p. 542.
68. Intimidation from the orthodox Hindu side resulted in Viresalingam's cook and family priest ceasing their services, and many reformers did not attend the wedding because of such threats: Viresalingam, *Caritramu*,

vol. 1, pp. 189, 191; Viresalingam, 'Vivaha Caritramu', in *KVKG*, vol. 7, pp. 20–2.

69. Viresalingam, *Caritramu*, vol. 1, pp. 190, 196; Viresalingam, 'Vivaha Caritramu', in *KVKG*, vol. 7, p. 23; Prakasa Row, *Kayastha Samachar* 7, no. 4 (1903): pp. 294–6.
70. Viresalingam, *Caritramu*, vol. 1, pp. 160–1; Viresalingam, 'Vivaha Caritramu', in *KVKG*, vol. 7, p. 11; Prakasa Row, *Kayastha Samachar* 8, no. 5 (1903): p. 413.
71. Venkataraya Sastri, *Vedamu Venkataraya Sastrulavari Jivita Caritra Sangrahamu*, pp. 36–7; Viresalingam, *Caritramu*, vol. 1, pp. 152–8.
72. Viresalingam, *Caritramu*, vol. 1, pp. 172, 184–5, 187, 197–9; Viresalingam, 'Vivaha Caritramu', in *KVKG*, vol. 7, p. 12; Prakasa Row, 'Widow Marriage', p. 542; Venkatappayya, *Caritra*, vol. 1, p. 61.
73. Viresalingam, *Caritramu*, vol. 1, pp. 197–9, 281–2; Viresalingam, 'Vivaha Caritramu', in *KVKG*, vol. 7, pp. 18–20, 23–4, 25; Prakasa Row, *Kayastha Samachar* 8, no. 4 (1903): pp. 296–7.
74. Prakasa Row, *Kayastha Samachar* 8, no. 4 (1903): pp. 298–301, 294; Viresalingam, *Caritramu*, vol. 1, pp. 204–9.
75. Viresalingam, *Caritramu*, vol. 1, pp. 215–19, 230, 242, 246; Viresalingam, 'Vivaha Caritramu', in *KVKG*, vol. 7, p. 31; Prakasam, *Yatra*, p. 89; Venkatappayya, *Caritra*, vol. 1, p. 36; Prakasa Row, *Kayastha Samachar* 8, no. 4 (1903): pp. 299–301.
76. *The Madras Mail*, 12 September 1882, p. 3.
77. *Indian Law Review* 6 (Madras Ser.): pp. 381–96; Viresalingam, *Caritramu*, vol. 1, p. 235; Prakasa Row, *Kayastha Samachar* 8, no. 4 (1903): p. 298.
78. *Hindu Desabhimani* in *Madras Native Newspaper Reports*, October 1882; *Vizag Observer*, no. 20, and *Purusharthapradayini*, nos. 4, 5 and 6, in *Madras Native Newspaper Reports*, July 1883.
79. *The Madras Standard*, 27 April 1883, p. 3; *The Madras Mail*, 25 April 1883, p. 2, and 26 April 1883, p. 3.
80. Viresalingam, *Caritramu*, vol. 1, pp. 196–266; Prakasa Row, *Kayastha Samachar* 8, no. 5 (1903): p. 414.
81. Five per cent of Hindu girls in Madras Presidency, but 11 per cent of Brahman girls, married before the age of 10; and 3.3 per cent of Brahman girls 10 to 14 were widowed, compared to less than 1 per cent of all girls 10 to 14. The marriage percentages before the age of 10 are from 1881: *Imperial Census of 1881* (Presidency of Madras) (Madras: Government of India, 1883), vol. 1, pp. 70–3, and the widow percentages from 1891: *Census of India*, 1891 (Presidency of Madras) (Madras: Government of India, 1893), XIII, pp. 146–7.
82. Gurunatham, *Viresalingam*, p. 101; Viresalingam, 'Vivaha Caritramu', in *KVKG*, vol. 8, pp. 41–2.

83. Viresalingam had given many of the bridegrooms allowances in their college days to permit them to continue their educations, and the marriages themselves usually cost more than they ordinarily would have for boys of that status—thus expectations were raised but the benefits after marriage were not very great. Viresalingam mentioned only a few bridegrooms who were dissatisfied but the situation was obviously more serious. The old reform association was dissolved, and a new one was constituted specifically to exclude some bridegrooms and to counter the demands of the married couples. Viresalingam, *Caritramu*, vol. 1, pp. 278–9; Gurunatham, *Viresalingam*, pp. 115–17.
84. Viresalingam, *Caritramu*, vol. 1, pp. 325–75; Gurunatham, *Viresalingam*, pp. 104–12; Prakasa Row, *Kayastha Samachar* (Allahabad) 8, no. 5 (1903): pp. 415–17. For the satire Viresalingam published, see Kandukuri Viresalingam, 'Dambhacarya Vilasanamu', *VV*, 13 March 1886, and Ramapati Rau, 'Grantha Racana', in *Yuga Purusudu*, p. 211. Lakshminarasimham's initial reaction was to burn *Viveka Vardhani* at a public demonstration, although he later apologized for this outburst; see Viresalingam, *Caritramu*, vol. 1, pp. 347–54.
85. *The Indian Social Reformer* 16 (1905): pp. 548, 560.
86. Gurunatham, *Viresalingam*, pp. 180–1. In the 1880s, journals were still the main outlet for Telugu authors, and Viresalingam published scholarly works on Telugu poetry in his journal until he was forced to discontinue it in 1890 because of competing journals and government pressure. Then he and his friend Nyapati Subba Rao started a monthly journal which Viresalingam edited, *Cintamani*. From 1891 on this journal featured novels published serially, and although a few novels had been published just prior to this time (including one by Viresalingam), Telugu novels really originated with this journal's encouragement (Venkata Rau, *Andhra Vacana*, pp. 139–41). Telugu journals founded in 1885 in Madras competed with *Viveka Vardhani* in its last years: *Andhra Prakasika* was closely allied with the Madras Mahajana Sabha, a political association formed in 1884, and the Brahmo Samaj leader in Madras, Mannava Buccayya, began *Hindu Jana Samskaram*, which represented the interests of social reform in Madras. Other specialized journals began in 1885 and 1891. The type of men who edited these journals changed for most Telugu journals from 1885 to 1891, a change coinciding with the decline of social reform. The new editors were not Western-educated Telugu scholars but members of the educated elite who practised journalism as a profession. Educated as lawyers or teachers, these men were more attuned to the new currents in politics than the older editors. The Madras Mahajana Sabha got publicity for its efforts from the English-language *The Hindu*, but *Andhra Prakasika* (Telugu) and *Swadesamitra* (Tamil) became regional-language journals

allied with the Sabha: *The Hindu*, 21 January 1885, p. 5; *The Madras Mail*, 18 September 1885, p. 4. *Andhra Prakasika* soon outstripped *Viveka Vardhani* and the *Andhra Bhasha Sajivani* in circulation, but it concentrated solely on political issues. Buccayya was a friend of Viresalingam, and his *Hindu Jana Samskaram* combined political and social comment and equalled *Viveka Vardhani's* circulation: *Madras Native Newspaper Reports*, January to December 1885 (Madras Record Office). The literary journal *Amrta Granthamali* of Nellore began in 1885 and the Rajahmundry Prarthana Samaj journal *Satya Samvardhani* began in 1891: *Amudrta Grandha Cintamani* (Nellore), no. 9 (1887); Sivudu, *Samsmrti*, p. 31. For the new editors, *The Hindu*, 8 April 1895, p. 4; Sivudu, *Samsmrti*, p. 31.

87. Prakasam, *Yatra*, p. 252.
88. Much later, in the beginning of the twentieth century, this process stimulated an interest in a political guarantee—an Andhra state—for the continuation of the Telugu cultural revival. See John G. Leonard, 'Andhra Movement', *Journal of Commonwealth Political Studies* 5, no. 1 (March 1967), pp. 60–77.
89. Viresalingam, *VV*, July 1880, in *KVKG*, vol. 8, p. 485; Kandukuri Viresalingam, 'Desabhimanamu', *VV*, July 1881, in *KVKG*, vol. 8, p. 555; Kandukuri Viresalingam, 'Sangha Duracara Nivaranamunaku Stri Vidya Yavasyakamu', *VV*, March 1885, in *KVKG*, vol. 8, pp. 639–40.
90. Kandukuri Viresalingam, 'Stri Punar Vivaha Visayakopanyasamu', in *KVKG*, vol. 7, pp. 13, 48.
91. Viresalingam, 'Stri Punar . . .', in *KVKG*, vol. 7, pp. 5, 48, 56.
92. Kandukuri Viresalingam, 'Desabhimanamu', *VV*, July 1880, in *KVKG*, vol. 8, pp. 482–3.
93. Viresalingam, 'Desabhimariamu', *VV*, July 1880, in *KVKG*, vol. 8, p. 482.
94. Viresalingam, 'Stri Punar . . .', in *KVKG*, vol. 7, pp. 6–16.
95. Kandukuri Viresalingam, 'Hindu Matamulu', in *KVKG*, vol. 7, p. 3.
96. Kandukuri Viresalingam, 'Kalamu Yokka Viluva', *VV*, March 1880, in *KVKG*, vol. 8, p. 460; Kandukuri Viresalingam, 'Vaidyulu', *VV*, February 1881, in *KVKG*, vol. 8, p. 510; Viresalingam, *VV*, October 1881, in *KVKG*, vol. 8, p. 562.
97. Kandukuri Viresalingam, 'Isvara Datta Pustakamulu', in *KVKG*, vol. 7, p. 22; Viresalingam, 'Stri Punar . . .', in *KVKG*, vol. 7, pp. 6, 11.
98. Viresalingam used the phrase 'common folk' or 'ordinary people' (*samanya janulu*) which has a vulgar connotation in Telugu. Our use of 'the masses' expresses the social distance which Viresalingam felt separated him from the masses of illiterate people.
99. Kandukuri Viresalingam, 'Rajakiya Pathasalalu', *VV*, March 1881, in

KVKG, vol. 8, p. 526; Kandukuri Viresalingam, 'Kulina Brahmana Vivahamulu', *VV*, August 1885, in *KVKG*, vol. 8, p. 647; Viresalingam, *VV*, July 1880, in *KVKG*, p. 489.

100. Viresalingam, *VV*, July 1880, in *KVKG*, vol. 8, p. 485; Kandukuri Viresalingam, 'Desabhimanamu', *VV*, July 1881, in *KVKG*, vol. 8, p. 555.
101. Kandukuri Viresalingam, 'Sangha Duracara Nivaranamunaku Stri Vidya Yavasyakamu', *VV*, March 1885, in *KVKG*, vol. 8, pp. 639–40.
102. Viresalingam, 'Isvara Datta Pustakamulu', in *KVKG*, vol. 7, p. 22.
103. Kandukuri Viresalingam, 'Desa Bhasalu', *VV*, October 1881, in *KVKG*, vol. 8, pp. 556–66.
104. Kandukuri Viresalingam, 'Desabhivrddhi', *VV*, January 1883, in *KVKG*, vol. 8, p. 597.
105. Kandukuri Viresalingam, 'Patupaduta', *VV*, November 1884, in *KVKG*, vol. 8, p. 633.
106. Kandukuri Viresalingam, 'Vidyadhikula Yokka Krtyamulu', *VV*, June 1883, in *KVKG*, vol. 8, p. 607.
107. Viresalingam, *VV*, October 1881, in *KVKG*, vol. 8, p. 566.
108. Kandukuri Viresalingam, 'Vidyadhikula Yokka Krtyamulu', *VV*, March 1882, in *KVKG*, vol. 8, pp. 577–8; Kandukuri Viresalinga, 'Andhra Bhasabhivrddhi', *VV*, June 1882, in *KVKG*, vol. 8, pp. 580–1.
109. Viresalingam, *VV*, November 1886, in *KVKG*, vol. 8, p. 667; *The Hindu*, 12 January 1885, p. 6.
110. Viresalingam, *VV*, March 1882, in *KVKG*, vol. 8, pp. 577–8; Kandukuri Viresalingam, 'Desa Bhasa', *VV*, November 1886, in *KVKG*, vol. 8, p. 670.
111. Viresalingam, *VV*, June 1882, in *KVKG*, vol. 8, pp. 580–1; Viresalingam, 'Vidyadhikula Yokka Krtyamulu', *VV*, March 1882, in *KVKG*, vol. 8, pp. 577–8; Viresalingam, *VV*, January 1883, in *KVKG*, vol. 8, p. 600.
112. Kandukuri Viresalingam, 'Stri Vidyabhyasamu', *VV*, February 1884, in *KVKG*, vol. 8, p. 624; Viresalingam, *VV*, November 1886, in *KVKG*, vol. 8, p. 667.
113. Viresalingam, *VV*, June 1882, in *KVKG*, vol. 8, p. 667.
114. Viresalingam, *VV*, November 1884, in *KVKG*, vol. 8, p. 633; Viresalingam, *VV*, November 1886, in *KVKG*, vol. 8, p. 667.
115. Viresalingam, *VV*, July 1881, in *KVKG*, vol. 8, p. 554; Kandukuri Viresalingam, 'Janmantaramu', in *KVKG*, vol. 7, pp. 9–10
116. Viresalingam, *VV*, March 1882, in *KVKG*, vol. 8, p. 577; *The Hindu*, 12 January 1885, p. 6; Kandukuri Viresalingam, 'Desiya Mahasabhalu, Dani Yuddesamulunu', in *KVKG*, vol. 8, pp. 1–6.
117. Viresalingam, *VV*, November 1884, in *KVKG*, vol. 8, p. 633; Kandukuri Viresalingam, 'Kulacara, Matacara Samskaranamu', *VV*, April 1887, in

KVKG, vol. 8, pp. 674–7; Viresalingam, 'Desiya Mahasabha . . .', in *KVKG*, vol. 8, pp. 21–46.

118. Viresalingam, *VV*, November 1886, in *KVKG*, vol. 8, p. 667.
119. Viresalingam, 'Desiya Mahasabha. . .', in *KVKG*, vol. 8, pp. 8–17.
120. Viresalingam, *VV*, November 1886, in *KVKG*, vol. 8, p. 667.
121. *The Hindu*, 15 July 1893, p. 3; Government of Madras, *General Index to Proceedings, Government of Madras*, 1894 (Madras, 1893), p. 339.
122. Cilakamarti Lakshminarasimhan gives an amusing description of the educated elite travelling from one district conference to another: *Caritramu*, pp. 127, 165–75.
123. *The Hindu*, 3 July 1895, p. 6; *The Madras Times*, 10 June 1895, p. 4; for a description of how social reform issues were treated in the different conferences, see Viresalingam, *Caritramu*, vol. 2, pp. 56–8.
124. *The Hindu Weekly Edition*, 11 April 1907, pp. 9–10; *The Indian Social Reformer*, 15 (1905), pp. 436–7.

11

Conjugality and Hindu Nationalism

Resisting Colonial Reason and the Death of a Child-Wife*

TANIKA SARKAR

At the risk of provoking startled disbelief, I propose to place ideas about Hindu conjugality at the very heart of militant nationalism in Bengal.[1] Historians have seen the centrality of debates around colonial laws relating to women and marriage in the discourse of liberal reformers. Thus far, however, they have not located these themes within early Hindu nationalism.

I will examine three interlocking themes in this chapter. First, I believe that in the last four decades of the nineteenth century a fairly distinct political formation had emerged, which could loosely be called revivalist-nationalist. This was a mixed group of newspaper proprietors, orthodox urban estate-holders of considerable civic importance within Calcutta, and pandits as well as modern intellectuals whom they patronized. Such people used an explicitly nationalist rhetoric against any form of colonial intervention within the Hindu domestic sphere. Their rhetoric marked them off from the broader category of revivalist thinkers who did not necessarily oppose reformism in the name of resisting colonial knowledge. At the same rime, the revivalist-nationalist group's commitment to an unreformed Hindu way of life

*From Tanika Sarkar, *Hindu Wife, Hindu Nation: Community, Religion and Cultural Nationalism* (Delhi: Permanent Black, 2001), pp. 191–225.

separated them from liberal nationalists of the Indian Association and Indian National Congress variety. Needless to say, the groups spoken of here were not *irrevocably* distinct or mutually exclusive. Yet, despite the overlaps, there was clearly a distinctive political formation of nationalists who contributed to the emerging nationalism a highly militant agitational rhetoric and mobilizing techniques that were built around a defence of Hindu patriarchy.

The second theme involves exploring why the revivalist-nationalists chose to tie their nationalism to issues of conjugality, which they defined as a system of non-consensual, indissoluble, infant marriage.

And, finally, in relation to the third theme, we need to dwell upon the arguments they fabricated. We find that the age of consent issue forced a decisive break in their discourse. It made it imperative for revivalist-nationalists to shift to an entirely different terrain of arguments and images, moving from the realm of reason and pleasure to that of discipline and pain. My elaboration of these themes is intended to widen the context of early nationalist agitations and provide them with an unfamiliar genealogy.

A few words are necessary to explain why, in the present juncture of cultural studies on colonial India, it is important to retrieve this specific history of revivalist-nationalism, and to work with a concept of nationalism that incorporates this history. Edward Said's *Orientalism* has fathered a received wisdom on colonial studies that has proved to be as narrow and frozen in its scope as it has been powerful in its impact. Said's work proceeds from a conviction about the totalizing nature of a Western power-knowledge which gives to the entire Orient a single image with absolute certainty. Writings of the Subaltern Studies pandits and of a group of feminists, largely located in first-world academia, have come to identify this singular structure of colonial knowledge as the originary moment for all possible kinds of power and disciplinary formations. Going hand in hand with 'Orientalism', this concept is seen by such academics to reserve for itself the whole range of hegemonic capabilities. This unproblematic and unhistoricized 'transfer of power' to structures of colonial knowledge has three major consequences: first, it constructs a monolithic, unstratified colonized subject who is powerless and without an effective or operative history of his/her own. The only history that she is capable of generating is 'derivative'. As a result, the colonized subject is absolved of all complicity and culpability in the makings of structures of exploitation over the last two hundred years of Indian colonial history: the subject's only culpability lies in the surrender to colonial knowledge. As a result, the lone political agenda for a historiography of this period shrinks into native contestations of colonial knowledge—since all power supposedly flows from this single source. Every species of contestation, by the same token, is taken to be equally valid. Today, with the triumphalist growth of aggressively communal and/or fundamentalist identity politics in our country, such a position comes close to indigenism. In fact it comes close to being intellectually Fascist in its authoritarian insistence on the purity of indigenous epistemological and autarkic conditions.

The Saidian magic formula has weird implications for the feminist agenda as well. The assumption that colonialism had wiped out all past histories of patriarchal domination, replacing them neatly and exclusively with Western forms of gender relations, has naturally led on to an exclusive identification of patriarchy in modern India with the project of liberal reform. While liberalism is made to stand in as the only vehicle of patriarchal ideology (since it is complicit with Western knowledge), its opponents—the revivalists and the orthodoxy—are vested with a rebellious, even emancipatory agenda, since they prevented colonisation of the domestic ideology. And since, for such academics, colonized knowledge is regarded as the exclusive source of all power, all thar contests it is supposed to possess an emancipatory possibility for women. By easy degrees, then, we reach the position that while opposition to widow immolation was complicit with the colonial silencing of non-colonized voices and, consequently, was an exercise of power, the practice of widow immolation itself was a contestatory act outside the realm of power relations since it was not sanctioned by colonialism. In a country where people will still gather in their lakhs to watch and celebrate the burning of a teen-aged girl as sati, such cultural studies are grim with political implications.

It is apparent that colonial structures of power compromised with—and indeed learnt much from—indigenous patriarchy and upper-caste norms and practices which, in certain areas of life, retained considerable hegemony. This indubitable fact opens out a new context against which to revaluate liberal reform. Above all, we need to remember that other sources of hegemony, far from becoming extinct, were reactivated under colonialism and opposed the liberal-rationalist agenda with considerable vigour and success. The historian cannot view the colonial past as an unproblematic arena within which all power was on one side and all protest on the other. It is necessary to take into account a multi-faceted nationalism (and not simply its liberal variant), all aspects of which were complicit with power and domination even when they critiqued Western knowledge and challenged colonial power.

II

A summary of controversial legislative activity pertaining to Hindu marriage in the late nineteenth century will help map our discursive field. The Native Marriage Act III of 1872 was, for its times, an extremely radical package which prohibited polygamy, legalized divorce and laid down a fairly high minimum age of marriage. It also ruled out caste or religious barriers to marriage. Predictably, the proposed bill raised a storm of controversy. Its jurisdiction was eventually narrowed down to such people as would declare themselves to be not Hindus, not Christians, not Jains, not Buddhists and not Sikhs. In short, its scope came to cover the Brahmos alone, whose initiative had led to its inception in the first place.[2]

Furious debates around the bill opened up and problematized crucial areas of Hindu conjugality—in particular the system of non-consensual, indissoluble infant marriage whose ties were considered to remain binding upon women even after the death of their husbands. This polemic hardened in 1887 when Rukma Bai, an educated girl from the lowly carpenter caste, refused to live with her uneducated, consumptive husband, claiming that since the marriage was contracted in her infancy it could be repudiated by her decision as an adult. She was threatened with imprisonment under Act XV of 1877 for non-restitution of conjugal rights. The threat was removed only after considerable reformist agitation and the personal intervention of Victoria.[3] The issue foregrounded very forcefully the problems of consent and indissolubility within Hindu marriage.[4]

In 1891 the Parsi reformer Malabari's campaign bore fruit in the Criminal Law Amendment Act 10 which revised Section 375 of the

Penal Code of 1860, and raised the minimum age of consent for married and unmarried girls from 10 to 12.[5] Under the earlier penal code regulation a husband could legally cohabit with a wife who was 10 years old. The revivalist Hindu intelligentsia of Bengal now claimed that the new act violated a fundamental ritual observance in the life-cycle of the Hindu householder—that is, the 'garbhadhan' ceremony, or the obligatory cohabitation between husband and wife which was meant to take place immediately after the wife reached puberty. Since puberty, in the hot climate of Bengal, was quite likely to occur before she was 12, the new legislation meant that the ritual would no longer remain compulsory. If the wife reached puberty before attaining the age of consent, then obviously garbhadhan could not be performed. This in turn implied that the 'pinda', or ancestral offerings, served up by the sons of such marriages would become impure and that generations of ancestors would be starved of it. The argument provided the central ground for a highly organized mass campaign in Bengal. The first open mass-level anti-government protest in Calcutta and the official prosecution of a leading newspaper were its direct consequences.[6]

This summary might be taken to suggest, Cambridge School fashion,[7] that nationalist initiative was actually a mere reflex action, following mechanically upon the legal initiatives of the colonial state. This was far from being the case. Not only was colonial initiative itself generally a belated and forced surrender to Indian reformist pressure, Hindu revivalist reaction against both was ultimately constituted by a new political compulsion: it was coterminous with a recently acquired notion of the colonized self which arose out of the 1857 uprising, the post-Mutiny reprisals, Lyttonian discriminatory policies in the 1870s, and the Ilbert Bill racist agitations in the 1880s. These experiences collectively modified and cast into agonizing doubt the earlier choice of loyalism that the Bengali intelligentsia had made, fairly unambiguously, in 1857. Our understanding of responses to colonial legislation can make only very limited and distorted sense unless they are located within this larger context.

Whereas early-nineteenth-century male liberal reformers had been deeply self-critical about the bondage of women within the household,[8] the satirized literary self-representation of the Bengali 'baboo' of later decades recounted a very different order of lapses for himself: his was a self that had lost its autonomy and now willingly hugged its chains.

Rethinking about the burden of complicity with colonialism hammered out a reoriented self-critique as well as a heightened perception about the meaning of subjection. It is no accident that even the economic critiques of drain, deindustrialization and poverty would come to be developed by the post-1860s generations.

With a gradual dissolution of faith in the progressive potential of colonialism, a dissolution that accompanied political self-doubt and the failure of indigenous economic enterprises,[9] there was also a disenchantment with the magical possibilities of Western education. Earlier reformers had been led to look hopefully at the public sphere as an arena for the test of manhood, of genuine self-improvement. But now, with activities shrinking into parasitic petty landlordism and tenure-holdings, or to mechanical chores within an oppressive and marginalized clerical existence, the *bhadralok* household increasingly resembled a solitary sphere of autonomy, a site of formal knowledge where—and only where—education would yield practical, manipulable, controllable results. The Permanent Settlement had generated a class of parasitic landlords with fixed revenue obligation whose passivity was reinforced by uninhibited control over their peasants' rent. The gap between a fixed sum of revenue and flexible rent procurement in a period of rising agricultural prices cushioned an existence of fairly comfortable tenure holding. The Rent Acts of 1859 and 1885, however, breached that security. Organized tenant resistance of the late nineteenth century led to heightened anxieties and uncertainties among the landed gentry. The household, consequently, became doubly precious and important as the only zone where autonomy and self-rule could be preserved.[10]

In the massive corpus of household management manuals that came to occupy a dominant place in the total volume of printed vernacular prose literature of these years, the household was likened to an enterprise to be administered, an army to be led, a state to be governed[11]—all metaphors rather poignantly derived from activities that excluded colonized Bengalis. Unlike Victorian middle-class situations, then, the family was not a refuge after work for the man. It was their real place of work. Whether in the Kalighat bazaar paintings[12] or in the Bengali fiction of the nineteenth century, workplace situations remain shadowy, unsubstantial, mostly absent. Domestic relations alone constitute the axis around which plots are generated, in sharp contrast with, for example, Dickensian novels.[13]

The new nationalist worldview, then, reimaged the family as a contrast to and a critique of alien rule. This was done primarily by contrasting two different versions of subjection—that of the colonized Hindu male in the world outside, and that of the apparently subordinated Hindu wife at home. The forced surrender and real dispossession of the former was counterposed to the allegedly loving, willed surrender and ultimate self-fulfilment of the latter.[14] It was in the interests of this intended contrast that conjugality was constituted as the centre of gravity around which the discursive field on the family organized itself. All other relations, even the mother–child one (which would come to take its place as a pivotal point in later nationalist discourse) remained subordinated to it up to the end of the nineteenth century. It was the relationship between the husband and wife that mediated and rephrased, within revivalist-nationalism, the political theme of domination and subordination, of subjection and resistance as the lyrical or existential problem of love, of equal but different ways of loving.

The household generally, and conjugality specifically, came to mean the last independent space left to the colonized Hindu. This was a conviction that was both shaped and reinforced by some of the premises of colonial law. English legislators and judges postulated a basic division within the legal domain: British and Anglo-Indian law had a 'territorial' scope and ruled over the 'public' world of land relations, criminal law, laws of contract, and evidence. On the other hand, there were Hindu and Muslim laws which were defined as 'personal', covering persons rather than areas, and ruling over the more intimate areas of human existence—family relationships, family property and religious life.[15] Early nationalists chose to read this as a gap between on the one hand the *territory* or the *land* colonized by an alien law, and on the other the *person*, still ruled by one's own faith. This was a distinction that the Queen's Proclamation of 1859, promising absolute non-interference in religious matters, did much to bolster.[16] Even in subjected India, therefore, there could exist an interior space that was as yet putatively inviolate.

Far from trying to hegemonize this sphere and absolutize its control, colonial rule, especially in the post-1857 decades, tried to keep its distance from it, thus indirectly adding to the nationalist conviction. The earlier zeal for textualization and codification of traditional laws was gradually replaced by a recognition of the importance of unwritten and varied custom, of the inadvisability of legislation on such matters, and of urging judicial deference, even obedience, to local Hindu opinion.[17] Towards the end of the century, a strong body of Hindu lawyers and judges came to be formed whose conformity to Hindu practices (Hindutva) was often taken to be of decisive importance in judicial decision-making, even though their professional training was in Western jurisprudence, not in Hindu law.[18] There was, moreover, an implicit grey zone of unwritten law whose force was nevertheless quite substantial within law courts.[19] Take a Serampore court case of 1873, for instance, where a Hindu widow was suing her brothers-in-law for defrauding her of her share in her husband's property by falsely charging her with 'unchastity'. Her lawyer referred frequently to notions of kinship obligations, ritual expectations from a Hindu widow and moral norms and practices of high-caste women.[20] Clearly, these arguments were thought to possess value in convincing the judge and the jury, even though overtly they had little legal significance. Far from laughing peculiarly Hindu susceptibilities out of court, English judges, even the Privy Council, seriously rationalized them. Referring to the existence of a Hindu idol as a legal person in a different law suit, an English judge commented: 'Nothing impossible or absurd in it . . . after all an idol is as much of a person as a corporation.'[21] Legal as well as ritual niceties about the proper disposition of idols were seriously debated, and sacred objects were brought into courts of law after due ritual purification of the space.[22] The introduction of a limited jury system between the 1860s and the 1880s in Bengal further strengthened the voice of local Hindu notables, and, consequently, of local usages and norms. An official recommendation of 1890 curtailed the powers of the jury in many directions but left the powers of settling marriage disputes intact in their hands.[23]

Nor did colonial legislators and judges form a unified, internally coherent body of opinion on proper Hindu norms and practices which they would then try to freeze. A substantial debate developed over a proposal in 1873 to transfer the cognisance of cases connected with marriage offences, especially adultery, from criminal to civil courts. While Simson, the Dacca commissioner, recommended the repeal of penal provisions against adultery, Reynolds, the magistrate of Mymensingh strongly demurred: 'I have always observed with great aversion the practice of the English law in giving damages in cases of adultery and seduction, and wanted it to remain a criminal offence.'[24] About cases of forfeiture of property rights by 'unchaste widows', there was a clear division between the high courts of Allahabad on the one hand and those of Bombay, Madras and Calcutta on the other.[25] The divisions reflected the absence of any monolithic or absolute consensus about the excellence of English legal practice as a model for Indian life.

These decades had in England seen profound changes in women's rights *vis-à-vis* property holding, marriage, divorce, and the rights of prostitutes to physical privacy,[26] Englishmen in India were divided about the direction of these changes and a significant section felt disturbed by the limited, though real, gains made by contemporary English feminists. They turned with relief to the so-called relative stability and strictness of Hindu rules. The Hindu joint-family system, whose collective aspects supposedly fully submerged and subordinated individual rights and interests, was generally described with warm appreciation.[27] Found here was a system of relatively unquestioned patriarchal absolutism which promised a more comfortable state of affairs than what emerged after bitter struggles with Victorian feminism at home.

The colonial experience, in its own way, mediated and reoriented debates on conjugal legislation in England. There were important controversies: the best known being between John Stuart Mill and James Fitzjames Stephen on the issue of consensus *vs* force and authority as the valid basis for social and human relations. Stephen, drawing on his military-bureaucratic apprenticeship in India, questioned Mill's premise of complementarity and the notion of the companionate marriage.[28]

There was no stable legal or judicial model that could, therefore, be imported into India. Prior to the Judicature Act of 1873 there were four separate systems of courts in England, each applying its own form of law, and these were often in conflict with each other.[29] In any case, the prolonged primacy of case-law and common-law procedures within England itself made English judges in India agree with Indian legal and nationalist opinion that customs, usages and precedents were far more valid sources of law than legislation.[30]

A general consensus about the differentiated nature of colonial law, then, postulated a fissure within the system wherein Hindus could insert their claims for a sectoral yet complete autonomy, for a pure space. The specific and concrete embodiment of this purity seemed to lie more within the body of the Hindu woman rather than the man—a conviction shaped, no doubt, by the growing self-doubt of the post-1857 Hindu male. Increasingly, irony and satire, a kind of black humour, became the dominant form of educated middle-class literary self-representation. There was an obsessive insistence on the physical manifestation of this weakness. The feeble Bengali male physique became a metaphor for a larger condition. Simultaneously, it was a site of the critique of the ravaging effects of colonial rule. 'The term Bengali is a synonym for a creature afflicted with inflammation of the liver, enlargement of the spleen, acidity or headache.'[31] Or, 'Their bones are weak, their muscles are flabby, their nerves toneless.'[32] Or, 'Bengal is ruined. There is not a single really healthy man in it. The digestive powers have been affected and we can eat but a little. Wherever one goes one sees a diseased people.'[33] Through the grind of Western education, office routine[34] and enforced urbanization, with the loss of traditional sports and martial activities, the male Bengali body was supposedly marked, maimed and completely worn down by colonialism. It was the visible site of surrender and loss, of defeat and alien discipline.

The woman's body, on the other hand, was still held to be pure and unmarked, loyal, and subservient to the discipline of shastras alone. It was not a free body by any means, but one ruled by 'our' scriptures, 'our' custom. The difference with the male body bestowed on it a redemptive, healing strength for the community as a whole. An interesting change now takes place in the representation of Hindu women in the new nationalist discourse. Whereas for liberal reformers she had been the archetypal victim figure, for nationalists she had become a repository of power, the Kali rampant, a figure of range and strength.[35]

What were the precise sources of grace for Hindu women? A unique capacity for bearing pain was one. So was the discipline exercised upon her body by the iron laws of absolute chastity, extending beyond the death of the husband, through an indissoluble, non-consensual infant form of marriage, through austere widowhood, and through her proven capacity for self-immolation. All these together imprinted an inexorable disciplinary regimen upon her person that contained and defined her from infancy to death.

Such discipline was not entirely confined to the normative or conceptual sphere. Bengal, with the exception of the Central Provinces and Berar, and Bihar and Orissa, had the highest rate of infant marriages—a custom that cut across caste and community lines and did not markedly decrease even after the Act of 1891.[36] Before it was banned, Bengal had also been, as we know, the heartland of the practice of sati. The Hindu woman's demonstrated capacity for accepting pain thus became the last hope of greatness for a doomed people. As we saw, Bankimchandra linked sati with national regeneration:

> I can see the funeral pyre burning, the chaste wife sitting at the heart of the blazing flames, clasping the feet of her husband lovingly to her breasts. Slowly the fire spreads, destroying one part of her body and entering another. Her face is joyful. . . . The flames burn higher, life departs and the body is burnt to ashes. . . . When I think that only some time back our women could die like this, then new hope rises up in me, then I have faith that we, too, have the seeds of greatness within us. Women of Bengal: You are the true jewels of this country.[37]

Bankim had plenty of reservations on other aspects of Hindu conjugality,[38] but he seemed to identify with it at its most violent point of termination, through a highly sensualized spectacle of pain and death, a barely disguised parallel between the actual flames destroying a female body and the consuming fires of desire.

III

There were two equally strong compulsions and possibilities in the construction of Hindu womanhood—love and pain—which produced deep anxieties within early nationalism.

The accent on love had, from the beginning, underlined acute discomfort about mutuality and equality. Pandit Sasadhar Tarkachuramani, the doyen of Hindu orthodoxy, argued that a higher form of love distinguished Western from Hindu marriages. While the former seeks social stability and order through control over sexual morality, the latter apparently aspires only towards 'the unification of two souls'.

'Mere temporal happiness, and the begetting of children are very minor and subordinate considerations in Hindu marriage.'[39] The revivalist-nationalist segment of the vernacular press, polemical tracts and manuals translated the notion of marriage of souls as mutual love lasting practically from cradle to funeral pyre. This uniquely Hindu way of loving supposedly anchored the woman's absolute and lifelong chastity.[40] Yet the very emphasis on love, so necessary as a critique of alien oppression and misunderstandings of the Hindu order, was a double-edged weapon: once it was raised, sooner or later the question of the mutuality of such love was bound to arise. Was it equally binding on both partners? If not, and since Hindu males were allowed to be polygamous, could its jurisdiction on women be anything more than prescriptive? Particularly if marriage was imposed on her at birth, without the question of her consent or choice?

Nothing in the Hindu shastras would confirm the possibility of mutually monogamous ties. To redeem this absence there appeared, for the first time in the history of Hindu marriage, a wave of polemical literature that valorized, indeed insisted on, male monogamy: 'We find tracts that advise widowers never to remarry.'[41] Manuals advocating self-immolation for the adult widow now simultaneously advise that child widows should be remarried; they have no obligation towards a husband whom they have not, as yet, come to love.[42] Not just sacred texts but custom too now allows a wide spectrum of castes to make a second marriage possible for men if the first wife is barren or bore no sons.[43] Yet in the absence of a shastric or custom-based injunction against polygamy, and given the reluctance among Hindu revivalist-nationalists to invite reformist legislation, male chastity was fated to remain normative rather than obligatory, while the woman's chastity was not a function of choice or willed consent. This was a compromise that became fundamentally difficult to sustain.

Through much of the 1880s we find a studied silence on this uncomfortable equation within the Hindu marriage and a self-mesmerizing repetition of its innately aesthetic qualities. The infant-marriage ritual is drenched in a warm, suffusing glow. 'People in this country take a great *pleasure* in infant-marriage. The *little bit* of a woman, the infant bride, clad in red silk, her back turned towards her boy husband. . . . The drums are beating, and men, women and children are running in order to glimpse that face . . . from time to time she breaks forth into *little* ravishing smiles. She looks like a *little lovely doll*' (italics mine).[44] The key words are little, lovely, ravishing, pleasure, infant and doll.[45] They are inserted at regular intervals to make the general account of festivities draw its warmth from this single major source—the delight-giving and delighted infant bride. The community of 'men, women and children' that forms for the occasion is bonded together by a deeply sensuous experience, by great visual pleasure, by happiness. The radiant picture of innocent celebration is rounded off through the cleverly casual insertion of the phrase 'boy husband'. Yet infant marriage was prescriptive only for the girl. The groom of the 'lovely doll' could be, and frequently was, a mature, even elderly man, possibly much-married already. A strategic and organizing silence lies at the heart of this image of desire and pleasure.

Even if the quality of Hindu love was assumed to be 'higher', Hindu marriage was still placed firmly within mainstream developments in the universal history of marriages which had supposedly trodden a uniform path from the 'captive' stage to fairly permanent, often sacramental, systems. Consent-based alternatives, whether in ancient Indian or in class-based modern Western traditions, were dismissed as aberrations or minor variations.[46] A long editorial, significantly entitled 'The Bogus Science', questioned the sources and authenticity of reformist knowledge: the nature of their evidence, of deduction, of arrangement of proof.[47] A powerful eugenics-based argument against infant marriage (infant marriages produce weak progeny) was countered by a climatic view of history:[48] irrespective of the age of the parents, a tropical climate was in any case bound to produce weak children: reformers were thereby accused of casuistry or weak logic. And since the penal code had earlier laid down 10 as the minimum age of consent, how would raising it to 12 ensure genuine consent? 'A girl of fourteen or sixteen is not capable of legally signing a note of hand for 5 rupees and she is, *ipso facto*, a great deal more incompetent to give her consent to defile her person at twelve.'[49] It was also considered more than a little dishonest to place such importance on the woman's consent in this one matter since, within post-marital offences, 'in the case of the wife the point does not turn on consent, for, if that had been the case, there would have been no such offence as adultery in the Penal Code'.[50] A high premium was thus placed on the rule of rationality in the defence of Hindu marriage.

Hindu rationality was represented as more supportive than reformist or colonial projects. Given the physical and economic weakness of women, an indissoluble marriage tie had to be her only security. This contention conveniently overlooked the fact that, in a polygamous world, indissolubility was binding, in effect, on women alone. A clear-eyed kulin brahmin widow had remarked: 'People say that the seven ties that bind the Hindu wife to the husband do not snap as they do with Christians or Muslims. This is not true. According to Hindu law, the wife cannot leave the husband but the husband may leave her whenever he wants to.'[51] It was also maintained that consent was immaterial since parents were better equipped to handle the vital question of security than an immature girl.[52] Security also largely depended upon perfect integration with the husband's family, so the sooner the process began, the better it was for the girl.[53]

Hindu marriage, in the rather defensive discourse of the 1880s, then, was more pleasurable and more beautiful, kinder and safer, more rational, and guaranteed by a sounder system of knowledge. In any case, it was essentially a part of universal developments in the history of civilizations: differences in marriage systems between the Hindu and the non-Hindu were played down, if not obliterated.

The Rukma Bai episode of 1887 made it imperative at last to rewrite this narrative of love and pleasure in the language of force. The earlier lyricism in relation to such 'love' had already been ruptured from time to time to underline and recuperate the basic fact of non-consensuality. At a meeting convened at the palace of the Shova Bazar Raj, Rajendralal Mitra had insisted: 'in it [Hindu marriage] there is no selection, no self-choice, no consent on the part of the bride. She is an article of gift, she is given away even as a cow or any other chattel.' Approving laughter greeted his exposition and he went on: 'There is in Hinduism not the remotest idea of choice and whoever changed any small part of it was no Hindu.'[54] Rukma Bai's action violently foregrounded the sexual double standards and made a mockery of the notion of the loving heart of Hindu conjugality. A lot of the debate centred around the vexed question of whether a woman could sue for separation from an adulterous husband. 'Among the Hindus, unchastity on the part of the husband is certainly a culpable offence but they set much higher value upon female chastity': its erosion would lead to the loss of family honour, growth of half-castes and the destruction of ancestral rites.[55] Bare, stark bones that formed the basic foundation of Hindu marriage now began to surface, threatening to blow the edifice of love away. 'A good Hindu wife should always serve her husband as God even if that husband is illiterate, devoid of good qualities and attached to other women. And it is the duty of the government to make Hindu women conform to the injunctions of the Shastras.'[56] The basis of conjugality now openly shifts to prescription.

Rukma Bai had forced a choice upon her community—between the woman's right to free will and the future of the pristine essence of Hindu marriage: the two could no longer be wedded together as a perfect whole. Revivalist-nationalists had to treat the two as separate, conflicting units, and indicate their own partisanship.

That came forth in no time at all. 'It is very strange that the whole of Hindu society will suffer for the sake of a very ordinary woman.'[57] Or, 'kindness to the female sex cannot be a good plea in favour of the proposed alteration.'[58] Interestingly, the episode had shown up another fault in the image of the Hindu community. Rukma Bai belonged to the carpenter caste, where divorce had been customary. Whose custom must colonial law recognize now? Was Hinduism a heterogeneous, indeed, self-divided, self-contradictory formation, or was it a unified monolithic one? The revivalist-nationalist answer, once again, was unambiguous. 'The Brahmin caste occupies the highest position and all laws and ordinances have been formed with special reference to that. All the other castes conduct themselves after the fashion of the Brahminical castes.'[59] Or, 'it is true that divorce obtains among some low-caste people and the government should be really doing an important duty as a ruler if it should make laws fixing and negotiating the uncertain and unsettled marriage customs of the people.'[60]

The debate prised open the imagined community along lines of caste and gender and delineated the specific contours of the revivalist-nationalist agenda. This could no longer base its hegemonic claims on its supposed leadership of the struggle of a whole subjected people for autonomy and self-rule in their 'private' lives. Its nationalism became more precisely defined now as the rule of brahmanical patriarchy. Its rationality was based on the forced and absolute domination of upper-caste male standards, not universal reason leading towards freedom and self-determination for the dispossessed. If it aspired to detach Hindus from colonized reason and lead them to self-rule, it would only do so by substituting for it a brahmanical, patriarchal reason based on scripture-cum-custom, both of which were disciplinary and oppressive for the ruled subjects—as was the colonial regime in the sphere of political economy. The contestation of colonization was no simple escape from or refusal of power: nor had colonialism equally and entirely disempowered all Indians. Resistance was an agenda itself irrevocably tied to schemes for domination, an exercise of power that was nearly as absolute as that which it resisted.

IV

Curiously, one possibility within Hindu marriage had not occurred to reformists or to Bengali Hindu militants—the possibility of the sexual abuse of infant wives. There had been, from time to time, the occasional stray report. The *Dacca Prakash* of June 1875 reported that an 'elderly' man had beaten his child-wife to death when she refused to go to bed with him. Neighbours had tried to cover it up as suicide but the murder charge was eventually proved. The jury, however, let off the husband with a light sentence.[61] The *Education Gazette* of May 1873 had reported a similar incident when the 'mature' husband of a girl of 11 'dragged her out by the hair and beat her till he killed her' for similar reasons. He was let off with a light sentence as well.[62] Reporting remained sporadic and the accounts were not picked up and woven into any general discussion about Hindu marriage as yet. The controversy over the right age of consent continued to hinge on eugenics, morality, child rearing and family interests.

In 1890 Phulmonee, a girl of 10 or 11, was raped to death by her husband Hari Maiti, a man of 35. Under existing penal code provisions, however, he was not guilty of rape since Phulmonee had been well within the statutory age limit of 10. The event, however, added enormous weight and urgency to Malabari's campaign for raising the age of consent from 10 to 12. The reformist press began to systematically collect and publish accounts of similar incidents from all over the country. Forty-four women doctors brought out long lists of cases where child-wives had been maimed or killed because of rape.[63] From the possible effects of child marriage on the health of future generations, the debate shifted to the life and safety of Hindu wives.

Phulmonee was the daughter of the late Kunj Behari Maitee, a man from the 'Oriya Kyast' caste, who had been a 'Bazar Sircar' at Bow Bazar Market. It was a well-paid job and it seems that, by claiming 'Oriya Kyast' status, the family was aspiring to a superior caste position in consonance with their economic viability: Maitees were otherwise categorised as a low Sudra group. The family frequently referred to its specific caste practices in court with some pride. They said that while they adhered to child marriage, they forbade cohabitation before the girl's menstruation and that, in this respect, Phulmonee had not come of age. Their version was that the newly married couple had been kept apart according to caste rules, and that Hari, on a visit to his in-laws, had stolen into Phulmonee's room and had forced himself upon her, thereby causing her death. Hari Maiti, however, insisted that since their marriage she had spent at least a fortnight at his house and they had slept together all the time. He made no mention of caste rules against pre-menstrual cohabitation. It seems, then, that caste customs remained loose and flexible, and that each family would allow considerable manipulation within them.

Even though Hari Maiti had insisted that on the last night they had not had intercourse, medical opinion was unanimous that the girl had died of violent sexual penetration. If the court accepted that Hari was right and that Phulmonee had slept with him earlier, then it could go a long way to show that since nothing untoward had happened earlier, on the fatal night in question Hari would not have had any reason to suspect that more vigorous penetration might lead to violent consequences. He would, in fact, have been able to seem convinced that intercourse was perfectly safe. The English judge, Wilson, clearly indicated that he chose to accept Hari's version, thus exonerating him from the charge of culpable homicide. The charge of rape, in any case, was not permissible since the penal code provisions ruled out the existence of rape by the husband if the wife was above the age of 11. The judge was equally opposed to any extension of the strict letter of the law, in this case to devise exemplary punishment for a particularly horrible death: 'Neither judges nor juries have any right to do for themselves what the law has not done.'

The judge built up his case on the hypothetical argument that the couple had slept together earlier. He chose to ignore the version given by the women in the girl's family—of Radhamonee, Bhondamonee and Sonamonee, the mother, aunt and grandmother of the girl.

> I think it is my duty to say that I think there exists hardly such solid and satisfactory ground as would make it safe to say that this man must have had knowledge that he was likely to cause the death of the girl . . . You will, of course, in these, as in all matters, give the benefit of any doubt in favour of the prisoner.
>
> The weight of concern is, very blatantly, on the exoneration of the man rather than on the fate of the woman. The law itself was shaped so as to preserve custom as well as the male right to the enjoyment of an infantile female body.

What needs to be particularly noted here is that, throughout the trial, the judge was saying nothing about a husband who insisted on sleeping with a child, or about the custom which allowed him to do so with impunity. Above all, he was not making any judgmental comparison between the ways of husbands, Eastern or Western. In fact, he bent over backwards to exonerate the system of marriage that had made this death possible: 'Under no system of law with which Courts have had to do in this country, whether Hindu or Mohammedan, or that formed under British rule, has it ever been the law that a husband has the absolute right to enjoy the person of his wife without regard to the question of safety to her.'[64]

Both the Hindu husband and the Hindu marriage system are generously exempted from blame and criticism. There is, in fact, an assertion about a continuity in the spirit of the law from the time of the Hindu kingdoms to that of British rule. A significant body of English medical opinion confirmed the clean bill of health that the colonial judiciary had advanced to the Hindu marriage system. Even in a strictly private communication, meant for colonial officialdom alone, the secretary to the Public Health Society wrote to the Government of Bengal:

> The council direct me to lay special stress upon the point . . . that they base no charge against the native community.

They reverently cited the work on Hindu law by Sir Thomas Strange to evoke, in near-mystical terms, the supreme importance of his marriage rules to the Hindu, and the inadvisability of external interference with them.

> The council admit that our native fellow subjects must be allowed the fullest possible freedom in deciding when their children should be ceremonially married. That, in the constitution of Hindu society, is a matter with which no Government could meddle and no Government ought to meddle.

They proceeded to review the considerable medico-legal data on sexual injuries inflicted on child wives and concluded that, whatever the weight of evidence on the matter, the system of infant marriage must continue unabated. The age of commencing cohabitation could be raised *only if Hindus themselves expressed a great desire for change* (emphasis mine).

Contrary to received wisdom, then, there is hardly here a vision of remaking the Hindu as a pale image of his master, nor of designs of total change and reform. Macaulay's notorious plan of recasting the native as a brown sahib was not necessarily uniformly dominant for the entire spectrum of colonial rule. Even when dominant, it had to make crucial negotiations with other imperatives and value preferences and, above all, with the everlasting calculations of political expediency. If, at the time of Macaulay, the Anglicist vision of a Westernized middle class had appeared as the strongest reservoir of loyalism, soon enough other alternatives emerged and were partially accommodated, modifying the earlier formula and crucially mitigating its reformist thrust. Our moment of the 1890s comes after a long spell of middle-class agitation over demands on constitutional rights, of Indianization of the services, of security against racial discrimination and abuse. It comes after the outburst of white racism over the Ilbert Bill issue, when the educated middle class was temporarily vested with the possibility of standing in a position of judicial authority over Europeans. Empowering the Indian through Westernization, consequently, came to be envisaged as the most threatening menace to colonial racial structures.[65] It was a moment when the slightest concession to Indian liberal reformism would be made most unwillingly and only in the belief that it represented a majority opinion.

The new legislation was conceived after the reformist agitation had convinced the authorities that the 'great majority' was ready for change.[66] After the Phulmonee episode, revivalist-nationalists were maintaining a somewhat embarrassed silence; this was broken only after the proposed bill came along. During the interval the reformist voice alone was audible. Since this, for the moment, looked like the majority demand, political expediency coincided temporarily with reformist impulse and the government committed itself to raising the age of consent. At the same time, official opinion in Bengal did not extend the terms of the specific reform to larger plans for invasive change. On the contrary, it displayed a keenness to learn from the codes of Hindu patriarchy. Did a recognition that they were confronted with the most absolute form of patriarchal domination evoke a measure of unconscious respect and fellow feeling among the usually conservative, male English authorities, rather than the instinct for reform? As the secretary to the Public Health Society put it: 'The history of British rule and the workings of British courts in India manifest a distinct tenderness towards . . . the customs and religious observances of the Indian people.'[67]

There was still the mangled body of 'that unhappy child, Phulmonee Dassee', a girl of 10 or 11, sexually used by a man whom she had known only a few weeks, 29 years her senior, a man who had already been married (aunt Bhondamonee's evidence in court). There was the deposition of her mother Radhamonee: 'I saw my daughter lying on the cot, weltering in blood. Her cloth and the bed cloth and Hari's cloth were wet with blood.'[68] There was unanimous medical opinion that Hari had caused the death of a girl whose body was still immature and could not sustain penetration. She died after 13 hours of acute pain and continuous bleeding, The dry medical terminology somehow accentuates the horror more than words of censure:

> A clot, measuring 3 inches by one-and-a-half inches in the vagina . . . longitudinal tear one and three quarters long by one inch broad at the upper end of the vagina . . . a haematoma three inches in diameter in the cellular tissue of the pelvis. Vagina, uterus and ovaries small and undeveloped. No sign of ovulation.[69]

Phulmonee's was by no means an isolated case. Dr Chever's investigations of 1856 mentioned at least 14 cases of premenstrual cohabitation that had come to his notice, and the subsequent finding incorporated in Dr McLeod's report on child marriage amply corroborated his data.[70] We may presume that only such cases as would have needed police intervention or urgent medical attention entered the records. These were, then, cases of serious damage that resulted from premature sexual activity. An Indian doctor reported in court that 13 per cent of the maternity cases that he had handled involved mothers below the age of 13. The defence lawyer threw a challenge at the court: cohabiting with a pre-pubertal wife might not have shastric sanction, yet so deep-rooted was the custom that he wondered how many men present in court were not in some way complicit with the practice.[71]

The divisional commissioners of Dacca, Noakhali, Chittagong and Burdwan deposed that child marriage was widely prevalent among all castes, barring the tribals, in their divisions. The commissioner of Rajshahi division found that only in Jalpaiguri district 'Mlechhes and other aboriginal tribes do not favour child marriage . . . amongst the Muhammadans and Rajbungshis, females being useful in field work, are not generally married until they are more advanced in age'. On the whole, the practice was more common among lower castes. The average age of marriage for upper-caste girls was slowly moving up to 12 or 13 due to the relatively large spread of the new liberal education among them, and, ironically, to the growing pressures of dowry which forced parents to keep daughters unmarried till they could put together an adequate amount of dowry.[72] In fact, the compulsion to delay marriage till the dowry could be collected would have found a convenient ally in the new liberalism. Among the lower castes, on the other hand, emulation of brahmanical orthodoxy rather than of liberal values would be a more assured way of claiming pure ritual status. Wherever infant marriage prevailed, there was no way of ensuring that cohabitation would be delayed till the onset of puberty.

While both scriptural and customary injunctions were too strongly weighted in favour of early marriage to allow a raising of the age of marriage for girls, certain parts of the shastras did prescribe against pre-pubertal cohabitation among married couples. Nobinchandra Sen, poet and district magistrate of Chittagong, suggested that this injunction could be reinforced with legislation. Official opinion tried to distinguish between two distinct levels in marriage; the wedding ceremony itself was interpreted as a sort of a betrothal, after which girls remained in their parents' homes. It was only after the onset of puberty that they went through a 'second marriage' and went off to live with their husbands. A group of medical reformers' (Indian as well as European doctors who advocated changes in marriage rules on strictly medical grounds) as well as administrators advised legislation to ban marital cohabitation, before the performance of the second marriage. They hoped that there was sufficient shastric as well as customary sanction behind the practice.[73]

It was soon clear, however, that too much was being made of the 'second marriage'. It was not generally taken to constitute a distinct separate stage within marriage as a whole. While there was widespread recognition that girls should begin regular cohabitation only after they attained puberty, the custom was customarily violated. Once the marriage had been performed, domestic (especially female) pressure pulled the wife into the husband's family. In any case, it was difficult to decide exactly at what age girls attained puberty or make sure that no girl was sent off to her husband any earlier. Viable legislation would have to spell out a definite age at which puberty started rather than indicate a general physical condition.

The definition of puberty proved to be the stumbling block. According to custom, it was equated with the onset of regular menstruation. And here, revivalist-nationalists were treading delicate ground. While they wanted to oppose the proposed age of 12, they could not push the age too far back, since they had not opposed the earlier penal code ban on marital cohabitation before the girl was 10. If they now chose to construe the earlier ban as an oppressive intrusion which had already interfered with Hindu marriage practices, then they could no longer sustain their present agitational rhetoric to the effect that the current intervention was the first fundamental violation of Hindu conjugality, and therefore spelt the beginning of the end of the only free space left to the Hindu. Without this sense of a new, momentous beginning of doom, the pitch of the highly apocalyptic rhetoric would fall flat. If the new legislation were to be seen as merely a part of a long-drawn-out process, then opposition to it could hardly invest itself with a life-or-death mission. They therefore insisted that 'true puberty' only occurred between the of ages of 10 and 12. Even if menstruation occurred earlier, it was a fluke and not a regular flow. The earlier penal code regulation had not therefore interfered with the garbhadhan ceremony. Since, in the hot climate of Bengal, menarche was sure to start between 10 and 12, further raising the age of consent would constitute the first real breach in ritual practice.

Reformers argued that puberty sets in properly only after 12. In this, they used a different notion of puberty. While revivalist-nationalists unequivocally equated puberty with menarche, medical reformers argued that puberty was a prolonged process and menarche was the sign of its commencement, not of its culmination. The beginning of menstruation did not indicate the girl's 'sexual maturity'—which meant that her physical organs were developed enough to sustain sexual penetration without serious pain or damage. Until that capability had been attained, they argued, the notion of her consent was meaningless.

It is remarkable how all strands of opinion—colonial, revivalist-nationalist, medical-reformer—agreed on a definition of consent that pegged consent to a purely physical capability, divorced entirely from free choice of partner, from sexual, emotional or mental compatibility. Consent was put into a biological category, a stage when the female body was ready to accept sexual penetration without serious harm. The only problem lay in establishing when this stage was reached.

It would be simplistic, however, to conclude that there was complete identity of patriarchal values between reformers and revivalists. Whatever their broader views, reformers always had to struggle along with a minimalist programme since nothing else would have the remotest chance of acceptability either with the legislative authorities or in Hindu society. We only have to remind ourselves about the explosive protests that this legislation provoked. Reformist campaigning for legislation was more a consciousness-raising device, a foregrounding of issues of domestic ideology than pinning effective hopes of real social change to acts. Nor was the minimalist programme of insisting on the woman's physical safety an insignificant matter, under the circumstances. Revivalist-nationalists on the other hand, grounded their agenda on the most violently authoritarian regime of patriarchal absolutism. Their insistence upon self-rule in the domestic sphere coincided with their insistence that the Hindu girl should sacrifice her physical safety, and even her life if necessary, to defend the community's claim to autonomy.

As the reformist campaign gathered momentum and as the government, by the end of 1890, seemed committed to Malabari's proposals, Hindu militants were faced with two options. They could accept a radical reorientation of their earlier emphasis: that is, they could admit of a basic problem within present marriage practices and then separate them from past, supposedly authentic, norms. This way, they could still maintain their distance from reformers by insisting on reform from within in place of alien legislation from outside. While this would have amounted to an honourable face-saving device, it would still have implied an assault on the totality and inviolability of what had so far been exalted as the essential core of the system. Worse still, it would have amounted to a surrender to missionary, reformist and rationalist critiques of Hindu conjugality. On the other hand, it could come to terms with the phenomenon of violence and build its own counter-campaign around its presence. If difference was found to lie not in superior rationality, greater humanism, pleasure or love, but rather in pain and coercion, then these constituents of difference should be admitted and celebrated.

V

The Age of Consent Bill could have reasonably been faulted on many counts. It was an unbelievably messy and impractical measure. The reporting and verification of violations were generally impossible in familial situations. Even if the girl—provided she survived—and her parents were willing to depose against the husband, neighbours, whose evidence was crucial in such cases, usually protected the man. Proving the girl's age was fairly impossible in a country where births, even today, are not often registered. Medical examination was often inconclusive. Where matters did eventually reach the court, the jury and British judges, fearful of offending custom, rarely took a firm stand. In 1891 the mother of a young girl had pressed for legal action in such a case and the girl herself gave very definite evidence in court. On the basis of a dental examination the English magistrate, however, could not be absolutely certain that she was not over 12. The husband was consequently discharged.[74] Unnerved by the massive anti-bill agitations, the government hastened to undermine the scope of the act. Five days after its enactment. Lord Lansdowne sent circulars instructing that enquiries should be held by 'native Magistrates' alone, and in any case of doubt prosecution should be postponed.[75]

The nationalist press referred to these problems from time to time but used them as auxiliary arguments rather than as central ones. Certain other kinds of political criticism found a stronger resonance. There was a powerfully articulated fear about the extension of police intrusion right into the heart of the Hindu household.[76] There was also strong opposition on the grounds that an unreformed and unrepresentative legislature should not legislate on such controversial matters[77]—a criticism that sought to link the anti-Bill agitation with (Moderate) Congress-type constitutional demands. These protests too remained rather marginal to the true core of the Hindu revivalist-nationalist debate, which was carried on by hardliners like the newspapers *Bangabashi, Dainik O Samachar Chandrika* and *The Amrita Bazar Patrika.*

Hindu nationalists started on a very familiar note that had been struck on all sorts of issues since the 1870s: a foreign government was irrevocably alien and immune to the meaning of Hindu practices. And where knowledge does not exist, there power must not be exercised. A somewhat long illustration from the *Dainik O Samachar Chandrika* sums up a number of typical statements on the matter.

> That a woman should, from her childhood, remain near her husband, and think of her husband and should not even think of or see the face of another man . . . are injunctions of the Hindu Shastras, the significance whereof is understood only by 'sattvik' [pure] people like the Hindus. The English look to the purity of the body. But in Hindu opinion she alone is chaste and pure who has never even thought of one who is not her husband. No one who does not see with a Hindu's eye will be able to understand the secret meaning of Hindu practices and observances. . . . According to the Hindu the childhood of a girl is to be determined by reference to her first menses and not to her age . . .[78]

The first point made here is a methodological one that disputes the attempt to comprehend any foreign system of meaning through one's own cognitive categories (and immediately proceeds to do so itself by generalizing on English attitudes about the body and the soul). The meaning of Hindu female childhood is then made different through a different arrangement of medical, sexual, moral and behavioural conditions. While revivalist-nationalists do not, as yet, insist on complete autonomy in the actual formulation and application of personal laws, they do claim the sole and ultimate right to determine their general field of operations. The claim is justified by breaking up and dispersing the sources of Hindu conjugality among numerous and ever-shifting points of location. Some could be based on written texts, some located in oral traditions, yet others in ritual practice, and—most problematic of all—a whole lot could be simply embedded in an undefinable, amorphous, diffused Hindu way of life, accessible to Hindu instincts alone. The intention is to disperse the sources of Hindu law and custom beyond codified texts, however authoritative or authentic those might be. Even an ancient authority like Manu, who advocated 16 as the upper limit of marriage age for girls, was dismissed as someone who wrote for the colder northern regions—where puberty came later. Charak and Susruta were dismissed even more summarily as near-Buddhists who had scant regard for true Hindu values. The process of wide dispersal renders Hindu customs opaque and infinitely flexible, to the point of being eternally elusive to colonial authorities.

The crucial emphasis lay in the reiteration that the proposed law was the first of its kind to breach and violate the fundamentals of Hinduism. The argument could only be clinched by derecognizing the importance of earlier colonial interventions in Hindu domestic practices. Sati, it was argued, was never a compulsory ritual obligation and its abolition therefore merely scratched the surface of Hindu existence. The Widow Remarriage Act had a highly restricted scope, simply declaring children born of a second marriage to be legal heirs to their fathers' properties.[79] Reformers replied that the new bill was no unprecedented revision of custom either, since the penal code had already banned cohabitation for girls before the age of 10. Since girls could attain puberty before that age, the sanctity of the garbhadhan ceremony had already been threatened. Hindu revivalist-nationalists retaliated with a reference to the elusive sources of Hindu custom and a notion of the Hindu 'normalizing' order which could be grasped by pure-born

Hindus alone: 'It seems they [the reformers] do not know the meaning of *Adya Rim* [real menses]. Mere flow of blood is no sign of *Adya Ritu*. A girl never menstruates before she is ten and even if she does the event must be considered unnatural.'[80] This took care of the 1860 Penal Code provision against cohabiting with a girl under 10. An 'authentic' Hindu girl, according to revivalists, does not reach puberty before she is 10. The earlier ban had therefore not really tampered with Hindu practices. Were the ceiling to be extended to 12, a serious interference would occur. The meaning of physicality itself is constituted differently and uniform biological symptoms do not point to a universal bodily developmental scheme, since Hindus alone know what stands for the normal and the abnormal in the body's growth.

The insistence that the English were about to commit a primal sin against Hinduism, that an unprecedented attack was going to be mounted on the last pure space left to a conquered people, was necessary to relocate the beginnings of true colonisation here and now—so that a new chronology of resistance could also begin from this moment, redeeming the earlier choice of loyalism. 'The Indians have felt for the last two centuries that India is no longer theirs, that it has passed into the hands of the Yavanas. But the Indians have, up to this time, found solace in the thought that though their country is not theirs, their religion is theirs.'[81]

Or, even more forcefully and explicitly, 'No, no, a hundred battles like that of Plassey, Assay, Multan could not in terribleness of effect compare with the step Lord Lansdowne has taken.'[82] With the possibility of protest in the near future, apocalyptic descriptions of subjection became common: 'The day has at length arrived when dogs and jackals, hares and goats will have it all their way. India is going to be converted into a most unholy hell, swarming with hell worms and hell insects. . . . The Hindu family is ruined.'[83]

It was this language of resistance and repudiation that gave the Age of Consent controversy such wide resonance among the Bengali middle class. The *Bangabashi*, in particular, formulated a rhetoric in these years with phenomenal success,[84] becoming in the process the leading Bengali daily, changing over from its weekly status, and pulling a whole lot of erstwhile reformist papers into its orbit for some time. Even Vidyasagar, the ideal-typical reformer figure, criticized the bill.[85]

The response of a fairly pro-reform journal, the *Bengalee*, epitomizes the way in which the new agitational mood reacted on a potentially reform-minded, yet largely nationalist, intelligentsia. It had supported the bill quite staunchly up to the end of January 1891, after which there seemed to occur an abrupt change of line. In February, after reporting on 'an enormous mass protest meeting, the largest that had ever been held', it started to find problems with the legislation—albeit more of a constitutional kind, with reflections upon the unrepresentative nature of the legislature.[86] In March it covered yet another mammoth protest meeting and then redefined the grounds of its own opposition. 'It is no longer the language of appeal which opponents of the Bill address to the rulers of the land. . . . However much we may differ from the opponents of the measure, we cannot but respect such sentiments.'[87]

We therefore turn to the 'language' of the opponents, to the *Bangabashi*. Here was a radical leap from mendicant appeals, from oblique and qualified criticism and from guilt and shame-ridden self-satirization, here was the birth of a powerful, self-confident nationalist rhetoric. 'Who would have thought that a dead body would rise up again? Whoever thought that millions of corpses would again become instinct with life?'[88] There was an exhilarating sense of release in the naming of the enemy.

> The Englishman now stands before us in all his grim and naked hideousness. What a grim appearance. How dreadful the attitude . . . The demons of the cremation ground are laughing a wild, weird laugh. Is this the form of our Ruling power? Brahmaraksharh, Terror of the Universe; Englishmen . . . do you gnash your teeth, frown with your red eyes, laugh and yell, flinging aside your matted locks . . . and keeping time to the clang of the sword and bayonet . . . do you engage yourselves in a wild dance . . . and we . . . the twenty crores of Indians shall lose our fear and open our forty crores of eyes.[89]

Very confidently, almost gleefully, every former trapping of rationalization was peeled away from the core message. Admittedly, sanction for infant marriage came from Raghunandan alone, who was a late and local authority. It might well lead to other deaths.[90] It did, in all likelihood, weaken future progeny and lead to racial degeneration; but 'the

Hindu prizes his religion above his life and short-lived children'.[91] Hindu shastras undoubtedly imposed harsh suffering on women: 'This discipline is the pride and glory of chaste women and it prevails only in Hindu society.'[92] There were yet other practices that might bring on her death.

> Fasting on *Ekadashi* [fortnightly fasting—without even a drink of water—to which widows are meant to ritually adhere] is a cruel custom and many weak-bodied widows very nearly die of observing it . . . it is prescribed only in a small 'tatwa' of Raghunandan. Is it to be banned, too, for this reason, and the guardian of the widow arraigned in front of the High Court and pronounced guilty by the Baboo jurors?[93]

There would be other Phulmonees who would die similar violent deaths through infant marriage. Yet:

> the performance of the garbhadhan ceremony is obligatory upon all. Garbhadhan must be after first menstruation. It means the first cohabitation enjoined by the shastras. It is the injunction of the Hindu shastras that married girls must cohabit with their husbands on the first appearance of their menses and all Hindus must implicitly obey the injunction. And he is not a true Hindu who does not obey it . . . If one girl in a lakh or even a crore menstruates before the age of twelve it must be admitted that by raising the age of consent the ruler will be interfering with the religion of the Hindus. But everyone knows that hundreds of girls menstruate before the age of twelve. And garbhas [wombs] of hundreds of girls will be tainted and impure. And the thousands of children who will be born of those impure garbhas will become impure and lose their rights to offer 'pindas' [ancestral offerings].[94]

Even in translation the power of the voice comes through. The repetitive short sentences joined by 'ands', the frequency of the word 'must', the use of vast and yet vaster numbers to build up inexorably towards a sense of infinite doom—all add up to an incantatory, mandatory, apocalyptic mode of speech that is the typical vehicle for a fundamentalist millenarianism. All external reasoning has been chipped away, just the bare mandate is repeated and emphasized through threats and warnings. This is an immensely powerful, dignified voice, aeons away from timid mendicancy or morbid self-doubt. This is the proud voice of the community legislating on itself total defiance of foreign rule and alien rationalism. It speaks the authoritative word in the appropriately authoritarian voice. The Hindu woman's body is the site of a struggle that for the first time declares war on the very fundamentals of an alien power-knowledge system. Yet it is not merely a displaced site for other arguments but remains, at this moment, the heart of the struggle. Bengali Hindu revivalist-nationalism, at this formative moment, begins its career by defining itself as the realm of unfreedom.

This contestation of alien reformism and rationalism, this defence of community custom, represses the pain of women whose protest was drowned to make way for a putative consensus. It is no longer possible to resurrect the protest of Phulmonee and of many, many other battered child-wives who died or nearly died as a result of marital rape. We have, however, several instances when cases were lodged at the initiative of the girl's mother, sometimes forcing the hand of the male guardians—for those times a rare demonstration of the woman's protest action. We also have a court deposition left by a young girl who was severely wounded and violated by her elderly husband.

> I cannot say how old I am. I have not reached puberty. I was sleeping when my husband seized my hand. . . . I cried out. He stopped my mouth. I was insensible owing to his outrage on me. My husband violated me against my will. . . . When I cried out he kicked me in the abdomen. My husband does not support me. He rebukes and beats me. I cannot live with him.

The husband was discharged by the British magistrate. The girl was restored to him.[95]

Notes

1. I use the term 'militant nationalism' in a somewhat unconventional sense here: not as a part of a definite and continuous historical trend but as a moment of absolute and violent criticism of foreign rule that was developed by a group of Hindus in the late 1880s and early 1890s, largely over Hindu marriage controversies. Certain newspapers, especially the *Bangabashi*, took the lead in mobilizing protest, organizing mass rallies, and provoking official prosecution. That particular group, however, soon withdrew from the scene

of confrontation. In the Swadeshi Movement of 1905–8, the *Bangabashi* would remain quiescent, even loyal to the authorities. I owe this piece of information to Sumit Sarkar. For an excellent study of the newspaper, see Amiya Sen, 'Hindu Revivalism in Bengal' (Ph.D. thesis, Delhi University, 1980).

2. Charles H. Heimsath, *Indian Nationalism and Hindu Social Reform* (Princeton: Princeton University Press, 1977), pp. 91–4; Ajit Kumar Chakraborti, *Maharshi Debendranath Tagore* (Allahabad, 1916; Calcutta, 1971), pp. 406–35.
3. The act of 1877 was a colonial intervention to tighten up the marriage bond which the Hindu orthodoxy strongly defended on the grounds that it coincided with and reinforced the true essence of Hindu conjugality.
4. See Dagmar Engels, 'The Limits of Gender Ideology: Bengali Women, the Colonial State, and the Private Sphere, 1890–1930', *Women Studies, International Forum*, vol. 12, 1989.
5. Heimsath, pp. 147–5.
6. See extracts from *Bangabashi* and *Dainik O Samachar Chandrika* between 1889 and 1891 in *RNP*.
7. For this version of Cambridge historiography on Indian nationalism, see J. Gallagher, A. Seal and G. Johnson, *Locality, Province and Nation* (Cambridge, 1973).
8. I have discussed this in 'Hindu Household and Conjugality in Nineteenth-Century Bengal', paper read at the Women's Studies' Centre, Jadavpur University, Calcutta, 1989.
9. N.K. Sinha, *Economic History of Bengal* (Calcutta, n.d.), vol. I.
10. See my Introduction within the present volume [*Hindu Wife, Hindu Nation*].
11. See for instance Prasad Das Goswami, *Amader Samaj* (Serampore, 1896); Ishanchandra Basu, *Stri Diger Prati Upadesh* (Calcutta, n.d.); Kamakhya Charan Bannerji, *Stri Shiksha* (Dacca, 1901); Monomohan Basu, *Hindur Achar Vyavadhar* (Calcutta, 1872); Chandranath Basu, *Grahasthya Path* (Calcutta, 1887); Bhubaneswar Misra, *Hindu Vivaha Samalochan* (Calcutta, 1875); Tarakhnath Biswas, *Bangiya Mahila* (Calcutta, 1886); Anubicacharan Gupta, *Grihastha Jivan* (Calcutta, 1887); Narayan Roy, *Bangamahila* (Calcutta, n.d.); Chandrakumar Bhattacharya, *Bangavivaha* (Calcutta, 1881); Pratapchandra Majumdar, *Stri Charitra* (Calcutta, n.d.); Purnachandra Gupta, *Bangali Bau* (Calcutta, 1885); and many others.
12. See the preponderance of this theme in the collection of W.C. Archer, *Bazaar Paintings of Calcutta* (London, 1953).
13. See, for instance, plots in the novels of Bankimchandra, *Bankim Rachanabali*, vol. I.

14. Prasad Das Goswami, op. cit.
15. See, for instance, Sir William Markby, Fellow, Balliol College and erstwhile judge in Calcutta High Court, *Hindu and Mohammadan Law* (1906; reprinted Delhi, 1977), pp. 2–3.
16. See frequent reference to the Queen's Proclamation in the agitational writings in the nationalist press, *RNP*, 1887–91.
17. Markby, op. cit., for a convergence of the views of this Orientalist scholar-cum-colonial judge with Hindu legal opinion; and c.f. Sripati Roy, *Customs and Customary Law in British India*, Tagore Law Lectures, 1908–9 (reprinted Delhi, 1986), pp. 2–6.
18. See J.D.M. Derrett, *Religion, Law and the State in India* (London, 1968).
19. For a clarification of the notion of unwritten law, see Robert M. Ireland, 'The Libertine Must Die: Sexual Dishonour and the Unwritten Law in the 19th Century United States', *Journal of Social History*, Fall 1989.
20. *The Bengalee*, 7 March 1873.
21. Markby, op. cit., p. 100.
22. This relates to a case involving the disposition of a Shalgram-shila in the case of Surendranath Bannerjee *vs* the chief justice and judges of the High Court at Fort William, July 1883. See an account in Subrata Choudhary, 'Ten Celebrated Cases Tried by the Calcutta High Court', in *High Court at Calcutta, Centenary Souvenir 1862–1962* (Calcutta, 1962).
23. Sharmila Bannerjee, *Studies in the Administrative History of Bengal, 1880–1989* (New Delhi, 1978), pp. 151–5.
24. Cited in *The Bengalee*, 26 April 1873.
25. See extracts from *Murshidabad Patrika, Dacca Prakash* and the *Education Gazette* in April 1875, *RNP*.
26. See Phillipa Levine, *Victorian Feminism, 1850–1900* (London, 1987), pp. 128–43. Also see Holcombe, *Wives and Property—Reform of the Married Women's Property Law in 19th Century England* (Oxford, 1983).
27. Markby, op. cit., p. 100.
28. Mendus and Rendall (eds), *Sexuality and Subordination, Interdisciplinary Studies of Genders in the 19th Century* (London: RKP, 1989), p. 133.
29. See also Holcombe, 'Victorian Wives and Property: Reform of the Married Women's Property Law, 1857–82', in Martha Vicinus, *A Widening Sphere: Changing Roles of Victorian Women* (London: Methuen, 1977).
30. Markby and Sripati Roy, op. cit.
31. *The Amrita Bazar Patrika*, 4 February 1873.
32. *The Hindoo Patriot*, 16 August 1887.
33. *The Amrita Bazar Patrika*, 28 January 1875, *RNP* Bengal, 1875.
34. See Sumit Sarkar, 'The Kalki-Avatar of Bikrampur: A Village Scandal in Early Twentieth-Century Bengal', in Ranajit Guha (ed.), *Subaltern Studies VI* (Delhi, 1989).

35. See 'Nationalist Iconography' in this volume [*Hindu Wife, Hindu Nation*].
36. *Report of the Age of Consent Committee, 1928–29,* Government of Bengal (Calcutta, 1929). For some statistical observations on this matter, see pp. 65–6.
37. *Kamalkanter Daptar*, op. cit.
38. Tanika Sarkar, 'Bankimchandra and the Impossibility of a Political Agenda' in this volume [*Hindu Wife, Hindu Nation*].
39. *Bangabashi*, 9 July 1887, *RNP*, 1887. For a critical discussion of such views see Rabindranath Tagore, *Hindu Vivaha* (*c.* 1887). Rabindranath himself, in this extremely convoluted logical exercise, grants a practical purpose to infant marriage purely for better breeding purposes but, in the process, Hindu conjugality is denied all effective or spiritual pretensions. *Rabindranath Rachanabali*, vol. 12 (Calcutta, *c.* 1942).
40. Chandrakanta Basu, *Hindu Patni and Hindu Vivaha Bayas O Uddeshya*, cited in *Hindu Vivaha*, op. cit., also by the same author, *Hinduttva*, op. cit.
41. See for instance Prasad Das Goswami, op. cit., Bhubaneshwar Misra, op. cit., Kalimoy Ghatok, *Ami* (Calcutta, 1885).
42. Monomohan Basu, op. cit.
43. Ibid.
44. *Sulabh Samachar O Kushadahe*, 22 July 1887, *RNP*, 1887.
45. Far from invariably evoking a sense of superiority and disgust among Englishmen, the spectacle would very often arouse similar sentiments. Compare a description of a marriage procession by an English tourist with our earlier account: 'It was the prettiest sight in the world to see those gorgeously dressed babies . . . passerbys smiled and blessed the little husband and the tiny wife'; John Law, *Glimpses of Hidden India* (Calcutta, *c.* 1905).
46. *The Hindoo Patriot*, 25 July 1887.
47. Ibid., 16 August 1887.
48. Ibid., 12 September 1887.
49. Ibid., 1 August 1887.
50. *Surabhi O Patrika*, 16 January 1887, *RNP*, 1887.
51. Nistarini Devi, *Sekaler Katha*, first published serially in *Bharatbarsha* between 1913 and 1914. Jana and Sanyal (eds), *Atmakatha* (Calcutta, 1982), p. 11.
52. Chandrakanta Basu, op. cit.
53. *The Hindoo Patriot*, 19 September 1887.
54. Cited in *The Hindoo Patriot*, ibid.
55. *Dainik O Samachar Chandrika*, 22 June 1857.
56. *Bardhawan Sanjivani*, 5 July 1887, *RNP*, 1887.
57. *Dhumketu*, 4 July 1887, *RNP*, 1887.
58. *Sambad Prabhakar*, 30 June 1887, *RNP*, 1887.

59. *Bangabashi*, 25 June 1887, *RNP*, 1887.
60. *Nabibibhaker Sadharani*, 18 July 1887, *RNP*, 1887.
61. *Dacca Prakash*, 8 June 1875, *RNP*, 1875.
62. *Education Gazette*, 11 May 1873, *RNP*, 1873.
63. Heimsath, op. cit.
64. Bengal Government Judicial JC/171, Proceedings 96–102, 1892, Nos 101–2. File JC/17–25. Honourable Justice Wilson's charge to jury in the case Empress *vs* Main Mohan Maitee, Calcutta High Court. Report sent by Arcar, Clerk of the Crown, High Court, Calcutta, to Officiating Chief Secretary 90B, no. 6292-Calcutta, 8 September 1890.
65. See Mrinalini Sinha, *Colonial Masculinity: The 'Manly Englishman' and the 'Effeminate Bengali' in the Late Nineteenth Century* (Manchester: Manchester University Press, 1995), pp. 33–69.
66. Bengal Government Judicial NF JC/17/, Proceedings 104–17, June 1893. From Simmons honorary secretary, Public Health Society of India to chief secretary, Government of Bengal, Calcutta, 1 September 1890.
67. Ibid., C.C. Stevens; officiating chief secretary 908, to secretary, home department, Government of India, Darjeeling, 8 November 1890.
68. Letter from Simmons, op. cit.
69. Bengal Government Judicial, J C/17/, op. cit.
70. Ibid.
71. *McLeod's Medical Report on Child Wives*, Bengal Government Judicial, ibid.
72. Ibid.
73. Ibid.
74. *The Bengalee*, 21 March 1891.
75. *Dagmar Engels*, op. cit.
76. *Surabhi O Patrika*, 16 January 1891, *RNP*, 1891.
77. *The Bengalee*, 21 March 1891.
78. *Dainik O Samachar Chandrika*, 14 January 1891, *RNP*, 1891.
79. *Nabayug*, 15 January 1891, *RNP*, 1891.
80. *Dainik O Samachar Chandrika*, 15 April 1896, *RNP*, 1896.
81. *Nabayug*, op. cit.
82. *Bangabashi*, 21 March 1891, *RNP*, 1891.
83. Ibid.
84. See Amiya Sen, op. cit.
85. Mentioned in *The Bengalee*, 7 March 1891.
86. *The Bengalee*, 28 February 1891.
87. Ibid., 21 March 1891.
88. *Bangabashi*, 28 March 1891.
89. Ibid.
90. *Dainik O Samachar Chandrika*, 15 January 1891.

91. *Bangabashi*, 25 December 1890.
92. *Dainik O Samachar Chandrika*, 14 January 1891.
93. Ibid., 11 January 1891.
94. Ibid.
95. *The Bengalee*, 25 July 1891.

12

Rebellious Wives and Dysfunctional Marriages

Indian Women's Discourses and Participation in the Debates over Restitution of Conjugal Rights and the Child Marriage Controversy in the 1880s and 1890s*

PADMA ANAGOL

Introduction

A historic landmark in the social legislation of nineteenth-century British India was the Age of Consent Act of 1891, the culmination of the long-drawn debates on restitution of conjugal rights, divorce and child marriage of the 1880s.[1] On 19 March 1891, the Indian Penal Code and the Code of Criminal Procedure were amended so that the Age of Consent for girls was raised from 10 to 12 years making sexual intercourse with unmarried and married girls below 12 years rape and punishable by 10 years' imprisonment or transportation for

*Revised and extended version of Padma Anagol, 'The Age of Consent Act (1891) Reconsidered: Women's Perspectives and Participation in the Child Marriage Controversy in India', *South Asia Research*, vol. 12, no. ii (November 1992): pp. 100–19. The author is grateful to Sage Publications for permission to reprint some sections of the article.

life. According to the well-known reformer and historian of nineteenth-century India, S. Natarajan, this Act was the last measure of reform in India effected by influencing British public opinion, the first measure of reform by which Indian public opinion was aroused, the first time Indian leaders harnessed the potential of the Indian masses, and the first time that politics and reaction were successfully linked.[2] It is, therefore, little wonder that the Age of Consent controversy has become a major case study for social and cultural historians of India.

The historiography on the Age of Consent is impressive. Over a period of 50 years a vast body of scholarly literature has become available on this subject. American cultural historians of the 1960s were eager to point out the importance of social legislation for the emergence of nationalism in modern India. Charles Heimsath, for example, argued that the real importance of the Bill was in terms of the nationalist movement and the popular support won for Hindu orthodoxy; these strands are being re-investigated and re-confirmed in greater detail by the latest scholarly works which use post-colonial and poststructuralist theories.[3] However, the works most pertinent to this study are those that have resulted from the second wave of feminism in the 1970s. This saw a new shift in several disciplines, accentuating the absence of gender as a category in previous scholarship and showing a determination to remedy this through a new treatment of old issues.[4]

Later studies analysed how the category of woman was manipulated as a sign in the cultural contest for legitimation between the colonizer and the colonized, and are valuable additions to modern Indian social history.[5] However, the conspicuous irony about these analyses emanating from 'gender studies' is the scant attention paid to women's perceptions and participation.[6] It is hard to believe that a social reform movement and the by-products of colonialism such as education, access to legal and administrative institutions, new opportunities of travel and the vernacular and English print technology would not have been accessed by women. And this observation throws doubt on the conclusions of post-colonial studies which seem eager to obscure women's agency lest the study of the latter disrupt their preferred programme of homogenizing imperial policies as a relentless and brutal exercise of power over the colonized. Sumit Sarkar has rightly pointed out that the very notion that colonial rule might have provided some good for men or women is masked by Saidian scholarship's insistence on the malevolent nature of imperialism besides repeating the crime of objectifying women by employing them as a site over which to debate the nature of colonial power.[7] Some current studies have shown how there was more reaction than reformist zeal amongst Bengali men during the passing of the Act. Discussing Bengal's reaction over the debates opened by the Phulmonee Dassee case, Tanika Sarkar has demonstrated how Bengali men had effectively forced the creation of a 'state within a state' by insisting that the household space remain a zone of autonomy and self-rule for the Hindu male.[8] If official voices, and reformist and reactionary male discourses are analysed it begs the question: why not women's voices? Surely it is pertinent to ask how did women act or react to a Bill that was meant for their welfare? How did they counter the rising tide of reaction expressed by their menfolk against their empowerment?[9] Was there a movement of self-assertion building in certain parts of India among women which could have threatened Indian men into reacting against the onslaught on their hold of patriarchal practices?

This study attempts to answer some of these questions. It addresses the problem of the invisibility of women in Indian history by charting the growth of feminist consciousness among the *bhaginivarg* (sisterhood) in Maharashtra on the issue of marital reforms. More significantly, the oppositional discourse created by women is contrasted with that of the dominant male discourses, highlighting the differences between them. In the first section of this article the focus is on the origins of consciousness among women on the issue of child marriage in contrast to the discourse of the state and Indian men. The popular participation of women in the agitation against child marriage and their lobbying techniques for legislation to raise the Age of Consent are the focus of the discussion in the second section.

Birth of Indian Feminism: Nineteenth-century Maharashtra

Indian feminism grew out of the women's movements of the late nineteenth century, reaching full maturity in the early twentieth century.

Indian women's subjectivities were forged within the context of colonialism; and they had a choice now, of selecting from a wide array of discourses on tradition and modernity. The rise of feminism in India was made possible through a combination of factors: the presence of a colonial economy, the opportunities thrown up by the social reform movement which allowed for a re-questioning of Hinduism and presented new choices of religion such as Christianity and the hope of forming new sects and cults, and the new web of modernizing impulses, which interacted with the contending circumstances and criteria of sex, race, status, class, caste and religion.[10] In western India women chose and applied gendered critiques to the older religion and some embraced conversion to other religions such as Christianity as a way of expressing their discontent with Hinduism's misogynist view of womanhood whilst others remained within it. Christian feminists had made a clean break with the Indian past by rejecting Hinduism on the basis of a gendered approach to religion. They had fruitfully applied the 'welfare' and 'mission' rhetoric of Christianity to assert themselves in breaking with traditional roles and legitimating their entry into public professional roles. Their refusal to belong to any one church as well as their rejection of clerical mediation along with funding from non-Indian sources had given them autonomy to create a unique brand of Indian feminism and also provide leadership to the women's movement.[11] However, Christian feminist leaders were able to sustain women's interests only as long as the active phase of the reform movement lasted. Their alignment to mission Christianity, which at this time equated Christianity with civilizing values and modernizing impulses with the West, meant that they denounced nationalism and its growth. Eventually, it had two effects; firstly, it prevented them from effectively countering the nationalist ideologies of the early twentieth century with new strategies for enrolling women into their movement that had hitherto promised emancipation with conversion. Secondly, it paved the way for the leadership of Ramabai Ranade who in due course marginalized Christian feminists with a takeover of the women's movement.

Although Hindu women questioned Hinduism and Hindu customs and rituals, unlike their Christian counterparts, they did not reject it. This meant working within the structures of Hindu society and its limitations.[12] Several Hindu feminist leaders overcame the hindrances of working within Hindu society through a strategy of assimilation and accommodation. Separate female institution-building programmes by women were to prove to be the vehicle for the movement of Hindu women's embracing of modernity and in the development of the Maharashtrian women's movement. First, it enabled women to mobilize in pursuit of the goal of their own welfare. Secondly, it contributed immensely to the transformation of women's public roles. This was made possible by the astute leadership of the far-sighted women who founded these organizations. Their feminism, which embodied the ability to 'assimilate and accommodate', kept the larger Hindu society's criticism of their programmes to a minimal level.

By the early half of the 1870s, around 50 to 70 women were gathering in the hall of the Prarthana Samaj every Saturday to listen to lectures given by prominent reformers. However, not only did they listen but they also learnt the art of oratory in their own right, leading to the formation of the Striyancha Sabha (Women's Society), in the 1880s.[13] This organization conducted weekly meetings for women only, where educated women would read essays, give public lectures and impart instruction in various subjects to other women. The content of the lectures and essays reveals an overriding desire to combat popular prejudices against female education in Maharashtra,[14] whilst simultaneously making women understand the advantages of learning. By the 1880s, as the movement grew stronger, women in other areas, such as the towns of Dhulia, Poona, Nasik and Solapur, were forming similar groups, and the process of women instructing their fellow women gathered pace. While the women read the glories of ancient Hindu literature, they also read Western literary, philosophical and explicitly feminist texts that dealt with the position of women with Kashibai Kanitkar, Rakhmabai, Anandibai Joshi and Ramabai Ranade revealing their admiration for and the influence on them of the writings of George Eliot, Jane Austen and Mill's *Subjection of Women*. The rise of new women's institutions emboldened by the new feminist strategies of accommodation and assimilation saw to the mushrooming of Stri Sabhas in various towns.[15]

These women's networks were further strengthened by the transformation of older social events and ceremonies that predated the feminist movement such as the women's ritual known as *halad-kunkum* held mainly in western and southern India, and other social gatherings, such as *kirtans*, where learned men and women delivered sermons from religious books or from ancient myths usually accompanied by musical instruments. These rituals and ceremonies provided a framework, which the women's movement could build on to bring their new message about the need for female education, women's rights to property and inheritance, the evils of child marriage and enforced widowhood to a wider audience too. Female reformers, like Annapurnabai and Ramabai Ranade, now expanded the participants' horizons even further by incorporating educational schemes within them, such as readings, lectures and essay contests.[16]

Greater political capacities began to be expressed by women and this period saw the establishment of the first independent women's organization, the Arya Mahila Samaj,[17] which specifically highlighted women's needs and aspirations. The Arya Mahila Samaj was Pandita Ramabai's brainchild but women like Ramabai Ranade and Kashibai Kanitkar worked hard to popularize it among Hindu women. Furthermore, not only did they carry out door-to-door canvassing in order to persuade women to attend the group's meetings, but also, when Pandita Ramabai departed for England in 1883, they became President of its Poona and its Bombay branches respectively.

Certainly, the issues surrounding *samajik sudharana* (social reform) aroused many shades of opinion amongst women, necessitating an outlet for the expression of their views. An ideal medium for them to communicate with one another was through the mode of print periodicals, which provided a place where they could discuss their problems in 'Letters to the Editor', armed with the knowledge that their identity would be protected and thus solicit solutions from the journal's readers on a variety of gender-related social reform issues. Journals, such as those produced by the 'Women's Press' in Maharashtra, conducted by and for women in the Marathi language, allowed for the development of the notion of bhaginivarg within a larger women's collective.[18] By providing a space where women could freely discuss the issue of social reform and its implications on every aspect of women's lives, including education, domestic economy, religious and national identities, urban versus rural life, the conduct of religious rituals and widowhood, as Susie Tharu and K. Lalita have previously asserted, the 'women's periodicals' were a key instrument in the transformation and progress of the women's movement in India.[19] Indeed, such was the importance of the issue to many of its female readership, that many of the women's journals devoted whole issues to the subject. Even a superficial survey of the Marathi literary scene reveals the enthusiastic entry of women in appreciable numbers: many of them welcoming the 'condition of women' as a moot question posed within the social reform movement, which they adapted and wrote about in their literary ventures. Writing had thus given women the opportunity to *recast themselves* as modern women, rather than being *recast by men*, thus preparing themselves for the rapid changes brought by the colonial world.

The period of the Maharashtrian women's renaissance was between 1860 and 1920 and their writing demonstrates a strong Western influence, as they utilized genres such as essay writing, novels and short stories to disseminate their message of reform. The massive growth in publication during this period gave them new ways of expressing themselves and communicating that had never been open to them before. A strong business sense is not only demonstrated by their awareness of what the market wanted but also reflects their awareness of the value of the work they were producing; indeed, many promising women writers including the 'isolated' Tarabai Shinde held the copyrights to their own works, indicating a much higher level of alertness in business and public ventures.[20] In this area of publishing at least, women were able to assert themselves in a way that would have been unthinkable in the past. Although very different forms, the campaigning journalism of the women's press, the domestic science treatises and the school textbooks are notable, therefore, in demonstrating an increased self-confidence in building a distinct women's identity.

Although more traditional Indian genres, such as the ballad and religious poetry (Bhakti hymns), continued to exist, the new forms allowed women to create 'resistance' literature, in the form of treatises and tracts which used inversion techniques and role reversals to explore gender relations, aimed at suggesting a different, more egalitarian world. Maharashtrian women resorted to a rich vocabulary in the Marathi language to express ideas that are now considered feminist terms and enrich the Indian feminist lexicon with concepts and terms such as the following: bhaginivarg (sisterhood); *strihak* (women's rights); *strivarg* (womankind or womanhood); *strianubhav* (women's experience); *bandhivasan* (bondage); *dasyatva* (slavery); *mokaleek* (independence or freedom); *strijati* (female sex); *purushjati* (male sex); *purusharth* (manliness and masculinity).[21] These phrases occur regularly in the colloquial and formal texts written by Maharashtrian women and the most significant of the magazines within the broader women's press of the time, *Arya Bhagini*, literally uses the concept of *bhagini* (sisters) in its title—a telling sign of the times. The invention of this feminist lexicon reveals the nature of the advanced state of late nineteenth-century feminist thought and speaks volumes regarding the realization of 'selfhood' and the formation of women's subjectivities in western India. An instance of the maturity of the feminist movement in late nineteenth-century India is provided by women's public participation in the Age of Consent debates of the late 1880s and early 1890 to which we will turn shortly.

Dysfunctional Marriages and Women's Recourse to Law Courts

Women's self-authorization programmes were not restricted to writing alone, in fact they spilled over in the public sphere whereby they accessed knowledge of state procedures such as 'petitioning' and law courts in claiming their rights to property, livelihood, remarriage, mobility and custody of children.[22] Analysis of court records proves that the women's movement of the late nineteenth century was advanced enough when we see them utilizing the instruments of colonial economy, especially their recourse to the law courts for restitution of conjugal rights, divorce, separation, maintenance and remarriage.

The problems of dysfunctional marriages had been attended to by women throughout the nineteenth century through recourse to the law courts in the Bombay Presidency. The history of suits for the restitution of conjugal rights in India reveals that women were ready to use British law as a resource to improve their position and assert their rights in marriage. In a pattern, which would be further developed in the late nineteenth century, it also reveals that Indian male recognition of the empowering nature of colonial law for women was quickly followed by successful attempts to check its effectiveness by lobbying the colonial authorities. Restitution of conjugal rights was the only relief offered by British law to all Indian communities in cases of marital disharmony, whether they were Hindus, Muslims, Parsis or any other religious community;[23] suits for the restitution of conjugal rights were unknown in pre-colonial India. Scripture-based Hindu law did not sanction it, although customary laws did incorporate less formal ways of dealing with marital disputes. The concept of restitution of conjugal rights was, in fact, an importation from English Ecclesiastical law. Blackstone's summary of this legal suit in Britain allowed suits for the restitution of conjugal rights to be brought whenever either the husband or the wife was 'guilty of injury or subtraction, or lives separate from the other without any sufficient reason in which case they will be compelled to live together again'.[24] Although the law governing the restitution of conjugal rights was grafted onto the existing Indian Penal Code in the nineteenth century with little modification,[25] the form that it subsequently took in this period was wholly controlled and shaped by Indian interpretations of marital rights and obligations.

For Indian Parsis and Muslims, marriage was regarded as a contract; for Hindus, however, it was a religious union, although it was not a sacrament according to Ecclesiastical law as the Christian tradition defined it, because Hindu men continued to take second and third wives. Furthermore, these ties were not forged between consenting adults as arranged marriages, especially in the period under study; they were often agreements between families, not agreements between the couple themselves. Indeed, the notion of consent often did not arise, as the spouses were usually betrothed as children if not infants. Importing the concept of restitution of conjugal rights and applying it to Hindus was therefore entirely inappropriate; as lawyers and judges continually pointed out during this period, suits for the restitution of conjugal rights did not formally constitute part of any of the major religions in India, despite the fact that all of them did make reference to the broad duties involved in cohabitation and duties. In cases of severe disagreements between couples, the most common practice was for the wife to voluntarily flee to her natal family or be driven to seek their help by the husband. In the 150 case studies conducted for this study, separation had normally already taken place before the cases came up in court, with women often recounting their tales of gratitude to members of their extended families for care and maintenance.[26]

In the mid-nineteenth century, Indian law recognized two kinds of matrimonial suits for the purpose of obtaining conjugal rights. The first was for Restitution of Conjugal Rights (Act XV of 1877, Schedule 11, Article 35), available to both parties, that is, husband and wife. But the second was restricted to the husband claiming the society of his wife, namely recovering his wife from a person harbouring her with ill-intent (Act XV of 1877, Schedule 11, Article 34). Sections 259 and 260 of the Code of Civil Procedure of 1882 provided comprehensive regulations for the execution of decrees of both suits. Section 260 of the revised Code of 1877 provided that if a spouse refused to comply with a decree given in a suit of restitution of conjugal rights then he or she could be dealt with by imprisonment or attachment of property, or both. These decrees interfered extensively with customary law and, in the later nineteenth century, were arbitrarily used against women. Formerly, women could seek the help of the extended family in cases of violence against them by husbands but the wording of Section 259 meant that the extended family could not interfere, especially if the person 'harbouring' her was a distant relative; for example, an uncle instead of a 'parent'. Section 260 also worked against women with a little property in the form of *stridhana*. However, it is a testimony to women's resilience and determination that they increasingly resorted to the first form of suit, restitution of conjugal rights, knowing full well that the husband would rather agree to a maintenance grant than give up the privilege of making polygamous arrangements.

The origin and history of ecclesiastical jurisdiction reveals clearly that suits for restitution of conjugal rights had been entertained from the first introduction of English law in India. Matrimonial disputes amongst the various settlers of Bombay had been frequently brought and uniformly heard in the Supreme Court of Bombay (from 1823 to 1856) and prior to this, the Mayor's Courts (until 1823) that preceded the Supreme Courts. The Recorder's Court of Bombay lists a total of eight cases heard from 1800 to 1856; two involved the Armenian community, five were of Parsis and one concerned a Muslim couple. It is a point worth noting that seven out of the total of eight cases for the restitution of conjugal rights were brought by the wives against their husbands.[27] The wives demanded that the husbands should take them back and treat them with 'conjugal kindness'; if they refused, alimony should be provided to them. In six of a total of seven cases heard in the Recorder's Court of Bombay between 1800 and 1856, the court granted alimony to the wives. This inventory of facts crystallizes the manner in which the British courts were upholding the right of the Indian wife for a maintenance grant in the case of a failed marriage and were holding men to their marital duties. This situation was not to the liking of Indian patriarchs and soon the winds of change were to blow with the rise of Indian lawyers speaking on behalf of their male clients who wished to engage in polygamous relations or keep mistresses without their rebellious wives getting any kind of maintenance from them.

In 1856, the Privy Council was to hear the most celebrated case in the history of the restitution of conjugal rights. This was Ardaseer Cursetjee v. Perozeboye, a dispute between a Parsi couple from Bombay. Ardaseer's astute Indian lawyer brought a suit challenging Ecclesiastical jurisdiction over Indians.[28] The set of arguments proposed by the Bar in London reveals a great sensitivity towards safeguarding the rights of Indian women. A point in case is the set of arguments used in defence of the wife, Perozeboye, by Charles Jackson. He argued against exercising Ecclesiastical jurisdiction over Hindus, Muslims and Parsis and for suits to reinstate conjugal rights amongst Indians to be refused. However, he also argued that women should have access to legal remedy in cases of gross marital neglect by husbands by adapting the law of alimony. He further demonstrated that wives and husbands could not be forced to cohabit as the notion was anomalous to Asian marriage laws; furthermore, it was only Christian marriages that treated the woman as part of the man (Canon law considered a man and his wife as one person), thus meaning that the case could only be dealt with by Ecclesiastical courts and not by the civil courts. In India, no such principle existed in either Islamic, Hindu or Zoroastrian laws, meaning, he argued, that in such instances 'Native married women are *femme soles* and the Supreme Court at Calcutta treat them so'.[29] According to this reasoning, Ardaseer was guilty on three counts, of having forcibly evicted his wife from the house, refusing to take her back and having failed to maintain her—all these facts of abandonment and cruelty meant that there was nothing 'to prevent his wife from bringing an action against her husband for damages, or a suit for a maintenance past and present'.[30]

The force and conviction of these arguments was enshrined in the final judgement given by the Right Hon. Lushington of the Privy Council who upheld Jackson's argument that the courts in India, on the Ecclesiastical side, should not entertain such suits, but that the British state was obliged to provide legal remedies to subjects in suits arising in matrimonial matters; Perozeboye was therefore directed to apply for adequate relief in a civil court against her husband. Two facts emerge forcefully in this history of the legislation on the restitution of conjugal rights that were to have far-reaching implications and consequences. Early nineteenth-century cases show that suits for restitution were brought by wives against neglectful and cruel husbands in the hope that, if they were not taken back, at least the court would grant them maintenance rights. In the precedent created by the Ardaseer case, we also find that British legal experts were reluctant to apply Ecclesiastical laws to the Indian situation; moreover, the gendered arguments also reveal their anxiety to create safeguards for the protection for married Indian women. Since marriage in India was deemed more a contract than a sacrament, wives were encouraged to apply on the Equity side of Ecclesiastical Courts for maintenance and alimony from uncaring husbands. After this groundbreaking case, in which the Privy Council ruled that Ecclesiastical law could not be strictly applied to non-Christian suits for restitution of conjugal rights, these cases increasingly came to be entertained on the civil side of the courts in India. The early history of conjugal relations, especially case law as it emerges in modern India, demonstrates that it is difficult to sustain the view that 'English law was an instrument of oppression'.[31]

Instead, the argument here is that, in the late nineteenth century, English law as interpreted by Indian legal scholars and reformers becomes a tool for oppressing women and was a creation of Indian male agents with little assistance from their British counterparts who were mostly pressurized by the 'trial' of Indian newspapers into consenting to Indian orthodox opinion. Firstly, the Privy Council judgement that Indian marriages were more contractual than sacramental in character was turned on its head by Indian legal experts, who argued the reverse; that Hindu unions were religious and hence sacraments and it was actually Christian ones which were more contractual in nature. Following this new definition of Hindu marriages, the Privy Council's understanding and ruling of Indian wives' status as *feme soles* was overturned by conservative Indians who re-defined the position of Indian wives as *feme covert* and bound the Hindu woman in the person of the

Hindu male (i.e., her husband). Secondly, the early law enshrined in Privy Council rulings had instituted restitution of conjugal rights as a marital remedy to 'protect' the 'rights' of wives. By subverting the emphasis onto 'duties' of wives in the later nineteenth century, Indian elites overturned the implications of this legal remedy especially in the Rakhmabai case. Originally acting as a force for the empowerment of Indian women, British law was manipulated by Indian male elites who successfully contrived to turn it into a source of women's oppression.

In the nineteenth century, considerable obstacles stood in the way of women attempting to redress marital injustices. Ill-treated and abandoned wives fortunate enough to have the support of parents or the extended family looked to the civil courts to intervene and resolve marital disputes. As divorce was disallowed under the British interpretation of Hindu law, women resorted to the strategy of seeking the dissolution of their marriages on technical points of law. For example, a suit by a Hindu mother, as the guardian of her infant daughter, in favour of a declaration that the alleged marriage of the daughter with the defendant was null and void, was held to be a suit of a civil nature and was adjudicated upon.[32] Similarly, there were attempts to set aside marriages which had already taken place, on various grounds, for reasons such as the bride having been given away by her mother and not her father or by her stepmother when her paternal grandmother was alive, or having been married to a person belonging to a different caste, or her husband marrying a second wife, having previously agreed that if such a marriage occurred, the first marriage should be considered dissolved.[33] Non-Brahmin wives also sought divorce, but due to the operation of the colonial re-interpretation of Hindu law, it was increasingly difficult for women to exercise this option.

If we judge by statistics alone, the cases which annually came before the civil courts in the Bombay Presidency (including subordinate, district and high courts) between 1881 and 1885 consisted of 727 suits for enforcing decrees for the restitution of conjugal rights and 81 suits for the dissolution of marriages. The latter were usually between Christian husbands and wives, while the former involved Hindus and Muslims. Not all of these suits were by deserted wives seeking legal remedies to their dysfunctional marriages. Guardians and parents of young girl-wives brought quite a few of these cases to the court in their anxiety to protect them; presumably they followed the technical route described in the previous paragraph.

Given the factors that militated against women seeking legal redress, it is surprising that so many cases came to court. Achieving a remedy through civil courts was not a popular method, especially for women who had very few resources or did not know that Act XV, Schedule II, of 1877 provided an unwilling wife the option of serving six months' imprisonment in a civil jail instead of acquiescing to her conjugal duties. Mahipatram Rupram, a district judge, recorded that *vakils* (pleaders) never provided this vital information to female clients, despite the fact that they were forfeiting at least one source of income.[34] Furthermore, Rupram shows how it was only the wide publicity given to the Dadaji *vs.* Rakhmabai case in the vernacular newspapers that alerted the public in the remoter parts of Maharashtra to the fact that a wife could actually choose imprisonment in preference to the company of her husband. The anxiety of Indian male lawyers to restrict women's access to knowledge that could potentially have empowered them speaks volumes of their fear of women undertaking independent action. It is also an indicator of their desire to maintain the status quo that privileged men by containing the legitimate claims of rebellious wives in a society where the traditional power networks were being eroded as the colonial courts grew in influence. A by-product of this was the empowerment of women, who increasingly sought the British law courts which were determined to uphold the popular perception that the Raj stood for the 'rule of law' and justice. It was precisely the Maharashtrian women's acts of assertion that led to a backlash from the indigenous male population.

An interesting trend in the assertive acts of women is that many female clients preferred to use the criminal courts, as they were less expensive and more effective than the civil courts. Maharashtrian wives were also aware of the fact that, even if they applied for restitution of conjugal rights and won the case, the civil courts could not, in a practical sense, enforce their decree. By practising polygamy, a husband could always informally defy court orders by taking new wives and ignoring or maltreating his previous wife.[35] In their replies to the government regarding changing the laws that governed suits over the restitution of conjugal right and separation, Mahipatram Rupram and

M.G. Ranade pointed out that even illiterate women knew they could obtain payments as alimony from their husbands by applying to a magistrate;[36] moreover, many of these applications were likely to be successful. Between 1881 and 1885, a total of 2,874 wives brought cases against their husbands before the criminal courts of the Bombay Presidency, demanding redress in the form of maintenance payments for the ill-treatment they had suffered. Without doubt, one can say that 2,874 cases in four years reflects on the dysfunctionality of Indian marriage arrangements.

Not all of the suits quoted above were brought by adult wives; some of the cases were lodged by the parents of neglected child-wives. The statistics were compiled by M.G. Ranade, a celebrated social reformer and seasoned legal expert, who argued that 'the large majority of the cases under chapter thirty-six are undoubtedly due to the neglect of marital duties by husbands towards their wives'.[37] He uncovered considerable evidence of women's dissatisfaction with contemporary marriage laws; moreover, he recognized that they were not inclined to see the status quo continue, especially when they perceived the Raj as a good government that looked after its subjects irrespective of gender. Ranade's close observations and his everyday interactions in the courts led him to become a prominent advocate of divorce, although he stood alone and unsupported by his fellow-reformers.

Given indigenous and colonialist constructions of the Indian woman as passive, even a few isolated cases of women resorting to the courts would be highly significant. Yet the statistics on matrimonial disputes are considerably higher. If we combine civil and criminal cases, thousands of women every year sought legal redress to improve the quality of their domestic lives in the Bombay Presidency. Contemporary Indian men were quick to realize the subversive nature and veiled implications of the assertive acts of women. When we understand the constraints on women actually bringing a case to court, it is clear that Indian women were resisting a system of marriage that perpetuated maladjusted conjugal unions; in other words, what we witness during this period amounts to a great rebellion of wives against ill-treatment or abandonment. By signalling autonomy and self-determination, women's actions led to the resident patriarchs of nineteenth-century India formulating a formidable and negative response persuading us to seek explanations within Indian societal structures rather than viewing it as simply a tussle between metropolitan claims of unreserved masculinity versus Bengali effeminacy as some scholars have suggested.[38] The significance of this wives' rebellion needs to be understood if we are to properly assess the nature of debates set off by the Rakhmabai and Age of Consent controversy.

Counter Discourses of Women on Child Marriage

If Indian wives were quietly exercising their rights in the courts to maintenance and alimony in cases where there was gross neglect of conjugal duties by husbands, as a result of the national publicity over what became known as the 'Rakhmabai case', the 1880s were to bring changes in the marital remedies available to warring couples. For good reasons, the Rakhmabai case became one of the most publicized legal disputes of the later nineteenth century, and it was to have far-reaching consequences. Out of the contentious debates over the restitution of conjugal rights and divorce in the Rakhmabai case, there arose the greatest social reform issue of the nineteenth century, the child marriage controversy.

Unlike Indian men, who were aroused on a mass scale by the publication of 'Notes on infant marriage and enforced widowhood' in August 1884 by Behramji Malabari, a Parsi journalist and reformer from Bombay, the first signs of the bhaginivarg or women's collective coming together is discernible during the Rakhmabai-Dadaji episode. Rakhmabai, a product of the emerging women's movement in Maharashtra, was the daughter of Jayantibai and Janardhan Pandurang. She became an heiress to a modest fortune from her natural father, Janardhan Pandurang, on the remarriage of her mother, Jayantibai, to Dr Sakharam Arjun, an eminent surgeon and well-known reformer of Bombay.[39] In 1884 Dadaji Bhikaji filed a suit for the restitution of conjugal rights in the Bombay High Court. He was married when he was 20 to Rakhmabai, who was then 11 years old. The marriage was not consummated as Rakhmabai reached puberty in her mother's home at a much later age, by which time the marriage had broken down irrevocably. Dadaji's contention was that his in-laws coveted Rakhmabai's inheritance and had therefore contrived to keep the spouses apart.[40] Considering the facts that her stepfather and mother had independent means of income and were wealthy and that Dadaji himself had not bothered to claim marital rights for over 15 years, neither of his contentions were convincing. Rakhmabai's narrative of events differed dramatically from her husband's. She claimed that it was Dadaji's inability to earn an honest livelihood, his immoral lifestyle, his refusal to educate himself and his ill-health (he was in the intermediary stage of tuberculosis) which prevented her from living with him.[41]

She also explained the various occasions on which her acute aversion towards him had been formed:

> He abused my relatives including my mother in language, which was shameful. He set at defiance the efforts made by my father and grandfather to educate him and took to ways which a woman's lips cannot utter. Mr Dadajee went through every course of dissipation till my aversion for him was firmly settled.[42]

Significantly, Rakhmabai did not stress the factor of incompatibility which other Maharashtrian women were utilizing as an instrument in negotiating more rational marital arrangements, but instead placed her emphasis on complaints that an average traditional Hindu family could relate to, such as the life-chances of a bridegroom and his economic prospects. She pointed out that even a caste panchayat would agree, on the basis of textual precepts, that a man had to provide for his wife in order to claim her person because Hindu marriages were *contractual* in nature as the arrangement had been made between the family elders rather than by her as a child-bride or Dadaji as a young groom. An interesting shift in the male debates on Hindu tradition was the highly selective process of picking up those points of objection from Rakhmabai's statements that diverted the debate from the *duties of a husband* to that of the *duties of a wife* and inverting her statement that her marriage was more *contractual* in character than *sacramental*.[43] The case took four years for a final resolution through two legal suits.[44] In the second suit the ambivalence in the judicial discourse was evident when, accommodating the massive reaction that had been expressed in the media, the court ruled that Rakhmabai would have to face imprisonment if she refused to fulfil her wifely duties.[45] Rakhmabai chose imprisonment rather than live with her husband.[46] Her defiant act was publicized by the astute nationalist B.G. Tilak and other conservatives as showing the evil consequences of an English education, and was coupled with the sensational cry of 'Hinduism in danger'.[47]

The case of Rakhmabai was intricately interwoven with the Age of Consent debates. The question of the consummation of marriage was of material importance to the restitution of conjugal rights. The ecclesiastical laws in English courts did not, as a rule, order a wife to go back to her husband when the marriage had never been consummated. However, in the case of Rakhmabai, this was overruled by citing the custom of infant marriage in India whereby the girl-bride remained in her natal home until puberty when she was handed over to her husband's family in fulfilment of her marital obligations.[48] In this sense the second verdict was the state's recognition of the cultural laws that governed Hindus, but the colonial government's retraction was read by feminists as a devious alliance between the imperial state and the Indian male. Expressing her disappointment, Pandita Ramabai wrote, 'They (the government) have promised to please the males of country at the cost of women's rights.'[49] On the other hand, Rakhmabai's defiance of the court order was understood by Maharashtrian orthodoxy as an educated women's refusal to abide by the time-honoured Hindu tradition of remaining under her husband's protection.[50]

Between June and September 1885, Rakhmabai published a series of letters in the *Times of India*, on the subjects of infant marriage and enforced widowhood, under the pseudonym of 'The Hindu Lady'.[51] Her letters sparked a major conflagration among all sections of Maharashtrian society and were discussed minutely in the newspapers (including the women's press) right up to the end of 1885. Following the controversial Dadaji *vs.* Rakhamabai case, the Government of India considered amending Section 260 of Article 14 of the Code of Civil Procedure of 1882 in so far as its provisions related to the execution of decrees for the restitution of conjugal rights and divorce. Leading Indian judges and administrators were requested to give their opinions, while no woman, however prominent was consulted on an issue that so directly concerned women's well-being.[52] Nevertheless, Maharashtrian women voiced their opinions through their own press, through literary writings and letters in the Anglo-Indian press, and by enlisting the support of British feminists. Rakhmabai followed closely the reaction to Malabari's 'Notes', which prompted her to express not only her own personal views but also the perspectives of the bhaginivarg or the women's organizations she was part of at the time. While acknowledgeing the gratitude of Indian women to Malabari for his exertions, she constructed a gendered critique of child marriage startlingly different from that of Malabari.

In her first letter Rakhmabai wrote that child marriage had ruined her life:

> I am one of those unfortunate Hindu women, whose hard lot it is to suffer the unnameable miseries entailed by the custom of early marriage. This wicked practice has destroyed the happiness of my life.[53]

Her observations were also drawn from the lives of female friends, thus formulating general propositions based on the combined experiences of women. She began her analysis with the statement that the institution of child marriage cut across caste and class considerations and adversely affected all age and sex groups, but 'women', she concluded, were its 'greatest victims'.[54]

Infant marriage, according to women, was the most persistent obstacle to the psychological development of the female sex, stultifying a women's personality through the denial of higher education. The issue of female literacy preoccupied the attention of Maharashtrian women throughout the second half of the nineteenth century. The need for and nature of education, and the obstacles to its achievement were such an integral part of women's consciousness that it ended in splitting them into two groups—traditionalists and moderates—according to the ideology they professed.[55] However, the relevant strand for discussion here is: why was child marriage viewed as the greatest hurdle in the mental development of the female sex? Women believed that the structure of Indian marital relationships based on clan, caste and kin cramped the physical space and liberty of expression of women.

Giving graphic details of the lifestyle of a girl before and after marriage, Rakhmabai drew an accurate picture of how the imposition of a code of behaviour, forms of women's speech and a strictly regimented life, robbed the girl-wife of all incentive to develop individuality. In her opinion, control through the hierarchical relationships of the in-laws' home aimed, 'to make the girl as docile as a beast and as submissive as a slave'.[56] If the girl was married at the age of seven or eight the domestic code actively cajoled her to please rather than displease, to agree rather than disagree and divest her speech and thinking processes from the use of argument and dialogue. Writing about how she became aware of *stri-sudharana* (improvement in the position of women), a prominent feminist leader from Amravati, Yashodabai Joshi, recalls the oppressive atmosphere of her in-laws' home which she refers to as 'just plain slavery'.[57] The control exercised by in-laws was so absolute that without their permission not even a pre-pubescent girl-wife residing at her parent's home could go to school.

This belief reverberates in numerous letters to the editors of women's magazines, besides the memoirs and semi-fictional writings of women written during the late nineteenth century.[58] Contrasting the picture of a girl-wife with that of a boy-husband, Rakhmabai further noted that child-marriages 'do not entail on men half the difficulties which they entail upon women'.[59] According to her, men enjoyed full marital and physical freedom, and religion and custom did not interfere in any way with their liberty. In her opinion:

> Marriage does not interpose any insuperable obstacles in the course of their studies. They marry not only a second wife, on the death of the first, but have the right of marrying any number of wives at one and the same time, or any time they please. If married early, they are not called upon to go and submit to the tender mercies of a mother-in-law; nor is any restraint put upon their actions because of their marriage. But the case for women is the very reverse of this.[60]

Men, she argued, protected the interests of a male child, whether it was over the right to education or remarriage, and actively connived in prohibiting the mental development of women. Unlike the modernizing discourses of liberal men who argued that the education of women would gradually lead to the abolition of child marriage, women argued, to the contrary, that it was precisely the institution of child marriage which placed obstacles in the way of female literacy.

If we turn to the male liberal discourse on the Age of Consent issue, a totally different picture emerges. In the 'Notes' circulated by Malabari, he constructs a powerful picture of Indian society, characterized by incapacitated adults, sickly children, over-population, and acute poverty leading to epidemics. The consequences of child marriage in his view were:

> The breaking down of constitutions and the ushering in of disease. The giving up of studies on the part of the boy-husband, the birth of sickly children, the necessity of feeding too many mouths, poverty and dependence. . . .[61]

He insisted that the state had to address the question of child marriage on the purely economic grounds of 'over-population in poverty'. Eugenics and public health were powerful strands of argument in such indigenous discourse as seen in attempts to reform cultural practices. Management of the nation's health was an integral part of liberal discourse on child marriage as early as the 1890s, and the 1920s debates over the Age of Consent simply re-opened debates built on this strong tradition, contrary to what some scholars have suggested in their works.[62] M.G. Ranade, an influential reformer and a feminist, preferred to argue for legislation mainly on the grounds of checking the reproduction of a weak race and hence the economic ruin of India. He argued that early marriage led to premature consummation and resulted in the physical deterioration of the race; it diverted the attention of youths from their studies, checked enterprise and filled the country with weaklings bred of over-population.[63] He also argued for state interference on the ground that Indians were incapable of self-help due to their bondage to the past.

What is of significance to the discussion here is the singular absence in the indigenous male discourse of a gendered critique for the raising of the Age of Consent. It could be argued that elites of progressive opinion used public health arguments as a tactical move especially in cases such as M.G. Ranade, a sympathizer and friend of the women's movement in Maharashtra, in order to manoeuvre the state into overcoming its promise of non-interference in domestic matters. However, opinions expressed by liberals on other vital questions of women's education used the same 'rejuvenation of the race' theories. Dr Kirtikar, President of the Pathare Prabhu Reform Society, for example, argued in several lectures that the only reason why a woman was entitled to education was because she was the 'mother of the Indian race', and hence had to have a good knowledge of health and hygiene in order to raise strong and healthy children.[64]

The failure to admit gender inequalities is blatantly exposed by another trend in Indian liberal discourse. Liberals and conservatives alike argued that women themselves were active proponents of the institution of child marriage and opposed all reform. An Inamdar of Dharwar, Tirmal Rao Venkatesh, skilfully drew a picture of the origins of infant marriage as a recent phenomenon, owing entirely to the 'whims of females, belonging to rich families, who not only put up, but compel their male members to bring about infant marriages', simply as he put it, for the sake of enjoying the fun and pleasure of going through the ceremonies attendant upon such marriages.[65] However, it was the non-interventionists or 'reform from within' group, who successfully framed women as the chief culprits. The gist of their arguments was that women in India were conservative by nature, that they imbibed the claptrap of Hindu tradition more effectively than men, first in their parents' and subsequently in their in-laws' home, and that by the time they reached middle age they personified orthodoxy itself. Therefore, legislation would make no difference and child marriage would only disappear with modernization.[66] It would be no exaggeration to conclude here that women were fighting a dual battle—one was to stem the anti-legislationist arguments of their own menfolk and the other was to convince the state of the need for such social legislation.

In contrast to this discourse stood women's own views. They agreed that many women did block reforms but, by studying the conservative attitudes of women, they concluded that centuries of conditioning brought on by man-made shastras could not be wiped out in a few years. Reform-minded women were consistent in their opinion that Hindu men jealously guarded their rights through the connivance of Brahmanical priests. As Krupabai put it: 'Men treated women as mere appendices to their own great selves'; an educated bride was also by no means welcome to a man because, 'The fact of his wife being in any way above him will be gall wormwood to his inflated, self-satisfied nature.'[67] This male conspiracy, she contended, led to the situation where:

> a majority of our women resort to the most pernicious habit of gossiping about their neighbours, and quarrelling among themselves. Poor souls! They are not to be blamed; they know of no higher mode of existence;

> there is nothing to occupy their minds, no interest is taken in them: they are treated as toys and humoured with gilded trinkets or any such trifles.[68]

How did women react to this situation? Krupabai maintained that women are born and brought up to think themselves inferior, and they finally learnt to extract pleasure from housekeeping and dressing up.[69] Even though women were inured to their pitiful existence, she argued for the abolition of infant marriages altogether as the only way women could in practice share men's freedom and rights.[70] Rakhmabai summed up this view when she wrote: 'Reduced to this state of degradation by the dictum of the shastras, looked down upon for ages by men, we have naturally come to look down upon ourselves.'[71]

Women, therefore, pleaded that state intervention was not just desirable but essential. They believed that abolition of child-marriage would enable them to take advantage of higher education and that this would restore a necessary sense of dignity and pride in women's ability to plead their own cause.

A significant trend in the women's literature of the time entailed a proposed restructuring of the institution of marriage. Thus arose an analysis of 'why' and 'how' the Hindu marriage system maintained such absurd customs as infant and child-marriage. The reasons proposed by them were radically different from those of Indian men. There was no engagement with shastric injunctions on the primacy of the marriage consummation ceremony or *garbhadana* (literally, 'gift of the womb') which characterized the arguments of the indigenous male sections. Instead, they traced child marriage to the financial considerations of the boy's parents, the anxiety of the girl child's parents due to the low status accorded to the female sex, and the psychological need for a woman to be a mother-in-law in order to gain access to power in a Hindu joint family.

Taking up the issue of monetary transactions during marriages, they condemned the system of *hunda* (dowry) as the main reason why parents of male children succumbed to the institution of child marriage. Parents of female children constantly worried about them and were in the habit of sounding out the marriage negotiator who was either the family priest or a close relative. The latter found a suitable groom; the prospects of finding a better groom were relatively dependent on the size of the dowry. The anxiety of parents about a girl remaining unmarried led them to marry her off early or, if poor, they would wed their daughters to widowers, forcing them to become second or third wives to elderly men.[72] Women empathized with a girl child's status within a household which led them to view women who promoted child marriage with a degree of tolerance. Many women held the opinion that a girl-wife did not enter her husband's house to be the sole mistress but as the lowest in the hierarchy of family members and occupied the humblest position. The only way a woman could exercise any power was to bear sons and arrange their marriages as soon as possible in order to reach the exalted status of the mother-in-law.[73] Moving away from the utilization of the shastras in their arguments for the abolition of infant marriages and raising the Age of Consent was the single most radical stand taken by women during the Age of Consent controversy and whilst it marks the maturity of their feminism it also stands starkly in contrast to male discourses which fell back on the use of shastras whether the males in question were reformist or reactionaries in their perceptions of this question.

Another strand in women's arguments was their insistence that raising the age of marriage for girls alone would not be effective in practice: the age of consent for boys had to be raised too. This argument centred round the inability of a young husband to face the wrath of the conservative members of his family even as he bravely encouraged the education of his girl-wife. Personal narratives and the biographical and semi-fictional writings of women discusses the economic dependence of youthful husbands on their extended family and how these ties effectively prevented them from protecting their wives' efforts to educate themselves.[74] Autobiographical accounts of women who participated in the Age of Consent agitation clearly reflect how women were left to their own devices in countering the opposition of in-laws without the support of their husbands. Ramabai Ranade recalled in an autobiography which became a classic of Marathi literature, how- about 14 widowed aunts, cousins, and a sister-in-law, along with her step-mother-in-law in the vanguard, formed an orthodox camp within the household to torment her when she persisted in educating herself.[75] Their allegations that she was neglecting her household duties were unjustified as she rose at dawn in order to make time for her education. It was the unanimous view of women writing on this subject that, in the face of such formidable circumstances, only a very few courageous young women would continue to educate themselves. If, instead, girls were married after the age of 14, they would benefit from the extra time within their parents' home and their chances of a higher education would be greatly increased.

The indifference of Indian men to the suffering the female sex endured on account of child-marriage was angrily noted by women. Writing in Marathi journals, women expressed their shock and disgust at the cowardice of men in facing reality. Their studied discourtesy and contempt for 'reformers' correspondingly forms an important factor in women's implicit belief in the efficacy of the colonial government. After the replies of leading men to Malabari's proposals had been published, women wrote at length expressing their annoyance, not at the 'opinions of the old-fashioned, credulous and religious older generation', which they felt were comprehensible, but at the opinions of young learned men who aped modern ideas only as far as dress and diet were concerned while they were actually worse than conservative people in their views.[76] The reference here was to the 'reform from within' group who opposed legislation. Among women a special phrase had been coined for hypocritical reformers—*Potepurte sikhalele lok* (literally, those who gain a Western education not for self-improvement but merely to look after their stomachs).[77] 'Sati', argued one woman, would never have been abolished, left to the Indians, but was the greatest favour done by the British government, saving thousands of lives of women from the agonies of the fire.[78] She, and others like her, urged the government to show the same firmness of conviction over the Age of Consent issue.

When we consider whether or not male reformers advocated state intervention it is enlightening to allude to Tarabai Shinde's emphatic invective: to her all social reform societies were 'fake' and the work of male reformers as much use as a 'spare tit on a goat'.[79] It is remarkable that although considered a pioneer of women's rights in western India, even the modernizing Malabari did not support social legislation at first. In the 'Notes' circulated in 1884, Malabari did not invoke the aid of the legislature on the issue of child marriage except in a benign form. He proposed a system of incentives and disincentives to be offered by the government that would include suggestions such as 'no married [male] student shall be eligible to go up for University examinations, five years hence', and the public sector 'may prefer the unmarried to the married, all other qualifications being equal'.[80] Given the absence of divorce, women argued that there were many extenuating reasons explaining why wives deserted their husbands, or committed suicide or homicide. Even though, with good reason, women hesitated about writing explicitly on the subject of divorce, the statistical analysis of the previous section reveals that many abandoned or neglected wives sought separation and maintenance for themselves and their children. In marked contrast to Malabari's proposals, Rakhmabai recommended divorce as the primary means of resolving domestic tensions within a marriage that had broken down irrevocably.[81] At the height of conservative reaction from indigenous quarters, Indian women advocated some radical measures that represented a potential revolution in Indian conjugal affairs. Indian women's valorization of the achievements of colonial benevolence should not be read as a simplistic admiration for an alien government but stemmed from their observations that their own menfolk held in the thraldom of the Indian past would not move forward to share the benefits of British rule with the members of the other sex.

A solidarity between Hindu, Christian and Jewish Indian women is discernible over the Rakhmabai case and the Age of Consent controversy. These episodes also provided the first instances when British feminists successfully allied with Indian women. The uniting ground was the realization that it was the rights of women that were at the heart of the debate, rather than a tussle between traditionalists and reformists, native and English masculinity, and Western and Eastern religion as the rhetoric used by the Indian men seemed to imply. Maharashtrian women enlisted the support of British feminists both for guidance as well as to mobilize strength for propaganda purposes. It has been argued that in the nineteenth century European medical men were effectively performing the function of maintaining the image of the physical and moral superiority of the ruling race.[82] Their counterparts, the imperial medical women, were also, in effect, performing a similar function. Much of the medical evidence cited by Indian women in support of the agitation came from European female doctors who gave lectures on eugenic theories of weak and sterile populations issuing from the Indian race due to the ill effects of child marriage.[83] At Rakhmabai's request, Dr Edith Pechey-Phipson, a prominent doctor in charge of several hospitals in Bombay and one of the celebrated pioneers of the medical education campaign for women in Britain, assumed leadership of this movement and along with a few influential Indian women they formed 'The Hindu Lady Fund' to raise Rs 5,000 for costs incurred by Rakhmabai over the second suit.[84] Pandita Ramabai launched a scathing attack on the government's inertia, through letters and articles in influential newspapers while the Indian National Association publicized her case in England. Rakhmabai struck up a longstanding friendship with British feminists who eventually helped her to leave India in March 1889 to pursue a medical education in London.[85] Indian women's reliance on imperial feminists significantly reflects their loss of faith in Indian men.

Conjugal Incompatibility and Child Marriage

One of the prime concerns of women in their programme of restructuring Hindu marriage relations arose from their analysis of the unhappiness of Indian wives within the system of arranged marriages and the absence of choice of partners. They linked wives' discontent to the prevalent institution of child marriage. Malabari had made a fleeting reference in his 'Notes' to unhappy unions in Indian marriages due to child marriage, though he did not go on to argue that the government should intervene on this ground. The replies of eminent men whose opinion was solicited to his 'Notes' were silent on this issue, except for the well-known reformer R.G. Bhandarkar, who insisted that there were no 'ill-assorted marriages' in India.[86] Liberal discourse did not wish to publicly acknowledge the existence of unhappiness in child marriages.

We should turn for a moment to the women's views to see whether they considered incompatibility and ill-treatment to be the main effects of child marriage and, if so, what remedies they proposed. Among women there was a unanimity of opinion about child and arranged marriages creating tensions between couples. There was no genuine affection between a husband and wife in India, wrote a woman to *Arya Bhagini*, because both were too young to know the meaning of love and merely accepted a mechanical imposition of the duties and obligations on them.[87] Gulabbai recalled what a farce her whole marriage was to her:

> When I was 11 years old I was married to my husband who was then 13 years of age. When they sent me to my in-laws, I remember crying my heart out the whole day. He used to go to school and to me it appeared he was making merry the whole day and when he returned home he was immersed in play with his friends. We started to live together with the fact thrown upon us that 'he is a husband and I am a wife', there was nothing beyond this. . . . What happiness can one see in such a relationship.[88]

Many women wrote about the bewilderment that a young girl experienced with the onset of puberty and the sudden enforcement of sexual duties. The mental immaturity of the girl-wife, they argued, built up resentment within her and allowed conjugal strife to set in.[89] Incompatibility was usually a result of child marriage, wrote Girijabai in a compilation of her essays and lectures. The girl-wife's immaturity created a barrier to communication between them and her husband (who was usually older than her) could not rationally convince her of anything that he considered important. For this reason alone she stood for restraining girls below 14 and men below 20 from marrying.[90]

If a union of minds was unlikely in this set-up then what was the solution? Instead of child marriage, women showed a strong preference for adult marriages and choice of partners rather than arranged marriages. They attributed domestic strife to the discontent and unhappiness of young wives, and came up with the radical suggestion that choosing a spouse should not be men's prerogative alone but that women should be consulted too.[91] This was the main reason why *swayamvar* (the ceremony by which a woman chose her spouse in an open competition between male suitors and supposed to have been in vogue in ancient India) was enthusiastically proposed, rather than as a cultural defence, as was the case with revivalist and nationalist discourse. The 'golden age' theories were utilised in more skilful and complex ways in women's emancipatory programmes than has been understood by contemporary scholarship.[92]

The Marathi journal *Masik Manoranjan* interviewed various prominent Maharashtrian women activists who had participated in the Age of Consent agitation. Among these, it is worth discussing the views of Kashibai Kanitkar who was an important member of the Arya Mahila Samaj and a highly regarded author in the Marathi literary scene of the late nineteenth century. She is reported to have said that 99 per cent of marriages were unhappy ones, but that the degree of unhappiness could be considerably reduced by raising the Age of Consent. According to her if human beings were married at a very young age they would later on say, 'I was deceived, I was cheated', and rebel against the marriage bond.[93] Her opinion was that no girl should be below 14 and no boy below 20 at the time of marriage, and that both sexes should have the freedom to choose their partners so that in the event of a breakdown in their marriage, 'they will not point fingers at others but at themselves'.[94] Her argument was that the responsibility in such a vital issue as marriage should be shouldered by adults alone rather than by children.

Women were acutely aware of the romantic notion of Indian womanhood propagated by Orientalist and revivalist discourse, but contested it strongly. The *Subodh Patrika*, the official organ of the Prarthana Samaj, reported the views of the famous Indologist, Max Müller, on the issue of child-marriage. At the height of the agitation, he had idealized Indian marriages, believing that love and affection were generated in infant marriages through the mere fact of the child-spouses growing up together in one home. Thus he implicitly endorsed the idea that domestic harmony reigned in arranged marriages. The growing women's collective, the bhaginivarg, took him to task by writing to the women's press disputing his findings. The editor of the women's magazine *Arya Bhagini* criticized him for his lack of firsthand experience of India and his excessive reliance on a textual knowledge of the East thus:

> Max Muller saheb is living in a foreign country and will do so forever. He has no first-hand knowledge of an average Indian nor of the behaviour and conduct of our men. Therefore the statements made by the saheb are not uniformly applicable to everyone of us. Among cases of child marriage only around four or five couples out of a hundred live in a state of mutual love and harmony. And around ninety couples do not experience this state of love and affection; instead there is constant bickering and quarrelling in the home.[95]

The analysis of child-marriage led women to believe that it was the cause of domestic unrest and of misery to child wives, and so they called for the regulation of conjugal relations through raising the age of consent.

Public Participation of Women: Meetings and Memorials

The first memorial proposed by women from the Bombay Presidency was done through the collaboration of British feminists in Bombay and London. In the middle of 1890 the work of a Women's Committee supporting the Age of Consent Bill in Bombay was reported in leading newspapers. This Committee consisted of influential English and Maharashtrian women.[96] Their counterpart in London was Millicent Fawcett who lobbied through the Indian National Association for legislative action by the government as an 'act of conscience'.[97] The Women's Committee decided to send a memorial addressed to the Queen with 2,000 signatures of Maharashtrian women. The signatories' social position and caste were to be indicated, too, but in order to protect their interests, their identity was to remain confidential and was not to be revealed to the press.[98]

The memorial pleaded for 'the necessity for legislation in the interests of child-wives and other female minors'. The remedy they sought was that 'the criminal law in India may be so altered as to protect at least girls under fourteen from their husbands as well as from strangers'.[99] The petitioners pointed out the absurdities and anomalies in the criminal law of 1860 which fixed the Age of Consent for British girls at 12 and for Indian girls at 10. They argued that in India girls did not normally attain maturity before 14, basing their contention on the medical evidence produced by European women doctors in India. Impressive statistics were harnessed as evidence for the grievous consequences of early consummation, which resulted in child retardation and maternal mortality.[100] They pointed to the anomaly in the law whereby a girl of 18 could not validly consent to grievous harm to her person, but she could to rape. Also a girl under 12 could not validly consent to the removal of jewels from her person, but she could to 'the theft of her honour'.[101] Finally, they argued that the Queen's 'keen maternal interests' in her subjects should influence her to take action to redeem the status of her weakest subjects—the women of India—and make the law in India conform to the English law.

Between the despatch of the first memorial (December 1890) and the deliberations of the Viceregal Council on the Bill (March 1891) a great deal of activity was reported among Indian women. At least eight women's meetings are reported to have been held in western India and one in Bengal to consider aspects of the Bill and to pass resolutions and write new petitions. Mrs Ghosal of Calcutta, under the pseudonym of 'Srimati' (Mrs) informed the *Statesman* that at a private meeting of middle-aged Hindu ladies, a unanimous verdict was passed in favour of Sir Andrew Scoble's Age of Consent Bill. She said, 'Trustful of the government, the ladies hail any legislation that aims at an amelioration of the nameless doom to which among others, the married girlhood of India are subjected'.[102] The average attendance at these meetings varied between 75 and 250 women. The gatherings were always in urban centres like Pune, Bombay, Amravati and Ahmadabad, and consisted entirely of educated, middle-class women. It seems likely that the women were galvanized into action due to the massive reaction to the Bill.

An innovation in male agitational techniques as a result of the reaction to the Bill was the holding of public meetings of gigantic proportions by men organized on a caste or professional basis. Unscrupulous methods were used to recruit large numbers both for meetings and petitions.[103] While women successfully adopted the new form of constitutional agitation of holding public discussions, they condemned the methods of their male opponents. An important item on women's agenda was to inform the government of the unscrupulous practices used by the anti-legislationists. Orthodox Hindus in Maharashtra did apparently feel the women's meetings to be a threat. Tilak, the leader of the opposition, writing in the *Kesari* and *Mahratta*, registered the unity of women over the Bill, but tried to dismiss their memorials as ineffectual.[104] Some sensational vernacular papers, representing reactionary views, reported that anti-legislationist groups intended to break the influence of liberal women by organizing their wives and sisters to hold counter-meetings.[105] However, no reports of such subversive meetings by women are recorded and this merely suggests the fears of orthodoxy in the face of a united feminist collective.

If the opposition in Maharashatra felt the threat posed by women's public participation, the reverse was true too. The unprecedented traditionalist group's agitation against the Bill prompted women from differing faiths to unite on an issue which they increasingly saw as a gendered one. Typically, in one such meeting, the speaker, while arguing a case for firm commitment and unity among women said, 'The question concerns our most vital interests rather than those of *men*.'[106] Likewise, a woman writing under the authority of a 'mother of several children' said that allowing a husband or stranger to have sexual intercourse with a pre-pubescent girl was an outrageous act. She added:

> Women as a sex, were subject to and underwent far more excruciating pains and miseries and risks of the worst kind happening in child-bearing and child-birth, than man, the opposite sex, had ever conception of . . .[107]

Therefore, she cautioned against listening to the views of men as they were not a reliable index of what women went through, and advised a severe punishment for men indulging in premature cohabitation. Women thus turned the age of consent controversy into a sex-specific case where the experience of women was privileged over the textual interpretations offered by men.

Two kinds of public participation were evident among women. They joined either as members of caste- or religious-affiliated women's bodies or under the umbrella of secular women's organizations.[108] The proceedings of the women's meetings, as well as their petitioning, revealed no further collaboration with British feminists during the passage of the Act. However, there is no indication of disagreement between them. One obvious explanation for this is that the leadership of these organizations was entirely controlled by Indian women; another is that the firmness and confidence exhibited by them made outside help superfluous.[109]

The difference between the first memorial drafted with the help of British feminists and addressed to the Queen and the later petitions gives a clue to the unique aspects of the objectives and participation of Indian women under the supervision of their own feminist leaders. In the first memorial under the guidance of British women, the proposed minimum age of consent for girls was 14 years. By February 1891, when no response had been received to their memorial, women leaders like Rakhmabai Modak and Dhaklibai Sukthankar thought that the reason for the non-response to their first memorial was that 14 years appeared too high an age limit to the imperial government and hence all of their subsequent petitions proposed 12 years as the minimum age.[110] A second difference can be discerned in the construction of arguments for raising the age of consent. While the first memorial concentrated on the anomalies of the Penal Code, the later petitions personalized the issue as one concerning the strijati. The 514 petitioners from the Arya Mahila Samaj argued that while representations against the Bill were by male oppositionists, as far as women were concerned, 'the feeling in favour of the Age of Consent Bill among the female classes is indeed very general wherever the object of the Bill is correctly understood'.[111] Thus not only did the issue concern the strijati alone, but it also had the full consent of the women of Maharashtra. The tone of the later petitions was also marked by a caution which is missing in the first memorial. While some petitions requested guarantees against the misuse of the criminal process (by vesting it exclusively in magistrates), others asked for a less severe punishment in the case of husbands found guilty of breaching the Act.[112]

Finally, the question that arises from this study is why and how was agency uniquely vested in Maharashtrian women? The question is especially pertinent as the existing historiography explicitly or implicitly denies such agency to Bengali women of the same period. Several external factors contributed to the development of women's consciousness in Maharashtra. The social reform movement took a different course there from that in Bengal. In Bombay the social reform movement was more circumspect and less revolutionary. Under the guidance of the Prarthana Samajists, it was eager to change public opinion and developed practical ways of relating their convictions and practices to the existing social structure and thus found a readier public acceptance. In Bengal it was fiery and did not therefore establish a popular base as seen in the Brahmos who, no doubt, created an integrated new philosophy of life but separated themselves from society at large.[113] The specific case of the Age of Consent debate is a good illustration. In Bengal the debate hinged on the control of female sexuality and Bengali women's sexual nature.[114] On the west coast in the hands of B.G. Tilak, the debate became a nationalist issue. Even for reformers like K.T. Telang the aim was to show that social reform must precede political reform. Scholars like Bhandarkar, who cited scriptural sanction for the postponement of the garbhadana, sought to eventually prove that such a delay in holding a religious ceremony was granted in the texts and therefore implied no 'loss of religion' to the ordinary scripture-abiding Hindu and no 'danger to Hinduism' as far as the larger society was concerned. The lines on which the debate was conducted through indigenous male discourse necessarily sharpened the differences for women. Clarity marked the debate by women on the Age of Consent as they realized that it was a gender issue rather than a national or religious one.

Yet another important difference was the slow but sure building of a regional discourse within Maharashtra during this period. There is evidence of anxiety in the way Maharashtrians painstakingly distinguished themselves from Bengalis. After the publicizing of the Phulmonee case, when a Bengali husband killed his pre-pubescent wife in the act of intercourse, Bengal was reported as being a culturally backward region of India in the vernacular newspapers of western India. Even the progressive groups in western India cited the speeches of R.C. Mitter or Sir Stuart Bayley and believed the many allegations made about Bengali women's sexuality. Their rationale was that in a region like Bengal, where purdah was rife, and women were not allowed to look at men other than their close blood relations, it was only natural that Bengali women were full of sexual thoughts and craved the company of their husbands before puberty.[115] On the other side of the coin they represented Maharashtrian women as purdah-free and upheld the region's cultural practices which made consummation of marriage before puberty an exception.[116] The tone and colour of the debates in Maharashtra at once freed women from defending their sexuality and simultaneously set up an agenda on which they could participate on equal terms. This is epitomized in the arguments used by female petitioners who agreed that consummation of marriage before the girl reached the age of 12 was indeed rare in Maharashtra but who also argued that the government had to recognize the existence of the practice in other regions of India and make provisions against it.[117]

Conclusions

In significant ways women's perceptions and their participation in the child marriage debates of the 1890s challenged the social reformist ideology and practice of the nineteenth century. Their position in the debates was an expression of the tensions between their new-found aspirations for education, individuality, and desire for a change in conjugal relations on the one hand and the unchanging balance of power within home, family and society on the other. In their personal lives women attempted to translate the public debates about the role and position of women into practice at home where these relations were actually played out, and here they encountered insuperable obstacles. This led them to move their personal anxieties into a public arena with the child marriage debates.

The Age of Consent debates gave them the opportunity to bring into public prominence their frustration in translating social reform ideals into the domestic sphere. It was precisely their attempt to change their role and position in the domestic realm which enabled them to create a gendered critique of child marriage and armed with the knowledge of the true nature of Indian gender inequality as a creation of indigenous conditions they were equally clear about the *potential* of colonial power to rectify it. Women's discourses on marriage and marital reforms show that they were concerned with gender oppression rather than with colonial oppression and hoped to tap into the possibility of invoking state aid in ending their misery and pain. Their articulation of the cumulative experiences of women allowed them to contextualize their problems, thus enabling them to counter the dominant, male discourse which relied on textual interpretations of the shastras. Women's enduring contribution to the social reform movement and the women's movement of the late nineteenth century therefore is their insistence of the use of a *context-over-text* argument in the way they approached the Age of Consent issue.

The maturity of the Maharashtrian women's movement becomes clearly demonstrable in the Age of Consent controversy. Their attack on the shastras is the most important marker in their progression towards feminism, binding them into a community of women with common interests. The utilization of their women's collective, the bhaginivarg, in marshalling the arguments of gender-specific issues via the women's press is yet another milestone in their progress towards sexual equality. The third and equally important achievement was their insistence on strianubhav (women's experience) as a primary category of analysis of women's subordination rather than a harking back to an imagined past. The bhaginivarg had developed a clearly feminist perspective by relating to the everyday misery of belonging to the strijati, be it a child-wife or widow. The construction of a critique on the 'condition of the strijati' based on either their own personal experiences or the everyday existence of their *bhagini* (sisters) bonded Hindu, Jewish, Christian women together. Another remarkable feature of nineteenth-century Indian feminism was that women's discourse on social reform was based on humanitarian ideals, rather than the arguments used by male social reformers who constantly sought the sanction of the shastras for it. The differences in the arguments proposed by male reformers from those of their female counterparts also highlights the inescapable conclusion that it would be an affront to call Hindu women reformers' function a 'mediating role' in late nineteenth-century and early twentieth-century Maharashtra. Far from it, their constant contestations of men's role in holding women back as well as their separate women's organizations reveal an independent and assertive role in which men played a minimal part.

Some contemporary scholars have argued that simply because the government had not consulted women's opinions on the restitution of conjugal rights or the Age of Consent it is perfectly all right to dismiss women's voices as being beyond the terms of the debate. Such an argument is unsustainable. By studying the viewpoints and public participation of women in social debates such as the Age of Consent we are now in a position to observe subaltern perceptions of the Raj. One of the richest insights into how the colonial state was viewed by subordinated groups is provided through a study of women's assertion and resistance. Fear, submission and deference—the more readily associated reactions of Indian women towards their menfolk—are missing when it comes to their attitudes to the state. Whilst claiming recognition of their rights, women appeal to the state as the supreme arbiter of justice. Women's adulation of the Raj and their firm belief in the state's will to do good can be read as a sign of how the state was utilized as a tool to counteract patriarchal injustices. The Raj is seen as a humanitarian resource and the final arbiter—wherein the state is registered as the sovereign authority, far more so than the patriarchal head of the household. Women had used the opportunities supplied by colonialism by signing petitions, lobbying sympathetic male officials, joining secular and religious organizations and organizing meetings and rallies. The greatest impact women's crusades in the late nineteenth century had can be discerned in their persuasion of the government to legislate in favour of women. Highlighting of the insensitivity of men and the double standards embedded within men's thinking on sexuality caused an outrage that stimulated the movement well into the twentieth century for legal reform, for the case of women doctors and for women's suffrage.

What this chapter offers is an argument to look at women's counter-discourses over the question of marriage reform against the backdrop of their actions in their movements of self-assertion through their recourse to the colonial courts in the crucial decades prior and leading up to the 1890s—that is, the centrality of women's extensive resorting to and accessing of the British law courts for the resolution of their dysfunctional marriages, their seeking of alimony and maintenance and divorce on technical points in the courts. By concentrating on women's agency and contrasting it with the Indian male reformist and revivalist discourse it should be clear that if the Hindu patriarchal system felt it was under siege during the child marriage controversy, it was because of the real threat posed by the actions of their own womenfolk rather than the unreserved expression of English masculinity over the native one. The oppositional discourse of the female subject in creating her own identity and initiating her own desires via the law courts and subsequently in her creation of the bhaginivarg and their successful lobbying with the government had led to Tilak's attempt to shore up patriarchy. Male hostility to women's public participation as seen over the Age of Consent agitation also explains why Tilak's nationalist programme had such ready appeal in Maharashtra.

Maharashtrian women's participation in the popular agitation over the Age of Consent debates of 1891 effectively takes Indian women's popular protests back into the nineteenth century.[118] Women's organized protest during the passage of the Bill was an instance of the process through which they overcame religious, caste and class distinctions. The realization that the Age of Consent was an issue relating to the well-being of the strijati united them. Women's groups in the reformist era did not possess a clear-cut ideology or managerial skills like the women's organizations of the 1930s. However, it was precisely their non-adherence to nationalist and political reformist ideologies which gave them the necessary space and freedom to unite on a gender-specific basis.[119] This also provides a case study for the differences in women's responses in various British colonies such as Kenya over the clitoridectomy issue.[120] In India female pressure groups gave their opinions unsolicited and tried to persuade the government by their lobbying techniques even though the sexual politics of the colonial government prevented consultation with women. It would be an affront to our foremothers' words and actions if scholarship left unrecognized their contribution towards raising the Age of Consent.

Notes

1. The Age of Consent refers to the age at which the law recognized that an individual was eligible to give consent to sexual intercourse.
2. S. Natarajan, *A Century of Social Reform in India* (London, 1959), pp. 82–3.
3. C.H. Heimsath, 'The Origin and Enactment of the Indian Age of Consent Bill, 1891', *Journal of Asian Studies*, 21:4, 1962, pp. 491–504.
4. In 1982, Meredith Borthwick argued that the Age of Consent Bill provided a case-study in which Bengali women came to public prominence as symbolic objects rather than as a group speaking on their own behalf. See her article, 'The *Bhadramahila* and Changing Conjugal Relations in Bengal', in M. Allen and S.N. Mukherjee (eds), *Women in India and Nepal* (Canberra, 1982), p. 116.
5. Dagmar Engels drew attention to the opposition between two gender systems in which the male control of female sexuality in Bengal was threatened by the dominant ideology of Victorian sexual values: 'The Age of Consent Act of 1891: Colonial Ideology in Bengal', *South Asia Research*, 3:2, 1985, pp. 107–34. Most recently Mrinalini Sinha has argued that the evaluation of Bengali masculinity was a crucial element in the rationalization of empire: 'The Age of Consent Act: The Ideal of Masculinity and Colonial Ideology in Nineteenth-Century Bengal', in T.K. Stewart (ed.), *Shaping Bengali Worlds, Public and Private* (Michigan, 1989), pp. 99–127.
6. Two exceptions are the works of Geraldine Forbes and Barbara Ramusack who have studied women's participation for a later period (the Sarda Act, 1929). See Forbes, 'Women and Modernity: The Issue of Child-Marriage in India', *Women Studies International Quarterly*, 2, 1979, pp. 407–19;

Ramusack 'Women's Organisations and Social Change: The Age of Marriage Issue in India', in N. Black and A.C. Cottrell (eds), *Women and World Change: Equity Issues in Development* (London, 1981), pp. 198–216. However, both these works assume that Indian women's participation in child marriage agitations began only with the Child Marriage Restraint Act of 1929.

7. Sumit Sarkar, 'Orientalism Revisited: Saidian Frameworks in the Writing of Modern Indian History', *Oxford Literary Review*, 16, 1994, p. 220.
8. Tanika Sarkar, 'Rhetoric against Age of Consent: Resisting Colonial Reason and Death of a Child-wife', *Economic and Political Weekly*, 28:36, 4 September 1993, pp. 1869–71 and 1874.
9. The now familiar argument about a 'lack of sources' does not hold good here as there is ample evidence to the contrary. Many newspapers, both English and vernacular, carried reports of women's meetings, letters, articles and details of their memorials. The major source for earlier studies has been the 'Legislative Council Proceedings', which contain women's petitions as well as speeches by Indian members of the Legislature, listing the numerous activities of women in support of the Bill. See Krishnaji Lakshman Nulkar's speech in *Extract from the Abstract of the Proceedings of the Council of the Governor-General of India*, 19 March 1891. Appendix A24 (hereafter cited as *Proceedings*).
10. Padma Anagol, *The Emergence of Feminism in India, 1850–1920* (Ashgate, 2005).
11. For more details see ibid., especially Chapter 2 titled 'Discriminating Converts: Christian Women's Discourse and Work'.
12. For details see ibid., especially Chapter 3 titled 'Beyond Kitchen and Kid: Hindu Women's Discourse and Work'.
13. *Subodh Patrika*, a Marathi weekly and the literary mouthpiece of the Prarthana Samaj regularly reported the proceedings every week from the 1880s onwards.
14. See Gangutai Bhandhari's speech, *Subodh Patrika*, 6 February 1881, p. 163; Durgabai Joshi's essay, *Subodh Patrika*, 13 February 1881, pp. 167 and 171.
15. Ramabai Ranade's Hindu Ladies Social Club, Yashodabai Joshi's Vanita Samaj in Amravati, Girijabai Kelkar's Bhagini Mandal in Jalgaon and the pioneering Shri Saraswati Mandir of Solapur are instances of this awakening. See Chapters 2 and 3 in Anagol, *The Emergence of Feminism in India, 1850–1920*.
16. Sarojini Vaidya, *Shrimati Kashibai Kanitkar: Atmacharitra ani charitra* (Mrs Kashibai Kanitkar: Autobiography and Biography) (Bombay, 1979); see p. 14 for *halad-kunkum* and pp. 89 and 177 for *kirtans* and its new use. Also Ramabai Ranade, *Himself: The Autobiography of a Hindu Lady*, trans. Katherine Gates (New York, 1938), p. 116.

17. Pandita Ramabai had brought various women's groups under the umbrella organization of the Arya Mahila Samaj.
18. I have identified 10 Marathi journals run by *kartris* or 'women-editors' that collectively encompass the women's press of the late nineteenth and early twentieth centuries. The periodicals were meant for an audience of women and came from different parts of Maharashtra. They are: *Arya Bhagini*, edited by Anandibai and Manakbai Lad; *Saubhagya Sambhar*, edited by Sarubai Goa from Kolhapur; *Swadesh Bhagini*, edited by Tarabai Navalkar from Bombay; *Subhodini*, by Godubai Shinde from Nipani; *Strisaundarya Latika*, by Mrs Penkar from Bombay; *Bhamini Prakash*, by Chimabai Kadam from Poona; *Maharashtra Mahila*, by Manorama Mitra of Bombay; *Grihini Ratnamala* by Sitabai Sawant in Bombay; *Striyanchi Maithrini* by A.A. Abbott, a female missionary; and finally *Simanthini* for which I have no details. The runs vary greatly but their life-span approximately begins in the late 1870s and ends around the 1920s.
19. *Women Writing in India*, vol. 1 (New York, 1991), pp. 167–9.
20. This information is culled from Catalogue of Books printed in the Bombay Presidency starting from the Quarter Ending 30 September 1867 to Quarter Ending 31 December 1896.
21. For an analysis of feminist vocabulary in nineteenth-century Maharashtra, see Anagol, *The Emergence of Feminism in India, 1850–1920*.
22. For details, see ibid., especially Chapter 4 titled 'Women's Assertion and Resistance'.
23. Paras Diwan, *Law of Marriage and Divorce* (Allahabad, 1991), p. 283.
24. Cited in Rakhmabai, *Indian Law Reports* (hereafter *ILR*), 10 Bom., 312, 1885.
25. 'The Indian Divorce Act, 1869', Section VII, Clause 32, reproduced in Diwan, *Law of Marriage*, p. 749.
26. For more details, see Chapter 6 titled 'Women as Agents: Contesting Discourses on Marriage and Marital Rights', in Anagol, *The Emergence of Feminism in India, 1850–1920*.
27. The eighth was a warring Muslim couple disputing the validity of the marriage. These statistics are compiled from E.F. Moore, *Reports of Cases Heard and Determined by the Judicial Committee and the Lords of Her Majesty's Privy Council on Appeal from the Supreme and Sudder Dewanny Courts in the East Indies* (Bangalore, 1858), Hereafter *Moore's Indian Appeals*.
28. 'Ardaseer Cursetjee v. Perozeboye, 12 and 14 April 1856', ibid., vol. 6.
29. '*Femme sole*' is better understood in relation to its sister concept the '*femme covert*'. In nineteenth-century English law the wife was regarded as the 'property of her husband' because the doctrine of coverture declared that the legal personality of the woman was merged in her husband's after marriage. A '*femme covert*' often referred to a married woman who could

not alienate her property including that which had come to her before marriage, nor sign contracts, or make a will without the consent of her husband. However, a degree of autonomy was embedded in the term '*femme sole*' which was defined as: 'A wife with a separate estate could deal with *that* [sic] property as if she were unmarried, or what the law called a *feme sole*.' This quote and information is from Mary L. Shanley, *Feminism, Marriage and the Law in Victorian England* (Princeton, 1989), pp. 25–6.

30. Ibid., p. 372.
31. Amongst a host of scholars, see in particular Sudhir Chandra, *Enslaved Daughters: Colonialism, Law and Women's Rights* (New Delhi, 1998).
32. See the letter of Dayaram Gidumal, Acting Assistant Judge, Ahmedabad, to the Secretary to Government, 15 September 1887, 'Proposed amendment'.
33. Ibid., p. 173.
34. See his confidential letter dated 6 August 1887, 'Proposed amendment'.
35. See the reply of Tirmal Rao Venkatesh Inamdar, retired Judge, Court of Small Causes, Dharwar, 14 August 1887, in 'Proposed amendment'.
36. See their replies in 'Proposed amendment'. Ibid.
37. Reply by Rao Bahadur Mahadev Govind Ranade, to the Chief Secretary to Government, 19 September 1887, 'Proposed amendment'.
38. Mrinalini Sinha, 'Potent Protests: The Age of Consent Controversy, 1891', in *Colonial Masculinity: The 'Manly Englishman' and the 'Effeminate Bengali' in the Late Nineteenth Century* (Manchester, 1995), pp. 138–80.
39. Jayantibai lost claims to her first husband's property as the Widow Remarriage Act of 1856 disallowed remarried widows from inheriting their previous husband's property. See Lucy Carroll, 'Law, Custom and Statutory Social Reform: The Hindu Widows' Remarriage Act of 1856', *Indian Economic and Social History Review*, 20:4, 1983, pp. 363–88.
40. 'An Exposition of Some of the Facts of the Case of Dadaji vs. Rakhmabai', *Law Tracts* (Bombay, 1887), pp. 1–13.
41. 'Rukhmabai's Reply to Dadajee's "Exposition" ', reprinted from the *Bombay Gazette*, 29 June 1887, *Law Tracts*, Bombay, 1987.
42. Ibid., p. 3.
43. The emphasis is mine.
44. There was a third legal suit, too—a libel action by Dadaji against the *Bombay Gazette*, which had investigated the lifestyle of Dadaji and his uncle and validated Rakhmabai's version. On 5 July 1888, the Bombay High Court dismissed Dadaji's claims on sufficient evidence that he had suppressed information. Realizing that he would lose any further suits, he negotiated an out-of-court settlement with Rakhmabai whereby she paid him Rs 2,000 (a large fortune for the 1880s) on the assurance that he would take no further legal action against her. This version of events,

from a Marathi biography of Rakhmabai and based on new information, is the more credible because Dadaji's sudden interest in claiming his marital rights from Rakhmabai followed the news of her sole inheritance to a considerable estate from her natural father. The eventual resolution of the case also indicates the monetary considerations in marital disputes. See Mohini Varde, *Dr. Rakhmabai: Ek Arth* (The Saga of Dr Rakhmabai) (Bombay, 1982), pp. 85–92.

45. In 'Dadaji Bhikaji v. Rakmabai', *ILR*, 10 Bom. 301,1886, pp. 572–9.
46. Rakhmabai spent a day in prison according to her own testimony to a friend. In Varde, *Dr Rakhmabai*, p. 62.
47. '*Hindudharmavar ghav ghalnaren navin trikut*' (The New Confederacy of Three in Assaulting Hinduism'), *Kesari* (Marathi), 20 September 1887, p. 2
48. *ILR*, 10 Bom. 301, p. 575
49. Letter to Dorothea Beale, 22 May 1887, in A.B. Shah (ed.), *Letters and Correspondence of Pandita Ramabai* (Bombay, 1977), p. 175.
50. Rumours abounded among conservative groups that women were being encouraged to defy their guardians by male reformers so that attendance at the female schools run by Pandita Ramabai would increase significantly, *Hindu Punch*, 12 February 1891, reported in the Bombay Native Newspaper Reports (hereafter *NNR*), 14 February 1891.
51. It was a common feature among women during this period to use pseudonyms, probably prompted by fear of the awesome reaction in Maharashtra against the abolition of child marriage. However, the pseudonyms indicated their gender and were validated by citing their marital status or class. It was a clever strategy to say, for example, 'from a mother of three children', thus privileging their experience over that of men. It at once gave them a superior position to quote the evil consequences of child marriage on women as opposed to men.
52. This pattern was repeated in the Age of Consent controversy too.
53. 'A Hindu Lady', 'Infant Marriage and Enforced Widowhood', *Times of India*, 26 June 1885, p. 4.
54. 'Infant Marriage', p. 4.
55. See Chapter 3 in Anagol, *The Emergence of Feminism in India, 1850–1920*.
56. 'Infant Marriage', p. 4.
57. Yashodabai Joshi, *Amchi Jivanpravas* (The Journey of Our Life Together), (Pune, 1965), p. 18.
58. Champubai Madhavrao Nadkarni, Letter to Editor, *Arya Bhagini* (Marathi), 28 July 1891; Dhakbai Trimbhakran Desai, Letter to Editor, ibid., 1 November 1891; also opinions of Ahalyabai Morevale, Krishnabai and Lanibai Dhurandar, ibid., January 1893.

59. 'Infant Marriage', p. 4.
60. Ibid.
61. B. Malabari, 'Notes on Infant-Marriage and Enforced Widowhood', p. 3, in Government of India, Home Department, *Selections from the Records*, Serial No. 3, V/23/49/22.
62. See M. Michel, 'The Sarda Act, Political Strategy and Trends in Discourse in the Child-Marriage Debate in India during the 1920s', unpublished M.A. dissertation (Hannover, 1989), p. 121.
63. M.G. Ranade, 12 February 1885, *Selections from Records*, p. 92.
64. Dr K.R. Kirtikar, *An Address on the Occasion of the Second Anniversary of the Saddaharma Samaj of Thane*, 20 July 1883.
65. Letter, 30 December 1884, *Selections from Records*, p. 55.
66. See the reports and letters of Pandurang Balibhadra, Narayan Bhikaji, Deputy Collector, Nasik; Dr Bhikajee Amroot Chobhe, Assistant Surgeon, Pune, in *Selections from Records*, pp. 49, 63–5, 143.
67. K. Satthianadhan, 'Female Education', in *Miscellaneous Writings of Krupabai Satthianadhan* (Madras, 1896), p. 19.
68. Ibid., p. 21
69. Ibid., p. 27.
70. K. Satthianadhan. 'Hindu Social Customs', in *Miscellaneous Writings*, pp. 25–31.
71. 'Infant Marriage'.
72. See articles by Anandibai Lad on 'Lagnyachi chali' (Marriage Traditions), and 'Laukar lagna kamyachi chal' (The Custom of Child-Marriage), in *Arya Bhagini*, March 1886.
73. Pandita Rambai, *The High-Caste Hindu Woman* (London, 1888), especially chapters 2 and 3.
74. S.M. Nikambe, *Ratanbai: A Sketch of a Bombay High Caste Hindu Young Wife* (London, 1895).
75. R. Ranade, *Amchya Ayushyathil kahi atavani* (A Few Reminiscences of Our Life) (Bombay, 1963), pp. 42–68.
76. See 'Samajik sudharana' (Social Reform), *Arya Bhagini*, June 1891, p. 51.
77. 'Gaud Saraswat Brahman Stri' (pseudonym) (A Gaud Saraswat Brahman Lady), 'Letter to the woman-editor', *Arya Bhagini*, p. 52.
78. 'Eka susiksit stri kadun' (By an Educated Lady), 'Gulabbai ani Sevatibai yancha bodhapar samvad' (Instructive Debates Between Gulabbai and Sevatibai), *Arya Bhagini*, July 1891, pp. 60–1.
79. Tarabai Shinde, *Stripurushtulana* (Women and Men: A Comparison), 2nd edn, ed. S.J. Malshe [1st edn, 1882] (Bombay, 1975), p. 18.
80. Malabari, 'Infant Marriage in India, Paper 1', in *Infant Marriage and Enforced Widowhood*, p. 2.

81. Rakhmabai, 'Infant Marriage', p. 4.
82. D. Arnold, 'Medical Priorities and Practices in Nineteenth-Century British India', *South Asia Research*, 5:2, 1985, pp. 167–83.
83. Dr E. Pechey-Phipson, *Address to the Hindus of Bombay on the subject of Child Marriage*, Bombay, 11 October 1890, *IOL Tracts 799*.
84. British and Indian women included Mrs Greton Gary, Dr Edith Pechey-Phipson, Mrs Lyttleton, Mrs Portman, Lady Cowasjee Jehangir, Mrs Bhaunagari; From Varde, *Dr. Rakhmabai*, p. 64. See details as reported in *Jame-Jamshed*, in *NNR*, 16 March 1887.
85. See Varde, *Dr. Rakhmabai*, pp. 97–114, for details.
86. R.G. Bhandarkar, 24 February 1885, *Selections from Records*, pp. 133–4.
87. 'Eka susiksit stri kadun' (By an Educated Lady), 'Gulabbai ani Sevatibai yancha bodhapar samvad' (Instructive Debates between Gulabbai and Sevatibai), *Arya Bhagini*, pp. 52–3.
88. Ibid..
89. Kashibai, the female biographer of Anandibai Joshi, records the fearful delusions of the nine-year-old Anandibai who refused to enter her husband's bedroom for days because she thought there was a tiger there! K. Kanitkar, *Sou. Da. Anandibai Josi yance caritra* (Biography of Mrs Dr Anandibai Joshi) (Pune, 1888), p. 2. Gangutai recalled her intense repulsion at the term *naura* (husband) due to a childhood experience of sexual assault. G. Patwardhan, *Chakoribaher: Ek atmakatan* (Beyond the Courtyard: An Autobiography), (Pune, 1974), pp. 2–3.
90. G. Kelkar, 'Tarunpide va samajik sudharana' (The Younger Generation and Social Reform), in *Grihini Bhushan, Bhag Dusra, Puspahar* (Guide-Books for Women, Part Two, A Garland of Flowers) (Jalgaon, 1921), pp. 72–84.
91. Anandibai Lad, 'Laukar lagna karnyachi chal', *Arya Bhagini*, p. 5; and K. Satthianadhan, 'Female Education', *Miscellaneous Writings*, pp. 16–17.
92. It is, therefore, simplistic to state that all women who rejected the 'Golden Age' theory (the orientalist notion of a supposedly glorious ancient Indian past) became feminists and those who did not remained in the traditional mould, as has been argued by Uma Chakravarti, 'Whatever Happened to the Vedic Dasi? Orientalism, Nationlism and a Script for the Past', in K. Sangari and S. Vaid (eds), *Recasting Women: Essays in Colonial History* (New Delhi, 1989), pp. 27–87.
93. Quoted in S. Vaidya, *Srimati Kasibai Kanitkar: Atmachiritra ani charitra* (Mrs Kashibai Kanitkar: Autobiography and Biography), (Bombay, 1979), p. 23.
94. Ibid., pp. 231–2.

95. 'Eka susiksit stri kadun, 'Gulabbai ani Sevatibai bodhpar samvad', *Arya Bhagini*, September 1981, pp. 78–9.
96. Lady Reay and Dr Pechey-Phipson were the British representatives; the Indian women were Rakhmabai Modak, Pandita Ramabai and Dr Rakhmabai.
97. *Induprakash*, 22 December 1890, p. 3.
98. The memorial itself was published in verbatim in all the leading newspapers: *Maratha*, 14 December 1890, and *Induprakash*, 6 October 1890.
99. Memorial of 1,600 women of India to Queen Victoria, sent by W. Lee Warner, Secretary to the Government of Bombay, 30 December 1890, in 'Papers Relative to the Bill to Amend the Indian Penal Code and the Code of Criminal Procedure, 1882', *Proceedings*, April 1891, Appendix N.
100. The memoralists also suggested the likelihood of a sterile population resulting from child-marriage: see Memorial of Lady Doctors in India, signed by Monelle Mansell and 49 others, 22 September 1890, *Proceedings*, Appendix A15.
101. Memorial of 1,600 women of India, *Proceedings*.
102. *Induprakash*, 16 February 1891, p. 3.
103. The most publicized of these demonstrations were the Tulsi Bagh and Madhav Bagh meetings in Bombay. Leaflets carried such sensational messages as 'Violate your religion or suffer transportation for life'; 'Government interferes in domestic delicate matters'. On the basis of such slogans the anti-legislationsits were able to collect 10,000 signatures in a day. *Gujarati, NNR*, 21 February 1891 and *Vartahar, NNR*, 21 February 1891.
104. *Kesari*, 24 February 1891, *NNR*, 28 February 1891; *Mahratta*, 30 November 1890, *NNR*, 6 December 1890.
105. *Pune Vaibhav*, 7 December 1890, in *NNR*, 13 December 1890. Other vernacular newspapers which condemned women's meetings and participation were *Jagad-hitechchu, Vartahar* and *Hindu Punch*, reported in *NNR*, 7 March 1891.
106. 'Correspondence, Poona News', *Induprakash*, 2 March 1891, p. 4.
107. *Induprakash*, 8 December 1890.
108. Examples of the first kind are Zoroastrian Women's Club, the Bene-Israelite Women's Organisation, Nitiprasarak Mandal and the Native Christian Women's Society. Among the second type were the Arya Mahila Samaj of Bombay and the Aryan Ladies' Association.
109. The new-found confidence was expressed by some women in dropping their pseudonyms during this agitation, like Rakhmabai and Krupabai.
110. Petition from the Aryan Ladies' Association, Pune, by 65 Hindu and 23 Bene-Israel women, *Proceedings*. Also petition of certain Parsi and

Native Christian women, Pune, 23 February 1891, to the Governor-General of India, signed by 128 Parsi and 83 Native Christian women, in *Proceedings*, Appendix A12.

111. A petition from Dhaklibai Sukthankar, Secretary, Arya Mahila Samaj, Bombay, 4 March 1891, to K.L. Nulkar accompanied by a 'Memorial of 514 Native Ladies', of Bombay and Pune, *Proceedings*, Appendix A18.
112. A memorial adopted by 60 high-caste Hindu women from Ahmadabad. Reported in *Times of India*, 25 February 1891, p. 5.
113. Other details of these variations are to be found in Heimsath, *Indian Nationalism and Hindu Social Reform*, pp. 14, 86–7, 104–8.
114. See Engels, 'The Age of Consent Act', pp. 122–4.
115. *Sudharak*, in *NNR*, 24 January 1891; *Subodh Patrika, NNR*, 21 February 1891; *Indian Spectator, NNR*, 14 February 1891.
116. This was common ground, shared by both pro-and anti-legislationists, in Maharashtra.
117. Petition from Secretary, Arya Mahila Samaj, Bombay, *Proceedings*.
118. Contrary to the assumption of historians who have suggested that it was not until the passing of the Sarda Act of 1929. Cf. Forbes, 'Women and Modernity', p. 413, and Ramusack, 'Women's Organisations and Social Change', p. 203.
119. Adherence to nationalist ideals and allegiance to nationalist leaders probably shackled women's organization to a lukewarm ideology of women's emancipation, where they were neither feminists nor suffragists. The stand-point of the All India Women's Conference in the child marriage issue of 1929 is discussed in Forbes, 'Women and Modernity', pp. 414–15.
120. For a refreshing analysis, see S. Pedersen, 'National Bodies, Unspeakable Acts: The Sexual Politics of Colonial Policy-Making', *Journal of Modern History*, 63:4, 1990, pp. 647–80.

119. [illegible]